Motivation and Personality is the first book to be devoted primarily to content analysis systems for assessment of the characteristics of individuals, groups, or historical periods from their verbal materials. Manuals for using the various systems, theory and research regarding the background of the systems, and practice materials are included to create a book that is both reference and handbook.

Motivation and personality:
Handbook of thematic content analysis

Motivation and personality: Handbook of thematic content analysis

Edited by
CHARLES P. SMITH
City University of New York, Graduate School

In association with
John W. Atkinson
David C. McClelland
Joseph Veroff

 CAMBRIDGE
UNIVERSITY PRESS

Published by the Press Syndicate of the University of Cambridge
The Pitt Building, Trumpington Street, Cambridge CB2 IRP
40 West 20th Street, New York, NY 10011, USA
10 Stamford Road, Oakleigh, Victoria 3166, Australia

First published 1992

Printed in the United States of America

Library of Congress Cataloging-in-Publication Data
Motivation and personality : handbook of thematic content analysis /
Charles P. Smith, editor ; in association with John W. Atkinson,
David C. McClelland, Joseph Veroff.
    p.   cm.
  Includes bibliographical references and indexes.
  ISBN 0-521-40052-X
  1. Motivation (Psychology) – Testing.   2. Personality and
motivation.   I. Smith, Charles P., 1931-   .
  BF503.M665   1992
  153.8'014–dc20   91-23786

A catalog record for this book is available from the British Library.

ISBN 0-521-40052-X hardback

Contents

PART II.   CONTENT ANALYSIS SYSTEMS

Contents   vii

Contributors

John W. Atkinson, Ph.D.
Professor Emeritus of Psychology
University of Michigan
Ann Arbor, MI 48109-1346

Gloria Baker-Brown, M. A.
Vancouver Health Department
Vancouver, BC, Canada V6M 2E1

Elizabeth J. Ballard, Ph.D.
Lecturer
Vancouver Community College
Vancouver, BC, Canada V5Y 2Z6

Susan Bluck, B. A.
Program in Social Ecology
University of California
Irvine, CA 92717

Camilo Castellon, M.A.
Psychotherapist, CLUES
220 South Robert Street
St. Paul, MN 55107

Russell A. Clark, Ph.D.
Deceased, 1958; formerly with the
Office of Naval Research

Richard deCharms, Ph.D.
Professor of Education and
    Psychology
Washington University
St. Louis, MO 63130

Brian de Vries, Ph.D.
Assistant Professor of Family
    Sciences
School of Family and Nutritional
    Sciences
University of British Columbia
Vancouver, BC, Canada V6T 1Z4

Robert A. Emmons, Ph.D.
Associate Professor
Department of Psychology
University of California, Davis
Davis, CA 95616

Sheila C. Feld, Ph.D.
Professor
School of Social Work
University of Michigan
Ann Arbor, MI 48109-1285

Jacqueline Fleming, Ph.D.
Consulting Psychologist and
Adjunct Associate Professor
Barnard College, Columbia
    University
New York, NY 10025

Carol E. Franz, Ph.D.
Postdoctoral Research Fellow
in Human Motivation
Radcliffe College
(continued on p. x)

ix

Research Associate, Center for
  Health and Advanced Policy
  Studies
Boston University
Boston, MA 02215

Steven E. Hanna
Department of Psychology
University of Western Ontario
London, Ontario, Canada N6A 5C2

Joseph M. Healy, Jr., Ph.D.
Clinical Care Assessment Dept.
Harvard Community Health Plan
10 Brookline Place West
Brookline, MA 02146

Roger W. Heyns, Ph.D.
President, William and Flora
  Hewlett Foundation
525 Middlefield Road
Menlo Park, CA 94304

Matina S. Horner, Ph.D.
Executive Vice President
TIAA/CREF
730 3rd Avenue
New York, NY 10017

Laura A. King, Ph.D.
Department of Psychology
Southern Methodist University
Dallas, TX 75275

Richard Koestner, Ph.D.
Assistant Professor
Department of Psychology
McGill University
Montreal, PQ, Canada H3A 1B1

Edgar L. Lowell, Ph.D.
Executive Director (retired), John
  Tracy Clinic
Professor Emeritus
University of Southern California
Los Angeles, CA 90024

Dan P. McAdams, Ph.D.
Professor of Human Development
  and Psychology
The School of Education and Social
  Policy
Northwestern University
Evanston, IL 60208-2610

David C. McClelland, Ph.D.
Distinguished Research Professor of
  Psychology
Boston University
Boston, MA 02215

James R. McKay, Ph.D.
Investigator, Addiction Research
  Center
Research Assistant Professor of
  Psychology in Psychiatry
University of Pennsylvania School of
  Medicine
Philadelphia, PA 19104

Christopher Peterson, Ph.D.
Professor
Department of Psychology
University of Michigan
Ann Arbor, MI 48109

Franziska Plimpton, Ph.D.
Child Psychologist in Private
  Practice
Rebhalde 20
CH 6340 BAAR, Switzerland

Christopher J. R. Roney, Ph.D.
Postdoctoral Fellow
Department of Psychology
Columbia University
New York, NY 10027

Peter Schulman
Research Coordinator
Department of Psychology
University of Pennsylvania
Philadelphia, PA 19104

Martin E. P. Seligman, Ph.D.
United Parcel Service Foundation
  Term Professor in the Social
  Sciences
University of Pennsylvania
Philadelphia, PA 19104

Charles P. Smith, Ph.D.
Professor
Ph.D. Program in Social-Personality
  Psychology
City University of New York,
  Graduate School
New York, NY 10036

Richard M. Sorrentino, Ph.D.
Professor
Department of Psychology
University of Western Ontario
London, Ontario, Canada N6A 5C2

Abigail J. Stewart, Ph.D.
Professor of Psychology and
  Women's Studies
Director, Women's Studies Program
University of Michigan
Ann Arbor, MI 48109

Siegfried Streufert, Ph.D.
Professor of Behavioral Science and
  Psychology
College of Medicine
Pennsylvania State University
Hershey, PA 17033

Peter Suedfeld, Ph.D., F.R.S.C.
Professor
Department of Psychology
University of British Columbia
Vancouver, BC, Canada V6T 1Y7

Philip E. Tetlock, Ph.D.
Professor
Department of Psychology
University of California, Berkeley
Berkeley, CA 94720

Joseph Veroff, Ph.D.
Professor of Psychology
Research Scientist, Survey Research
  Center
University of Michigan
Ann Arbor, MI 48109-1346

Joel Weinberger, Ph.D.
Assistant Professor
Derner Institute
Adelphi University
Garden City, NY 11530

David G. Winter, Ph.D.
Professor
Department of Psychology
University of Michigan
Ann Arbor, MI 48109-1346

Preface

This is the first book devoted primarily to the presentation of nonclinical coding systems for the assessment of characteristics of persons and social groups. These systems have been empirically derived, refined, and validated, and may be applied with high interscorer agreement in research in the behavioral and social sciences and in the applied areas of education, business, and health.

Rapidly expanding beyond its original conception as a source of a few well-established motive scoring systems, this volume became a more general handbook for researchers who wish to employ content analytic methods to measure motives, attributional and cognitive styles, and psychosocial orientations. Although the early-developed motive scoring systems are included here, with various revisions and updatings, most of the systems are of more recent origin, and many are published here for the first time. The influence of the Murray tradition is evident in many of the systems; however, some derive from other research traditions and are not thematic in the sense of employing stories or the analysis of themes in stories.

Readers will discover that problematic aspects of earlier research have been addressed, important new research has been carried out, and significant advances have been made in the theoretical conceptions underlying both method and content. Limitations of the method, and problems that remain to be solved, are identified and discussed.

Part I provides a context for the scoring systems by presenting a theoretical background and a discussion of such issues as (a) the determinants of thematic apperception, (b) the relation of thematic methods to self-report inventories, experience sampling, and other contemporary approaches to the assessment of motivational and personality processes, (c) the role of motivational configurations and moderator variables, (d) the use of thematic measures in survey research, and (e) thematic analysis of preexisting or naturally occurring verbal materials. Throughout the volume issues concerning reliability and validity are discussed.

Part II presents fourteen different coding manuals, each introduced by a

xiii

chapter that describes the development of the system, reviews major research findings, and discusses measurement issues. Because of the necessary brevity of these introductory chapters, some may require background knowledge to be fully appreciated.

Part III is devoted to practical methodological considerations such as how to obtain material to score and how to learn the scoring systems. Practice materials and "expert" scoring are provided for scorer training. Recommended pictures are reproduced for use in story collection.

As I read and reread the contributions to this book, I had a growing sense of intellectual excitement that I think our readers will share if they read even several chapters and begin to see the rich mosaic that they form. Imagine the application of the same general method to such different areas as power, intimacy, fear of rejection, personal causation, and conceptual complexity, to name but a few. Somehow a qualitatively different impression of the range and power of this method arises when these approaches are taken together rather than in isolation. They confirm and augment, complement and refer to each other in such a way as to constitute a lively extended family of personal and socially relevant attributes and dispositions – a family that extends to a considerable portion of the domain of the behavioral and social sciences – to cultural anthropology and psychohistory, to sociology, economics, and political science. Perhaps this use of content analysis, still full of promise for the future, has begun to come of age.

Finally, the editors regret that the illness and death of our esteemed friend, Heinz Heckhausen, precluded the inclusion of his important work in this volume, and that other commitments prevented the inclusion of material on fear of failure by Richard Teevan, Robert Birney, and their associates.

Acknowledgments

This project is the result of the combined efforts of the authors, editors, and persons who have given advice and support, including the perceptive suggestions of anonymous reviewers. My editorial associates have contributed extensively not only to this volume, but to the development of thematic apperceptive research as we know it today. John W. Atkinson first suggested a publication of this type, and his outstanding theoretical contributions are evident throughout the final product. I am happy to have an opportunity to acknowledge not only his editorial contributions but also his role as an unsurpassed mentor during my graduate education at the University of Michigan. David McClelland took the initiative to get this project underway, further expanded its conception, and worked closely with me to see it to completion. He modestly declined to be listed as coeditor, so I can only acknowledge his innumerable contributions and say that it has been especially rewarding to work with him. Joseph Veroff has been a source of support and thoughtful advice during and since my graduate school years. He has worked closely with me in making his own major contributions to this volume, and in sharing editorial decisions. In an unofficial capacity, colleagues at other institutions including Norman T. Feather, Carol Franz, David Reuman, Peter Suedfeld, and David Winter have given generous editorial assistance in many ways. My wife, Judith, has also made unofficial contributions of major proportions affecting virtually every aspect of the project.

Helpful suggestions and support have been provided by too many colleagues and former colleagues to name; those who have been especially helpful include Alan Gross, Ian McMahan, Samuel Messick, Suzanne Ouellette Kobasa, David Rindskopf, and Richard Smith. For insights regarding the Thematic Apperception Test and countless other matters, I am deeply grateful to my friend and former colleague, Silvan Tomkins. Linda Bastone and Joyce Blanchette gave much needed competent help with the preparation of the references and the manuscript. I am indebted to the City University Graduate School for facilities and support, especially for the work of Peter Harris and his staff in preparing photographs and camera-ready material.

An important role in providing "expert scoring" of the practice stories was played by Caroline McLeod, Joseph Scroppo, and Joel Weinberger. Robert Wesner gave valuable advice about publishing considerations, as did Robert Kidd. At Cambridge University Press it has been a distinct pleasure to work with Julia Hough as editor and with Russell Hahn as production editor. Their expert advice, given with patience and good nature, has made an important contribution to the quality of this volume.

City University of New York, Graduate School   Charles P. Smith
March 1991

1 *Introduction: inferences from verbal material*

CHARLES P. SMITH

OVERVIEW

This handbook deals with the use of content analysis for making inferences about the characteristics or experiences of persons or social groups. In this chapter the ancestry, conception, and gestation of this volume are briefly described. The particular approach to content analysis of the contributors is characterized; highlights are reviewed; integrative themes are identified; a trend away from single-variable research is documented; and some not-so-obvious implications of the contents for the debate about the cross-situational consistency of behavior are noted.

Conception

The initial impetus for the book was provided by requests to the contributors for copies of their scoring systems and practice materials. Soon the plan expanded to include information about current research, and a section on theoretical and methodological issues. Part I deals with the determinants of thematic apperception, reliability and validity, the relation of thematic analysis to other contemporary methods of conceptualizing and measuring person variables, and the use of thematic methods in survey research and for the analysis of archival and naturally occurring verbal materials. Part II presents fourteen different scoring systems for the assessment of motives, attributional and cognitive orientations, and psychosocial orientations. With one exception, these systems are applicable to verbal material from both sexes. Each system is introduced by a concise chapter describing the development of the system and key studies. (Because of their brevity, some of these prefatory chapters may require some background knowledge to be fully appreciated.) Part III provides guidelines for research, and materials for scorer training and data collection.

I wish to thank David McClelland, Ian McMahan, and Peter Suedfeld for their helpful comments on an earlier draft of this chapter.

I

Table 1.1. *Topics investigated by means of various scoring systems (chapter numbers in parentheses)*

Academic achievement
Classroom climate (23)
Determinants of grades (9, 13, 23)
Graduation rates (23)
Volunteering in class (19)

Avoidance motivation
Fear of failure (2, 9)
Fear of rejection (13)
Fear of success (11)
Fear of weakness (19)
Avoidance of uncertainty (29)

Careers
Leader careers (27)
Managerial success (5, 35)
Occupational mobility (6, 9)
Women's careers (33)

Inner life (private personality)
Affiliative thoughts (15)
Daily affect (4)
Experience sampling (4, 15)
Feelings of autonomy, self-determination
   (23, 31, 33)
Mood shifts (25)
Secrets and fears (33)
Well-being versus distress (4, 15, 31)

Personality development and change
Age and conceptual complexity (27)
Change in psychotherapy (25)
Child-rearing practices (9, 17)
Motive development (3, 21)
Origin training (23)
Parent–child interaction (19, 23)
Parental expectations (35)

Personality and social processes
Attitude change (27)
Groupthink (21, 27)
Interpersonal attraction (27)
Leadership (19, 27, 35)
Political activity (19, 25)

Stress and coping
Adaptation to life changes (31)
Coping capacity (33)
Distress in cancer patients (33)
Helplessness (25)
Responses to stress (27, 31, 33)

Gender differences
Fear of success (11)
Intimacy (15)
Personal causation (23)
Responsibility (35)

Goal setting
Occupational choice (9)
Personal goals (4)
Realism of goal setting (5, 9, 29)
Short-term and long-term goals (9)

Methodology and measurement
Archival analysis (7, 9, 21, 27)
Computer simulation (2)
Controlling for verbal fluency (11, 19,
   21, 27, 37)
Relation of self-report and content analysis
   measures (3, 4, 11, 23, 25)
Reliability and validity of thematic measures
   (2, 8, 9, 21, et al.)
Sampling verbal material (7, 27, 37)
Storytelling instructions (9, 19, 21, 37)
Storytelling stimuli (pictures, verbal cues)
   (6, 21, 23, 37)
Use of thematic measures in survey
   research (6)

Physical health and illness
Agency and illness (5)
Death from heart disease (7)
Elevated blood pressure (5, 33)
Immune system functioning (5, 17, 21)
Pessimistic style and illness (25)
Release of catecholamines (5)
Severity of illness (5, 25)

Table 1.1. *Continued*

Societal characteristics and trends; ideology	Psychosocial adjustment
Child-rearing practices in different societies (9)	Alcohol and/or drug abuse (4, 15, 35)
Economic development of nations (7, 9)	Career, family role adaptation (35)
Entrepreneurial activity in different cultures (9)	Concern about sexual identity (19)
Homicide rates (19)	Divorce (21, 31)
Modal personality (7)	Expression of aggression (21, 35)
Periods of war and peace (7)	Job satisfaction (6, 15)
Political ideology (27)	Marital happiness (5, 6, 15, 19)
Roles of marriage, parenthood, and work (6)	Major life changes (31)
The Protestant ethic (6, 9)	Medical school adjustment (5)
Treatment of events by mass media (7)	Uncontrollable events (25)
	Studies of important persons
	Novelists, scientists, revolutionaries (27)
	Political leaders (7, 27)
	Supreme court justices (7, 27)

Scope and provenance

The scope of the book is conveyed by the range of scoring systems and the topics investigated by means of these systems. The achievement, affiliation, and power motive systems are included in essentially their original form. Other previously published systems are included in *revised* form, including those for personal causation, explanatory style, intimacy motivation, motivation to avoid success, and (an alternative approach to) power motivation. Research employing the remaining systems has been published, but the following coding systems themselves have not been published previously: affiliative trust–mistrust, conceptual/integrative complexity, uncertainty orientation, and systems for assessing three psychosocial orientations: stances toward the environment, self-definition and social definition, and responsibility.

The theoretical provenance of these systems is equally broad; they reflect the influence of Murray (achievement, affiliation, power), Adler (power as fear of weakness), Erikson (stances toward the environment; affiliative trust–mistrust), Kelly and Schroder (conceptual/integrative complexity), Heider (explanatory style), Buber, Sullivan, Maslow, and Bakan (intimacy), White, Heider, and Kelley (personal causation and the origin concept), Rokeach, Raynor, and Trope (uncertainty orientation), Sartre and de Beauvoir (self-definition).

Readers familiar with some of the original scoring systems may be surprised by the amount of recent research that has been carried out on topics of contemporary interest. Some categories into which these topics fall are listed in Table 1.1.

Extensive as it is, however, this book does not attempt to include clinically oriented systems of content analysis such as those of Karon (1981) or Westen (1991), nor does it present the work of researchers such as Martindale (1990) and Simonton (1987, 1990) whose content analytic studies are not oriented toward the use of previously validated individual difference measures of particular person variables.

The synergistic effect of bringing the contributions together

When all of the chapters were in place it became clear that the separate contributions taken together complemented each other and contributed to a general understanding of both the thematic method and current issues in theory and research in the behavioral and social sciences. In part these emergent qualities arise because motive measures are juxtaposed with measures of styles and what we have called *orientations*. Together these measures yield a more balanced and integrated approach to personality structure and process. In addition to being of importance in their own right, some of the nonmotive measures are moderators of motive expression and others complement motive measures in providing insights into phenomena of general interest, such as political leadership. In contrast to the hundreds of isolated studies that have employed thematic apperceptive measures with little cumulative impact, the contributions included here add up to a relatively coherent body of knowledge concerning a wide variety of personal and social phenomena.

THE PRESENT APPROACH TO THEMATIC CONTENT ANALYSIS

Key terms and concepts

Of the many possible applications of content analysis, the one represented by the systems in this volume involves "coding" or "scoring" verbal material for *content* or *style* for the purpose of making inferences about, or assessing, the characteristics or experiences of persons, social groups, or historical periods. The term *thematic* is used loosely in the title to signify this particular use of content analysis. *Thematic* connotes the analysis of storylike verbal material, and the use of relatively comprehensive units of analysis such as *themas* (Murray, 1943), *themes* (Holsti, 1969), or combinations of categories (Aron, 1950). While many of the systems included here reflect the Murray tradition, others do not and are not thematic in the sense just described. For example, some assess style rather than content, and some do not employ storylike material.

For the most part, throughout this book, terms such as *thematic apperceptive measure* or *picture-story exercise* have been used rather than *Thematic Apperception Test* or *TAT* in order to distinguish the modified procedures that have been developed from Murray's (1943) published test. Some of Murray's terms are used, however. For example, most readers will recognize the lowercase italicized *n* as Murray's abbreviation for "need."

The terms *projective* and *fantasy* usually associated with thematic apperception, receive relatively little use in this volume. Suffice it to say that these terms have excess clinical and theoretical connotations that are not a necessary part of most of the approaches included here (cf. D. G. Winter, 1973, p. 35). As deCharms (chapter 23) puts it: "Although the thought sampling technique has roots in the concepts of the unconscious and projection, we avoid these terms in favor of construing the thought sample as a nonself-conscious description of the way a person experiences her world."

It is probably safe to say that most of the contributors think of their work as involving some sort of "thought sampling," to use Murray's (1943) felicitous term, and that they select verbal material to be representative of a person's characteristic thought content or style (under the particular conditions in which the verbal material is produced). Even when the verbal material takes the form of imaginative stories, however, most authors have not used the term *fantasy*, possibly because of Holt's (1961) cogent demonstration that TAT stories lack the characteristics of fantasy as represented by reveries or daydreams.

Most, if not all, of the coding systems included in this volume work with "manifest," rather than "latent," symbolic, or disguised content. (The interpretation of symbols may be necessary when more conflictual motives, such as sex, are being assessed; cf. Clark, 1952.) For the most part, an attempt has been made to limit inferences that go much beyond the words used in order to attain high intercoder reliability. However, the conceptual/integrative complexity system (chapter 28) "requires the judgment of trained coders, who may have to make subtle inferences about the intended meaning of authors."

Derivation of scoring categories

In most uses of content analysis, coding categories are either identified in advance of obtaining verbal material on the basis of theoretical or practical considerations, or they are derived by classifying responses after they are produced by finding the descriptive categories into which most responses fit. In contrast, most systems in this book have identified coding categories either by determining the effects on imagery of *theoretically relevant experimental manipulations*, or by comparing the responses of theoretically relevant naturally occurring groups that differ in the strength of a characteristic. In their early work on hunger, Atkinson and McClelland (1948) showed that the content of imaginative stories varied systematically with hours since last eating. They discovered, however, *that the kinds of imagery changes that occurred with increasing hunger were not necessarily the changes they would have expected*. Thus, in subsequently deriving scoring systems for achievement and other "psychogenic" needs, they let the effects of their experimental manipulations determine the scoring categories. *Whatever kinds of imagery changed as a result of the manipulations defined the effect of the motive on thematic apperception and constituted the scoring categories.*

The derivation of categories for the motive-to-avoid-success scoring system represents an interesting variation of this procedure. Fleming and Horner (chapter 11) conceive of fear of success as an avoidance motive subject to conscious denial. Their results suggest that the arousal of such an inhibitory tendency may produce a *decrease* rather than an increase in diagnostic imagery categories. They also find less fear of success imagery in response to strong, as compared with weak, achievement cues.

The sensitivity of a content analytic measure to theoretically relevant manipulations represents one kind of validation of the measure. A second kind of validity (construct validity) involves the demonstration that thematic scores are related as expected to a network of theoretically relevant dependent variables.

A few of the scoring systems included here have been derived by what might be called progressive refinement of theoretically derived categories. In those systems, (e.g., conceptual/integrative complexity), the empirical results of predictions from such categories have led to revisions of both the initial theory and the scoring categories derived from the theory.

Is thematic content analysis worth the effort?

Because content analysis is a labor-intensive method, why not use a more simple and direct way of obtaining the desired information? Because associative thought tends to be more spontaneous and less self-critical than self-report, thematic apperception or other thought samples may reveal thoughts and feelings about which the subject is unwilling or unable to report, though few today would go so far as to say that thematic apperception provides "an X-Ray picture of [the] inner self" (Murray, 1943, p. 1). In addition, content analysis of preexisting verbal material permits nonreactive assessment of persons who are not available for testing (e.g., the famous or the deceased). For additional discussions of the advantages and limitations of content analytic methods, the reader is referred to chapters 3, 6, 7, 11, 21, 23, and 25. Persuasive testimony to the value of the method is provided by the remarkably rich mine of findings reported in this volume, some of which are mentioned in the sections that follow.

HIGHLIGHTS: PART I

Part I deals with general issues in thematic research beginning with Atkinson's presentation of a theory of motivation that supplies a *conceptual foundation* for the thematic apperceptive measurement of motivation. The theory provides an explanation for issues concerning internal consistency, test length, the effect of one story on the next, the measurement of temporary states versus relatively stable dispositions, and the effect on imaginative thought of a hierarchy of motives. Atkinson's conception is responsive to some of the concerns expressed early on by Feshbach (1961), Lazarus (1961), and others regarding the effect on thematic apperception of conflict, inhibition, and displacement.

Further understanding of the properties of thematic measures is provided by McClelland, Koestner, and Weinberger (chapter 3), who compare self-report measures of motives ("self-attributed motives") such as those obtained from the Personality Research Form (PRF; D. N. Jackson, 1974) with motives measured from imaginative thought ("implicit motives"). The former "predict immediate responses to structured situations," whereas the latter predict "spontaneous behavioral trends over time because of the pleasure derived from the activity itself." The authors conclude that "there is evidence that implicit and self-attributed motives are acquired in different ways at different times of life, respond generally to different types of incentives, function differently in guiding behavior, and are associated with different physiological correlates."

Emmons and King (chapter 4) broaden the discussion even more in an integrative review of the relation of thematic analysis to other current approaches to research in personality and social psychology. With respect to method, they consider the relation of information obtained from imaginative productions to that obtained by other approaches to the contents of consciousness, including personal memories, personal goals, naturally occurring thoughts (e.g., experience sampling methodology), and, more generally, "the private personality" (cf. Singer & Kolligian, 1987). They demonstrate that information obtained by other methods can be used to validate thematic measures as well as complement information obtained by thematic methods. With respect to theory, they relate the approaches to motivation, pattern, and coherence included in this volume to the approaches taken by theorists who deal with related concepts, including "nuclear scripts" (Tomkins, 1987), "core conditional patterns" (Thorne, 1989), "core conflictual relationships" (Luborsky, 1977), and "core organizing principles" (Meichenbaum & Gilmore, 1984). Emmons and King also compare approaches to personal goals, including "current concerns" (Klinger, 1978), "personal projects" (Little, 1983), "life tasks" (Cantor & Langston, 1989), and "personal strivings" (Emmons, 1989) and propose a way of thinking about the relation of personal goals to motives.

In chapter 5, McClelland demonstrates the desirability of considering *motive combinations* for the prediction of such varied phenomena as choice of work partners, risk taking, persistence, personal and marital adjustment, success in business careers, and health (including high blood pressure, the release of catecholamines, impaired immune functions, and severity of illness). Four moderator variables are shown to play an important role when used in conjunction with motive measures. *Uncertainty orientation*, described in chapter 29 by Sorrentino, Roney, and Hanna, contributes to the understanding of the relation of achievement motivation to performance. *Stances toward the environment* – see chapter 31 by Stewart & Healy – help to explain, among other things, the relation of power motivation to control of anger, heavy drinking, and organizational membership. *Activity inhibition* helps to explain whether the power motive will be expressed for selfish purposes or for the good of others, and *responsibility* – see chapter 35 by Winter – improves the prediction of long-term success in business management as well as other behavioral manifestations of the power motive.

Veroff (chapter 6) reviews studies in which thematic apperceptive methods for measuring achievement, affiliation, power, and intimacy motives have been used in survey research on a cross section of the American population. Survey topics include mental health, marriage, parenthood, work, and Catholic–Protestant motivation differences. Results from similar surveys done in 1957 and in 1976 are compared. Veroff discusses various problems that can arise, and recommends procedures and pictures (see appendix II) for the use of thematic apperceptive measures in survey research.

The further extension of the method "to analyze archival historical materials, personal and cultural documents, and everyday verbal material such as conversations, reported dreams, and even transcriptions of television programs" is described by Winter (chapter 7). By using preexisting or naturally occurring verbal material, an investigator can study persons or groups that cannot or will not be tested directly, that are too large to be tested (whole cultures), or in whom testing may arouse unwanted reactions. Problems in history, political science, and economics become amenable to study by this approach. For example, achievement motivation has been related to economic development (see chapter 9), and integrative complexity (chapters 27 and 28) has been related to professional eminence, political leadership and ideology, and conflict and war. Explanatory style (see chapters 25 and 26) has also been related to the functioning of political leaders as well as to accounts of events in newspapers and to therapy transcripts.

Compared with the early development of many thematic measures, there is an *increased complexity in current theory and research*. Regarding earlier research, reservations had been expressed from both clinical and personological perspectives about the thematic apperceptive measurement of single variables taken out of the context of the rich information provided in a set of stories about the story writer (Carlson, 1989; Henry, 1961). And D. E. Hunt (1980) called for a conception of the whole person "to remind us of the context within which the single variable part operates" (p. 448).

It is true that many of the approaches taken in this book are neither clinical nor personological, and that they do not attempt to make use of all the information contained in each story. Reflecting the influence of experimental and differential psychology, research with these systems has tended to assess one or more nomothetic variables in groups of subjects. However, the approaches of McAdams (chapter 15), Winter (chapters 7, 21, and 35), and Suedfeld, Tetlock, and Streufert (chapter 27) have been used extensively for the study of particular individuals, and the research of Peterson (chapter 25) and his associates extends to clinically relevant studies of individuals. Winter's discussion of idiographic studies of individuals shows that thematic scoring systems may be used "to make inferences about . . . particular individuals, as part of a systematic psychobiography or personality portrait." Winter reviews studies of political leaders that have employed several of the motive measures included in this volume, as well as the conceptual/integrative complexity, and explanatory style coding systems.

Moreover, the present volume reveals a clear trend away from single-variable research. As McClelland (chapter 5) puts it: "To do justice to the complexity of personality we need to consider many aspects acting simultaneously. We investigate motives one at a time primarily to validate our measures and learn about them, not because we think they act in isolation. Furthermore, different tasks arouse different motives or motive combinations. So we need to know what cues in the situation elicit different motives." He points out that combinations of motives reveal properties of persons that are not predictable from motives considered separately.

Atkinson (chapter 2) takes into account a *hierarchy of motives* in the individual as they interact with situations over time. He considers both approach and inhibitory tendencies, and employs computer simulation to accommodate the complexity of a model in which many aspects of the person and the situation are considered simultaneously over time.

McClelland, Koestner, and Weinberger (chapter 3) show that the inclusion of self-report measures of motives (self-attributed motives) *together with* thematic measures can improve the prediction of some types of behavior. For example, "the n Achievement variable by itself gives a poor indication of the area of life in which a person will strive to do better or be entrepreneurial. Self-attributed motives, plans, and goals are needed to show the direction in which the achievement motive will turn." Similarly, Emmons and King (chapter 4) recommend the use of a variety of methods *in addition to* the storytelling method for studying personal goals and "the private personality." Veroff (chapter 6) illustrates the value of multiple-variable analyses in survey research, and Winter (chapter 7) recommends multiple-variable assessment in the study of texts.

Veroff also calls attention to the important role of the social context in prediction and understanding. He employs context as a moderator in his analysis, and he uses pictures depicting relatively universal social situations in order not to neglect the context in which members of a particular gender, social, or age group express a given motive.

The general issues discussed in part I are followed in part II by coding systems that fall into three classifications: motives, attribution and cognitive orientations, and psychosocial orientations.

Motive scoring systems

The motive scoring systems fall into three clusters relating to achievement, affiliation, and power.

ACHIEVEMENT-RELATED SYSTEMS. Theory and research regarding achievement-related motives are presented in chapters on the achievement motive, the motive to avoid success, and uncertainty orientation. In chapter 9, McClelland and Koestner describe the original development of the achievement motive scoring system and report cross-cultural replications and studies showing that the same scoring categories are applicable for females as well as for males. Recent research developments include studies of contingent paths to future goals, careers and occupations, self-concept, health, and collective levels of achievement motivation. Theory and research on the achievement motive are also discussed in chapters 2, 3, 6, and 7, and reliability issues are discussed in chapter 8.

Achievement situations may arouse not only the motive to approach success but *avoidance* motives as well. Atkinson (chapter 2) conceives of motivation to avoid failure as an inhibitory tendency that weakens, at least temporarily, the expression of the achievement tendency. Another such avoidance tendency is motivation to avoid success. Fleming and Horner (chapter 11) believe this type of motivation may be particularly likely to be aroused in women in competitive situations and should be taken into consideration in order to make sense of the behavior of women in such situations. Horner and Fleming (chapter 12) present a new version of the fear-of-success scoring system that was developed, in part, as a response to questions raised about the original system (Horner, 1968).

Also relevant to the understanding of achievement behavior is *uncertainty orientation* (chapter 29), which acts as a moderator variable influencing the relation of achievement motivation to risk taking and performance. The influence on achievement behavior of such situationally aroused factors as fear of failure, fear of success, and uncertainty orientation helps to make sense of some of the apparently conflicting findings in the literature on achievement motivation.

Yet another perspective on achievement tendencies is provided by the theory of *personal causation*. In chapter 23, deCharms describes another type of motivation that affects achievement behavior, as well as situational factors that enhance or diminish sought-after origin experiences.

AFFILIATION-RELATED SYSTEMS. Three systems concern affiliative tendencies: affiliation, intimacy, and affiliative trust–mistrust. The *n* Affiliation scoring system (chapters 13 and 14) was developed to measure a motive to establish, maintain, or restore positive affective relations with another person or persons. A great deal of research supports the construct validity of the measure, especially if it is interpreted to reflect not so much a tendency to approach affiliation as a tendency to avoid rejection.

To get at the positive, approach aspects of affiliative motivation, McAdams (chapters 15 and 16) developed a measure of intimacy motivation. Intimacy refers to a "recurrent preference or readiness for experiences of warm, close, and communicative interaction with other persons." Although this is a relatively recent system, a large body of research supports its construct validity. For example, intimacy scores are related to psychosocial adjustment, affiliative thoughts, feelings and behavior, and self-disclosure.

Reflecting Erikson's ideas about the development of *basic trust* during the oral period, the affiliative trust–mistrust system (chapters 17 and 18) assesses the strength of two kinds of feelings or sentiments about affiliative relationships: *trust* refers to seeing relationships as positive and enjoyable, *mistrust* to regarding relationships with negativity and cynicism. The system was developed to measure affiliative thoughts and feelings associated with the functioning of the immune system. Two independent subscales for trust and mistrust were derived. Construct validity studies show separate and combined subscale scores to be associated with such things as affiliative life changes, immune function, self-reported health, and parental feeding practices in the oral stage.

POWER-RELATED SYSTEMS. In developing the original *n* Power scoring system, Veroff (chapter 19) conceived of the power motive as a concern with having the means to influence others. Types of imagery characteristic of power motivation in males were identified and later cross-validated with females. Scores for *n* Power were found to be related to assertive behavior under certain conditions, and in national surveys Veroff found power to be related to marital problems, parent–adolescent relationships, and concern over sexual identity. He interpreted the pattern of results as indicating that the scores reflected *fear of weakness* more than a positive desire for power.

A subsequent measure of the power motive was developed by Winter (chapter 21) to assess a *positive* concern with having an impact on other people. Winter tells how the revised measure was derived and why thematic apperception is a particularly appropriate way of assessing this motive. The measure is applicable for males and females and for a wide range of ages, ethnic groups, and cultures. Power is considered a relatively stable disposition whose expression depends on other personality and situational factors (including social structure and culture). Possible origins of power motivation are considered, and key validity studies are reviewed showing the relation of the power motive to occupations, aggression, profligate behavior, and stress and illness. Winter and Veroff recommend the use of both power measures in future research in the expectation that power-related phenomena will be more fully understood by determining approach, avoidant, or ambivalent orientations toward power.

Scoring systems for attribution and cognitive orientations

Included in this section are the coding systems for personal causation, explanatory style, conceptual/integrative complexity, and uncertainty orientation.

PERSONAL CAUSATION. Heider's (1958) seminal ideas concerning internal versus external locus of causality influenced the conception of both personal causation and explanatory style. According to deCharms (chapter 23), every person experiences himself or herself as a cause, that is, has *origin* experiences. DeCharms discusses the relationship of the origin concept to other concepts such as locus of control and intrinsic motivation. The origin concept refers to a personal disposition when used to describe individual differences in the extent to which people seek origin experiences. However, "the measure . . . was developed primarily to gauge *changes* in experience, *not as a personality measure.*" In a large project teachers were trained to enhance personal causation in inner-city children. The treatment produced significant increases in origin scores and in the percentage of students graduating from high school.

EXPLANATORY STYLE. For Peterson (chapter 25) the term *style* refers to cross-event consistency in the explanations that individuals give for good or bad events. Such styles play an important role in the reformulated theory of learned helplessness by accounting for more or less debilitating reactions to uncontrollable events. Peterson describes the content analysis measure of explanatory style and its relation to a self-report measure of explanatory style. With the former, a wide range of verbal material can be analyzed to provide information about persons who may differ in social class, gender, ethnicity, and psychopathology. In one study, explanatory style for bad events was found to be relatively stable over a 50-year age span ($r = .54$). Construct validity studies have dealt with predictions of mood shifts in psychotherapy, depressive symptoms, precursors of physical illness, and success of presidential candidates.

CONCEPTUAL/INTEGRATIVE COMPLEXITY. As described by Suedfeld, Tetlock, and Streufert (chapter 27), *conceptual/integrative complexity* most closely resembles a cognitive style in its emphasis on the structure, rather than the content, of thought. The authors assume that complexity can be modified by experience and motivation as well as by organizational climates. They are less concerned with complexity as a trait than with state complexity – "the level of differentiation and integration shown in thought and behavior in a particular situation and context." A vast body of research on complexity and metacomplexity is cited that employs nonarchival and archival content analysis to study attitudes, communication, performance in work situations, social policy decisions, aging, political ideology, and many other topics.

UNCERTAINTY ORIENTATION. Sorrentino, Roney, and Hanna (chapter 29) challenge the premise that all people are motivated by a need to know and understand. They propose that some persons (the uncertainty-oriented) "are primarily motivated to seek clarity through mastery of uncertainty, while the certainty-oriented are motivated to maintain clarity by adhering to what is already known." Uncertainty orientation is assumed to function as an unconscious screening device affecting the way in which a person engages a situation. For example, in an early study, Sorrentino and Hewitt (1984) found that uncertainty-oriented persons chose tasks that provided information about their ability, while certainty-oriented persons chose tasks that gave no new information about ability. Subsequent studies dealt with issues in social cognition, social comparison, social categorization, and memory and recall. The authors conclude that "current theorizing in many of these areas only accounts for the behavior of uncertainty-oriented persons. Certainty-oriented persons behave quite differently and do not conform to the rational model of human behavior."

Scoring systems for psychosocial orientations

In consultation with Stewart and Winter, the remaining three scoring systems – psychological stances, self-definition, and responsibility – were classified as psychosocial orientations.

PSYCHOLOGICAL STANCES. Research by Stewart and Healy (chapter 31) on psychological stances toward the environment grew out of earlier research on stressful life events. Four stances are identified reflecting concern with dependency–receptivity, autonomy, assertiveness, and integration. In one sense, the stances "define a continuum at one end of which the individual is depicted as at risk of being entirely submerged in the environment, and at the other end of which the individual is depicted as in some stable and neutral relation to the environment." While most people experience some concerns characteristic of each stance, one or another may predominate. The content analysis system has been used in the study of adaptation to life changes such as graduation, marriage, parenthood, and divorce. The innovative framework presented in chapters 31 and 32 has provocative implications not only for personality growth and adjustment but also for the ways in which motives are expressed by individuals in whom different stances predominate (cf. chapter 5).

SELF-DEFINITION AND SOCIAL DEFINITION. In chapter 33 Stewart describes research on self-definition and social definition conceived as a personal style. "The measure . . . aims to assess the degree to which an individual is inclined to accept social definitions, or to attempt to create personal self-definitions." A distinctive feature of Stewart's approach is that this variable is measured not by means of content, but by means of *narrative style*. Regardless of content, "stories told by the 'self-defining' criterion group were characterized by explicit causal statements, and by a sequence of 'reasons' . . . resulting in effective actions or plans for action. . . . Stories told by the 'socially defined' criterion group were characterized . . . by causelessness . . . , a sequence of actions resulting . . . in feelings or mental states, and ineffective actions." The self-defining person regards herself or himself as capable of effective action and does not take inappropriate responsibility for events.

Women high in self-definition had distinctive family backgrounds (e.g., employed mothers) and reported engaging in more activities that were counternormative for women. Longitudinal studies revealed a connection between self-definition and social definition assessed in college and later career patterns in women and counternormative behaviors (e.g., dual-career families) for men. Self-definition was also shown to be related to coping capacity and coping strategies and to lower emotional distress in patients with cancer. As might be expected, some environments are more likely than others to support and strengthen self-definition.

RESPONSIBILITY. Winter (chapter 35) regards responsibility as a feeling of "inner obligation to do what is right." The measure is unusual in that it was developed to serve as a moderator variable. Responsibility is conceived of as "a complex cluster of cognitions (beliefs and values) that act to channel, shunt, or even block the ways in which all motives are expressed" (e.g., channeling men's and women's power motivation into constructive behaviors, such as leadership, rather than profligate behaviors, such as drinking to excess). Research is reported regarding the socialization of responsibility and the relation of responsibility to the expression of power and aggression.

CROSS-SITUATIONAL CONSISTENCY OF BEHAVIOR

Numerous chapters discuss, or have implications for, the question of whether *relatively stable personality dispositions* are expected to lead to behavior that is consistent across situations. These implications will be considered first for motive dispositions and then for orientations and styles.

The following points provide a framework for the discussion: (a) because the term *consistency* tends to have value connotations, it may be preferable to speak of behavior as being more or less variable across situations; (b) there is some variability of behavior over time *even under similar conditions* (with some persons being more variable than others); (c) there is a great deal of situational specificity of behavior and only a modest degree of generality attributable to some types of person variables; (d) an adequate theory requires a statement of the situational factors affecting the behavioral expression of dispositions; (e) cognitive assessments of the situation mediate the effects of situations on the activation and expression of dispositions; and (f) cross-situational variability will be affected by the status of *all* of a person's dispositions, not just the one on which the researcher happens to be focusing.

Motives and variability

The following points regarding motives and consistency are either stated or implied by various chapters.

1. An individual's assessment of situational factors, such as expectancies and incentives, affects the activation and expression of motive dispositions.

2. Striving for the satisfaction of a motive may lead to different behaviors in different situations (i.e., inconsistency). For example, depending on the perceived difficulty of a task, strong achievement motivation may be manifested *as either high or low persistence* (see chapter 9).

3. Behavior in the *same* situation may vary during a period of time. That is, even given a stable personality and a constant environment, behavior is expected to change (see chapter 2; also Reuman, 1982). For example, a person who is reading may stop and make a telephone call without any change in the external situation.

4. The expression of one motive is affected by the extent to which others are aroused. For example, a person who is usually affiliative may not stop to chat with his neighbor if he is very hungry.

5. Motives affect the kinds of situations (activities, careers) people choose to be in. For example, a person with a strong intimacy motive should more often be in situations that permit a feeling of intimacy than a person with a weak intimacy motive. (For evidence, see chapter 15.)

Thus, motivation theory leads to the expectation of variability of thought and behavior (i.e., inconsistency) both across situations and within similar situations over time. It also leads to the expectation that a person will engage repeatedly in motive-relevant behavior (consistency). The apparent paradox is resolved by assuming that: (a) behavior that is inconsistent at the phenotypic level may be consistent (serve the same purpose) at the genotypic level, and (b) behavior will tend to be consistent because people, if free to choose, tend to be repeatedly in the same types of situations. Furthermore, because motivation is assumed to affect the amount of *time* one spends in motive-relevant activities, *over the long term*, motives should predict consistency of behavioral outcomes such as cumulative achievement (see Atkinson, 1974) or career success (see chapter 3, this volume).

Orientations, styles, and consistency

The dispositions classified in this handbook as cognitive and psychosocial orientations and cognitive and attributional styles tend to reflect personality structure more than dynamics, though two of the systems (origin and uncertainty orientation) have an explicitly motivational component. Styles and orientations tend to function by affecting information processing and/or by regulating the expression of motives. For example, uncertainty orientation involves a cognitive assessment of degree of uncertainty in a situation followed by approach or avoidance of uncertainty.

Although the approaches to orientations and styles differ in many respects, there are some commonalities among them. First, like the motive variables, the manifestation of these dispositions is regarded as a function of the situation as well as the person. For example, persons differ in the extent to which they seek origin experiences, and situations differ in the extent to which they permit origin experiences. The role of the situation is given particular emphasis by Suedfeld, Streufert, and Tetlock (chapter 27), who are primarily concerned not with conceptual/integrative complexity as a relatively stable trait, but with *state* complexity in a particular situation and context.

Second, these dispositions are not regarded as immutable; they are thought to be altered by such factors as important events, training, or psychotherapy. Third, like motives, at least some of these dispositions influence individuals' choice of situations. For example, women high in self-definition were more likely to engage in political action and choose unconventional careers than women low in self-definition. Finally, although the concept of a *style* implies cross-situational consistency of functioning, there is a recognition that some people are more consistent across situations in thought and/or behavior than others (see, e.g., chapter 25).

We might have expected that constructs reflective of cognitive or personality structure would lead to relative consistency of thought and behavior across situations whereas dynamic constructs would lead to more variable behavior. Instead we find, in the approaches described here, similar implications for cross-situational consistency for both types of variables – namely, thought and behavior are, to a considerable extent, situationally determined (and therefore variable), but, to the extent that the same kinds of situations are selected repeatedly and construed in a characteristic way, a substantial amount of consistency is also expected. Somewhat different aspects of thought and behavior are involved, however, for motives, styles, and orientations.

In sum, considering the fact that dispositions are not immutable, and that situations are what they are construed to be, and that thought and behavior are a function of *all* of a person's dispositions, we find that the question about whether behavior is or is not cross-situationally consistent, like the question about heredity versus environment, implies a simpler answer than is possible.

WHITHER THEMATIC ANALYSIS?

The research and theory presented in this volume answer some, but not all, of the questions about the thematic apperceptive method that have been raised over the years. There remains a need to understand more completely the determinants of thematic apperception and to use that understanding to devise more effective uses of the method.

In developing a more complete theory of the measuring instrument, it may be possible to take advantage of research in cognitive psychology on such relevant concepts as propositional and narrative thinking (Bruner, 1986; Howard, 1991), episodic and semantic memory (Kinsbourne, 1987; Tulving, 1983), analytic and syncretic cognition (Buck, 1985), priming (Tulving & Schacter, 1990), construct availability and accessibility (Higgins, 1990), and automatic, unintended thought (Uleman & Bargh, 1989). Similarly research on affect, such as that of Isen (1987) on the effects of mood on subjective probabilities, memory, and creativity, seems highly relevant. It is hoped that one effect of the body of work presented here will be to stimulate thought about possible contributions from other areas of psychology to the measurement of person variables by means of content analysis.

PART I

General issues

2 Motivational determinants of thematic apperception

JOHN W. ATKINSON

Thematic apperceptive measurement of motivation now has a solid conceptual foundation, something it lacked when David McClelland led the vanguard in establishing its validity (McClelland, Atkinson, Clark, & Lowell, 1953). A new theory of motivation (Atkinson & Birch, 1970, 1974, 1978) has overcome the conceptual limitations of both statistical test theory and traditional motivational theories by emphasizing the temporal continuity of behavior and its underlying motivational structure. I will show how old puzzles about thematic apperception have been resolved and the old vision of its promise reawakened by reconsidering the method within the new theoretical framework.

Skepticism about the scientific worth of this projective method has been sustained by two arguments. One is the criticism that the Thematic Apperception Test (TAT) n Achievement (need for achievement) score lacks acceptable reliability when one considers the lack of internal consistency among scores obtained from one story and the next in the set from which an individual's total n Achievement score is obtained (Entwisle, 1972). Reliability is considered the *sine qua non* of validity according to the presumptions of test theory. The other argument derives from the inherent complexity of the relationship between the strength of a motive and its behavioral expression, something about which we became very much aware in the course of developing the theory of achievement motivation (Atkinson & Feather, 1966; Atkinson & Raynor, 1974, 1978). To observers not committed to resolving the puzzle of the motivation of behavior, the symptoms of the complexity of the problem are mistakenly treated as no more than a

This chapter was written during my term as a visiting fellow at the Educational Research Center of the University of Leyden, in 1980. My sincere thanks are extended to its director, Hans Crombag, for making it possible for me to study and to interact with others in a context so close to my present theoretical interests.

Originally published as: Atkinson, J. W. (1982). Motivational determinants of thematic apperception. In A. Stewart (Ed.), *Motivation and society* (pp. 3–40). San Francisco: Jossey-Bass Inc., Publishers. Reprinted by permission of the author and the publisher.

21

bewildering set of inconsistencies that violate an unquestioned presumption. One should expect consistency in different behavioral expressions of anything considered a stable personality trait. Given our present theoretical perspective, we can see that the first issue is really an instance of the second. So in focusing on the critical issue of test reliability in the discussion that follows, I speak to both.

According to the logic of traditional test theory, each behavioral incident (such as the successive stories in a Thematic Apperception Test) is treated as a discrete and independent incident in the life of an individual. It is gratuitously presumed that individual differences in some temporally stable and transitutional personality trait (for example, the achievement motive) imply comparable temporal and transitutional consistencies in behavior. All this can be summed up in the simple expression, obtained score = true score ± random error, where the true score (or expected behavior) corresponding to a particular strength of motive is presumed to be constant in each of the successive stories of a Thematic Apperception Test. Substantial variability in the obtained scores is then attributed to substantial random error of measurement.

In contrast, the principles of the dynamics of action, to which we shortly turn, were introduced to explain variable behavior, a simple change from one activity to another even in a constant environment (Atkinson & Birch, 1970). When applied to the question of what is expected in the successive stories of a Thematic Apperception Test, the new theory of motivation specifies how a *stable* personality disposition, strength of achievement motive, is expected to be expressed behaviorally in systematically *variable* amounts of time thinking and/or writing about achievement in successive stories even before consideration of the question of random error in measurement. That, simply put, is why the new motivational principles have provided a coherent explanation of how it is possible for the test as a whole to have construct validity without reliability as traditionally defined. Computer simulations of thematic apperceptive measurement of achievement motivation based on the new principles have shown that the expected amount of time an individual spends imagining achieving during the whole temporal period of a four- to six-story test can provide a valid measure of the strength of the motive being expressed without test reliability as it is conventionally defined (Atkinson, Bongort, & Price, 1977). The more important outcome of this work has been to expose flaws in the foundation of classical test theory, long taken for granted as something akin to a settled creed (Atkinson, 1981).

The point of computer simulation of a motivational problem is simple enough. It is to apply the relatively simple principles of the theory of motivation to antecedent conditions that are too complex to think about without the deductive capacity of the computer. Thus, for example, we may ask the question: How much time should these thirty individuals who differ in strength of achievement motive spend thinking about achievement in response to each picture in this set of six pictures? The program applies the principles of the dynamics of action to deduce the systematic changes in the motivational state of each hypothetical subject and, in so doing, to spell out precise behavioral implications for each subject. The results may then be treated as equivalent to data collected using a perfectly reliable measuring instrument. This spells out the theoretically expected result prior to consideration of the error of measurement that one normally confronts in empirical research. In the case of computer simulations of thematic apperceptive measurement of motivation, we use the simulated results (given an advanced motivational psychology) to comprehend and interpret the results of many earlier empirical investigations.

THE DYNAMICS OF ACTION AND THEMATIC APPERCEPTION

The basic concepts of the new dynamics of action (see, for example, Atkinson & Birch, 1978) can be conveyed as easily in reference to the stream of imaginative thought and behavior as to the stream of overt action. Both are characterized by continuity rather than by the discreteness of the episodes of traditional reactive psychology, and both are characterized by change.

The *kind* of activity (or *content* of the stream) changes from one to another and still another, even when a person's immediate environment is constant for a substantial period of time, as on a rainy Saturday morning at home or a sunny Sunday afternoon at the beach (Atkinson & Birch, 1978, pp. 24–26). This variability is an essential characteristic of operant or voluntary behavior. It is *emitted*, as Skinner has always argued, rather than *elicited* as a reaction to a given environment or stimulus situation. The dynamics of action is a theory of operant behavior. It *explains* the otherwise mysterious behavior-controlling influence of the immediate environment (the discriminative stimuli) in Skinner's radically empirical behaviorism.

So also does the *content* of thought change in what is otherwise a continuous stream of thought, even when the person is continuously exposed to the same immediate environment or stimulus situation. McClelland (1973) called attention to the operant character of imaginative behavior in his continuing effort to get personologists to distinguish the potential value of imaginative (operant) behavior from that of explicitly self-descriptive (respondent) behavior in measuring motives (McClelland, 1958a, 1980). In a recent scanning of William James's *Principles of Psychology* (1890), I was amazed to see how thoroughly and eloquently he had anticipated the "new" view, which stresses continuity in behavior and in the underlying structure of the motivational state, in his introspective analysis of the stream of con-

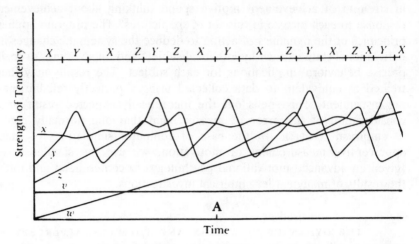

Fig. 2.1. An example of a stream of overt action or imaginative behavior and the systematic change in the strength of tendencies that produced it (see text). (Adapted and extended from Seltzer, 1973)

sciousness. James wrote: "*Within each personal consciousness thought is sensibly continuous.* . . . Consciousness . . . does not appear to itself chopped up in bits. Such words as 'chain' or 'train' do not describe it fitly as it presents itself in the first instance. It is nothing jointed; it flows. A 'river' or a 'stream' are the metaphors by which it is most naturally described. *In talking of it hereafter let us call it the stream of thought, of consciousness, or of subjective life*" (pp. 237–239).

But what of the "sudden *contrasts* in the quality of successive segments of the stream of thought" that James acknowledged. His reply: "The things [*contents*] are discrete and discontinuous; they do pass before us in a train or chain, making often explosive appearances and rending each other in twain. But their comings and goings and contrasts no more break the flow of the thought that thinks them than they break the time and the space in which they lie. . . . The transition between the thought of one object and the thought of another is no more a break in *thought* than a joint in a bamboo is a break in the wood" (p. 240).

The kind of stream of behavior (or of thought) that we have been generating, employing a computer program for the dynamics of action while holding both personal and situational (or environmental) influences constant, is shown in the continuous line with the various segments *X*, *Y* and *Z* along the top of Figure 2.1. This could be the observable stream of operant imaginative behavior produced in a given setting by a particular person when presented a particular picture in a Thematic Apperception Test.

Below the observable stream of behavior, to which we apply our method of motivational content analysis, is the continuous yet systematically chang-ing motivational state of the individual. It is composed, in this simple case, of increases and/or decreases (or mere persistence) in the strength of separate tendencies to do (or to imagine) the different hypothetical behav-iors v, w, x, y, and z. The strongest among the competing tendencies is expressed in the content of the stream of behavior.

We have confidence in employing computer simulations to comprehend what is happening from moment to moment in thematic apperception because we know that the principles of the dynamics of action adequately encompass what is known about (1) the behavioral effects of previous reward and punishment in animal research and (2) the experimental facts concerning individual differences in achievement-oriented behavior (Atkinson & Birch, 1970, 1974, 1978). Furthermore, computer simulation has already been used effectively to analyze other problems: how the con-tent of thought can motivate overt action (Birch, Atkinson, & Bongort, 1974); why the preference of persons motivated to achieve has always peaked when subjective probability of success is somewhat less than .50 rather than exactly .50 (Kuhl & Blankenship, 1979; Revelle & Michaels, 1976); the relationship between both consummatory value of success and substitution to task difficulty (Blankenship, 1982); the motivational deter-minants of decision time as it is influenced by the way content of thought may be implicated in deciding (Kuhl & Atkinson, 1986); and most important of all for our present discussion, the motivational determinants of allocation of time among competing alternatives in operant behavior (Atkinson & Birch, 1978, pp. 306–312, 362–366) as described in the Matching Law of de Villiers and Herrnstein (1976). In other words, the new theory and its computer program (Bongort, 1975; Seltzer, 1973; Seltzer & Sawusch, 1974) were not especially constructed to explain thematic apperceptive measure-ment of motivation.

The key to understanding the discussion that follows is to recognize the most fundamental difference between traditional conceptions of motivation, which define what we have called "the episodic paradigm," and the new "stream of behavior paradigm" (Atkinson & Birch, 1978, p. 375). Since the early theory of achievement motivation (Atkinson, 1957; Atkinson & Feather, 1966) was simply an application of the more general cognitive theories of Tolman, Lewin, and the decision theorists to the domain of achievement-related activity, we shall refer to it to make our points. According to that theory the strength of the tendency to achieve success in a particular activity (T_S) was considered the product of the strength of motive to achieve (M_S), the strength of expectancy or subjective probability of succeeding in a given activity (P_s), and the incentive value of success of that activity (I_s), that is, $T_s = M_S \times P_s \times I_s$.

Call to mind the ring toss game. The individual is confronted with a stimulus situation defining alternative activities that differ in difficulty (P_s).

The "traditional" conception said, in effect, that as soon as the individual was exposed to the ring toss game there would be elicited, *instantaneously*, a number of competing tendencies whose different strengths would remain static (as defined by the product of the three determinants) except for the kind of *random* moment-to-moment oscillations proposed by Cartwright and Festinger (1943). These "wobbling" effective tendencies would determine the individual's moment-by-moment preferences. The tendency that was expected to be strongest in its static level, according to the product of its three determinants, would probably, but not necessarily, win out in the competition for behavioral expression because of the random oscillations. The role of random oscillation both in this cognitive theory and in traditional *S-R* behavior theory (Hull, 1943) is comparable to the role of random error of measurement in classical test theory, as expressed in the simple equation, obtained score = true score ± error (de Groot, 1969). What is observed in behavior is not always quite what was expected to happen.

In the new conception, the dynamics of action, the interaction of personality (M_S) and immediate environment ($P_s \times I_s$) – a specification of what Lewin had summarized as the product of personality (P) and environment (E) in his classic equation for predicting behavior, $B = f(P, E)$ – determines *the arousability* of the tendency (T_s), and not its initial and static strength. The arousability, or rate of arousal of a tendency, is represented by the different initial slopes of the curves for tendencies y, z, v, and w in Figure 2.1. Stable individual differences in personality (a motive) and/or the effects of the immediate environment, given previous learning experiences in that environment (as in operant conditioning), are now coordinated with the arousability of the inclination to engage in a certain kind of activity, not its expected static strength in a given setting.

Our notion is that the magnitude of *instigating force* (F) for a particular activity accounts for how rapidly a tendency to engage in that activity (T) is aroused and strengthened on a given occasion. One is *exposed* to the instigating forces of a particular situation. The other important factor is time, the duration of exposure to the instigating force (t). Thus, in the dynamics of action, the old idea $T_s = M_S \times . P_s \times I_s$ is replaced by a new idea, $F_s = M_S \times P_s \times I_s$, for the simplest case.

Returning to Figure 2.1, we see that when a tendency becomes dominant (that is, becomes the strongest among simultaneously aroused and competing tendencies) it is expressed in behavior. This expression of a tendency in behavior, as in catharsis, is what reduces its strength. The *consummatory force* (C) of the activity depends, we think, on two factors: the nature of the activity and the strength of the tendency being expressed in that activity. We speak of the *consummatory value* of a particular activity (c), having in mind that the tendency to eat is reduced more rapidly by one kind of food than by eating some other kind, that succeeding reduces the tendency to achieve more than failing, and so on. We generalize this idea and presume that all activities have some consummatory value (c). They differ only in degree. So-called goal activities presumably have more consummatory value than so-called instrumental or preparatory activities. And, as mentioned already, we consider the strength of the tendency being expressed in the activity as the other important determinant of the consummatory force (C) of an activity, that is, $C = c \times T$. The instigating force (F) and the consummatory force (C) produce changes in the strength of a particular tendency (T).

The newest thing we have learned from empirical research guided by computer simulation is that the consummatory value of success (c_s) is greater when one succeeds at an easy task than when one succeeds at a difficult task (Blankenship, 1982). In everyday terms, this means that tendencies to achieving activities are more "turned off" or satisfied by a success when P_s at the task is .70 than when P_s at the task is .30. According to the theory of achievement motivation, the instigating forces for these two tasks – easy and difficult – are equivalent.

Given our conception that the change in the strength of a tendency depends on these two forces, one representing the effect of the stimulus situation and the other the effect of the occurrence of the activity itself, that is, $dT/dt = F - C$, and continuing to refer to Figure 2.1 as if it represented the stream of imaginative activity instigated by a particular picture in a Thematic Apperception Test, we have the following three implications. When $F > C$, the strength of a tendency (T) will increase. This is the case at the outset for T_y, T_z, and T_w in Figure 2.1. They are instigated by cues of the picture to which the individual is exposed but are not, as yet, being expressed in imaginative behavior, so $C = 0$ for each of them. When $C > F$, the strength of a tendency (T) will decrease. This is shown most clearly for T_y, shortly after activity y is initiated. Finally, when $F = C$, the strength of the tendency (T) will tend to become stable. This is the case for T_x, which is being expressed in activity x at the beginning of our interval of observation.

Given these implications, combined with our notion that $C = c \times T$, we should expect that in a given situation a particular tendency expressed in behavior will rise or fall in strength, but that sooner or later, if the activity continues, the strength of the tendency will become stable. Why? Because if $F > C$ at the outset and T increases, then C will also increase (because $C = c \times T$). Or if $C > F$ and T decreases as a result, then C will also decrease. In both cases, sooner or later $F = C$ and at a level equivalent to F/c for that activity. (The expression $C = F$ may be written $c \times T = F$, which is equivalent to $T = F/c$. A tendency, T, will increase rapidly and ultimately become stable at a high level when F is strong but will increase less rapidly and become stable at a lower level when F is weak.) This guarantees variability of behavior in a constant environment without any need to introduce the concept of random oscillation as in the traditional, episodic

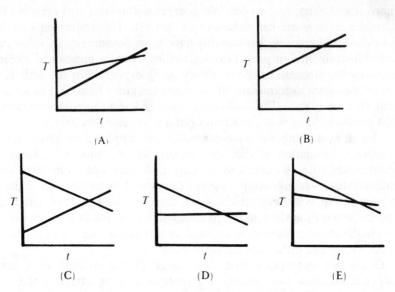

Fig. 2.2. Ways in which a change in the relative strength of two tendencies can come about during an interval of time (see text). (From Atkinson & Birch, 1970, 1974, 1978)

theories. Sooner or later some other initially subordinate tendency will become dominant, unless no other activity is instigated in a particular situation – a very unlikely prospect.

In fact, the conceptual analysis of a simple change from one activity to another *in a constant environment* is what suggested the new conception of the functional significance of exposure to "a stimulus" (that it controls the rate of arousal of a tendency and not its static level) and of the functional significance of "the response" of traditional psychology (that it influences the rate of diminution of a tendency). The logic of the principle of a simple change in activity can be simply stated in reference to the several logical possibilities shown in Figure 2.2 (Atkinson & Birch, 1970, Ch. 1).

A living individual is always doing something when an observer takes note. The dominant tendency (in Skinnerian terms, "inclination") is expressed in behavior. That activity A is already in progress implies that initially

$$T_{A_i} > T_{B_i},$$

where B is the next activity to occur. When, at some point in time, activity A ceases and B is finally initiated,

$$T_{B_f} > T_{A_f}.$$

In every instance shown in Figure 2.2, the time (t) to change from A to B (which represents a measure of persistence of A and latency of B) is given by the simple equation

$$t = T_{A_f} - T_{B_i}/F_B.$$

All measurable aspects of behavior that reduce to the questions *which activity* will occur and *when* can be deduced from the principle of a change in activity (Birch, 1972): initiation of an activity, persistence of an activity, and choice among alternatives (as shown in the *initial* preference for y instead of z in Figure 2.1). To get beyond a single change in activity and to generate a stream of operant behavior, one must assume that there are temporal lags in the initiation and cessation of the full consummatory force of an activity. In addition, one is more continuously exposed to cues producing the instigating force for the dominant tendency that is motivating the ongoing activity than to cues instigating other activities instead. Being exposed to an instigating force for something less than 100 percent of the time when another activity is occurring is equivalent to being exposed continuously to an instigating force having a somewhat lower average magnitude, as shown in Figure 2.1. These last two concepts, consummatory lags and selective attention, allow us to deduce the additional behavioral measures that can be taken from the molar stream of operant behavior: relative frequency, operant level (or rate) of an activity, and most important for our discussion, the allocation of time among various activities – that is, the percentage of time spent expressing one tendency (as in a TAT story) instead of others.

The principle of a change in activity specifies both how variations in persisting strength of an already aroused tendency and how the rate of its arousal, attributable to direct exposure to some stimulus, jointly influence the expression of the tendency in imaginative behavior. Look again at Figure 2.1, and compare the fate of T_z, having greater initial strength, and T_w for an explanation of why experimental arousal of a tendency prior to a Thematic Apperception Test, as in the earliest validation studies, should then immediately influence the content of imaginative thought in response to pictures. And while considering the figure again, notice that a comparison of the slopes of T_y and of T_z provides a model for thinking about the well-documented effects of strongly cued versus weakly cued pictures on thematic content (Atkinson, 1958a; McClelland, Atkinson, Clark, & Lowell, 1953).

There is more to the dynamics of activity. Changes in activity can occur for negative as well as positive reasons. So far, in focusing on the tendency to perform an activity or *action tendency* (T), we have attended either to the motivational implications of prior reinforcement for some activity in a given situation or to the effect of being exposed to stimulation for some activity that has been intrinsically enjoyable in the past. But prior punishment, frustration, rejection, failure – any negative outcome of an activity in a given setting – can be the antecedent of subsequent *inhibitory force* (I). This would cause the arousal of a tendency *not* to do the activity, a *negation* tendency (N), which would produce resistance to the activity by opposing and dampening the resultant action tendency $(\bar{T})$, which is what ultimately gets expressed in behavior. The resultant action tendency is simply represented as $\bar{T} = T - N$. One may recall the conflict between tendency to achieve (T_s) and to avoid failure (T_f) in the early theory of achievement motivation $(T_{res} = T_s - T_f)$.

The conception of resistance has some interesting new implications for thematic apperception. But I will put off discussing resistance in order to simplify my discussion of why we may have validity without reliability in thematic apperception and the meaning of the n Achievement score. In what follows I shall refer often to Figure 2.1. Consider Figure 2.1 an illustration of what might be expected in the stream of imaginative behavior "emitted" by an individual having a stable achievement motive (M_Y) of given strength. It will be a determinant of F_y, the rate of arousal of T_y, as would any other determinant of the instigating force to achieve, for example, future orientation (Raynor, 1969, 1974). The imaginative activity y in the figure represents the kind of concern about competition with standards of excellence that we tried to identify and code with the manual for TAT n Achievement (Atkinson, 1958a, Ch. 12; McClelland, Atkinson, Clark, & Lowell, 1953, Ch. 4).

To begin with, note that T_x, T_y, T_z, and T_v are assumed already to be aroused even before individual subjects are exposed to the first picture. Here is the very basic initial premise of the dynamics taken from Freud – the wish (tendency) once aroused will persist long after the source of its instigation is gone. So our subjects are already active in two senses when we turn our attention to them. They are engaged in some activity and also actively aroused and motivated to do many other things (in this case only three) even before exposure to the first picture of our TAT. Only T_w, which begins at zero strength, reminds us of the traditional presumption that the organism is at rest, awaiting a stimulus to goad it to react. Note that T_v persists unchanged in strength throughout the whole duration of exposure to the first picture and the writing of the first imaginative story. (This particular tendency is not instigated directly during exposure and writing, nor are many others we might have introduced but at the cost of complication. Nor is T_v increased indirectly by *displacement*, or decreased indirectly by *substitution*. These are important topics we shall take up later.)

Notice that T_y is not expressed in imaginative behavior continuously. It shares the stage with other concerns, x and z, which come up from time to time. The total amount of time expressing T_y (concern over achievement) is represented by a summation of the line segments y. The percentage of time spent thinking about achievement is represented by this total time thinking about y divided by the total time spent thinking about x, y, and z, all the other activities that occurred during the interval of the first four-minute story.

In this case, the person with a certain strength of motive, considered a stable characteristic of personality (M_Y), is expected to spend about 37 percent of the total time expressing achievement-related concern in the stream of imaginative behavior. Were the index we obtain using our present scoring system equivalent to a perfect clock, the obtained n Achievement score would be proportional to this 37 percent. But put aside the possible question of inadequacies in our present technology; that is an issue, but not the vitally important issue. We have a theoretical basis for expecting the person with a stable M_Y (which is identified in the graph with F_Y, the slope of the curve for T_y) to express achievement-related concern 37 percent of the time. One can imagine that if the motive (M_Y) were weaker, then the slope of the curve corresponding to F_y would be less steep than the one in the figure (more like that of z), the initial expression of y in the stream of thought would be delayed, and each occurrence would be of shorter duration and less frequent. In other words, the percentage of time thinking about achievement (y) would be less. In contrast, we can visualize the effect of a stronger motive (M_Y). The initial slope of T_y would be steeper, describing a more rapid arousal of the tendency. The latency of the initial achievement-related activity would be shorter than shown here. The absolute level of T_y when expressed would be higher, implying deeper involvement in the subject. The number of separate occurrences of y would be greater and the average duration longer. In sum, our subject with the stronger motive would spend more time thinking about achievement.

Now look again at the initial and final strengths of the competing action tendencies at the extreme left and right sides of Figure 2.1, respectively. At the end of the first story, and therefore at the very beginning of the second story, whatever the incentive characteristics of the second picture, T_x is stronger than it was at the beginning of the first story. So are T_z, T_y, and especially T_w. The rank order of the strengths of tendencies was T_x, T_y, T_z, T_v, T_w at the outset of the first story. But it is $T_x = T_w$, T_z, T_y, T_v when the picture for the second story is presented. So even if that second picture were *exactly equivalent* to the first one in its motivational properties (that is, if its effect were the same on the various instigating forces for v, w, x, y, z as the first picture), the content of the stream of imaginative behavior would nevertheless be different. Probably the most noticeable difference would be the early and repeated expressions of activity w, which didn't occur at all in the first story because there had been no persistent carryover from previous experiences to give T_w some initial strength for the first story.

In this hypothetical example, both determinants of the instigating forces – personal (motives) and environmental (incentives) – are presumed constant. Yet the expected imaginative behavior would be different. In other words, the assumption of stability in personality throughout the temporal interval of two successive imaginative stories does not imply an equivalent constancy in the expected behavior even if the picture stimuli were identical. This expected behavior corresponds to the *true score* in the equation of traditional test theory: obtained score (what you see and measure) = true score (what you expected to see) + random error. According to the conventional logic, individual differences in stable dispositions of personality (P) imply comparably stable and consistent differences in the expected behavior (true score). This would be observed in successive samples of behavior (tests) were it not for random error. Each test, subpart of a larger test, or item on a test, is assumed to be a discrete and independent episode in the life of a person. The variations in behavior from moment to moment are attributable to error of measurement. It is assumed to be independent from one test to the next, normally distributed, with mean zero.

The fundamental flaw in this logic is the unjustified leap from stable differences in personality to the expectation of comparably stable differences in behavior.

The very same point is easily made if one divides Figure 2.1 in half at point A on the abscissa, as if this point corresponded to the end of the first story and the beginning of a second story responding to an equivalent picture stimulus. The time spent thinking about y (achievement) is here *expected to be* 40 percent greater in the second story than in the first story though the personality disposition (M_Y) and the pictures influencing F_y (the arousal of T_y) have both remained constant.

Here, then, is the basis for the main theoretical conclusion from twenty-five computer simulations of thematic apperceptive measurements of individual differences in strength of motive under varied conditions: The construct validity of the total score does not require internal consistency (reliability). The computer input consisted of individual differences in strength of achievement motive for samples of eighteen to thirty hypothetical subjects for whom other determinants of the stream of imaginative behavior were held constant. Hypothetical subjects differed in strength of achievement motive, but were assumed equivalent in strength of competing motives or in the sum of the strengths of all motives. The incentive characteristics of pictures in a set of five to twelve differed, but were the same for all subjects in a given study. Certain parameters, such as selective attention, the consummatory lags at initiation and cessation of activities, and the relative magnitude of achievement versus other incentives in the pictures, were varied from one study to another so as to sample a range of conditions.

Table 2.1. *Expected time spent expressing tendency to achieve according to computer simulation*

Subject	Motive strength	Computer time units per picture minutes					
		A	B	C	D	E	Total
4	High (1.5)	12	8	11	24	25	80
16	Medium (1.0)	2	19	16	9	19	65
24	Low (0.5)	15	9	9	14	10	57

Source: From Atkinson, Bongort, and Price (1977, p. 13).

The simulated time spent thinking about achievement in each of a set of stories was treated as the *n* Achievement score for that story. The expected test reliability, as measured by coefficient alpha taken as an estimate of the average of all corrected split-half reliabilities for a given test (Cronbach, 1951), was computed using the simulated behaviors the way one would use the actually obtained scores in empirical research. The expected construct validity of the total time spent thinking about achievement in all the stories (the theoretically deduced *n* Achievement score for each hypothetical subject) was computed by correlating this simulated measure with the individual differences in strength of motive fed into the computer as input for the simulation. The expected internal consistency reliability could be as low as .07, .08, or .09 (with an errorless measuring instrument) and the construct validity of the conventional measure of individual differences in strength of motive could be as high as .90, .85, or .85, respectively. Table 2.1 shows why.

Table 2.1 shows the theoretically deduced or expected time spent expressing "concern over achievement" in response to each of five pictures for hypothetical subjects who are strong, moderate, and weak in strength of achievement motive (as defined by the computer input). These data come from one of our earliest simulations, which had produced an alpha of .08 (internal consistency reliability) and a construct validity of .85 as defined above. The personalities of the three hypothetical subjects are constant, but the expected behavior in successive stories (the true scores of traditional test theory) obviously are not. Our conclusion, succinctly stated, was this:

The theory of motivation specifies how a *stable* personality disposition, strength of motive, will be expressed behaviorally in *variable* amounts of time spent thinking and/or writing about achievement. It tells us specifically how, under various conditions, the "truly expected" time spent expressing the tendency to achieve will vary in a sequence of consecutive incidents. . . .

Basic theory about the underlying psychological process is logically prior to any application of traditional test theory. One must, in other words, have some sound theoretical basis for expecting a certain "true score" on a given test before one introduces the whole logic of test theory, which has to do with the implications of random error in the effort to measure accurately. With thematic apperception, it has been a mistake to assume that the "true score" (some [expected] behavioral manifestation) should be constant just because the strength of the underlying trait (motive) is presumed constant. One needs a theory to get from personality to something measurable, viz., behavior (Atkinson, Bongort, & Price, 1977, p. 24].

The fundamental fallacy in the application of classical test theory to the assessment of individual differences in personality is the unstated presumption that the central problem of motivation – explaining how personality is expressed in behavior – had already been solved and that the solution was a simple one. I had implicitly accepted that presumption in an early display of interest in test reliability (Atkinson, 1983) and in an earlier effort to view thematic apperceptive measurement of motives within the context of a theory of motivation (1958b). It is this long-taken-for-granted but mistaken presumption about what one should expect to observe that has sustained the argument that there are no stable, transsituational differences in personality because the correlations among various behavioral manifestations of the same trait are so low (Mischel, 1968). We have tried to challenge that argument by showing how modest the *expected* correlations are among such behaviors as risk preference in a ring toss game, arithmetic performance alone in a room, a Thematic Apperception Test, and so forth in computer simulations of how individual differences in achievement motive should be expressed in a variety of behaviors and settings (Atkinson, 1981; Reuman, Atkinson, & Gallop, 1986). The essence of that argument is apparent in the expected variability from story to story in Table 2.1.

The point at issue in this confrontation between the "statistical" framework of traditional test theory and the "psychological" conception of motivation is to define the proper relation between the two. Are they to be viewed as alternative theories of motivation between which we must choose to move the science ahead? Or does the dynamics of action, which purports to be a general theory about the basic process of motivation, provide a basis for defining conditions under which the premises of traditional test theory should and should not hold? We have pointed out, both here and elsewhere (Atkinson & Birch, 1978, p. 378; Atkinson, Bongort, & Price, 1977), that if an individual engages in a particular activity, such as solving arithmetic problems or describing one's behavior on the typical personality inventory, for a sustained period, the strength of the tendency sustaining that kind of activity will become stable. Under these conditions, assuming constancy in the relevant personality traits, such as arithmetic ability or one's conception of self, the assumption of equivalent constancy in the expected behavioral expressions of the trait (the true scores on successive subtests) is justified. It obviously is not justified in reference to a constantly changing stream of operant behavior.

It is in the context of sustained performance of mental tests and self-descriptive tests of personality that high internal consistency is typically achieved. And in reference to thematic apperception, where there may often be very little internal consistency in the content of the stream of imaginative thought, we have found that alpha based on the number of words per story is .96. This measure refers to imaginative-verbal productivity in each of eight stories over a period of 32 minutes when the actually obtained alpha for the empirical *n* Achievement in those eight stories was .57 (Atkinson, Bongort, & Price, 1977, p. 25).

THE MEANING OF THE TOTAL TAT *n* ACHIEVEMENT SCORE

The most important generalization to come from the new dynamics of action supports its claim of being a theory of operant behavior. It has to do with allocation of time among competing activities in a given setting. Initially developed mathematically in reference to the simple case of two competing activities (Atkinson & Birch, 1970, pp. 101–107), it was extended to the case of multiple alternatives (Sawusch, 1974) and has since been supported by the results of computer simulations under varying conditions (Atkinson & Birch, 1978, pp. 145–146, 364–366; Atkinson, Bongort, & Price, 1977, p. 177). The generalization is stated:

$$\% \text{ time spent in activity } A = \frac{F_{A/c_A}}{F_{A/c_A} + F_{B/c_B} + \ldots F_{N/c_N}}$$

where $F_A, F_B, \ldots F_N$ refer to magnitudes of the instigating forces for activities $A, B \ldots N$; $c_A, c_B \ldots c_N$ refer to the consummatory values of those activities, and the ratio F/c in each case refers to the asymptotic strength of the tendency $T_A, T_B \ldots T_N$, in a given setting. The latter is the level at which the strength of the tendency would become stable if the activity were to continue uninterrupted for a sustained period of time.

This theoretical generalization corresponds in form to the Matching Law in operant behavior (de Villiers & Herrnstein, 1976) according to which the relative strength of a particular response (when there are multiple alternatives) equals or matches its relative frequency of reinforcement. The consummatory values of activities in animal studies of operant conditioning, such as pressing a bar or pecking at a spot, are so similar that we assume they would cancel out in the time allocation generalization. What is left, then, is the implication that in operant behavior the magnitude of instigating force for an activity depends upon the frequency of prior reinforcement of that activity. We had already presumed this in showing how the new dynamics of action is related to the long historical development concerning the law of effect (Atkinson & Birch, 1970, Ch. 5).

The same principle applies to allocation of time among competing alternatives in the stream of operant imaginative behavior. As we proceed, recall that the earlier theory of achievement motivation (Atkinson & Feather, 1966) and its more recent elaboration by Raynor (1969, 1974) to include "future orientation" is now taken to be an hypothesis about the components or determinants of instigating force ($F_s = M_S \cdot P_s \cdot I_s$ in the simplest case). For the moment let us presume that the consummatory values of different kinds of imaginative activity (achievement, affiliation, power, and so forth) are reasonably equivalent. Assuming this, the time allocation rule may be simplified to read:

$$\% \text{ time spent in activity } A = \frac{F_A}{F_A + F_B + \ldots F_N}.$$

If we suppose that F_A represents the instigating force to achieve, F_B the instigating force for affiliation, and so on, we can consider the meaning of the thematic apperceptive n Achievement score (that is, the percentage of time spent in activity A) in a new light.

Consider an experiment in which the average strength of achievement and affiliation motives can be considered equal in two random samples of college students. Now suppose that the same Thematic Apperception Test is administered to each subject in one group in the context of working alone in a room providing only a strong incentive to achieve and to each subject in the other group in the context of working to achieve but in the presence of an audience that, presumably, provides an additional incentive for approval.

Intuition suggests that the average n Achievement score should be rather high and constant across conditions, but that the average n Affiliation score (often taken as a measure of the need for social approval in achievement settings) should increase in the audience condition. The principle of time allocation (above), which takes into account the influence of the strength of instigating force for achievement or affiliation (in the numerator) *relative to* the influence of the sum of all instigating forces produced by incentives in the situation (in the denominator) implies something different. The effect of the audience should be to increase time spent thinking about social approval (n Affiliation) but to decrease time spent thinking about achievement (n Achievement) in comparison with the alone condition. Kawamura-Reynolds (1977), employing this logic, found that the average n Achievement score decreased from 4.83 (alone) to 3.86 (audience), while the n Affiliation score increased from 2.75 (alone) to 3.36 (audience). Neither trend by itself was statistically significant, but the combined effect of both was (see also Atkinson & Birch, 1978, p. 345).

These results help to begin to concretize the interpretive problem spelled out in the principle concerning allocation of time among competing alternative activities. Time, like money, cannot be spent twice. And if the amount to spend is limited, twenty minutes for a sample of thematic apperception and twenty-four hours in a day, an increase in time allocated to one kind of activity must be accompanied by a compensatory decrease in time allotted to others.

One may consider the interpretive problem faced by Veroff, Depner, Kulka, and Douvan (1980) when confronting trends in thematic apperceptive *n* Achievement, *n* Affiliation, and *n* Power scores obtained from national samples in 1957 and 1976. In addition to teasing apart the personal (motive) and situational (incentive) determinants of the motivational state at a particular time, we must now be aware that time spent thinking about achievement, for example, depends also on the number and strength of competing alternatives. This conception should apply as well to "thought samples" obtained from literature in societal studies (for example, McClelland, 1955, 1958c, 1961). The new idea does not solve the problem of what to make of an increase or decrease in *n* Achievement for an individual, or a society, over a period of years; perhaps, by identifying the determinants, it will at least clarify the nature of the interpretive problem.

If one were to assume for simplicity that other determinants of tendencies to achieve, affiliate, gain power, and so forth produced by the test situation and pictures are reasonably equivalent among subjects engaged in thematic apperception, one might rewrite the generalization about allocation of time so that it refers only to the systematic effect of the strength of motives as determinants of differences among people in the magnitude of the various instigating forces:

$$\% \text{ time spent in activity } A = \frac{M_A}{M_A + M_B + \dots M_N}.$$

These are obviously very strong and unwarranted assumptions given the number of variables known to influence the magnitude of an instigating force (for instance, probability of obtaining the goal, incentive value of the goal, future orientation). They are made here to simplify the discussion of the new insight about the meaning of the *n* Achievement score (taken as an indicator of time spent thinking about achievement).

In the past we have rather glibly taken individual differences in *n* Achievement score to mean individual differences in absolute strength of motive to achieve. Now we can see that we are dealing with the problem of a hierarchy of motives suggested by Murray (1938) and McClelland (1951) and popularized by Maslow (1954). The measure obtained from thematic apperception should always provide a useful basis for predicting other differences in behavior that also depend upon the *relative* strength of achievement motive within an individual (initiation and persistence of achievement activities, preference for them over other kinds of activity, time spent achieving in everyday life, and so forth) but not necessarily differences in behavior that depend upon differences in *absolute* strength of motive, such as choice among achievement tasks that differ in difficulty (Hamilton, 1974; Schneider, 1978) or level of performance in an achievement task engaged in constantly for a period of time (Atkinson & Reitman, 1956). Individuals who differ greatly in absolute strength of achievement motive (in the numerator in the above equation) might, nevertheless, obtain the same thematic apperceptive *n* Achievement score if they also differed in a certain way in number and/or strength of competing motives (in the denominator). For example, the ratio $1/1 + 1 + 1$ is equivalent to $3/3 + 2 + 1 + 3$ is equivalent to $2/2 + 1 + 1 + 1 + 1$. All equal $1/3$ and imply spending the same percentage of time (that is, having the same *n* Achievement score for) thinking about and engaging in achievement-related activities. Yet the strengths of achievement motives are 1, 3, 2. In light of this, it is important to note that some of the repeatedly obtained empirical results (for instance, those concerning TAT *n* Achievement and risk preference or performance level) imply that variations among individuals in strength of achievement motive (numerator) must not be as highly correlated with the sum of the strengths of all of their competing motives (denominator) as suggested in the examples above.

Here is a new problem to engage the interest of psychometricians: to specify the conditions under which variations in time spent imagining achievement or engaging in achievement-related behavior can unambiguously be attributed to individual differences in the strength of that motive, or at least to the overdetermined numerator, the instigating force, in the time allocation ratio.

In the first simulation of time spent in an activity as a function of the strength of tendency to do it (the numerator, ranging randomly from 1 to 9) versus the sum of the strengths of *other* competing tendencies (ranging randomly from 3 to 27 to comprise a major part of the denominator), Sawusch (1974, p. 436) found time spent correlated .69 with strength of tendency for that activity and $-.57$ with the sum of the strengths of *other* competing tendencies. The correlation between these two normally distributed components of personality ($N = 80$) was by design not significant, .08. In some of the computer simulations of thematic apperception described earlier, the sum of all competing tendencies *including* the tendency to achieve was held constant among the hypothetical subjects so that individual differences in strength of achievement motive would be the only possible source of variation in time spent thinking about achievement. To the extent that individuals vary substantially in the sum total of the strengths of their competing tendencies, represented in the denominator of the time allocation principle, it would seem that correlations between the strength of a particular tendency (numerator) and percentage of time expressing it in behavior should be lower. Dato de Gruijter (1980) has analyzed the problem mathematically. Assuming that the mean and variance of the strengths of several motives in a sample of persons is the same and that they are independent, the numerator in the time allocation ratio becomes more highly correlated with the overall ratio itself, as the number of the subjects' other competing motives increases. Under the assumed conditions, his analysis showed that strength of motive to achieve (M_A) in the numerator would be expected to correlate .70 with percentage of time doing A if there were only one competing motive, .82 if there were two competing motives, .86 if there were three, and around .90 or higher if there were four or more. This corroborates one result of a preliminary exploration by Virginia Blankenship (reported in Atkinson, 1980) for the special case of four independent motives, all equal in mean strength and variance. Her results also showed that strength of achievement motive (M_A) and the idealized thematic apperceptive *n* Achievement score, as defined by the time allocation ratio, increased to .92 when its strength was correlated -1.00 with one of the other motives. In this case, the strength of that other motive would be correlated $-.92$ with the idealized *n* Achievement score. And the correlation of M_A and idealized *n* Achievement score dropped to .82 when M_A was correlated $+1.00$ with one of the alternatives.

These early explorations, referring to very special and often idealized conditions, open up a line of inquiry that must be followed if we are to have an adequate psychometrics of measures obtained from the stream of operant imaginative behavior.

THE EFFECT OF RESISTANCE

The theory of achievement motivation (Atkinson & Feather, 1966; Raynor, 1969, 1974) presumes that the challenge to achieve is always accompanied by the threat of failure, the other possible outcome in a test of one's competence. So let us again use the model of achievement motivation to introduce the new conception of resistance in the dynamics of action and to see how it might influence thematic apperception. I say *might* because I mean to confine this preliminary discussion to one of at least two plausible possibilities. It is the possibility that the effect of arousal of a tendency to avoid failure on the content of imaginative thought is analogous to its effect on the stream of overt instrumental achievement-related action. That is, the avoidance tendency always functions to dampen or suppress expression of the positive tendency. The other possibility, and one that is perhaps more consistent with Heckhausen's (1967) success in obtaining measures of both "hope of success" and "fear of failure" from the manifest content of thematic apperception, is that *thoughts* about succeeding and failing both are positively instigated (as in the discussion to this point), but the content of the thoughts, success versus failure, have exactly opposite motivational implications for overt action. This second possibility requires the more elaborate kind of analysis we have already undertaken, but in reference to simpler problems: cognitive control of action (Birch, Atkinson, & Bongort, 1974) and motivational determinants of decision time (Kuhl & Atkinson, 1986).

The discussion of the first alternative will provide a model that might be applied more generally to suppression of manifest sexual content in imaginative behavior (as in Clark, 1952), or of aggression, or of achievement-related content in the stories of conflicted women (see Horner, 1974; Lesser, Krawitz, & Packard, 1963).

The treatment of the arousal and expression of a tendency to avoid failure in the dynamics of action is analogous to the treatment of arousal and expression of a tendency to achieve. Corresponding to arousal of an action tendency (T) by exposure to an instigating force (F) is the arousal of a tendency not to engage in an activity, a *negaction tendency* (N), when the consequences of the activity in that situation have been negative in the past. This is attributable to exposure to an inhibitory force (I). The tendency not to do something (N), a disinclination to act, will produce resistance to the activity. It opposes, blocks, dampens; that is, it subtracts from the action tendency to determine the *resultant action tendency* $(\bar{T} = T - N)$. It is the resultant action tendency that competes with the resultant action tendencies for other, incompatible activities for expression. And now we may add a refinement to what was said earlier. It is the resultant action tendency $(\bar{T})$ that influences the consummatory force of the activity in which it is expressed, that is, $C = c \times \bar{T}$. Similarly, the resistance to an action tendency, produced by the opposition of a negaction tendency (as represented in $\bar{T} = T - N$), constitutes an analogous *force of resistance* (R), which diminishes in a comparable way the strength of the negaction tendency.

The argument by analogy, which is developed more fully elsewhere (Atkinson & Birch, 1970, 1974, 1978), explains why the suppressive negaction tendency (N) increases but eventually becomes stable in strength. In Figure 2.3 we see what happens when the immediate environment, and/or the picture stimulus in thematic apperception, produces both instigating and inhibitory forces for the same activity, B, to succeed $(F_{B,s})$ and to avoid failure $(I_{B,f})$. A hatched line shows arousal and linear growth of the action tendency, $T_{B,s}$ (as in the earlier Figure 2.2, which had ignored the problem of resistance). Simultaneously, below, another hatched line shows the trend in the growth of the tendency *not* to engage in activity B, the negaction tendency, $N_{B,f}$. As soon as N_B is aroused, it resists T_B to determine the strength of the resultant action tendency $(\bar{T}_B = T_B - N_B)$ as depicted in the solid curve, $\bar{T}_B$. This process of blocking the expression of T_B – resistance –

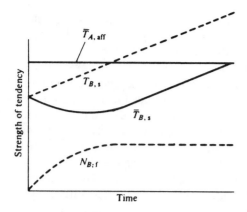

Fig. 2.3. The dynamics of a simple change from an affiliative activity to an achievement-related activity. Resistance attributable to a tendency to avoid failure (N_f) will, in time, be overcome by the tendency to achieve success (T_s) when an individual is exposed to instigating force to achieve success (F_s) and inhibitory force to avoid failure (I_f) (see text). (From Atkinson & Birch, 1978, p. 132)

produces a force of resistance (R) analogous to the consummatory force (C) that occurs when an action tendency is expressed in action. So N_B will increase as long as $I_B > R_B$, but as N_B becomes strong and produces more resistance, R_B becomes stronger. The initial difference between I_B and R_B favoring growth of N_B diminishes. In time $R_B = I_B$, so N_B becomes stable, as shown in Figure 2.3.

The effect of the resistance attributable to a negation tendency is always a temporary suppression of the action tendency. It delays the initiation of activity B for a period of time. The duration of the delay, or suppression, is the amount of time the action tendency T_B would require (given the magnitude of F_B) to become strong enough to compensate for the maximum strength of N_B. This continued growth in the strength of T_B is shown in the figure. Quite obviously the "temporary delay" or suppression of activity B will be relatively short or long depending upon the magnitude of the inhibitory force, I_B, which defines the level at which the disinclination to act will stabilize.

In reference to overt achievement-related action, the dynamics of action recovers the conflict between tendencies to succeed and to avoid failure, but does not view it as static. Viewing the product of motive to avoid failure (M_F), subjective probability of failure, and incentive value of failure as now determining the magnitude of the inhibitory force to avoid failure (I_F), which defines the arousability of the negation tendency (N_F) and ultimately the level at which its strength will become stable, we have this important new implication: No matter how strong the motive to avoid failure relative to the strength of achievement motive (i.e., $M_F > M_S$), the resultant tendency to achieve success ($\overline{T}_S = T_s - N_F$) will sooner or later become dominant and be expressed in the stream of behavior.

Let us apply this idea that the negative tendency temporarily suppresses the positive tendency to the stream of imaginative behavior in thematic apperception. It implies that the conflicted person should inhibit expression of achievement-related content during the early period of a sustained stream of imaginative behavior but should begin to express it later when he has overcome the resistance. This would mean that the typical short four-story Thematic Apperception Test of n Achievement may be yielding a measure that is sensitive to individual differences in the relative strengths of motive to achieve (M_S) and motive to avoid failure (M_F) rather than only to individual differences in M_S.

To excite interest in the task of studying the various logical possibilities and complexities by the method of computer simulation, I refer to one of the intriguing results from one of our very earliest explorations of how the combination of an instigating force (F_X) and an inhibitory force (I_X) for the same activity X would influence the way subjects allocate time to that activity. The effect of an inhibitory force was to increase the latency of activity X, that is, to delay the initial occurrence of activity X in the stream of operant behavior but to increase both its frequency and the time spent in activity X once the activity had been initiated the first time in the face of resistance. The effect was most pronounced when the inhibitory force was very strong relative to the instigating force (Atkinson & Birch, 1974; 1978, pp. 64–67).

These two possible effects of an inhibitory force might combine to produce certain trends in a long Thematic Apperception Test. In the early stories of a longer set, the time spent expressing concern over achievement would favor those in whom the achievement motive was clearly dominant, $M_S > M_F$. Expression of this concern would be suppressed among those in whom $M_F > M_S$. But then as the sequence of stories continued, the previously bottled-up expression of tendency to achieve in the latter would begin, and if the test were sufficiently long, those expressing this concern latest in the test would be those who were literally most inhibited, most conflicted about it. One might therefore expect the following: the n Achievement score obtained from stories early in the test will correlate positively with some other behavioral manifestation of achievement motivation: the n Achievement scores obtained from stories in the middle of the test will not correlate with this behavioral criterion at all; and the n Achievement scores obtained from stories very late in the test will correlate negatively with this behavioral criterion.

This may explain why Reitman and Atkinson (1958) found that n Achievement scores obtained from the first four of eight stories were positively related to fourteen minutes of arithmetic performance alone in a room but scores from the last four of eight stories were not. And the effect described may explain why clinical psychologists have argued that the more significant material (given their special interest) emerges late rather than early in the standard Thematic Apperception Test.

DISPLACEMENT AND SUBSTITUTION

Two other important motivational concepts deserve comment. Lazarus's (1961) critical arguments concerning our early use of thematic apperception helped to keep our thinking focused on the importance of the basic psychoanalytic concepts of displacement and substitution.

Displacement refers to the possibility that the arousal of one impulse might have a general effect and indirectly cause arousal of another related impulse. Substitution refers to the possibility of the same kind of interaction among tendencies but in reference to the process of consummation or diminution in the strength of a tendency. In the context of the principles of the dynamics of action, these concepts provide a theoretical basis for use of more general terms such as "achievement motive" and "tendency to achieve" in description and discussion of individual differences in personality.

In retrospect it is clear that our earliest use of the terms "achievement motive", "affiliative motive", "power motive," and the like was based on the presumption of a *basic personality structure* acquired early in life, and in part describable in terms of a limited number of general motivational dispositions that could be attributed to common life problems that arise for everyone, everywhere, in early childhood (McClelland, 1951, pp. 341–352). Later, in the initial statement of a theory of achievement motivation (Atkinson, 1957), the motive to achieve (M_S) was conceived as a relatively general and stable disposition that would (as in a ring toss game) influence the strength of a number of separate tendencies to succeed (T_s), a *family* of functionally related tendencies each member of which might vary in strength depending upon the subjective probability of success (P_s) and incentive value of success (I_s). The latter variables were considered relatively transient situational determinants of motivation. The basic idea was that a family of functionally related tendencies would generally be stronger in one person than another. It was convenient to use the family name, such as "motive to achieve" and "tendency to achieve," in describing individual differences in personality and motivational state. In a sense the concept of a general motive was a convenient fiction. Now, however, we can find more theoretical justification for the concept of a family of functionally related tendencies in the concepts of displacement and substitution. Let us begin with the latter.

Among the different ways in which a simple change from one activity to another can come about, as shown earlier in Figure 2.2, one in particular, graph (E) deserves our attention. Here, the initially dominant tendency is becoming weaker as the initial activity continues because, presumably, the consummatory force of that activity is greater than the instigating force of the stimulus situation. But why is there also a declining trend for the initially subordinate tendency? It is not being expressed in behavior. We might presume that it would persist at its initial strength, as in graph (D), if there were no instigating stimulus in the immediate environment or that it would increase in strength when there was an instigating stimulus, as in the other graphs. The last pattern (E) would seem impossible unless certain tendencies, or the activities they motivate, were functionally related so that what happened to one directly might have a similar but indirect effect on the other. We know from common observation that the aroma of a steak broiling over a charcoal fire increases not only the tendency to eat the steak but to eat other foods as well; and we know that eating the steak reduces not only the tendency to eat more steak but tendencies to eat other foods as well.

We refer to the capacity of one activity to reduce the tendency for another activity as its *substitute value* for the other. The indirect reduction in the strength of a tendency for one activity, T_y, by the behavioral expression of another, T_x, that is, the degree of substitution, will depend upon the magnitude of the consummatory force of the activity that is occurring (C_x) and the degree of relationship between the two activities. In a more detailed and technical discussion of this (Atkinson & Birch, 1970, Ch. 2), we have supposed that the closeness of the relationship between two activities can depend upon their association in the person's history; their symbolic equivalence (both proposed by Freud); their being two instances of essentially the same kind of consummatory activity; or their being alternative means to the same or similar goals or effects. Whatever the cause of the functional equivalence of the two activities, we represent the magnitude of the indirect or substitute consummatory force on T_y that is attributable to behavioral expression of T_x this way: $C_{xy} = C_x \cdot \gamma_{xy}$.

The magnitude of the indirect or substitute force C_{xy} depends upon the magnitude of the direct consummatory force C_x and the degree of relationship (0 to 1.00), γ_{xy}, between the two activities. Since C_x depends upon the consummatory value of activity x (c_x) and the strength of resultant tendency $(\bar{T}_x)$ being expressed at the time, that is, $C_x = c_x \cdot \bar{T}_x$, the *substitute consummatory value* of one activity for another is given by the expression $c_{xy} = c_x \cdot \gamma_{xy}$. Thus, for example, success in one activity may provide an indirect or *substitutive* effect on the tendency to succeed in another activity, as Blankenship (1986) has recently demonstrated: Success at a difficult task has the indirect effect of also reducing the tendency to succeed at easier tasks.

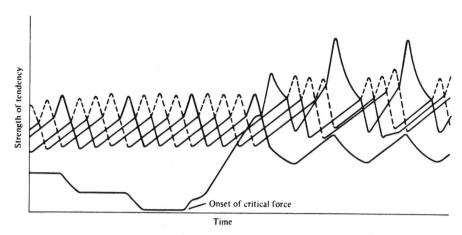

Fig. 2.4. Effect of substitution. The occurrence of activity x indirectly reduces T_y, which persists from an earlier setting, because the degree of relationship between activities x and y is .20. Once a strong instigating force for activity y is introduced, and activity y is initiated, then T_x is reduced by substitution, and it never again attains dominance (see text). (Based on Atkinson & Birch, 1978, p. 69)

How substitution might influence the stream of overt or imaginative operant behavior is shown in Figure 2.4. Consider the lower curve as T_y; it has been aroused previously. At the outset there is no instigating stimulus for y in the immediate environment. The occurrences of activity x in the stream of behavior reduce the strength of T_y because it is here assumed that γ_{xy}, the degree of relationship between the two activities, is .20. At a certain point in time the instigating stimulus for activity y is introduced. It produces a strong F_y, and so T_y begins to increase rapidly, though one can still see the substitutive effect of activity x on T_y before activity y is initiated for the first time. Then this more strongly instigated of the two alternatives $(F_y > F_x)$ begins to produce a strong, indirect substitute force C_{yx}, which reduces T_x. Activity y replaces activity x in the stream. To use a concrete example, one might think of eating potato chips until the host brings on the peanuts, which are preferred.

Here, in Figure 2.4, we provide a formal conceptual foundation for the argument about the importance of "alternative behavioral manifestations" of the same motive that was introduced by Frenkel-Brunswik (1942) and emphasized by McClelland (1958a, 1980). One must not, as Wittenborn (1955) also argued, expect too much from simple correlational analysis at the phenotypic surface of behavior.

Displacement, the indirect instigation of an activity, is treated in a comparable way. Displacement depends upon the magnitude of the instigating force that is directly attributable to exposure to an instigating stimulus in the

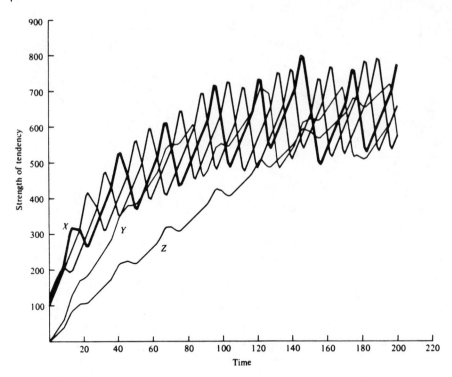

Fig. 2.5. Displacement and substitution. Three activities are directly instigated by forces in the immediate environment; one of these, activity x, is functionally related to both y and z; the tendencies for these activities are increased by displacement and diminished by substitution (see text). (Figure contributed by Virginia Blankenship; from Atkinson & Birch, 1978, p. 68)

environment and the degree of relationship between the two activities. Thus the indirect or displaced force, F_{xy}, should depend upon the magnitude of the force that is directly instigated, F_x, and the degree of relationship between the two activities (0 to 1.00) as represented in δ_{xy}. That is, $F_{xy} = F_x \cdot \delta_{xy}$. We represent the degree of relationship between two activities with different symbols in reference to instigation (δ_{xy}) and consummation (γ_{xy}) in order not to beg the question. Are tendencies organized into families in the same way in references to their arousal and their reduction? That point is illustrated in Figure 2.5. Here we have a stream of behavior in a constant environment producing three different instigating forces, among them F_x. It is assumed, concerning instigation, that the degree of relationship between activity x and activity y (for which there is no stimulus in the environment) is .60, and that the degree of relationship between activity x and activity z

(also without a stimulus) is .40. Neither activity is directly instigated, but there is nevertheless continuous exposure to indirect or displaced instigating force equal to .60 F_x for activity y and .40 F_x for activity z. With respect to substitution, a .20 degree of relationship is assumed between x and each of the other activities y and z. This means that whenever activity x occurs, there are indirect consummatory forces equal to .20 C_x influencing (that is, reducing) the strength of both T_y and T_z. One observes the arousal of T_y and T_z by displacement, the occasional reductions attributable to substitution, and the initial expression of T_y at about 80 on the time scale and of T_z at about 170 on the time scale.

Thus broadened to include these more general and indirect effects, we systematically embrace the concept of *a family of functionally related tendencies* that will ordinarily tend to increase and decrease together in strength relative to other families of tendencies. The members of the same family will, in other words, tend to have a common fate. It can simplify our discussion of effects to use the family name, a class term, such as "tendency to eat," "tendency to achieve," or "tendency for power," that embraces all the specific action tendencies affected by displacement and substitution, rather than trying to list exhaustively and in precise detail (which is probably impossible) what happens to the strength of each specific action tendency. This means that when we say the tendency to achieve is aroused by administering a test of ability in a given situation, we mean, specifically, that the effect of the direct instigation to achieve on the test spreads (that is, is displaced) and thus indirectly influences the strength of a whole family of functionally related action tendencies. When the cues of a particular picture in a Thematic Apperception Test presented immediately afterward produce a direct instigating force that arouses a very specific achievement-related concern, we need only combine the notions of a previously aroused and persisting family of tendencies and instigating force of the immediate stimulus to understand what we learned very early about the combined effects of prior situational arousal of motivation and picture cues on thematic content (Atkinson, 1958b; Haber & Alpert, 1958; McClelland, Atkinson, Clark, & Lowell, 1953, Ch. 7).

The more general terms "motive to achieve," "motive for power," and so forth are used in reference to the corresponding family of instigating forces. Individual differences in strength of achievement motive are differences among individuals in the arousability of the tendency to achieve. The concepts of displacement and substitution take us from the specifics of particular life situations to description of the more general motivational implications for an individual and the convenience of using more general terms in descriptions of personality.

A new conception of the problem of motivation (namely, to explain the stream of operant behavior) and its solution (the dynamics of action) have provided a theoretical foundation for response to critics of thematic apperceptive measurement of motivation. I hope that the new conception outlined here will provide the systematic guide needed to suggest new and better ways of realizing the promise of content analysis of imaginative thought for understanding motivation and personality.

3   How do self-attributed and implicit motives differ?

DAVID C. McCLELLAND, RICHARD
KOESTNER, AND JOEL WEINBERGER

From the beginning of the work on the achievement motive (McClelland, Atkinson, Clark, & Lowell, 1953), it has been apparent that motive dispositions as coded in imaginative thought from stories written to pictures differ from motive dispositions with the same name as measured in self-reported desires or interests. The authors of the studies on achievement motivation wanted to demonstrate that the variable they had identified in fantasy functioned like an animal drive in the sense that it energized, directed, and selected behavior. In this tradition (cf. Melton, 1952) it was particularly important to show that a motivational disposition that these authors labeled *n Achievement* (for the need to achieve) would select behavior or facilitate learning just as hunger would facilitate a rat's learning a maze. When McClelland et al. examined a self-reported desire for achievement, they observed that it did not facilitate learning in the same way that *n* Achievement did and so concluded that self-reported desires do not function like motives. An early study (deCharms, Morrison, Reitman, & McClelland, 1955) showed that the two measures of achievement motivation were uncorrelated and that their behavioral correlates were different. For these reasons deCharms et al. urged that the two measures be distinguished in future research by referring to the variable identified in fantasy as *n* Achievement (for the need to achieve) and the self-reported desire for achievement as *v* Achievement (for valuing achievement).

The recommendation that the two types of motive measures be carefully distinguished has not generally been followed in psychology for a variety of reasons. Ever since Murray's (1938) orginal study of motives, it has been commonly assumed that questionnaries and projective tests are simply

This research was funded in part by fellowships granted from the Seaver Institute.

Originally published as: McClelland, D.C., Koestner, R., & Weinberger, J. (1989). How do self-attributed and implicit motives differ? *Psychological Review*, *96*, 690–702. Copyright 1989 by the American Psychological Association. Reprinted without abstract by permission of the publisher.

49

alternative ways of getting at the same variable (see, e.g., Campbell & Fiske, 1959). Furthermore, it has seemed unreasonable not to call a strong self-reported desire for achievement a need or a motive (Edwards, 1954; D. N. Jackson, 1974). Moreover, the fantasy-based measures of variables like *n* Achievement did not appear to satisfy the psychometric requirements of a good measure (Entwisle, 1972) whereas the questionnaire measures did. More recent evidence has suggested that when a picture-story exercise is administered properly, the motive variables obtained from it have satisfactory test–retest reliability (Koestner & Franz, 1989; Lundy, 1985; McClelland, 1980; D. G. Winter & Stewart, 1977b), yet many psychologists remain convinced that the distinction between motives and values is unnecessary and confusing (J. Raven, 1988). A current reason for rejecting the distinction derives from the cognitive revolution in psychology, which turned attention away from the interest in unconscious and mechanistic models of motivation aroused by the earlier Freudian (e.g., Freud, 1940) and Hullian (e.g., Hull, 1943) conceptions, respectively. Modern investigators have focused more on information processing and on the way in which motivational thoughts are converted into action (e.g., Heckhausen & Kuhl, 1985; Weiner, 1972, 1986). And these processes could best be followed by asking subjects to report consciously on their desires, intentions, goals, and reasons for action (Kreitler & Kreitler, 1976; Kuhl, 1986). From this point of view, the problem was to explain the story-based motives in such cognitive terms, rather than to consider them to be separate and distinct.

A further consequence of the cognitive reorientation of motive theory has been to call into question the use of the term *value* to describe self-reported motives. For *value* is a term that has come to be used to describe normative beliefs about desirable goals and modes of conduct (Chaiken & Stangor, 1987; Rokeach, 1973, 1979). To avoid misunderstanding, we abandon the term *value* to describe attitudinal or self-reported motives and refer to them as *self-attributed motives*. For convenience, the motive measures derived from the picture-story exercise will continue to be labeled in the traditional way as *n* Achievement, *n* Power, and so on. We will consider them *implicit* needs in the sense that the person is not explicitly describing him- or herself as having the motive. In contrast, the self-reported, attitudinal motive measures are labeled *san* Achievement, *san* Power, and so on to indicate that they are *self-attributed* needs of various types.

Relabeling helps to avoid some types of misunderstanding, but it does not clarify the issue of whether it is important to distinguish between motives measured in these different ways, and if it is, then why. We have recently completed research (Koestner, Weinberger, & McClelland, 1991) that we believe does help to explain why these two types of motive measures have often yielded different results. To provide a background for the clarification that we believe these results bring to the field, it is first necessary to review briefly why it has been considered necessary to treat implicit and self-attributed motives as different variables (cf. McClelland, 1985a). The findings are then described in terms of how they shed light on these differences and how they provide more general insights into the way in which behavior is motivated.

THE RELATION OF IMPLICIT AND SELF-ATTRIBUTED MOTIVES

Measures of self-attributed and implicit motives seldom correlate significantly with one another. This fact was reported first in 1953 by McClelland et al., was confirmed in 1956 by Child, Frank, and Storm, and has been reported many times since (Atkinson & Litwin, 1960; Heckhausen, 1980; Heckhausen & Halisch, 1986; D. S. Holmes & Tyler, 1968; Korman, 1974; Kreitler & Kreitler, 1976; McClelland, 1958a). As a recent example, in the two studies referred to later in Figures 3.1 and 3.2 involving college students, the correlations between *n* Achievement and *san* Achievement were −.21 and .15, respectively; between *n* Power and *san* Power, the correlations were .08 and .05, respectively; and between *n* Affiliation and *san* Affiliation, the correlations were −.06 and −.08, respectively. In these studies, the self-attributed motive measures were obtained from the D. N. Jackson (1974) Personality Research Form (PRF) scales.

Few facts in psychology are as well established as this one, yet psychologists have had difficulty in dealing with it. They have generally reacted in one of two ways: (a) by concluding that the story-based motive measures are worthless (Campbell & Fiske, 1959; Entwisle, 1972) or (b) by concluding that the reason for the lack of correlation is that the self-report measures have not been designed properly (J. Raven, 1988). Over the years many attempts have been made to develop questionnaire measures of *n* Achievement and other motives (Edwards, 1954; Gjesme & Nygard, 1970; Gough & Heilbrun, 1975, 1983; Hermans, Petermann, & Zielinski, 1978; D. N. Jackson, 1974; Kreitler & Kreitler, 1976; Mehrabian, 1969, 1970; J. Raven, Molloy, & Corcoran, 1972), yet none of them has proved to be consistently related to story-based motive measures. The most common reaction to this failure has been to gloss over it and to treat the self-report measures as if they were assessing the same variables as the story-based measures, despite the lack of correlation between them (Weiner, 1980, 1986). And the hope still persists that asking a person just the right questions will yield a measure of implicit motives (J. Raven, 1988).

Another way to react to this lack of correlation is to take it seriously, to insist that, at a minimum, psychologists should not call by the same name two measures that do not correlate with one another (McClelland, 1980). Perhaps there are two qualitatively different kinds of human motivation, both of which are important; what needs explaining is how they differ, and how they relate to each other.

IMPLICIT AND SELF-ATTRIBUTED MOTIVES INFLUENCE
DIFFERENT CLASSES OF BEHAVIOR

McClelland (1980) has summarized evidence that implicit motives predict spontaneous behavioral trends over time, whereas self-attributed motives predict immediate specific responses to specific situations or choice behavior. The story-based measures of motives have been demonstrated to have greater validity for predicting long-term trends in behavior than have self-reported desires as recorded in questionnaires. For example, n Achievement was shown to predict entrepreneurial activity over time in the United States (McClelland, 1965) and in India (McClelland, 1987b). The inhibited power-motive syndrome, likewise scored in stories, was shown to predict managerial success in a major U.S. company over 16 years (McClelland & Boyatzis, 1982) and elevated blood pressure in an adult sample of graduates of a prestigious college over 20 years (McClelland, 1979). The amount of intimacy motivation in imaginative stories written by individuals at age 30 predicted marital happiness and overall psychosocial adjustment 17 years later (McAdams & Vaillant, 1982). In several of these instances, a variety of self-report measures of similar motives had no predictive validity over time. See especially, Bray, Campbell and Grant (1974) for the failure of a variety of questionnaire measures of motivation to predict managerial success over time.

Although self-attributed motives have at times appeared to relate to long-term trends in behavior, the results may often be as easily explained in terms of the effects of such behavioral trends on self-attributions as the reverse. For example, Kreitler and Kreitler (1976) reported a significant relationship between cognitive orientation toward achievement and final grades received by the subjects in the academic year preceding the date of the study. Kreitler and Kreitler described such results in terms of the *predictive power* of the cognitive orientations, but it seems just as likely that the cognitive orientations and self-attributions were a result of the grades received (i.e., those who did well ascribed achievement motivation to themselves).

To take another example, D. N. Jackson (1974) has validated the self-attributed motive scores obtained on his PRF scales against peer ratings that are presumably based on behavioral trends over time. But here again, if people have achieved, they are likely to attribute achievement motivation to themselves. The observer also notices their many achievements and rates them high on achieving behavior, so the person's self-reported achievement motive correlates with the observer's judgments of their achievements. Moreover, people who see themselves as achievement oriented are likely to express this to others who then dutifully report it on rating measures. That is, people form opinions about themselves that they report in direct measures (as on the Jackson PRF) and in conversations with others. These others therefore come to know and report these opinions when they are asked to make judgments in the form of peer ratings (McClelland, 1972). It is therefore possible to conclude that self- and other-judgments are influenced by the same achievement behavior and self-concept, not that self-reported achievement drive *predicts* achievement behavior over time as independently judged by others.

On the other hand, self-attributed motives, like other attitude measures, seem to predict behaviors best when the attitude and behavior measures show what Ajzen and Fishbein (1977) have termed a high degree of *correspondence*; that is, when both are closely matched on specificity and are assessed within a short time of one another. (For a review of the relation between attitudes and behavior, see Zanna, Higgins, & Herman, 1982.) Thus, behavioral intents in a Prisoner's Dilemma game predict very well what choices the players will make in that well-defined situation (Ajzen & Fishbein, 1970). Also, Kreitler and Kreitler (1976) reported that childrens' statements about the degree of their curiosity correlates with a number of specific behaviors characteristic of curiosity in a well-defined classroom test situation. Similarly, Bandura (1982) reviewed a variety of studies indicating that self-efficacy judgments tailored to a specific domain of functioning are highly predictive of performance in that domain. But as Ajzen and Fishbein (1970) pointed out, "the longer the time interval between the statement of intention and the actual behavior, the lower the correlation between intent and behavior will tend to be" (p. 469). Thus, the relationship between setting a goal to get a higher grade and actually getting a higher grade over several months tends to be low, especially when previous grade-point level is partialed out (Locke & Bryan, 1968).

So, generally speaking, implicit motives appear to be better at predicting behavioral trends over time and self-attributed motives, like most attitude measures, appear to be better at predicting immediate choices. Adopting a distinction introduced by Skinner (1938), McClelland (1980) referred to the spontaneous behavioral trends as *operants* and the immediate choice behaviors as *respondents*. Skinner used these terms to distinguish between occasions in which the stimulus for a response could be identified (respondent behavior) or could not be identified (operant behavior). In the case of respondent behaviors, the strength of a response is measured in terms of its *intensity* (latency or amplitude) in reaction to a known stimulus. In contrast, operant behaviors are measured in terms of the *frequency* of a response over time.

In a direct test of the usefulness of this distinction, Constantian (as reported in McClelland, 1985a) used two measures of the affiliation motive – one, the traditional picture-story measure of implicit *n* Affiliation and the other a typical self-attributed measure of the need for affiliation (*san* Affiliation). The affiliative motive is defined as the desire to establish, maintain, or restore warm relationships with other people (Atkinson,

Heyns, & Veroff, 1954; Boyatzis, 1973). Constantian found that *n* Affiliation correlated more strongly than *san* Affiliation with an operant measure
of affiliative behavior (whether the person was found to be talking with
someone when he or she was beeped randomly throughout several days).
Note that the operant behavior was without identifiable stimuli, a type of
spontaneous behavior varying in frequency over time that involved a readily
available response (e.g., talking to someone). In contrast, the *san* Affiliation
measure correlated more strongly than the *n* Affiliation measure with affiliative choices – with reporting that they would rather go to a movie with
someone than go alone, live with others than live alone, and so on.

Heckhausen and Halisch (1986) found similar results in an extensive
study. First, they reported the usual lack of correlation between an *n*
Achievement TAT measure and *san* Achievement questionnaire measures.
More important, they found different behavioral correlates for each variable. The *n* Achievement score correlated with the number of job-related
activities that subjects reported they had successfully and spontaneously
carried out – an operant measure. The *san* Achievement scores correlated
with a number of respondent measures, such as setting higher levels of
aspiration and reporting that they had higher levels of ability. Such findings
serve to underline the importance of maintaining the distinction between
self-attributed and implicit measures of motive dispositions, inasmuch as the
two types of measures correlate differently with other behaviors in ways that
are potentially of theoretical importance.

COMBINING SELF-ATTRIBUTED AND IMPLICIT MOTIVES FOR THE PREDICTION OF BEHAVIOR

Separate measures of self-attributed and implicit motives may be combined to yield a better understanding and prediction of certain types of
behavior.' If the measures were of the same variable, this would not be
true. McClelland (1985a) and Parsons and Goff (1980) suggested that implicit motives as reflected in the TAT measures might provide a general
orientation toward certain types of goals but that self-attributed desires
often reflect social norms that help define more narrowly the areas in which
those goals are to be accomplished. Thus, *n* Achievement is associated
with a concern to do things well – a kind of general process goal that in
time, assuming no special self-conscious types of achievement goals, may
lead people into entrepreneurial activity (McClelland, 1985b). Although
explicit desires for achievement are often also measured in general terms
(cf. Edwards, 1954; D. N. Jackson, 1974), they much more readily combine
with explicit goals of trying to do well in some particular socially accepted
domain, such as in school or on the job. Hence, knowing the strength of
both explicit and implicit motives can improve prediction of performance.

For example, Raynor and Entin (1982b) measured among college students both *n* Achievement and the extent to which they saw doing well in a particular course as related to their future career success. That is, for some students, but not others, doing well in the course was seen as a subgoal to later achievement. Results showed that students high in *n* Achievement did better in the course than those low in *n* Achievement only if they saw doing well in it as instrumental to reaching a long-term achievement goal. Thus, *n* Achievement provided an impulse toward doing something well. The conscious achievement goals (doing well in the course and career success) defined the particular area in which this impulse expressed itself. So measures of both types of motives improved prediction of performance over what either predicted alone.

Self-attributed motives, more often than implicit motives, are allied to explicit goals that are normative for a particular group and that channel the expression of implicit motives for members of that group. Realization of this fact provides an answer to the frequent criticism that achievement motivation theory is ethnocentric because it appears to emphasize individualistic striving in a way that is not appropriate to the way older people (Maehr & Kleiber, 1981), people from other cultures (Gallimore, 1981), or women (Parsons & Goff, 1980) define achievement or success. This criticism is valid in the sense that the *n* Achievement variable by itself gives a poor indication of the area of life in which a person will strive to do better or be entrepreneurial. Self-attributed motives, plans, and goals are needed to show the direction in which the achievement motive will turn.

So individuals in different cultural groups can still be concerned with doing something well (their achievement motive), but that *something* is defined by the motives and goals that the individuals attribute to themselves, as determined in part by what is considered important in the group to which they belong. An early illustration of this point was provided in a study by French and Lesser (1964), in which they determined whether college women were oriented toward a career or toward a traditional role as a wife and mother. They found that *n* Achievement in career-oriented women was significantly associated with doing better at an academic task like anagrams, but not with doing better at a social task that involved listing the number of different ways in which they could make friends if they moved into a new community. In contrast, among the women oriented toward the traditional women's role, those with higher *n* Achievement performed better at the social task of how to make friends, but did not perform better at the anagrams task. Self-attributed motives or purposes here defined the type of task at which a woman high in *n* Achievement would do better. So it is useful in understanding and predicting behavior to measure both implicit motives and self-attributed motives, with their associated explicit goals, because they often give specific direction to the implicit motives.

THE RELATION OF SELF-ATTRIBUTED AND IMPLICIT MOTIVES TO ENVIRONMENTAL INCENTIVES

Recent research that we have undertaken (Koestner et al., 1991) pointed to another distinction between self-attributed and implicit motives that we believe will help explain the other differences just reviewed. The research was undertaken because of hints in the literature that implicit motives are chiefly activated by incentives experienced in doing something, whereas self-attributed motives are usually activated by explicit, often social, incentives such as rewards, prompts, expectations, or demands. For example, it is relatively well established (McClelland, 1985b) that those scoring high in *n* Achievement do better at challenging tasks (those with a moderate probability of success) than do those low in *n* Achievement, because such tasks provide the maximum incentive of feeling good from doing something better. Conversely, such individuals often do worse than those with low *n* Achievement when the challenge incentive is not present in the task – that is, when the task is very easy (Atkinson, 1958c). And if performance is totally under the direction of external prompts or demands (as when an experimenter keeps telling subjects to "Hurry up!"), subjects high in *n* Achievement do not do significantly better than those low in *n* Achievement (Wendt, 1955).

On the other hand, those who score high on a self-attributed motive measure have been shown to be more influenced by salient external social demands. In the very first study of *san* Achievement (then called *v* Achievement) by deCharms et al. (1955), it was demonstrated that people high in *san* Achievement were more likely to change their views of the quality of paintings to be more in line with expert opinion than people low in *san* Achievement or high in *n* Achievement. Furthermore, Patten and White (1977) showed that under normal testing conditions, high *san* Achievement did not lead to better performance on a laboratory task, but if an external demand for achievement was added, those high in *san* Achievement did perform better than those low in *san* Achievement (see McClelland, 1985a).

A number of studies have recently been carried out that were designed to compare directly the effect of social and task incentives on the performance of those who score high on a self-report versus a picture-story measure of the same motive. The general hypothesis that guided the research was that salient social incentives would combine with self-attributed motives to influence performance, whereas task incentives would influence performance in conjunction with implicit motives or needs.

In the first such study (Koestner et al., 1991), college students were presented with 32 picture–word pairs for 5 s each. In one condition, they were asked simply to try to associate the pairs, as they would be asked to recall them later. In another condition, an achievement incentive was introduced by making repeated references to ways of retaining or recalling the

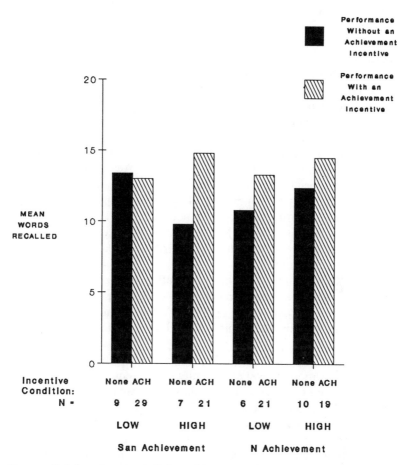

Fig. 3.1. Relation of words recalled to achievement values, achievement motive, and an achievement incentive.

words better. After a period of about 5 min during which the subjects filled out a background questionnaire, the subjects were asked to try to recall the picture–word pairs and to list the words they had seen.

A story-based measure of *n* Achievement was obtained in the standard way (McClelland, 1985b) at the outset of the session. In addition, the D. N. Jackson (1974) Personality Research Form was administered after the picture-story exercise. It provides in self-report format a measure of the subject's interest in or self-attributed desire for achievement – here labeled *san* Achievement.

Figure 3.1 presents the results in terms of the mean number of words recalled by subjects classified by *san* Achievement, *n* Achievement, and incentive condition. As Figure 3.1 illustrates graphically and as an analysis of variance (ANOVA) confirmed statistically, introducing an achievement incentive improved overall recall (main effect of incentive, $p < .05$). This indicates that introducing the achievement incentive was effective in improving performance. The most striking result confirms the hypothesis that the performance of those high in the self-attributed desire for achievement will be most influenced by an external social incentive. The interaction term in the ANOVA is significant ($p = .02$), showing that those high in *san* Achievement do significantly better under the influence of an achievement incentive than do those low in *san* Achievement. In fact, those high in *san* Achievement actually do worse than those low in *san* Achievement ($p < .05$) when there is no special achievement incentive. Such a result helps explain why under normal testing conditions people high in self-attributed need for achievement often do not perform better, a fact that has been reported a number of times previously (McClelland, 1985b). They need to be told that the performance relates to their self-attributed goal of doing better before they, in fact, do better.

On the other hand, when the classification is made in terms of the implicit motive measure – *n* Achievement – the same interaction term in the ANOVA is not at all significant. Those high in *n* Achievement are no more stimulated to perform well by the achievement incentive than are those low in *n* Achievement.

In a second part of the experiment, these subjects worked at word-finding puzzles that varied in level of difficulty or challenge. This task had no special incentive condition. The results showed a significant *n* Achievement × Difficulty Level interaction ($p = .035$, in the predicted direction), indicating that those subjects who were classified as high in *n* Achievement performed relatively better on the difficult than on the easy puzzles, whereas low-*n* Achievement subjects showed the reverse pattern. The subjects' level of *san* Achievement did not interact with difficulty to affect performance. Together, these studies provide support for the hypothesis that the implicit motive for achievement is affected by task incentives (such as the challenge of a more difficult puzzle) to influence performance, whereas self-attributed achievement motivation will affect performance under the influence of social incentives (such as are made explicit by the way an activity is described).

Another experiment (Koestner et al., 1991) sought to determine if the results obtained for the two types of achievement motives would also occur for the two types of power motives. The need for power is defined as the desire to have impact on others by influencing, persuading, helping, arguing with, or attacking them (McClelland, 1975; D. G. Winter, 1973). The question was whether an introduced social incentive to show power would affect those high in *san* Power more than it would those high in *n* Power. This study also used college student subjects for whom the *n* Power scores from stories and a *san* Power measure from the Dominance or Leadership

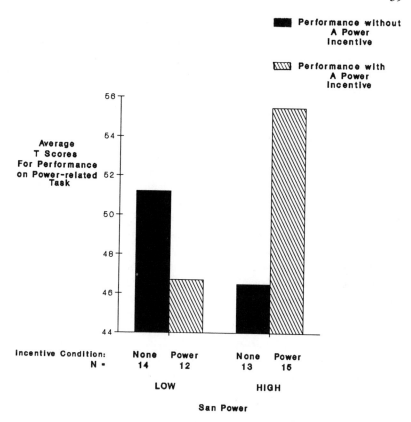

Fig. 3.2. T-scored performance on the power-related task by incentive condition and level of self-attributed power motivation. The means have been adjusted for the covariate (*n* Power).

scale of the D. N. Jackson (1974) PRF were obtained. The subjects were presented with a social perception task (Sternberg, 1986) consisting of pictures of two people. The subjects were instructed to figure out the relationship between the people in the picture. For some pictures, the task was to determine the affiliative relationship between a man and a woman, and for other pictures, the task was to determine the power relationship between two adults in an office or in a factory setting. The subject was to decide which one was the boss. For each picture, the subject could find out if he or she had been correct by looking at the answer on the back of the sheet. Here, we will be primarily concerned with performance on the power-related task, as it has been shown that people high in *n* Power are more sensitive to power stimuli and perform better at power-related tasks (McClelland, 1985b).

One half of the subjects were simply told how to perform the task – the no special incentive condition. The other half was told that a high score on the social perception task would indicate that they were in a better position to influence or manage others. This explanation was expected to trigger the power motive in those high in *san* Power but not in those high in *n* Power. As expected, the subjects high in *n* Power performed significantly better than did subjects low in *n* Power on the power-related task (picking who was boss in the pictures), both in the no incentive and power incentive conditions, but differences in *n* Power bore no relation to performance on the affiliation task. In other words, the nature of the task incentive combined with *n* Power to influence performance as expected.

On the other hand, the social power incentive influenced performance of those high in *san* Power, as shown in Figure 3.2. Because *n* Power was significantly related to performance on the power task, its influence has been covaried out in the performance means shown in Figure 3.2. The interaction between social incentive condition and *san* Power is significant ($p = .02$), indicating that those high in *san* Power do better than those low in *san* Power when there is a social power incentive but not when it is not present. Again, no such relation appears for performance on the affiliative portion of the social perception task. Introduction of the power incentive does not improve the performance of those high in *n* Power more than the performance of those low in *n* Power.

The overall conclusion is the same as it is for the results in Figure 3.1. Explicitly introduced incentives generally affect performance more for those varying in the strength of self-attributed desires than they do for those varying in the strength of implicit motives as measured in the picture-story exercise. In common-sense terms, those who believe that they are interested in leadership and in influencing others are more apt to respond to an instruction that says the task is related to those goals than those who do not attribute those goals to themselves.

A further study (Koestner & Zuckerman, 1989) shows how varying the nature of the salient social incentive influences whether those high in *san* Achievement or *san* Power are more motivated to work on a task. College student subjects worked for a time on a word maze and then were given success or failure feedback in terms of how much of a task they had mastered (mastery or achievement feedback) or how well they had done compared with others (competitive or power feedback). The experimenter then told them the experiment was over, left them free to do what they liked, and recorded the percentage of them who continued working on the task on their own. Such persistence has often been considered a measure of intrinsic motivation (Deci, 1971; Lepper, Greene, & Nisbett, 1973; Ryan, 1982). One might regard intrinsic motivation as a better measure of motivation than performance that is influenced by skill independently of motivation. As Figure 3.3 shows, a greater percentage of those high in *san* Achievement

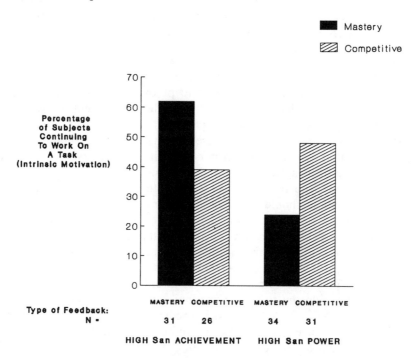

Fig. 3.3. Percentages of subjects high in *san* Achievement or *san* Power continuing to work on a task after mastery or power feedback on performance.

continued to be interested in the task after mastery than after competitive feedback, whereas the reverse was true for those high in *san* Power; more of them continued to work on the task after power feedback than after achievement feedback. The interaction chi-square is significant ($p < .03$). People high in the implicit motive measures n Achievement and n Power were not differentially affected by the explicit mastery or power feedback.

The results of these studies suggest that implicit motives are more apt to be aroused by task incentives than by explicit social incentives, whereas self-attributed motives are more apt to be aroused by explicit social incentives or demands than by incentives implicit in a task experience. Four experiments are not enough to establish such generalizations firmly, nor are we prepared to believe that the reverse of these propositions would never be true – that, for example, an implicit motive could never be aroused by explicit social pressures (see French, 1955). Nevertheless, even as preliminary generalizations, the results appear to be theoretically important because they help explain other differences that have been found between the two types of motives and lead to a more comprehensive understanding of the nature of human motivation.

EXPLANATION OF THE RELATIONSHIP OF IMPLICIT
AND SELF-ATTRIBUTED MOTIVES TO DIFFERENT CLASSES
OF BEHAVIOR

To begin with, these results provide a ready explanation of why implicit motives have generally been found to predict operant behaviors and self-attributed motives have been found to predict respondent behaviors. For, if the primary incentive for carrying out an activity is in the activity itself, then the person implicitly interested in that incentive should continue to carry out that activity. Thus, a person high in *n* Achievement should continue to perform a task that provides a moderate challenge (Atkinson & Litwin, 1960), the primary incentive for that motive; and a person high in *n* Affiliation should continue to interact with people spontaneously (Constantian, reported in McClelland, 1985a), inasmuch as being with people is the primary incentive for *n* Affiliation.

By way of contrast, if the incentive lies in an external social demand, then the person with a strong self-attributed motive will perform the task well to the extent that the external demand or incentive for doing it is salient and is perceived as relevant to the self-attributed motive. As noted earlier, behavioral intents or attitudes are best at predicting behavior in immediate social situations in which the social norms and expectancies of success for various acts are all known and explicit (Ajzen & Fishbein, 1980). The problem with predicting from them to long-term behavioral trends lies in the fact that the external social incentives may not always be salient enough to elicit the behavior. For this reason, recent research on achieving distant goals has stressed the importance of setting proximal subgoals that sustain commitment to performing in the service of a long-term goal (Bandura, 1982, 1986).

The way in which these two types of motives influence behavior in everyday life can be illustrated by research on the relation of *n* Power and *san* Power to success in a managerial position. Managing others successfully involves influencing others or having an impact on them, which has been defined as the natural incentive for *n* Power. People high in *n* Power should enjoy the many opportunities for making decisions and having an impact that the managerial job offers. And, in fact, they have been shown to be more successful managers (McClelland & Boyatzis, 1982).

What about people high in *san* Power? They have a strong desire to be a leader and rise to a managerial position. They may have joined the company because they saw that there was ample opportunity for advancement. If they rise to a managerial position, they will doubtless try to behave as they think a manager should and demand the respect a manager should have. But for their *san* Power to influence their decision making, they will have to see at every point just how that decision relates to their advancement. However, in managerial jobs there is a lot of discretion as to what people actually spend their time doing. That is, the job entails operant activities in which there are no moment-to-moment social explanations as to how this or that activity relates to one's explicit goals. So people high in *san* Power are no more likely than others to succeed in a managerial job (Bray et al., 1974). People high in *n* Power, on the other hand, seize every opportunity to spend their time doing what they enjoy doing – making decisions and influencing others – which is what the managerial job requires.

The distinction between task and social incentives also explains why McClelland (1980) came to the erroneous conclusion that self-attributed needs were not motives because they did not drive, direct, or select behavior. The conclusion correctly summarized early research on the implicit motives because the experiments were done primarily under neutral conditions when no explicit social incentives to do well had been introduced (Atkinson & Litwin, 1960). In fact, the relation between *n* Achievement and performance tended to disappear when subjects were explicitly urged to do well (McClelland et al., 1953). According to the present understanding, under these conditions subjects high in *san* Achievement would tend to do well, but that relation was not checked in these early studies. In any case, Figures 3.1 and 3.2 clearly show that self-attributed motives result in better performance if they are explicitly aroused by appropriate incentives. So they do act like implicit motives under certain conditions. That is, if explicity aroused, they drive behavior (i.e., energize it), direct behavior (i.e., focus attention on the relevant activity), and select behavior (i.e., produce better learning or performance). However, implicit motives may energize behavior more in the sense that they lead to more frequent activity of a certain type because it is pleasurable, even in the absence of specific social demands.

EXPLAINING THE WAY IMPLICIT AND SELF-ATTRIBUTED MOTIVES COMBINE

If implicit motives are aroused by incentives present in tasks or activities and self-attributed motives are triggered by explicit social incentives, the presence of both types of incentives should summate to facilitate performing the act. Including both *n* Affiliation and *san* Affiliation maximizes prediction of operant affiliative activities (talking to people) in the Constantian study cited by McClelland (1985a), presumably because sometimes the initiative for the interactions is personal, coming from those high in *n* Affiliation who take pleasure in interaction), and sometimes the initiative is social, coming from the other person (evoking a response from those high in *san* Affiliation in line with their commitment to be nice).

Knowing that there are different types of incentives also contributes to an understanding of how self-attributed motives influence the area of activity in which an implicit motive expresses itself. For explicit social incentives are often more differentiated and specific as to what is demanded or expected. In the French and Lesser (1964) study referred to earlier, n Achievement promotes better performance in making friends in a new community in those women who want primarily to be good wives and mothers. In this instance, the interest in being a good wife and mother directs the implicit achievement motive into the activity of making friends, which is instrumental to being a good wife and mother. In the same study, if the achievement goal is to have a successful career, that directs the implicit achievement motive into the activity of doing better at an anagrams task, which is presumably instrumental to showing that one is more qualified for a successful career.

Motives and incentives can conflict and undercut as well as combine and facilitate performance. Suppose that a person high in a particular self-attributed need is confronted by a conflicting or inappropriate incentive. That analysis was actually performed in the first study reported here. Subjects were classified not only as to san Achievement and n Achievement, as in Figure 3.1, but also as to san Power. When the achievement incentive was introduced in this study, those high in a self-attributed power need actually performed significantly less well in recalling words than they did when there was no stated external incentive. It was as if they were reacting by feeling that because the stated incentive of doing better did not interest them (because they were high in san Power), they would not put much effort into recalling the words. For these people, an explicit achievement incentive actually undercut performance. Deci and Ryan (1987) reported a large number of studies that have shown how explicit incentives can undercut intrinsic interest in performing a moderately challenging task.

Furthermore a conflict between an implicit and a different self-attributed motive can lead to compromise behaviors. In the Constantian study of spontaneous affiliative behavior, as reported in McClelland (1985a), some subjects were high in n Affiliation and also in an explicit desire to spend time alone. Their n Affiliation did not express itself in chatting with people but found an outlet in writing letters to people, which also satisfied the desire to be alone. So having measures of both implicit and self-attributed motives helps explain a variety of behaviors that could not be accounted for by either measure alone.

IMPLICATIONS

To return to the observation that started the discussion, one might infer that the two motive measures do not correlate because they are built on different types of incentives and were probably acquired in different ways, often at different stages in a person's developmental history. Suppose we assume, in line with the argument so far, that implicit motives are based on incentives involved in doing or experiencing certain things and that self-attributed motives are built around explicit social incentives or demands. If that is the case, then one might also infer that the implicit motives are built on associations with innately triggered affective experiences, called *natural incentives* by McClelland (1985b) and *primes* – for primary emotional experiences – by Buck (1985). In contrast, self-attributed motives would require a relatively well-developed concept of the self and of others, and some ideas acquired during socialization as to what is valuable or important. It would also follow that it should be possible for implicit motives to develop without symbolic conceptualization in language, whereas self-attributed motives would require linguistic conceptualization of ideas about the self and what the culture explicitly defines as important and valuable.

This distinction suggests a number of important implications:

1. The implicit motives seem more likely to be built on affective experiences with natural incentives early in life, before the development of language, than are self-attributed motives that would develop later, after concepts of the self, others, and what is valuable have been acquired. The evidence that natural or innately pleasurable incentives exist has been summarized by Buck (1985) and McClelland (1985b). Recent research has even suggested that there may be specific hormones or hormone profiles that reflect the specific affective arousal associated with different natural incentives (McClelland, 1987a). For example, the power motive is hypothesized to be based on the natural incentive of "having impact," as in aggression, which has been associated with more norepinephrine release. One might think of the implicit motive as a kind of conditioned emotion in which the emotion releases a hormone (norepinephrine) that is associated at least centrally with reinforcement and "pleasure" (Olds, 1977). If this were the case, then people high in *n* Power when involved in an "impactful" experience should show a greater release of norepinephrine than people low in *n* Power. This has been shown to be true: Students high in *n* Power respond to experiencing the impact of an important examination with a greater release of norepinephrine than do those low in *n* Power (McClelland, Ross, & Patel, 1985).

Another study showed that affiliative arousal through presentation of a romantic film is associated with increased dopamine release for those high in *n* Affiliation, but not for those high in *san* Affiliation (McClelland, 1989). Central dopamine release has also been linked to reinforcement (Wise, 1980) and could reflect a positive emotion that gets conditioned to affiliative cues forming the basis for *n* Affiliation.

2. It should be possible for implicit motives like *n* Achievement or *n* Power to develop in animals without language so long as the species responds to the natural incentives on which these motives are based. For example, Festinger (1943) has shown that the white rat prefers a moderately

challenging to an easy path to food, suggesting that it is responding to the natural incentive on which *n* Achievement is based. Thus, it should be possible to measure individual differences in the strength of the responsiveness to this incentive by exposing rats to a variety of such challenging situations. Furthermore, a strong achievement motive might well be developed in the rat by pairing a number of cues with experiencing this incentive.

3. Because the implicit motives are apparently built on direct experiences of affect also characteristic of animals, it seems likely that these motives are mediated by more primitive midbrain structures than are the self-attributed motives that would be subserved by the highly developed cerebral cortex, in which language is processed. As a consequence, implicit motives should show closer connections with physiological systems controlled by midbrain structures, such as neurohormone release, than do the self-attributed motives. McClelland (1987a) has summarized some evidence suggesting that this is the case. The fact that the implicit motives appear to be more directly associated than the self-attributed motives to neurohormone release tends to support the hypothesis that the implicit motives are mediated through midbrain structures governing the autonomic nervous system.

4. Even though stories written to pictures obviously involve the use of language (and hence the cerebral cortex), it seems likely that they are more successful than self-reports in reflecting implicit motives because they provide a more direct readout of motivational and emotional experiences than do self-reports that are filtered through analytic thought and various concepts of the self and others. Here we follow Buck (1985) in his distinction between analytic cognition and syncretic cognition. Syncretic cognition is knowledge by acquaintance, as in reacting appropriately to a familiar face or feeling angry. Analytic cognition is knowledge by description, in which people interpret what they see or feel using linguistic concepts. Buck argued that the "direct subjective experience of emotion" in syncretic cognition allows subsequent cognitive analysis of the experience. This paves the way for self-regulation, "for verbally mediated control of emotionality." It "allows behavior to be under the control of principles of logic and reasoning that are mediated by language" (Buck, 1985, p. 398). The distinction he made between the two types of cognition describes very well the difference between the two types of motives. Self-attributed motives involve analytic thought in the sense of people making complex judgments as to the degree to which certain statements apply to them. And the imaginative stories from which implicit motives are coded reflect motivational and emotional themes in the person's life, unevaluated as to their appropriateness in terms of concepts of the self, others, and what is important.

5. The cognitive, information-processing model of human motivation in terms of needs, plans, and goals describes the way self-attributed motives function much better than the way implicit motives function. Self-attributed

motives are characterized by organized thought; they start with an explicit goal that a person wishes for, then wants, then becomes committed to pursuing in various ways (Heckhausen & Kuhl, 1985; Klinger, 1975, 1987a). Klinger, Barta, and Maxeiner (1981) have studied empirically the varieties of current concerns that people report in interviews or on questionnaires. Most of the concerns have to do with unattained goals of unfinished business. The more committed people are to a goal or the more salient it becomes, the greater the likelihood that they will feel frustrated and unhappy at some point for their slowness or failure in reaching it.

The situation is different with implicit motives because they are aroused by affective experiences intrinsic to an activity and not by explicit references to unmet goals. Thus, in the example given earlier (McClelland, 1989), a romantic film arouses those high in *n* Affiliation, which leads to greater release of dopamine, presumably because dopamine release is associated with affiliative arousal (McClelland, Patel, Stier, & Brown, 1987). The same experience does not lead to a release of dopamine for those high in *san* Affiliation because it was not acquired in connection with affective affiliative arousal but in connection with explicit understandings of the importance of affiliation to the self. So *san* Affiliation should be aroused by reminding the person that he or she has important unmet needs for affiliation. And that type of arousal should be predominantly negative, leading to physiological signs of increased anxiety, such as increased skin conductance or the release of cortisol (Lundberg & Frankenhaeuser, 1978). Thus, the physiological correlates of arousing the two types of motives may differ because of the different ways in which they are aroused.

It is especially important to realize that failure to meet a goal is not so obvious to those with a strong implicit motive. Observers may infer that a person who scores high in *n* Achievement has a goal of doing better, but that person is not necessarily aware that he or she has such a goal: There is no correlation between *n* Achievement and the explicit desire to achieve. Hence, it is not obvious to such a person when a goal is not being met. In describing how an implicit motive functions, it is not appropriate to speak of wishing, wanting, and committing oneself to the goal that we recognize as the natural incentive for that motive. Instead, we conceive of the motive as leading to an activity that is the incentive for that motive. Thus, people high in *n* Achievement may have learned through experience to seek out certain activities that provide the pleasure of moderate challenge. But they do not necessarily know that they have a goal of doing better. It follows that they know less about what is guiding their behavior than do people with an explicit achievement need. And they are therefore less able to plan appropriate corrective action when things go awry.

6. The distinction between the two types of motives is very similar to a distinction made by memory theorists (e.g., Kinsbourne, 1987) between explicit and implicit, or episodic and semantic memory. The difference

between the two types of memory is illustrated by the fact that although amnesiacs cannot voluntarily recall an experience, thus showing a failure in episodic memory, it can readily be demonstrated that the experience influences their subsequent performance. Their semantic or implicit memory is intact. Conscious goal setting is analogous to episodic recall: It involves a voluntary act. And implicit motives are more like semantic memory: They automatically influence behavior without conscious effort. They are like rules that guide behaviors that have been acquired on the basis of repeated affective experiences. Voluntary goal setting, like conscious recall, provides a means of escape from automatic processing – an escape that may involve overriding, stronger responses (Kinsbourne, 1987) contained in the general rule or implicit motive. Thus, conscious motives, intentions, and current concerns can override more primitive automatic functioning, at least temporarily (Bargh, 1984; Logan, 1980; Posner & Snyder, 1975). Although the override may be only temporary – witness the failure of many New Year's resolutions – it provides greater flexibility in adaptation, particularly when difficulties arise. In evolutionary terms, a conscious motivational system has been built on top, so to speak, of a more primitive motivational system. The evolutionary advantage of such an arrangement is obvious because the more primitive, automatic motivational system is not well equipped to make plans or to set specific goals that can take into account contextual circumstances. As noted earlier, self-attributed goals often serve to guide implicit motives into specific channels.

DEVELOPMENT OF SELF-ATTRIBUTED AND IMPLICIT MOTIVES

We finish our discussion of the two kinds of motives by considering recent empirical findings concerning their developmental origin. If implicit and self-attributed motives differ in the ways postulated, then they should have different antecedents in child rearing. The implicit motives should be more often built on early, prelinguistic affective experiences, whereas the self-attributed motives should be more often built on explicit teaching by parents and others as to what values or goals it is important for the child to pursue. Such instruction can occur only after the child can comprehend linguistic communication and organize its meanings into such constructs as self, others, and social norms. Allport (1937) also argued that there were two types of motivation, one characteristic of early infancy and the other of adult self-directed behavior. However, he did not believe that motives developed in infancy could continue to influence adult behavior in the way that we contend that early developed, implicit motives continue to guide thought and action in later life.

Some empirical fingings on the child-rearing antecedents of the two types of motives are summarized in Table 3.1. They come from a follow-up study of children whose mothers were extensively interviewed on their child-

Table 3.1. *Correlations of child-rearing variables with implicit and self-attributed motives in adulthood*

Child-rearing variable	Correlation with	
	n Achievement	*san* Achievement
Scheduling of feeding	.33*	.06
Severity of toilet training	.41***	−.10
Early tasks set for child	−.10	.31**
	n Power	*san* Power
Permissiveness for sex and aggression	.31**	.08
Punishes aggression to parents	−.17	.32**
Frequency mother spanks	−.07	.39**
	n Affiliation	*san* Affiliation
Mother unresponsive to infant crying	.27*	.02
Child told not to fight back	.11	.27*

Note. N = 76–78.
* p < .05.
** p < .01.
*** p < .001.

rearing practices in 1951 when their children were 5 years old (Sears, Maccoby, & Levin, 1957). In 1977–1978, when the children had become 31-year-old adults, they were given both a version of the picture-story exercise from which implicit motives were scored (see McClelland & Pilon, 1983) and a self-descriptive adjective checklist that can be scored for *san* Achievement, *san* Power, and *san* Affiliation (Gough & Heilbrun, 1983). (The scoring keys for *san* Achievement and *san* Power contain a number of the same adjectives that were eliminated to prevent overlap in the measures of the two motives.)

Table 3.1 shows the early-rearing practices that were significantly correlated with adult implicit motives (McClelland & Pilon, 1983), along with those child-rearing practices that correlate significantly with adult self-attributed motives. The different origins of the two types of motives fit the theory quite well. Setting high standards early in life for moderately difficult mastery of internal states is associated with adult *n* Achievement but not with adult *san* Achievement. Learning when to be hungry and when and where to defecate and urinate should provide some intrinsic pleasure from self-mastery in all children. And parents who emphasize the importance of these learnings apparently succeed in developing an affectively based interest in mastering challenging tasks that lasts into adulthood. On the other hand, setting explicit tasks for the child to learn and perform is significantly associated with adult *san* Achievement but not with adult *n*

Achievement. Explaining what tasks a child is to carry out certainly involves more linguistically coded information than does teaching a child when to be hungry by scheduling feeding, and probably more than is involved in consistently putting the child on the toilet and demanding performance. Furthermore, in this sample at this period in history, toilet training was reported to be complete for the majority of children by 19 months (Sears et al., 1957) so that the learning occurred before language comprehension was developed as highly as would be necessary to understand what was involved in carrying out instructions to perform various tasks. The later emphasis on carrying out tasks, however, did develop a self-attributed need to achieve that persisted into adulthood.

The picture for the power motives is similar. Permissiveness about sex and aggression is associated with adult *n* Power but not with adult *san* Power. And permissiveness means that the parent allows or ignores the behavior without saying much about it. Thus, the children who experience the innate pleasure of having impact through sex and aggressive play grow up with a strong implicit *n* Power but have not coded this into a strong explicit desire for power, for the parents have not been saying things like "It's good to hit me." On the other hand, spanking and punishment for aggression are usually accompanied by explicit statements forbidding the child to do something and explaining why he or she is being spanked for violating a prohibition. This should lead to an explicit linguistically coded understanding of the following sort: "If I do such and such, I will be spanked," which should readily translate into a proposition like "Punishment – the exercise of power – is the way to control behavior." So adults, whose mothers reported that they had spanked them a lot at age 5, are more likely to grow up attributing a desire to exercise power to themselves but not necessarily with a strong implicit need for power because they may have been interrupted in their experiencing pleasure from "having impact."

The findings are less reliable in the area of affiliation motivation, but they point in the same direction. The only significant correlation with adult *n* Affiliation is again based on a very early experience. Overall, children whose mothers said they were unresponsive to them as infants when they cried grew up to have higher *n* Affiliation, although this relationship did not appear in all subgroups (McClelland & Pilon, 1983). Because *n* Affiliation contains a strong element of fear of rejection (see chapter 13, this volume), this correlation makes sense. Children who experienced insecurity in the primary affiliative relationship very early in life are apt to grow up with an implicit fear of rejection, although they have not explicitly coded this need as represented in the *san* Affiliation score. On the other hand, if the mothers said they explicitly told their children not to fight back – in other words, to be nice – the children were more apt as adults to attribute to themselves a desire to be compliant and nice to others, as represented by a higher *san* Affiliation score.

So the data can be reasonably interpreted to support the generalization that implicit motives are acquired earlier in life on the basis of important nonverbal affective experiences, whereas the self-attributed motives are acquired later, after the development of language, on the basis of more explicit instructions as to what is important from the parents. The key theoretical point is that the implicit motives appear to have been acquired on the basis of affective experiences and so remain aroused by them later in life, rather than by salient social incentives. Similarly, the self-attributed motives were acquired from social, linguistically conceptualized instructions and remain responsive to them in adulthood.

Although it may seem surprising that early childhood experiences would have an observable effect in adulthood, more than 25 years later, it should be remembered that the values that parents express, which develop self-attributed motives, are doubtless stressed over and over again as the child grows up. And McClelland (1942) has suggested a number of reasons why early, prelinguistic, affectively based associations might persist, because later, more cognitively elaborated experiences do not directly contact or replace them.

The influence of early childhood experiences on the development of motives, of course, does not preclude the possibility of motives being acquired later in life in response to similar experiences. In fact, numerous attempts to develop the implicit motive to achieve in adulthood support the conclusion that courses that emphasize experiencing positive affect in the course of mastering challenging tasks are more successful than those that emphasize a more cognitive approach to altering the self-image (McClelland, 1985b). Thus, it seems likely that the educational experiences that contribute to developing the two types of motives in early childhood would also contribute to developing them later in life.

CONCLUSION

There is evidence that implicit and self-attributed motives are acquired in different ways at different times of life, respond generally to different types of incentives, function differently in guiding behavior, and are associated with different physiological correlates. Small wonder that measures of them generally do not correlate. However, there is still the question of why, over time, they do not tend to become more congruent. We are all familiar with individuals who express a desire to act in a certain way but seem unable to do so consistently. That is, their self-attributed and implicit motives are discordant. For such people, as Buck (1985) argued, analytic thought should provide the opportunity to regulate emotion and motivation. Because the correlation between the two types of motives is essentially zero, this does occur for roughly one half of the population whose self-attributed and implicit motives are similar. As for the other half of the population, systematic experience-based self-observation, as in psychotherapy or motivation training courses (Miron & McClelland, 1979), may bring the two types of motives into alignment. For example, managers may discover that although they believe they have a strong desire to manage others (*san* Power), they are not doing well at managing because they do not enjoy having impact on others (low *n* Power). And this discovery enables them to take corrective action either by learning to enjoy doing what the job requires or by changing their conscious aspirations.

But whatever the reasons for discordance between implicit and explicit motives, it can certainly lead to trouble. It was precisely symptomatology that had no basis in self-attributed motives that led Freud to get interested in implicit motives. He, like other psychotherapists since, has stressed the importance of discovering the implicit motives by getting down to basic feelings through an analysis of dreams and associative networks. Our picture of implicit motives is consistent with his view in the sense that we assess such motives in fantasy and believe that they are based on innate types of affective arousal and are more primitive than the elaborate system of explicit goals, desires, and commitments that are characteristic of self-attributed motives. We also believe, as he did, that through self-observation and analysis, greater congruence between the two types of motives can be achieved. So an understanding of how implicit and self-attributed motives function is not only theoretically important, it has important practical implications for psychological adjustment.

4 *Thematic analysis, experience sampling, and personal goals*

ROBERT A. EMMONS AND LAURA A. KING

Many of the contributions to this volume focus on the identification of thematic lines in people's lives through the analysis of imaginative productions, a venerable tradition begun by Christiana Morgan and Henry Murray (1935) over 50 years ago. The scope and breadth of the knowledge that has accrued in this area are unquestionably impressive. At the same time, there is no reason to restrict our sources of knowledge about an individual's motivational tendencies to fantasy material collected under experimental conditions. McClelland (1985b) defined a motive as a "recurrent concern for a particular goal state, based on a natural incentive, that energizes, orients, and selects behavior" (p. 590). This definition captures the pervasive impact of motives on human experience. Moreover, it suggests that one may find clues to an individual's motive tendencies in a vast array of aspects of experience, none of which can be seen as untouched by the individual's motivational constitution. A second implication of McClelland's definition of motive is that an important source of the idiosyncratic unity, coherence or internal lawfulness in personality is provided by motivation (McClelland, 1981). Motivation has long been viewed as a force underlying pattern and meaning in human life (e.g., Murray, 1938). Interest in motivation implies an interest in recurrent pattern. Explorations in motivation can be seen as explorations in the spontaneous expressions of the individual as well as in thematic coherence. Motive impulses find expression through a variety of outlets and all of these outlets are potentially useful to research in human motivation. Thus, a wide range of techniques is available to the researcher intent on depicting the motivational aspects of a person.

There are several methodologies examining the contents of consciousness that are potentially useful to such an exploration. In this chapter, we will review the possibilities of a number of contemporary methodologies and

We wish to thank Charles Smith, David McClelland, Rebecca Eder, and Dan P. McAdams for their helpful comments on an earlier draft of this chapter.

73

consider their relation to the technique of thematic analysis. This chapter will focus on three levels of inquiry that have proved useful in research. First, means of accessing naturally occurring thought will be considered as they pertain to the uncovering of motivational themes. Second, various approaches to thematic coherence will be examined. Last, we will consider the role that may be played by personalized goal units in the search for a more complete understanding of human motivation. Throughout this discussion, opportunities for innovative applications of thematic analysis will be emphasized. Our review is meant to be less exhaustive than suggestive, for we view the possible venues of motivational inquiry to be innumerable given the appropriate methodological and theoretical considerations. The works to be described here should be taken as models for future research in motivation, utilizing in addition to imaginative stories, a variety of motive-relevant aspects of experience. In addition, we will suggest throughout instances in which aspects of experience that have been employed as criterion variables might prove useful as indicators of motivation in their own right. Presumably, naturally occurring thought, personally significant memories, and idiographically generated goals share at least as intimate a link with the individual's motive configurations as a sample of storytelling.

ASSESSING MOTIVATION VIA THOUGHT STREAMS

Atkinson (1982; reprinted as chapter 2 of this volume) has contended that motives determine how much time a person will devote to thinking about a particular content area. A number of techniques have been developed for exploring spontaneously generated thought (for reviews, see Klinger, 1978; Singer, 1988; and Singer & Kolligian, 1987). Singer and Kolligian have provided an exhaustive review of methodologies for studying "the private personality" – the ongoing stream of consciousness, including emotion, fantasy, imagination, and cognitive variables such as schemata, scripts, and prototypes. Methods for studying ongoing thought include using retrospective questionnaires, having subjects "think aloud" during problem solving, and having them keep track of each time they think of a particular topic or every time an event occurs during their daily routine (Klinger, 1978). Although these procedures are well suited to a number of investigations, they do not lend themselves directly to the study of naturally occurring spontaneous thought (Klinger, 1978; Singer, 1988). In addition to these techniques, researchers have employed an Experience Sampling Method (ESM) by which subjects' daily activities may be periodically interrupted using unobtrusive electronic pagers or "beepers" (Hormuth, 1986; Klinger, 1978; Larson & Csikszentmihalyi, 1983; Singer, 1988). The beepers cue subjects to focus on the thoughts and behaviors occurring just before the beep. Generally, beepers are programmed to cue subjects at random times during the time period in which they are awake. After the cue, thoughts and behaviors may be described narratively by subjects or they may be recorded in questionnaire scales designed for the procedure.

Hormuth (1986) has reviewed the potential role of ESM in the study of individuals. The ESM provides a great deal of information regarding the single case, while, at the same time, allowing for aggregation of data. Both of these treatments of thought sampling data have proved useful (e.g., Klinger, 1977; Klinger, Barta, & Maxeiner, 1981). The ESM has been used to investigate mood variation and the "topology of daily life" (Hormuth, 1986). The ESM would appear to be an especially promising technique for the study of the impact of motivation on thought and behavior because it taps precisely the type of thoughts and behaviors considered most likely to be influenced by motivation.

McClelland (1980, 1981, 1985b; McClelland, Koestner, & Weinberger, chapter 3, this volume) contrasts operant with respondent behaviors and thoughts. Operants are behaviors and thoughts that occur spontaneously, without an obvious provoking stimulus. Respondents are conscious, thoughtful behavior requiring self-reflection. Constructing an imaginative story in response to a picture is an example of an operant behavior. Implicit motives, or those assessed through content analysis of thematic apperceptive stories, should be expected to correlate only with criteria that involve spontaneous behaviors, not self-conscious choices. Because it taps into the naturally occurring stream of behavior, the ESM is particularly suited to the study of these operant dependent variables.

McAdams and Constantian (1983) successfully employed the ESM in research on implicit affiliation and intimacy motivation. Fifty college students, having previously written imaginative stories to pictures, wore electronic pagers for a period of 1 week. These students were beeped seven randomly determined times each day. Upon being beeped, students stopped whatever they were doing and completed a brief questionnaire in which they reported thoughts, feelings, and behaviors. These thoughts were later coded for interpersonal content.

Intimacy scores, obtained from the thematic apperceptive measure, were positively correlated with the frequency of interpersonal thoughts. The ESM also provided McAdams and Constantian with information about spontaneous behaviors and feelings. Compared with those who scored low in intimacy motivation, subjects scoring high in intimacy motivation were more likely to be found writing letters or talking to people and to report feeling positive affect when engaged in interpersonal encounters. In this case, the ESM was used to provide criterion measures with which to validate intimacy motive scores. In addition, the ESM provided information about the discriminant validity of the intimacy scoring system compared with the n Affiliation scoring system. McAdams and Constantian (1983) found that individuals high in n Affiliation who were beeped when alone were more likely to wish for some company than those high in intimacy motivation who were alone. This finding supports the theoretical distinction that has been made between the intimacy motive and *n* Affiliation (McAdams, 1982b). The study by McAdams and Constantian demonstrates the utility of using the ESM to validate motive measures, in particular in demonstrating that the motive being measured predicts naturally occurring thoughts, behaviors, and feelings.

Although in this example, thoughts provided a dependent variable predicted by motive scores, research to be discussed later has utilized thought samples as predictors of outcome variables. In addition, the ESM has proved useful in demonstrating the motivational character of constructs that are not tied to the social motive tradition (e.g., current concerns, studied by Klinger, 1978). It is plausible that investigators might gain more information from thoughts as the actual indicators of motivation. Thoughts themselves could be content analyzed for motivational themes, much the same as personal documents might be (Alexander, 1988). Spontaneous thoughts would seem to be the most direct way to tap motivational pattern and coherence. After all, it seems sensible that the amount of time an individual spends thinking about a particular content area would be an indicator of the individual's preoccupation with that topic.

Both Hormuth (1986) and Singer (1988) concur that the ESM can be used to access coherence in personality. For instance, Singer has suggested that a number of potentially related sources of coherence (to be discussed) be studied within ongoing thought sequences in order to clarify the nature of their organization via naturally occurring thought. Singer reports results indicating that thematic life patterns may be reflected in thought samples. Adolescents with long-standing interpersonal conflict tended to have more thoughts about simulated conflict than those who did not have such a long-standing pattern. The utility of experience sampling in highlighting resonant patterns in thought, linked to situational cues and previous experience, is yet another way in which this methodology can serve an important role in studies in motivation.

McClelland (1981) asserts that personality psychology should seek out not merely superficial behavioral consistency but, more meaningfully, coherence or "lawfulness" at a more "genotypic" level. Thus, we should strive to uncover those attributes of the person that render inconsistencies meaningful, that illustrate the internal logic and thematic pattern that exist within experience throughout life. Because motives are sources of pervasive and enduring concern, they should provide a means of gaining access to this coherence, and studies have supported this contention. For instance, with regard to autobiographical material, McAdams (1982b) found that individuals high in intimacy motivation tend to have selective recall for interpersonal memories compared with those low in intimacy motivation. As was the case with thought samples, it would be both possible and interesting to utilize the dependent variable in this study, personally significant memory, content analyzed for motives, as an indicator of motivational themes in its own right. Alexander's (1988) methodologically oriented paper details techniques for extracting motivational themes from personal materials, such as autobiographical documents (see also, Winter, chapter 7, this volume). It may be possible to apply these methods to personal memories collected for the purpose of assessing motives.

INTERACTIONAL THEMES

A number of related approaches have shared an interest in identifying recurrent interpersonal themes or motivational tendencies, as expressed in narrative accounts of personal experience. Thorne (1989) has proposed that "core conditional patterns" motivate individuals to perceive and construct experience in familiar ways. These conditional patterns are statements phrased in if–then rules linking behaviors to conditions and they usually contain wishes, often but not always frustrated. For example, an individual might identify a core conditional pattern as "Whenever I need help from others, they let me down." This concept bears considerable resemblance to Tomkins's (1987) "nuclear script" concept. Scripts may be characterized as recurrent, affectively charged, dynamic sequences (Alexander, 1988; Tomkins, 1987). Two related constructs are the "core conflictual relationship theme" (Luborsky, 1977) and "core organizing principles" (Meichenbaum & Gilmore, 1984). After reviewing transcripts from the psychotherapeutic sessions of individuals who had and had not experienced improvement within the therapy, Luborsky identified overarching relationship themes that are repeated throughout the individual's life and, importantly, within the process of therapy. The link between these core conflictual relationships and Freudian transference and repetition compulsion is readily apparent. According to Luborsky, individuals who showed improvement were more likely to have mastered their core conflictual relationships within therapy. For example, one improving client, whose core conflictual relationship theme was "I need to be given assurance that . . . I am okay" (p. 378), demonstrated mastery over the conflict after experiencing it within the confines of therapy. Because core conflictual relationships have been found to persist throughout therapy, attention to these themes allows the therapist to identify and deal with important, enduring, idiographic concerns.

Meichenbaum and Gilmore (1984) define core organizing principles (or "cops") as cognitive structures, outside of conscious awareness, that explain and predict behavior. Cops represent overlearned "tacit knowledge" that influences behavior automatically or an individual's "set" in approaching the world. Meichenbaum and Gilmore give as an example a man who overreacts to daily hassles because of a history of being humiliated and feeling victimized. This individual used his experiences and feelings to construct an approach to life that guided his behavior and, eventually, the behavior of those around him. Although the language of core organizing principles remains largely cognitive, these cognitive structures are described by Meichenbaum and Gilmore as based on learning and deprivation, similar to treatments of the development of motives (e.g., McClelland, 1985b). In addition, their potential value as a link to motivational structures increases because their influence on behaviors is largely implicit.

The broad theoretical constructs of core conditional patterns, core conflictual relationships, and core organizing principles are different in a number of ways, because they have been developed to answer diverse questions about behavior, affect, and cognition. Nevertheless, these constructs, as well as a number of others, share an emphasis on coherence throughout human life. Notably, they contain reference to motivation as well. For instance, Thorne (1989) describes core conditional patterns as motivating the individual toward familiar contingencies. Thorne further states that the more complex patterns include the element of a wish or desire. Luborsky (1977) states that conflictual relationships "get expressed when wishes are activated" (p. 387). Meichenbaum and Gilmore (1984) illustrate how various needs, such as the need for approval, reveal the ways in which situations are perceived and behaviors are selected.

At the core of these conceptualizations is the idea that thematic pattern and continuity throughout human life are provided by needs that are never completely satisfiable (cf. Aronoff & Wilson, 1985) and persist as a source of activity. Consistencies as well as inconsistencies emerge as a result of efforts toward thematically similar ends. Thematic analysis within and among these structures would provide enormous information about the relevance of certain types of motives for a number of outcomes. The means by which they are collected and studied provide additional areas of untapped potential for thematic analysis. Thorne (1989) conducted a small scale exercise in which individuals actually identified patterns for themselves from among their own memories. Luborsky (1977) painstakingly examined psychotherapy transcripts. Both types of data would be of interest of investigators of motivation. Lastly, these core principles may require more fine grained analysis given that they may conflate a need with the strategy typically used to achieve the object of the need.

PERSONAL GOALS

Just as thematic analysis need not be limited to imaginative stories told to specific stimuli, motivational constructs need not be limited to high level motive dispositions or abstract theoretical structures. In recent years, a considerable literature has developed around the study of human motivation via personalized action units or personal goals. Examples of such units include current concerns (Klinger, 1971, 1975, 1977, 1987b), personal projects (Little, 1983, 1989), life tasks (Cantor & Langston, 1989; Cantor, Norem, Niedenthal, Langston, & Brower, 1987), and personal strivings (Emmons, 1986, 1989). A current concern may be defined as the state an organism occupies between becoming committed to pursuing a goal and either gaining it or abandoning it (Klinger, 1977). Personal projects are sequences of personally relevant action (Little, 1989). Life tasks are consensually defined problems individuals are currently working on, typically tied to normative life transitions (Cantor et al., 1987). Personal strivings are relatively enduring, idiographically coherent patterns of goals that represent what an individual is typically trying to do (Emmons, 1986, 1989). Similarities and differences between these constructs are discussed by Cantor (1990) and Klinger (1989). All of these units have proved valuable in research. Their various applications and their potential relations are addressed in a recent review by Emmons (in press).

Goal perspectives on motivation share the basic assumption that goals influence ongoing thought and behavior as well as emotional reactions. Thus, much like motives, their impact on experience is pervasive. Unlike social motives, however, goals are thought to be accessible to conscious awareness, though they may not be represented in consciousness while an individual engages in active pursuit (Emmons, in press). An additional commonality in these perspectives is that subjects have been asked to rate their goals (life tasks, current concerns, personal projects, or personal strivings) on various nomothetic dimensions such as importance, difficulty, and ambivalence. These dimensions have been used to predict thought as well as well-being (e.g., Emmons & King, 1988) enabling the goals perspective to benefit from both nomothetic and idiographic techniques.

Although most of these goal units purport to be motivational in some sense, their proposed relations to social motives vary. For instance, current concerns were developed as an alternative to social motive research, in reaction to the equivocal results apparent in studies employing thematic apperceptive measures of motives to predict naturally occurring behaviors and thoughts (Klinger, 1978). On the other hand, the relations that might exist between personal strivings and motive dispositions have been addressed theoretically and empirically (Emmons, in press; Emmons & King, 1989; Emmons & McAdams, 1991) and these explorations will be considered later. The concepts of current concerns and personal strivings will be the focus of the remainder of this discussion. Two questions will be addressed: First, to what extent can these goal units be considered motivational? Second, how can these units be used in a thematic analysis of motivation?

Because the concept of current concern was developed as a reaction to motive disposition research, it is a logical starting point in this last portion of our discussion. Klinger (1971, 1975, 1977, 1987b) has argued that motivational effects on thought content as reflected by thematic apperceptive stories can be better accounted for in terms of current concerns than motive dispositions. Accordingly, Klinger (1966) concluded that motive dispositions are too broad to predict moment-to-moment thought. In contrast, current concerns may be very broad or very narrow. Their time frame may be transient or lifelong. In combination with environmental external cues or internal symbolic cues, current concerns predict naturally occurring thought. For example, Klinger has demonstrated in a number of studies that current concerns, gleaned from interviews with subjects or from questionnaires, sensitize individuals to attend to, recall, and reflect cues related to their current concerns. In addition, Klinger, Barta, and Maxeiner (1980) found that whether a given concern was reflected in spontaneous thought could be predicted by a number of characteristics of the concerns. For instance, current concerns were more likely to appear in thought if they were not routine and if little time remained for action on the goal. The intensity of the individual's sense of commitment to the concern, the amount of unexpected difficulties in the pursuit of the goal, and the goal's instrumentality for the accomplishment of other goals all predicted thought about the goal (Klinger et al., 1980). In summary, current concerns have proved useful in predicting spontaneous thought and studies have supported the status of this concept as motivational as well as cognitive.

The current concern approach is not without its disadvantages, however. Whereas a number of studies indicate that the concerns are indeed motivational, their relevance to the issue of coherence remains troublesome. This problem is exacerbated by the absence of both a specific time frame and a clearly delineated level of abstraction in the formulation of concerns. For instance, current concerns may include such trivial goals as picking up one's dry-cleaning and such broad long-term goals as making a meaningful contribution to humanity. Thus, concerns include terminal goals that will be dropped upon their completion as well as goals that will provide a source of pattern throughout life. Given this wide variation, concerns may not lend themselves readily to an investigation of coherence as a continuous phenomenon. In this regard, personal strivings may provide the preferred level of analysis.

As mentioned previously, personal strivings represent an individual's characteristic goals. As such, they occupy a level of abstraction below broad social motives but above concepts like current concerns or personal projects. For instance, the current concern, "to finish the paper I've been working on" might be subordinate to the personal striving, "to succeed in my academic endeavors," and in turn this striving might be subordinate to an overarching need to succeed. Compared with concerns, strivings are more enduring. They are thought to render subordinate goals functionally equivalent for the individual (Emmons, 1989). Importantly, strivings are similar to social motives insofar as they refer to a person's goals rather than their actual success at those goals (Emmons, 1986).

Research using the personal striving construct has been reviewed by Emmons (1989) and only the most relevant aspects of this research will be discussed here. Generally, investigations utilizing this construct have indicated that, like current concerns, strivings are both motivational and cognitive and that these units may serve as predictors for important personality variables. In addition, these investigations have demonstrated that it is possible to operationalize traditionally significant motivational processess (e.g., intrapsychic conflict) using personalized goals.

In experience sampling studies, characteristics of personal strivings have been found to predict naturally occurring mood and thought (Emmons, 1986; Emmons & King, 1988). Daily negative affect has been related to ambivalence about one's goals, as well as to conflict between goals. Daily positive affect has been related to goal characteristics of value, importance, and past fulfillment (Emmons, 1986). In a study of the impact of personal striving conflict on well-being (Emmons & King, 1988), subjects completed a matrix in which they rated the effect that success in each of their goals would have on every other goal. Subjects' daily thought and behavior samples were then coded for their relatedness to each of the subjects' goals. Results indicated that subjects were more likely to think about those goals that conflicted with other goals, and yet they were unlikely to act on them. Using the relationship between thoughts, behavior, and conflict within subjects, inhibition and rumination scores were computed for each subject and found to correlate with measures of psychological distress (Emmons & King, 1988). As well as illustrating the effect of two components of conflict, rumination and inhibition, on well-being, this personalized approach to motivation also employed the ESM as a predictor, not just as a dependent variable, and conducted the thematic coding of thoughts using idiographically determined categories – the individual's idiosyncratic strivings.

PERSONAL STRIVINGS AND MOTIVE DISPOSITIONS

Recently, work on personal strivings has adopted a method for coding goals with regard to the type of underlying motive disposition they seem to tap. The rationale behind this procedure involves the hierarchical ordering of implicit motives and explicit goals. Motives can be seen as clusters of recurrent prototypical goals in a fashion analogous to conceptualizing traits as clusters of prototypical behaviors (Emmons & McAdams, 1991), with personal strivings occupying the lower level of the hierarchy. Thus, personal goals occupy a place below social motives on a hierarchy of control (Powers,

Table 4.1. *Personal strivings categorized as social motives*

Motive	Striving
Achievement	"Push myself to attain my goals"
Affiliation	"Meet new people"
Intimacy	"Take others' needs into consideration"
Power	"Persuade others that I am right"

Source: King, 1989.

1973). This hierarchy can be construed in a number of ways. The higher levels may be seen as less cognitive, less accessible to awareness and hence less self-conscious, less malleable, and less informed by situational particularities. On the other hand, the next level, personal strivings, may be seen as infused with the influences of motive dispositions, of beliefs and values, and of situational opportunity. Thus, personal strivings may be viewed as at once cognitive and motivational, as "secondary process" reflections of abstract, basic needs. Given the pervasive impact of motives on spontaneous thought and behavior, it seems reasonable to expect motives to find expression in individualized, self-generated goals.

The guide for the coding of strivings into motive content categories is based on published thematic motive scoring systems included in this volume. The criteria for scoring each goal as relevant to a specific motive were also closely tied to the definitions of each motive as described in a number of investigations (Emmons & McAdams, 1991). For example, *n* Power has been defined as the need to have influence on one's surroundings and it has been tied to the natural incentive of impact (McClelland, 1985b). The criteria for scoring a striving as power-related include the following concerns: (a) establishing or maintaining power; (b) having impact, control, or influence over others; (c) seeking fame or public attention; (d) comparison and/or competition with others; (e) dominating, persuading, or convincing others; and (f) arousing emotions in others (Emmons & McAdams, 1991). Table 4.1 contains examples of the types of goals that have been categorized as pertinent to the various motives. After coding is completed, each subject is assigned a score for each motive, which indicates the number of strivings (or proportion, if subjects generate an uneven number of strivings) they generated that were relevant to the motive. Thus, using this procedure, the list of strivings given by the subjects are treated as relatively operant responses elicited by the open stem, "I typically try to . . ."

Within this perspective, several issues regarding the relations between motives and motive-relevant goals have been addressed; however, a few criticisms that can be foreseen in reaction to this scheme also deserve comment. We will first address these problems and then present a summary of a recent study employing thematic coding of personalized goals. The most basic problem facing our attempted integration is that goals are based on self-report and conscious choice, regions argued (McClelland, 1981) to be of limited relevance in motivational inquiry, given the previously described operant–respondent distinction. Distinctions have been drawn between self-attributed or explicit needs and social motives or implicit needs. McClelland, Koestner, and Weinberger (chapter 3, this volume) compared motive scores obtained from content analysis of imaginative stories and motive scores derived from self-report questionnaires such as the Personality Research Form (PRF; D. N. Jackson, 1984). They concluded that explicit and implicit needs predict different criterion variables, with implicit motive scores fulfilling the three defining functions of a motive. Projective measures provide an open response format, conducive to spontaneous nonconscious activity. Self-report questionnaires limit response options and require self-reflection.

Thus, self-report and projective measures would seem to tap two essentially independent systems (McClelland, 1985b). Further, McClelland (1981) has admonished motivational researchers against the use of self-reports since they are likely to be tempered by considerations of impression management. In addition, although motivation need not be wholly or dynamically unconscious, motive dispositions function via implicit channels and therefore they are not necessarily available to self-report (McClelland, 1981). Thus, in order to tap motivational material, information must be collected in a manner that does not severely limit response possibilities and does not require self-reflection by subjects. These concerns would seem of vital import to our proposed system in which conscious goals share an implied relationship with underlying motives.

The comparisons between thematic measures and questionnaire measures of motives are not wholly applicable to the present discussion of personalized goals for a number of reasons, however. These comparisons have tapped self-report only as it is represented by forced-choice questionnaires, which severely limit an individual's range of response. Goal units are idiographically defined, the only limitation being that the goals listed meet a certain level of abstraction. Generating this list may not be as unrestricted as storytelling, but it is clearly less constraining than a scale item.

Constructing a striving list does require some self-reflection, however. Ultimately, the importance of this fact depends on one's view on a critical, though possibly unanswerable, question: To what extent do people know what they are doing? Generally, goals have been taken at face value, as reflections of individuals' perceptions of the dynamic tendencies in their own lives. The assumption is made that individuals do have at least some access to what they typically try to do. This assumption presents a dilemma to our proposed integration of the two classes of motivational data.

One response to this issue is to place the strivings within the context of other spontaneously generated responses. In requiring subjects to generate lists of strivings, we are asking them not to tell us if they possess a given motive configuration but to create a list of their own ideas about what they are doing. Whether these goals reflect reality is irrelevant. Like a personal diary, they are subjective and potentially erroneous, but they are just as potentially useful to the investigator interested in studying motivation. Still, the fact that striving lists do require self-reflection requires that issues of self-deception and impression management be considered as possible extraneous factors in the final list itself. Addressing this issue, Klinger et al. (1981) assert that people may sometimes misrepresent their goals but there is no evidence to indicate that this is typical or common. The coherence that exists in human life would seem to support the assertion that there is a connection between different levels of abstraction.

The issues of self-deception or impression management only serve to illustrate further the ultimate usefulness of a goals perspective to studies of motivation. Without examining the motivational units or goals that are accessible to self-conscious expression, we would be unable to gauge the extent to which an individual's motive dispositions are reflected in his or her awareness. Clearly, the possible relation between one's implicit and explicit motivation is a significant topic for motivational psychology. Examining goals as well as motives allows us to ask important questions, whose implications are certain to impact upon both areas of research.

No doubt, a number of other challenges may be raised in response to the integration of goal and motive perspectives. Integration does not imply subsuming one set of constructs by the other, but rather exploring the links between them as well as their ability to differentially predict criteria. A recent study by Emmons and McAdams (1991) serves to shed light on some of the issues addressed thus far, as well as to illustrate the potential that exists in this integrative approach.

Emmons and McAdams (1991) employed the personal striving coding system to examine the relation between motive dispositions and idiographic strivings. Subjects wrote stories to thematic apperceptive pictures, completed a list of personal strivings (coded according to the procedure just outlined), and completed the PRF, a questionnaire measure of motive dispositions. Interrater agreement for the striving categories and thematically coded motive scores were 88% and 88 to 94%, respectively. Because striving categories were systematically correlated with their corresponding thematic apperceptive motive, Emmons and McAdams concluded that the ends an individual is trying to achieve correspond with the thematic lines that appear in their imaginative stories. The PRF subscales, interestingly, were related to their corresponding thematic apperceptive motive scores, though inconsistently. Finally, motives assessed via strivings were also

Table 4.2. *Self-reported goals of a subject high in* n *achievement*

Be successful in everything I do
Be an understanding and caring person
Be a patient worker
Help my friends and family when I'm needed
Enjoy life
Express my opinions on an issue when in a discussion
Push myself to my fullest potential
Keep up with latest fashions
Look at life without anxiety
Follow through with my promises and goals
Do not draw too much attention to myself

Source: Emmons and McAdams, 1991.

inconsistently related to PRF scores. These results indicate that the striving lists ought to be considered examples of operant behaviors in which motives are indeed allowed expression. Because strivings do require self-reflection and because they occupy awareness, they may also be considered to serve as schemata. Table 4.2 illustrates the thematic quality that pervades a goal list of an individual who scored high in thematically coded *n* Achievement. The theme of achievement is apparent.

Examining both levels of motivation increases our understanding of thought, feeling, and behavior. The integration of goals and social motives through the combination of narrative thematic analysis and thematic categorization of goals is a new endeavor that presents a number of possibilities for research. Although viewed as fairly persistent, because they occupy a lower level on the hierarchy, strivings may be more likely to shift than motive dispositions. Thus, tracking the channeling of motives through goals throughout the life-span might provide insight into the ways in which individuals negotiate their enduring needs within changing situational constraints and opportunities. This integration would allow us to examine both the foreground of specific changes and the background of general patterns that are characteristic of human life. Such an approach would allow for an examination of that which varies and that which brings meaning to variations in human experience. Because goals can be viewed as both personal and situational (Graham, Argyle, & Furnham, 1980; Read & Miller, 1989), the fit that exists between situations and motives may be examined using goals, providing a contextual analysis of the impact of motives on a number of variables. Goals can be used to provide information about the interplay of motives within the individual. Looking at the types of relationships (i.e., instrumentality or conflict) that emerge between goals that are prototypical of various motives may provide a more fine-grained analysis of the issue of conflict and of the well-established contribution of motive dispositions to both psychological (Malley, 1989; McAdams & Bryant, 1987) and physical (Jemmott, 1987; McClelland, 1989) well-being, as well as to other issues central to human adaptation.

5 *Motivational configurations*

DAVID C. McCLELLAND

Almost from the beginning of research on motives measured in imaginative story content, there has been a continuing interest in how various motive combinations affect behavior (Atkinson, 1958a; Murray, 1938). Over the years a number of different motive configurations have been identified to help explain the ways in which people differ. Sometimes the way in which the configuration has been defined has developed out of theoretical considerations, sometimes out of simple curiosity, and sometimes out of a need to explain findings that are confusing when viewed from the standpoint of only one particular motive.

To do justice to the complexity of personality, we need to consider many aspects acting simultaneously. We investigate motives one at a time primarily to validate our measures and learn about them, not because we think they act in isolation. Furthermore, different tasks arouse different motives or motive combinations. So we need to know what cues in the situation elicit different motives. A task requiring cooperation may appeal to people high in both achievement and affiliation motivation whereas a competitive task may appeal to those high in achievement and low in affiliation motivation (Sorrentino & Sheppard, 1978).

This chapter first reviews research on specific motivational configurations and on moderator variables that affect the relation of motives to behavior. Then the relation of motive configurations to illness is examined. The chapter concludes with a discussion of methodological issues involved in identifying motive configurations and the statistical analysis of data involving multiple motive variables.

RESEARCH ON SPECIFIC MOTIVE COMBINATIONS

Achievement and affiliation motivation

In an early exploratory study, using 127 male clinical psychology trainees, Groesbeck (1958) split *n* Achievement and *n* Affiliation scores at the median,

87

thus generating four motive configurations: high in both motives, low in both motives, and high in one and low in the other. (The tetrachoric r between n Achievement and n Affiliation was .24.) He then determined the extent to which individuals in each of these groups were characterized by a large variety of personality measures obtained from self-reports, peer ratings, and staff ratings. He found that people in the various motive groupings differed from each other in a number of ways, many of which could not be predicted from the correlates of n Achievement and n Affiliation considered separately. In fact there were "twelve significant correlates of the motive configurations . . . which were not related to either motive measure alone" (Groesbeck, 1958, p. 395). For instance, those who were high in both motives felt they were socially responsible and were judged to be conscientious and serious, whereas those low in both motives were considered to be generous and considerate. Those low in n Achievement and high in n Affiliation were considered to be cautious and were less often chosen for intimate friendship. The impression is unmistakable that the motive configurations yield personality portraits that differ from each other and on dimensions not associated with each of the motives considered separately.

The fact that Groesbeck's subjects were male clinical psychology trainees may limit generalization from this study, because they may have had clusters of interests not typical of people in general. For this reason it is particularly interesting that Sorrentino and Sheppard (1978) obtained results that were similar in some respects. These authors studied the way in which motive configurations affected racing times for swimmers competing either individually or as members of a team. Like Groesbeck they found that subjects high in both achievement and affiliation motives were more conscientious and socially responsible in the sense that they swam faster in *group* competition than other people, whereas those who were high in n Achievement and low in n Affiliation swam faster in *individual* competition.

French (1956) found that subjects high in n Achievement and low in n Affiliation chose competent people as work partners rather than friends, whereas the reverse was true of those high in n Affiliation and low in n Achievement. French (1958b) also found that subjects with the former motivational configuration performed better when they were given feedback on how well they were doing, whereas those with the latter configuration performed better when they were told how cooperative they were.

Power and affiliation motivation

Among those high in n Power, McClelland (1975) identified a group of people who were also high in n Affiliation and low in Activity Inhibition (a moderator of motive combinations to be discussed). These people appeared interested in developing a kind of personal enclave, "which gives them a feeling of warmth, strength, and security. For them the family often becomes a kind of fortress; inside it they feel safe, and the whole outside world they view as potentially threatening. They get inspiration from the mother or religious sources, and their attachment to family members is their security and their strength" (McClelland, 1975, p. 281). He also found this motive pattern in the popular literature of countries like Italy and Mexico, in which the culture is frequently characterized as one in which security is sought in a closely knit family system.

On the other hand, high *n* Power and high *n* Affiliation represents an infrequent configuration because the two motives are negatively correlated (McClelland, 1985b). In an analysis of popular literature over time, McClelland (1975) found that the combination of high *n* Power and high *n* Affiliation is frequently followed by a drop in *n* Affiliation, because of the conflict between the two motives. The drop in *n* Affiliation tends to be accompanied by reformist movements on behalf of the disadvantaged that are fueled by increased socialized power motivation. For high power motivation expresses itself more in terms of thinking about the welfare of others when *n* Affiliation is low than when it is high (McClelland, 1975, pp. 346–59, 412).

Zeldow, Daugherty, and McAdams (1988) also found evidence that power and intimacy motivation conflict. Medical students high in both motives were "more depressed, neurotic, fatalistic and self-doubting than were their classmates" (Zeldow et al., 1988, p. 182). They reason that the heavy time demands and pressures of medical school make it difficult for students to achieve their goals of doing an outstanding job and also taking time to be intimate with others. On the other hand, the high intimacy, low power–oriented students demand less of themselves and were found to be best adjusted.

Achievement motivation and motivation to avoid failure

Atkinson (1957) proposed a theory in which risk-taking behavior was jointly determined by the motives to achieve success and to avoid failure. To test implications of the theory empirically, he employed *n* Achievement as the measure of the motive to achieve success and the Test Anxiety score (Mandler & Sarason, 1952) as a measure of the motive to avoid failure. To insure relatively clear-cut motive groups, he and his students at the University of Michigan classified subjects as above or below the median on each score. Then a person high in *n* Achievement and low in anxiety could be considered to be primarily motivated to achieve success, whereas a person high in anxiety and low in *n* Achievement could be considered to be motivated primarily to avoid failure. A simpler way to express this relationship is to subtract the standardized Test Anxiety score from the standardized *n* Achievement score to yield a resultant achievement motivation score. Many of the behavioral correlates reported for the achievement motive by the Michigan group were obtained using the theoretically derived resultant achievement motivation score (Atkinson & Raynor, 1974, 1978, Raynor & Entin, 1982b).

Atkinson and Feather (1966) summarized some of these results by pointing out that the achievement-oriented person (high n Achievement, low motive to avoid failure) is attracted to realistic challenges, starts out as somewhat more optimistic about his or her chances of success, is persistent when it makes sense to continue, but quits sooner when chances of success seem low. The failure-threatened personality (high motive to avoid failure, low n Achievement) on the other hand "resists activities in which his competence might be evaluated." If forced to work he chooses tasks he knows he can succeed at or tasks no one could succeed at so that he can get credit for trying.

Using somewhat different pictures in Germany, Heckhausen developed both n Achievement and fear of failure scores and by subtracting the latter from the former created a Net Hope of Achievement score, which has been used extensively in German studies of achievement motivation (Heckhausen 1963, 1967, 1980).

Implicit and self-attributed motives

Those who developed thematic apperceptive measures of motives have pointed out repeatedly that these measures generally do not correlate significantly with self-reports of motive strength (Atkinson & Litwin, 1960; McClelland, 1980; McClelland, Atkinson, Clark, & Lowell, 1953). McClelland, Koestner, and Weinberger (1989; chapter 3, this volume) have recently reviewed this issue again and tried to clarify the differences between motives measured in thematic apperception ("implicit" motives) and motives measured by means of self-report inventories ("self-attributed" motives). Granted that they are different, it becomes of interest to combine them in various high–low categories. For example, McClelland (1985a) has shown that using both types of measures of affiliation motivation improves predictions of spontaneous affiliative behavior over the predictions by either measure alone. The reason appears to lie in the fact that implicit motives are apt to generate spontaneous behavior and self-attributed motives lead to behavior in response to specific motive-related demands (see chapter 3). In the study referred to, the measure of spontaneous affiliative behavior was the frequency with which a student reported he or she was talking to someone when "beeped" by a pager at random intervals. Talking to another student can be initiated by the person paged (reflecting a strong implicit affiliative motive) or by the request of another student, in which case a person with a strong self-image of being affiliative would be apt to respond. So being strong in both types of motives should predict talking to another student better than being high on either one alone.

However, not much has yet been done with the typologies that result from combining implicit and self-attributed motives. For example, it is not known how differently people high in *n* Achievement would behave who either know or do not know that they have a strong need to achieve.

Uncertainty orientation

Sorrentino, Short, and Raynor (1984), in a study of 239 female college students, introduced a personality modifier of the relationship of resultant achievement motivation to behavior – namely uncertainty orientation. To measure uncertainty orientation they scored stories written to a sentence lead for the frequency with which people mentioned concern about or efforts to reduce conflicts and uncertainties. To measure certainty orientation, they used the acquiescence-free self-report measure of authoritarianism (Byrne & Lamberth, 1971). By subtracting the latter from the former they obtained a resultant measure of uncertainty orientation. They found that only among those high in uncertainty orientation was resultant achievement motivation associated with such classical behaviors as performing better at tasks of intermediate difficulty or tasks that had to be completed before the subject could move on to something else. Certainty-oriented people showed none of the usual relationships of resultant achievement motivation to behavior. Thus, they concluded that it was important to include a cognitive trait to understand better the relation of motivation to performance. The current status and measurement of Uncertainty orientation is presented in chapters 29 and 30 of this volume.

Power motivation at different levels of maturity

McClelland (1975) studied how *n* Power expressed itself in adults who showed different stages of maturity in modes of adaptation to the environment, as the measure has been more recently described by Stewart (see chapter 31). McClelland added standard scores for *n* Power to standard scores for a given mode of adaptation to the environment and correlated the totals with a variety of behaviors. He found, for example, that men high in *n* Power tended to read more power-oriented material if they scored high on the intake mode of adaptation, to control their anger if they scored high on the autonomy mode of adaptation, to drink more heavily if they scored high on the assertive mode of adaptation, and to belong to more organizations if they scored high on the generativity mode of adaptation. In other words combining the power motive with modes of adaptation helps explain a lot of behaviors that are theoretically supposed to occur at various stages of development according to theorists like Erikson (1963), building on earlier contributions by Freud.

Inhibition as a moderator of power motivation

McClelland, Davis, Kalin, and Wanner (1972) found that in comparison with men low in power motivation, those high in power motivation tended to drink alcohol more heavily, but only if they were also low in what the authors termed Activity Inhibition. The measure of this variable was simply a count of the number of times the word "not" appeared in a set of stories. It was called Activity Inhibition because "not" is most often used to indicate that an activity is stopped or is not performed, whereas "n't" is a softer expression often used to negate a state of being (as in "he isn't happy") rather than an action. Men high in n Power and high in Activity Inhibition expressed their power motivation through joining organizations and serving as officers in them. Furthermore, the quality of their power-related stories was different: People in the stories were described as concerned about using power for the good of others or some cause. Thus, a scoring system for this type of power motivation was developed that was called s Power for social-ized power motivation. It contrasted with power-related stories in which the power was exercised for selfish reasons, for the glory of the person using power (called p Power for personal power motivation). People high in p Power or high in n Power and low in inhibition not only drank more, but they were characterized by reckless driving and chasing women and behaving assertively in less socialized ways.

Later the p and s Power scoring systems were dropped and replaced by the classifications on which they were based (namely high n Power and low Activity Inhibition and high n Power and high Activity Inhibition). Because the latter people were drawn to organizational leadership, a more intensive study was made of whether men high in n Power and Activity Inhibition would turn out to be successful managers in business organiza-tions (McClelland, 1975). It was predicted that they would be because managers by definition are required to influence others (high n Power) to get things done, and it seemed reasonable to suppose that if they did this in a controlled way (high Activity Inhibition) they would be more successful than if they did it in an uncontrolled impulsive way (low Activity Inhibition).

The expectation was confirmed, but it was also discovered that prediction of managerial success was improved if it was also required that the n Affiliation score be low (McClelland & Burnham, 1976). This was rational-ized on the grounds that men who were interested in being liked by people (high n Affiliation) would be less likely to be able to make hard managerial decisions. Thus, a *leadership motive syndrome* was defined as at least a moderately high n Power score (T score 45 or more), which was higher than the n Affiliation T score, combined with an Activity Inhibition score above the median. Men characterized by this motive configuration created a better organizational climate in business units (McClelland, 1975), were promoted over a 16-year period to higher levels of management in the American

Telephone and Telegraph Company (McClelland & Boyatzis, 1982), and had more successful marriages (McClelland, Colman, Finn, & Winter, 1978). McClelland (1975) also associated this motive configuration, as scored in national popular literatures, with mobilization of more of a nation's resources for use by the government.

D. G. Winter (1990d) has recently shown that combining *n* Power with a thematic apperceptive measure of responsibility (D. G. Winter & Barenbaum, 1985b) yields a configuration very similar to the leadership motive syndrome. This "responsible power" measure also predicts just as well long-term success in management and has the advantage of more directly suggesting the motivational combination important for management than the rather indirect measure involving the relation of Activity Inhibition to socialized power imagery. (For further information about the responsibility measure, see chapters 35 and 36 of this volume.)

MOTIVE CONFIGURATIONS AND HEALTH

Power motivation and illness

After an initial indication that the leadership motive syndrome predicted high blood pressure (McClelland, 1979) and reported severity of illness (McClelland, Floor, Davidson, & Saron, 1980), subsequent studies showed inconsistent relationships among these variables (Blumenthal, Lane, & Williams, 1985; Fontana, Rosenberg, Marcus, & Kerns, 1987; McClelland, Alexander, & Marks, 1982).

The number of power-related life changes or stresses in combination with high *n* Power had also been found to be related to illness severity (McClelland et al., 1982; McClelland & Jemmott, 1980). So attention shifted to the stressed power motive syndrome defined as an *n* Power T score of 45 or more, lower *n* Affiliation T score, and the number of power or total stresses above the median. The stressed power motive syndrome has been found to be more consistently related to illness severity, although in some cases part of the relationship is due to the fact that more life stress is also associated with more illness. In a study of 47 normal adults (McClelland, Abramson, et al., 1990), a significant correlation between the stressed power motive syndrome and illness severity is accounted for by the fact that stress by itself is highly related to reported severity of illness. However, number of life stresses is not related to number of colds reported ($r = .11$), so the significant correlation between stressed power motive syndrome and colds reported ($r = .30$) is beyond what can be expected from mere stress by itself.

It has been theorized (McClelland, 1989) that people with strong power motives would want to have their way, to control events and have impact on the environment. Blockage of this power drive in the form of internal inhibitions or life stresses would arouse them physiologically leading to sympathetic activation and release of catecholamines (e.g., epinephrine, norepinephrine). This relationship has been confirmed (McClelland, Ross, & Patel, 1985). The increased circulation of catecholamines might impair immune functions such as salivary immunoglobulin A, as demonstrated by McClelland et al. (1985). And impaired immune functions might make the person more susceptible to illness. Jemmott and McClelland (1989) have summarized evidence showing that levels of salivary immunoglobulin A (S-IgA) reflect resistance to upper respiratory infections. The stressed power motive syndrome has been shown in several studies to relate to lower levels of S-IgA (Jemmott & McClelland, 1989), thus accounting for the fact that individuals characterized by the stressed power motive syndrome are more susceptible to colds. The stressed power motive syndrome has also been shown to relate to lower levels of another important immune function, natural killer cell activity (Jemmott et al., 1990).

Affiliative motive configurations and illness

Among college students a dominant affiliative motive (n Affiliation T score higher than n Power T score) was associated with reports of less severe illness, particularly when combined with low Activity Inhibition and low stress (McClelland & Jemmott, 1980). So a relaxed affiliative motive syndrome was defined as dominant n Affiliation combined with an Activity Inhibition score below the median. The relaxed affiliative motive syndrome has been found to relate to higher levels of S-IgA (Jemmott & McClelland, 1989) and to lower illness severity. In another adult sample (McClelland, Abramson, et al., 1990) the relaxed affiliative syndrome correlated $-.22$, $N = 47$, $p < .15$ with severity of illness reports.

An unstressed affiliative motive syndrome has also been defined as dominant n Affiliation combined with a number of life change events below the median. It has been found to relate to higher levels of the S-IgA immune function (Jemmott & McClelland, 1989) and also to a lower frequency of colds reported as one would expect ($r = -.35$, $N = 47$, $p < .05$) in the sample studied by McClelland, Abramson, et al. (1990). The unstressed affiliative motive syndrome has also been shown to relate, though less certainly, to higher levels of natural killer cell activity (Jemmott et al., 1990).

Agency and illness

McClelland (1989) used implicit motive scores to get a measure of the extent to which a person was oriented toward agency or communion, following a distinction introduced by Bakan (1966). It was theorized that people high in the power or achievement motives would be agentically oriented in the sense that they were assertive in trying to master the environment. In contrast, those high in *n* Affiliation should be more oriented toward communion in the sense of wanting to be with people and cooperate with them. So an agency syndrome was defined as being high in *n* Power, high in *n* Achievement (T score of 47 or more), and low in *n* Affiliation (T score below 50). People meeting two of these three criteria were classified as characterized by the agency syndrome. Agency was weakly associated with less illness reported at the outset of a behavioral medicine treatment intervention (McClelland, 1989) and also predicted that adults in mid-life would have fewer serious illnesses in the 10 years after the agency assessment was made (McClelland, 1989).

But both relationships were much stronger if the number of life stresses was taken into account. People characterized by high agency and low stress had good health, whereas those who were either low in agency, or high in agency and high in life stress, were much less healthy. Furthermore agentic individuals less often smoked and more often exercised (McClelland, 1989), which reflects an assertive attitude toward achieving health and may explain why they were healthier.

Six-week behavioral medicine interventions that emphasized coping and relaxation increased agency motivation significantly as contrasted with a control intervention (McClelland, 1989). The measure of increase in agency was the sum of scores of +1 for any gain in T scores for *n* Power or *n* Achievement or loss in T scores for *n* Affiliation from before to after treatment. Furthermore, the greater the agency gain score the greater the reduction in symptoms of illness from before to 6 months after treatment.

METHODOLOGICAL ISSUES

Configurations versus linear additive combinations of characteristics

It can be argued that clustering variables into types, configurations or dichotomies is not methodologically sound (Mendelsohn, Weiss, & Feimer, 1982). As compared with multiple-regression or analysis of variance techniques it apparently loses information. It does not show, as these techniques would, the extent to which each of the variables combine or their interaction contributes to predicting a third variable. For example, when *n* Power and Activity Inhibition are combined by adding scoring weights into an index of socialized power motivation, we cannot discover the extent to which *n* Power, Activity Inhibition, and their interaction contribute to predicting work accomplishment. Either an analysis of variance or a multiple-regression approach would answer such questions, which are presumably questions one might want to ask of the data.

However, J. Block and Ozer (1982) have made it clear that the traditional additive combination approach yields different results and answers different questions from those the pattern approach seeks to answer. For example, if Groesbeck (1958) had used the additive linear approach in trying to understand the relation of combinations of n Achievement and n Affiliation to various personality variables, it is unlikely that he would have discovered a number of the results he reports. The reason is that the characteristics of people with various combinations of these motives are quite different and do not reflect in any orderly way the characteristics of people high in one or the other of these motives. New characteristics appear from the combinations of motives that were unrelated to the motives taken one at a time.

To return to the question of what motive combinations predict work accomplishment, n Power correlated .07 and Activity Inhibition .02 with work accomplishment in a sample of adults (McClelland & Franz, in press). These two components of socialized power motivation correlated $-.26$ with each other. Neither multiple regression nor analysis of variance would indicate that the combination of these components, as represented in the s Power syndrome, would be significantly related to work accomplishment as reported by McClelland and Franz (in press). As J. Block and Ozer (1982) point out, the weakness of additive linear analysis is that it is atheoretical. In this instance a theory stated that the components of the syndrome could not combine in a way in which one substituted for the other. That is, it did not seem theoretically correct to call a person high in s Power who had a low n Power score but a very high Activity Inhibition score so that the sum of the two variables would define him or her as high in s Power.

McClelland and Boyatzis (1982) found that sums or products or other linear combinations of the variables in the leadership motive syndrome did not predict long-term success in management as well as simple high–low breaks on the critical variables in the syndrome. Apparently it is a question of being high on one characteristic plus being high or low on another that makes up a syndrome, not *how* high the person is on the component characteristics. Thus adding the extent of increases in n Achievement and n Power and decreases in n Affiliation after therapy does not yield an agency change index that predicts symptom reduction as well as simply summing shifts in the agentic direction.

Perhaps an analogy from another area can contribute to understanding such results. Imagine using an analysis of variance or multiple-regression technique to predict the power of a compound made up of a combination of oxygen and hydrogen to dissolve sugar. The conclusion would be that neither oxygen nor hydrogen nor their interaction would have the power to dissolve sugar. For it is these variables only in a particular combination that produce water that dissolves sugar. As J. Block and Ozer (1982) conclude, pattern or syndrome analysis is better designed than linear additive analysis to "carve nature at its joints and provide conceptual and predictive advantages."

Multiple determinants of action

Pointing to the value of combinations of motivational variables for predicting behavior does not resolve questions like what combinations are most useful or how many variables of what type should be included in a syndrome. However, both McClelland (1951) and Atkinson (1974) have also conceived of the multiple determinants of action in terms of additive or interactive combinations of variables. Thus, both think of motives, schemata or beliefs, and abilities or skills as independent determinants of action which combine to produce action. McClelland (1985a) has explicitly used a multiple-regression model to show how the affiliative motive, beliefs about one's need for affiliation, and perceived interpersonal skill combine to predict spontaneous affiliative activity. Yet it has just been argued that a configurational rather than a linear regression approach to understanding the relation of implicit and conscious needs for affiliation to action might yield more information. Also variables like stress are usually considered to be part of the environment in equations involving the multiple determinants of action. Yet in some of the research just discussed, stress is combined with power motivation to yield a configuration that predicts illness. When is it more useful to include a determinant of action like life stress in a configuration or to treat it as an independent determinant of action in a regression equation? Sometimes theory will provide an answer to such questions, sometimes not. But it is worth pointing out that the configurational approach, while useful, is not the answer to all questions surrounding combinations of determinants of action.

Standardization problems

Because the configurational approach does not employ sums or differences in characteristics, it necessarily has to establish criteria for deciding that a person is characterized by a particular motive configuration. Usually this has been done by correcting raw motive or other scores for protocol length and T-scoring the resultant measures so that they can be directly compared. Then the T score is classified as above or below the mean or the median and as higher than the T score the person receives on another variable in an ipsative comparison. Because samples have often been relatively small, in order to get enough cases of a given type, individuals have been classified as "relatively high," say, in *n* Power or *n* Affiliation, meaning they have a T score of 45 or more. Furthermore, if the configuration requires that a person be higher on one motive than on a second motive, it has seemed reasonable to set an upper limit on how high the person can score on the second motive and still qualify for inclusion (McClelland et al., 1982). The rationale has been that while an *n* Affiliation T score of 66 might be higher than an *n* Power score of 65, it did not seem reasonable to conclude the person was showing really dominant *n* Affiliation unless *n* Power was relatively low (i.e., below a T score of 50).

Decisions about cutting points for inclusion in configurations have been fairly consistent but have always been made within the particular sample being investigated. Furthermore, because a particular sample may yield few instances of a critical configuration, the criteria have sometimes been liberalized slightly to obtain a larger number of instances of the configuration. The rationale for this procedure has been that the population sampled, the testing conditions, and even the pictures used to elicit stories have varied from study to study. So one can properly talk about high and low only in terms of a particular study. The other possible implication of this procedure is that the results are not really comparable from one study to another. High in *n* Power for one study may mean a score of eight or more and in another a score of five or more. The fact that the mean *n* Power is significantly different for the two studies is difficult to interpret. It may signify that the testing situation or the pictures produced higher *n* Power scores, in which case it is appropriate to define "high" differently in the two groups. On the other hand, if there is a "true" difference in *n* Power due to differences in the people tested, then it would be more appropriate to pool the results from both studies and set a common cutting point for deciding who is high in *n* Power.

These problems are worrisome, particularly when cutting points vary from study to study. The problems arise because there is no standard set of results on a large sample of people who wrote stories to the same set of pictures. The reason such standardization has not been carried out is that somewhat different pictures have been considered appropriate to elicit particular motives in different samples of people. But that argument does not get rid of the problem that motive patterns identified in different studies are not, strictly speaking, precisely comparable. In a way it is surprising, in view of the lack of standardization, that results have been as consistent as they have generally been reported to be.

Stability of configurations

Much of the research using the configurational approach has treated syndromes as if they were stable personality characteristics. Thus, when the leadership motive syndrome predicts managerial promotions 16 years later (McClelland & Boyatzis, 1982), it has been assumed that this is because the syndrome is a stable personality characteristic that has sponsored behaviors that, over time, have led to the person's promotion. Or when agency motivation predicts fewer major illnesses over the succeeding 10 years, presumably it is because people with this characteristic have behaved in ways over time that have enabled them to lead healthier lives.

Yet little or nothing is known about the stability of motive patterns over time. In an examination of all the motive configurations listed in this section on a sample of adults (see McClelland & Franz, in press), only the un-stressed affiliative motive syndrome showed significant stability over a 10-year period in mid-life ($r = .33$, $N = 46$, $p < .05$). This result is probably due to the fact that motive stability is greater when there are few life changes (Koestner & Franz, 1989). Good data on stability over shorter periods of time are not available at this time. Lack of stability may be due to the fact that any element in the configuration, such as stress, can obviously vary from one time period to another or to the fact that small numbers of people in most samples meet the criteria for a configuration (usually around 20%). In such cases, regression toward the mean could easily undermine or reverse a significant relationship. For example, the agency motive combina-tion is defined as being high on two motives and low on another. Regression effects due to chance variability would tend to bring the high scores down and the low score up, weakening any correlation between agency scores at any two time periods. The problem of stability of motive configurations is in need of further study.

Whatever the weaknesses of research to date on identifying particular motive configurations, it is clear that future research must continue to make use of them if it is to make headway in accounting for the complexities of human behavior. Although what has been accomplished in this area to date is clearly exploratory, it has been sufficient to demonstrate over and over again that motive configurations yield better explanations of behavior than a motive alone or in linear combinations with other variables. What is needed now are more careful definitions of motive configurations employing larger samples and standardized measures together with the usual tests of their reliability and validity.

6 *Thematic apperceptive methods in survey research*

JOSEPH VEROFF

By and large, survey research has come to mean asking people questions about their lives or attitudes in a fixed-alternative format. To introduce projective methods into survey research would appear to be an improper marriage of methods. This paper focuses on studies that fostered such marriages. Two in particular (Veroff, Atkinson, Feld, & Gurin, 1960; Veroff, Depner, Kulka, & Douvan, 1980) have yielded exciting information about the nature of motives in the American population – information unavailable through other methods. I review these studies in the hope of generating interest among other researchers in doing similar studies in the future, or helping researchers already interested in doing such studies to meet the challenges unique to the survey setting.

In a certain sense the use of the projective method of assessing motives in survey research is merely an extension of a technique that has long been used in survey research. In order to get spontaneous revelations from respondents, researchers have often asked respondents to talk about issues with regard to an unknown third person rather than directly about themselves. Examples of such measures can be found for the following: psychological defense (D. R. Miller & Swanson, 1960); attitudes toward mental illness (Star, 1955); orientations toward marriage (Gurin, Veroff, & Feld, 1960); and adolescent feelings about peer pressure versus adult authority (Douvan & Adelson, 1966). These ad hoc procedures for specific attitudes have been quite common. Less common are survey projective measures of more general dispositions that have had a history of the usual validation procedures. Such a measure is the topic of this paper.

MEASURING MOTIVES IN SURVEY RESEARCH

In 1956, Gerald Gurin, Sheila Feld, and I undertook a survey of the American people's experiences of well-being or distress in their lives, their reactions to important social roles, and ways in which they dealt with psychological problems. The results of this research were published as *Americans View Their Mental Health* (Gurin et al., 1960). At the suggestion of John Atkinson, we also included in that survey a version of the thematic apperceptive measures of motives that were extant at that time, measures inspired by the study of the achievement motive spearheaded by McClelland and his associates (McClelland, Atkinson, Clark, & Lowell, 1953). The rationale for including these measures was to have a framework for thinking about well-being that was rooted not just in a general descriptive account of how Americans were faring, but in a scientific examination of how that experience was related to some basic motivational dispositions.

Quite apart from the ways in which the motive assessments could help us understand the experiences of psychological well-being or distress, we were frankly interested in the ways in which these motives were expressed in a population more heterogeneous than those groups we had been investigating in our work on motives. That is, in the past the bulk of research on motives focused on college students or other easily available subject populations. To have an assessment of these motives in a cross-section of the American population was an exciting prospect in itself.

The new venture was not a simple undertaking. Nor would it be for anybody who contemplated a similar project in a community or other cross-sectional survey. Many problems were encountered and would still be encountered today. I will enumerate them and discuss them in the hope that anyone who plans such a study can profit by our experience. All of these problems stem from the issue of how a researcher deals with a very heterogeneous sample. In previous research on motives, knowing that one was dealing with a specific homogeneous sample (college sophomores, high school seniors, seventh-graders) allowed the researcher to adapt a simple strategy for data collection, one tied to the sample's characteristics. In a survey one deals with people with varying verbal capacities, from widely different social contexts, and from all parts of the age spectrum. How do you deal with such heterogeneity with a single tool and obtain commensurate results? We will present some answers to this question. (For a complete discussion of these problems, see Veroff et al., 1960.)

Picture selection

If, in the projective assessment of motives, one is to use the standard technique of providing a picture to which a respondent tells a story, then what pictures would be appropriate for all ages and subcultural differences? This was a very difficult question to answer, especially when we wanted to assess not just one motive but three. Our solution was to get pictures that represented relatively universal social situations that most people encounter in their lives. We used different pictures for men and women because we thought that we could not fully transcend the gender difference in how important motives in peoples' lives are expressed. For each gender, then, we had at least one picture of the following: (a) people at work, (b) people in a group setting of the same sex, (c) two persons (an older person with a younger person most commonly seen as a child of the woman or man), (d) a man and a woman,[1] and (e) a single person in a work setting. It was important to cover all these contexts because if we omitted a major context, we would perhaps be neglecting the very context in which one or the other gender and a given social or age group expressed a given motive.

The fact that we were dealing with different age groups, however, presented an enormous problem. We resolved it by selecting pictures of people who were neither very young nor very old. The settings in the pictures are very light on detail, which makes them relatively ambiguous.

We also had to overlook other discrepancies between pictures and respondents of different social backgrounds and decided to err in the direction of the majority. It would have been very difficult to come up with a set of pictures that would duplicate the experience for both blacks and whites. We showed pictures of whites to all respondents. There is no way one can tell whether this arbitrary decision was the best, but research findings from the 1957 survey based on these biased pictures yielded sufficiently interesting and meaningful results for most groups that we felt that the hunches we had about the pictures were reasonable.

The set of pictures that was used is reproduced in the Appendix of this volume. There is some evidence from Veroff, Feld, and Crockett (1966), that an achievement motive score derived from pictures of situations slightly *different* from the one that the person is actually in, are particularly diagnostic of achievement motivation.

Interviewer effects

In a survey one most often employs a group of interviewers, each of whom can be a person with a distinct stimulus value for the particular respondents that he or she interviews. In the national surveys, however, we were fortunate to have control over some of the variables involved. All the interviewers were middle-aged white females. Nevertheless, within that set there can be differences that could affect the quality of motive responses. To handle this we conducted a study of interviewer effects. We assessed the degree to which particular interviewers affected the motive scores of individuals (assuming that motive score distributions were randomly assigned to interviewers). With that assumption we found that there were no significant interviewer effects on the achievement or affiliation motive scores; however, there was a slight, but significant, effect on power motive scores (Veroff coding system: see chapters 19 and 20). If we assume that the power scoring system measures reactions to people's interest in maintaining control, then subtle pressures by the interviewer to respond in a certain way could very well have affected the momentary arousal of the power motive and hence led to higher power motive scores in certain respondents. Thus, with this caution that the power motive scores may be somewhat attributable to interviewer effects, we felt reasonably assured that we were getting commensurate assessment from the interviewers on the various motives.

Placement of motive assessment in the survey

Because we were aware from previous research that the motive assessment could be affected by the immediate prior condition, we were concerned that the set of questions asked immediately before the motive assessment be relatively neutral. Thus, the motive measure was placed very early in the survey. Subjects were given a few questions about some of the experiences in their daily lives such as participation in leisure activities or in organizations as a way to begin the survey as a lead into the motive assessment procedure. The cover story for the projective assessment was that we were trying to get at respondents' reactions to different life situations through the story technique. In future studies using motive or other projective assessments in survey research, we suggest that this precaution also be adopted and that the projective assessment appear relatively early in the sequence of assessment and not be preceded by questions with affective content.

Verbal fluency of respondents

In prior studies of motives we were always dealing with a highly verbal population, and a population who could write. In these survey settings we were dealing with a more heterogeneous population, one in which we had no guarantee that people could write or speak fluently. We clearly had to rely on oral transmission of stories. We decided not to use a tape recorder largely because of expense. We thus had to depend on interviewers being speedy transcribers and in some instances faithful recreators of stories from shorthand notes, once the interview was completed. If there is money available, the tape-recording procedure would be preferable. Respondents are occasionally put off by the storytelling procedure and unable to give free imaginative content. Interviewers are instructed, however, to take what they are given. If respondents said, "I don't know," then interviewers were asked to repeat the question, or if respondents gave just description, interviewers were asked to say, "is there anything more?" There is a problem in allowing interviewers total freedom for deciding when to probe for more information from a respondent. Therefore, with the set of questions that was devised for keeping the flow of a story going, the interviewers were asked not to probe unless the person did not give or felt they could not give any imaginative response whatsoever. The instructions given by the interviewer were as follows:

Another thing we want to find out is what people think of situations that may come up in life. I'm going to show you some pictures of these situations and ask you to think of stories to go with them. The situations won't be clearly one thing or another – so feel free to think of any story you want to. (Show picture 1.) For example, here's the first picture. I'd like you to spend a few moments thinking of a story to go with it. To get at the story you're thinking of I'll ask you questions like: Who are these people? What do they want? and so on. Just answer with anything that comes to mind. There are no right or wrong answers.

The following questions were asked for each story:

     1. Who are (is) the persons (person) – what are (is) they (she/he) doing?
     2. What had led up to this – what went on before?
     3. What do they want – how do they feel?
     4. What will happen, how will it end?

These are adaptations from the standard procedures that were used for written protocols (see appendix 1 of Atkinson [1958a] and chapter 37 of the present volume).

With this provision for not probing even if respondents gave minimal imagery, approximately 12% of the respondents gave such short responses that not much in the way of imaginative content could be coded. We had to establish clear criteria for codable protocols. Judgments were made about whether the responses to each one of these questions reflected any imaginative content. If in two stories a person did not answer one question, or did not respond with imaginative content, or if in one story a person did not respond to two of the questions, then none of the respondent's stories were considered for analysis. We did find that those people whose stories were considered not usable were from less-educated groups.

We were also aware that some respondents, although they did give us codable protocols, could generate some bias because they told especially short stories. We correlated story length and motive scores for achievement, affiliation, and power and found that the correlations, ranging between .21 and .28, were significant for the large samples (597 men; 774 women) with whom we were dealing. We reasoned that verbal fluency was affecting these correlations, and entered a correction factor to remove the correlation of story length from the scores for the motives. We suggest that anyone who is assessing a heterogeneous population in surveys should be alert to this story length problem and apply a correction for story length to the scores for the motives, if it is needed.

Scoring reliability issues

Whenever one goes to a community population, imagery will emerge from responses to pictures that will be different and unusual. This presents some problem for maintaining coding reliability. Therefore, it is important in dealing with coding of stories from surveys to train coders not only to the usual set of stories, like those in appendix I of this book, but also from types of stories that come from respondents in their surveys. Very often there are much more minimal stories than those in the back of this book. Some coding conventions will have to be pragmatically devised for each study as it comes along. For each of the three motives we developed additional coding criteria that helped maintain a reasonable reliability for each of the motives. These criteria are listed in *Marriage and Work in America* (Veroff & Feld, 1970, pp. 370–371).

THE 1957 NATIONAL SURVEY

In spite of these difficulties, the results from using the motive assessment in a national survey were richly rewarding and impossible to obtain in more circumscribed research. Besides giving us demographic norms for the various motives for different groups (black–white differences, Catholic–Protestant differences, occupational differences, age differences, and so on), we are also permitted to see how motives relate to various other aspects of peoples' lives controlling for different types of social contexts. More often than not, social context interacted with a basic relationship that a motive had to behavior. Thus, there is an enormous advantage in getting a large-scale heterogeneous population.

Let me give you some ways in which the 1957 survey has proved useful for understanding motives in different groups and permitted us to do unique, rather complicated analyses. One of the first analyses emerging from the national survey tested Catholic–Protestant differences in need for achievement. McClelland (1961) had been arguing from Weber (1930) that Protestants have stronger need for achievement than Catholics. In our national survey we were able to test that proposition and found that controlling for various factors, there was no Catholic–Protestant difference in the achievement motive. If anything, Catholics have higher scores under certain conditions; we found that middle-aged Catholic men have higher need for achievement than middle-aged Protestant men. From that research McClelland's hypothesis has been virtually abandoned for modern-day American life. Previous studies showing a difference were judged to be peculiar to special groups studied.

With the full array of respondents' occupations provided by the survey and knowing the occupations of respondents' fathers, Crockett (1962) was able to develop measures of occupational mobility and found evidence that men who were upwardly mobile relative to their fathers did have higher achievement motives than those who were not upwardly mobile. This type of finding is much harder to get at in more restrictive samples.

With a variety of age groups available in the survey data, Baruch (1967) was able to show that the achievement motive of college-educated women was perhaps dampened during their twenties but became much greater later on. Her explanation took into account the fact that in 1957 this generation was part of a more traditional sexist society and middle-class women were not encouraged to fill occupational roles when they finished college. Rather they were expected to raise and nurture a family. After children, careers were possible.

A multitude of results were available through Veroff and Feld's (1970) examinations of how motives interact with the roles of marriage, parenthood, and work. Being able to control for different role situations that people were in (e.g., being a young parent as opposed to being a middle-aged parent; or being a high-school-educated husband as opposed to being a college-educated husband; or being in very professionally oriented work as opposed to being a service worker or a farmer) enabled us to test the impact of different role demands on the expression of different motives. The results from the study appear in the book *Marriage and Work in America* (1970). Just to give some flavor for the kinds of results that were available in that monograph the following can be stated:

1. Age of children in the life cycle of parenthood is an important conditioner needed to understand ways in which parenthood relates to the power motive.
2. Reactions to the marital role are not correlated with the motive for affiliation but with the motive for power.
3. It is very clear that the type of work men do has impact on motive satisfaction, particularly affiliative satisfaction.

THE 1976 NATIONAL STUDY

In redoing *Americans View Their Mental Health* in 1976, Veroff, Douvan, and Kulka (1981) reintroduced a second testing of the national study of motives 19 years later. The same general procedures were used, which allowed us to compare motives assessed in 1957 with those assessed in 1976. We were able to recode the 1957 stories using a new coding scheme that was devised since the initial study was done. Coding for the Winter version of the power motive (see chapters 21 and 22) was conducted along with the Veroff version.[2] We were able to compare the changes in motives for men and women during the generation through the 1950s to the 1970s, controlling for the changes in the educational level and the age distribution of the population shifts during that time. Veroff et al. (1980) summarized these comparisons. The most dramatic was that fear of weakness increased in both men and women across the generation. Another result was that the affiliation motive decreased in men but not in women. These results can help us interpret ways in which the national character has shifted over that generation. The drop in the affiliation motive in men was disconcerting and not readily predictable. The interpretation given to this is that men have increasingly been concerned about competition in the work place and less interested in the community orientation. It would be exciting to have additional replications after 1976 to see whether these trends have continued.

With repeated surveys there is also another potential use of the data. Some important developmental findings can now be suggested independent of cohort or history effects. If one has scores plotted against age in two different generations and the same results emerge, then there is some chance that the relationship reflects an underlying developmental trend. Such developmental findings occurred in Veroff, Reuman, and Feld's (1984) analysis of motives across the life cycle. They found that women's affiliation motive is high in the younger ages and low in older ages in both 1957 and 1976. This argued for a developmental decrease in the affiliation motive over the life-span for women. Similar analyses yielded a middle-age surge in the power motive for men. Otherwise there were few persistent parallel results for the other motives. This analysis also permits one to look for cohort effects. One striking result was that men born in the 1920s were extremely high in the achievement motive in their young adulthood but extremely low at middle-age.

The 1976 survey was analyzed for motive effects on well-being in the same way that Veroff and Feld (1970) did in the 1957 survey. Veroff and Smith (1985) ignoring cohort and period interpretations of the 1976 data depicted motive effects for people at different ages. The most interesting result from that work was the fact that while leisure was an expression of the achievement motive among older men, it was not at all a channel for achievement interests of young adults. This of course could be a cohort phenomenon but for the moment it stands as an interesting result that had been suggested by other research (Maehr & Kleiber, 1981). It took a heterogeneous sample found in a survey to attack the problem systematically. Veroff and Smith (1985) also found that the correlates of "motives" as measured through projective assessment and the correlates of "values" as measured through conscious choices were not the same in the analysis of their data (see McClelland, Koestner, & Weinberger, 1989; chapter 3 of this volume).

The most exciting use of the data from the two surveys comes from finding ways in which the motive scores are related to certain kinds of behaviors or feelings very differently in the two different studies. One of them had to do with job satisfaction. We found that the achievement motive measure in the 1957 survey was negatively related to job satisfaction, but in the 1976 survey it was positively related to job satisfaction. Different explanations for these contradictory results are possible: Perhaps the achievement motive assessment is different in the two years; perhaps the meaning of job satisfaction is different in the two years; or perhaps the relationship between the two is different in the two years. All three explanations are plausible. The one that we considered most likely is that important concerns about achievement were more frustrated in the 1950s and more gratified in the 1970s. A follow through on such results can tell us as much about the nature of the achievement motive as it does about the relationship of the achievement motive to work.

ARE THERE SHORTCUTS FOR MEASURING MOTIVES IN SURVEYS?

To get assessments of needs for achievement, affiliation, or power through thematic apperceptive assessment in these surveys was an enormous effort. Much time and concern for control had to be invested in this work. Researchers connected to the studies obviously thought it was worth it, but we have to face the fact that not all researchers will be as invested. Are there shortcuts to getting measures of motives through more convenient means? A number of us (Veroff, McClelland, & Ruhland, 1975) undertook a survey study to assess the validity of a questionnaire measure of the achievement motive. We used a variety of techniques in a Detroit survey, in addition to the standard projective measure. Some involved very short projective techniques such as completing the sentence "In the future . . . ," a technique that had been used by Rogers and Neill (1966) on Colombian farmers and found to be predictive of how successful they were as farmers. Others involved multiple-choice procedures modeled after the work of Atkinson and Moulton (1969), using the Atkinson model for risk taking (Atkinson, 1957) as a basis for determining multiple-choice alternatives that reflected high resultant achievement motives. Others were more behavioral, namely persistence and choosing challenging alternatives. There was some validation for the multiple-choice assessment. Although it correlated with the projective assessment and with other tasks given to respondents in that survey, it was not a reasonable substitute for the thematic apperceptive measure, which has yielded the most complex and rewarding set of results.

SUMMARY

If using the projective measure is so complicated, why bother? We think the results speak for themselves. We have gained insights about national character through the use in repeated surveys. Moreover, we have taken advantage of the heterogeneity of the survey samples to examine the different motives contextually, to see how different life experiences of people affect motivational striving in different ways. And finally, the fact that the same projective measure is used in repeated surveys allows us to test general propositions about the nature of the motives, especially those dealing with how these motives shift over the life-span and historical time.

NOTES

1 This was the only picture that was common to both men and women. Thus, gender differences could be directly assessed on this picture, but only on this picture.
2 Dan McAdams has also coded the 1976 stories for the motive for intimacy (see chapters 15 and 16).

7 Content analysis of archival materials, personal documents, and everyday verbal productions

DAVID G. WINTER

The scoring systems described in this book are usually applied to written thematic apperception materials obtained by the direct testing of groups or individuals. Veroff (chapter 6) has described how they can be adapted for use in survey research, which greatly expands their applicability. This chapter describes how they have been used to analyze archival historical materials, personal and cultural documents, and everyday verbal material such as conversations, reported dreams, and even transcriptions of television programs.

WHY USE HISTORICAL MATERIALS?

Problems of direct testing

Often we want to make psychological inferences about people and groups to whom we lack access, groups that cannot be studied by any kind of direct testing or survey interviewing. Prominent persons such as authors or political leaders usually cannot be tested; and when they can, ethical considerations would make it difficult to disclose the results. Large groups or cultures are too amorphous and too expensive to study by direct testing. And (to adapt a quotation from Glad, 1973) by their deaths, historical figures and groups have taken with them their achievement and power motivation, their integrative complexity and their explanatory style. There are also situations where testing, even with thematic apperception methods, is possible but undesirable because it arouses test-taking or self-presentation sets, suspiciousness, defensiveness, or anxiety (Lundy, 1988). In all these circumstances, people must be studied indirectly or at a distance if they are to be studied at all. Thus many researchers have adapted the scoring systems described in this book for use with naturally occurring verbal materials such as letters, speeches, popular literature, and interviews.

Advantages of historical materials

While historical materials may be the only way to study some problems, they may also have advantages when studying people who could be tested directly. First, personal documents such as letters or diaries are (at least from the point of view of the research) completely nonreactive – not even subject to the nuances of test administration situations that can plague the validity of thematic apperceptive methods (Lundy, 1988). Second, as D. G. Winter (1991) found, scores from historical materials may have temporal reliability and validity that are even higher than more traditional methods. For example, he reports a study of leadership among Naval officers demonstrating that motive scores based on "ordinary" verbal material (in this case, critical-incident interviews) predicted leadership performance far better than did scores based on thematic apperceptive methods.

Fianlly, using historical materials expands the range of possible studies, permitting, for example, retrospective study of personality development and change in response to external events. (Stewart, Franz, & Layton, 1988; and Espin, Stewart, & Gomez, 1990, are recent examples; see Allport, 1942, for a general discussion of the use of personal documents.)

Plan of this chapter

This chapter reviews some of the applications of the scoring systems described in this book to materials other than those obtained from direct testing of individuals. I include not only historical materials but also materials that can be obtained in the present, from the kinds of ordinary people whom we typically study in motivation and personality research. These studies will be reviewed by the variables studied and, within variable, by type of historical materials used. At the end, I discuss some general issues and problems raised by these materials and suggest some guidelines for their use.

MOTIVES

Many researchers have applied the achievement, affiliation, and/or power motive scoring systems to historical materials. Sometimes they want to elucidate the motivational basis of broad historical trends and cultural developments. Other times they seek to understand general processes and relationships but choose to focus on certain strategically placed groups such as political leaders or prominent authors. Finally, some researchers have begun to use at-a-distance analysis of historical materials to suggest more "idiographic" analyses of particular individuals. I will review each kind of study in turn.

Studies of historical trends and cultural developments

ACHIEVEMENT MOTIVATION AND ECONOMIC DEVELOPMENT. The earliest and most widely known applications of the motive scoring systems to historical materials are undoubtedly the many and varied studies collected by McClelland in the analysis, *The Achieving Society* (1961). Marshaling a wide range of evidence, McClelland demonstrated links between a society's achievement motivation and its subsequent rate of economic development.

McClelland first demonstrated this thesis by studies of individual cultures or nations over time. Berlew (1958; see also McClelland, 1958c) had shown that as the level of achievement imagery in various categories of Greek literature declined over the period 900–100 B.C., Greek economic development (as measured by the extent of trading area) first peaked and then declined. Cortés (1960) found a similar pattern in Spain: a decline in achievement motivation in literature from 1200–1730, with a peak and then a quick decline in economic activity during the late 1500s.

Although provocative, both of these studies do not demonstrate full covariance of motivation and economic activity because they do not show that achievement motivation increases before economic growth begins. However, two later studies fill this gap. Bradburn and Berlew (1961) scored achievement motivation in English drama, accounts of sea voyages, and street ballads from 1400 through 1830. They found two "waves" of high achievement motivation – in the late 1500s and again in the late 1700s, each preceding periods of faster economic development in England (as measured by coal shipped to London). DeCharms and Moeller (1962) found that levels of achievement motivation in U.S. children's school readers from 1810 through 1950 were closely related to the rate of inventions, as measured by the number of patents issued per million population.

The centerpiece of the *Achieving Society* research, however, was McClelland's collection of second-, third-, and fourth-grade school readers from 23 countries for the period 1920–1929 and 40 countries for the period 1946–1955 (to which he later added scores for China for the first period, and the People's Republic of China and Taiwan for the second period; see McClelland, 1963).[1] In each sample, national achievement motivation scores were significantly correlated with subsequent (but not prior) economic growth, adjusted for initial level ($r = .53$ and $.43$, respectively, $p < .01$ in each case; see McClelland, 1961, chap. 3). In the 1976 reprint of *The Achieving Society*, McClelland reports (p. C of the "New Introduction") that the latter correlation is still significant ($r = .39$, $p < .05$) when economic development is measured over the longer period of 1952–1967. National achievement motivation levels are also related to more specialized economic development statistics such as incremental capital/output ratios (pp. 422–423) and wealth-adjusted airline passenger miles flown per capita (p. 316).

McClelland also supported his hypothesis by relating motivation scores of folktales from 52 preindustrial cultures collected by Child, Storm, and Veroff (1958) to cultural characteristics as recorded in the Human Relations Area Files. Cultures scoring high in achievement motivation, for example, have larger percentages of full-time entrepreneurs and lower percentages of religious "experts" (the religious individualism implied by Weber's "Protestant ethic"?) and use hunting or agriculture, rather than "gathering," as the principal method of getting food.

Diaz (1982, cited in McClelland, 1985b, pp. 452–456) scored corporate annual letters to stockholders from American and Japanese automobile manufacturing companies for 1952 through 1980. Comparing the two American companies (General Motors and Chrysler), he found that both (relative) achievement motive scores and (relative) power motive scores of a given year predicted (relative) market share in subsequent years. Comparing the two Japanese companies (Toyota and Nissan), he also found that relative achievement motivation positively predicted subsequent relative market share. The effect of power motivation, however, was the reverse of the American case: Relative power motivation was negatively correlated with subsequent relative market share. Taking these two results together, it seems clear that achievement motivation predicts economic performance in both countries. Power motivation, however, predicts performance positively in the United States (in relative terms, at least) and negatively in Japan.

Perhaps these differences only reflect national differences in the structure of the automobile industry or the broader economy. On the other hand, they may help to explain the decline of the American automobile companies relative to the Japanese (see Halberstam, 1986). In any case, it is worth noting that in a secondary analysis of *The Achieving Society* data, Southwood (1969) found that high power motivation was often the *result* of prior economic growth. That is, national economic gains between 1937 and 1954 correlated .34 ($N = 40$, $p < .05$) with national power motive level in the 1946–1955 children's readers.

Two other studies also involved achievement motivation as it relates to social change, modernization, and economic development: Henley (1967) studied motivation in popular fiction, and Straus and Houghton (1960) scored newspaper editorials.

POWER AND AFFILIATION MOTIVATION AND WAR. In a later analysis, McClelland drew on many of the data sets just described to construct a general theory relating shifts in power and affiliation motivation to war and peace (McClelland, 1975, chapter 9). Based on the Bradburn and Berlew (1961) English data (scored for power motivation by Giliberto, 1972), and the U.S. data of deCharms and Moeller (1962), supplemented with motive scores of hymns and popular novels, McClelland suggested that periods when power and affiliation motives were both high were usually followed in

10 to 25 years by some kind of religious or secular crusade. Typically, affiliation motivation levels then dropped, leading to a war 10 to 25 years later. After wars, power motivation generally fell and affiliation rose, which led to peace until power increased again and the cycle repeated.

Supporting this general historical model with cross-national data from the children's readers described earlier, McClelland also found that high power motivation and low affiliation motivation, combined with high Activity Inhibition (the Leadership Motive Pattern, or LMP), led to relatively greater percentages of gross national product being spent for government in general and military forces in particular. Moreover, the same LMP was associated with higher national death rates from heart disease and hypertension, thus confirming laboratory studies relating inhibited power motivation to cardiovascular stress and reduced immune system functioning (McClelland, 1985b, pp. 441–444).

Thus the historical and cross-national materials suggest, in convergence with individual data, that the power motive (particularly if linked with low affiliation motivation) is related to violence and aggression against other nations and health problems within the person. (In this respect the power motive resembles Freud's death instinct, which ultimately kills the self but which can be directed outward for a time, leading to homicide and destruction.)

As a contrast, high historical levels of achievement motivation in the United States were often followed by times of *internal* dissent, violence, and rebellion rather than external war. Feierabend and Feierabend (1966) confirmed this finding with the 1946–1955 cross-national sample of children's readers from *The Achieving Society*.

Southwood (1969) pinpointed this relationship as applying especially to countries with low educational levels, which were therefore presumably lacking in opportunity. Perhaps achievement motivation makes people more ambitious, therefore restless and more easily frustrated with social and political obstacles to the realization of their ambitions.

D. G. Winter (1989c) tested aspects of McClelland's general model by scoring three sets of historical materials: (a) the Speech from the Throne that British sovereigns give at the opening of each session of parliament (also called the "Sovereign's Speech" or "Queen's [King's] Speech"); (b) the direct government-to-government communications between Great Britain and Germany in the July 1914 weeks of crisis immediately before the outbreak of World War I; and (c) the statements and letters exchanged by President Kennedy and Premier Khrushchev during the Cuban Missile Crisis. He found that combined power minus affiliation motivation scores were significantly higher in years just before Britain entered a war, as compared with years during which Britain stayed at peace; they also increased significantly from the beginning to the end of the World War I crisis, but *decreased* significantly from the beginning to the end of the Cuban Missile

Crisis. Finally, he found that British wars tended to *end* only after power motive levels had declined.

OTHER STUDIES WITH CULTURAL DOCUMENTS. As noted, Child et al. (1958) collected and scored folktales from 52 preindustrial cultures. Relating these scores to other characteristics of the cultures, as recorded in the Human Relations Area Files, McClelland (1985b, pp. 438–440) found that cultures scoring high in the affiliation motive tended to *value interpersonal networks* more highly. In these cultures, for example, people depend more on other people for help, and they are more endogamous and/or less neolocal (daughters marry and live closer to their family of origin). They care more about individual people, as reflected in low levels of spouse abuse and infanticide. The *Achieving Society* data indicate that affiliation-motivated nations have slightly lower death rates from homicide, suicide, and "stress-related" conditions such as ulcers, cirrhosis of the liver, and hypertension. This confirms laboratory studies of the positive effects of affiliation motivation on health (McClelland, 1985b, pp. 366–368).

The cultural correlates of high power motivation include having a cold climate and a simple social–economic structure that deemphasizes lineal descent (McClelland, 1985b, pp. 461–464). In the American historical data, power motivation tended to peak following times of high unemployment. One theme that brings together all of these structural features and historical conditions is an emphasis on individual assertiveness, without either the constraints or supports of elaborate institutional structures.

SCORING TELEVISION PROGRAMS. D. G. Winter and Healy (1983) adapted the achievement, affiliation, and power motivation scoring systems for use with television programs, films, and other "real-time" presentations. Scores are expressed as the percent of alternate 15-second units of time in which motive imagery is present. As yet little research has been done with this procedure.

Studies of "strategic" persons and groups

UNITED STATES PRESIDENTS AND WOULD-BE PRESIDENTS. Donley (1968) and Donley and Winter (1970) began the systematic study of motives of American presidents by scoring the first inaugural addresses of twentieth-century presidents for achievement and power motivation. D. G. Winter and Stewart (1977a) added affiliation scores. Finally D. G. Winter (1987b) rescored these addresses and added previous presidents back to George Washington and forward through Carter and Reagan. D. G. Winter's (1991) review and extension of these studies suggest that presidential motive scores correlate with presidential behaviors and outcomes in predictable ways:

power-motivated presidents are rated as "great" but are likely to involve the country in war; affiliation-motivated presidents seek peace but are vulnerable to the influence of self-seeking subordinates and hence scandal; and the idealistic restlessness of achievement-motivated presidents often leads them to frustration in the amorphous mire of political intrigue and bargaining.

D. G. Winter (1976, 1988c) also scored the announcement speeches of candidates in the 1976 and 1988 elections, relating their scores to aspects of campaign strategy and performance (D. G. Winter, 1982). He found a significant correlation between (a) congruence of motive profile between president and American society of the time and (b) the president's margin of election victory (D. G. Winter, 1987b). This result suggests hypotheses for future research on leadership and the election process.

SUPREME COURT JUSTICES. Aliotto (1988) studied the motives of U.S. Supreme Court justices by scoring transcripts of their testimony at confirmation hearings. (Such transcripts exist for 15 justices confirmed during the period 1925–1984.) She found that writing majority opinions (a dependent variable reflecting justices' prestige and impact on the Court and society) was, as predicted, positively correlated with power motivation and negatively correlated with achievement and affiliation. (The latter two negative relationships offer an interesting confirmation of the laboratory findings of Sorrentino, 1973.) Achievement-motivated justices cast relatively fewer concurring votes or dissenting votes (versus joining the majority without comment). When they do concur or dissent, however, they are more likely to write a separate opinion. Aliotto interprets this finding as a reflection of their concern with excellence rather than prestige or visibility. In contrast, affiliation-motivated justices, who are also less likely to concur or dissent, tend *not* to write separate opinions when they do. Presumably this reflects their concern with agreement and being liked.

WORLD POLITICAL LEADERS. Hermann (1979, 1980b) scored affiliation and power imagery in press conference transcripts of 45 world leaders, and related leaders' scores to their foreign policy orientations. As predicted from laboratory studies, affiliation-motivated leaders pursue a cooperative and interdependent foreign policy, whereas power-motivated leaders are more independent and confrontational.

SOVIET LEADERS. Hermann (1980a) further illustrated these relationships in a study of the motives of Soviet Politburo members in the late 1970s. Members scoring high in affiliation and low in power were relatively more favorable to détente than members with the opposite motive pattern.

Schmitt (1990) studied the motives of general secretaries of the Communist Party of the Soviet Union, from Lenin through Gorbachev, in relation to societal motives expressed in contemporary Russian literature. He found evidence that the motive profiles of a general secretary tended to anticipate (rather than follow) changes in societal motive levels.

AFRICAN LEADERS. Along the lines of her previous research on motivation and foreign policy role-orientation, Hermann (1987) scored interview transcripts from twelve heads of government in sub-Saharan Africa and related the results to their foreign policy roles and styles.

D. G. Winter (1980) scored interview transcripts from 22 political leaders from southern Africa, including heads of state, cabinet ministers, and exiled nationalist guerilla leaders. As expected from laboratory studies, power-motivated leaders were rated by a panel of experts as more likely "to initiate, support, or continue armed conflict." Interestingly, these ratings of propensity for violence were unrelated to ratings of power motivation made by these same expert judges, though one might have expected that they would be, on the basis of shared method variance.

MAJOR NIGERIAN ETHNIC GROUPS. LeVine (1966) collected dream reports from 342 adolescent males from the four principal ethnic groups of Nigeria: Hausa, Ibo, and Northern and Southern Yoruba. His principal finding was that the Ibo boys scored highest in achievement imagery, significantly higher than the pooled other three groups. (Mother's education and religion were not related to achievement motive scores.) Because LeVine viewed his results as generalizable to the four groups in question, his study is really intended as an assessment of "national character" or "modal personality" (see Inkeles & Levinson, 1969) by sampling "ordinary" verbal material from individual people.

When LeVine asked the boys to write essays on the topic, "What is a successful man?" he found no ethnic differences in "achievement value motifs." One explanation for the discrepancy between these two results is that the dreams were spontaneously generated, whereas the reports elicited structured responses to an assigned topic. On the other hand, differences in the actual scoring systems used, as well as differences in the treatment of data (dichotomous versus interval scoring, and length corrections for the reports but not the dreams; see LeVine, 1966, pp. 95–116) may also account for the differences in results.

"Idiographic" studies of individuals

In recent years, several researchers have used motive scoring of historical materials to make inferences about the motives of particular individuals, as part of a systematic psychobiography or personality portrait.

D. G. Winter and Carlson (1988) explored how the motives expressed in Richard Nixon's first inaugural address (high achievement and affiliation, average power) could be used to resolve some of the paradoxes of Nixon's personal and political behavior. For example, they suggest that Nixon's twists and changes of political beliefs – from liberal populist in college to postwar "Redhunter" to guest of Mao Zedong in 1972 – can be understood as a manifestation of the tendency for achievement-motivated people to modify actions on the basis of results of previous actions. More systematically, they validated Nixon's overall motive profile by gathering accounts of his motive-related behavior from the published memoirs of his principal associates, as well as Nixon's own autobiographies. They found that Nixon shows almost all of the correlates of achievement and affiliation motivation, as would be expected by his very high scores on those two motives. Further, he shows only some correlates (slightly fewer than half) of the power motive, again as would be expected by his (average) score. (See also D. G. Winter, 1991, for additional discussion of Nixon's motive profile.)

D. G. Winter (1991) used motive scores from John F. Kennedy's first 13 press conferences and principal speeches to illustrate two aspects of Kennedy's power motivation: It increased in response to threatening situations, and it was significantly related to working longer hours (as well as how Kennedy actually spent those hours). In contrast, when Kennedy's achievement motivation was high, he spent less time at work, perhaps as a reflection of an "efficiency" orientation or even distaste for the work of the presidency (see the studies of presidents discussed previously).

More recently, D. G. Winter (1989b) analyzed the motive scores of Soviet President Mikhail Gorbachev (see also Winter, Hermann, Weintraub, & Walker, 1991). (Like both George Bush and Richard Nixon, Gorbachev showed a motive pattern of high achievement, high affiliation, and average power.) Hermann used power and affiliation motive scores, as well as other personality characteristics measured at a distance, to construct a personality portrait of Reagan (1983), Syrian leader Hafez al-Assad (1988), and Gorbachev (1989). Along these same lines, Snare has constructed portraits of Libyan leader Muammar Kaddafi (in press) and post-Khomeini Iranian leaders (1990). In another quantitative idiographic study, N. Winter (1990) scored selected speeches of Mussolini and found a significant increase in power motivation and decrease in affiliation after the 1937 meeting with Hitler that marked the beginning of their close relationship.

Social-psychological use of motive scores

Recent studies of conflict escalation by D. G. Winter (1987a, 1987c) involve a novel use of scoring of historical materials for motive imagery. Winter compared how the mass media of each side in a conflict report (and distort) the statements of leaders of each side. Thus, during the last weeks before the outbreak of the U.S. Civil War, Southern pro-secession newspapers exaggerated the power motive imagery in their reports of Abraham Lincoln's speeches and diminished the power motive imagery in their reports of Jefferson Davis's speeches, while Northern pro-Union newspapers showed the reverse pattern. Winter suggested that this pattern of mutual distortion could be an important dynamic of conflict escalation. Along those same lines, D. G. Winter (1987c) observed a similar pattern in British and German newspapers and diplomatic dispatches during the July 1914 crisis that led up to World War I, but did *not* find such a pattern in U.S. and Soviet media during the Cuban Missile Crisis in 1962 (D. G. Winter, 1988a). Here motive scores, traditionally variables of personality, are used to study the social psychological processes of conflict escalation and resolution.

INTEGRATIVE COMPLEXITY

The integrative complexity measure developed by Suedfeld and his colleagues (see chapters 27 and 28) has been applied to archival material and personal documents in many different studies, offering both "real-world" confirmations of laboratory results and also psychological explanations of important social and political processes.

Integrative complexity and effective functioning

Several studies suggest that high integrative complexity is associated with more effective functioning. In a study of the correspondence of five eminent English authors, Porter and Suedfeld (1981) found that stressful events such as war and personal illness (the latter suggesting diminished functioning) were negatively related to integrative complexity, whereas age (and presumably "maturity") were positively related.

LIFE AND DEATH. Unexpectedly, Porter and Suedfeld found a significant and substantial relationship between integrative complexity and number of years of life remaining. Following up on these results, Suedfeld and Piedrahita (1984) examined the correspondence of 18 eminent persons during the last decade of their lives. They found declines in integrative complexity during the last 5 years of life among those who died of protracted illness or old age; but among persons who died suddenly (e.g., by accidents, contagious diseases, or heart attacks), there was a sharp decline only in the year before death. This fascinating finding – that integrative complexity is somehow intimately linked to life itself – suggests hypotheses for future research in fields such as gerontology and psychoimmunology.

PROFESSIONAL EMINENCE AND SUCCESS. Suedfeld (1985) related integrative complexity scores from 85 American Psychological Association presidential addresses to various indexes of eminence, while Suedfeld, Corteen, and McCormick (1986) scored the official dispatches and orders of

Confederate General Robert E. Lee and the Union generals who opposed him in several major Civil War battles. When Lee scored higher than his opponent, he was usually victorious against heavy odds (e.g., at Antietam); but when he scored lower than his opponent, he lost (e.g., at Spotsylvania).

Overall, these results using historical materials support laboratory findings relating integrative complexity to effective functioning in a variety of situations.

Integrative complexity and the political process

GAINING OFFICE AND HOLDING OFFICE. As might be expected from the previous discussion of general functioning, integrative complexity is related to getting and holding political office; but the relationships are more complicated and interesting than one might expect.

First, Tetlock (1981b) found that presidents show gains in integrative complexity between their campaign speeches and their early presidential speeches, followed by declines as the next election approached. Suedfeld and Rank (1976) showed that successful (e.g., George Washington, Lenin) and unsuccessful revolutionary leaders (e.g., Alexander Hamilton, Trotsky) both showed relatively low levels of integrative complexity during the revolution, but only the successful leaders increased their integrative complexity *during* the postrevolutionary period of consolidating power. Taken together with Tetlock's results, this suggests that flexibility or the ability to vary integrative complexity – to adapt it to the political situation – is important in attaining and holding political office.

IDEOLOGICAL POSITION. Several studies suggest a negative relationship between integrative complexity and conservative political ideology and positions, for example, among U.S. Supreme court justices (Tetlock, Bernzweig, & Gallant, 1985), senators (Tetlock, 1981a, 1983b), and members of the British House of Commons (Tetlock, 1984), which is consistent with the well-documented relationship between authoritarianism (or dogmatism) and cognitive simplicity (see Brown, 1965, chapter 10).

CONFLICT ESCALATION. A large body of research suggests that low levels of integrative complexity lead to conflict and war, whereas higher levels facilitate the peaceful resolution of conflicts. Suedfeld and Tetlock (1977) compared communications and statements from two crises that ended in war (1914, and the 1950 Korean crisis) and three peacefully resolved crises (the 1911 Moroccan crisis, the 1948 Berlin Airlift, and the 1962 Cuban Missile Crisis). Similar results were reported by Suedfeld, Tetlock, and Ramirez (1977) for the Middle East and by Raphael (1982) for Berlin. Several studies (Porter & Suedfeld, 1981; Suedfeld, 1981; 1985) suggest an inverse relationship between international tension and low integrative complexity, even among people who are not directly involved with foreign policy decision making. One explanation for all these results may be that low integrative complexity is associated with defective, "groupthink"-dominated decision making (Tetlock, 1979). A recent study by Suedfeld and Bluck (1988) suggests a more complicated pattern of integrative complexity shifts before surprise attacks, such as at Pearl Harbor.

EXPLANATORY STYLE

The optimistic explanatory style (see chapters 25 and 26) involves explaining "bad" events by factors that are external, specific, and temporary. In laboratory research, it is related to feelings of zest, persistence, and good performance. In contrast, the pessimistic style, where bad events are seen as the result of internal, global, and enduring factors, leads to depression, avoidance, and failure. These findings have been confirmed in a few studies using historical material.

Optimistic and pessimistic styles

LYNDON JOHNSON AND VIETNAM. H. M. Zullow, Oettingen, Peterson, and Seligman (1988) report a study of Lyndon Johnson's explanatory style during the course of the Vietnam War. As would be predicted from the laboratory findings, Johnson had a highly optimistic style during the Gulf of Tonkin "incident" and during the American military buildup that followed. Then when the limits of American power (and success) became clear during the Tet offensive, and Johnson decided not to seek reelection, his explanatory style score moved down into the pessimistic or depressive range.

EAST AND WEST BERLIN. H. M. Zullow et al. (1988) report a comparative study of explanatory style in accounts of the 1984 Winter Olympics in East Berlin and West Berlin newspapers. Although East Germany won six times as many medals as did West Germany, the East Berlin accounts displayed a markedly less optimistic explanatory style. These differences are consistent with other comparative data that suggest greater frequencies of depressive behaviors in East Berlin as compared with rates in West Berlin, and they are certainly consistent with the extraordinary political changes that swept East Germany during late 1989 and 1990.

PRESIDENTIAL CANDIDATES. H. M. Zullow and Seligman (1990) studied explanatory style in speeches of the two major candidates in American presidential elections from 1900 through 1984. In general, the more "optimistic" candidate wins the election, or at least comes very close, especially when the initial polling results at the time of the nominating conventions are taken into account.

METHODOLOGICAL ISSUES AND PROCEDURES IN THE USE OF HISTORICAL MATERIALS

Researchers who decide to use historical materials should consider several issues. (Many of these topics were originally discussed by McClelland in a research note on "Coding historical source materials for motivational variables" [1975, appendix 4], which should also be consulted.)

Selecting and processing materials

The suggestion that materials selected for coding should be similar in form, purpose, and style may seem obvious; yet it is often ignored and sometimes must be violated. We can only compare one president with another by scoring speeches or other statements prepared for "similar" occasions. On this basis Donley (1968) and Donley and Winter (1970) chose to score first inaugural addresses. Yet the nature, occasion, and purpose of the inaugural address have changed in the 200 years between George Washington's speech to a few thousand citizens in New York City to George Bush's message instantly seen by millions on television. Standards of style, vocabulary, and nuances of meaning are also different. Comparisons of "war" and "nonwar" crisis communications from 1914 and 1962 may be compromised by differences in format (telegrams vs. letters) and the effects of translation, as well as differences in style over 48 years. Still, researchers should select material that is as comparable as possible, across whatever variations (one leader or country or era vs. another, preinaugural vs. postinaugural, war outcome vs. peace outcome, etc.) are to be studied.

EFFECTS OF SPEECHWRITERS AND SELF-PRESENTATION.   When prepared materials are scored for motives or any other psychological characteristic, skeptics might ask whether the results reflect the author's "real" personality or that of the speechwriters. Or perhaps the scores are only positive self-presentation (even disinformation). Do political speeches tell us about the personality of the leader or the styles of the speechwriters? (Of course, speechwriters are generally selected for their ability to express what the leader wants to say, especially in the case of important speeches.)

Using more spontaneous interview material may reduce (though it does not fully eliminate) this problem, because many "spontaneous" interviews are carefully prepared, even "scripted." Yet in a larger sense, these questions may not matter. Whatever their status, prepared texts do exist as the author's (leader's) words; they are taken as the author's words, and they have effects as the author's words. For the present I assume that the scores are a reasonable guide to the speaker's personality, with the caution that the "real" question is whether they are useful in predicting or interpreting the author's behavior.

ADAPTING THE SCORING SYSTEMS. Scoring systems originally designed for use with thematic apperceptive stories must sometimes be adapted for use with other kinds of material that is not broken up into 100- to 300-word stories or other natural units. In scoring motivation, many researchers follow the practice of Berlew, who scored only achievement imagery, dropped the subcategories, and counted the number of images per unit length (page, 10-line segment of poetry, etc.). Recently, D. G. Winter (1991) codified these and other modifications in the process of developing an integrated manual for scoring achievement, affiliation intimacy, and power motivation in verbal "running text."[2]

The scoring manual for integrative complexity (chapter 28) needs little adaptation for scoring historical materials, because it is based on the paragraph as the unit of analysis. Likewise, the procedures for extracting material and scoring it for explanatory style are readily applicable to historical materials.

TRANSLATION. The research that has been done on the effects of translation on motive scores (Hermann, 1980a, p. 352, n. 2; D. G. Winter, 1973, pp. 92–93) suggests that translated documents yield about the same scores as originals, so long as the translation was careful.

CORRECTING SCORES FOR LENGTH. In most historical materials there are no natural divisions into short units of text, analogous to the stories obtained with thematic apperceptive techniques. In most cases, therefore, motive scores must take account of the length of text. In thematic apperceptive stories, this is often done by regressing score on length to derive predicted motive scores given length of text. These are then subtracted from actual scores, and the residuals (often after standardization) are used as length-corrected measures (see D. G. Winter, 1973, p. 146). Dividing raw scores by the length of the stories does not always correct for length, in that the correlation of length with the resulting quotient scores is not necessarily zero.

In most historical materials, however, any factors causing variation in text length (including the researcher's selection) are assumed to be random – that is, to have nothing to do with score. Any correlation between the resulting quotient scores and length is therefore assumed *not* to be an artifact. Thus the usual procedure with historical materials is to express results in terms of score per unit length (per page, per 10 lines, per 1,000 words, etc.).[3]

Constructing dependent variables

Perhaps the most enjoyable and creative aspect of analyzing historical materials involves developing dependent variables. Often there is little precedent, and the disciplinary precedents that exist may be misleading or unsuitable. Some examples include the following: First, what is economic growth? Per-capita gross national product, which is the measure traditionally used, may involve various problems and distortions. McClelland (1961) sought a measure that would reflect more strictly the capacity to use modern technology, and so (in that preconservation era) measured per capita consumption of electricity.

Second, which presidents had the most scandal-prone administrations? Most people would immediately think of Nixon, Harding, and perhaps Truman; but how can "scandals" be measured in precise and objective ways? D. G. Winter and Stewart (1977a) constructed a crude measure from the work of historians, by consulting a major scholarly review of presidential scandals and political misconduct and simply counting the number of pages per year devoted to each president.

Third, during which years did Great Britain enter a war? This requires a definition of war and an accurate historical list. D. G. Winter (1989c) constructed such a list from several standard scholarly sources.

Only general advice can be given: Consult colleagues in the relevant fields for whatever "lists" or at least complete compilations of material already exist. Search the library. Then get immersed in the material, trying to construct objective definitions or codes.

EXISTING SOURCES OF HISTORICAL MOTIVE SCORING DATA

Sometimes individual reports of research using historical materials or personal documents include motive scores for the individuals, groups, or nations that have been studied. Certain sources have especially valuable data and so deserve special mention. McClelland (1961, pp. 461–463) gives motive scores obtained from the children's readers of modern nations, and scores obtained from folktales for preindustrial cultures (p. 491). McClelland (1975, appendix 4) gives additional historical material for the United States and Great Britain. I have compiled motive scores for the individuals and groups that I and several other researchers have studied using historical materials, as well as some of McClelland's earlier scores (D. G. Winter, 1990b).[4]

CONCLUSION

Using archival historical materials is an enjoyable way to apply psychology to history and political science, and economics. For example, the well-documented connections between achievement motivation and economic growth, on the one hand, and power motivation and war, on the other, suggest a psychological basis for Kennedy's (1987) theory of great power growth and decline. At the same time, historical materials, personal documents, and everyday verbal material also offer valuable ways to test basic psychological theory, using the world (or at least the library) as a "laboratory" (see Simonton, 1981). I hope that this brief survey will lead other researchers to pursue these methods and materials.

NOTES

1 The collection of stories from these readers that McClelland actually used (21 stories per country per time period), translated into English and with all identifying information removed, is available to scholars at the Henry A. Murray Research Center of Radcliffe College, Cambridge, Massachusetts, 02138.
2 The running text manual and practice materials are available at cost from the author, Department of Psychology, University of Michigan, Ann Arbor, Michigan, 48109.
3 I am indebted to Robert Rosenthal for discussion and advice on this point.
4 This compilation is available from the author, Department of Psychology, University of Michigan, Ann Arbor, Michigan, 48109.

8 *Reliability issues*

CHARLES P. SMITH

> Our highest allegiance is to psychology, which can best be served not by
> rash rejection of the projective techniques when the literature is replete
> with fascinating results or on the other hand by a loyal but naive faith in
> any given instrument, but by a serious examination of the ways in which
> a variety of difficult practical and research problems can be solved.
> – Jerome L. Singer (1981, p. 298)

Psychologists tend to be either for or against projective techniques – either
convinced that they provide valuable and perhaps unique information or
convinced that objective evidence does not justify their continued use. In
short, there is a tendency toward "all or none" thinking. There is also a
tendency to lump all "projective" techniques together even though almost
25 years ago, in an annual review chapter, Fisher (1967) urged that "we
must stop reviewing projective tests as if they were an entity. They are often
without meaningful overlap" (p. 166).

This chapter will deal primarily with the reliability of thematic apperceptive measures of motives, because those measures have received the most
critical attention. Much of the discussion should be applicable to thematic
apperceptive measures of nonmotive variables, however, and, to a lesser
extent, to nonthematic content analytic measures. (Information regarding
the reliability of each coding system included in this volume is given in the
chapters introducing those systems and will not be summarized here.)

The position taken here is that the reliability of many of these motive and
nonmotive measures is indeed relatively low, but not as low as critics have
alleged, and that there are steps that can be taken to minimize the problem. The organization of this chapter is simple: First, critical reviews are
summarized; second, responses to the critics are summarized and new views
and new evidence are presented; third, recommendations are made for
maximizing reliability in future research.

The author is indebted to Carol Franz, Alan Gross, Ian McMahan, David Reuman,
David Rindskopf, and Richard Smith for helpful discussions of these issues.

126

CRITIQUES

Over the years a number of reviews and critiques have appeared that have questioned the adequacy of the reliability of projective measures in general and thematic apperceptive measures in particular. For example, Murstein (1965b) states that "projective techniques have lower reliabilities than multiple-choice paper-and-pencil tests because, in addition to the usual sources of error, they add new ones. These include ... scorer reliability, the influence of a response on succeeding responses, ... and the ofttimes peculiar distributions of scores" (p. 189). Murstein believes that "the questionable validity of many projective techniques is in part the inevitable consequence of the low reliability of these measures" (p. 216).

Because most critics have accepted that satisfactory *interscorer agreement* is possible with the types of coding systems included in this book, only representative critiques of internal consistency and stability will be reviewed. (Interscorer agreement of $r = .85$ or higher has typically been reported for most of the coding systems included in this book. For further information, please refer to chapter 37.)

Klinger

Klinger (1966) finds reported test–retest correlations for need for achievement to be "generally low or nonsignificant" and questions whether the *temporal stability* of *n* Achievement scores is adequate to reflect stable motivational dispositions. Klinger comments that H. H. Morgan's (1953) test–retest correlations of .56 and .64 "seem exceptional" and suggests that "the instability of the scores might contribute to the frequent failure to find *n* Ach related to long-term nonfantasy indices of performance" (1966, p. 300). Unfortunately, Klinger fails to mention two important studies of stability, those of Haber and Alpert (1958) and Heckhausen (1963).

Entwisle

Entwisle (1972) reviewed studies of "fantasy-based achievement motivation" and found homogeneity reliability to be "typically in the range .30 to .40" (p. 389) – too low, she concludes, to permit adequate predictive validity (e.g., consistent relationships between *n* Achievement scores and grades).[1] Furthermore, Entwisle conjectures that it is probably not feasible to improve the homogeneity reliability of thematic measures by increasing the number of stories obtained.

Because low reliability limits validity, Entwisle speculates that when significant relationships had been obtained between *n* Achievement scores and grades they may have been due to variations in story length. (Entwisle seems unaware that the need to adjust motive scores for differences in story length was recognized almost from the outset of research on achievement motivation, e.g., Atkinson, 1958a, p. 837).

Fineman

Fineman (1977) makes many of the same points as Klinger and Entwisle and identifies few additional references relevant to the reliability of thematic apperceptive measures. Unaccountably, Fineman omits consideration of the two studies that report the highest temporal stability of *n* Achievement scores, namely those of Haber and Alpert (1958) and H. H. Morgan (1953).

REPLIES

Critique of the critiques

Reliability concerns expressed by Entwisle (1972) and other critics have been responded to on various grounds. Before presenting these responses, however, I review *the treatment of the evidence* by Entwisle and other critics. Some of the following material is adapted from a reply to Entwisle prepared by Brody and Smith (1972).

The main point is that Entwisle may *underestimate* both the internal consistency and test–retest reliability of *n* Achievement. For one thing, she treats all studies as if they were equally informative, although some have serious methodological deficiencies (e.g., Mitchell, 1961). Fully 46% of the publications cited in table 4 of her review of published studies either report no interscorer agreement (Birney, 1959; Klinger, 1968) or comparatively low interscorer agreement (Krumboltz & Farquhar, 1957; Lindzey and Heinemann, 1955; Lindzey & Herman, 1955; Weinstein, 1969). In fact, Lindzey & Heinemann (1955, p. 39) explicitly state that they do not view their interscorer agreement of .64 as satisfactory. Two studies cited for low equivalent-forms reliability (Klinger, 1968, and Reitman & Atkinson, 1958) did not employ equivalent forms. Two studies (Kagan & Moss, 1959; Lowell, 1950) cited for low test–retest reliability employed fewer than four pictures on each occasion. Studies that employed long intervals between testing (3 to 10 years) are averaged in with studies that employed much shorter intervals. No mention is made of a study by Heckhausen (1963) in which a correlation of .53 was obtained for scores from the same six pictures administered 5 weeks apart.

Of the studies done at the time of Entwisle's review, three were most appropriately designed and executed, in my opinion. In the first, Atkinson (1950) administered eight pictures in one session and obtained a correlation of .48 between four pictures that had been used in earlier research and four new pictures selected on a priori grounds to be reasonably equivalent. (See McClelland, Atkinson, Clark, & Lowell, 1953, pp. 186–194 for a summary of this study.)[2] From Atkinson's eight pictures, two sets of three pictures selected for equivalence were administered to college students by Lowell (1950) 1 week apart. The obtained equivalent-forms correlation of .22 is unexpectedly low, a result somewhat mitigated by the fact that *only three pictures were used in each form*, and scores from the two· forms agreed in placing 72.5% of the subjects above or below the combined median.

In the second study, a research project under the direction of David McClelland, H. H. Morgan (1953) developed three alternate *12-picture* forms from pretested pictures and administered them 5 weeks apart to high school students. He allowed 2.5 minutes for the writing of each story. Interscorer reliability was .89. Stability correlations of .56, .56, and .64 were obtained.

In the third and most impressive study, Haber and Alpert (1958) first used an objective procedure to select pictures and then administered two six-picture forms 3 weeks apart. They obtained a correlation of .54 for subjects tested on both occasions under a relaxed orientation, and a correlation of .45 for subjects tested first under a relaxed orientation and second under an achievement orientation.

As noted, Klinger (1966) discounts H. H. Morgan's (1953) study and omits mention of the study by Haber and Alpert (1958), and neither of these studies is mentioned in Fineman's (1977) review.

The considerations that have been mentioned previously suggest that Entwisle's estimate of the reliability of "fantasy" *n* Achievement (.3 to .4) is too low, and that the appropriate figure is more like .5. The evidence also suggests that reliabilities tend to be higher when more stories are obtained.

Reliability and validity

In a response to Entwisle to clarify issues regarding the relation of reliability and story length to construct validity, Reuman, Alwin, and Veroff (1984) employed a causal modeling approach. They point out that true relations among constructs may not be apparent from obtained correlations if the measures differ in their reliability. Reuman et al. (1984) investigated the relation of thematic apperceptive *n* Achievement scores and story length to job satisfaction in adult males. Their results demonstrated that "when a tau-equivalent measurement model does not fit the data well, coefficient alpha underestimates the reliability of the composite measure" (p. 1352). They also found that the achievement motive construct was positively related to work satisfaction whereas story length was not, with the first relationship being significantly greater than the second, thereby "demonstrating the discriminant validity of the achievement motive construct and the story length construct with respect to the work satisfaction construct" (pp. 1356–1357). The authors concluded that:

TAT *n* Achievement is sufficiently reliable to detect significant covariation where it is expected on theoretical grounds. On the other hand, we conclude that TAT *n* Achievement and TAT story length are not equivalent or interchangeable constructs, even though they are quite strongly positively related. Entwisle (1972) argues that TAT *n* Achievement only predicts academic performance by virtue of its association with story length, which she believes represents verbal achievement or academic socialization. The evidence for discriminant validity that we present here suggests that TAT *n* Achievement is not simply an unreliable measure of verbal achievement or academic socialization. Furthermore, the hypothesis that correlated error variance accounts for a significant proportion of the covariation between TAT *n* Achievement and TAT story length was tested and disconfirmed. (pp. 1359–1360).

Replies regarding internal consistency

ATKINSON. On the basis of a theory of motivation called the *dynamics of action*, developed by Atkinson and Birch (1970, 1978), Atkinson (1982) challenges the assertion that low internal consistency necessarily entails low validity. Because the theory is complex, the following summary necessarily oversimplifies, and the reader is urged to read Atkinson (1982, reprinted as chapter 2, this volume) for a fuller exposition.

Atkinson points out that the emphasis of traditional test theory on interitem consistency is related to the assumption that tests or test items are unaffected by preceding events (e.g., answering one item does not affect the answer to the next). In contrast, the dynamics of action assumes that thought and behavior are part of a continuous stream and that successive events are not discrete.

The dynamics of action shows how stable motive dispositions can affect the allocation of time to various activities. As applied to storytelling, the theory implies the following sequence:

1. A person begins a picture-story task with tendencies to engage in various actions that have carried over from the preceding activity.

2. The stimulus properties of the first picture represent, to some extent, expectancies and incentives relating to the satisfaction of one or more motives.

3. These expectancies and incentives interact with motive dispositions to produce instigating forces that increase the strength of action tendencies. (Expectancies and incentives may also produce inhibitory forces whose effects on storytelling are too complex to summarize. See chapter 2.)

4. The strongest of the competing action tendencies is expressed in behavior (e.g., in the amount of story time devoted to motive-relevant content).

5. The expression of a tendency in behavior (e.g., writing achievement-related story content) is assumed to *reduce*, to some extent, the strength of the tendency.

6. After a standard interval of time (e.g., 4 minutes), the next picture is presented and impacts the person's action tendencies at the level they had reached at the end of the preceding story.

7. Time spent in a particular type of imaginative activity (e.g., writing achievement imagery) summed over all stories, indicates the amount of time that particular action tendency (achievement) was predominant. Thus, time spent writing achievement content is the equivalent of a true (errorless) *n* Achievement score.

8. The time that a particular tendency is stronger than all other tendencies is, in part, a function of the strength of other motives in the person. (To give an extreme example, achievement might be stronger or weaker than all of the person's other motives.).

An important implication of the dynamics of action, therefore, is that the *n* Achievement score does not measure the absolute strength of the motive to achieve but rather its strength *relative* to that of other motives. "The measure obtained from thematic apperception should always provide a useful basis for predicting other differences in behavior that also depend upon the *relative* strength of achievement motive within an individual (initiation and persistence of achievement activities, preference for them over other kinds of activity, time spent achieving in everyday life, and so forth)" (Atkinson, 1982, p. 24).

Atkinson, Bongort, and Price (1977) explored the implications of the dynamics of action for thematic apperception by means of a computer program that models the theory. In a series of computer simulations, using parameter input values derived from the theory, they showed that the amount of time spent imagining achievement in simulated storytelling was highly correlated with individual differences in input strength of achievement motive. Thus, time spent (i.e., overall achievement-related content) was shown to be a valid measure of motive strength. This was the case for various simulations even when the alpha values for story by story intercorrelations ranged as low as .07. *These results demonstrated that consistency among items (stories) is not a necessary prerequisite for the validity of total scores.*

A hypothetical example may clarify this point. We might follow two persons who differ in the strength of the motive for food and record the proportion of time spent eating during every 15-minute interval throughout a party. We would not necessarily expect the person with the stronger food motive to eat more food during each and every 15 minute interval than the person with the weaker food motive. However, *over the course of the entire evening* we would expect the person with the stronger motive to spend more time consuming food. The assumption of stable personality dispositions does not necessarily imply consistency of behavior each time behavior is sampled.

It is not clear whether the theory of action implies that a longer period of time (i.e., a greater number of intervals) will produce a more accurate (reliable) measure of tendency strength. Within limits this clearly appears to be the case from the simulation data (e.g., five stories are more valid than two). Although simulations employed tests varying in length from 5 to 12 pictures, many other parameters were varied along with picture length, so it may not have been possible to report whether there was a monotonic improvement in validity as the number of pictures increased. The report (Atkinson et al., 1977) does indicate that for at least some simulations, scores from Pictures 7 through 12 had lower validity than scores for Pictures 1 through 6. Such effects might be expected as a result of inhibitory forces (see chapter 2). We know from actual (as opposed to simulated) studies that subjects become tired and uncooperative after writing for a time, so that it has not been feasible to obtain more than about six written stories in a single testing session. On the other hand, because inhibitory forces delay the expression of action tendencies, the early pictures in a set may under-estimate the strength of the achievement motive in persons in whom the motive to avoid failure is strong. As Atkinson puts it: "the typical short four-story Thematic Apperception Test of *n* Achievement may be yielding a measure that is sensitive to individual differences in the relative strengths of motive to achieve (M_s) and motive to avoid failure (M_f) rather than only to individual differences in M_s" (1982, p. 29).

Although the theory of action shows that internal consistency is not necessary for a valid thematic measure of motive strength, it does imply that a measure of motive strength should have a reasonable degree of *temporal stability*. Thus, one might expect reasonably good test–retest correlations between equivalent forms given under similar conditions, even though internal consistency need not be high.

REUMAN.   Reuman's (1982) investigation of the implications of the theory of action for the variability of motive-relevant imagery also suggests that a longer measure should provide a more accurate estimate of motive strength than a shorter measure. In addition, Reuman's results provide empirical support for Atkinson's contention that a measure can be valid even though it has low internal consistency.

KARON.   Karon (1981) makes some similar points regarding internal con-sistency. He agrees that the assumption of classical mental test theory that items are independent is arbitrary and does not apply to the Thematic Apperception Test in which a need may be expressed (and partially satis-fied) in one story and therefore not expressed in the next. Without the assumptions of random error and parallel items, "there is no necessary mathematical relationship between internal consistency and validity" (p. 105). Karon points out that a test that is valid must be reliable and, refer-ring to a theorem of mental test theory (Gulliksen, 1950), recommends that: "Students who work with the TAT . . . may take the highest validity coefficient . . . , square it, and report this estimate of a lower bound to the reliability, which indeed it is. That this lower bound to the reliability, so estimated, is frequently higher than the internal consistency directly measured, is simply evidence of the fact that mental test theory, with its assumption of random error uncorrelated with anything, does not apply to their domain" (p. 106). (See also Karon, 1966, p. 227.)

MCCLELLAND. McClelland (1985b, pp. 208–213) agrees that there are good reasons to expect that scores for one story may not be highly correlated with scores from the next. Rather than add scores from different stories to obtain a *total* score which is then related to some criterion variable, McClelland suggests using each story as a separate variable in a multiple-regression analysis, thus permitting each story to make its distinctive contribution to the prediction of the criterion variable.

Fleming and Horner used a variant of this approach in the development of the revised measure of the motive to avoid success (see chapter 11) and report substantial improvement in prediction obtained by multiple-regression as opposed to summed story scores.

Replies regarding stability

WINTER AND STEWART. D. G. Winter and Stewart (1977b) in their own review of the test–retest reliability of thematic apperceptive measures of need for achievement and need for power found the median reported test–retest correlation to be .28. They noted that one plausible reason for low retest agreement is that having told one set of stories, subjects may think that new and different stories are expected on the next occasion (cf. also Karon, 1981; McClelland et al., 1953, p. 211; Tomkins, 1961).

To test this possibility, D. G. Winter and Stewart (1977b) conducted a study in which college students wrote stories about four pictures and then 6 to 8 days later wrote stories about the same four pictures, but with additional retest instructions. Two different retest groups were told either: "Do not worry about whether your stories are similar to or different from the stories you wrote before. Write whatever stories you wish"; or "Try to write stories as different as possible from the ones you wrote before in class." The test–retest correlation for n Power scores was .58 ($p < .01$) for the first group and .27 (n.s.) for the second group. (For the difference between the two correlations $p \sim .06$). As the authors note, these results are similar to those obtained by Heckhausen (1963) whose retest instructions were: "Write down immediately what goes through your mind, regardless of whether you already wrote that the first time" (p. 79). As mentioned earlier, Heckhausen's test–retest correlation was .53 ($N = 42$). Winter and Stewart conclude that the problem of low temporal reliability "can be substantially resolved by instructing subjects at the retest . . . not to worry about whether their stories are similar or different" (p. 439).

LUNDY. Additional evidence is provided in a study (Lundy, 1985) in which 47 high school students (a more heterogeneous sample than that of Winter and Stewart) wrote stories to four pictures and were retested 1 year later with instructions that they could tell stories that were the same as or different from those told before. Of the six pictures used for the retest, three were the same as were used initially. Scores were corrected for story length. The retest correlation was .48 for the need for intimacy and .56 for the need for affiliation. Because retest correlations for the same pictures did not exceed retest correlations for new pictures, Lundy concluded that the retest correlations could not be attributed to recall and repetition of previous stories. (While it may be reassuring to know that stability was not due simply to memory of previous responses, the finding raises a question about how the Winter–Stewart instructions work. If they permit subjects to repeat stories, but the subjects do not do so, why do the instructions improve stability?)

KOESTNER, FRANZ, AND HELLMAN. Koestner, Franz, and Hellman (1991) have identified another factor that affects the stability of thematic apperceptive motive scores (corrected for story length). Their subjects were retested after a period of 8 months. Test–retest correlations for n Power were .55 for subjects who had experienced few recent life changes and $-.01$ for those who had experienced many recent life changes. The difference is significant ($z = 2.264$, $p < .025$, two-tailed). Comparable correlations for n Intimacy (.74 and .49) were in the same direction but the difference was not significant ($z = 1.493$, $p = .15$, two-tailed). The authors infer that recent life changes affect stability by causing a temporary shift in motive levels.

Aggregation

Although reported alphas for thematic apperceptive measures of motives tend to be low, interitem (i.e., interstory) correlations are not lower than those of self-report inventories with high alphas. The inventories simply have more items. As Green (1981) has noted, "on a 50-item test with a reliability of .90, the average item intercorrelation is only .15" (p. 1005). From this perspective individual stories (considered as items) are neither better nor worse samples from their relevant universe than are items from inventories. In principle all that would be needed to improve alpha would be an increase in test length, that is, more stories (assuming that additional items have equivalent cue properties and that responses to previous items do not alter responses to additional items). However, as both critics and advocates of thematic measures have agreed, there appear to be limits on the number of stories that can be obtained from a subject, and if one goes much beyond four stories, later stories appear to reflect different determinants than earlier stories (see, e.g., Karon, 1981; Reitman and Atkinson, 1958).

One way around this problem is to allow less time for writing each story, as H. H. Morgan (1953) did in obtaining 12 stories in a single session. Another way would be to obtain stories over a series of occasions in which testing conditions were similar. The latter approach is suggested by Epstein's (1979) demonstration that reliability may be increased by averaging measures taken on different occasions (see also Rushton, Brainerd, & Pressley, 1983). This procedure is illustrated by data obtained in one of my classes following an example given by Epstein. Each of 15 students recorded his or her 30-second pulse count in four consecutive class sessions. The correlation between pulse data from the first and second sessions was only .52; but data from sessions one plus three were correlated .85 with data from sessions two plus four. The correlation obtained between only the first two occasions gives the (presumably correct) impression that pulse is relatively sensitive to situational influences. By adding only two more occasions, however, one obtains a much stronger reliability estimate – one that conveys a sense of relatively stable individual differences. As Epstein points out, this effect occurs because averaging reduces error of measurement. As scores are averaged over occasions, the standard deviations become smaller; within-subject variance is reduced and a more stable score is obtained for each individual.

This approach was followed in a study of n Achievement reliability by Smith, Krogh, and McMahan (1991) who obtained 20 stories each from female juniors in a Catholic high school over 10 occasions during the course of a semester. Story writing was introduced as a part of the English course and the teacher gave the story writing instructions. To prevent satiation only 2 5-minute stories were obtained during each class session. Attendance was excellent and complete data were obtained on 49 of the 53 students. Verbal rather than picture cues were used in order more easily to develop similar (parallel) items representing four types of achievement situations: academic (e.g., "A young woman sitting in a classroom looking thoughtfully into space."), performance (e.g., "A student rehearsing for her school play."), career (e.g., "A woman in a laboratory looking into a microscope."), and future orientation (e.g., "A student telling a girlfriend her plans for the future.").

After scoring the first 4 stories, the first two authors discussed and reconciled their differences; they then scored the last 16 stories independently. The product moment correlation between total scores for the 16 stories from the two coders was .93. (Great care was taken with scoring, because satisfactory agreement was a prerequisite for subsequent analyses.) The number of words in stories 1 and 2 were correlated with the n Achievement scores for those pictures. Since neither correlation was significant, no correction of scores for story length was made.

Other measures in addition to n Achievement were obtained in the study, but only the results pertaining to reliability will be summarized here. The finding of most relevance was an increase in reliability from an r of .10 between story 1 and story 2 to an r of .57 between the sum of the 10 odd stories and the sum of the 10 even stories. For the total (20 story) score alpha was .68.

Although obtaining 20 stories is not a practical solution to the reliability question, the study clearly demonstrates that increasing test length improves the reliability of a thematic apperceptive measure as it does for a self-report inventory. Because the alpha for the five career cues alone was .53, it may be possible to develop alternate sets of four cues each that could be administered on two occasions that would yield alphas in the .5 to .6 range.

CONCLUSIONS AND RECOMMENDATIONS

Conclusions

Reliability estimates for thematic apperceptive measures tend to be considerably lower than reliability estimates for "objective" self-report inventories. Literature reviews have exaggerated this difference, however, by estimating the modal reliability of thematic measures from studies that are not methodologically sound, from studies not designed with reliability considerations in mind, and from studies that employ inappropriate cues, have unsatisfactory interscorer agreement, obtain too few stories, or have lengthy test–retest intervals. Moreover, most of the critiques fail to consider, much less weigh appropriately, some of the most impressive reliability studies.

Studies that have (a) reported high interscorer agreement, (b) used an appropriate rationale for picture selection, and (c) used six or more pictures, have reported alphas and stability correlations in the .5 to .6 range. Although this attainment is modest, this degree of reliability is sufficient to permit valid theory-based research, even though it is not sufficient for making predictions and decisions about individuals. Even this degree of reliability cannot be attained, however, without some effort. The steps that need to be taken to insure optimal reliability are detailed in the recommendations given in the next section.

Subsequent to the critiques reviewed at the outset of this chapter, and partly because of them, theoretical and empirical advances have been made that provide an improved understanding of factors affecting the reliability of thematic apperceptive measures. For example, stability may be expected to be higher for persons who have not experienced major recent life changes than for persons who have, and internal consistency is no longer regarded as a prerequisite for the validity of composite scores. Even though internal consistency is not essential, an investigator must still attempt to obtain scores that contain the least possible amount of measurement error and that demonstrate satisfactory stability, when stability is assumed. (An emphasis on stability should not overshadow the fact that one of the strengths of the thematic apperceptive method is its sensitivity to change, either in the conditions of testing or in the subjects. The use of the method to assess changes in subjects due to training is illustrated by the work of deCharms as reported in chapter 23.)

Recommendations

Several things may be done to optimize the reliability of a thematic apperceptive measure.

REDUCE ERROR OF MEASUREMENT AS MUCH AS POSSIBLE. Options include:

1. Reduce coding errors. Strive for the highest possible degree of inter-scorer agreement (preferably .85 or higher).
2. Sample items (cues) as broadly as possible over the domain (cf. Murstein, 1965b, p. 203).
3. For sufficient test length obtain at least six stories. If possible aggregate stories over occasions (e.g., two alternate four-story forms).
4. If stories are collected on more than one occasion, make testing conditions as similar as possible, separated by an appropriate interval (e.g., 1 week). Use the instructions of D. G. Winter and Stewart (1977b) for retest occasions. (See chapter 37 for a discussion of data collection procedures.)
5. Assessing recent life changes will permit screening out subjects who have experienced major life changes; or entering life change scores into data analyses; or carrying out analyses both with and without subjects who have extreme life change scores.

INCREASE THE VARIABILITY OF THE SCORES AS MUCH AS POSSIBLE. Like any other correlation coefficient, a reliability coefficient is a function of the variability of the scores. Variability, in turn, is a function of the subject population and the characteristics of the measure.

6. Obtain scores from as heterogeneous a population as is consistent with the purpose of the research (e.g., high school students rather than college students).

7. Select pictures that produce the greatest dispersion of scores; avoid distributions of scores that are badly skewed. Pictures eliciting an intermediate, or intermediate to high, percentage of imagery (approximately 50% to 80%) seem to produce the most desirable distributions of scores (see section on picture selection and cue characteristics in chapter 37). Interstory correlations also will be greater if item difficulty (i.e., percentage of imagery) is in the intermediate range. If two cues elicit very different amounts of imagery (e.g., 10% and 90%), the maximum correlation between them is drastically limited. Such items scored dichotomously could have a maximum correlation of only .11 (Gorsuch, 1983, p. 292). Item difficulty is itself a function of the cue and the subject population, so it is necessary to pretest new cues or old cues used with new populations.

Because interstory correlations tend to be low for thematic measures, rather than add scores to obtain a composite score, it may be advantageous to enter picture scores (corrected for length, if necessary) into a multiple-regression equation to predict a dependent variable. In using this approach one should be aware of the assumptions underlying this statistical technique (e.g., linearity, interval scale scores) as well as the desirability of using relatively large samples and the importance of cross validation.

POWER. The relation of reliability to the power of statistical tests is complex (Zimmerman & Williams, 1986). However, it is safe to say that researchers should estimate effect size and determine the appropriate sample size in order to maximize the chances of finding an effect if it is there. For example, many correlations between thematic measures and criterion variables are in the .3 range. (Interestingly, $r = .3$ is regarded as a *medium* effect size by J. Cohen, 1988.) With such an estimate, and the desired degree of power (e.g., .80), one can use Cohen's tables to determine the sample size for the particular statistic one plans to use. In the past inadequate sample size has almost certainly contributed to the lack of consistent results from one study to another. Not only will adequate samples permit more effective tests of hypotheses, they will contribute to the credibility of content analytic research by providing results that are more likely to be replicable.

NOTES

1 Entwisle was apparently unaware that 14 years earlier Atkinson (1958b, p. 605) had spelled out reasons for not using grades as a criterion (see also Atkinson & Reitman, 1956/1958, p. 287).

2 Using a table of cell means, Entwisle (1972) estimated the alpha for these eight pictures to be .37. Atkinson subsequently calcuated alpha from the raw data and found it to be .57 (Atkinson et al., 1977).

PART II

Content analysis systems

9   *The achievement motive*

DAVID C. McCLELLAND AND
RICHARD KOESTNER

This chapter is intended to tell how and why a thematic apperceptive measure of achievement motivation was developed and to explain the significance of the measure for current theory and research. Because space does not permit a systematic review of the hundreds of studies on this topic or an explication of the increasingly complex and technical theoretical developments, we have provided a list of major books dealing with achievement motivation at the end of this chapter.

DERIVATION OF A FANTASY MEASURE

The development of a measure of the need for achievement, labeled *n* Achievement or *n* Ach, using Murray's (1938) nomenclature, began with attempts to arouse achievement motivation by telling young men that performance tests they were taking would yield information about their general intelligence and leadership abilities, and then giving them feedback on how well or poorly they had done (McClelland, Atkinson, Clark, & Lowell, 1953). The unique effects of this type of arousal were examined in brief imaginative stories the men wrote afterward because previous research on hunger had demonstrated that such stories sensitively reflect varying degrees of motive arousal (Atkinson & McClelland, 1948).

To arrive at an empirically justified system of content analysis, a scoring system was developed based on the differences between stories written under achievement arousal versus neutral testing conditions. Unlike previous scoring systems, which rated stories for psychogenic motives based on dictionary definitions (Murray, 1938), no characteristics were included in the scoring scheme, regardless of how theoretically justified they might be, unless they appeared more often in the stories of subjects exposed to motive arousal than in stories written under neutral testing conditions.

The characteristics that appeared more often following achievement arousal took the form of "thoughts about performing some task well, of sometimes being blocked, of trying various means of achieving, and of

143

experiencing joy or sadness contingent upon the outcome of the effort. Together, the sum total of these different kinds of imaginative response in the set of stories written by a particular person constitute that person's *n* Achievement score, presumably an indicator of the strength of achievement motivation in the person at the time" (Atkinson, 1977, p. 30). Achievement motivation can be defined as a concern with "doing things better, with surpassing standards of excellence" (McClelland, 1985b, p. 190).

It was reasoned further that individuals who scored high according to this system under neutral testing conditions could be considered to be in a state of chronic achievement arousal. That is, they would have a need or disposition to think in achievement-related terms even when there were no cues in the situation calling for achievement. Consequently, valid measures of individual differences in *n* Achievement can only be obtained under neutral testing conditions. Both French (1955) and Smith (1966) have shown that *n* Achievement scores obtained under different conditions have different properties, and Lundy (1988) has reviewed a large number of studies employing the *n* Achievement measure and has found that significant results were obtained in about two-thirds of the reports, and that in many of the cases where significant results were not obtained, there was reason to believe the stories had not been written under neutral conditions.

Achievement arousal has been reported to have the same effects on imaginative thought in Germany (Heckhausen, 1963), Poland (Krol, 1981), and Brazil (Angelini, 1959), as well as in non-Western cultures such as in Japan (Hayashi & Habu, 1962), India (Mehta, 1969), and among the Navaho (McClelland et al., 1953). From the theoretical point of view, successful cross-cultural replications are of crucial importance, because they demonstrate that the effects of arousing the achievement motive on associative thought are the same regardless of social, cultural, or linguistic definitions of what constitutes success or achievement. These definitions of what constitutes achievement do differ by age, sex, and culture as many have pointed out (e.g., Maehr, 1974), but what is constant across these groupings is the notion of *doing something better* (whatever it may be). This has led McClelland (1985b, p. 249) to suggest that the motive might better have been called the *efficiency* motive (since that implies doing something better) rather than the achievement motive (which refers to the content of what is achieved, which varies by cultural grouping).

Despite the initial impression that the empirical derivation of the imagery categories was demonstrable only for males (McClelland et al., 1953), successful replications of the effect of achievement arousal on fantasy have also been obtained with female subjects (Schroth, 1988; Stewart & Chester, 1982). Furthermore, the behavioral correlates of individual differences in *n* Achievement among women are similar to those found for men (McClelland, 1985b; Stewart & Chester, 1982). Consequently, the scoring system presented in chapter 10 is used for both males and females, though it may be advisable to elicit stories by means of different pictures or verbal cues for males and females (see chapters 6 and 37). As Horner's (1974) work suggests, however, the strength of achievement-related *avoidance* motives may be different for women and men and may need to be considered in accounting for the achievement-related behavior of women, at least under certain conditions (see chapter 11 by Fleming and Horner).

Measurement issues

The scoring system for *n* Achievement is presented in chapter 10, and practice materials for learning to use the system are included in appendix I. Instructions and pictures or other cues used to elicit stories have varied somewhat depending on the age, sex, and cultural background of the subjects. Information on cues and test administration may be found in chapter 37. In chapter 6, Veroff describes the use of the fantasy measure of motivation in survey research.

Research has shown that the scoring criteria are sufficiently objective to yield interscorer agreement in the 85% to 95% range after training (Atkinson, 1977; Feld & Smith, 1958). Chapter 8 summarizes information on the internal consistency and test–retest reliability of the *n* Achievement measure, and in chapter 2 Atkinson presents a theoretical conception of the determinants of thematic apperceptive imagery that casts a new light on issues of reliability and validity.

As to validity, the fantasy measure qualifies as a measure of motivation because, like hunger, achievement motivation has been shown to *energize* the organism (Mücher & Heckhausen, 1962; Raphelson, 1957; Wendt, 1955), to *orient attention* to related stimuli (McClelland & Liberman, 1949), and to *select behavior* or promote learning of moderately difficult activities (Clark & McClelland, 1956; Karabenick & Yousseff, 1968; Raynor & Entin, 1982b). As noted in the sections that follow, validity studies have shown the achievement motive to be related as theoretically expected to measures of perception, memory, instrumental behavior, level of performance or effort, choice, future orientation, and long-term accomplishment.

Relationship of fantasy n Achievement to other measures of achievement motivation

The expected positive relationships have been found between the thematic apperceptive *n* Achievement score and other measures of achievement motivation in expressive behavior, namely, the French Test of Insight (French, 1958a), and graphic expression (Aronson, 1958), but fantasy *n* Achievement has not been related consistently to a wide variety of self-report measures of one's own achievement motivation (McClelland, 1980). Chapter 3 in this volume presents a review and explanation of these findings.

THEORETICALLY RELEVANT CORRELATES OF n ACHIEVEMENT

Preference for intermediate difficulty

The definition of n Achievement implies that people who are high on this dimension will be drawn to activities that are moderately difficult. That is, if the incentive is "to do better," or the anticipated satisfaction is to be gained from doing better, neither a very easy nor a very difficult task would provide much opportunity for gratification. Numerous studies (Weinstein, 1969) indicate that people high in n Achievement (especially when also low in fear of failure) prefer moderately difficult tasks defined in various ways, such as choosing to throw a ring at moderate distances from a peg (Atkinson & Litwin, 1960; McClelland, 1958b), choosing moderately difficult puzzles (Raynor & Smith, 1966; Smith, 1963, 1969b), choosing moderately difficult college majors (Isaacson, 1964), or aspiring to moderately difficult vocations (Mahone, 1960; Morris, 1966).

Atkinson (1957) proposed a theoretical model to explain the relation of n Achievement to risk preferences. He suggested that the strength of preference for various activities is a joint function of the motive to achieve success (Ms), the expectancy or subjective probability of success (Ps), and the incentive value of success (Is), where incentive value is defined as one minus the probability of success $(1 - Ps)$. In other words, it is assumed that the value of success is directly proportional to the difficulty of attaining it. According to this formula, if probability of success is moderate (e.g., Ps = .50), the product of Ps (.50) $\times$ Is $(1 - Ps$ or .50) is maximal, explaining why moderately difficult tasks offer the largest weighted positive incentive value. Atkinson further assumes that motivation to avoid failure is also aroused whenever motivation to achieve is aroused. In the model, motivation to avoid failure is a function of the motive to avoid failure (Maf) $\times$ Pf $\times$ If. Choice depends on the *relative* strength of these approach and avoidance motives. If Ms > Maf, then tasks of intermediate difficulty elicit the strongest resultant approach tendencies; if Maf > Ms, tasks of intermediate difficulty elicit the strongest resultant avoidance tendencies.

Kuhl (1978) has emphasized the importance of considering *subjective* standards of difficulty in the elaboration of this risk-taking model. Such emphasis seems warranted given the fact that studies have found that individuals with high n Achievement initially estimate tasks as easier than people with low n Achievement (McClelland et al., 1953; Reeve, Olson,

& Cole, 1987). In addition, research suggests that the relationship of achievement-related motives to goal setting is affected by the age of the subjects (Smith, 1969b), the nature of the task (skill or chance), and the arousal conditions under which goal setting is assessed (Raynor & Smith, 1966; Smith, 1963).

Persistence

In an early study, Atkinson (1953) found that individuals high in *n* Achievement recalled more uncompleted than completed tasks under achievement-oriented conditions, presumably because they were more persistent than those low in *n* Achievement in trying to complete a task or do it well. Deriving hypotheses from Atkinson's risk-taking model, Feather (1961) showed that persistence in working at a task characteristic of persons *relatively* high in *n* Achievement (Ms > Maf) as compared with those *relatively* low in *n* Achievement (Maf > Ms) depended on the perceived probability of success at the task. Thus, individuals with Ms > Maf persisted longer when unable to solve an "easy" task than when unable to solve a "difficult" task, whereas individuals with Maf > Ms showed the opposite pattern.

The explanation in terms of the Atkinson model lies in the fact that for a task initially perceived as easy (Ps > .50), failure moves the probability of success *toward* intermediate difficulty (Ps = .50), thereby arousing more approach motivation (and more persistence) in those with Ms > Maf and more avoidance motivation (and less persistence) in those with Maf > Ms. For a task that is perceived as difficult to begin with (Ps < .50), lack of success will move the subjective probability of success further away from the moderate difficulty level, thereby decreasing the approach motivation and persistence of subjects relatively high in *n* Achievement and decreasing the avoidance motivation and increasing the persistence of subjects relatively low in *n* Achievement. Subsequent studies elaborating on the relationship of achievement-related motives to persistence were carried out by Brown (1974), Smith (1964), and Weiner (1965).

Atkinson's early conception of the determinants of achievement-related behavior is now embedded in a full-scale theory of motivation and action (Atkinson, 1983; Atkinson & Birch, 1970, 1978) in which turning from persistence at one activity to the initiation of a new activity becomes a central problem for the theory of motivation.

Personal responsibility and knowledge of results

Besides optimal challenge, several other factors have been found to affect the relation of *n* Achievement to task preferences, performance, and persistence – namely, personal responsibility for the performance outcome and knowledge of results or of how well one is doing. Only if people with high n Achievement feel personally responsible for a performance outcome under conditions that emphasize individual problem solving are they likely to derive any satisfaction from doing something better (McClelland, 1961; Short & Sorrentino, 1986). Thus, they do not perform better when pressured externally to do better (Atkinson & Reitman, 1956; McClelland, Koestner, & Weinberger, 1989; Schroth, 1988; Smith, 1966; Wendt, 1955), or when performance outcomes are due to chance, as in gambling (Hancock & Teevan, 1964; Littig, 1963).

People high in n Achievement also do better as compared with people low in n Achievement if they can get performance feedback on how well they are doing (French, 1958b). This would explain their tendency to perform better on teaching machines (Bartmann, 1965) and their preference for occupations like selling (McClelland, 1961) or hobbies like carpentry or model building (Kagan & Moss, 1962) that give immediate feedback on how well they are doing. It may also explain the curious fact that while monetary rewards do not operate as an incentive for persons high in n Achievement, they do value money more than others for the information it gives on how well they are doing (McClelland, 1985b). Interest in how well one is doing may also explain the preference of those high in n Achievement for surrounding themselves with experts (French, 1956).

Future orientation

McClelland (1961) and Raynor and Entin (1982a) have reviewed the extent to which people with a strong achievement motive are more future-time-oriented. In particular the extent to which succeeding on a task is important for moving on to attain future goals affects how hard and efficiently people high in n Achievement work (Raynor, 1974). For example, students with a strong achievement motive will get better grades in a course than those with a weak achievement motive *if* they perceive the course as a necessary means to achieving a future goal (Raynor & Entin, 1982a). If they see the course as irrelevant to future goals, they do not get better grades than those low in n Achievement. In more general terms, n Achievement facilitates performance along contingent paths to goals.

Achievement motivation and work

Men high in n Achievement are more interested and involved in their occupations than others (Veroff, 1982), are more upwardly mobile (Andrews, 1967; Crockett, 1962; McClelland & Boyatzis, 1982), and often make more money at work (Cummin, 1967; McClelland & Franz, in press).

Such relationships appear for women if they are career-oriented (Elder & MacInnis, 1983; Jenkins, 1987).

Because the job requirements of entrepreneurship appear to match the interest that those high in *n* Achievement have in challenging tasks, personal responsibility, and performance feedback, it was theorized and confirmed empirically that people high in *n* Achievement should be drawn to entrepreneurial occupations and should perform better in them (McClelland, 1961, 1987b; McClelland & Winter, 1971; Tessler, O'Barr, & Spain, 1973). Following this line of thought, McClelland (1985b) has summarized evidence that training courses in achievement motivation can improve the performance of small business entrepreneurs. High *n* Achievement has also been shown to relate to more enterprising activity in farming (Ray & Singh, 1980; Rogers & Neill, 1966; Rogers & Svenning, 1969; Sinha & Mehta, 1972), in taking college courses (Andrews, 1966), and in searching for work among the unemployed (Sheppard & Belitsky, 1966).

School achievement

The relation of *n* Achievement to school performance has been the object of considerable study and debate (Entwisle, 1972; Klinger, 1966). No consistent relation has been found (McClelland, 1985b). However, on theoretical grounds, one would expect a relationship *only* when conditions in a school setting are "achievement motive congenial" (Heckhausen & Krug, 1982) – that is, when they provide optimal challenge and permit personal responsibility or self-determination. For example, O'Connor, Atkinson, and Horner (1966) showed that children high in *n* Achievement performed better in classes in which challenge was optimal because the children were all of about the same ability level, but they did not do better in heterogeneous classes in which the challenge was too high or too low because of wide discrepancies in ability level. And McKeachie (1961) showed that students high in *n* Achievement performed *less* well in classes emphasizing high standards and competition among students, presumably because the "achievement motive congenial" requirement of self-determination was violated by external achievement pressure. So the presumption is that the achievement motive will predict school success only when the school environment provides optimally challenging activities, performance feedback, and the opportunity for self-determination in working on tasks.

Self-concept and acceptance by others

Highly achievement-motivated people also appear to be recognized for their ability to get along with others (Feld, 1967; Lifshitz, 1974; Teevan,

Diffenderfer, & Greenfeld, 1986). Furthermore, they have a more positive and stable self-concept (Hamm, 1977; Srivastava, 1979) and show signs of maintaining better health over time (Koestner, Ramey, Kelner, Meenan, & McClelland, 1989; McClelland, 1979).

Development of achievement motivation

Much effort has gone into studying the origins and development of achievement motivation (McClelland, 1985b; Smith, 1969a). In general there are two schools of thought: One conceives of achievement motivation as developing out of early socialization experiences surrounding a natural incentive centering in the pleasure derived from mastering a challenging task. Thus, parental stress on mastering a feeding schedule in infancy or toileting in early childhood has been found to be associated with adult achievement motivation levels (McClelland & Pilon, 1983). The resulting achievement motive may also be partly dependent on innate differences in ability to experience such pleasure (see Cortés & Gatti, 1972) and may be acquired prelinguistically, so that it is not explicitly represented in the developing self-image. In this view, what develops is the expanding experience of what constitutes a challenging task. This line of thought is developed more fully in chapter 3.

Another view is more cognitive in its focus and suggests that the achievement motive develops along with children's ability to understand and conceptualize their successes and failures (Heckhausen, 1967; Veroff, 1969).

Collective levels of achievement motivation

The n Achievement scoring system has been used to code popular literature such as children's stories, popular fiction, public speeches, folktales, and hymns in an effort to estimate collective levels of motivation (McClelland, 1961; D. G. Winter, 1987b). Generally, higher levels of n Achievement in popular literature have preceded increases in rate of economic growth and lower levels of n Achievement have preceded economic decline. This was found to be true in ancient Greece, in Spain in the Middle Ages, in England from the 16th to 18th century, and cross-nationally roughly from 1925 to 1958 (McClelland, 1961). The explanation presumably lies in the presumption that high collective achievement motivation levels reflect a higher level of entrepreneurial activity in the culture, which translates in time into more rapid rates of economic growth. D. G. Winter (1991) has developed a system for scoring n Achievement and other motives in preexisting verbal material (running text).

CURRENT APPROACHES TO THE STUDY OF ACHIEVEMENT
MOTIVATION

Since the publication of *The Achievement Motive* (McClelland et al.,
1953), research has led to major changes in the original theory (e.g., the
discrepancy-from-adaptation-level theory has long been abandoned) and in
the understanding of the conditions under which motives are expressed
in thought and behavior. Criticisms (e.g., Klinger, 1966) and alternative
perspectives (e.g., Weiner, 1980) have stimulated improvements in measurement procedures (see chapters 6, 8, and 37) and a greater appreciation of
the role of other motives and dispositions that come into play along with
the achievement motive (see chapter 5 on motivational configurations).
Methodological and theoretical issues have been discussed in an extensive
review by McClelland (1985b).

One contemporary framework for understanding the measurement of the
achievement motive as well as other motives and their effects on behavior is
provided by the theory of the dynamics of action (Atkinson & Birch, 1970,
1978). In that approach, the functional significance of fear of failure is also
spelled out. For another view, also including consideration of fear of success
in women (Horner, 1974), discussion of how the overall intensity of motivation affects the efficiency of performance, and analysis of how the different
effects of motivation on persistence (how long) and efficiency (how well)
account for so-called over- and underachievement in tests and academic
achievement, see Atkinson and Raynor (1974). Other contemporary collec-
tions of theoretical analysis and empirical evidence concerning achievement
motivation are to be found in Atkinson (1983), D. R. Brown and Veroff
(1986), and Kuhl and Atkinson (1986). The research of Blankenship on
substitution, the consummatory value of success, and the use of computer
simulation in motivational research may also be found in these volumes and
in Blankenship (1982).

BOOKS DEALING EXTENSIVELY WITH ACHIEVEMENT
MOTIVATION

Atkinson, J. W. (Ed.). (1958). *Motives in fantasy, action and society*. Princeton, NJ:
Van Nostrand.
Atkinson, J. W. (1964). *An introduction to motivation*. Princeton, NJ: Van
Nostrand.
Atkinson, J. W. (1983). *Personality, motivation, and action*. New York: Praeger.
Atkinson, J. W., & Birch, D. (1978). *An introduction to motivation: Second edition*.
New York: Van Nostrand.
Atkinson, J. W., & Feather, N. T. (Eds.). (1966). *A theory of achievement motiva-
tion*. New York: Wiley.
Atkinson, J. W., & Raynor, J. O. (Eds.). (1974). *Motivation and achievement*.
Washington, DC: Winston (Halsted Press/Wiley).

Brown, D. R., & Veroff, J. (Eds.). (1986). *Frontiers of motivational psychology.* New York: Springer-Verlag.

Fyans, L. J., Jr. (Ed.). (1980). *Achievement motivation: Recent trends in theory and research.* New York: Plenum.

Heckhausen, H. (1967). *The anatomy of achievement motivation.* New York: Academic Press. (Original work published in 1965)

Heckhausen, H., Schmalt, H.-D., & Schneider, K. (1985). *Achievement motivation in perspective.* New York: Academic Press.

Kuhl, J., & Atkinson, J. W. (1986a). *Motivation, thought and action.* New York: Praeger.

McClelland, D. C. (1961/76). *The achieving society.* Princeton, NJ: Van Nostrand. (Paperback edition, 1967, New York: Free Press. Reissued with a new preface, 1976, New York: Irvington)

McClelland, D. C., Atkinson, J. W., Clark, R. A., & Lowell, E. L. (1953/1976). *The achievement motive.* New York: Appleton-Century-Crofts. (Reissued with a new preface by J. W. Atkinson, 1976, New York: Irvington)

McClelland, D. C., & Winter, D. G. (1969/1971). *Motivating economic achievement.* New York: Free Press. (Paperback edition with afterword, 1971)

Rosen, B. C., Crockett, H., & Nunn, C. Z. (1969). *Achievement in American society.* Cambridge, MA: Schenkman.

Smith, C. P. (Ed.). (1969). *Achievement-related motives in children.* New York: Russell Sage Foundation.

Veroff, J., & Feld, S. (1970). *Marriage and work in America.* New York: Van Nostrand–Reinhold.

Veroff, J., & Veroff, J. B. (1980). *Social incentives: A life span developmental approach.* New York: Academic Press.

10 *A scoring manual for the achievement motive*

DAVID C. McCLELLAND, JOHN W. ATKINSON,
RUSSELL A. CLARK, AND EDGAR L. LOWELL

RELATION OF SCORING CATEGORIES TO THE ADJUSTIVE BEHAVIORAL SEQUENCE[1]

Our classification of many of the aspects of the behavior and experiences of characters in imaginative stories reveals an implicit acceptance of the kind of descriptive categories elaborated by many different psychological theorists in conceptualizing adjustive overt behavior. Thus, we perceive the behavioral sequence originating when an individual experiences a state of need or a motive (N). (The symbols in parentheses are used throughout to denote the various scoring categories.) He may also be anticipating successful attainment of his goal ($Ga+$) or anticipating frustration and failure ($Ga-$). He may engage in activity instrumental (I) to the attainment of his goal, which may lead to the attainment of the goal ($I+$) or not ($I-$). Sometimes his goal-directed activity will be blocked. The obstacle or block (B) to his progress may be located in the world at large (Bw) or it may be some personal deficiency in himself (Bp). He may experience strong positive and negative affective states while engaged in solving his problem, for example, in attempting to gratify his motive. He is likely to experience a state of positive affect ($G+$) in goal attainment, or a state of negative affect ($G-$) when his goal-directed activity is thwarted or he fails. Often someone will help or sympathize with him – [nurturant press (Nup)] – aiding him in his goal-directed behavior. This, in brief, is our analysis of the behavioral

"A Scoring Manual for the Achievement Motive" was originally published as chapter 4 of McClelland, D. C., Atkinson, J. W., Clark, R. A., & Lowell, E. L. (1953). *The Achievement Motive* (pp. 107–138). New York: Appleton-Century-Crofts. *The Achievement Motive* was reissued in 1976 by Irvington Publishers, Inc., New York, NY. The scoring manual is reprinted here with minor modifications by permission of the authors and Irvington Publishers, Inc. The present abridged version of the scoring manual was published as chapter 12 in Atkinson, J. W. (Ed.). (1958). *Motives in Fantasy, Action and Society* (pp. 179–204). Princeton, NJ: Van Nostrand. It is reprinted with minor modifications by permission (copyright by John W. Atkinson).

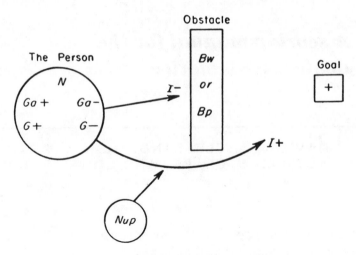

Fig. 10.1. Position of the scoring categories in the adjustive behavioral sequence.

sequence. It is presented schematically in Figure 10.1. Note that the five states an individual may experience (Need, Positive or Negative Anticipatory Goal States, Positive or Negative Affective States) are located within the person in this diagram. Instrumental Activity is denoted by the arrows suggestive of trials and errors in the problem-solving attempt. A Block (which may also be located within the person) is denoted as a barrier that must be overcome if the goal is to be attained. The symbol for Nurturant Press is another person with an arrow in the direction of the goal indicating aid of some sort. And finally, the goal is indicated by a plus sign. The goal defines whether or not the various anticipations, affective states, instrumental acts, and so forth of the person are achievement-related or are related to some other motive. Presumably these categories may be used to describe the behavioral sequence no matter what the goal of the individual. For this reason, major attention must be directed to the definition of what constitutes an achievement goal.

DEFINITION OF ACHIEVEMENT IMAGERY (AI)

The scorer must first decide whether or not the story contains any reference to an achievement goal which would justify his scoring the subcategories (Need, Instrumental Activity, and so on) as achievement-related. By achievement goal is meant *success in competition with some standard of excellence*. That is, the goal of some individual in the story is to be successful in terms of competition with some standard of excellence. The individual may fail to achieve this goal, but the concern over competition with a standard of excellence still enables one to identify the goal sought as an achievement goal. This, then, is our generic definition of *n* Achievement. In the definitions of criteria for scoring Achievement Imagery that follow, it will become apparent that we include certain types of imagery in which there is no explicit statement in the story concerning competition with a standard of excellence. For these particular criteria it is our feeling that the evidence is sufficient for a fairly safe *inference* that competition with a standard of excellence is implicitly involved.

Competition with a standard of excellence is perhaps most clear when one of the characters is engaged in competitive activity (other than pure aggression) where winning or doing as well as or better than someone else is the primary concern. Often, however, competition with a standard of excellence is evident in the concern of one of the characters with how well a particular task is being done, regardless of how well someone else is doing. Any use of adjectives of degree (good, better, best) will qualify so long as they evaluate the excellence of performance. Stories are scored for Achievement Imagery *only* when one of the criteria listed below is met. Although competition with a standard of excellence is implicit in all three criteria, as pointed out above, the phrase is used to denote the first criterion in which concern over how well the activity is being done is most explicit.

1. *Competition with a standard of excellence. a.* One of the characters in the story is engaged in some competitive activity (other than pure cases of aggression) where winning or doing as well as or better than others is *actually stated* as the primary concern. Wanting to win an essay contest, or an apprentice wanting to show the master that he, too, can fix the machine, are typical examples.

b. If one of the characters in the story is engaged in some competitive activity (other than pure cases of aggression), but the desire to win or do as well as or better than others is *not explicitly* stated, then (1) affective concern over goal attainment, and (2) certain types of Instrumental Activity are considered as indicating that the desire to compete successfully with a standard of excellence is implicit in the story. Examples of (1) would be: "The boy wins the essay contest and feels *proud.*" "The boy loses the contest and becomes *bitter.*" "The boy *anticipates* the *glory* that will be his if he should win." An example of (2) would be: "The boy is working *very carefully* on his essay."

{Stories are not always scored for Achievement Imagery (*AI*) when the evidence of affective concern is largely negative. When a person is in achievement-related difficulty, it is normal to experience negative affect (*G*−). This is not enough to justify scoring Achievement Imagery. There must be independent evidence of a *positive achievement orientation*. The story must indicate, either by a direct statement of need (*N*) or by a sufficiently descriptive instrumental activity (*I*), that the person stays in the field and is realistically concerned about overcoming the deficiency. In most cases, both *G−* and *N* must appear, or *G−* paired with a *clear-cut* achievement-related instrumental act. The following story is an excellent example of *what not to score*. Here the person leaves the field – a fine example of a failure-avoidance motive but not of an achievement motive. (Score Doubtful Imagery.)

The young student *seems to be perplexed* with some problem and then finding no solution appears to daydream. The young student was asked a question about which he *didn't know the answer*, so he *felt rather discouraged and disgusted*. The student is *wondering whether school work is necessary "stuff"* or not. He hopes he *were doing something else*. He will continue in school, perhaps graduate; if not, he will soon quit school and look for adventure elsewhere perhaps in a trade school.

In the next story, there is negative affect following an obstacle, but there is no evidence of achievement concern in any statement of need nor is there any instrumental act which implies achievement concern. (Score Doubtful Imagery.)

Machine has broken down and is being fixed. Man fixing it is the boss of the shop. Other man is *worker who broke machine*. Boss has told worker to be careful in handling machine because it operates with difficulty. Man fixing the machine thinks breakage could have been avoided. The worker *is just plain angry because the damn thing broke* and is watching with disgust. The machine will be repaired. Worker will be fired if it happens again.

In the following two stories, there is both negative affect (regret) and a statement of need to overcome the obstacle. Both these stories are scored for Achievement Imagery and also for other categories.

Peter is in class and he has to write a quiz. The day before Peter *instead of studying for the quiz went to the movies* with some friends. Peter *thinks now how foolish it was to go to the movies*, he *wants now to know the answers for the quiz*. Peter will have a poor grade in his quiz and *should work harder to make up* his grade.

An engineer is taking an open book exam and he is *finding the exam too* difficult. The student is not stupid, but he has a girl and *didn't study as hard as he should have*. He *wishes that he had studied harder* and *wishes the correct answers*. He would cheat, but it is an honor exam and he has too much character. He will get a "D" in the exam and *will turn over a new leaf* and devote the proper time to study.}[2]

c. Often the standard of excellence involves no competition with others but meeting self-imposed requirements of good performance. In this case, in order to score for *AI* what is needed are words to the effect that a good, thorough, workmanlike job, and so forth is desired, or statements showing the affective concern or Instrumental Activity that will allow such an inference. Typical examples are: "The boy is *studiously* and *carefully* preparing his homework." "The boy is *worried* because he cannot quite grasp the meaning in the textbook assignment."

In the above criteria, distinction is made between statements of the *intensity* and *quality* of instrumental acts. Working hard or working fast would be evidence of concern over achievement only when excellence at the task demanded speed or intense effort. But one may work hard to complete a task for reasons other than personal achievement. For instance, "The boy is working hard to finish his homework," may indicate only that he wants to go out and play or perhaps that he is late with his term paper and is rushing to get it in. In neither of these examples is there evidence of concern over a standard of excellence, and so there is no basis for scoring Achievement Imagery. However, a statement such as "He is working slowly with great thoroughness" implies concern with accuracy, a standard of excellence. In this instance and in ones like it, Achievement Imagery would be scored.

2. *Unique accomplishment.* One of the characters is involved in accomplishing other than a run-of-the-mill daily task which will mark him as a personal success. Inventions, artistic creations, and other extraordinary accomplishments fulfill this criterion. There need be no explicit statement of concern over the outcome or direct statement that a good job is wanted when someone is working on a new invention or is in the process of doing something unique which will be generally accepted as a personal accomplishment. Here we make the inference that the individual is competing with a standard of excellence, and that unless his goal is reached he will also experience feelings of failure.

{The manual focuses attention chiefly on the distinction between the story in which two men are simply working at a machine versus two inventors in the process of developing something new and socially useful. The scorer, however, must be sensitive to what would constitute a unique accomplishment in other fields of endeavor. For example, a boy practicing at the piano versus the young composer struggling with a new composition, a reporter finishing an article versus a reporter getting the beat on everyone else, etc. In the story below, the unique accomplishment imagery is embedded in a story that is loaded with ideological content. It should be scored as a unique accomplishment in terms of the underlined imagery.

These two men are working with a machine, perhaps a printing press. It might be Tom Paine and an assistant *working on the publication of his famous booklet* advocating freedom for America. Oppression by the British has angered Paine into writing a pamphlet expressing the grievance of the Americans *which is destined to make history*. The two men are perhaps disturbed by the failure of their primitive press and are discussing possibilities of repairing it so that *their important document* can be published. The pamphlet of T. Paine *is destined to become one of the greatest of revolutionary documents* and was instrumental in arousing the colonists to fight for their freedom.}

3. *Long-term involvement.* One of the characters is involved in attainment of a long-term achievement goal. Being a success in life, becoming a machinist, doctor, lawyer, successful businessman, and so forth, are all

examples of career involvement which permit the inference of competition with a standard of excellence *unless it is made explicit that another goal is primary*, for example, food for the kids, personal security.

{If other motives are contributing to the striving toward a long-term achievement but are not primary, so that *some part* of the striving is attributable to *n* Achievement, Achievement Imagery should be scored.}

Often, one of the characters may be involved in attainment of some limited achievement goal, for example, a specific task. When rather routine and limited tasks or performances are shown definitely to be related to long-term achievement interests, Achievement Imagery *is* scored. Studying for an exam would *not* be scored unless there was evidence of concern over doing well or over the possibility of failure as outlined under criterion (1) listed above, *or* unless the exam were explicitly related to "going on to medical school" or "graduating from college" – both being long-term achievement goals. *The relationship of a specific task to a long-term achievement goal must be clearly stated and not inferred by the scorer when it does not fulfill criterion (1) above.*

It is worth noting that we are able to include long-term involvement as evidence of achievement motivation only because we have knowledge that in contemporary American society, success in the career usually demands successful competition with a standard of excellence. Not everyone can be a doctor, lawyer, successful businessman, or expert machinist. Attainment of these goals is accompanied by feelings of personal success which we believe to be historically related to the pleasure associated with independent accomplishment in early childhood, in which reward (hence pleasure) is contingent upon mastery, viz., doing a good job. *In scoring the stories of other cultures without knowledge of the culture, it would be necessary to adhere to the criterion of an explicit statement of concern over successful competition with a standard in order to define the achievement goals of that culture. Only with growing knowledge of the culture could other criteria be added which involve the inference that competition with a standard of excellence is inherent in certain cultural activities.*[3]

Only stories which fulfill at least one of these three criteria are scored for the achievement-related subcategories.

{The same phrase may be scored for Achievement Imagery and any other category. But the same phrase may *not* be scored for *two* subcategories.}

DOUBTFUL ACHIEVEMENT IMAGERY (TI)

Stories containing some references to achievement but which fail to meet one of the three criteria for Achievement Imagery are scored Doubtful Achievement Imagery (*TI*) and are not scored further for achievement-related subcategories. The *T* chosen as a symbol for this category indicates that most frequently the stories to be classified as doubtful are ones in which one of the characters is engaged in a commonplace *task* or solving a routine problem. Whenever there is doubt about whether or not one of the three criteria for Achievement Imagery has been met, and the story is not totally unrelated to achievement, it is classified *TI*.

UNRELATED IMAGERY (UI)

Stories in which there is no reference to an achievement goal are scored unrelated and not scored further. The difference between a story scored *TI* and one scored *UI* is simply that the *TI* story usually contains reference to some commonplace task goal and often contains other task-related sub-categories but fails to meet one of our three criteria for scoring Achievement Imagery, whereas the story scored *UI* fails to have any reference whatsoever to achievement.

The three imagery categories (*UI*, *TI*, and *AI*) comprise a continuum of increasing certainty that the story contains imagery related to achievement motivation. Often the scorer may feel that a story that must be scored *TI* because it fails to meet any one of the criteria for *AI*, should have been scored for *AI* and the other achievement-related subcategories as well. Our experience indicates that while undoubtedly some achievement stories are lost according to the present criteria, in the long run, rigid adherence to the stated criteria is the only means of assuring high scorer reliability. The rationale for distinguishing between stories with doubtful achievement imagery and those unrelated to achievement will become clear when the method of computing the *n* Achievement score is discussed.

STORIES ILLUSTRATING VARIOUS TYPES OF ACHIEVEMENT IMAGERY

Competition with a standard (AI)

1. One fellow is the supervisor and the other the machine operator. There has been trouble with the machine, and the supervisor is attempting to repair it. The machine operator has been turning out faulty equipment and after having been called down by the supervisor, he explained what he thought has been wrong. Upon inspection by the supervisor, this theory has been proven correct. The operator has his doubts about the ability of the supervisor to repair the machine. The boss realizes this and is determined to repair it. *He wants to prove that he is capable of making minor repairs.* The boss will do part of the repairs, but due to the technicalities of the machine will be unable to complete the job, and he will have to either call in the maintenance men or a specialized repair man from the outside.

2. An operation is taking place. The persons are the doctor, patient, nurse, and a

student. The patient must have been sick at one time to be on the table. The student is observing the doctor doing his job along with the nurse. The doctor is concentrating on his work. The student is attending the doctor's movements, the nurse probably thinking of her boy friend. *A good job is wanted by the doctor* and student. The doctor will complete the operation, give a lecture on it, the student will ask questions on the work, the nurse will take off on her other duties.

(The clearly stated desire to meet a standard of excellence enables one to score these two stories *AI* instead of *TI*.)

3. The boy is taking an examination. He is a college student. He is trying to recall a pertinent fact. He did not study this particular point enough although he thought it might be on the examination. He is trying to recall that point. He can almost get it but not quite. It's almost on the tip of his tongue. Either he will recall it or he won't. If he recalls it, he will write it down. *If he doesn't, he will be mad.*

(Evidence of affective arousal as a result of nonattainment of the achievement goal in this specific task situation is all that keeps the imagery from being considered *TI*.)

4. A group of medical students are watching their instructor perform a simple operation on a cadaver. A few of the students are very sure they will be called on to assist Dr. Hugo. In the last few months they have worked and studied. The skillful hands of the surgeon perform their work. The instructor tells his class *they must be able to work with speed and cannot make many mistakes.* When the operation is over, a smile comes over the group. Soon they will be leading men and women in the field.

(The instructor's interest in accuracy and perfection is evidence of a desire for mastery in this specific task.)

5. The student is *worrying about his two exams* coming up Friday, the first night of the May frolic. The student has spent most of his time previous to this, studying information for his research paper in English 108. He is *wondering how he can ever manage to study sufficiently enough to be able to pass the exams* while he is so preoccupied with thoughts of the Frolic. He will study "like mad" for a few hours, and then "knock off," hoping for the best.

(Note that it is the student's affective arousal [worrying] concerning the threat of not reaching his achievement goal [passing the exam] which leads to the decision to score this story *AI* and not the vigorous Instrumental Activity of the last sentence [studying "like mad"]. A distinction must be made between evidence of intense Instrumental Activity [working hard] and evidence of concern over mastery. Stories with only intense Instrumental Activity will not be scored *AI* unless one of the three criteria for Achievement Imagery is met.)

Unique accomplishment (AI)

6. Something is being heated in a type of furnace which appears to be of metal. The men are blacksmiths. The men have been doing *research* on an alloy of some type and *this is the crucial test* that spells success or failure of the experiment. They

want a specific type of metal. They are working for government interests. They may be successful this time. They have *invented* a metal that is very light, strong, durable, heat resistant, etc. A *real step in scientific progress*.

7. The boy is a student and during a boring lecture his mind is going off on a tangent, and he is daydreaming. The instructor has been talking about medieval history, and his reference to the knights of old has made the lad project himself into such a battle arrayed with armor and riding a white stallion. The boy is thinking of riding out of the castle, waving goodbye to his lady fair, and *going into the battle and accomplishing many heroic deeds*. The boy will snap out of it when the instructor starts questioning the students on various aspects of the lecture, and the boy will become frantic realizing he has not been paying attention.

8. Gutenberg and his assistant, Flogman, are working on an edition of the Bible. They are working hard to get as many printed as possible. Together *they have worked on Gutenberg's idea of a printing press and now, together, they are attempting to prove its worth*. Gutenberg thinks, "Will that fifth lever in the back of the joint hold up?" Flogman thinks, "If the Cardinal approves, we are in, but it is not likely that he will." The Cardinal disapproves, but the City Council approves, and Gutenberg and Flogman receive their contracts.

9. The boss is talking to an employee. The boss has some special job that he wants done, and this man is an expert in that particular phase. The boss wants the employee, an engineer, to start *working on a specially designed carburetor for a revolutionary engine*. The employee is thinking out the problem. The job will come off "O.K.," and the engine will *revolutionize* the automobile industry.

10. *Two inventors are working on a new type of machine*. They need this machine in order to complete the work on their new invention, the automobile. This takes place some time ago. They are thinking that soon they will have succeeded. They want to improve transportation. Their *invention* will be successful and they will found a great industrial concern.

Long-term involvement (AI)

11. *The boy is thinking about a career as a doctor. He sees himself as a great surgeon performing an operation*. He has been doing minor first aid work on his injured dog, and discovers he enjoys working with medicine. He thinks he is suited for this profession and sets it as an ultimate goal in life at this moment. He has not weighed the pros and cons of his own ability and has let his goal blind him of his own inability. An adjustment which will injure him will have to be made.

12. A boy, Jim Neilson, 18 years old, is *taking an examination for entrance in the Army Air Corps*. He has studied very hard in high school *hoping all along that he will some day be a fighter pilot*. Now that he sees how difficult the examination is, he is very worried that he may fail it. He is thinking so much about his failing it he cannot concentrate on the test itself. He will just barely pass the test and will later become a cadet, then finally a pilot.

(The first sentence of this story is an example of a specific task being related to a long-term achievement goal. The second sentence reiterates the long-term concern. There is also affective concern over the possibility of failing the test that would warrant scoring this story *AI*.)

13. The boy is a thinker, bored with his schoolwork he is attempting to do. His mind wanders. He thinks of his future. The boy has completed all but the last of his

high school career. The boy is eager to graduate. He has faith in his capabilities and *wants to get started on the job he has lined up, dreaming of advancements.* The boy will graduate ranking near the middle of his class. He will do all right on the outside.

14. The boss is inquiring about a story that the young man wrote in the paper. He had claimed evidence in a murder trial that didn't actually exist. Reporter reported false evidence, and the police have raised quite a stink about it. Public opinion is clamoring for conviction. The boss wants the reporter to find new evidence which will take pressure off the paper. *Reporter is thinking he'll lose his job if he doesn't.* Reporter will find new evidence but police get conviction anyway so pressure is off paper. Man doesn't lose job.

(Here there is concern about a long-term goal, the job. The specific task of finding new evidence is related to this long-term goal of the reporter.)

15. This is a father and a son. The father is an immigrant, and his son has stopped to see his father. *The son has been successful in his business* largely because of the training he received in his home as a child and youth. The old man is looking with a feeling of pride at his son and feels that he is very fortunate to have many things he himself never had. The son realizes this *pride* in his father's thoughts. The son will try to give his father some of the things he gave up in order to educate him.

{The following story is an example which is too specific to be scored long-term involvement.

There are two men here, John the younger, Bill the older. The machine on which John is working has broken in some way. Bill will try to fix it. John has worked in this lab only six months and is unfamiliar with the machine except to run it. John wants to learn to fix the machine. Bill wants the machine fixed so that he may do it himself (J.) next time. The machine will be fixed. John will go back to work. Bill will return to his supervising job.}

Doubtful Achievement Imagery (TI)

16. There are two men working in some sort of machine shop. They are making some sort of a bolt or something. One of the men's car broke down, and he has discovered that a bolt is broken. So, being a fairly good forger, he is making a new bolt. He is discussing with the other man just how he is making the bolt and telling him about all of the details in making this bolt. When he is finished, he will take the bolt and replace the broken bolt in the car with it. He will then be able to get his car going.

(This is an example of a specific task story in which there is no stated need for mastery and no evidence of affective arousal concerning the possibility of personal success or failure. There is, however, a specific achievement goal, namely, making the bolt. Therefore, the story is scored *TI* rather than *UI*.)[4]

17. Two workmen are trying to remove one lead pig from a small blast furnace. This action was to be completed months before, but only now did the necessary material arrive. One young man is showing the other just how to handle the pig, and perhaps a little theory is presented while they are waiting for the finished product. During the conversation, a distant bell is heard, the men quickly stop their work and prepare to adjust a number of tools before taking the pig from the furnace.

18. Jim is in the midst of deep thought trying to pick the answer to a problem on his exam out of the thin air. He is evidently having a difficult time with it. Jim probably didn't prepare himself too well for his exam and therefore doesn't have necessary things at his fingertips. Jim is trying to remember some formula. If he could just remember it, he could solve his problem immediately. Jim will skip to the next problem in a short while and then return to this one.

(Note that being in an exam situation is not scored *AI* in this instance, since there is no evidence of concern over the outcome either in the form of a stated need to do well, working carefully, affective arousal over the possibility of success or failure, and so forth.)

19. The persons are students in a school. They were studying until a distraction occurred which was the teacher who attracted their attention. The students were studying. The teacher had disciplined them for their actions in class telling them to study a story for repetition later. The students are looking at the teacher with dislike in their eyes. They don't think much of her this day and dislike her for her ways of teaching. The students will not do too well in the repetition exercise, and as a result further punishment will be applied.

(The achievement goal of the story is studying. There is no evidence of concern over mastery, perfection, or the possibility of failure, so the story is scored *TI*.)

20. An elderly man and young man with their heads together in conference. The older one is giving advice to the younger man perhaps on a matter of law. The young man, who has just entered the field of law, has come up with a difficulty in a recent case and has turned to the senior and wiser partner of his firm. They go over the situation and facts from which the elderly man will then advise. The advice will be taken by the young lawyer, and he will then proceed to form his case around the advice.

(Two lawyers are engaged in a specific, routine task, that of solving a particular problem. The mere mention of the profession of law is not sufficient to classify this story as a long-term involvement. Becoming a lawyer is not the goal of the story. Rather, the solution to a specific legal problem is the goal. Unless there is evidence that perfection, the best possible solution, and so on, is wanted, the story is scored *TI*.)

21. Doctor Ingersoll is making a very difficult operation on Frank Briston's left kidney. Another doctor and nurse are present. Frank has been a drunkard most of his life which has poisoned his kidneys. The doctor is concentrating on the operation. The nurse is thinking that it is futile to try to save him. He will just go to drink again. He will recover, but as the nurse thought he will die of drinking.

(A doctor performing a routine operation is scored *TI*, unless there is direct evidence of concern over mastery, perfection, and so forth.)

22. It looks like a painting that has not been completed. The boy in the bottom of the picture is the artist. The painting has been started but has not been completed. The canvas was prepared and the rough drawing made. The boy (in the lower

right-hand corner) is thinking about what to do next. He has already begun to shade in the left-hand side of the painting. The painting will be completed by the boy.

(The story is clearly not an example of a unique accomplishment. The boy is not creating a work of art. Rather he is engaged in the specific task of painting a picture, therefore, this story is scored *TI*.)

Unrelated Imagery (UI)

23. A young fellow is sitting in a plaid shirt and resting his head on one hand. He appears to be thinking of something. His eyes appear a little sad. He may have been involved in something that he is very sorry for. The boy is thinking over what he has done. By the look in his eyes we can tell that he is very sad about it. I believe that the boy will break down any minute if he continues in the manner in which he is now going.

24. The boy is daydreaming of some picture he may have seen or is projecting himself into the future, putting himself into the situation as it would be if he were a man. The boy has seen a movie. The boy is thinking of how he would like to be in the situation as seen. The daydream, if not too vivid or realistic, will be terminated so that he can engage in activity more related to his present needs.

25. An elderly man is talking to a much younger man in the study of the older man. A problem has presented itself in which the older man needs the younger man's help or advice. The younger man is listening to what is being said and seriously thinking over the situation at hand. A conclusion will be reached in which there will appear some of the advice of the younger man. But the older man will not accept everything presented by the younger.

(Here the solution of the problem is in no clearly stated way related to achievement, and hence it is scored *UI*. In Example 20 the solution of a problem related to achievement was the goal.)

STATED NEED FOR ACHIEVEMENT (N)

Someone in the story states the desire to reach an achievement goal. Expressions such as "He *wants* to be a doctor," "He *wants* to finish the painting," "He *hopes* to succeed" are the clearest examples. Very strong indications of the presence of the motive in phrases like "He is *determined* to get a good mark" are also scored. The accomplishment desired may be specific, "He wants to finish the invention"; may refer to personal status, "He wants to become a successful businessman"; or may be more general and altruistic, "He wants to be of service to mankind." Need is scored only once per story, even when it appears more than once in varying forms.[5] *Need is not inferred from Instrumental Activity.* It may seem quite obvious to the scorer that the characters who are working furiously toward an achievement goal must want to succeed. Need is scored, however, only when there is a definite statement of motivation by one of the characters.

Not all statements of desire that appear in an achievement-related story are evidence of the presence of Need (*N*). If, for example, an inventor "wants his assistant to hand him the hammer," *N* is not scored. The scorer may imagine the stated need satisfied and then determine whether or not an achievement goal has been attained. Obviously, having the hammer in hand is no personal accomplishment. If the inventor stated that, "He hopes to get the lever in place so that the machine will be complete," *N* would be scored. Having the machine completed is an achievement goal of the inventor. Another kind of statement of need which is *not* scored is a statement by one character which defines an achievement goal for another character. Examples of this are: "The teacher wants the students to study their lesson," "A man wants the machinist to fix his car," "The machine has probably gone on the 'bum' and now needs to be fixed."

Illustrative stories

(Note that all the examples which follow also fulfill one of the criteria for scoring Achievement Imagery.)

26. A man is experimenting with a new alloy of iron, while his assistant looks on. Many years of research have lead up to this situation. The two men have experimented and failed many times over but have stuck to their job. *Both men are hoping that at last they have succeeded* in making the strongest steel possible. They will test their alloy and find that it meets with their expectations. It will then be refined in great quantities for use the world over.

27. A young person *wishes to become a doctor*. He can visualize himself performing an operation. He received a toy doctor's kit for a present several years ago, and several of his friends are planning to be doctors. He is thinking of the pleasant or glamorous side of the picture and not the long years of study. He will be unable to pass pre-medical school. He decides to become a lab technician as he wants to stay in that field.

28. Watt and an assistant are working on the development of the steam engine. There has been a *need* for mechanical power, time, and labor saving machinery to increase production. A *need* for better and faster transportation. It looks as though they are fitting a valve or piston.

(*N* is *not* scored in this story, because the need stated does not refer to a need for achievement on the part of the characters but rather to a lack in the world.)

29. A skilled craftsman is working at his machine. A townsman *wanted* a basket woven in a certain way and asked the craftsman to make it. The craftsman is absorbed in his work and thinks that this will be another fine product worthy of his reputation. He will work far into the night until it is finished and display it with pride the next day when the townsman calls for it.

(*N* is *not* scored in this story, since the statement of need for a basket by the townsman defined the achievement goal of the craftsman. When the townsman's need was satisfied, i.e., the basket handed to him finished, he did not experience feelings of personal accomplishment. Had the *craftsman* "wanted a basket woven in a certain way" and then gone on to weave it, *N* would be scored.)

INSTRUMENTAL ACTIVITY WITH VARIOUS OUTCOMES (I+, I?, I−)

Overt or mental activity by one or more characters in the story indicating that something is being done about attaining an achievement goal is considered Instrumental Activity and is scored *I+*, *I?*, or *I−* to indicate whether the outcome of the Instrumental Activity is successful, doubtful, or unsuccessful. {Covert or mental activity such as *thinking* about how to attain the goal, *planning, scheming*, etc., should be scored *I* if instrumental to the attainment of an achievement goal.} Instrumental Activity is scored only once per story even though there may be several instrumental acts stated. The outcome symbol scored reflects the net effect of all the instrumental acts which have occurred. *There must be an actual statement of activity within the story independent of both the original statement of the situation and the final outcome of the story.* If the first sentence of a story describes such a situation as "Two men are working on a new invention" and there is no further statement of Instrumental Activity in the story, *I* would *not* be scored. Neither would *I* be scored if a story went on with no statement of Instrumental Activity and ended "They will finish the invention." {Instrumental Activity appearing in the initial clause of the first sentence which is sheer description of the picture is not scored – e.g., "Here are two men working." Nor is Instrumental Activity inferred from the final clause of the last sentence which states the outcome – e.g., ". . . and he goes on to college." However, a clear-cut statement of an instrumental act appearing either later in the first sentence or earlier in the last sentence may be scored. Just avoid scoring *I* when it is sheer initial statement of situation or final statement of outcome of the story. This does *not* mean to avoid first and last sentences *in toto*.}

The instrumental act sometimes may be successful even though the overall outcome of the *story* is not a success. Also, a statement of Instrumental Activity within the story in the past tense may be scored so long as it is more than a statement of the outcome of previous instrumental acts. For example, after the statement of the situation "Two men are working on an invention," a statement such as "They have *worked diligently* night and day in the past with repeated trials yielding only failures" may appear. It would be scored *I* and then +, ?, or −, depending upon the rest of the story. However, if after the statement of the situation, a statement such as "They completed two important phases of their work yesterday" appeared, *I* would *not* be scored. This is considered as a description of the outcome of previous acts with no word indicating actual striving. {A statement of Instrumental Activity in the future tense may also be scored so long as it is more than a statement of outcome. For example, "They will succeed" would *not* be scored *I+*, while "They will continue to work diligently and will succeed" would be scored *I+*.}

Stories illustrating successful Instrumental Activity (I+)

30. James Watt and his assistant are working on the assembly of the first steam engine. They are working out the hole for a slide valve of the first successful steam engine. All previous experiments have failed. Successful use of steam has not been accomplished. If the slide valve works, the first compound steam engine will be harnessed. *James Watt is pulling the pinion in place for the slide valve.* His assistant is watching. The purpose is to make a pinion to hold the yoke in place which will operate the slide valve. If the slide valve works satisfactorily, they will perfect it for use in factories and for use on the railway. *It will work.*

(Not until the end of the story do we learn that the Instrumental Activity which occurred earlier in the story is successful.)

31. A boy is dreaming of being a doctor. He can see himself in the future. He is hoping that he can make the grade. It is more or less a fantasy. The boy has seen many pictures of doctors in books, and it has inspired him. *He will try his best* and hopes to become the best doctor in the country. He can see himself as a very important doctor. He is performing a very dangerous operation. He can see himself victorious and is proud of it. He gets world renown for it. He will become the *best doctor in the U.S.* He will be an honest man too. His name will go down in medical history as one of the *greatest men.*

32. The two men are mechanics and are *making parts* for a racer. They have found a future in driving midget cars at various tracks and are intent on trying their skill. They are thinking about the money they will get when they enter the races. A superior racing car is wanted by both men. They will eventually go to the races and will make their money. The car will just be another homemade job, but the fans will enjoy seeing the hometown boys come through.[6]

Stories illustrating Doubtful Instrumental Activity (I?)

33. The older man is a well-known pianist giving the younger man lessons in advanced piano. He is not satisfied with his student at the moment. In the past, *the young man has worked hard* on the piano, *studying long hours*, and all his family noticed how well he was doing. He is *thinking hard and trying hard* to put into his music just what his teacher wants him to. Just because he has a famous teacher, it doesn't necessarily mean that he will be famous. *He may not do very well or also he may.*

34. The boy is in an art studio. He is probably learning to be a sculptor. Behind him is a picture of a sculptor at work. *By looking at work done before his time and by great artists, he can learn much* from their styles and mistakes. He is probably

thinking someday he'll be doing great artistic work like that. The boy wants all the information he can get to better himself. *He will observe and then go to work* on some artistic work himself. He may accomplish something great and maybe not. Anyway, he is learning.

(In these two examples the outcome of the Instrumental Activity is scored doubtful, because the writer presents alternatives of both success and failure without choosing between them.)

35. The men are metal workers and they are working on a new tool for the shop. They need a sharp-edged tool and are doing work which requires tempering. A tool for the shop has worn out or broken and needs to be replaced. In the period that this picture depicts, tools couldn't be purchased, but must be made in the shop. The men are probably wondering if their work will be flawless or if the tool will replace the one that has broken. *After the metal has been removed from the flame, it will be dipped into some cold water.* Doing this repeatedly serves to temper and harden the new tool.

(In the above example the outcome of the Instrumental Activity is scored doubtful, because the writer does not present an ending to his story.)

Stories illustrating unsuccessful Instrumental Activity (I−)

36. The scene is a workshop. Two men are doing a very important job. They are grinding an important cog for a new jet engine which will attempt a flight to the moon. The inventor who doesn't want to let his secret out has hired these two men to work secretly for him. They are not very well known, but if the job is a success, they will be famous. They are both very tense, each knowing that one little mistake will mean *months of hard work* lost and wasted. When they are finished, they find that the piece is too small for the engine, and they have *failed* and must start again.

37. The boy is thinking that he does not know whether he can cover the material the night before the test. His roommate, seen at the right, is working. The boy is trying to decide whether to go to bed or to study all night. He has been swamped with work and has been delayed from study until a late hour because of another activity which he could not miss. He finds that the work is difficult and hasn't enough time for it. If I stay up, I'll miss much in reading later. If I go to bed, I'll get up early but maybe won't have time to finish the work. He wants to get the work covered thoroughly to pass with a good grade. He goes to bed and *gets up early and studies*. Then he covers the work, but not well enough and consequently he *doesn't do well* on the test and *shoots his average out the window*.

ANTICIPATORY GOAL STATES (GA+, GA−)

Someone in the story anticipates goal attainment or frustration and failure. The Anticipatory Goal State is scored positive (*Ga+*) when someone is thinking about the success he will achieve, expects that the invention will work, dreams of himself as a great surgeon. The Anticipatory Goal State is scored negative (*Ga−*) when someone is worried about failure, is concerned over the possibility that the invention won't work, expects the worst, or is wondering whether or not he will succeed. Both *Ga+* and *Ga−* may be scored in the same story, but each may be scored only once. The *Ga−* category includes all achievement-related anticipations that are not clearly positive. Thus, doubtful statements such as, "He is wondering what the outcome will be" are scored *Ga−*.

Achievement-related anticipations must be related to the achievement goal of the story. {Distinction between *instrumental thought (I)* and *goal anticipation (Ga+)*. When a person is thinking or planning or wondering *how* to attain the goal, score *I*. When he is dreaming or pondering about the completion of his task, e.g., when he has a mental picture of the circumstances which define the attainment of the goal, score *Ga+*. Recollecting a past goal state or goal activity is also scored *Ga+* since we have no past-oriented category for thought processes.}

Stories illustrating positive Anticipatory Goal State (Ga+)

38. A research man is forming a bar. Both men are extremely interested in the operation. These two men are working together on a research problem. They have been working tirelessly up to now to get the correct ingredients for the material being used now. They are feeling satisfied with their work. A stronger metal is desired by both men. The experiment has been a successful one. They will attempt to sell their new discovery *with a feeling of surety that they will become rich*. This work has meant much in their lives.

39. The older man is advising the younger one on the choice of occupation. The older man is a doctor and *he sees prospects in the young man to become a great surgeon*. The younger man has just returned from the Army, and he is disappointed with the attitude of the civilians and has given up hope of being a surgeon. The young man is thinking that it is useless to become a great healer if people are going to fight wars which amount to nothing more than mass murder. The older man will convince him that the world is not as bad as he believes, and he will return to medical school.

(Note that the Anticipatory Goal State need not refer to the person who is ultimately going to achieve the goal in question. In this story the old doctor is anticipating a successful future for the young man.)

Stories illustrating negative (or doubtful) Anticipatory Goal State (Ga−)

40. A father is telling his son not to worry while in college because his health is more important, but to become a professional man and carry on in his father's footsteps. The son has flunked a few exams and feels very bad about it. His father has noticed his unusual behavior and thinks he should talk with his son. *The boy thinks he just can't make it through college*, but he really wants to. His father wants him to continue and become a professional man. The boy will go back to college full of resolution for better studying, and he won't let the work get the best of him, for "it is not life that matters, but the courage you bring to it."

41. Two men trying out their invention for the first time. One man is tightening the last bolt on the machine before the test, while the other is giving the machine a careful eye check. These two men worked in a factory where the machines were constantly breaking down, so they decided to invent a new process for doing the work. A new machine is wanted by the factory owner, and the people who are successful will receive a boost in pay. *The two men are thinking now whether or not their efforts and time have been spent in vain.* The invention will work, and the men will receive their reward – a story-book ending.

42. The boy is doing homework. He is a student at some college. He is encountering a very difficult problem. Perhaps he has not been faced with anything as difficult as this problem. The boy is searching for a solution. *He wonders if he will succeed in solving this and future problems of college curriculum.* He will probably solve this situation but become permanently baffled by other situations.

(The above anticipation is doubtful in nature, and according to the present system would be scored *Ga−*.)

43. The older man has just told the younger one that he has a very important job he wants him to do. The younger man has had a very good record in his previous work, and the older man believes that he is the only one capable of doing the job. *The younger man is wondering if he is capable of performing this* task, and he *realizes what the results will be if he fails.* The older man knows that he is asking a great deal, but feels the younger man will come through "O.K." The young man will have a great deal of trouble with this, but he is very determined and will succeed.

(In the above story a doubtful anticipation is followed by a clearly negative anticipation. In the next sentence, a positive Anticipatory Goal State appears, "feels the younger man will come through 'O.K.'" The story would be scored both *Ga−* and *Ga+*.)

OBSTACLES OR BLOCKS (BP, BW)

{*Bp* stands for "block within the person"; *Bw* stands for "block in the world," i.e., external to the person.}

Stories are scored for obstacles when the progress of goal-directed activity is blocked or hindered in some way. Things do not run smoothly. There are obstacles to be overcome before the goal may be attained. The obstacles may be a previous deprivation, i.e., failure, which must be overcome before further progress towards the goal is possible, or the obstacle may be a present environmental or personal factor. If the obstacle is located within the individual (lack of confidence, a conflict to be overcome, inability to make decisions, responsibility for some breakdown in equipment, or some past failure), it is scored Personal Obstacle (*Bp*). When the block to be overcome is part of the environment, i.e., when it may be located in the world at large such as: "The invention was almost finished when the gasket broke," "His family couldn't afford to send him to medical school," "Competition was too keen for him"; or *when there is some doubt about whether it is located in the individual or in the world*, Environmental Obstacle (*Bw*) is scored. Both *Bp* and *Bw* may occur and be scored in the same story, but each is scored only once per story.

It is necessary to make a distinction between "apparent obstacles" which really define the achievement goal of the story and real obstacles to ongoing goal-directed behavior. If a story began with the statement "The skilled craftsman is fixing with great care the old antique which broke," *Bw* is not scored, since the breakdown which has already occurred defines the achievement goal of the story. However, if the craftsman has the chair nearly finished when the wood snaps, then *Bw* is scored. In this latter case, the breakdown interrupts goal-directed activity in progress. This distinction is made only in the case of *Bw*. Indications of past failures are scored *Bp* whether or not they interfere with the immediate goal-directed activity.

Stories illustrating Personal Obstacle (Bp)

44. A new man is being taught how to run a machine in a factory. He is interested in the work, but he is nervous. He has been hired quite recently and has *made a mistake*. The foreman is helping him to realize what he has done. The new man is hoping that with practice he will become a skilled worker. The foreman is bored teaching him. He is required to do this every day as work hands come and go, and he feels he is wasting his time. The foreman will show the man how to do the work and then will walk off. The hired man will look around to see if anyone is watching. Then he will start to do the required work as best he can.

45. A boy is daydreaming. He is a student who knows he has to study. *In the past he has had poor marks*. Now he realizes he must study harder or else his schoolwork will just be a waste of time. He thinks of the last mark and what will happen if he doesn't improve. This man will really study and prove to himself he is not a failure but will make good.

46. Father is giving advice to his son. The son has been faced with some *trying situation or problem*. Perhaps he *is trying to decide whether to stay in college or accept a business position*. The son wants guidance. His father is trying to utilize his greater experience in life in order to help his son. The father will probably persuade the son to stay in college and reap the advantages of a higher education that he was deprived of.

(The block to overcome in this last story is the problem of coming to a decision.)

Stories illustrating Environmental Obstacle (Bw)

47. Two workmen in a small garage. They have just completed an experiment which they hope will revolutionize the rubber industry. They have been conscious of the need for better rubber. They have worked for years at this and now have their results before them. They are wondering if success is theirs. They want success because of the remuneration to get them back on their feet. They will not be successful. *They have not the equipment needed for rubber improvements*. The

improvement of rubber by merely adding a compound and heating is over. They will not give up.

48. Lawyer and client in conversation. The younger man came in for advice. He had a going business and was prospering, but a *new industry is driving his product off the market*. "Shall I be forced to give up?" "Shall I sue?" "What are my chances of success?" The lawyer explains that competition is legitimate and can't be sued. The man will go out and instead of selling, will convert his industry to a specialty along the same line only one which is not jeopardized. He will try to sell out.

49. Student is sitting at his desk worrying over his grades. *He has had poor high school preparation for college*, and as a result poor semester grades. He wishes he could settle down and make a go of his college without constant failing. He eventually makes a go of his college after finding courses in which he is interested.

(In this last example the obstacle is scored *Bw* and not *Bp*, because it seems clear that the high school was to blame for the inadequate preparation and not the student.)

NURTURANT PRESS (NUP)

Forces in the story, personal in source, which aid the character in the story who is engaged in ongoing achievement-related activity are scored Nurturant Press (*Nup*). Someone aids, sympathizes with, or encourages the person striving for achievement. The assistance must be in the direction of the achievement goal and not merely incidental to it. For example, "The experienced machinist is trying to straighten things out for the apprentice and is encouraging him." Press must always be considered from the point of view of the character or characters in the story who are striving for achievement.

Stories illustrating Nurturant Press (Nup)

50. *An old experienced man is giving a young green kid a little helpful advice on how to improve his work*. The kid has been slow and has had a little trouble getting into the swing of things, and the old gentleman has noticed it. The kid is thinking maybe the old boy has some good ideas, and it may help him improve and maybe even impress someone enough for a raise. The kid will take all the advice to heart and go back to work with better methods or ideas suggested by the older man.

51. The young boy is dreaming of what he hopes to do for the future. He is thinking of a great surgeon who saved his father's life and wishes to become such a man. His father needed an emergency operation. He watched the surgeon save his father's life. He is thinking he must work hard to reach his goal. But he is sure that is what he wants to do in life. He will see the surgeon again and *will be encouraged in his ambitions by the great man*.

AFFECTIVE STATES (G+, G−)

Affective (emotional) states associated with goal attainment, active mastery, or frustration of the achievement-directed activity are scored *G*. When someone in the story experiences: (1) a positive affective state associated with active mastery or definite accomplishment ("He *enjoys* painting," "He is *proud* of his accomplishment," "They are very *satisfied* with their invention"), or (2) *definite objective benefits* as a result of successful achievement which allow the inference of positive affect ("His genius is acknowledged by millions," "The people are proud of the inventor," "Fame and fortune were his," "He received a raise in pay"), $G+$ is scored. $G+$ *indicates more than mere successful Instrumental Activity.* "He works his way through college and becomes a doctor" is scored $I+$. Positive Affect ($G+$) would be scored only when a statement of positive affect was included, for example, "He becomes a successful doctor and experiences a deep sense of satisfaction," or if there were *adequate* indications of objective benefits associated with his success from which positive affect might be inferred with little doubt, such as, "He becomes a *famous* surgeon." This is another example of an arbitrary distinction which was necessary to make in order to insure an objective scoring system. {*Objective benefits.* A descriptive statement, in a word or phrase, of the objective state of affairs accompanying success or failure sufficient to warrant your inference that the outcome falls in the upper 10% ($G+$) or lower 10% ($G-$) of all possible outcomes for that sort of activity should be scored G. For example: "He becomes a doctor" (no $G+$), "He becomes a successful doctor" (no $G+$), "He becomes a famous doctor" (yes $G+$), "He becomes a very successful doctor" (yes $G+$), "He fails" (no $G-$), "He fails and is a broken man" (yes $G-$).}

Positive affect may occur within the story, or it may be associated with the outcome of the story. *It is scored only once per story and should only be scored when there is a definite statement of positive affect associated with the achievement-directed activity or a statement of objective benefits above and beyond the statement of successful instrumental activity.* {*Affective states.* Any affective word, positive or negative, associated with *activity*, *attainment*, or *nonattainment* will be scored $G+$ or $G-$ unless it is scored $Ga+$ or $Ga-$. $G+$ can come in the *middle* of the story when positive affect regarding *progress toward the goal* is evinced. For example: "He is interested in his work."}

When someone in the story experiences: (1) a negative affective state associated with failure to attain an achievement goal ("He is disturbed over his inability," "He is discouraged about past failures," "He is disgusted with himself," "He is despondent, mad, and sorry"), or (2) *the objective concomitants of complete failure and deprivation* which allow the inference of negative affect ("He became a drunken bum," "He became the laughing stock of the community"), $G-$ is scored. As in the case of positive affect, negative affect must not be inferred merely from the unsuccessful outcome of instrumental activity. Negative affect may occur within the story or at the end, but it is scored only once per story. {$G-$ can be scored on the basis of negative affect over an *obstacle which causes lack of progress toward the goal.*} Both positive and negative affect may appear in the same story, in which case both are scored.

Mere mention of famous persons is not sufficient evidence for scoring *G+*. The Affective State categories are only scored when associated with the achievement-related activities of the story, as is the case with all subcategories.

Stories illustrating positive affective state (G+)

52. This is the story of the invention of a machine. One man is showing another one of his new inventions. The man approves but is recommending that some changes be made. The inventor has spent the greater part of his life working on this invention. At last he finds that his work and dream is realized. *The men are both happy* due to the new discovery. The inventor is not interested in money that can be made out of it but only the benefit it will be to mankind. The inventor, on the advice of his friend, will sell the invention to a manufacturer. He will receive little reward and will die a sick man.

(Note that *G−* would also be scored in this story because of the negative concomitance associated with the outcome.)

53. A father is talking to his son. *He is telling him that he is proud of him because he is doing so well in school.* He wants his son to stay on the ball and keep getting good marks. He just knows his son will be a very successful businessman. The son has just come home from college after pulling honors all through the year. He never goes out and is always in his room studying. He never partakes in sports. They are both dreaming of what the son will be in the future, a successful businessman. The son can just see himself as the president of the biggest baby rattle company in the U.S. The boy will become meagerly and puny because of his studying. He will never have any fun out of life. He will always be a mope. Is it worth it?

54. Goodyear and his young son are getting near the end of the experiment on uses of rubber. They have been pressing different objects from rubber. They spilled a tub of rubber on the stove. Goodyear is thinking that now he is close to his goal. *They will be hailed in later years as great inventors and saviors of our country.*

(The above story is an example of our practice of scoring so-called *objective benefits* as indicating the presence of *G+*.)

Stories illustrating negative affective state (G−)

55. This is the night before the big economics exam, and Johnny Jones is worried. He's got to get an A. He has been taking it easy all year and now wants to bring his average up with a good grade. He is *thinking what a damn fool he has been,* and why didn't he study the months before. He must get an A or he will have to take the course over. If he has to take the course over, he knows his father will give him the devil for not working hard the first part of the year.

(Note that the phrase "Johnny Jones is worried" has a future reference and so would be scored *Ga−* rather than *G−*.)

56. The older man is about 60, and the younger man, his son, who is a writer, about 30. He is trying to encourage his son to continue. He is successful in writing. The father is a well-known writer who struggled to get where he is. The son so far has had very little work accepted, and it doesn't seem as if he ever will. The father knows that if the boy tries, he can do it. The young man has his doubts but is beginning to feel that perhaps his father is right. The boy will struggle some more. He will get work accepted, but some will come back. Because he *feels inferior to his father*, he has an emotional block and is never as successful as he might otherwise have been.

57. The man is a professor of astronomy, and the younger person is a student. They have just discovered a new planet that is headed for the earth and will end the world. These two men have been fearing this for many months and have just proved their findings. They are thinking that the earth will soon be no more and that all life must end. They want to find a way to escape from this so that they may save a few people on earth and become heroes. The planet will change course. Their blunder will be discovered, and *they will become outcasts for putting people on earth in a dither*.

(This illustrates the scoring of *G−* for negative objective concomitances of failure.)

ACHIEVEMENT THEMA (ACH TH)

Achievement Thema (*Ach Th*) is scored when the Achievement Imagery is elaborated in such a manner that it becomes the central plot or theme of the story. Striving for an achievement goal and eventual attainment of the goal may be the central plot of the story. On the other hand, the plot may be primarily concerned with someone who is in need-related difficulty and never does succeed. In any case, the decision to be made by the scorer is whether or not the whole story is an elaboration of the achievement behavior sequence. If there is a major counter plot, or if there is any doubt about the achievement imagery being central to the plot, *Ach Th* is not scored. It does happen that *AI* and some of the subcategories will be scored in stories having another *leitmotif*. These stories are *not* scored *Ach Th*.

{To compute the *n* Achievement score, give +1 for Achievenment Imagery (*AI*), 0 for Doubtful or Task Imagery (*TI*), and −1 for Unrelated Imagery (*UI*). Subcategories can be scored only if *AI* has been scored. Each subcategory scored counts +1. Since each category may be scored only once, the maximal score possible for a single story would be +11 (*AI, N, I, Ga+, Ga−, Bp, Bw, Nup, G+, G−,* and *Th*). The *n* Achievement score for a particular person is the sum of the scores obtained on all of the stories written by that person.[7] N Achievement scores on different persons are only comparable when the scores are obtained from the same pictures.}[8]

Stories illustrating Achievement Thema (Ach Th)

58. The boy is contemplating running away from home. He has just been badly whipped, and being quite an introvert, he declines to show his emotions. This boy

has been reprimanded because he has failed to conform to social approval in regard to taking a small stone belonging to another lad who has evidently attached a good deal of sentimental value to it. The boy in the picture had recognized this stone as a diamond, and he likes it so much that he wants to obtain more. He is determined to leave and go to South Africa and *get a fortune* and is now laying mental plans for his lone expedition.

(This story is *not* scored *Ach Th*. Not until the last few lines is there any evidence to justify scoring it Achievement Imagery (*AI*). This Achievement Imagery is peripheral to the central concern of the story which appeared earlier.)

59. Father and son are discussing the future of the world. The boy has just returned from overseas combat duty, looking older and wiser than when he left four years ago. Before entering the Army, the boy never gave much time to his father and had spent most of it with the gang. Now he is changed and considers a talk with his father of extreme importance. They are discussing the peace treaties that are being drawn up, each wanting peace fervently. No matter how much they desire peace, the answer is not given them. They can only surmise as to the best way of concluding a lasting peace. Time will tell whether the son's generation will *do better than* the father's.

(Once more, the Achievement Imagery ("do better than") appears very late in the story and is hardly central to the plot of this story. Therefore, *Ach Th* would *not* be scored.)

60. The boy and his father have had a serious accident and the boy's father is being operated on. The boy and his father were having a quarrel about the boy's marks in school, and the boy accidentally caused an automobile accident by stepping on the gas pedal. The boy is thinking that if his father dies, he will be to blame. He fervently wants his father to recover and be well again so he can prove to his father that he can do schoolwork. The father dies on the operating table, and the boy makes a vow to himself that he will become a great surgeon and save lives. He does and saves many lives, but his conscience never lets him alone. At the height of his career he commits suicide.

(In this example the Achievement Imagery appears as a counter plot. Because there is a strong alternate theme, *Ach Th* is *not* scored.)

61. A young boy is daydreaming about the past wars in which doctors have participated. He is not sure of the course to follow. He cannot decide whether or not to become a doctor. He is thinking about John Drake, the great surgeon of World War I, and his great feats in it. He was certainly a remarkable man. The boy will finally become a famous surgeon himself and in turn will be an incentive to the future doctors of the world to work hard and be interested only in the welfare of mankind.

(By way of contrast, this story illustrates the Achievement Thema. No other interest is introduced.)

62. Father and son are having a serious talk. They are going into bankruptcy because of a railroad strike. They are trying to remedy the situation by borrowing

money from bankers. They do get some money but not as much as they need to get the business running successfully again. The business continues but does not make money as usual until ten years later.

(This example of *Ach Th* illustrates the fact that by Achievement Thema we do not necessarily mean a "success story." In this example the achievement-related activity central to the plot of the story is not very successful. Rather, the whole story is about an unsuccessful attempt to overcome achievement-related difficulties.)

NOTES

1 The scoring criteria presented in this chapter constitute "Scoring System C" (see McClelland et al., 1953, p. 147). Because square brackets were used in the original 1953 version, footnotes added by J. W. Atkinson in 1958 have been enclosed in braces { } and have been incorporated into the text. An additional note suggested by David C. McClelland has been added in the present version as well as an occasional note by the editor of this volume (C.S.). In stories used as examples throughout the text, *errors in spelling and grammar have been preserved intentionally*.

The same scoring criteria are used for stories written by males and females. Although the stories cited in the manual were all written by males, the practice materials in appendix I of this volume consist of stories written by both males and females. Additional practice materials may be found in appendix I of *Motives in fantasy, action and society* (Atkinson, 1958a).

2 Material in braces { } was added by John W. Atkinson in the form of footnotes in the version of this scoring manual included in *Motives in fantasy, action and society* (Atkinson, 1958a).

3 Italics added by John W. Atkinson (1958a).

4 Under *Definition of Achievement Imagery (AI)* it is stated that "Any use of adjectives of degree (good, better, best) will qualify so long as they evaluate the excellence of performance." Note, however, that the words in Example 16 "being a fairly good forger" do *not* qualify as *AI*. The use of the word *good* in a description of a person's *ability* (being good at something) is not scored for *AI* as it would be in a description of a person's motivation (*wanting* or *trying* to do a good job). (Editor's note, C.S.).

5 Need is sometimes scored if a phrase such as "Fame and fortune." or "A good grade." is clearly an answer to the question "What is wanted?" That is, the story writer is saying: "The inventors *want* fame and fortune." or "The student *is hoping for* a good grade."

6 In the original manual this example was *not* scored for *I* because the entire first sentence was regarded as a statement of the situation. However, this appears to be an instance in which instrumental activity does occur *after the initial clause*; hence, the words *making parts* have been italicized, and the story serves as an example of *I*+. (Editor's note, with concurrence of David C. McClelland, C.S.)

7 In sets of pictures designed to measure several motives, scores for *n* Achievement will tend to be low because of the number of pictures not designed to elicit Need for Achievement. Many stories written to such pictures will be scored Unrelated Imagery (−1). This will give an incorrect impression that *n* Achievement scores

are low, in terms of raw scores. However, if scores are converted to T scores within the sample receiving the same set of pictures, the problem is resolved. (Note suggested by David C. McClelland, personal communication, July, 15, 1990. The editor, C.S.)

8 And under the same conditions. (Editor's note, C.S.).

11   *The motive to avoid success*

JACQUELINE FLEMING
AND MATINA S. HORNER

This chapter describes the origin of the concept of the motive to avoid success (fear of success) and reviews research that has responded to criticisms of the early work on this topic. The next chapter presents a revised scoring manual for the Motive to Avoid Success.

THEORETICAL FOUNDATIONS

While research on the Need for Achievement (Atkinson, 1958a; McClelland, Atkinson, Clark, & Lowell, 1953) provided the model for the conceptualization of a motive to avoid success, it had one major difficulty. The research, while conclusive for male subjects, proved inconsistent for females (French & Lesser, 1964; Lesser, 1973). To explain the inconsistency, the concept of fear of success was proposed (Horner, 1968, 1972, 1974). The explanation, that a person might fear success as well as hope for it in achievement-oriented situations, is fully consistent with expectancy value theory as it relates to the concept of achievement motivation. The first studies of fear of success (Horner, 1968) showed that the expectation (not necessarily in awareness) of negative consequences as a result of the pursuit or attainment of success aroused anxiety in female subjects. Similar expectations were significantly less evident in male subjects. Although some subsequent studies found a considerable amount of fear-of-success *imagery* from males as well (see Tresemer, 1976), the predictive consequences were still far more debilitating for females.

Horner introduced the concept of fear of success as an additional variable to be considered in studying gender differences and the behavior of women in competitive achievement situations, and made the following assumptions. Fear of success is a learned, latent, stable characteristic of the personality acquired early in life in conjunction with the learning of sex role standards and other learned motives; is more prevalent and much more easily aroused in women than in men; is not equally important for all women; is much more

179

strongly aroused in competitive achievement situations reflecting intelligence and leadership ability than in noncompetitive settings; will function, *once aroused*, as a negative inhibitory tendency acting to reduce the expression of the positive tendency to achieve; and is presumed to interact with other motivational and personality variables as a complex function of motive strength, incentive value, and probability of success (see Horner, 1974).

Because fear of success is subject to conscious denial, content analysis is assumed to be the most effective way available to disclose its presence and unearth the function of what may initially appear to be an irrational, counterintuitive dilemma.

HISTORICAL BACKGROUND

The 1968 measure of fear-of-success imagery

To explore the possibility of a fear of success, Horner (1968) asked female subjects to tell stories in response to a set of six verbal leads. The last cue depicted a female being highly successful: "After First Term Finals, Anne Finds Herself At The Top Of Her Medical School Class." A matching male cue was administered to the male subjects. A subject was designated as having fear of success if his or her story contained any one of the seven categories developed by Scott (1958) to assess fear in a thematic apperceptive story. Only 10% of the male subjects projected fear-of-success imagery, while 62% of the female subjects responded to the success cue with fear-of-success imagery. Female subjects who were high in fear of success demonstrated performance decrements on achievement tasks in the presence of males, confirming the motivational nature of negative imagery. Women low in fear of success performed better in this condition.

It became apparent that there were a number of problems with this first exploratory method of assessment (Horner, 1973): utilization of only an imagery present/absent scoring system, with no finer differentiation; dependence on only one "success cue"; concern that this method tapped attitudes toward success, not motivational dynamics; and increasing evidence that the imagery measure produced no interpretable pattern of results (e.g., Tresemer, 1976; Zuckerman & Wheeler, 1975). Therefore, a new scoring system was developed based on the method and strategy for developing coding systems for other motives (e.g., Atkinson, 1958a; McClelland et al., 1953; D. G. Winter, 1973).

DERIVATION OF A REVISED SCORING SYSTEM

The objective of the experimental manipulation was to arouse the motive to avoid success in one group of women by allowing each of them to compete successfully against a man (Horner, 1973). Their subsequent performance and imagery were compared with that of a nonaroused group. Also, the scoring system was anchored in its ability to predict actual behavior.

Subjects

The initial subject pool was 211 male and female undergraduates at a large New England university. Males were, however, omitted from all derivation analyses because fear of success had been shown to be most easily aroused in women. This choice was no less appropriate than the choice of male subjects for the derivation of the need for Achievement scoring system for similar reasons. The final comparison was based on the stories of 31 females in the arousal condition and 28 females in the nonarousal condition.

Procedure

In the Time I neutral condition, all subjects received a Cue Interpretations Task. (Specific instructions used for this and other tasks can be found in Horner, 1973.) Subjects were asked to tell stories to the following five cues:

> Carol is looking through the telescope.
> Joan seems to be particularly pleased.
> Diane has just received word that she is one of three students in the state to get a perfect score on the LSAT (Law School Admissions Test).
> Linda is looking out at the sunset.
> Barbara is in the midst of a heated argument.

Subjects then took a Scrambled Words Test, with 5 sets of 24 scrambled words, and completed a basic information questionnaire.

After 4 weeks, subjects in the Time II arousal condition were paired with male subjects. The arousal was carried out by placing the female subjects in a situation in which they were competing with males. Subjects were assigned to pairs that consisted of one female and one male. They were told that they were paired with a subject who was their equal in the verbal task on which they were about to compete. The Scrambled Words Test from Time I provided an estimate of verbal abilities for making realistic assignments.

Subjects then received the arousal task: A Two-Step Arithmetic Task, labeled "Memory and Intellectual Productivity: Arithmetic Problems." Each pair competed for 10 minutes. Following the competition, while subjects worked on a filler task, the protocols were collected and scored by the experimenter who always reported the *female* member of the pair to be the winner of the competition.

A parallel "Cue Interpretations Task" consisting of the following five cues was given immediately following the success manipulation:

> Sue is looking into her microscope.
> Judy is sitting in a chair with a smile on her face.

After first term finals, Ann finds herself at the top of her medical school class.

Carol is walking along the beach late in the day.

As a leader of a group of men and women, Nancy has the final say on all decisions of the group.

The Generation Anagram Task, the actual performance task, described as a measure of ability to think quickly and efficiently, followed next.

A Post Experimental Questionnaire and Debriefing concluded the arousal session.

Subjects in the Time II nonarousal condition received the same measures. However, the experimenters adopted a relaxed manner and told students that they were gathering general norms for a college population. Subjects were not paired, and there was no success feedback. Subjects in the non-arousal group were also asked about their experience by means of a post-experimental questionnaire and were then debriefed.

Protocol analysis

There were two kinds of cues in the apperceptive battery: neutral cues and highly structured cues. The major focus of comparison involved the three neutral cues in each condition, that is, cues not highly structured with respect to achievement or power (Cues 1, 2, and 4 in each set). Cue 3 in each condition was a "success" cue and Cue 5 in each condition was a "power" cue. The rationale for focusing on neutral cues is that scoring criteria should be appropriate for scoring ambiguous thematic apperceptive pictures. Stimuli of different levels of ambiguity are associated with advantages and disadvantages, so that a range of ambiguity levels is usually preferred (Murstein, 1965a, 1965d). However, the use of lower levels of ambiguity may be preferable for scoring system development in view of evidence that under arousal, expressions of approach–avoidance conflict may be displaced toward lower ends of the stimulus dimension (Epstein, 1966). The three neutral stimuli represent two levels of ambiguity; the microscope/telescope cues moderately suggest achievement, while the sunset/beach and smile/pleased cues are not at all achievement relevant. A reanalysis of these data revealed highly structured cues to be less predictive (Fleming, 1982; Fleming & Watson, 1980).

A research team identified a preliminary scoring system with 43 categories that appeared to differentiate story themes written to the three neutral cues in the arousal and nonarousal groups. Scoring of these categories from stories written in the Time I neutral condition were used to predict performance in the Time II arousal condition. The categories obtained in Time I were entered into a regression equation with performance change as the criterion.

T scores were produced for both the Scrambled Words Test given in Time

I and the final 3 minutes of word production in the Anagram Task given in Time II. The final 3 minutes of anagrams was chosen because it requires more effort to produce words in the final minutes of the test (McClelland et al., 1953). A change score for each individual was calculated based on the difference in performance from Time I to Time II.

Results

To determine which of the 43 categories were to be included in a regression analysis, a series of one-way analyses of variance were performed. Of those approaching significance, the regression analysis revealed 6 categories, which added to the prediction of a performance decrement.

The 6 categories remaining from the original 43 made up the first version of the fear-of-success scoring system by Horner, Tresemer, Berens, and Watson (1973), now referred to as Version A. The scoring manual was further revised and expanded by Horner and Fleming (1977) into a 113-page manual, Version B.

Version C of the scoring manual, presented in the next chapter, includes revisions based upon reanalyses of the original data. First, Contingent Negative Consequences was excluded from the scoring categories, leaving five categories remaining in the system. A reanalysis by Fleming and Watson (1980) revealed an error: that Contingent Negative Consequences did not contribute to prediction. Version C of the scoring manual is also distinguished in not recommending the weighting of the scoring categories, because different populations have produced different weights (Fleming & Watson, 1980; Horner, 1973; Marshall & Karabenick, 1977).

The final categories are briefly defined as: (a) Noncontingent Negative Consequences – when tension, deprivation, or disaster comes about through the impingement of some external force. (b) Interpersonal Engagement – when two or more specific persons are clearly involved or occupied with each other in the story. (c) Relief – when a relative tension or deprivation state is suddenly alleviated, often in a manner incurring surprise. (d) Absence of Instrumental Activity – when there is no statement of instrumental action taking place in the story, that is, no purposive activity toward attaining a goal. (e) Absence of Mention of Others – when no other character or group is mentioned in the story.

Fear-of-success scores should be controlled for story length (see chapter 37). The reanalysis by Fleming and Watson (1980) revealed that correlations with story length ranged from .213 to .420, and that correcting for story length improved prediction substantially.

Fear-of-success scores decreased somewhat under competitive arousal (Fleming & Watson, 1980). Although the result was nonsignificant, the mean fear-of-success scores decreased in the Arousal Group (from Time I to Time II) from 2.29 to 1.65 ($t = 1.20$, n.s.). This trend is contrary to expectation, but may occur in groups of women and perhaps men where resultant approach tendencies may be stronger than resultant avoidance tendencies. An avoidance motive, such as fear of success, does not necessarily increase under arousal. The present finding is consistent with two reports of fear-of-success scores that dropped under arousal in black women (Duncan, 1974; Fleming, 1978) and shows that the decrease can occur regardless of race. However, there are other reports that fear-of-success scores increase under different arousal conditions (Jackaway & Teevan, 1976; Shinn, 1973). The usual procedure for isolating imagery in apperceptive scoring systems is to compare the changes in mean category levels from neutral to arousal conditions. Those categories that consistently increase under arousal become the basis for the scoring system. But because there is evidence that avoidance motives may behave differently under arousal (Epstein, 1966; Kenny, 1964), this method was not used in the development of a fear-of-success scoring system. The unusual shifts in fear-of-success motive scores under arousal conditions fit the unexpected behavior of avoidance motives.

An inverse relationship was found for fear-of-success and achievement relevance of projective stimuli (Fleming, 1982; Fleming & Watson, 1980). In general, for approach motives the amount of imagery increases with the appropriate drive relevance. But when the apperceptive stimuli were ranked according to achievement relevance, fear-of-success scores were substantially lower to achievement-related cues of high and moderate achievement relevance than to those of low relevance. For example mean scores to the Time I Telescope were −.36 and to Pleased were .52. Furthermore, the differences are stronger under achievement arousal such that fear-of-success scores are lowest when obtained in response to drive relevant cues under arousal: Microscope, −.68, and Smile, .84. These findings, then, provide further support for the idea that avoidance motives may behave differently.

The present scoring system would benefit from *exact* replications (of which there are none) as well as from other validation studies, such as that by Marshall and Karabenick (1977), that examine scoring categories, beta weights, and their implications. Because small sample studies that employ regression procedures may not generalize to other populations, replications are particularly important.

Although there are other paper-and-pencil measures of fear of success, shared variance with the new projective measure is not high (Canavan-Gumpert, Garner, & Gumpert, 1978; Griffore, 1977; Piedmont, 1988; Sadd, Lenauer, Shaver, & Dunivant, 1978; Shaver, 1976; Zuckerman & Allison, 1976). Studies using other measures of fear of success report different, but not necessarily incompatible, patterns of prediction. This should not be surprising because these measures tap different levels of the mind and often employ different experimental procedures. The reader is referred to chapter 3 by McClelland, Koestner, and Weinberger for a discussion of the relationship between self-report measures and projective measures.

The Zuckerman and Allison (1976) scale and the Pappo (1972) and N. E. Cohen (1974) scales have a large enough body of literature to assess scale validity. Studies using the Zuckerman and Allison scale find fear-of-success scores to be higher in females than males in three of five samples and evidence for the validity of the Fear of Success Scale was indicated by approach–avoidance reactions following success feedback, but not following failure feedback (Zuckerman & Allison, 1976; Zuckerman, Larrance, Porac, & Blanck, 1980). However, these studies did not produce convincing performance results, perhaps because no particular competitive manipulations were employed. The empirical evidence generated by the Pappo and Cohen scales leaves little doubt as to the promise of the instruments in clarifying the fear-of-success phenomenon. Five different studies showed that success fearers became debilitated when close to success, but rallied after failure (Canavan-Gumpert et al., 1978). These studies found no sex differences in fear-of-success scores, but the most notable sex difference in performance was that same sex competitors are the most debilitating to males. Other real-life correlates found using the Cohen scale showed that success-fearing students were more often characterized by spotty academic records, withdrawal from school, changing of majors, indecision about future careers, and derogation of competence.

RELIABILITY

Interscorer reliability

Intercoder reliabilities of 90% or better have been obtained with the new scoring procedures (e.g., Fleming, 1978; Marshall & Karabenick, 1977; Stewart, 1975).

Internal consistency reliability

From the psychometric point of view, good internal consistency of test items is a necessity if those items are to be combined additively. The real issue, however, is accuracy of prediction. Fleming and Watson (1980) found that the categories of the fear-of-success scoring system produced an alpha coefficient of .293, but accounted for 46% of the variance in performance change in a regression equation (see also Fleming, 1982).

Also, fear-of-success scores for the five cues given in Time I produced an alpha coefficient of $-.15$, but, when entered separately in a regression equation with aroused performance as the dependent variable, they accounted for 49% of the variance in performance change ($R = .698$). The consequences for prediction when cue scores are combined additively are, relative to a regression analysis, disastrous. The reanalysis of Horner's validation study showed that the standard procedure of summing scores across all five projective cues given in Time I resulted in dramatic losses in predictive power compared to the previous results from a regression analysis: from 49% to 12% (Fleming, 1982; Fleming & Watson, 1980). The simple r using the additive combination of all five cue scores was only $-.34$ ($p <$ .10). This result is from the 31 female subjects in the arousal group and the criterion was performance change from the neutral to the arousal session in which each woman received success feedback in competition with a man. Because most of the motivation literature has relied on the summation of cue scores, these findings suggest the compelling hypothesis that the magnitude of the findings in published research may be sharply underestimated.

Test–retest reliability

No retest reliability coefficients have been reported. However, in the validation study, the correlation between Time I and Time II scores was a substantial .49 ($p < .005$) for the arousal group, but was only .13 for the nonarousal group. Note that Time II for the nonarousal group was a very relaxed condition, as opposed to achievement-oriented conditions for all other groups. Shinn (1973) found that fear-of-success scores were well correlated from Time 1 to Time 2 for women ($r = .51$, $p = .001$) but not for men ($r = .02$, n.s.). Because the Time 2 scores were obtained under arousal conditions for women, the conditions for optimal retest reliability were not met. It appears that retest coefficients are quite sensitive to testing conditions, as well as to the instructional set that D. G. Winter and Stewart (1977b) have identified as a major factor in determining retest reliabilities.

VALIDITY

The studies reviewed here have used either Version A or Version B of the new, empirically derived scoring system for the motive to avoid success. Version C, which omits one scoring category and does not use scoring weights, is not yet in wide use. None of the following studies used the 1968 measure of fear-of-success *imagery* that we now consider invalid.

Experimental performance

Three basic experimental designs have been employed. First, four studies investigating the performance of women in the mere *presence of men with no competitive manipulation* found effects. Three found fear of success negatively related to performance in testlike conditions (Duncan, 1974; Fleming, 1977; Shinn, 1973), while one found fear of success positively related to performance in a relaxed, nontest setting (Fleming & Watson, 1980). Second, two studies employed experimental designs involving direct *competition against males* with *no performance feedback*. Beldner (1979) found fear of success negatively related to performance in competition with men among School of Education women. No effects were found in competition with women. Jackaway (1974) did not find the predicted performance decrement among fear-of-success women in direct competition against a man. Third, results from all three of the studies involving *competition* in paradigms using *success feedback* found predicted negative effects on the performance of women (Fleming, 1978; Horner, 1973; Karabenick, 1977). Middle class black women were the only exception (Fleming, 1978).

In the few performance studies that included males, there was no indication that fear of success has a negative effect on competitive performance among white males (Karabenick, 1977; Shinn, 1973), but there is evidence of performance inhibition among working-class black males (Fleming, 1974). In all of these studies, Version A of the scoring system was used to score stories obtained from males in response to cues using male names.

Sex differences in fear-of-success scores

Very few of the studies using the empirically derived scoring system have included male subjects. Three of the five studies reporting fear-of-success scores for both sexes found significantly higher scores in females (Esposito, 1977; Jackaway & Teevan, 1976; Shinn, 1973). The Jackaway and Teevan study also found a significant increase in scores from neutral to arousal conditions for females, but not males. Shinn found no sex differences in a neutral session (i.e., given in same-sex classes), but a significant difference in favor of females in a second arousal session (in a coed classroom setting). Studies by Marshall and Karabenick (1977) and Esposito (1976) found a trend toward higher scores in females that did not reach statistical significance. Thus, the evidence from these studies suggests that fear-of-success scores *tend* to be higher among females under nonarousal conditions, but are more often *significantly* higher under arousal conditions. Note that the studies reporting a decrease in fear-of-success scores under arousal conditions did not include a comparison with male subjects.

Vocational aspirations

Several studies of fear of success and vocational aspirations among women find flight from career persistence in favor of marrying and having children among high fear-of-success women (Stewart, 1975); depressant effects on SES level and educational level of vocational aspirations in high fear-of-success women (Esposito, 1976, 1977); and avoidance of traditionally masculine careers in high fear-of-success women (Beldner, 1979; Fleming, 1978). Two studies of male aspirations found modest but significantly positive correlations with high fear of success and high levels of occupational aspirations among both high school and college age males (Esposito, 1976, 1977), suggesting effects in opposite directions for females and males.

Academic performance

Four studies have investigated the motive's relationship to academic performance (Beldner, 1979; Fleming, 1976; Kripke, 1980; O'Leary & Hammack, 1975). Only Beldner found the expected negative relationship to actual grade point average among women. Fear of success seems to have much less impact on grades than on experimental performance or career choice across samples.

Other correlates

Other correlates of fear of success include less fear of success in non-traditional women (O'Leary & Hammack, 1975); career conflicts and the expending of energy in pursuits that were not important or interesting among high fear-of-success college students (Jenkins, 1979); passivity in the face of crisis among high fear-of-success adult women (Stewart, 1975); an association between high fear of success and suffering from anorexia nervosa (Gilbert, 1986); and evidence of inconsistent parenting among children with high fear of success (E. F. Cherry, 1977).

Conclusions

Studies using the revised projective scoring system for fear of success provide more compelling evidence that fear of success can influence behavior under certain conditions compatible with expectancy-value theory. Furthermore, in accordance with the two possible theoretical resolutions of avoidance motivation (inhibition or redirection), the female results suggest redirection, whereas the male results suggest inhibition. The new scoring system suggests an interpretation of fear of success as the problematic expression of instrumental action. That is, such individuals harbor achievement drives but inhibit them in certain situations. Such individuals may perform well under relaxed or nonthreatening conditions but poorly in threatening conditions perceived as competitive, challenging, or masculine (see Fleming, 1982). According to a review by McClelland (1985b), fear-of-success individuals are most likely to inhibit achievement performance in the presence of a person of greater power. Conflict over the expression of achievement drives is the hallmark of the motive.

SUMMARY

The new, empirically derived scoring system, now in its third revision, Version C (see chapter 12), represents an improvement over the 1968 measure of fear-of-success imagery. The motive was isolated in fantasy using an experimental paradigm in which each of a group of women competed successfully against a man. The scoring system uses an increased number of projective stimuli and levels of ambiguity. Unlike other projective scoring systems, the fear-of-success measure has a firm grounding in behavioral prediction. Unlike approach motives, fear-of-success scores were found to decrease under experimental arousal in some samples of women, and fear-of-success scores to individual cues were inversely related to the achievement relevance of the projective stimulus. Like most other thematic measures, this one has low internal consistency. However, high internal consistency of cue scores was not necessary to obtain maximum prediction to performance in a regression equation. Indiscriminate summation of cue scores results in dramatic losses in predictive power.

From the available evidence, the new empirically derived measure of fear of success shows more convincing predictive validity than the earlier instrument. The new scoring system suggests an interpretation of the fear-of-success phenomenon as the conflicted expression of instrumental action in achievement situations.

12 *A revised scoring manual for the motive to avoid success*

MATINA S. HORNER AND
JACQUELINE FLEMING

The following pages describe a new, experimentally derived scoring system for the motive to avoid success. This new system differs from the original (Horner, 1968) present–absent scoring system for "fear-of-success *imagery*" in several ways. (a) It is an *empirically* derived scoring system based upon a series of studies designed to arouse and isolate the motive to avoid success in fantasy (Horner, 1973; see also Atkinson, 1958a; McClelland, Atkinson, Clark, & Lowell, 1953). (b) It does not depend on a gross assessment of the tone of the manifest content in a thematic apperceptive story but involves the scoring of subtler story sequences. (c) Verbal leads that are highly structured with respect to success and failure cannot be used with this system. It requires the use of neutral/ambiguous verbal leads or pictures that are more likely to reflect *spontaneous* motivation or naturally occurring concerns. (d) The new scoring criteria do not revolve around the avoidance of success per se but are more generally concerned with the avoidance of instrumental competence.

Comprising the present scoring system are the following five scoring categories for which the appropriate scoring weights are given in parentheses:

Noncontingent Negative Consequences	(+1)
Interpersonal Engagement	(+1)
Relief	(+1)
Absence of Instrumental Activity	(+1)
Absence of Others	(−1)

A single story may be scored for any or all of these categories. Each of the categories is explained in order.

NONCONTINGENT NEGATIVE CONSEQUENCES (+1)

Stories are scored for negative consequences when there is *movement* or a progression in the story toward a situation that can be interpreted as worse than the original situation. The initial state can be positive, neutral, or even slightly negative as long as the overall development or outcome of the story reflects a more negative state. The final situation must be seen as having a negative *consequence*, either explicitly stated or easily inferred, for anyone in the story such as death, disaster, injury, failure, loss, frustration, hopelessness, disappointment, or negative affect. The general definition, then, is (a) evidence of movement; (b) toward a situation worse than the original one; (c) brought about by the impingement of external forces; (d) which is interpreted as having a negative consequence for someone in the story. Thus, to score for negative consequences one looks for a sequence of events with a negative outcome rather than the mere presence of negative content.

Noncontingent negative consequences are scored when an event comes about through the impingement of external forces, which usually meet one of the following criteria. Italics have been added to call the attention of the reader to phrases that make a story scorable for a particular category.

1. External forces: caused or inflicted by others

She is angry over her grade because it was unjustly given to her. She is thinking how *unfair a professor she has*.

Carol got so angry that she went back to the house and with all her strength *she grabbed the girl and flung her across the room*. The girl, whose name was Helen, hit her head and was knocked out cold.

Diane is now wondering why that weird man hiding in the bushes is staring at her. Diane will *get raped*.

2. External forces: accidents

When Carol returned the telescope was gone. When she looked out the window she saw it lying on the ground *broken all in little bits*.

At the end she arrives at the doctor's office, but *with a sprained leg*.

She kept on watching Bozo, that is, until *the TV blew up*! Judy is still sitting there glued to the chair.

3. External forces: forces beyond one's control

She feels she has plenty of time. She will sketch the drawings carefully at first, and *as time runs out*, she will be *tense* and make more hurried drawings and copy details from her textbook.

Now, though, she is a technician and looking at a patient's tissues. She liked Mrs.

Smith and was hoping that she wouldn't find what she was now looking at. *These tissues were definitely cancerous.*

Barbara got to her desk and started typing. When she had finished typing and took her hands off the keys, *the typewriter started typing all by itself.* The typewriter typed the same beat, rhythm, and length she had typed. Barbara was frightened and ran out.

Hand in hand, they both turn and walk down the beach. Each tries to hold on to this moment. For tomorrow Tom leaves for Vietnam. Linda heads for school. *Neither wants the other to leave*, each walks silently with nothing to say.

(Note that in the last example the causes of the unwanted separation are out of their control. The negative consequence for Tom is Linda heads for school; the negative consequence for Linda is Tom leaves for Vietnam.)

Do not interpret motives. Score the language actually used in the story. "*She* ruined the experiment" is an active statement and is not scored as noncontingent. "The experiment *was ruined*," without other statements connecting this outcome to an actor, is a passive statement and is scored as noncontingent.

Joan comes walking into the Social Science Center looking very pleased. She has been up most of the night writing a paper for history. She had put a great deal of work into it and was confident of a good grade. She reached into her pocketbook for the paper *only to find it missing*. Retracing her steps, she found the neatly typed paper lying in a mud puddle. Very upset, she returned to the building and found her instructor.

(Note that this story does not say "she lost the paper" and is therefore scored as noncontingent negative consequences.)

The movement and/or negative consequences usually involve three general classes of outcomes.

1. Outcome: misfortune and disaster

Most negative outcomes can be classified as involving some sort of misfortune such as failure, injury, punishment, quarrels, accidents and the like. For example:

... but unfortunately there was no film in the camera.

This time she managed to get there, but the door wouldn't open.

Disasters are a subcategory of misfortune and usually involve death, ruination, natural disaster, or acts of God or all-powerful forces. These stories sometimes have a bizarre quality.

It is a slide from her sister's blood. Her sister has too many cells and has leukemia.

Carol went up to the Martians and asked them their names. But they weren't very greetful, so they disintegrated her.

2. Outcomes: increase in tension

An increase in tension is indicated by negative affect or fear of an outcome.

She has been in the building speaking with Paul. . . . Paul is my fiance. . . . Why is she smiling so wryly? And why is she so dressed up and acting so confident? I feel *tears on my cheek.*

3. Outcomes: deprivation

Deprivation is defined as having something that one wants removed, taken away, or withheld.

. . . She feels sad though, because everyone is already dead and she will be alone for the rest of her life.

"Probably" or "maybe" statements should be scored as if the events happened. On the other hand, conditional "if . . . then" statements where the real outcome is in doubt are not scored. Similarly, any story in which the outcome (and thus the nature of the negative consequence) is unclear should not be scored.

Movement toward misfortune/disaster, increased tension, or deprivation often occurs quite suddenly and is encapsulated in a single sentence. Frequently it is the very last sentence that gives the story a downward turn and, regardless of what the rest of the story was like, this is enough for scoring negative consequences. For example, the very last sentence of an otherwise positive story:

The experiment was ruined.

A number of negatively toned stories are not scored for negative consequences because there is no evidence of movement. These stories usually begin and end on a negative note, but the original situation remains unchanged or the plot line does not develop:

Standing atop a rocky cliff, she watches the sun float down behind the trees. It's beautiful and majestic and breathtaking, but Linda can't feel it. She feels nothing, only . . . "I want to die." She can't even think of anyone to write a suicide note to. No one cares enough – no one wants to take on the responsibility of sitting down and listening to her problem. Her parents would kill her if they knew she was pregnant. Joe won't admit it to himself, but exists in a stoned stupor since she told him Friday. Well, it's Monday night. Oh! Am I going to kill me and extinguish another life?

(Note that here the story begins with Linda wanting to die and does not really progress. The body of the story is taken up with lamenting over the reasons for her predicament.)

In contrast, the following story develops from bad to worse as indicated by the movement toward increased tension:

Linda is looking out at the sunset, wondering what really is going on. Why was I born? How can I serve a useful purpose in life?. . . If Steve were still at her side, she's sure she wouldn't be as confused as she is now. But he's gone, a mistake of her own, just as she feels her life is but one big mistake. The sunset should make Linda feel calm, but unfortunately *her depression grows*.

Descriptive statements of difficulties, blocks, hardships, or disasters that merely function to set the stage for the rest of the story are *not* scored. These generally occur in the first sentence and are followed by improvements in the situation or some more definitive negative consequences:

Linda is all alone and yes, she is lonely. Today was just a perfect day at the beach and now it has to come to an end. The flaming, orange sun slowly sinks behind the ocean. Its bright and brilliant rays shine down upon the water. The sun is going to find peace and rest just like Linda's brother who was *killed in Vietnam*.

(Note that Linda's loneliness is setting the stage for the rest of the story and, though negative, is not scored as a negative consequence. It is the final statement of the story that *is* scored.)

A number of stories contain numerous fluctuations up and down, and we have termed these "zigzag" stories. If there are several shifts between positive and negative movements such that the overall story development does not suggest clearly negative consequences, the story is not scored. The following story illustrates the oscillation phenomenon:

Anne is happy. Sort of. She is in the lunchroom with lots of people, but doesn't feel them around her. She feels separate. She's happy like usual, but not really because nothing good has happened today. Al didn't speak to her at breakfast. Nobody wants to be with her, help her. She's happy, because that's the only way she can go on living. If she's happy about the myriad wonderful little things, then the big ones don't hurt so much. Al will smile at her at lunch. That won't make any difference. She feels like a pawn, a body to him. He's cold, hard. She wants to help him, but can't.

It is fairly common to see stories in which the outcome is negatively toned but is not clearly perceived as having a negative consequence for someone in the story. Usually the event is only moderately negative, but in some cases even a clearly negative event will not be interpreted as such.

Carol is looking through the telescope. Her younger brother, Teddy, is waiting for a chance to look through it. But Carol is fascinated by the boy in the window of the house next door. Teddy wants to look at the mountain that is near their house. After waiting 20 minutes, Teddy finally pushes Carol away and gets his chance.

(Note that the negative event for Carol – being pushed away – is stated matter-of-factly and there is no explicit or implicit statement that the event constitutes a misfortune, leads to increased tension, or is perceived as a deprivation.)

INTERPERSONAL ENGAGEMENT (+1)

Interpersonal engagement is scored when there is evidence that two or more people are actively involved with each other on an interpersonal level. There are three aspects to this engagement: there must be instrumental activity toward an affiliative or interpersonal goal; there must be evidence of clear involvement between two or more people present in the story; and interpersonal involvement must comprise a major goal in the story – that is, an interpersonal or affiliative goal must be as important as an achievement, task, or power goal.

Instrumental activity toward an affiliative goal

This subcategory refers to overt acts, interchanges, or thoughts of a problem-solving nature by one or more of the characters that are directed toward an interpersonal or affiliative goal. This is a necessary (but not sufficient) condition for scoring interpersonal engagement. The actions may be directed toward positive goals (e.g., wanting to become closer to another, seeking advice or consolation) or they may be directed toward negative or threat-oriented goals (e.g., breaking off a relationship, seeking revenge, etc.). Sometimes the existence of these goals is not clearly stated and must be partially inferred. There are four types of actions or interchanges that qualify as instrumental activity toward an affiliative goal.

(1) VERBAL MODE: DIALOGUE. Sometimes stories having interpersonal aspects are written in dialogue form, which clearly makes the interchange between two or more people conspicuous.

Barbara told her mother that she never wanted to see that man again. "He can stay in his little office and rot for all I care," she screamed. Her mother realized that Henry was a work bug, but she also knew that Barbara loved him and he loved her. "Listen, dear, Henry only works so hard so he can make enough money to marry you," Barbara's mother replied. "So he gets rich, but in the meantime he completely neglects me," Barbara sobbed. "I think instead of being so self-centered you should try to help Henry." Finally after much talk and consideration, Barbara went back to the office at the end of the day.

(Note that the interchange between mother and daughter clearly has an interpersonal aspect – advice and consolation.)

(2) VERBAL MODE: DESCRIPTIONS OF ACTIVE VERBAL INTERCHANGES. Common verbs showing interpersonal engagement include tell, ask (a question, for a date), say, suggest, announce, urge, invite, listen discuss, talk to, call, and phone.

She has just *discussed* some very intimate thoughts with a friend and felt encouraged by the understanding and love her friend shows.

Her friends *called* her and *asked* her to meet them for lunch.

(3) NONVERBAL MODE: VERBS DESCRIBING INTERACTIONS. Common verbs include wait for, come by, pick up, flirt with, approach, meet, join, visit, kiss, date, take out, help, share, settle an argument, receive.

Diane decided to stop by my house where Theresa *was paying me a visit*.

She and her friend will *share* an apartment.

When her boyfriend entered the room, she *received a marriage proposal*.

(4) NONVERBAL MODE: Other interchanges include overt or mental actions toward an affiliative goal. Any other verb that does not in itself convey an interchange or interaction between people may be sufficient if the goal of the action is affiliative.

Carol is a young woman who has just had an argument with her husband over his outlandish spending of money on model trains. She is very angry and walking fast. She becomes tired, stops and thinks about the situation. She loves her husband and since they aren't in desperate need of the money, she *decides* it isn't worth the anger.

Judy is *assessing the relationship* with her friend, wondering if they will be able to continue working cooperatively through the years.

It is fairly common to see stories in which communications are conveyed from one person to another by *letter*. Interchanges via the written word rather than two people directly are considered instrumental activity and are scorable.

Judy received a letter from her brother in California and he is *telling* her about the first day on the job and how many mistakes he has made. She feels lonely that he has gone out there since he was her only sibling, but he felt that he had to start to live on his own away from their parents. *He has also invited her* to come out and spend some time with him when he gets settled and she is smiling with happiness.

There are a number of affiliative or interpersonal stories that cannot be scored for interpersonal engagement because there is no activity toward an affiliative goal.

Diane is by herself walking back from Barney's. Her little sister's birthday is coming up and she has neglected to buy a birthday card. Diane is thinking it would be nice to go home and see her sister rather than mail the card. She will slip on the ice, break her leg and get to go home for the rest of the semester.

(Note that denial of an action – "neglected to buy" – does not qualify as activity toward a goal.)

Instrumental activity toward an interpersonal goal is *not* indicated by the passive voice (". . . she has *been asked* to the formal dance by Ralph

Jones...."), statements of wishes, hopes, or desires ("Her friends now *want* her to help them..."), or statements of intention or obligation ("Now she will *have to* tell her roommate it's her turn on the couch this weekend.")

Involvement

In addition to the presence of instrumental activity toward an affiliative or interpersonal goal, there must be some indication that two or more characters are actively involved with each other on an interpersonal level, rather than being involved in a relationship or exchange that is largely non-interpersonal. An active interaction or interchange must take place. When the story is romantic, the interpersonal nature of the involvement/interaction is immediately obvious and the presence of instrumental activity is sufficient to indicate an active concern and thus interpersonal engagement: "He asked her for a date" or "He proposed marriage." However, when the story is not strictly romantic, more evidence is necessary to show that the relationship between two people – family members, co-workers, colleagues – is more than just routine. Such evidence may be an indication of *intimacy* in the relationship (e.g., friendship, togetherness), explicit evidence of *emotional involvement*, or some indication that the relationship has some *effect* on one or both parties. The following story is an example of a nonromantic relationship where there is instrumental activity toward an interpersonal goal and evidence of interpersonal involvement:

> *Diane has had a frustrating fight with her friends* and can't relate her points to be given equal validity so she's frustrated. Mary, Donna and Sue all were saying how stupid getting upset over fellas is. Each has been to the point of never... They want her to be cool and aloof and be in control of the situation. Diane agrees (rather is forced to do so) and *will follow her friend's example just for peer acceptance.*

In the next story, there is no evidence that the characters are involved on an interpersonal level:

> Sue is in biology class and she is looking at a slide of bacteria. She realizes she must be able to identify correctly every form, or she will flunk the exam. She needs a good mark if she is to continue in the course. Mr. Potter, her professor, has warned her about her need for a good grade, and he feels she can achieve much more than she already has.

(Note that, although the professor gives Sue a warning, it is strictly in the line of duty and is not accompanied by an interpersonal reaction.)

In a number of stories there is no real clue as to the relationship between two people except for the fact that they are discussing interpersonal, personal, private, or intimate issues. Such affiliative, interpersonal discussions are sufficient indication of an interpersonal relationship or involvement:

Judy, what are you so happy about? Did Tom finally call you? No, but Ken did and he's taking me to the movies tonight. I think Tom's so mad at me he'll never call back and I don't even care. What did you do that made him so mad? I can't tell you, but I will say that Ken helped me plan it. Oh, it must have been pretty mean if Ken helped you. Yeah, and you know what.

Major goal

The major goal or *one* major goal of the story must be explicitly affiliative or interpersonal. There may well be other themes in the story that exist along-side an affiliative orientation as long as interpersonal engagement is a well-developed aspect of the story:

Anne had to do a project for science. *She asked some of her brothers to help her.* They told her what books to get and material she would need. So she got everything. They told her what pages to read in what books. And when she finished reading and making things she had the best project of the science classes. So she won first prize. Anne was so happy that her brothers had told her what to do and read that *she let them have the medal.*

In the following example, interpersonal engagement is not scored because the affiliative/interpersonal aspects of the story are considerably less developed than the major theme. In some cases actions that could be interpreted as having an interpersonal goal clearly do not when seen in context.

Judy is thinking about the beautiful day she spent yesterday. She remembers how she and Jack went to the mountains and sat and watched the snow come down and cover the trees and ground. She remembered how happy it made her feel when it snowed. She loved the snow. Then she remembered how they went sliding down a hill on a toboggan. This was a great thrill – to enjoy the new snow.

(Note that, although Judy and Jack do a number of things together, Judy seems much less interested in Jack than in the snow.)

RELIEF (+1)

Relief is scored when there is *movement* from a state of relative tension or deprivation to a relief of that tension that takes place without the instrumental intervention of the character involved. There must be no clear statement that an individual's efforts led to the positive outcome. If there are indications of goal-oriented striving or instrumental activity, the rewards, affect, or sense of relief must be out of proportion to the amount of effort expended. The movement toward relief of tension often occurs suddenly, dramatically, or magically and often in a manner incurring surprise. Also, many stories seem to end in a symbolic "whew!" with the sense of "at long last" or seem to have the quality of a great breakthrough, burden lifted, or a longing satisfied.

It has been so long that Judy was sick that she became discouraged, pale and thin. She bore the pain daily, but she occasionally broke down to tears when the pain intensified. *Suddenly* she walked into out room and sat down in a chair, smiling. "It's gone," she said. "The pain is gone, and I'm healthy again."

The tests were passed back to all the chemistry class. Joan's paper finally reached her. She was afraid to turn it over. She thought to herself and wondered if she had studied enough. Joan finally got the courage and turned her paper over. To her amazement, she had gotten an A on the exam.

Joan is married to Jean and for many years they've been trying to have children. Well, today she just returned from the doctor's and found out that she was pregnant. She feels beautiful sensations as she and her husband have longed for a baby ever since they were married. In nine months Jean and Joan will bring a baby boy into the world!

As in the case of negative consequences, the condition that there be movement in the story means that the assessment of relief must be made upon the overall story development with respect to a given theme or sub-theme, rather than a discrete sentence or statement of relief. Thus, statements such as "She feels relieved to be sitting home" or "it seems relaxing to her after such a busy, hectic day" are not scorable in and of themselves. Relief, then, refers to a story *sequence* as opposed to a particular aspect of manifest content.

ABSENCE OF INSTRUMENTAL ACTIVITY (+1)

In scoring a story for this category, the judgment to be made is whether or not instrumental activity is present. Instrumental activity is defined as any overt act, thoughts of a problem-solving nature, or mental activity by one or more characters in the story indicating that something is being done about attaining a goal. There are various goals, such as achievement, power, affiliation, or task goals, that may be stated or easily inferred. In addition, any overt (or mental) action can be scored for instrumental activity as long as there is evidence that the activity is of a purposive nature.

... Four years of your life *doing hard work, trying to get to this end with good grades to get into law school* ...

The phone rang. *He went to answer it.*

He *decided to ask her out for the following Saturday night.*

Absence of instrumental activity is scored when there is no statement of any instrumental act ("thinking" or "doing") toward attaining a goal within the story. By convention, absence of instrumental activity is also scored when the only instrumental activity appears in the first clause of the initial sentence and is merely a description of the picture or repetition of the verbal cue. However, a clear-cut statement of an instrumental act appearing later in the first sentence may be scored. Thus, avoid scoring restatements of the cue material, but not first sentences *in toto*.

In the matter of an instant the bare branches of the trees were transformed from their stark presence into a multitude of tiny veins endlessly reaching toward the vibrances of the hues which were above them. The rich, warm colors of the sun provided a feeling of pulsating life for Linda as she lay beneath the trees gazing into the sunset. It would seem that climbing these massive branches should deliver her into the warmth of the sun, yet she knew that even the uppermost reaches of the tallest tree could not serve to make her one with heaven.

Carol is looking through the telescope wondering where the man in the moon is. Her mommy always talks about him, but poor little Carol never does get to see him. And when she's lonely like tonight and needs a friend, she really wishes she could see him and have a nice chat. But again, Carol has never heard the man in the moon talk back. She can only hear of him through grownups. Carol can't wait until she grows up so that she may find and see the great big man in the moon.

Verbs indicating covert or mental activity (thinking, wondering, wishing, imagining) and passive activities (looking, watching, noticing, waiting) are difficult to score. Special care must be taken to determine whether or not the action is purposive, that is, whether something is done about attaining a goal. For example, "she was watching television" is not instrumental activity, but "She was watching an educational program that the teacher advised the class to see" is. Similarly, "John is looking through his telescope at a star" is not instrumental, whereas "John is looking through his telescope to see if there are any meteors, falling stars, or even a few flying saucers" is.

Instrumental activity is not to be confused with descriptions of actions or statements of final outcome. Although such descriptions often include the presence of verbs, they merely describe a situation or state of affairs rather than the action itself. For example, the statement "She made a contribution to the world" is not instrumental activity because only the outcome or effect of the person's actions has been described. On the other hand, "She was working on her project which would be a contribution to the world" or "She was thinking about the solution to the problem which would make a contribution to the world" is instrumental activity because the actual activity is explicit. Likewise, "She finished the paper" does not constitute instrumental activity, whereas "She wrote all night until the paper was finished" does. Other descriptive statements, such as ". . . while driving back from the beach . . . ," ". . . on her way to class . . . ," ". . . she has just come back from a visit with the assistant principal . . . ," or ". . . she finally put him down, set him in his place . . ." are not instrumental activity. Instrumental activity within the story can occur in the past or future tense as long as it is more than a statement of the outcome.

Statements describing interactions among people where the action and/or goal is not specific (such as help, meet, visit) are usually not adequately focused toward a goal to meet the requirements of instrumental activity. However, such interactions may qualify under Interpersonal Engagement. For example, "John is helping Susan" is not an example of instrumental activity, but "John is helping Susan focus her microscope" is instrumental activity because purposive action has been specified. Also *not* indicative of instrumental activity are: the subjunctive mood ("would" or "should"); statements embedded in conditional phraseology (if . . . then, perhaps, maybe); wishes and desires ("He *wants* to study hard to get good grades"), habitual or routine actions ("*Every day*, he gets up at 7 o'clock and dresses for work," or "He *usually* cooks his own dinner"); or statements of obligation rather than activity ("She *has to* write down what she observes" or "He *ought to* go the dentist"). The act of saying something to another person, asking a question, responding to a question or statement, and so forth, whether in the form of dialogue or descriptive verbal interaction (saying, telling, asking), is considered instrumental activity in the sense that conversation is instrumental to conveying information (e.g., "He *tells* her the good news," or "My father *says* I can't go"). Only when the content of verbal interaction is unspecified is instrumental activity not indicated ("He is saying *something*").

ABSENCE OF OTHERS (+)

Absence of others is a counterindicative category that is scored when there is no mention of another person or group of persons in the story besides the character in the picture or verbal cue.

When the label for a group is global, vague, or descriptive ("Her *class* has been studying insects . . ." or ". . . Now she will have a chance to prove herself to the *world*." "Power to the people."), then it is not treated as a mention of another person and Absence of Others is scored. However, a more explicit reference to the "members of the class" or "group of friends" indicates the presence of specific other people. Plural pronouns (e.g., we, they, us, them) indicate presence of others even when the referent is vague. Occasionally one finds a plural pronoun in a story when there is clearly no one else present besides the main character. Such grammatical inconsistencies look like slips of the pen and are common in children's stories. If there is indeed no plural referent for the pronoun, the story should be scored for Absence of Others.

Others may *not* be mentioned by implication or noted as missing. Thus, statements that the cue character is all alone or feeling lonely do mention other persons by their absence and are not scored in this category:

. . . and she's the only one there . . .

. . . and Carol was getting lonely . . .

These moods often came over her, feeling of loneliness, the absence of a true friend.

(Note that Absence of Others is much less likely to be scored when the thematic apperceptive stimulus depicts two or more characters.)

Animals (and other nonhuman characters) do not count as people unless they are personified in a story that is written about them or have clear effects on a character.

GUIDE TO RESEARCH WITH THE MOTIVE TO AVOID SUCCESS SCORING SYSTEM

Careful use of practice materials should enable the user to score fear of success with acceptable interscorer reliability for research purposes. After having read the scoring manual carefully and having studied the example stories, the user should test himself or herself by trying to recall the scoring definitions of each category without consulting the manual. Further test questions to consider are: (a) What is meant by "movement" in a story? For which scoring categories is movement a relevant consideration? (b) What is the difference between the way instrumental activity is treated in Interpersonal Engagement and Absence of Instrumental Activity? (c) What is the difference between a relief statement and a relief sequence? Check your answers carefully with the manual before you proceed to score. A set of practice stories and expert scoring for the stories is provided in appendix I of this volume.

Interscorer reliability

The degree of agreement between your scoring and that of the expert may be obtained by computing either agreement about categories scored or agreement about total story score or both.

CATEGORY AGREEMENT. For all stories from all subjects, identify all categories scored as *present* by you *and* by the expert. (Disregard plus or minus category weights.) Double the number of agreements between you and the expert, and divide that number by the total number of categories scored by you plus the total number scored by the expert. For example, for a single story that was scored by you for three categories (Relief, Absence of Instrumental Activity, and Absence of Others) and by the expert for four categories (Noncontingent Negative Consequences, Interpersonal Engagement, Relief, Absence of Others), you would have 2 instances of agreement (which doubled equals 4), divided by the number of categories scored by each scorer (3 + 4 or 7). The index is 4/7 or 57% agreement.

TOTAL STORY SCORE AGREEMENT. Compute a correlation between your total story score and the expert's for the practice stories in appendix I.

As D. G. Winter (1973) has pointed out, Category Agreement is the more conservative formula in that it does not count agreement on the absence of a category. We recommend that the user attain a Category Agreement score of *at least* .85 before scoring stories for research purposes. Scoring reliability should be reported for each research study.

Story collection and scoring

At least three or four stories, obtained either from pictures or neutral verbal leads should be used in determining a subject's total score. The only leads *not* recommended are highly structured, especially success-specific leads. Verbal leads used for development of the motive to avoid success scoring system are:

> Sue is looking into her microscope.
> Judy is sitting in a chair with a smile on her face.
> Carol is walking along the beach late in the day.
> Carol is looking through the telescope.
> Joan seems to be particularly pleased.
> Linda is looking out at the sunset.

The researcher may wish to make up a scoring sheet with a line at the top for the cue used to elicit the stories. The first column is headed "Subject Number," the next five columns are headed with the names of the scoring categories and their scoring weights, and the last column is headed "Total Score." Each row gives, for a particular subject, the categories present, if any, and the total score for that story.

There are two possible ways to obtain a final score. For *Categorical Scoring* the subject may receive only one score per *category*, no matter how many stories the subject has written. If imagery occurs in at least one story for a particular category, the category is scored as present. Scores are then summed across categories rather than across stories. The final score for the subject is computed by weighting each category with the appropriate weights given in the manual. Thus, scores may range from -1 to $+4$, regardless of the number of stories considered in the scoring process. For *Continuous Scoring*, a score is determined separately for each story and then scores are summed across stories. Thus, scores may range from -3 to $+12$ for three stories. Although there is no evidence as to which is the best method, Continuous Scoring does provide a wider range in scores. In any case, the method used should be reported.

Subjects who write longer stories have a tendency to receive higher fear-of-success scores. If the correlation between total number of words for all stories and fear-of-success score reaches .25, the researcher should correct the motive score for story length. Please consult chapter 37 of this volume for the details of how to adjust scores for story length.

13 *The affiliation motive*

RICHARD KOESTNER AND
DAVID C. McCLELLAND

DERIVATION AND ADMINISTRATION OF THE FANTASY MEASURE OF *N* AFFILIATION

Affiliative motivation is defined as a concern over establishing, maintaining, or restoring a positive affective relationship with another person or group of persons (Heyns, Veroff, & Atkinson, 1958). The system for scoring the need for affiliation (*n* Aff) from imaginative thought content (see chapter 14) was developed by comparing stories written by college men after they had been socially evaluated by their peers with stories written under neutral conditions (Atkinson, Heyns, & Veroff, 1954; Shipley & Veroff, 1952). Similar evaluative conditions were shown to arouse affiliative concerns in stories written by women (Rosenfeld & Franklin, 1966). The same scoring system is used for males and females.

The procedure for eliciting associative thought content that can be coded for *n* Affiliation is identical to that used for the achievement and power motives. This procedure is sometimes referred to as the Picture-Story Exercise (PSE) and requires subjects to write 5-minute stories to a series of four to six pictures like those of the Thematic Apperception Test (TAT). It is recommended that the PSE be administered by an experimenter who behaves in a relaxed, friendly, and approving manner (Lundy, 1988). It is also advisable to *avoid* administering the PSE immediately after an objective test or cognitive task (Lundy, 1988).

Three other methodological points regarding the assessment of *n* Affiliation need to be mentioned. First, if *n* Affiliation is assessed on more than one occasion it is important to use the administration instructions designed by

Preparation of this chapter was funded by a grant from the Fonds Pour La Formation De Chercheurs Et L'Aide A La Recherche (FCAR-Quebec). We would like to thank Joseph Veroff and Charles Smith for their comments on earlier versions of this chapter.

205

D. G. Winter and Stewart (1977b) that explicitly permit subjects to tell similar stories on the second testing. Failure to employ these instructions results in very low stability coefficients. Second, in calculating a subject's level of n Affiliation it is important to statistically control for the length of the story protocol because story length and the occurrence of n Affiliation themes are positively (and sometimes significantly) correlated. Third, self-report measures that purport to assess the strength of the affiliative motive should *not* be used in place of the fantasy measure as these two methods typically yield uncorrelated scores (McClelland, Koestner, & Weinberger, 1989; also reprinted as chapter 3 in this volume).

RELIABILITY, STABILITY, AND VALIDITY OF
FANTASY n AFFILIATION

Early studies noted that the need-for-affiliation scoring system was easy to learn and that high levels of interrater reliability could be obtained (Atkinson et al., 1954; Shipley & Veroff, 1952). The fantasy measure of need for affiliation appears to display sufficient temporal stability to be viewed as a dispositional construct. For example, Lundy (1985) reported a test–retest correlation of .56 over the span of a year with a sample of high school students. Koestner and Franz (1989) reported a test–retest r of .66 over the span of 8 months and a test–retest r of .30 over 10 years with two separate samples of men and women. It has generally been found that males and females possess comparable levels of affiliative motivation (Stewart & Chester, 1982). However, there is some evidence that level of affiliative motivation decreases across the adult life-span for women, whereas it remains stable for men (Veroff, Reuman, & Feld, 1984).

McClelland, Atkinson, Clark, and Lowell (1953) argued that in order to validate fantasy motive measures it is necessary to show that the particular motive functions like a biological drive in the sense of energizing, directing, and selecting behavior. That is, a strong affiliative motive should make one active in pursuing affiliative goals, sensitive to cues related to affiliation, and quick to learn what is necessary to reach an affiliation goal (Biernat, 1989). Various studies support the notion that people who are affiliative-motivated are more energized or activated in the sense that they are more likely to initiate affiliative interactions (Boyatzis, 1973; Constantian, 1981; Lansing & Heyns, 1959). The orienting function of affiliative motivation was confirmed by a study that showed that visual cues related to human faces were more salient to people with high rather than low n Affiliation (Atkinson & Walker, 1956); the selective function was supported by a study that showed that people who score high on n Affiliation are able to learn social networks more quickly than those who score low (McClelland, 1985b).

AFFILIATIVE MOTIVATION AND INTERPERSONAL RELATIONS

People who are high in n Affiliation spend more of their time interacting with others than do people with low affiliative motivation. Highly affiliative-motivated people visit their friends more frequently, make more phone calls, and write more letters than their peers who are low in n Affiliation (Boyatzis, 1973; Constantian, 1981; Lansing & Heyns, 1959). Even at work, affiliative-motivated people spend more time interacting with others (Noujaim, 1968). If they are randomly beeped during the day, people high in n Affiliation are more likely than others to be found interacting with someone (McClelland, 1985b) or if alone, to report wishing that they were with someone (McAdams & Constantian, 1983). Among college-aged women, affiliative motivation is positively related to interest in establishing long-term romantic relationships (Bickman, 1975).

Affiliative motivation also affects the way in which social interactions are conducted. High levels of affiliative motivation appear to predispose people to be sympathetic and accommodating toward others. Thus, affiliative-motivated individuals are more likely to place a high value on living in a peaceful world (Rokeach, 1973) and to express an interest in pursuing people-oriented careers (Exline, 1960; Sundheim, 1962). When they are asked by others to adjust their behavior, people with high n Affiliation are especially likely to comply with the request (Walker & Heyns, 1962). Such social accommodation may well have its roots in a desire to avoid inter-personal conflict (Exline, 1962), which is most clearly manifested in an aversion for competitive interpersonal endeavors (McClelland, 1975; Terhune, 1968). Moreover, if people with strong affiliative motivation are placed in an interpersonally competitive performance context, they are likely to perform worse than their peers (Karabenick, 1977).

Level of n Affiliation can also influence behavior in situations that are not directly social in nature. This is exemplified by research indicating that the affiliative motive often influences behavior in achievement settings. For example, compared with people who are low in affiliative motivation, those who are high prefer to work with friends rather than experts (French, 1956), prefer affiliative-oriented rather than competence-focused feedback (French, 1958b), and believe that goodwill is more important than reason in solving problems (McClelland, 1975). Furthermore, it has been shown that, under certain conditions, affiliative motivation can promote effective per-formance at achievement tasks. Thus, if the outcome of a task is related to an affiliative goal, men with high n Affiliation outperform those with low n Affiliation (Atkinson & Raphelson, 1956; deCharms, 1957; French, 1956). Similarly, McKeachie (1961) showed that college students with high n Affiliation achieved better grades than students with low n Affiliation in classes led by warm and friendly instructors. The potential role of affiliative motivation in fostering achievement is highlighted by the fact that among cultures that are primarily affiliative rather than achievement oriented (e.g., Hawaiians), n Affiliation is a better predictor of school performance than n Achievement (Gallimore, 1981).

AFFILIATIVE MOTIVATION AND SOCIAL SUCCESS

Given that people who are high in affiliative motivation spend more time interacting with others and do so in a generally accommodating and co-operative manner, one might guess that they would be popular among their peers. Surprisingly, the research evidence suggests that people with high n Affiliation are not only no more popular than people with low n Affiliation (Skolnick, 1966), they may even be relatively more *unpopular* (Atkinson et al., 1954; Crowne & Marlowe, 1964; Shipley & Veroff, 1952). This introduces a rather significant problem for the predictive validity of the affiliative motive. For both achievement and power motivation, high levels of the motive led to superior performance on motive-related variables. For example, n Achievement was shown to lead to greater entrepreneurial success and n Power led to greater managerial success (McClelland, 1985b). In contrast, affiliative motivation does not translate into higher levels of social success, at least not as measured in terms of peer popularity. More-over, there is no evidence that the quality of relationships established by affiliative-motivated people is in any way superior to that established by people with low affiliative motivation.

How can the apparent negative relation between n Affiliation and social success be accounted for? The explanation that has received the most attention is that the fantasy measure of n Affiliation may capture only the more dependent, deficit-motivated aspect of affiliative needs. Since its derivation, investigators have suspected that the fantasy measure of n Affiliation may represent fear of rejection (Boyatzis, 1973; Shipley & Veroff, 1952). This suspicion was rooted in the realization that the arousal conditions used to derive the scoring system for n Affiliation all involved rejection or potential rejection by peers. It is noteworthy that nearly all of the action correlates of n Affiliation (e.g., calling friends more frequently, avoiding conflict, performing badly under competitive conditions) could be explained by assuming that people are responding defensively to underlying concerns about being rejected rather than responding to a positive drive to be with others. In fact, if one assumes a defensive function for the affiliative motive, the association between n Affiliation and lack of popularity becomes more understandable. Perhaps high n Affiliation (read fear of rejection) is a *result* of a failure to establish fulfilling relationships.

A variety of other evidence indicates that people's scores on n Affiliation may primarily reflect their level of fear of rejection. Skolnick (1966) found that teenage girls who were quiet, submissive, and unassertive were most likely to develop strong affiliative motivation as adults. Two studies showed that fantasy *n* Affiliation is associated with greater social anxiety (Byrne, 1961; Mussen & Jones, 1957). Furthermore, in a longitudinal study of the early parenting origins of motives, McClelland et al. (1989, and chapter 3, this volume) reported that the single best predictor of adult levels of *n* Affiliation was early rejection by one's mother as reflected in the mothers' reports that they did not go to their children when they cried at night. Together, these findings suggest that the fantasy measure of *n* Affiliation should be conceptualized as an index of affiliative anxiety and concern about rejection.

Assuming that *n* Affiliation is really measuring affiliative anxiety allows one to makes sense of some otherwise incongruous findings. For example, Mason and Blankenship (1987) reported that college women with high *n* Affiliation who possess low self-control and who have experienced a great deal of life stress were more likely than other women to report having physically or psychologically abused their boyfriends. These authors speculated that women with high *n* Affiliation (read fear of rejection) resort to these violent methods in a desperate attempt to keep their relationships with their partners intact.

It is important to note that McAdams (1980, chapter 15, this volume) employed more positive arousal conditions (e.g., a warm, convivial party) to derive a fantasy measure of the need for intimacy, which he defined as "a recurrent preference or readiness for experiences of warm, close and communicative interactions with others." The intimacy scoring system (see chapter 16, this volume) focuses more directly on the quality of relationships rather than on the active striving to attain them. Intimacy motivation correlates only .32 with *n* Affiliation scores (McAdams & Powers, 1981) and appears to do a much better job of predicting indexes of relationship quality (McAdams, 1988).

SUMMARY

Affiliative motivation is defined as a concern over establishing, maintaining, or restoring positive relations with others. The fantasy measure of *n* Affiliation possesses excellent interrater agreement, very good test–retest stability, and a moderate degree of predictive validity. Affiliative motivation has been related to the amount of time spent interacting with others, with possessing a sympathetic and accommodating interpersonal style, and with performing well in achievement settings that offer affiliative incentives. Because affiliative motivation has been associated with social anxiety and lack of popularity among peers, it was suggested that it is best conceived as a measure of affiliative anxiety or fear of rejection. Future researchers interested in employing the fantasy measure of n Affiliation should consider simultaneously assessing intimacy motivation (see chapters 15 and 16), which appears to capture the positive, "approach" aspect of affiliative motivation.

14 A scoring manual for the affiliation motive

ROGER W. HEYNS, JOSEPH VEROFF,
AND JOHN W. ATKINSON

What follows is a revision of the scoring procedures developed by Shipley and Veroff (1952) for *n* Affiliation. These revisions are based on analysis of additional data obtained under very similar experimental conditions with different pictures and reanalysis of their data (Atkinson, Heyns, & Veroff, 1954). The definitions which follow *include* and extend those developed by Shipley and Veroff and purport to be a more general statement of what is meant by *n* Affiliation or motivation to be socially accepted. This revision, however, is probably not final. Future refinements are anticipated if the experience with the achievement motive is taken as an example. Therefore, this measure of the affiliation motive should be considered more as a research tool than as a formal test.

DEFINITION OF AFFILIATION IMAGERY (AFF IM)

The single most important decision the scorer of a particular imaginative story has to make is the one which enables him to identify a particular sequence of imaginative behavior as affiliation related. Said another way, the scorer must first decide whether or not there is any imagery in an imaginative story which would allow the inference that the person writing the story was at all motivated to affiliate. Minimal evidence of the motive, then, is what is meant by Affiliation Imagery.

Affiliation Imagery (Aff Im) is scored when the story contains some

This chapter was originally published as chapter 13 of Atkinson, J. W. (Ed.). (1958). *Motives in fantasy, action and society* (pp. 205–218). Princeton, NJ: Van Nostrand. It is reprinted here by permission (copyright by J. W. Atkinson).

Notes, added in 1958 by J. W. Atkinson, are amplifications and revisions of the text based on seminar discussions of difficult scoring decisions. The introductory passage of the scoring manual for the achievement motive (see chapter 10, this volume) serves to introduce the general meaning of the categories for *n* Affiliation as well.

211

evidence of concern in one or more of the characters over *establishing, maintaining, or restoring a positive affective relationship with another person. This relationship is most adequately described by the word friendship.* The minimum basis for scoring would be that the relationship of one of the characters in the story to someone else is that of friendship.

Certain interpersonal relationships, in and of themselves, do not meet this criterion. For example, father–son, mother–son, brothers, lovers, etc., are all descriptive of a relationship between two people, but they do not necessarily imply that the relationship has the warm, companionate quality implied in our definition of affiliation. These must be further characterized by concern about maintaining or restoring a positive relationship.[1] Sex, achievement, dominance, or other motives might better describe the nature of the relationship in cases of this sort when there is no explicit statement of the precise nature of the relationship.

Affiliative concern is also readily inferred from some statement of how one person *feels* about another or their relationship. Some statement of *liking*, or the *desire to be liked* or *accepted* or *forgiven* reveals the nature of the relationship.

The affiliative concern of one of the characters may be apparent in his *reaction to a separation or some disruption of an interpersonal relationship.* Feeling bad (negative affect) following a separation or disruption implies concern with maintaining or restoring the broken relationship. For example, sorrow in parting, shame or grief over some action that has led to a separation, or similar instances imply the desire to restore the affiliative relationship of the past.[2] But we must bear in mind that a sheer factual description of a disrupted interpersonal relationship is no guarantee that either member of the relationship wants it restored. Families are broken up, sons and fathers argue and part, lovers quarrel – these and many similar instances occur frequently with no evidence that there is a desire for restoration of the relationship or forgiveness. Such instances do not allow the inference of affiliative concern and are hence *not scored* as Affiliation Imagery.

When there is no statement in the story of a friendship relationship, nor an indication of feeling or wanting, there is a third kind of story content which permits the scoring of imagery. We infer the existence of affiliative feelings from generally accepted affiliative, companionate activities such as parties, reunions, visits, relaxed small talk as in a bull session.[3] In addition, friendly, nurturant acts such as consoling, helping, being concerned about the happiness or well-being of another are regarded as evidence of affiliative feelings provided they are not culturally prescribed by the relationship between the persons. Thus, for example, protecting the child on the part of the father to the son would not necessarily be indicative of affiliation, while the same sort of behavior between nonrelatives would be. There must, in these ambiguous instances, be evidence that the nurturant activity is not motivated by a sense of obligation.[4]

Also *not scored* are those instances in which the characters are engaged in what might normally be viewed as a companionate activity such as a fraternity reunion, but the affiliative nature of the situation is counter-indicated by elaborations of the story which *deny* the affiliative concerns of the characters, i.e., the whole story is about a business meeting, a debate in which tempers fly in an effort to maintain dominance, etc.

Excluded from our definition of Affiliation Imagery are descriptions of normally close interpersonal relationships which are not always characterized by companionship, mutual interest, and sympathetic understanding. In such cases when there is no additional support for the assumption that the relationship is an affiliative one, Affiliation Imagery is not scored. Heterosexual relationships are usually the most ambiguous on this score. *Dating behavior* may or may not imply affiliation. There must be evidence of the sort outlined above before it is scored Affiliation Imagery. Some dating stories which seem to involve concern over disruption are not scored if the relationship is not clearly established as an affiliative one. Concern over marriage, however, is a heterosexual relationship that normally implies more than sex and hence *is* scored Affiliation Imagery unless elaborated in such a way as to make it certain that there are not any affiliative concerns in this relationship.[5]

To summarize, Affiliation Imagery is scored when the relationship between two or more individuals is friendly. If the nature of the relationship is not spelled out this clearly for us by the author of the story, we must infer affiliative concerns by examining the way one or more of the characters[6] feel about the other or the relationship between them. Often the concern for affiliation is evident in a character's reaction to separation or disruption of a relationship. If there is no clear evidence of affiliative concern in statements about how the characters feel, we must examine their actions to see whether or not their behavior in the particular situation implies the kinds of feeling from which we might infer concern over establishing, maintaining, or restoring a warm, companionate interpersonal relationship. Loving, nurturing, and friendly actions on the part of one character towards another imply a desire that similar actions be reciprocated.

We realize that some things are escaping us and that some fairly doubtful instances may be included, but experience has taught us that scoring reliability is only possible by sticking to the written definitions of the categories and not scoring what doesn't clearly fit. When there is *reasonable doubt* of the fit of a particular instance it should be scored Doubtful Imagery. Re-examination of these provides a basis for clarifying category definitions. If the story clearly qualifies, Affiliation Imagery is scored and *then* a further analysis of the behavioral sequence related to the Affiliation Imagery is undertaken. It may be that no other category will be scored. Most often, however, one or more of the subcategories defined below will also be present when imagery is scored. Stories that clearly do not meet the stated criteria are scored Unrelated Imagery (U Im) and not scored any further. Doubtful Imagery stories are also not scored any further.

Illustrations of Affiliation Imagery

1. Two college *buddies* who haven't seen each other in a long time. A chance meeting and they are *glad to see each other*. It is probably a class *reunion* or frat founders day. They were very *close friends* in college. They are probably reminiscing. They will have an evening *together* and make arrangements for *future meetings*.

(This story is saturated with a number of bases for scoring Aff Im.)[7]

2. A younger man is approaching a man older than himself for help or advice on a problem. The younger man is *worried about his lack of acceptance in the new social group* he just became acquainted with. The young man seeks restoration of his confidence. He knows his problem. A short conversation will ensue in which the older man will restore the young man's confidence in himself.

(Here is concern over separation from an affiliative object, in this case a group.)

3. The people involved are a baby and his brother. The older fellow is baby sitting. The parents have gone out for the evening. The older fellow is *thinking of how nice it would be down at the corner with the gang*. He seeks escape. He will spend a lonesome, uneventful evening with the baby, but perhaps witnessing and experiencing many uneasy moments caused by the baby's crying.

(Once more concern over separation from the affiliative object, the gang.)

4. The boys are just *getting up from a fraternity dinner table*. The one standing with the glasses is the pledge. They have eaten dinner and the pledges entertained the actives with their jokes, etc. The pledge is wondering what might happen next and is relieved that dinner is over. He *wants to* complete training and *become an active*. He will probably complete his training and become a good leader.

(Here we have an example of convivial, companionate activity, and also the desire to affiliate.)[8]

STATED NEED FOR AFFILIATION (N)

This category is scored when someone in the story desires to affiliate with some other person or a group of persons. The bare statement of a need is provided by expressions such as "he wants to," "he hopes . . . ," "he is determined . . . ," etc. To identify the motivational state as that of *n* Affiliation, what is wanted must fit the general criterion of Affiliation Imagery, i.e., establishment, maintenance, or restoration of an interpersonal relation characterized by warmth, mutual liking, and understanding. Wanting understanding implies wanting a positive affective reaction from another person.[9] Selected examples follow: he wants to be forgiven (for some action which interrupted a friendly relationship), he wants understanding, he wants to marry his girl, he doesn't want to lose her, he wants to see the visitors he expects, he wants people to accept him and want him around, he wishes there were someone to chum with, he *longs for* the old companionship, he wants *to join* a fraternity, his only desire is to blow off steam and sound off with a bunch of guys in a bull session, they want to hold the spring prom.

Prayer for maintaining or establishing an interpersonal relationship is scored Need. Also scored Need is a statement of unrequited love.

These examples share this characteristic: what is wanted is a relationship with others, or the kind of activity (bull session, junior prom) in which there can be a relationship with others that is described by the words *friendly* or *accepting*.

INSTRUMENTAL ACTIVITY (I+, I?, I−)

This category refers to overt acts or thoughts of a problem-solving nature by one or more of the characters in the story directed towards establishing, maintaining, or restoring an interpersonal relationship characterized by friendship, mutual interest, and sympathetic understanding. They are scored I+, I?, I−, depending upon the ultimate outcome of the activity. The three symbols correspond to successful, doubtful, and unsuccessful instrumental acts. The decision concerning the outcome of a particular instrumental act must be postponed until the final outcome of the story is known. Instrumental Activity is scored only once per story even though several separate instrumental acts may appear. The outcome scored will be the overall outcome of all the instrumental acts in the story.

There are a number of types of instrumental acts which can be enumerated. Such acts as giving advice or helping another are not sufficient to warrant scoring I. These particular acts must be accompanied by evidence of concern for the feelings of the person being advised or helped. Certainly they should not be scored when they could be construed as instrumental to some other goal than that of a positive relationship, e.g., dominance or meeting obligations.[10]

The most clear-cut type of affiliative instrumental act consists of *convivial, companionate activities*: they decided to play a game of poker, they were having their usual Saturday night party, they were shooting the bull between classes, they went for a walk together and enjoyed each other's company.

Another common type of affiliative instrumental act consists of *acts or thoughts directed towards restoring a broken relationship*: he went for advice concerning his inability to get along with people, he thought about how he would ask for forgiveness, he asked for forgiveness, after three long years he decided to return to his wife.

Positive nurturant actions on the part of one person towards another are also viewed as affiliative acts, e.g., he tried to cheer up his friend, he offered sympathy. The assumption made is that such actions have previously been instrumental in establishing and maintaining a positive relationship with other persons.

By convention, neither the initial statement of a story nor the final statement of outcome is scored as an instrumental act. This convention is dictated by the fact that the writer of the story is asked the questions: What is happening? and What will be done? The scorer should look for statements of activity independent of an initial statement of a situation and final statement of an event in the story. The statement must be of someone actually *doing* something.[11]

A statement of Instrumental Activity *in the past tense* is scored so long as it is more than a statement of the results of previous acts. For example, "they went together to the movies yesterday" would be scored, while "they had a good time at the movies yesterday" would not be scored Instrumental Activity.[12]

Sometimes the activity scored instrumental will seem almost to be goal activity. The scorer should keep in mind that *all* activity which contributes to bringing about certain positive affective feelings (the actual goal of any behavioral sequence) is scored Instrumental Activity. Thus, "they shook hands warmly" may seem to be the goal activity itself. We, however, view the *warm feelings* of affiliation as the goal of the whole sequence. The handshaking is instrumental action, i.e., it is directed towards the production of those warm affiliative feelings, the goal state.

ANTICIPATORY GOAL STATES (GA+, GA−)

This category is scored when someone in the story anticipates goal attainment or frustration and deprivation. The Anticipatory Goal State is scored Positive (Ga+) when *someone in the story* is thinking of the happiness accompanying an affiliative relationship or some affiliative activity or is thinking of the activity itself, e.g., he is thinking of how nice it would be to be with the gang, his thoughts are with his friends, he is dreaming of the fun he had last summer with his friends,[13] he is dreaming of the day he will be initiated into the club. Note the difference between this kind of thinking and the kind of problem-solving thinking that is scored instrumental activity. In the illustrations just given, the thoughts of the character are not directed towards bringing about the affiliative relationship. Rather they contain imagery associated with the attainment of the goal state itself.[14]

The Anticipatory Goal State is scored Negative (Ga−) when someone is thinking of the pain of separation or rejection or the fact of possible future separation or rejection itself. For example, he is thinking of how much he will miss his parents; he is worried about how his friends will react to his behavior; he wonders whether or not he will be liked at college.

Conventions and special discriminations

1. Doubtful or uncertain anticipations are scored negative.
2. Often, the author of the story does not tell us directly what one of the characters is thinking. He may, however, describe the state of the person objectively in such a way that we are justified in inferring the state of anticipation, e.g., he is waiting expectantly for his friends to arrive (Ga+), he is nervous and uncertain as he walks into the fraternity (Ga−).[15]
3. The anticipations must be intimately related to the affiliation behavioral sequence in order to be scored. Both Positive (Ga+) and Negative (Ga−) anticipations may appear. They may both be scored, but each type of anticipation is scored only once per story.

OBSTACLES OR BLOCKS – PERSONAL (BP) AND ENVIRONMENTAL (BW)[16]

Categories Bp and Bw are scored when goal-directed activity is hindered or blocked in some way. Things do not run smoothly for the person concerned with establishing, maintaining, or restoring an affiliative relationship. The obstacle may be some previous separation or interference with an interpersonal relationship that must be first overcome, or the obstacle may be some contemporary environmental or personal factor.

Actual physical separation is the most frequent Environmental Obstacle (Bw), e.g., someone is alone and wants companionship, someone dies. However, two persons who might have been expected to affiliate may be in close physical proximity but separated by some flare-up or disagreement. Unless the fault is clearly attributed to the character concerned with affiliation, as in the case of misbehavior leading to a disruption of a relationship, disagreements are scored Bw.

Most frequently, Personal Obstacles (Bp) take the form of past actions or present attributes of one character which disrupt a relationship or prevent a positive relationship, e.g., he is ashamed of what he did and wants his friend to forgive him, his own inability to get along with others reduces the chances of his being accepted in the club, he doesn't have the same interests (as the affiliative object).

What has been said before is worth repeating here: the mere occurrence of some disruption to a relationship is not sufficient evidence of an affiliative behavioral sequence. Before Obstacle can be scored, it must be ascertained that some character in the story is concerned with restoring the positive affiliative relationship.

Both types of obstacles may be scored but only once per story for each.

AFFECTIVE STATES – POSITIVE (G+) AND
NEGATIVE (G−)

Affective (emotional) States associated with attainment of affiliative relationships, affiliative activities, or their frustration are scored G. When
someone in the story experiences the joys and satisfactions of affiliation,
e.g., he is happy over being accepted into the club, or companionate activity, e.g., they enjoyed the poker game, the Affective State is scored
Positive (G+). When the pain of separation or rejection is experienced,
the Affective State is scored Negative (G−), e.g., he feels *lonely*, he is
depressed over his inability to make friends, he *feels bad* about what he did
that led to his friends' anger.[17]

It should be noted that the Affective States (G+ and G−) differ from the
anticipations (Ga+ and Ga−) in being linked to the immediate circumstance
of the character in the story. The anticipations (Ga+ and Ga−) are Affective
States having a future reference. One may feel miserable at the moment of
being lonely or rejected by his friends (G−) or may feel anxious over the
possibility in the future (Ga−). Similarly, one may enjoy the conversation
with friends (G+) or think how nice it would be to have some friends in for
conversation (Ga+).[18]

Both Positive and Negative Affective States may appear in the same
story. They are both scored, but *each* is scored only once per story as in the
case of the anticipatory states.

Often the author of the story doesn't tell us directly how the character
feels. If the objective description of his current circumstance is so complete
and vivid as in the case of *he is the best liked person in the club* or *he doesn't
have one friend in the world*, the inference of Affective State is allowed and
G+ or G− is scored. This type of inference is very rare and should not lead
to a confusion between Successful or Unsuccessful Instrumental Activity and
Affective State. A simple statement of the outcome of Instrumental Activity
is not sufficient evidence to warrant scoring Affective State.

AFFILIATION THEMA (TH)

Thema (Th) is scored when the behavioral sequence in question is the
central plot or *leitmotif* of the imaginative story and does not share the stage
with any other behavioral sequence. When the Affiliation Imagery is so
elaborated that the whole story (independent of the number of subcategories
scored) is about establishing, maintaining, or restoring an interpersonal
relationship characterized by friendship, mutual interest, and sympathetic
understanding, Thema is scored.

The assumption made in scoring Thema at all is this. The subject is asked
to write a four-minute story in response to a picture. If his thoughts are
saturated with imagery concerning one particular goal for a period of four

minutes, it is assumed that his motivation for that particular goal is sufficiently strong to prevent competing associations in his imaginative story for that period of time. The Thema category, then, is an estimate of motive strength based on the unidimensionality of the associations which make up the imaginative story. If there is a strong alternative behavioral sequence in the story, Affiliation Thema is not scored. The scorer should keep in mind that Thema may be scored even though no other subcategory is scored. Thema is not, in other words, dependent upon the presence of instrumental acts, anticipations, or the outcome of a story. Occasionally a story is written in such a way that only Imagery and Thema are scored. The scoring of Thema in such an instance reveals that the story was saturated with imagery about affiliation none of which was stated in the form required for scoring the various subcategories. Similarly, it often occurs that several subcategories are scored in stories *not scored* for Thema since there was in the story a competing behavioral sequence, i.e., evidence of other kinds of motivation imagery.[19]

NOTES

1 In other words, the bare statement of the existence of a mother–child or father–child relationship is not grounds for scoring Aff Im. In addition, if the mother or father or child is doing something *affiliative* that might be *expected only* because she is the mother (father or child), don't score unless further Aff Im is given.

The following are instances of stories concerning parent–child relations, and explanations of the imagery scoring in each case.

> The son who left home at 18 to make a place for himself – the son has just returned. It is the first time his mother has seen him in 20 years. He got in a fight with his father when 18 – his father wouldn't allow him to go to college; he wanted him to stay in the small town and work at the gas station. Mother thinks how long it's been since she last saw him. How he's aged and how it's too bad he wasn't at home for his father's funeral. Son wishes he hadn't come home. He no longer knows his mother; she's a stranger to him. Son will stay in small town for a few weeks. Then say he has urgent business. Big city – leave and again pound the streets in the B.C. looking for a job.

The above story is not scored for Aff Im. There is no clear-cut indication of warmth of feeling on the part of either mother or son.

> A boy has gotten into an argument with his mother. He wanted to get married and she didn't like the idea. He is thinking that she doesn't understand and she is thinking he is too young. He still wants his mother's approval. He will finally get his mother's permission and will marry the girl.

The above story is scored for Aff Im. The son wants his mother's approval, this implies a need for a positive response from another person, and thus is a basis for scoring Aff Im.

> The guy is feeling low. It is mother and son. The son told his mother something that he did which wasn't very ethical. The boy got into trouble and didn't know how to get out of it. He kept getting in deeper and finally

was in too deep not to do anything more about it. The boy is feeling sad and disheartened. He wants his mother to do something, forgive him if she would. The boy will lose his job and the mother will forgive him. He will start anew and never more get into trouble.

The above story is similar to the one just before it, the child wishes forgiveness in this case rather than approval. The basis for scoring Aff Im is the same in both cases; there is an expressed need for a positive response from another person. Similar situations would be a child seeking understanding from a parent, being ashamed of hurting his parent, etc.

2 In other words, any word that implies feeling bad about some action that has led to separation, such as shame, guilt, would be the basis for scoring Aff Im.

3 However, not all bull sessions involve relaxed small talk. Thus mere mention of a bull session is not sufficient ground for scoring Aff Im. Sharing experiences, conversation which is an end in itself, i.e., nonproblem-solving oriented talk, can be considered the goal of the affiliation motive. Thus its occurrence constitutes a basis for scoring Aff Im.

The following story is scored for Aff Im; the phrase bull session is here clearly being used to describe relaxed small talk.

A discussion is being held in our house by a bunch of brothers – a bull session – all are amused – some walk in, others walk out – but all do not disagree seriously. Nothing in particular – *just a desire to "blow off" steam and "sound off" with a bunch of guys we all get along with fairly well.* Hard to say – women, girls, alcoholic beverages, nothing desired – just shooting off all talking – mostly one at a time but occasionally all at once. Nothing – will gradually break off when we move on to our studies or the sack – no hard feelings some blowhards and liars but all in good feelings.

The next story, on the other hand, is not scored for Aff Im since the point of the conversation is to solve a problem, to reduce anxiety and uncertainty about a threat.

A bull session in a fraternity house is going on. The people are brothers. The war in Korea led up to this situation. They are thinking of what the future will hold. They want a chance to do something along their line of study. Someone may be stirred up enough to enlist for fear of not getting a good deal.

4 There must, in other words, be explicit evidence of an affiliative concern to augment what might be no more than the acting out of a culturally defined role.

5 Mere mention of the existence of a marriage relationship is not sufficient grounds for scoring Aff Im. There must be concern about getting married, being happily married, etc. before Aff Im is scored.

The following story is not scored for Aff Im; marriage is mentioned, but nobody expresses concern about it.

Father is talking to his son – son is going to college. Son is just ready to leave for his first year at college. His father is thinking how his son is grown up so quickly. He wants (the father) to assure himself that his son will make the new adjustment at college and continue making his father proud of him. He will give his son some advice about buckling down, working hard at school and continue making his father proud of him – However, the son left alone at school will begin drinking, going out with girls and *finally get married in his first year* – after first flunking out.

The next story, on the other hand, is scored for Aff Im since there is concern about marriage. They were planning for the marriage, and are now arguing over just when it should occur.

> Apparently a tense moment, or a moment of clash has occurred between the man and his girl. They seem to be arguing over something. The two have gone together for some time and are *planning to be married* – it is the first time there has ever been a radical difference of opinion between them. They each have different plans – *The man feels he should go into the service before they are married and the girl wants to marry now*. They will work out a happy solution; some sort of a compromise on taking the step after they know definitely what will happen to him in the service.

6 It is important to note that the basis for scoring Aff Im can be the wishes, feelings, actions of *any* character, one or more, in the story. We do *not* attempt to determine with whom the author of the story seems to have identified, and then score only for the motives of that character.

7 The following story has the minimum basis for scoring Aff Im, the relationship described is one of friendship.

> The fellows are having an argument. The one on the left seems to be angry with the one on the right. The one on the right has done something the one on the left didn't like. The one on the right is puzzled by the accusation. The boys will *still be friends* after the argument.

8 The following story illustrates an instance where the normally convivial, companionate fraternity situation is presented as an aggressive situation, and thus Aff Im is not scored.

> An active is raising the devil with a pledge. These are two fraternity men as indicated above. The pledge has probably done something that irked the active. The active is thinking of doing something "dirty" for the pledge, i.e. the pledge is in for the devil. The pledge is very defiant. The pledge will probably get a bad opinion of the active from this incident and will probably have hostile feelings against him forever throughout activeship.

9 Wanting to nurture someone implies wanting to induce positive reactions and a warm relationship. The following story is scored for N.

> A grandchild is giving his grandmother a present for her 85 birthday. She is obviously pleased and surprised. When he was younger his grandmother always made cookies etc. He liked her and they became quite close. *So on her birthday he wants to give her something.* The grandmother is feeling very proud of her grandchild because of his thoughtfulness. *The grandchild is hoping she likes the gift.* She will accept the gift, thank and kiss him for it, and probably give him some of the cookies that he always liked.

10 Seeking help or advice is not scored *I* unless the help or advice sought concerns an affiliative problem. The following story is scored *I* since the help the boy seeks concerns his acceptance in the new social group.

> *A younger man is approaching a man older than himself for help or advice on a problem. The younger man is worried about his lack of acceptance in the new social group he has just become acquainted into.* The young man seeks a restoration of his confidence. He knows his problem. A short conversation will ensue in which the older man will restore the young man's confidence in himself.

The next story is not scored for *I* since it is not clear whether or not the problem the pledge wants help with is an affiliative one.

> Two people are having a serious conversation with each other. They are fraternity brothers and are probably talking about something very close to themselves or their house. A problem has developed or *perhaps one needs advice*. Maybe a pledge is talking to his big brother. *The pledge is thinking that in his big brother he can find understanding and worthwhile advice. The younger fellow wants to be put straight and make himself a better fellow and thus wants his big brother to help him in this*. The pledge will be enlightened and will proceed to develop into a worthwhile individual.

11 Instrumental Activity appearing in the initial clause of the first sentence which is sheer description of the picture is not scored, e.g., "Here are two men talking." Nor is Instrumental Activity inferred from the final clause of the last sentence which states the outcome, e.g., ". . . and he gets the girl."

However, a clear-cut statement of an instrumental act appearing either later in the first sentence or earlier in the last sentence may be scored. Just avoid scoring *I* when it is sheer initial statement of the situation or final statement of outcome of the story. This does not mean to avoid the first and last sentence *in toto*.

12 A statement of Instrumental Activity in the future tense is scored providing it is not a mere statement of outcome. The following story is scored Aff Im on the basis of the boy wanting forgiveness, and feeling guilty. The italicized statement concerns activity in the future that will avoid disruption to the affiliative relationship, or so it is hoped. Since the effect of this action is not clear, that is, we do not know if the caution will avoid disruption, I? is scored.

> It seems a father is telling his son what to do and what not to do. The boy appears to be guilty of doing something undesirable and is being reprimanded in a man-to-man talk. Apparently the boy did something that did not comply with the desire of the father. The son feels guilty and wants forgiveness by his father. *The son will be more cautious next time*. Probably no further punishment will be inflicted on the boy at this time.

13 Recollecting a past goal state or goal activity is also scored Ga+ since we do not have a past-oriented category for thought processes (at present).

> A college boy is home for spring vacation. He is standing in the doorway of a not now used summer cottage. The previous summer this boy met, dated, and fell in love with a girl whose parents were staying at this cottage near his home town. The girl is now far away in Hawaii and the boy is seeking to recapture the previous summer. *The boy dreams of last summer and longs for those happy days*. Does the girl still love him or does she think it a summer romance? He wishes he knew for sure. She writes that she does but it's been so long and she's young and pretty and so far away. The boy will turn, lock the door and leave. He will feel better somehow but the unanswered question will remain until she comes home.

14 When a person is thinking or planning or wondering *how* to attain the goal, *I* is scored. When he is dreaming or pondering about the completion of his Instrumental Activity, i.e., whenever he has a mental picture of the circumstances which define the attainment of the goal, score Ga.

15 Anticipations of success of a nurturant act would be scored Ga+.

> The persons in the picture appear to me to be older brother talking to his younger brother about an interesting experience. The older brother had, perhaps, been a star athlete and hence is relating an exciting anecdote. *The*

older brother feels that maybe his relating this experience will liven the younger boy's spirit because the latter is entering an important event or contest. The younger brother will give his all to follow in his brother's footsteps, whom his expression shows signs of idolization.

16 Bp stands for Block within the person, Bw for Block in the external world.

17 Any affective word associated with activity, i.e., they will work out a *happy* solution; attainment or nonattainment of a goal, i.e., he feels *happy*, will be scored G+ or G− unless it is scored Ga+ or Ga−.

18 While one may in general say that G+ and G− are linked to the immediate circumstances of the characters in the story, and that Ga+ and Ga− have future reference, a description by the author of the story of how a character will feel in the future, or has felt in the past, would be scored G, not Ga. Ga is scored when there is an anticipation by one of the characters of how he expects to feel.

The following story is scored G+. The author describes the affective outcome of a future I, a walk.

> A fellow is looking out the door, at leisure. He is a young fellow. It is spring, and he is wanting to go out in the open. He is waiting for his girl. He is thinking of going for a walk with her. He is waiting for her to come, so they can leave, but is in no hurry. His posture would indicate relaxation and expectancy to going out. *They will go for a walk and enjoy each other's company.* They like being together.

The next story is also scored G+. The author is describing the feeling of one of the characters in the past.

> The boy is the son of a deceased person probably father. He is thinking alone at the door. *The boy has had a very happy family life* and the death is a great shock. He is thinking of his childhood and also wondering of the future. He will go on in his father's business and try to make good.

19 The n Affiliation score is obtained for each story by counting +1 for each of the following categories: Affiliation Imagery (Aff Im), Need (N), Successful Instrumental Activity (I+), Positive Anticipatory Goal State (Ga+), Positive Affective State (G+), Environmental Obstacle (Bw), and Thema (Th). The maximum possible score in one story is +7. Both Doubtful and Unrelated Imagery are here scored 0. However, it is advisable to note all of the categories described even though in light of current evidence (See Atkinson, Heyns, & Veroff, 1954) not all of the categories should enter into the determination of the n Affiliation score. The question of whether to score and count all the categories, as in the case of n Achievement, or only those which indicate positive (approach) interest has yet to be answered definitively.

15 *The intimacy motive*

DAN P. McADAMS

The intimacy motive is a recurrent preference or readiness for experiences of warm, close, and communicative interaction with other persons. As one of a handful of basic human needs or general desires, the intimacy motive serves to energize, direct, and select behavior in certain situations. The motive is conceived as a relatively stable individual-difference variable in personality readily assessed via content analysis of imaginative narrative productions, such as stories told or written in response to the pictures of the Thematic Apperception Test (TAT).

At the center of intimate experience is the sharing of one's thoughts, feelings, and inner life with other human beings (McAdams, 1989). This quality of relating to others is described by Buber (1970) as the "I–Thou" experience, by Maslow (1968) in terms of "being-love," by Bakan (1966) as the "communal" mode of human existence, and by Sullivan (1953) as the "need for interpersonal intimacy." These authors emphasize that intimate experience involves joy and mutual delight in the presence of another, reciprocal and noninstrumental communication, openness and receptivity, perceived harmony or union, a concern for the well-being of the other, and a surrender of manipulative control and the desire to master in relating to the other. The person who is dispositionally "high" in intimacy motivation tends to be more sensitive and aware of opportunities for intimate sharing in everyday life than is the person relatively "low" in intimacy motivation. Individual differences, of course, are a matter of relative degree, in that virtually all people desire intimacy at one time or another in their lives. The person high in intimacy motivation, however, manifests a stronger and more pervasive desire over time, evident in characteristic thoughts, behaviors, and interpersonal experiences.

The thematic scoring system for assessing intimacy motivation in imaginative stories was developed in the late 1970s in the wake of dissatisfaction among some researchers (e.g., Boyatzis, 1973; McAdams, 1980) with the thematic apperceptive scoring system used to assess the need for affiliation (*n* Affiliation). The original intent was to design a new affiliation scoring

224

system that would emphasize the positive, hopeful aspects of human affiliation, eschewing the "fear of rejection" theme identified by some researchers as especially characteristic of *n* Affiliation (see chapter 13).

However, as intimacy research unfolded it became clear that the new evolving construct was different enough from *n* Affiliation to warrant a new name and theoretical retinue. The term *intimacy motive* was coined to emphasize the new construct's emphasis on the intensive, sharing quality of interpersonal experience described by Buber, Bakan, Maslow, and Sullivan. This emphasis differentiates it from the older *n* Affiliation system. Empirically, the two scoring systems tend to be positively correlated (+.25 to +.55).

Following the procedures designed by McClelland and his colleagues (Atkinson, 1958a; McClelland, Atkinson, Clark, & Lowell, 1953) for the derivation and validation of a thematic coding system to assess human motives, McAdams (1980) developed the scoring system for the intimacy motive through four arousal studies employing approximately 250 subjects. In each, college students and other young adults were administered the thematic apperceptive measure under relatively "intimate" conditions – during periods of warm, close, and communicative interaction with others – and the stories they produced were compared with those written by subjects under neutral conditions. In the first arousal study, college fraternity and sorority initiates wrote imaginative stories immediately after they were inducted into their organizations during friendly, joyful celebrations. In the second, college students attending a large dancing party volunteered to write imaginative stories. In the third, dating couples who scored extremely high on a self-report "in-love" scale were administered the storytelling measure. Stories written in these three arousal studies were compared with those written by students under neutral classroom conditions. In the fourth study, young adults wrote stories before (neutral condition) and after (arousal condition) an intensive series of games and discussions designed to promote intimacy and good cheer.

A small subsample of arousal and neutral stories were analyzed to derive thematic categories that consistently differentiated between the two conditions. The categories were then cross-validated through blind scoring of the remaining protocols. As a result, a 10-category scoring system for the intimacy motive was derived and cross-validated (see chapter 16). Each of the categories refers to the quality of interpersonal experience manifested by the characters in the thematic apperceptive story. The scorer determines whether each of the 10 categories is present in a given story. If a theme is present, the story gets a point, up to a maximum of 10 points per story, 1 for each of the 10 scoring categories. The broadest categories are "Relationship Produces Positive Affect" (+A) and "Dialogue" (Dlg). These two are called "prime tests" for intimacy imagery in that the presence of at least one of these two themes is a prerequisite for the scoring of the remaining eight themes in a given story. If the story manifests no +A and no Dlg, then it automatically receives a score of 0. A subject's intimacy motive score is the total across the number of stories written.

Scoring reliability for the intimacy motive system is very high, averaging +.90 for scorers who are trained with the scoring manual. Estimates of test–retest reliability are modest, though relatively high for thematic apperceptive measures. Lundy (1985) obtained a test–retest correlation of +.48 for intimacy scores from thematic apperceptive measures administered to high school students 1 year apart. Atkinson (1981; see also chapter 2, this volume) provides a thoughtful discussion of the problems of applying standard psychometric criteria for self-report tests, such as indexes of internal consistency and test–retest reliability, to thematic measures.

A growing body of published research supports the construct validity of the intimacy motive and its thematic coding system for the imaginative stories. Initial evidence for construct validity came from peer ratings. In two studies, subjects high in intimacy motivation were rated by their friends and acquaintances as significantly more "sincere," "loving," and "natural" and consistently less "dominant" compared with subjects low in intimacy motivation (McAdams, 1980; McAdams & Powers, 1981). Fourth- and sixth-graders scoring high in intimacy motivation, assessed via a simplified scoring system designed for this age group, were rated by their teachers as significantly more "friendly," "affectionate," "sincere," "cooperative," and "popular" than were students low in intimacy motivation (McAdams & Losoff, 1984). High-intimacy grade school students were rarely nominated by their classmates as a "disliked kid." In a study of nonverbal indexes of intimacy, subjects high in intimacy motivation showed more eye contact, smiling, and laughter in friendly one-on-one conversations than did subjects low in intimacy motivation (McAdams, Jackson, & Kirshnit, 1984). Asked to put on imaginative skits in a psychodrama group, subjects high in intimacy motivation worked to involve all group members in spontaneous and convivial exchange (McAdams & Powers, 1981). Compared with those low in intimacy motivation, high-intimacy subjects issued fewer commands, made more references to "we" and "us" as opposed to "I" and "me," positioned themselves in closer physical proximity to other group members, and allowed other group members to create their own scripts within the psychodrama rather than dictating exactly what everybody else should say and do.

Intimacy motivation has been associated with the quality of interpersonal interaction in everyday life. Employing the experience sampling or "beeper" methodology, McAdams and Constantian (1983) asked college volunteers to wear beepers for a week, during which time they were beeped seven times a day. After each beep, the subject completed an answer sheet recording what he or she was thinking, doing, and experiencing at the time of the beep. Over the course of the week, subjects high in intimacy motivation showed a much larger percentage of interpersonal thoughts (thoughts about other people and about relationships with people), a greater number of conversations, and a greater level of positive affect when in the presence of other people compared with subjects low in intimacy motivation. Zeroing in on particular daily experiences of friendship, McAdams, Healy, and Krause, (1984) asked college students to describe in detail 10 "friendship episodes" that occurred in their lives during the preceding 2 weeks. Intimacy motivation was positively associated with dyadic (as opposed to large-group) interactions, with greater levels of self-disclosure in conversations with friends, and with greater levels of listening. In describing the best friendship they ever experienced, students high in intimacy motivation said that they became very close to another person through episodes of self-disclosure or sharing one's innermost thoughts and feelings and that best friendships were terminated or strained by betrayals of trust, as when one friend disclosed the other's secrets to another (McAdams, 1984a).

A number of personality theorists suggest that the capacity for intimacy is a sine qua non of healthy human functioning in adulthood and should, therefore, be a predictor of psychological health and happiness. Although the intimacy motive assesses a "preference" rather than a "capacity" per se, it nonetheless appears to be associated with certain indexes of adaptive functioning. Zeldow, Daugherty, and McAdams (1988) found intimacy motivation to be positively correlated with a measure of the ability to experience pleasure ("hedonic capacity") in a sample of medical students. McAdams and Vaillant (1982) rescored thematic apperceptive stories written in 1950–1952, when male Harvard graduates were in their early 30s, for intimacy motivation and correlated those scores with indexes of psychosocial adjustment determined 17 years later, when the subjects were in their late 40s. Intimacy motivation predicted general psychosocial adjustment at impressive levels in this longitudinal study; in particular, intimacy was strongly associated with later job satisfaction and marital happiness.

McAdams and Bryant (1987) obtained nationwide thematic apperceptive data from the University of Michigan Survey Research Center collected in 1976 (see Veroff, Douvan, & Kulka, 1981). In a sample of more than 1,200 American adults, intimacy motivation was positively associated with certain indexes of subjective well-being. For women, intimacy motivation was positively correlated with self-reports of happiness and satisfaction with life roles. For men, intimacy motivation was related to low levels of strain (anxiety, drug and alcohol abuse, psychosomatic complaints) and less uncertainty in life. The results suggest that high levels of intimacy motivation are associated with happiness in women and with security in men. McAdams (1989) has suggested that intimacy tends to bring different psychological benefits for the sexes, providing men with "secure bases" for self-exploration and development and providing women with a greater sense of identity and the meaningfulness of the self.

In the area of sex differences, a recent reanalysis of thematic apperceptive stories written by over 1,500 subjects, mostly college students, shows that women score significantly higher on intimacy motivation than do men (McAdams, Lester, Brand, McNamara, & Lensky, 1988). The difference is relatively strong and consistent, revealing itself across various pictures employed in thematic apperceptive research. However, contrary to some claims (e.g., Pollack & Gilligan, 1982), men's lower intimacy motivation is not rooted in a higher "fear of intimacy" among men. Analysis of thousands of imaginative stories from different samples does not show greater levels of fear and violence themes in interpersonal stories written by men. Instead, men simply tend to write imaginative stories with fewer themes of intimacy than do women, which is in keeping with numerous theoretical and empirical suggestions in the recent psychological literature concerning differences between the sexes. The edge for females also shows up in thematic apperceptive stories written by fourth- and sixth-graders in McAdams and Losoff (1982).

Recent research has examined the way in which intimacy motivation, as well as other social motives such as the need for power (D. G. Winter, 1973), plays itself out in the person's own narrative rendering of his or her life. McAdams (1985b, 1990; McAdams, Ruetzel, & Foley, 1986) has proposed a life story model of adult identity in which social motives concerning human agency (e.g., power) and communion (e.g., intimacy) are viewed as prime determinants and reflections of the central "thematic lines" in a person's self-defining life story. People high in intimacy motivation tend to view significant events from their storied autobiographical past in intimacy terms (McAdams, 1982a), tend to construe the main characters in their current life stories as heroes and heroines of intimacy (McAdams, 1985a), and tend to see the script for the next "chapters" in their life stories as centering around close, warm, and communicative relationships with others. The intimacy motive, therefore, is reflected not only in one's daily thought and public behavior but in the internal self-defining myth by which people provide their lives with unity and purpose.

16   *The intimacy motivation scoring system*

DAN P. McADAMS

The scoring system for the intimacy motive is comprised of 10 thematic categories, 2 of which are labeled "Prime Tests" and 8 of which are sub-categories. The task of the scorer is first to determine the presence (+1) or absence (0) of Prime Tests 1 and 2 (+A and Dlg) in the story. If either or both of the Prime Tests are present, then the scorer should proceed through the remaining 8 subcategories, systematically detecting for each category its presence (+1) or absence (0) in the story. If neither Prime Test 1 nor Prime Test 2 is present, then all scoring of that story is terminated, and the story receives a score of 0. Each of the 10 categories receives either 1 point or 0. It is possible for the same phrase or sentence to be scored for the presence of more than 1 category. Each category can be scored only once per story. The total score for each story is simply the sum of the points for the 10 categories. Hence, the maximum score possible for each story is 10; minimum is 0.

PRIME TEST I: RELATIONSHIP PRODUCES POSITIVE
AFFECT $(+A)$

A relationship is defined as any meeting or encounter between (among) two or more human characters in the story in which there is interaction. The interaction may be anything from two people talking with each other, to a group of people dancing together at a party, to one person thinking about another person. All people mentioned by the writer of the story are considered "characters," regardless of whether they are present in the stimulus picture, and any situation in which the characters relate to each other in even the vaguest ways constitutes a relationship or interpersonal

This scoring manual was originally published as McAdams, D. P. (1984b). Scoring manual for the intimacy motive. *Psychological Documents*, No. 2613. (Abstracted in Vol. 14(1), 7.) The document may be ordered from Select Press, P. O. Box 9838, San Rafael, CA. 94912. A modified version of the original is printed here by permission of the author and Select Press.

encounter. For instance, "John remembers the afternoons he spent with his family" constitutes a relationship in the story even though John is only "remembering" them. On the other hand, "Two people sit on a bench; they are in separate worlds and do not notice each other" does *not* constitute a relationship, unless of course the two begin to interact in subsequent sentences of the story. Throughout this chapter, the terms *relationship* and *interpersonal encounter* will be used interchangeably.

In order to be scored (+1) for Prime Test 1, a story must manifest explicit evidence that the relationship, as previously defined, *precipitates, facilitates, or is decidedly connected with a positive affective experience on the part of at least one of the characters* in the story. In other words, positive affect is engendered because of the interpersonal encounter. There are five categories of phenomena that qualify as positive affect:

1. Feelings of *love* (romantic, platonic, or otherwise), warmth, closeness, affection, caring, trust, tenderness, sympathy, fondness, and so forth toward another (other) character(s) in the story.
2. Feelings of *friendship*, liking, camaraderie, brotherhood, fellowship, and so forth toward another (other) character(s) in the story, which includes using names to identify friendships as special bonds, such as *chums, buddies, pals, cronies, comrades, dear* (close, good) *friends*, and so forth (simply *friends*, however, does *not* qualify).
3. Feelings of *happiness*, joy, enjoyment, good cheer, excitement, merriment, delight, gladness, good spirits, hilarity, exuberance, rejoicing, glee, geniality, ecstasy, bliss, conviviality, mirth, and so forth experienced by at least one character in the story while engaged in an interpersonal encounter (generally an activity of some sort).
4. Feelings of *peace*, contentment, serenity, satisfaction, quietude, and so forth experienced by at least one character in the story while engaged in an interpersonal encounter.
5. *Tender behaviors* (always nonverbal behaviors – usually touching of some sort, or gestures) that generally denote positive affect in interpersonal contexts and that, in the context of the story, do in fact denote so – for example, smiling, caressing, laughing, kissing, holding hands, hugging, making love, and so forth.

There is also a sixth category of phenomena that qualifies as a special case of negative affect that connotes previous positive affect. Here, Prime Test 1 can also be scored for a character's feelings of *mourning* or *sadness* associated with the *separation* from or *loss* of another (other) person(s), the implication being that the interpersonal relationship must be associated with positive affect if its loss or suspension brings about sadness (e.g., grief, mourning, unhappiness, depression, melancholy). Only such feelings of sadness are scorable here, and then only in the context of interpersonal loss or separation. Hence, feelings of anger, frustration, irritation, disgust, anxiety, fear, and so forth do *not* qualify. A common manifestation of this special case that *is* scored for +A is found in stories in which one character "misses" another.

Generally, the relationship or interpersonal encounter must be seen by the writer of the story as an end in and of itself, rather than as an instrumental means in the service of some other end. In order to be scored (+1), the positive affect must stem from the interpersonal encounter itself, not from a goal to which the interpersonal encounter is a subservient means. Hence, characters must manifest positive affect because they are interacting with other people, not because the interaction is leading to some other goal state such as achievement, success, gaining prestige, building up influence, finishing a job, and so forth.

Examples of A+

the two *lovers* . . .

the *good friends* . . .

There is a true *affection* between the two, the feeling that exists between father and daughter.

Although it is raining outside and on the whole is a very dreary day, Nancy is still in a *good mood*. There is no particular reason for her *happiness*, just that things are going well for her with her job and with *her relationship* with the important people in her life.

She's acquired a certain *compassion* for him and wants to get to know him better.

They're just sitting there *enjoying being together*.

Each one is *content* with the other.

The man *loves* his family.

She is a *loving* wife.

As they were sitting there, they began to *feel better about their relationship*.

It was a very *jovial* seduction.

She is reminiscing about the *fun* they had *together* in Italy.

This is a *pleasant* Sunday picnic for the two people.

They greeted each other *warmly*.

They need to be alone, to talk about intimate matters, and to display physically their *caring*.

They sat, *hand in hand*.

Jack *enjoyed* Sue's company, but she didn't like him. [The relationship need only produce positive affect in one of the characters.]

She is *sad*. It is hard to accept the *loss* of a silent friend, one who will never tell your secrets but listen to them all. [Special case for negative affect.]

The man is looking at a picture of his family. The *sad* face is because they were all killed in an automobile accident. [Special case for negative affect.]

The man is very *excited* because he will be getting out of work in a couple of minutes and should be home in half an hour or so. Then he will be *with his family*.

He is rather *melancholy* because he *doesn't see them* as often as he would like. [Special case for negative affect.]

The two sat happily on the grass near the lake . . . They have come alone for the weekend . . . They are getting to know each other well. [Note that it is not always possible to score for +A, or any other category, on the basis of a key phrase or sentence that can be taken out of context. In this example, "The two sat happily" cannot be scored for +A until the scorer determines from the context of the story *why* the two are happy. If it becomes clear that the happiness stems from the interpersonal interaction itself, then the story is scored for the presence of +A, as would be done in this case. But, it is conceivable, and in fact common, that "The two sat happily" because they both succeeded in attaining scholarships for college, or recently robbed a bank, or experienced any of a number of different goal states that go beyond the relationship per se. In these cases, +A would not be scored.]

They felt both love and hate for each other. [Negative affects do not cancel out positive ones, and hence this example should be scored for +A.]

Examples not scored for A+

He is wishing he could leave his troubles behind and spend a few days with his wife and kids. [No affect here. To be scored for +A, the positive affect must be explicitly stated by the writer. "Wishing," "wanting," and "desiring" are not enough.]

He is complimenting her on her good looks. [No affect.]

She enjoys taking walks. So does he. [No interpersonal encounter is mentioned.]

He is married to a very happy woman. [The connection between the relationship of marriage and the affect of happiness is not clearly made by the writer. If the passage read, "The marriage made her happy," then it would be scored for +A.]

They had a good time at the party. [The good time is not explicitly tied to a relationship.]

He says, "Elaine is everything I've ever wanted in a wife." [No affect.]

Three farmers are sitting around a fire, shooting the bull. [No affect.]

The separation from Paul made her frustrated and upset. [Not special case for negative affect because the affect is not sadness and only sadness.]

The relationship made her sad. [Not special case for negative affect because no mention is made of loss or separation.]

John felt good because the business meeting went well. [Positive affect is connected with instrumental activity rather than an interpersonal encounter.]

The client *admired* his therapist. [Feelings of admiration, awe, adoration, reverence, respect, shock, surprise, approval, appreciation, thankfulness, idolization, fascination, gratitude, and other terms connoting *praise* or *wonder* are *not* considered positive affect for this category.]

He was infatuated with her. [Feelings of infatuation, lust, strong desire, interpersonal attraction, and the like are *not* considered positive affect for this category.]

He wants to have a friendly relationship with her. [Merely desiring or wishing for positive affect in an interpersonal encounter is not the same as experiencing it. Only the latter is scored for +A.]

They may be in love, then again they may not be. [Uncertain or hypothetical situations like this are *not* scored for +A. This should be considered a general rule to be applied to other categories as well.]

PRIME TEST 2: DIALOGUE (DLG)

Dialogue is defined as a particular kind of verbal (including written) or nonverbal *exchange of information* between (among) characters in the story. In order to be scored for Dlg, a story must manifest exchange of information that is at least one of three acceptable types: reciprocal and noninstrumental communication, discussion of an interpersonal relationship, or communication for the purpose of helping another person in distress.

Reciprocal and noninstrumental communication

This is verbal or nonverbal exchange among (between) characters that exists in the context of the story *for its own sake*, that is, the communication does not serve the purpose of furthering a particular goal or implementing a particular task. Such "communication for communication's sake" implies rapport, reciprocity, give-and-take, listening, and exchange. It may include phenomena as diverse as chatting about the weather to sharing ideas on the problems of society. In cases in which the writer of the story is not very explicit concerning the reciprocity and noninstrumentality of the characters' dialogue, the scorer should follow these scoring rules:

1. First, determine whether some kind of verbal or nonverbal communication exists. Any references to conversation or sharing ideas automatically qualifies here.

2. Then, if the writer makes explicit reference to the instrumental nature of the exchange – communication specifically engaged in for an outside purpose (e.g., interviewing, a business meeting, a lecture, sermon, therapy, giving instructions, making plans, etc.) – do *not* score for Dlg.

3. Third, if the writer makes explicit reference to "problems in reciprocity or agreement" in the dialogue (e.g., failure to communicate, a heated argument, one person not listening to another, one person is bored, the talk becomes a monologue, etc.) do *not* score for Dlg.

4. If the story meets Rule 1 and is not eliminated by Rule 2 or 3, then it is considered reciprocal and noninstrumental communication, and it is scored for Dlg.

Note: In some stories, the dialogue may start out in a reciprocal manner and then subsequently deteriorate (e.g., a pleasant conversation turns into a heated argument). In other stories, the reverse may be true (from argument to mutual dialogue). In these cases, the scorer should evaluate and score only the quality of communication as it is presented at the *end* of the story.

Discussion of an interpersonal relationship

This is, in fact, instrumental dialogue, the purpose of which is to consider and work through a particular aspect of the characters' relationship with each other. No other purpose for the discussion can be scored for Dlg here. If the writer makes explicit reference to problems in this discussion (see Rule 3), then the story is not scored for Dlg.

Communication for the purpose of helping another

This, again, is instrumental dialogue. This time the purpose of the communication lies in one person's attempt to help another, especially when the other is in trouble, feels bad, or has suffered a setback of some kind. Again, if the writer makes explicit reference to problems in reciprocity of communication (see Rule 3), then the story is not scored for Dlg.

Examples of Dlg

They found a spot to sit and *talk*.

He struck up a *conversation* with her.

They greeted each other warmly and sat by the Charles [River] for a while *reminiscing* about old times.

The old farmers are *swapping stories*.

. . . shooting the bull.

. . . making small talk.

She *told* him about the fight with her mother. He *listened*.

They *confide* in each other regularly.

Ann smiles sweetly to *return* the mood involved. [Nonverbal.]

She shook her head. Roy understood completely.

This picture depicts two people who are sitting by a river discussing their relationship. [Discussion of an interpersonal relationship.]

They had a *friendly argument* about the Red Sox and the Yankees.

He can't communicate with her unless they are riding or walking through the mountains. Then, they feel communion.

The girl is sitting there looking lonely. A guy feeling sorry for her and wishing for some company himself asks her if he may join her. She sheepishly says yes, and he proceeds to talk to her and try to cheer her up. [Communication for the purpose of helping another.]

They will listen to her and comfort her.

They had been exchanging letters for two years now.

Examples not scored for Dlg

They all got along well.

They have just realized that they are both in love.

They got to know each other better.

Jack came finally to talk. He didn't understand her wants and couldn't respond in the way she wanted him to. [Rule 3.]

She's interviewing the man for a human interest story. [Rule 2.]

They both have a lot to talk about, but instead she insisted that they walk the fields she played as a child.

He's asking her what she wants to do in the evening and so they plan their evening activities. [Rule 2.]

He asks her for a date. [Rule 2.]

He is very interested in her and is trying to show his interest by bringing her to this spot. He is presently trying to find out about this girl.

He is telling her about his childhood. She is thinking about the water. [Rule 3.]

CATEGORY 3: PSYCHOLOGICAL GROWTH AND COPING (PSY)

A relationship (as defined under Prime Test 1) is demonstrably instrumental in facilitating, promoting, or affording psychological growth, self-fulfillment, adjustment, coping with problems, self-actualization, self-realization, identity formation, self-esteem, psychological health, self-knowledge, enlightenment, spiritual salvation, inspiration, creativity, maturity, or the like.

Examples of Psy

Bev is continually becoming better adjusted to everyday life and how to handle it because of Harry.

He feels that she has changed his life. He has finally come to realize that he loves mankind.

A warm relationship with another person can be very comforting when trouble comes up.

When he is with his wife, whom he loves very much, he will think of a new design and solve the crisis.

She has made me what I am.

She has learned a great deal about life from him.

After talking with him, she regained lost patience and contentment.

In times of need, they depend on each other.

They will continue to walk. She will listen and stop trying so hard to let go. She then finds that she is more able to take it all in. She understands herself and nature in a new light.

Their walk in the mountains *together* seems to have shed new light on the problem.

Examples not scored for Psy

She helped him prepare the documents for the crucial diplomacy in Oslo. [Helping at a task rather than facilitating growth or coping.]

The parents had raised two fine children. [Too vague.]

The great works of Plato had changed Jim drastically, planting in him the seeds of an intellectual life. [No relationship.]

He taught her much about the history of Mayan culture. [Not *self*-knowledge.]

CATEGORY 4: COMMITMENT OR CONCERN (CC)

A character in the story feels a sense of commitment to or concern for another (others) that is *not* rooted in guilt or reluctant and begrudging duty. *Commitment* includes feelings of loyalty to and responsibility for another. *Concern* generally indicates a felt responsibility for another's welfare, usually leading to some kind of *helping* or humanitarian behavior, and sometimes personal sacrifice.

Note: Some passages that are scored for Psy may also be scored for CC, especially those in which a character in the story purposely takes an initiative in helping another person cope with a problem.

Examples scored for both CC and Psy

He will help her get through this difficult time.

John tries to comfort Susan, and after a while she begins to feel that her problems are not as bad as she had thought.

Henry is a sociologist trying to help people overcome drug addiction. He virtually saved Jill's life.

Examples scored for Psy but not CC

All examples listed previously under Psy are in this group.

Examples scored for CC but not Psy

She is devoted to her husband. [Loyalty.]

He feels responsible for their well-being.

Bob has committed himself to the relationship. He cannot back out now.

He wants to give them [his family] his best.

Everything he is working for is for them [his family].

Although the accident was not his fault, Joe feels responsible for them.

He will stay with the job and be bored rather than inflict pain on his loved ones.

The youngest grandson has taken his ailing grandfather outside for a walk and some fresh air.

The old man left his fortune to the poor family in Harlem.

He was outraged by the injustice inherent in apartheid and sought to change the governmental policies to more equalitarian ones. [Concern for human welfare.]

Examples not scored for CC

He didn't want to help the girl, but he knew that if he did nothing, he would be in trouble. So he gave her his car.

If she would not have spent the time with the ailing man, she would have felt guilty. That's why she took responsibility.

She would be loyal to him, unless of course he left town.

CATEGORY 5: TIME–SPACE (TS)

Two or more characters in the story are engaged in a relationship that *transcends the usual limitations of time and/or space*. This includes any explicit references made to the *enduring* quality of a relationship over an extended period of time or in the face of physical separation. If the writer merely reports objectively the length of time two people have known each other, then that time period should be greater than 6 months if the story is to be scored for TS. Furthermore, the category includes overt themes of "timelessness," "time standing still," "the eternal moment," and so forth, when employed by the writer in the context of interpersonal relationships.

Examples of TS

They have a kind of rapport that spans time and generations.

These *old* friends . . .

The three men in the preceding picture get together every year to hunt deer and shoot the bull.

They part with plans to meet again. Each one is content with the other, not knowing what their future together will bring.

They have been going together for a while now – nearly a year.

We talked it over and decided that he should take the job even though it meant that they would be separated for a while. He thinks of them often.

They have been married for a long time.

This moment together seemed to last a lifetime.

It seemed as if it were only yesterday when Jim and Randy had gone swimming together at Eden Pond.

. . . lasting friendship.

They talk secretly of the *future* together.

They didn't always have to be together to feel the tie between them.

Examples not scored for TS

The client took forever to be convinced.

Sue and Larry had known each other for only a month.

Jim and Barb were married. [Unless the writer refers to a "long marriage" in some way, this is not scored for TS.]

CATEGORY 6: UNION (U)

The writer makes explicit reference to the physical or figurative *coming together* of people who have at one time or another *been apart*. The emphasis is on unity, reunion, togetherness, oneness, reconciliation, synthesis, or integration. This category includes the coming together of people who are generally not found together by virtue of their dissimilarity (e.g., Republicans and Democrats are reconciled). It also includes characters who have recently come together in marriage (e.g., newlyweds) or are planning to do so (those becoming engaged).

Examples of U

This is a father and daughter who have come together after a long time.

She will end up back home and proceed with a reconciliation with her parents.

The *young woman* is sitting alone crying. While she is sitting there, an *old farmer* comes up to her as he walks through the fields and quietly asks her if it could be that bad.

After years apart, she came back to Switzerland to be with her grandfather.

Then she recognized an old friend from high school that she hadn't seen in years. They greeted each other warmly and sat by the Charles River for hours catching up on lost time.

They decided to get married.

The Irishman and the Mexican had become one with each other.

They are putting their relationship back together.

These two individuals very different in class, color, and age have met each other while riding in the mountains.

Examples not scored for U

The family went to the beach to celebrate the special occasion.

They had a happy marriage.

He felt at one with nature.

They were partners in the law firm.

They had lived together for a long time.

CATEGORY 7: HARMONY (H)

Characters find that they are in harmony with one another. They are "on the same wavelength," their actions are in "synchrony," one "understands" the other, they find something "in common," they share similar views, and so forth.

Examples of H

They found they *had much in common.*

She looks at him once and he *understands*, feels better; and looks out at the river.

They looked into each other's eyes and realized that they had to leave. [Also scored for nonverbal Dlg.]

. . . trapeze artists in *synchrony*. Each knows the exact movements of the others.

The two people are discovering a problem that they both share.

Usually she does not listen to her father. He is saying the same thing again, but she sees why this time.

These students met in section and through subsequent study sessions they became aware that they both avidly participate in crew.

They find each other very interesting to listen to. Each makes the other want to say something.

The only thing that both of them want is to be alone.

They realize that what they both are searching for is happiness.

They share an emptiness.

Horses were a kind of universal language of friendship for her, and she and the old man quickly struck up an amicable conversation in which for the first time she seemed to understand the thick brogue.

Examples not scored for H

They are both from France.

They did everything together. Bill handled the social aspects of things and Mary the business end.

They had a good time at the dance.

CATEGORY 8: SURRENDER (SR)

A character finds that interpersonal relations are subject to control that is in some way beyond him or her. He or she *surrenders to this outside force* (e.g., luck, fate, chance, society, God's will, etc.) or, minimally, does not struggle against the outside control. The absence of personal control over the vicissitudes of interpersonal relations, however, is *not* experienced with any anxiety or consternation. Rather, the character(s) may "go with the flow" of interpersonal events, acquiescing to the forces that he or she cannot control. Examples include quirks of fate, the unleashing of uncontrollable emotions, and accidental or chance meetings of people. It is essential to remember that the absence or loss of control must occur in the context of a relationship (as defined under Prime Test 1) if the story is to be scored for Sr.

Examples of Sr

A young couple *find themselves* deeply in love.

They accidently met on the road to Crown Point.

These two people *happen to meet* on a bench next to a river.

They are *helplessly* in love.

The man is under a lot of pressure. He must get his work done but all that he can think about is his family. [No control over his thoughts about his family.]

Her father misses her. But he knows and understands that his baby is no longer a baby and that he is not the only man in her life. [Surrendering to the inevitable.]

He accidently glanced at the picture on his desk of his wife and kids, and he has to stop his work.

Erma is in love with a train conducter she met when the circus train broke down and she had to travel Amtrak from Philadelphia to Memphis. [Relationship established by chance happening.]

Examples not scored for Sr

He could not control the car. [Not interpersonal.]

The army surrendered.

He suddenly realized that he was boxed in by his job, his wife, his kids, and all his other responsibilities. [The loss of personal control cannot be experienced as being "trapped" if the story is to score for Sr.]

They will become good friends.

CATEGORY 9: ESCAPE TO INTIMACY (ESC)

Character(s) in the story actively or mentally escape from a particular situation or state to another situation or state that affords the experiencing of happiness, peace, liberation, fulfillment, meaning, and so forth in the context of interpersonal relations. Characters may escape together, as in the case of a family leaving the city to take a vacation in the mountains or a group of meditators entering an altered state of consciousness together in order to escape the strains of everyday life. Or a character may escape by himself or herself. In the latter case, the escape or its concomitant goal state or activity must refer in some way to an interpersonal relationship if the story is to be scored for Esc (e.g., a young man escapes to the forest to think about his relationship with his lover or a woman leaves home in order to repair her decaying relationship with her parents in a more objective setting).

Examples of Esc

The two people were tired of being cooped up in the apartment so they decided to take a walk on the beach.

She is taking a walk to think out her problems with her boyfriend.

He is taking a break from his busy day to think about them.

Her father wants her to remain chaste and pure. But she will run off with her lover and they will become gypsies.

The walk home from school is usually her only time to be with herself and think about what she wants. Presently she is thinking about her brother and sister.

They left the party and came to the deserted parking lot. They had been phonies like the rest of them. Here they could be themselves.

The couple has no privacy. They need to be alone to share thoughts. . . . out on the river they can talk freely for a few minutes.

Examples not scored for Esc

He left the office to get a bite to eat.

Barbara had to get away from all the people. Suddenly she fled the crowded train station into a deserted warehouse. Ah! Alone at last!

At five o'clock the men all left work and went home to their wives, girlfriends, or whatever.

He wished that he could escape this stifling environment and spend a day with his family, but unfortunately he was trapped.

CATEGORY 10: CONNECTION WITH THE OUTSIDE WORLD (COW)

The outside world is defined as any or all aspects of the nonhuman world that exists outside the human body. Examples include all aspects of nature, the cosmos, animals, man-made environments such as streets and skyscrapers, the weather, and God or otherworldly forces. In order to be scored for COW, the story must manifest explicit evidence of a *connection* between one of the characters and the outside world. The connection must be one of two kinds: (a) a direct *interaction* with the outside world in which that world exerts a demonstrable effect upon the character's behavior, thought, or feelings; (b) a metaphoric *parallel* with the outside world in which the character or a relationship between (among) characters is seen by the writer as mirroring or being analogous to the outside world.

Examples of COW

. . . communion with nature.

. . . feel for the environment.

Their love like the weather is warm and light.

The heat is oppressive to him.

They love the way the morning air feels and smells.

They both had a lot of work to do but of course as soon as they got to the river they *felt the spring air* and began to watch the people around them.

She hated these rainy days in November! The kind of day where the first glance out the window brought disillusionment; the second anger.

The cold had sapped Mary's strength.

She liked the speed of the horses, the fresh air, and the countryside.

But the cool night breezes blew in their faces and they began to slow down and take all things into consideration.

Examples not scored for COW

It is a mild day in the springtime. The sky is bright blue.

They spent the morning out at the beautiful lake in Switzerland.

The air is turning warmer.

She was picking flowers.

DATA COLLECTION AND PRACTICE MATERIALS

Chapter 37 provides helpful information on data collection, data analysis, and scorer training. The practice stories presented in the appendix to this chapter were specially chosen because they contain a large amount of intimacy imagery. By contrast, the common practice stories in appendix I to this volume contain much less intimacy imagery. Information on how to order additional practice materials is also given in appendix III. A set of pictures used by McAdams to elicit imagery for intimacy and power is reproduced in appendix II of this volume.

APPENDIX TO CHAPTER 16

The following stories have been reproduced from original thematic apperceptive protocols collected mostly from college students. All spelling and grammatical errors have been faithfully preserved. The first 15 stories were written in response to a picture of an older man and a younger woman walking through a field with horses and a dog. Stories 16 through 20 were written in response to a picture of a sea captain and another man conversing on a ship. The final 10 stories were written in response to a picture of two people sitting on a park bench near a river. (See pictures in appendix II.)

Instructions

First, read through the scoring categories very carefully, paying particular attention to the examples illustrating each scoring concept. This should be done a number of times, at least until rudimentary definitions of all the scoring categories can be recalled readily.

Then, begin scoring the stories *one category at a time*, starting with the first category and determining its presence or absence in each of the 30 stories. Check your results with the expert scoring after each story, noting the explanations and recording all errors. Then start over with the second category and repeat this procedure until all ten categories have been scored. Do not trust your own memory or impressions. Refer to the manual, previously scored stories, and your own notes and records of errors whenever necessary.

The stories

1. This is a typical Minnesota farm. Except for the fact that there appears to be hills – a rare find in Minnesota. It's later afternoon & all of the chores are done. What better way to spend an afternoon than going through the countryside on horseback. Even if Mn. is the only state that is in a continuous season of winter, it does have a few beautiful sights. They left a few hours ago – & are now about 15 miles from home. They've stopped to walk for a while & just talk about things. It's always good to be out in the open. Then people aren't so inhibited – they say what they feel. These people – husband & wife, maybe?, cherish the moments like these where they can just appreciate nature. The city people can have their busy life. As for themselves, they'll never leave the countryside or give up the freedom they have in it.

2. In high school everyone laughed. Liza was taller and skinnier than Scott. He was sort of dumpy, but everyone thought he was hillarious. Now, after 15 yrs. of marriage, facing their middleage yrs together is wonderful. They compliment each other well. They live a simple but adequate life. They ride horses on the weekends or sit around a fire at home in the evening together. Neither feels that the other is perfect, but each loves the other very much & they are happy. They have no kids, but Liza teaches Sunday school & Scott is a children's dentist.

3. Karen is home for the weekend from school to visit her family. She went out into the meadow early in the morning to feel the morning air, hear the birds' songs and watch the sunrise. While she sat, she heard her grandfather leading two of their horses back up to the barn. Karen takes the opportunity to share in the wisdom of her grandfather and his years, and revel in the close relationship they have that she's missed so much since being away. They talk until lunchtime.

4. Joey is retarded and has spent much of his life in institutions. It is not that he couldn't live at a home, but his family is rejected him completely. He would probably spend the rest of his life in institutions also if it weren't for some workers that have taken a liking to him. Mary has been the kindest. She has done a lot to show Joey the surrounding beauty in the small mountain town where they live. She has been seen him grow in ways which can't be tested in any intelligence test. Being in the outdoors has given him a new outlook on life, even if it is only a 4 yr. old outlook. He seems to realize that life is worth living and is more than just an artificial institution. Joey has become a person.

5. I can't believe it. This guy, this clown who I've known for years and years, he's really someone special. Riding in the country like this, just to be alone – how beautifully innocent. For once I feel respect and admiration from a true friend. Even if he is a butterball. It'll be refreshing to spend more time with him. Maybe another

week. I can't get the poor boy's hopes up too much. Now I just wish that dog would get off my heels.

6. These two women have just come in from a ride through the woods. The day is beautiful, the scenery magnificent and the horses well behaved. They appreciate the chance to do this once in a while. Now they are feeling very good about everything. There minds are off the concerns of the day. They have fully appreciated each others company. The ride has prepared them to go back to school. The break was fine but the weekend is over and they will return. The time away from the school environment has made them more relaxed and whole. Now the books are not so oppressive and tiring.

7. Marilyn has rented the horses for the afternoon, but hardly wants to take the reigns from the owner. He's concerned for their – the horses – safety, and proposes sending along his beagle pup – for what protective purpose who knows. She explains for the upteenth time exactly where they're going and just exactly when they'll return. Reluctantly he gives her the reigns, quietly admonishing the horses not to do whatever horses aren't supposed to do . . .

8. The two people are out for a ride-walk together. The old man is a good friend of the girl. In fact the old man watched the girl grow up and now that she is all grown up the old man loves her very much. The girl is also very fond of the man because they are like best friends. The girl is about to go away so they are spending a beautiful spring day together. They are talking and thinking about all the good times they had when they were young. Right now they are heading home and the old man is giving the girl some advice or telling her how much he has enjoyed growing up with her.

9. "Boots" was a long-time horse trainer and a friend of the family. Young Marcia is a senior in high-school and having problems with her parents. She has always been freer to talk with Boots than her parents, because she could show her weaknesses easier. Marcia has a simple life planned and a dynamite guy she already's been dating could very soon become a permanent part of that life – though her parents don't realize that they're that serious yet. Marcia's parents are expecting her to go to college – she's a fairly good student, but Marcia just wants to get married and live forever after happily. Boots is telling her how important it is to be reconciled with her parents and says that he'll support her in her case.

10. The boy and his companion are good friends. They both share a common bond in love for horses. They have been riding hard for a while and they have decided to stop, walk, and let the horses rest. I think the companion is a girl, can't see well enough to tell for sure. The girl is older but this doesn't matter because they have the common bond that strengthens their friendship.

11. Colorado. Their dream. They had finally gotten away from the kids and the jobs and the clubs, and all of the rest of civilization – and taken that second honeymoon that they wished for for so long. People always wondered at their marriage. They'd been married 22 years, and they loved each other more and more each day. It showed, too. They were proud of each other – They helped each other, they challenged the other's ideas, and they accepted the other's failures. Now they were here, away from it all, not to work out the kinks necessarily, but just to deepen that love, that commitment, that they felt for each other, away from all the stresses and strains, and pressures of the world. And they were doing it doing the things they loved best – horsebackriding in the wilderness.

12. Many years ago a young woman died and left a husband and a small baby girl. The death of that woman changed both their lives drastically. The girl was sent off to an orphanage where she lived until she was fifteen years old. The father withdrew from the world and spent the rest of his life far up in the mountains with only his

horses and dogs and wildlife for companions. The young girl spent 15 years after leaving the orphanage seeking to find her parents. Her travels eventually led to her meeting an old man who had not seen another human being in nearly thirty years.

13. "How are you, Grandpa?" It had been a long since we'd seen each other. Even in my tennis shoes, I now towered over him. It was so good to be outside with him on this perfect day, exercising the horses as we had done when I was a child. Now I was taller, but the most important things about grandpa had not changed. Certainly he had also aged, but his joyful spirit had not departed. Never have I found another person with such a zest for living. It seems as if he will live forever. I know this is not the case, yet he has inspired me to remain young at heart no matter my age or circumstances. We free the horses in the lot and return to the house. Grandma awaits us with dinner and casual conversation; I am content.

14. It was a fantastic day and Jennifer decided to take the horse out for a run. She couldn't get over the smells in the field and the patches of flowers and the intense blue sky. It felt great to be outside again. She was really peaceful. Another girl came riding up and started talking to Jennifer. Jennifer had never seen this girl before but was some how intrigued by her. They talked all afternoon but never talked about their past experiences, only their ideas. They never exchanged ideas.

15. A Lord and his new bride are taking a ride and walk across part of his land in England. They had a short courtship, and she's not English. Nor has she ever been to England. He wants to show her how beautiful it is and always makes comparisons between her beauty and nature. He is sincere. He feels he has found true love a second time. His first wife passed away & now he found happiness with a younger woman.

16. The man has come to the admiral to ask him how his day is going and just make some pleasant conversation. The admiral is surprised but grateful that the man would be willing to overstep the rank of officer and civilian role boundaries to be kind. The admiral walks away feeling better than before the encounter.

17. It used to be that a captain of a ship was a romantic, adventurous occupation. Braving the high seas, battling storms and on and on. Now, it is like any other job, save that there is no time clock to punch in and out on. Yet some captains manage to make the job more than that. That is what Cptn. Phil Blankety-blank makes of his job. He loves to cruise the decks, talking to his crew and passengers as if he were just another crew member. Many times he gives unexpected tours of the ship to astonished passengers. Phil enjoys surprising people.

18. The ship is ready to leave. The great moment anticipated has arrived. The captain comes to the passenger dock, looks around and sees a man familiar to him. He is an inspector who has found error in the captains ability to run a ship. The captain quickly approaches the man, does not give him time to reply, but instead, argue strongly that he leave.

19. "Hello, welcome aboard." The captain holds out the key to the guest room to the man boarding the ship. The captain seems to understand the man's need of relaxation and solitude. His eyes pierce the gruff exterior & size up the suffering, overwhelmed person inside. Together they board the ship, & the captain leaves the man on his own. Througout the journey, the captain is available whenever the passenger desires comradship, yet he allows the guest his solitude, & leaves the option of companionship up to the guest.

20. When the man came board the ship he's been just any ordinary passenger. But the captain had talked with him several times and had found him interesting. By chance they discovered that he and the captain were brothers who had been separated when they were only 3 years old. As they said good-bye at the end of the trip, they

made arrangements to meet again. Each felt a little strange but very glad about finding a brother they'd never expected to meet.

21. Even though it was a rather cool day, John and Mary decided to go down to their favorite bench by the bridge and have their talk. Being by the water was quiet and peaceful, it was easy for them to speak honestly and openly. It has been a long while since they had seen each other and the atmosphere of the river was helpful in the way in brought them close again.

22. The two were strangers as they met. But Rudolph, a young man who had just lost a well-paying job, felt in the mood to have some unfamiliar company. So he joined the old fellow on the bench, and discussed unimportant experiences and issues. The old man has been jobless for years. They quickly form an understanding and are completely at ease. Rudolph temporarily forgets about the wife and two young children he will have to confront later that evening.

23. This is a married couple sitting on the banks of the river near their home. They both work full day and when the work is finished they want to enjoy each other. As it is evening after a meal, they are relaxing and discussing their day of work and the joys, sorrows and discoveries of the day. The mood is joyful in a serene way. They appreciate the chance to share with each other what is most important to them. After this they will go for a walk. Then sleep, and then wake up to a new day in which go about their work –

24. Many people came to the park during the fall and spring to see the birds wandering around the grounds or ducks in the river on their way south for the winter. During the summer, many children can be seen running through the well-tended grass. Young couples can be seen strolling hand in hand down the pathways, or lying in the grass enjoying their youth. But the men always come. It may seem sad to the outsider; older men seem to habitate park benches throughout the land. But to these people, it is a time of meeting. It is a fellowship or camerade of those who seem to get pushed out of the world's center ring. To the men, they are not sad here, because they are together. (lousy ending, real trite).

25. A girl walking along the river is confronted with a shabbily dressed man approaching her from the opposite direction. Normally wary of strangers, in this instance the girl feels no fear. Instead she senses his need for companionship, & feeling the same way herself, she returns his causal greeting. They chat & quickly discover they are both out for a short walk. Approaching a bench, they sit down, & slowly begin to open themselves up to one another in a way which is quite unusual for strangers. They sit there a long time, talking.

26. Laura and Bob had not seen each other for five years. They had a very unusual relationship that entered into an exploraton of theirselves and each other. Bob had been Laura's teacher for one year. During this time Bob shared his personal self while teaching in class and Laura was very attracted to him. Now there were together again sharing the highlights of their past five years. There was an excitement and spark that was generated between the two of them as they realted joys, pains and sorrows. They didn't know when they'd meet again but they felt secure that they would. And when this future encounter took place there would exist the same spark & communication knowing that a love bound them together.

27. In summer the town and countryside around it are full of tourists. The bridge is always crowded and all the benches full. But in the fall, they could walk along the river and see no one. There was a bench on the bank across the river from the town. So here they met, as they did every fall. This time was the last time though. They'd come to say good-bye. Yet even in this last meeting there was no sadness. For friends are friends no matter the distance between them.

28. Alone together, two friends share some time with themselves. The cold is no problem as they are quite warm inside. They are friends now but weren't always. For he is a bum and she a mere wanderer. Their chance meeting is enhanced by the oddly similar backgrounds. "Shall we go to your place" he says. "I don't have one" she replies.

29. Walking along the bridge one day, Mark saw this woman walking toward him. She was alone, and looked rather sad and seemed to be in dispair. The look on her face made Mark so curious about her that he couldn't resist not asking her what was wrong. They stood there talking for a while, when Mark noticed a bench on the river side. He invited the woman to sit down there where it would be quieter.

30. It was a cold day and looked as if it could snow anytime. Yet Richard thought it would be better for he and his friend to go for a walk. His friend John had just gone through the hardship of attending his sons funeral and he needed someone to talk to, as his wife had died several years ago. So they sat on a bench near the bridge that connected the main city to the suburbs of that city. And John just eased his mind with Richard listening intently.

Expert scoring

PRIME TEST I: +A

1. No.
2. Yes. "each loves the other very much and they are happy"
3. Yes. She has "missed" the relationship while away.
4. Yes. "Mary has been the kindest."
5. Yes. "a true friend."
6. Yes. "they are feeling very good about everything"
7. No.
8. Yes. "a good friend"; "loves her"
9. No.
10. Yes. "good friends"
11. Yes. "loved each other more and more deeply each day"
12. No.
13. Yes. "I am content."
14. No.
15. Yes. "found true love"
16. Yes. "to be kind"
17. Yes. "loves to cruise the decks, talking to his crew & passengers."
18. No.
19. No.
20. Yes. "*glad* about finding brother . . ."
21. Yes. "brought them *close*"
22. No.
23. Yes. "The mood is joyful in a serene way."
24. Yes. "hand in hand" (tender behaviors)
25. No.
26. Yes. "excitement and spark"
27. No. "friends" is not strong enough.
28. Yes. "warm inside"
29. No.
30. No.

PRIME TEST 2: DLG

1. Yes. "just talk about things."
2. No.
3. Yes. "they talk until lunchtime"
4. No.
5. No.
6. No.
7. No.
8. Yes. "talking about all the good times"
9. Yes. "She has always been freer to talk with Boots."
10. No.
11. No.
12. No.
13. Yes. "casual conversation"
14. Yes. "they talked all afternoon"
15. No.
16. Yes. "make some pleasant conversation"
17. Yes. "talking to his crew and passengers"
18. No.
19. Yes. " 'Hello, welcome aboard.' "
20. Yes. "talked with him several times"
21. Yes. "have their talk"
22. Yes. "discussed unimportant experiences and issues."
23. Yes. "discussing their days"
24. No.
25. Yes. "talking"
26. Yes. "communication"
27. No. "saying goodbye" does not score for Dlg.
28. Yes. They talk with each other.
29. Yes. "talking for a while"
30. Yes. "Richard listening intently."

CATEGORY 3: PSY

1. No.
2. No.
3. No.
4. Yes. Because of Mary, Joey "seems to realize life is worthwhile" and "Joey has become a person."
5. No.
6. Yes. "The time away from the school environment has made them more relaxed and whole."
7. Not considered for scoring because the story does not contain either of the two prime test categories. Hereafter, such cases will be omitted.
8. No.
9. No.
10. No.
11. Yes. "they challenged the other's ideas, and they accepted the other's failures."
13. Yes. "he has inspired me to remain young at heart no matter my age or circumstances."
14. No.
15. No.

16. Yes. "walks away feeling better than before the encounter"
17. No.
18. No.
19. No.
20. No.
21. No.
22. Yes. Interaction fulfills "need to have some unfamiliar company."
23. No.
24. Yes. "It is a fellowship or camerade of those who seem to get pushed out of the world's center ring."
25. Yes. Interaction fulfills "need for companionship."
26. No.
28. No.
29. No.
30. Yes. Interaction fulfills need to have "someone to talk to," in light of son's funeral.

CATEGORY 4: CC

1. No.
2. No.
3. No.
4. Yes. Mary exhibits helping behavior.
5. No.
6. No.
8. Yes. "giving the girl some advice."
9. Yes. Boots listens, gives advice, and says "he'll support her."
10. No.
11. Yes. "that commitment"; "they helped each other."
13. No.
14. No.
15. No.
16. No.
17. No.
19. Yes. Captain shows some compassion and concern by being open to the needs of passengers, etc.
20. No.
21. No.
22. No.
23. No.
24. No.
25. No.
26. No.
28. No.
29. Yes. Mark shows concern by "asking her what was wrong."
30. Yes. Richard helps John.

CATEGORY 5: TS

1. No.
2. Yes. "15 years of marriage"
3. Yes. She has been away for a long time, yet relationship is strong.

4. No.
5. Yes. "who I've known for years and years"
6. No.
8. Yes. The two have grown up together.
9. No.
10. No.
11. Yes. "married 22 years"
13. Yes. "as we had done as a child"
14. No.
15. No.
16. No.
17. No.
19. No.
20. Yes. "made arrangements to meet again"
21. Yes. "It had been a long while . . ."
22. No.
23. No.
24. No.
25. Yes. "sit there a long time, talking"
26. Yes. "not seen each other for five years"
28. No.
29. No.
30. No.

CATEGORY 6: U

1. No.
2. No.
3. Yes. A reunion with grandfather, after being away
4. No.
5. No.
6. No.
8. No.
9. Yes. Marcia is planning to get married.
10. Yes. Girl and guy come together because of "common bond."
11. No.
13. Yes. A reunion: "it had been so long since we had seen each other."
14. No.
15. Yes. "new bride"
16. Yes. Civilian and officer "overstep" "role boundaries" to come together.
17. No.
19. No.
20. Yes. Reunion of 2 brothers who have been apart.
21. Yes. "brought them close again" implies they have been apart.
22. Yes. *Young* man and *old* man come together.
23. No.
24. Yes. "men have always come" (together)
25. Yes. Girl and "shabbily dressed man" come together.
26. Yes. Reunion.
28. No.
29. No.
30. No.

CATEGORY 7: H

1. No.
2. Yes. "compliment [complement] each other very well"
3. No.
4. No.
5. No.
6. No.
8. No.
9. No.
10. Yes. "they *share a common bond* in love for horses."
11. Yes. A general sense that couple is in harmony.
13. No.
14. No.
15. No.
16. No.
17. No.
19. Yes. "the captain seems to understand the man's need of relaxation and solitude."
20. Yes. The two find something in common: They are brothers.
21. No.
22. Yes. "quickly form an understanding"
23. Yes. "They appreciate a chance to *share* with each other what is most important to them." (implying a shared interest)
24. No.
25. Yes. "quickly discover they are *both* out for a short walk" (common interest)
26. No.
28. Yes. "oddly similar backgrounds"
29. No.
30. No.

CATEGORY 8: SR

1. No.
2. No.
3. No.
4. No.
5. Yes. Writer is surprised at the "respect" and "admiration" he/she feels toward the clown. This reaction appears beyond his/her control.
6. No.
8. No.
9. No.
10. No.
11. No.
13. No.
14. Yes. An accidental meeting.
15. Yes. "His first wife passed away and now he found happiness with a younger woman."
16. No.
17. No.
19. No.
20. Yes. "*By chance* they discovered" they were brothers.

21. Yes. "atmosphere" brought "them closer again" implies surrender of control (being a passive vehicle of the atmosphere)
22. No.
23. No.
24. No.
25. Yes. Interaction unfolds spontaneously – no controlling.
26. Yes. "They didn't know when they'd meet again but they felt secure that they would. And when this future . . ."
28. Yes. "chance meeting"
29. Yes. accidental meeting.
30. No.

CATEGORY 9: ESC

1. Yes. They have escaped from chores to spend afternoon in the countryside together.
2. No.
3. No.
4. No.
5. No.
6. Yes. They have escaped the "school environment" to find happiness together in "a ride through the woods."
8. No.
9. No.
10. No.
11. Yes. They "had finally gotten away" to enjoy intimacy in Colorado – "their dream."
13. No.
14. No.
15. No.
16. No.
17. No.
19. No.
20. No.
21. No.
22. Yes. "Rudolph temporarily forgets about the wife . . ."
23. No.
24. No.
25. No.
26. No.
28. No.
29. Yes. Escape to bench on riverside "where it would be quieter"
30. Yes. "better for his friend to go for a walk."

CATEGORY 10: COW

1. Yes. "appreciate nature"
2. No.
3. Yes. "feel the morning air . . ."
4. Yes. "Being in the outdoors has given him a new outlook on life."
5. No.
6. No.

8. No.
9. No.
10. Yes. "love for horses"
11. Yes. "And they are doing the things they love best – horsebackriding in the wilderness."
13. Yes. "good to be outside with him on this perfect day"
14. Yes. "She couldn't get over the smells in the field . . ."
15. No.
16. No.
17. No.
19. No.
20. No.
21. Yes. "atmosphere of the river . . ."
22. No.
23. No.
24. Yes. "come to the park to see the birds"
25. No.
26. No.
28. No.
29. Yes. "quieter" on "river side"
30. No.

17 *Affiliative trust−mistrust*

JAMES R. McKAY

This chapter briefly describes the derivation of the affiliative trust−mistrust thematic coding system (McKay, 1988, 1991) and covers research done with it to date. The coding system assesses the strength of two types of sentiments about affiliative relationships: trust and mistrust. People who depict relationships as positive, enjoyable experiences that turn out well score high on the trust subscale. The mistrust subscale, on the other hand, assesses expressions of negativity and cynicism about relationships. Scores on the subscales can be considered independently or combined to form a measure of Trust versus Mistrust.

The trust−mistrust coding system (see chapter 18) was originally developed to measure thoughts and feelings about affiliative relationships (i.e., "object relations") that are associated with immune function. Object relations may be defined as "the residue within the mind of relationships with important people in the individual's life" (Greenberg & Mitchell, 1983, p. 11). Psychoneuroimmunology studies of the effects of bereavement, divorce, and social supports have shown that one's experiences with affiliation are related to physical health, including immune function. Specifically, good experiences with affiliative relationships tend to be related to better immune function whereas bad or painful experiences are associated with poorer immune function (cf. Bartrop, Lockhurst, Lazarus, Kiloh, & Penny, 1977; Kiecolt-Glaser et al., 1987). If actual experiences with relationships are associated with immune function, it seemed conceivable that thoughts and feelings about relationships might be as well.

Several motive coding systems, such as *n* Affiliation (Atkinson, Heyns, & Veroff, 1954) and the Intimacy Motive (McAdams, 1982b), assess degree of preference or readiness for establishing and maintaining positive relationships with others or experiencing warm, close exchanges. These thematic

Much of this research was supported by a MacArthur Foundation Grant to David C. McClelland. I would like to thank David McClelland for his invaluable assistance in all phases of the work described here and Dan McAdams for his helpful comments on an earlier draft of this chapter.

254

measures, however, do not capture and quantify negative thoughts and feelings about relationships. In studies of the relationship between motives and immune function, *n* Affiliation has not been strongly related to immune function unless combined with other measures (e.g., activity inhibition, stress, and *n* Power) to form motive syndromes (Jemmott, 1987). This may be because the *n* Affiliation measure does not address the more painful and disappointing aspects of relationships, which have been found to have important implications for health.

DERIVATION

In the studies used to derive the coding system (McClelland & Kirshnit, 1988; McKay, 1988, 1991), subjects saw a film about Mother Teresa of Calcutta, in which she gives aid and comfort to orphans and lepers. It was intended that the film would arouse various thoughts about affiliation and lead to changes in immune function. The goal of the study was to determine what kinds of thoughts about relationships, as reflected in thematic apperceptive stories, were associated with gains and losses in immune function. Before and after the film subjects provided samples of saliva which were assayed for concentration of S-immunoglobulin A (S-IgA), an immune cell that primarily serves to protect the upper respiratory tract from infection. A meta-analysis (Jemmott & McClelland, 1989) has indicated that higher concentrations of S-IgA were significantly associated with lower incidence of acute upper respiratory tract illnesses. After giving a second saliva sample following presentation of the Mother Teresa film, subjects wrote stories about four pictures that depicted people interacting in various ways. The method is described in full elsewhere (McClelland & Kirshnit, 1988; McKay, 1988).

Although exposure to the Mother Teresa film significantly increased mean S-IgA concentration, some subjects showed a decrease after the film. To determine what kinds of thoughts about affiliation were associated with increases and decreases in immune function, the stories written by the four subjects with the greatest postfilm gains in S-IgA were compared with stories written by the four subjects with the greatest drops in S-IgA. The only expectation guiding the content analysis was that "positive" and "negative" depictions of relationships might be associated with gains and drops, respectively, in S-IgA. Five themes emerged that consistently differentiated the two groups of subjects. Those in whom S-IgA levels increased wrote stories about relationships in which characters (a) did nice things for each other, (b) shared warm, positive feelings about each other, and (c) engaged in enjoyable activities together. Those whose S-IgA levels went down wrote stories in which characters (d) ended affiliative relationships, and (e) were deceitful or dishonest with each other (McKay, 1991).

The first three categories appeared to be capturing expressions of hopefulness and positivity about relationships, or *trust*, whereas the last two categories assessed cynical and negative thoughts, or *mistrust*. The coding system seemed to be assessing thoughts or judgments influenced by feelings, in other words "sentiments," rather than motives. Relative degree of trust versus mistrust was determined by subtracting the number of mistrust categories scored from the number of trust categories scored for each subject. Scores from the four picture protocols typically ranged from -5 to 6, with higher scores indicating a preponderance of positive imagery about relationships.

When the stories from the entire sample ($N = 31$) were coded, those whose S-IgA levels increased had significantly higher scores than those whose levels went down ($t(29) = 2.51, p < .02$). The coding system was then cross-validated on a second sample ($N = 32$). Once again, the stories of those with increased S-IgA had higher scores ($t(30) = 2.52, p < .02$). In both samples, the trust and mistrust subscales contributed about equally to the relationship between the measure and S-IgA shift. The stories in the first sample were also coded for n Affiliation, which was not significantly related to S-IgA shift.

Studies in which other types of affiliative arousal were used (Kelner, 1990) demonstrated that the relationship between S-IgA shift and trust–mistrust scores is not limited to arousal generated by the Mother Teresa film. One condition ($n = 32$) watched an edited version of Bergman's *Scenes from a Marriage*, a film about a deceitful husband and a trusting wife. A second condition ($n = 29$) spent 1 hour in a guided meditation on experiences of oneness. Postarousal trust–mistrust scores were correlated .34 with S-IgA shift in the first condition, .28 in the second, and .31 ($n = 61, p < .05$) for both conditions combined. In contrast, after being exposed to the control condition ($n = 28$) or to a condition ($n = 28$) in which subjects' friendliness was rated publicly by others (using a technique designed to arouse n Affiliation; see chapter 13), subjects' S-IgA levels did not rise, but fell – in the control condition significantly. In these two conditions the correlations between trust–mistrust and S-IgA change were nonsignificant ($r = -.13$ for both conditions combined). These results indicate that the correlation between trust–mistrust and S-IgA change depends on whether the conditions to which subjects are exposed also increase S-IgA levels overall.

PSYCHOMETRIC PROPERTIES

The psychometric properties of the affiliative trust–mistrust coding system were investigated with samples of subjects who had not been aroused experimentally. In one sample ($N = 30$, six stories per subject) the interrater reliability of the measure was high ($r = .94$), with agreement on the presence of individual categories ranging from .79 to .86. The test–retest reliability was .54 over a 7-month period in one sample ($N = 61$) and .43

over a 10-year period in another sample ($N = 42$). Principal components analyses done on two samples ($Ns = 49$ and 71) revealed that the two mistrust categories loaded heavily onto one component whereas the three trust categories loaded less stably onto two other components. Subscales formed by summing scores from the mistrust and trust categories were correlated $-.17$ ($N = 49$) and $-.05$ ($N = 71$) in two samples (McKay, 1988) and $.06$ ($N = 126$) in a third sample (Kelner, 1990). These analyses indicated that the trust and mistrust subscales are independent. Trust–mistrust scores are typically not correlated with the length of the thematic apperceptive stories and thus typically do not need to be corrected for story length. However, the trust and mistrust subscales are sometimes correlated positively with story length and, if so, should be corrected for length of the protocol (see chapter 37) when used separately. A full description of the categories and scoring procedures is given in the next chapter.

THEORETICAL BACKGROUND

Numerous theories link the feelings and thoughts adults have about relationships to early experiences with affiliation. Erikson (1963) has written on the origins of trust and mistrust in early infancy and how the outcome of this developmental stage affects subsequent development. Hazan and Shaver (1987) postulated that adult styles of attachment are determined in part by childhood relationships with parental figures, and are similar to the secure, anxious, and avoidant attachment styles identified in infants by Ainsworth and colleagues (Ainsworth, Blehar, Waters, & Wall, 1978). Adler (1985) and Masterson (1988) have argued that fear of abandonment and parental inadequacy during early childhood lead to mistrust in parental figures, which in turn plays a role in the development of various types of psychopathology, including personality disorders, later in life.

There are a number of ways in which affiliative trust–mistrust could be expected to be related to physical health. People with positive orientations toward relationships may have more social support, which has been linked to better health (S. Cohen & Wills, 1985). Moreover, they probably do not experience a great deal of stress and anxiety in dealing with others. Those who have mistrustful sentiments about relationships, on the other hand, do not feel safe or comfortable when involved with others, as they expect to be let down, deceived, or used (McKay, 1991). These expectations can lead to stress, anxiety, and loneliness, which have all been associated with decreased immune function (Jemmott & Locke, 1984; Kiecolt-Glaser & Glaser, 1986). Although the psychobiological mechanisms are not yet clear, there is some evidence that emotional distress leads to increased levels of cortisol and the catecholamines, which can have immunosuppressive effects (Jemmott & Locke, 1984).

CONSTRUCT VALIDITY

The construct validity of the coding system as a measure of individual differences in trust–mistrust was determined by correlating the scores of subjects who had not been aroused experimentally with their scores on other thematic coding systems, demographic variables, and self-reported behaviors and personality measures. Due to the independence of the two subscales, validity data on trust–mistrust as well as data on each subscale will be reported.

Trust–mistrust

Trust–mistrust scores have generally been moderately correlated with n Affiliation and Intimacy motivation. In research by Franz, McClelland, Koestner, and Weinberger (1990), for example, the measure was positively correlated with n Affiliation ($r = .35, p < .05$) and Intimacy motivation ($r = .22, p < .05$), using a sample of 82 adults. It was also correlated significantly with the extent to which the subjects listed relationships with those they are close to as positive and helpful rather than aggravating ($r = .29, p < .05$). Correlations summarized by Kelner (1990) indicate that people higher in trust than mistrust preferred friendly, polite, agreeable people and were interested in being involved in other studies of friendship and relationships among people. Negative affiliative life changes in the past year, such as family fights or divorce, were associated with lower trust–mistrust scores. In addition, major changes in the health area, such as from prolonged illness or drug consumption, were associated with lower scores. The finding that intimacy motivation and n Affiliation were not related to these variables provides support for the discriminant validity of the trust–mistrust measure.

Trust subscale

The thematic apperceptive stories of people with high trust scores contain descriptions of enjoyable interactions in which people do nice things for or with each other and share warm feelings. In studies reported by McKay (1988), the subscale was correlated .50 ($N = 70, p < .001$) with n Affiliation, .32 ($N = 70, p < .01$) with Intimacy, and .24 ($N = 70, p < .05$) with the Nurturance scale of the Personality Research Form (PRF), a self-report trait inventory (D. N. Jackson, 1966). The subscale was unrelated to the other 21 PRF scales, including the affiliation scale ($r = .05$, n.s.).

Kelner (1990) found that the trust subscale was associated with security of adult attachment. In a sample of 120 adults, endorsement of the secure attachment items from a measure developed by Hazan and Shaver (1987) to measure attachment styles was positively correlated with trust scores ($r = .27, p < .01$). Kelner (1990) also found that higher trust scores were associated with a greater interest in being involved in a study of networks of friends. Negative affiliative life changes in the past year were associated with lower trust scores. Somewhat surprisingly, however, the recent death of a loved one was associated with *higher* trust scores. One might speculate that in some cases death apparently brings people together and increases the sense of solidarity and support.

In general, these results provide support for the validity of the trust subscale as a measure of positive sentiments about relationships. Furthermore, the pattern of correlations and the categories themselves suggest that the subscale may more specifically be a measure of positive sentiments about caring for others, or being nurtured or cared for. The subscale is more highly correlated with *n* Affiliation than Intimacy, reflecting a "doing" as opposed to "being" orientation (McAdams, 1982b; chapter 15, this volume). Similarly, the subscale is significantly correlated with the PRF nurturance scale but not the affiliation scale. According to D. N. Jackson (1966), those with high nurturance scores tend to give sympathy and comfort and assist others, whereas those with high affiliation scores enjoy being with friends and maintaining associations. Thus the particular type of trust the subscale appears to be assessing is the belief that people can be counted on to take care of each other.

Mistrust subscale

The thematic apperceptive stories of those with high mistrust scores contain descriptions of failed relationships in which someone has cheated on, lied to, or abandoned his or her partner. According to Erikson and developmental psychopathologists like Adler (1985) and Masterson (1988), mistrust in the availability and resiliency of early caregivers leads to some or all of the following in adulthood: impulsivity, poor self-image, fear of abandonment, somatization, a sense of powerlessness, and difficulty understanding other people's perspectives (McKay, 1991). These predictions were tested by correlating subjects' mistrust scores ($N = 71$) with their scores on the PRF, a mood-adjective checklist, and the Interpersonal Reactivity Index, which includes a perspective-taking subscale (Davis, 1980).

The pattern of correlations that emerged supported the construct validity of the mistrust subscale. Those with high mistrust scores tended to be impulsive, as evidenced by high scores on impulsivity ($r = .28, p < .05$) and low scores on order ($r = -.33, p < .01$) PRF scales; defensive, suspicious, and wary of relationships, as evidenced by high defendance ($r = .25, p < .05$) and low affiliation ($r = -.29, p < .05$) PRF scores; and low in perspective-taking ability ($r = -.37, p < .01$). These people were also characterized by an external locus of control ($r = -.28, p < .05$) and little sense of resourcefulness ($r = -.26, p < .05$), suggesting feelings of powerlessness (McKay, 1991).

Kelner (1990) found that those high in mistrust like clever, cynical people and are not interested in participating in studies of friendship or of any other topic. Furthermore, changes in their health in the preceding year were associated with higher mistrust, as was the death of a loved one (Kelner, 1990). Interestingly, the occurrence of a death in the family was related to both higher trust and mistrust.

CHILDHOOD ANTECEDENTS OF TRUST–MISTRUST

According to Erikson (1963, pp. 249–250), trust–mistrust is first established early in life, during the oral stage. If affiliative trust–mistrust is reflecting the basic sense of trust Erikson and other psychodynamic theorists have referred to, then individuals whose mothers treated them in the oral period in a way that conveyed a sense of personal trustworthiness and a conviction that there was meaning in what they were doing should have higher trust–mistrust scores in adulthood.

Data from a study of early parenting by Sears, Maccoby, and Levin (1957) make it possible to test this hypothesis. The mothers' descriptions of their feeding practices in the baby's first year were rated on a scale of 1 (for feeding whenever the baby was hungry) to 9 (for feeding according to a strict schedule). It was reasoned that mothers who adhered to *either* feeding on demand or feeding on schedule (rated at either extreme on the feeding scale) could be considered to be building a sense of trustworthiness created out of their conviction in the meaning and appropriateness of their approach to parenting. On the other hand, mothers who were rated in the middle of the scale seemed more likely not to have had any firm conviction as to how they should relate to the baby, as they reported having responded first one way and then the other depending on circumstances. This behavior would seem less likely to have created in the baby that deep sense of trust in what to expect from the mother to which Erikson is referring. Accordingly, it was reasoned that the further the mother was rated as deviating from the mean rating (5 on the scale), the more likely it was that she would have fed her baby in a principled fashion, which resulted from her deep conviction as to how to treat a baby. Degree of deviation from the mean on the feeding scale was thus used to construct a Principled Feeding index, on which higher scores reflected greater deviation.

The children in the Sears et al. (1957) study were followed up and their trust–mistrust scores were obtained at age 31 and again at age 41. At 31, the correlation between the Principled Feeding index and overall trust–mistrust was .35, $N = 42$, $p < .05$. The relationship was somewhat stronger with the mistrust subscale ($r = -.33$, $p < .05$) than with the trust subscale ($r = .16$). By age 41, 81% of the 31 adults whose mothers had fed them in a principled way (rated at 1,2 or 8,9 on the scale of feeding practices) showed a positive trust–mistrust score as compared to 62% of the individuals whose mothers had fed them in a less principled way (chi-square $= 3.68, p < .10$). The trust subscale scores were positively and the mistrust subscale scores negatively associated with the Principled Feeding index. However, the relationship was significant only for the women at age 31 ($p < .001$) and only for the men at age 41 ($p < .01$). Although this result was not expected, it is consistent with contemporary personality theorizing (e.g., Gutmann, 1975), which has argued that issues of communion (security and trust in interpersonal relationships) are particularly salient for women in early adulthood and for men in later adulthood. Thus one could infer that an early principled approach to parenting, here represented by feeding practices, can lead to developing a sense of trust in adulthood at a time when the issue of trust in interpersonal relationships is particularly salient.

Parental practices in the oral stage other than feeding also undoubtedly play a role in the development of trust. The Principled Feeding index may have acted as a proxy variable, in that it likely reflected principled approaches to parenting in other areas besides feeding. The important point is that principled parental behavior in the oral stage was associated with trust–mistrust in adulthood.

AFFILIATIVE TRUST–MISTRUST AND HEALTH

Immune and health correlates

Previous studies reported in the literature suggest a relative abundance of trusting over mistrustful thoughts about relationships should be associated with better health. In a sample of 36 adults, trust–mistrust scores were highly correlated ($r = .50, p < .01$) with ratios of helper to suppressor T cells, a measure of immune function (McKay, 1991). Higher scores (e.g., the degree to which trust was greater than mistrust) were associated with higher ratios, which are thought to indicate better immune function. Trust–mistrust was more strongly related to suppressor cell percentages ($r = -.42, p < .01$) than to helper cell percentages ($r = .09$, n.s.). Self-report personality and mood measures, on the other hand, as well as n Affiliation, were not significantly related to immune function in this sample. In a larger sample of 49 adults, from which the sample of 36 was drawn, trust–mistrust scores were also significantly correlated with number of self-reported illnesses in the previous year ($r = -.31, p < .05$), with higher scores associated with fewer illnesses. In a second sample of 70 adults, however, trust–mistrust was unrelated to self-reported illness frequency in the previous year (McKay, 1988).

Further analyses revealed that the trust subscale was unrelated to immune or illness variables in the two samples described previously. Mistrust scores from the first sample, on the other hand, were strongly correlated with helper to suppressor T cell ratios ($r = -.48, p < .01$) and self-reported illness frequency over the past year ($r = .41$, $p < .01$), with higher levels of mistrust associated with lower ratios and more illness. Mistrust was more strongly related to suppressor cell percentages ($r = .41$, $p < .01$) than to helper cell percentages ($r = -.11$, n.s.). Mistrust was moderately correlated with self-reports of infectious illness in the past year ($r = .20$, $N = 70$, $p < .10$) in the second sample (McKay, 1988) and in a third sample ($r = .16$, $N = 125$, $p < .10$; Kelner, 1990).

Although postarousal trust–mistrust scores are associated with shifts in S-IgA during arousal experiments, baseline trust–mistrust and trust and mistrust subscales are generally not significantly correlated with baseline S-IgA (Kelner, 1990; McKay, 1988). These paradoxical results are discussed subsequently.

Prospective studies of Affiliative Trust–Mistrust and health

The relationship between affiliative trust–mistrust and later health has been examined in three prospective studies. Franz, McClelland, Koestner, and Weinberger (1990) used data from the sample of adults whose parents had been interviewed on child-rearing practices (Sears et al., 1957). Subjects completed a measure of ill health (Veroff, Douvan, & Kulka, 1981) that assesses physical and psychiatric symptoms. Affiliative trust–mistrust measured in 31-year-old adults in 1978 predicted overall self-reported health in 1988 ($r = -.33$, $p < .05$), with higher trust–mistrust scores associated with less ill health. Further analyses showed that only the mistrust subscale was significantly correlated with ill health ($r = .41$, $p < .01$). In this sample a count was also made of major illnesses, such as pneumonia, chronic back or neck pain, gynecological problems, surgery, cancer, phlebitis, or hospitalization for any reason, reported for the 10-year period between age 31 and 41. Of the 17 subjects with low trust–mistrust scores at age 31, 59% reported two or more major illnesses in the subsequent 10 years as compared to 30% of the 20 subjects with high trust–mistrust scores (chi-square $= 3.12$, $p < .10$).

Two other studies tested the extent to which affiliative trust–mistrust at the outset of behavioral medicine treatments predicted how much patients would gain from the treatment, as reflected in reduction in symptoms 6 months after the treatments had ended. In the first study (McLeod, Hellman, Budd, & McClelland, 1990), initial trust–mistrust was correlated $-.41$, $N = 34$, $p < .05$ with reduction 6 months later in positive psychiatric and physical symptoms as measured by a symptom checklist, the SCL90 (Derogatis, Lipman, Rickels, Uhlenhute, & Covi, 1974), after initial symptom level had been partialled out. Trust subscale scores were positively associated with symptom reduction ($p < .05$) but mistrust subscale scores were not. In the second study (McLeod et al., 1990), initial trust–mistrust scores were correlated $-.31$, $N = 47$, $p < .05$ with SCL90 symptom reduction 6 months after the end of treatment, again when initial symptom level had been partialled out. In this instance the mistrust subscale scores were related to symptom reduction ($p < .05$) whereas the trust scores were not. In both instances greater degrees of trust, or lack of mistrust, apparently enabled patients to gain more from the behavioral medicine treatments.

METHODOLOGICAL CONSIDERATIONS

The subjects in the studies described have been college age and adult men and women. Average trust and mistrust scores vary as a function of the nature of the pictures used to elicit stories, but in most samples the average mistrust score is about one-third of the trust score. For example, in a sample of 127 adults (Kelner, 1990), the following pictures were used: People looking upward, a couple picnicking by a mill, a trapeze act, a couple picnicking with a dog by a river, and a person alone under a lamppost (Murray TAT card 20). The mean trust score was 2.14 ($SD = 1.4$), the mean mistrust score was .72 ($SD = 1.22$), and the mean trust–mistrust score was 1.43 ($SD = 1.82$). In another sample of 70 adults (McLeod et al., 1990) in which pictures commonly used in health research were employed (ship captain, architect at a drawing board, couple on a bench, two women in a lab, and a trapeze act), the mean trust score was 1.10 ($SD = 1.04$), mean mistrust score was .40 ($SD = 1.13$), and mean trust–mistrust score was .60 ($SD = 1.01$). While the trust subscale and trust–mistrust scale scores are fairly normally distributed, mistrust scores are usually skewed. In the Kelner (1990) sample, for example, 61% of the subjects received mistrust scores of 0. This suggests that this subscale is sensitive to relatively strong mistrustful sentiments but not to lesser degrees of mistrust.

At this point, the affiliative trust–mistrust coding system has only been used to code stories written in response to thematic apperceptive pictures. Pictures that portray two people in some sort of interaction work best as they produce the greatest range in scores. Stories written to between four and six pictures usually provide sufficient material to code. It is also possible that the coding system could be used with other material, such as descriptions of present or past relationships, although it may have to be modified somewhat to do so.

CONCLUSIONS

The affiliative trust–mistrust coding system was originally devised to assess the kind of thoughts about relationships that are associated with changes in immune function following affiliative arousals. Construct validity studies of the coding system as a measure of individual differences suggest that it assesses feeling about the trustworthiness of relationships. Trust–mistrust scores were associated with lower helper to suppressor T cell ratios, and/or higher illness frequency in cross-sectional studies and were predictive of later illness frequency and illness symptoms in several longitudinal studies. The mistrust subscale is usually more strongly related to measures of health than the trust subscale, although often both sentiments contribute something to the relationship between trust–mistrust and health. These studies provide support for the idea that the coding system is assessing sentiments about affiliation that are related to physical health.

The trust–mistrust coding system appears to measure thoughts or sentiments about object relations rather than motives. Sentiments are likely to be somewhat more conscious than motives, which raises the question of why not assess them with questionnaires that are easier to score and often more reliable. The problem is that the kind of sentiments the affiliative trust–mistrust coding system assesses are not always amenable to self-report. Some people can be reluctant, or at times even unable, to express directly their hurt, despair, and lack of trust concerning relationships. A thematic coding system, such as trust–mistrust, may be a more effective way to get at people's underlying thoughts and feelings about object relations (Stricker & Healey, 1990). If this is the case, though, one might question the wisdom of using self-report measures to validate the trust–mistrust coding system. However, the self-report measures were used to assess personality characteristics that were expected to be associated with trust and mistrust, rather than reports of trust or mistrust per se. In the mistrust construct validity studies, for example, the subscale was correlated with measures of characteristics mistrustful people were predicted to possess, such as impulsivity, defensiveness, and poor perspective-taking ability, not with self-reports specifically of mistrust.

In addition, self-report personality and mood measures were not related to immune function in the studies reported here, whereas affiliative trust–mistrust was. For example, the UCLA Loneliness scale (Russell, Peplau, & Cutrona, 1980) was not related to helper to suppressor T cell ratios in the McKay (1988) study. In addition, the self-report scales of the Profile of Mood States (McNair, Lorr, & Droppleman, 1981), which suggest a positive or negative self-view or world view, were not correlated with gains in S-IgA during the affiliative arousal interventions (Kelner, 1990; McKay, 1988). None of these results is conclusive because the self-report measures were not designed to get at trust and mistrust directly, but they suggest that the trust–mistrust scores may tap sentiments at a deeper, less conscious level than that attained by self-report measures.

Several problems concerning the nature of the relationship between trust–mistrust and health are in need of further study. Perhaps the most major problem is that, although the coding system was derived from *changes* in S-IgA concentrations, neither subscale nor the trust–mistrust index was related to *baseline* S-IgA concentration in two subsequent studies. One possible explanation for this involves the stability of various immune measures. Helper to suppressor T cell ratios, which are relatively stable, are significantly correlated with nonaroused or "trait" trust–mistrust scores. Salivary IgA, however, is a more reactive immune measure, which might explain why it is not generally related to "trait" trust–mistrust but is consistently related to "state" trust–mistrust in arousal experiments when they succeed in creating a state that elevates S-IgA levels. It is also not yet clear to what degree trust–mistrust influences immune function or is simply correlated with it. Additional studies with multiple measures of immune function and health status are needed for a fuller understanding of the links between affiliative trust–mistrust, immune function, and health, as these relationships are clearly dynamic rather than static.

18 A scoring system for affiliative trust–mistrust

JAMES R. McKAY

The affiliative trust–mistrust coding system assesses the strength of two types of sentiments about affiliative relationships: trust and mistrust. People who depict relationships as enjoyable experiences that turn out well score high on the trust subscale. The mistrust subscale, on the other hand, assesses expressions of negativity and cynicism about relationships. Scores on the subscales can be considered independently or combined to form a measure of affiliative trust versus mistrust.

The coding system was designed to be used on written material generated in response to pictures such as those of the Thematic Apperception Test (TAT). Pictures with two or more people interacting in some way provide the best stimulus material. In order that enough material is generated to yield reliable scores, subjects should be given 5 minutes per picture to write stories in response to four to six pictures. Assessments can be done with groups of subjects, provided the environment is quiet and comfortable and the subjects are able to refrain from interacting. The scoring criteria for each category are presented, along with scoring examples.

POSITIVE SCORING CATEGORIES (TRUST SUBSCALE)

Affiliative action is taken (AT+)

This category is scored when a character makes affiliative overtures to another person (or persons), and the outcome, that is, the other person's response, is not specifically stated. The characters may already be in an affiliative relationship; however, action to initiate contact or help another is also scorable. Examples of this category include asking someone to dinner, buying someone flowers, complementing someone, helping with the dishes, initiating a conversation, and so forth. Several additional guidelines must be followed.

  1. Score only for described action, or action that is definitely planned, for example, "Jake decided to stop and buy a present for his wife on the way

266

home from work." Action that is merely considered or pondered is not scored, for example, "Jake was wondering whether he should call his wife."

2. To code for AT+, the affiliative action must be independent of both the original statement of the situation and the final outcome of the story. Usually this means the first and last sentences of a story cannot be scored for AT+; however, the second or third clause in a complex opening sentence may be scored. For example, if the following sentence appeared at the beginning of a story – "While they are walking together in the rain, Paul offered to take Marie to dinner" – it would be scored for AT+ on the basis of the second clause.

3. The action must be of a "positive" nature. That is, it must be to nurture an existing affiliative, caring relationship, or to initiate one. Affiliative action done strictly for one's own pleasure or gain, such as in stories about men soliciting prostitutes or seeking to seduce women purely for sexual release, would not be coded for this category.

4. The action must represent a departure from regular day-to-day activities. Thus, a story about a man who is eager to go home to see his family at the end of the workday, or after a business trip, would not be scored. However, a story about a man who works very hard, or extra hours, in order to support his family would be scored. In this example, the man is described as doing something extra, or "above and beyond the call of duty" for his family.

5. Score this category when a response is implied, but not directly stated. For example, a story in which a woman invites a man to go for a walk, and which later describes them sitting on a bench after the walk, would be scored. Obviously, they did go for the walk, but the story is mostly about the woman's affiliative overture. However, if the man's response was described as – "Yes, I'd love to go for a walk" – this category would not be scored (see the next section on SA+). Similarly, stories in which a parent takes her child out for a birthday treat would also be scored. The key point to remember is that this category is scored *when the emphasis is on the affiliative overture itself*, not the result.

6. This category may be scored more than once per story when affiliative actions are taken by different characters. Do not, however, score AT+ twice when two people engage in reciprocated affiliative action. This would be coded SA+ (seen next section).

7. "Asking for help" is not scorable. However, offers of help are, so stories in which someone comes to the aid of one who asks for help are scored. Also score AT+ when someone offers to help a friend or lover, but the offer is declined in a civil manner, because of "honor," or because the other person, for example, wanted to deal with the situation himself. In this case, the refusal does not constitute rejection.

8. Trips taken by characters to visit friends are scored for this category. However, it must be explicitly stated that they have gone on the trip to visit

friends. Thus, "Wendy has come to Scotland to see her father," would be scored, while "Gregory is his cousin from America," would not. In the latter case, it is implied that Gregory came from America to visit his cousin; however, this is not stated.

The portions of the following stories that are scored for AT+ are in italics:

Tim was my roommate in college. . . . Instead of going to Ft. Lauderdale that year, *Tim paid everyone's way at the Frat and favorite sorority to go on a caravan carriage hayride in Vermont.*

The two men are colleagues and friends. The man standing has a problem – a personal one – and *his friend is trying to help him, giving him advice and pointing out alternatives.*

He had seen her there that evening and he knew that he was falling in love. Oddly enough, his old best friend was back from school too, and just happened to be there. *He knew her well and introduced the two of them.*

(Here, the old friend helps his friend out by introducing him to a woman he's interested in.)

The man and woman are walking along at night in a big city. It's his mother and *he's taken her to dinner for her birthday.*

Mrs. Kavanaugh is listening to her nephew Robert. A few years back, Mrs. Kavanaugh had a falling out with her oldest brother – Robert's father. *Robert has approached Mrs. Kavanaugh in order to help bring an end to the family squabbling.*

Shared Affiliation (SA+)

This category is scored when people in an affiliative relationship share or reciprocate warm, positive feelings for each other, or engage in reciprocated affiliative behavior, for example, kissing or discussing their relationship. Stories in which couples are described as "in love," "happy together," "close," "getting along really well," and "enjoying each other" would all be scored for SA+. Do not score SA+, however, when one character "loves his wife" or is described as "in love" unless the feeling is clearly reciprocated.

Affiliative overtures that are reciprocated, for example, "John asked Linda if she wanted to get married and she said yes," or "His mom offered advice and he thanked her," are scored SA+. Similarly, score stories in which couples get married or make love.

Conversations by people in an affiliative relationship which pertain to their relationship and are beneficial in some way, either by nurturing each participant or enriching the relationship, are coded SA+. Do not, however, code SA+ for couples simply "talking together." Minor arguments or disagreements that are resolved and lead to more closeness are scored for SA+. Major arguments that threaten the relationship or that are not resolved are not scored (see the section on NRA−).

Other guidelines are as follows.

1. Stories about couples just sitting quietly together are not scored for SA+ unless there is an explicit reference to shared affiliation. Furthermore, do not score for simple descriptions of pictures without mention of shared feelings, for example, "Adam and his mother are walking down the street together," or "They are having a picnic together." In other words, positive affect in the relationship has to be mentioned or some word or phrase strongly associated with positive affect in order for SA+ to be scored. Do not score SA+ when phrases like "they had sex," or "they kissed" are associated with negative affect.

2. This category is coded both for shared affiliation that initiates new relationships and that nurtures or sustains existing relationships. Remember, score for shared affiliation between friends as well as lovers.

3. This category may only be scored once per relationship, per story.

4. Do not score when those in the affiliative relationship engage in some sort of joint activity, such as "going on vacation," or "working together to get dinner ready," unless the criteria outlined for SA+ are also clearly met. Cooperative or collaborative efforts such as these are coded differently (see the section on CA+). Also, do not score when a couple is talking about something entirely separate from their relationship, such as a movie, a course, politics, and so forth.

5. Shared affiliation that is described as in the past or present is scored as long as it is spelled out clearly. Do not score for probable action in the future, for example, "They'll probably get married."

6. Do not score when one person tells another how to handle a problem, what to do, and so forth.

The following examples are scored for SA+:

A man talking with his mother. They've been for a walk and are discussing the son's life away from home. He's also asking her about his family and what's been going on. . . . *They seem to be sort of reacquainting themselves to each other – tentative, but each one is interested in what the other has to say* . . .

A careless sunny day, an innocent cup of tea, a haphazard brush of her skirt against my arm, . . . these were all the forgotten backdrops, the sudden rush of sensation that quickly receded to gray or, should I say, the dazzling pink, of our first summer together. Nothing was certain which made the whole universe possible. *"Will you marry me?" I'd ask. "Yes, When?" she'd reply and I would say, "Yesterday perhaps?"*

Two people obviously attracted to each other are talking about their future, wondering what time is going to bring to them. . . . Communication is definitely a factor in relationships . . . they know what they are talking about and what points to agree and how to listen . . .

A young couple has decided to take a walk in the park with the girl's dog. The dog is roaming around while they are *kissing and talking*. The couple has not been going out for very long but *they are going to have their first sexual intercourse that evening*.

This is a mother and son. The son has told his mother of his plans to get married. She is quite pleased and offers advice and comments on marriage. *The mother and son enjoy an unusually close relationship* and she is genuinely concerned for his happiness. He tells her how his career is progressing, too. She approved of his fiancee and is very happy that they will live reasonably nearby . . .

Man, woman and dog at the lake. *These two people are discussing the need for more commitment in their relationship*. Commitment to God and to something deeper within themselves.

Collaborative Action (CA+)

This category is scored when two or more people in an affiliative relationship of some sort engage in an activity together that is good for the relationship, that is, that nurtures, sustains, or enhances it. Activities that are fun, or involve a shared ideology or common cause, or will promote the relationship in the long run are all scored for CA+. Examples include going on vacation, working together, seeing a marriage counselor, planning together to move, and going out together for a night on the town. *The emphasis here is on doing something together*, rather than on sharing feelings or discussing the relationship as in SA+. Lovemaking, though certainly a collaborative activity, is scored SA+ rather than CA+ because it involves an extremely intimate sharing of intense feelings.

There must be an affiliative relationship in the story in order to score it for CA+. Such stories involve family members, lovers, a man and a woman on a date, or good friends. Stories about groups or communities may also be scored for CA+ when it is stated explicitly that the members share a dream, hope, or common purpose. Thus a story about townspeople moving together to a new land to make a new life together would be scored.

Do not score CA+ in cases where people merely work together, or are doing something together without an explicit reference to friendship, mutual trust, or a desire to be involved with each other (i.e., stories without affiliation). Thus a story about two chemists working on a cure for cancer would not be scored for CA+, unless they were described as friends and the work somehow affected their friendship.

Score CA+ only for described action or the explicit planning of collaborative activities. Other guidelines are as follows.

1. To code for CA+, the collaborative action must be independent of both the original statement of the situation and the final outcome of the story. Usually this means the first and last sentences of a story cannot be scored for CA+; however, the second or third clause in a complex opening sentence may be scored. For example, a story that opened with "Paul and Mary are on a picnic" would not be scored unless there was another

statement like "They had planned the picnic the night before," or "They spent several hours rowing around the lake," in the remainder of the story. Similarly, "The families are traveling in wagons. They have decided to move to a safer area to raise their children," would be scored, on the basis of the second sentence.

2. Score CA+ for collaborative affiliative action that takes place in groups of all sizes, from dyads to whole communities. As long as the participants are engaged in some activity that will be good for them – for example, that will enhance their lives in some way, bring them closer together – score this category.

3. This category may only be scored once per couple or group, per story. It is scored more than once per story, however, when there is collaborative affiliative action between different groups of people in the same story.

4. Be very conservative: This is a "doing" rather than a "being" or "feeling" category. The expressions of feelings or shared goals are sometimes necessary for scoring this category, but never score in the absence of any action. Also, do *not* score for collaborative action that involves hurting others, or for brief references to eating together, for example, "They had just gone to Burger King," unless they are elaborated on.

The following stories are scored for CA+:

We're in Vermont and its a sunny day. The lake behind us is there for the taking and the dog, we fondly call him Spot, is just waiting for the go ahead. He loves to swim alongside *as we canoe across the lake.* But we just want to lie in the sun and enjoy each other. We've just finished lunch and will be relaxing in each other's arms for a few more hours.

It is 1914. A town has been razed and the people have been banished from its land by the Cossacks. The community leaders have advised all to gather their belongings as quickly as possible, for once the horsemen have struck they are bound to strike again. *At the crack of dawn tens of families gathered in the town square and set off into the unknown territories of the Pale* . . .

A small caravan is crossing the desert in the American Southwest. *The people are Mormons on their way to Utah to practice their religion as they see fit* . . .

It is so pretty up here isn't it Annie? *I just love England and I think we should move to this farm permanently after we retire. In fact, I think your idea about coming out here at least two months of every year is a splendid idea!* We could consolidate our dealings with the textile firms we normally buy from during a four-month period and run the business in the summer from our office here . . .

Coding for more than one positive category per story

The positive scoring categories are not mutually exclusive; some stories will be scorable for more than one of the categories. Stories of this sort contain separate imagery that fits the criteria for AT+, SA+, or CA+. For example, a story in which two people are talking about their relationship and in which the man later takes his brother out for his birthday would score for SA+ and AT+. Similarly, a story about a church group out on a picnic in which a woman asks a man over for dinner would be scored for CA+ and AT+ (or SA+ if he accepts the invitation).

Some of the more difficult stories to code involve couples "enjoying being together," or something to that effect, while doing something that is coded for CA+ (e.g., going on vacation). The question is, should these stories be coded for SA+ as well as CA+? The coder must decide whether the statement indicating shared affiliation is an integral part of the activity coded for CA+. If it is, SA+ is not scored. For example, "The couple are having a good time together on their vacation trip across Spain" would be scored for CA+ but not SA+, as a vacation would be expected to engender those feelings (in fact, that's why vacations are coded for CA+). However, if "They are very much in love," followed the example above, it would be coded for SA+. In general, *code CA+ for a description of the activity*, and *SA+ for an additional sentence describing shared closeness or love*.

Shared Affiliation (SA+) is scored for reciprocated affiliative behavior as well as reciprocated feelings. Score both SA+ and CA+ in stories in which one person invites another to do something, the other responds favorably, and the joint activity itself is described (and it fits the criteria for CA+) – for example, "John asked Ruth if she would go out with him on Friday. She was delighted and immediately accepted. They went out for dinner, and later went dancing at the new club."

Another coding dilemma crops up in stories in which one character does something that could be coded for AT+, like inviting a woman to go horseback riding, and later describes the couple enjoying a brisk ride together. Should this sort of story be coded for AT+ and CA+, or just SA+? (The woman apparently accepted the invitation.) The important point to remember in these cases is that SA+ is never coded for affiliative overtures unless a positive reply is clearly stated. So in this case, SA+ cannot be scored. Instead, AT+ and CA+ would be scored.

The following are examples of stories that are scored for AT+ and CA+:

A young couple was recently married and have *rented a cottage on a lake* [CA+]. The two people, along with their dog, are having a nice, quiet picnic, when the ants come. They march as in a parade and carry all the food away. Soon there is nothing around them but ants and the lady begins to panic. *Her husband helps her up into the tree* and stomps on the ants [AT+]. Soon they retreat and the man escorts his shaken bride back to the cottage. Tomorrow they will go sailing.

In this scene, two sisters are getting ready for their double date. The younger one is looking forward to it, but the older sister is not happy that her sister has to come too. *The older sister's boyfriend wanted to fix the younger sister up with his cousin so he suggested that all four of them go out on a date* [AT+]. The men will come to pick up the girls soon; and *they will go for dinner and then dancing* [CA+]. They will all have a good time, even the older sister.

The following example is scored for SA+ and CA+:

The scene looks as though the people are having a picnic under the old oak tree. The boy and the girl will go home later with their dog. *They are planning on taking a vacation to Europe later on in the summer* [CA+]. *The two met while shopping in a supermarket, he hit into her wagon purposely to introduce himself and she was eager to get to know him better* [SA+]. Now the two have a good relationship and go to their favorite place every weekend.

NEGATIVE SCORING CATEGORIES (MISTRUST SUBSCALE)

Cynicism (CYN–)

Stories that meet the criteria outlined in A or B are scored for CYN–.

A. Cynicism is scored when the behaviors or attitudes of characters in an affiliative relationship toward each other are *deceitful* or *dishonest*. This would include cheating on one's spouse or lover, killing off a family member to get his money, lying to a good friend, and so forth. Also score when a character's motivations for being in a relationship are extremely selfish or exploitative, for example, a man marries a woman for her money, or he wants the relationship because he will no longer have to pay money to prostitutes. Stories of this sort have a cynical feel, hence the name, and seem to disparage relationships. However, code for the presence of deceit, dishonesty, and so on, rather than the "feel" of the story.

B. This category is also scored in stories that present a hypocritical view of human nature, even though the stories are not primarily centered around affiliative relationships. In this type of story, people are presented (or present themselves) in a good light, for example, as well intentioned, upstanding, moral, and so forth. This portrayal, however, turns out to be false. In order to be scored, both the good or moral "front" and the actual intention must be clearly present. For example, a story about criminals smuggling drugs would not be scored; however, one about people claiming to be raising money for famine relief (a moral undertaking) who are actually going to keep the money for themselves would be scored for CYN–. In the first case, the criminals have not presented themselves in a favorable light, and thus cannot be viewed as hypocritical.

Hypocrisy can be conveyed in two ways. The characters are described as such, as in the example given in the preceding paragraph. Or the author's comments or observations are hypocritical, as in a story that begins with "See the happy artist?" and then describes a boring unsatisfying life. Another example of this would be a character who is described as a "success," either through good relationships or career, but subsequently engages in self-destructive behavior, for example, suicide, drunkenness, drug addiction, gambling and so forth.

Do not score stories in which characters who are not in an affiliative relationship (and thus cannot be coded for CYN– as outlined in section A) manipulate or exploit each other, unless there is a description of laudable behavior that turns out to be false. Thus an executive who has his secretary run errands for him would not be scored. However, if he gets the secretary to help him by falsely claiming to be tied up with charitable endeavors, CYN− would be scored.

Other points to be kept in mind are as follows.

1. This category may be scored more than once per story. Score CYN− every time a character behaves in a manner that meets the criteria as outlined in sections A and B.

2. Do not score AT+ or CA+ when the actions are motivated by deceit or selfishness, and thus are scored for CYN−. Other examples of AT+, SA+, and CA+ in the story that are not connected with behaviors coded for CYN− should be coded, however. An example of this sort of story would be one in which a good relationship (SA+) eventually falls apart when the husband starts sleeping around (CYN−).

3. "Cynicism" is not the same as "pessimism" or "hopelessness." Do not score a story for cynicism just because it is bleak. For example, in a hopeless story, a character may feel he will never be loved. In order for it to be cynical, he must also believe all women are dishonest and would only use him for his money, or something along those lines.

4. Do not score CYN− just because a relationship ends. Characters who are mad at each other or no longer in love are not scorable for CYN− unless they are involved in lying, manipulative behavior, deceit, and so forth.

5. Sometimes there can be a fine line between cynicism and humor. Do not assume, however, that because the story makes you laugh it is humorous, rather than cynical. Some cynical stories are very funny, but the humor has a hard, cruel edge to it.

The following examples contain passages that are scored for CYN−:

This is a young married couple leaving their house for a busy day. *He is checking with the wife to make sure she turned the gas off. Actually he knows she did* [1] but *he went back to the kitchen and turned it on with gloved hands. The mother-in-law is still asleep in the house. They will become very rich on her demise* [2]. He is asking the question to establish his innocence in his wife's eyes. However, *she saw him turn on the gas and has told the mother-in-law to leave the house. She intends to let the explosion take place and then charge her husband* [3].

(CYN− is scored three times in this story.)

Aunt Mildred is seen here discussing her plans for her nephew Nigel's future. *Nigel is going along with it all for now and tends to humor Aunt Mildred. She is filthy rich and last week she clued him in as to the contents of her will. He can't wait to get his greedy paws on the old bag's money* [1]. She is too healthy, he thinks. She'll probably live to be 90. "I've got to find a way to do in the old biddy so I can have her loot while I'm still young enough to enjoy it." Later, during dinner, *he puts poison in her mashed potatoes* [2].

(CYN– is scored twice here, once for Nigel's humoring his Aunt to get on her good side, and once for his killing her to get her money.)

The man by the window has just found out his *wife is cheating on him* [1] and his business is close to bankruptcy. Things do not look great. The man in the chair is telling him to look on the bright side. He reminds the standing man that he is not really wild about his wife and *has his own thing going on the side* [2]. If the business goes down, well then there are write offs and tax loops and all should be hunky dory. The man facing the losses gets a bit miffed at the sitting man. Who is he to tell him not to be depressed? Then he realizes the man is probably right and begins to question how he has approached his life up to this point. "What's it all about, Alfie?"

A navy captain is being confronted by a loanshark who is getting itchy about whether or not he will get paid. The captain had borrowed the money in order to *shut up a bimbo he had had who threatened to tell his wife of the misbegotten affair* . . .

. . . Doreen and Edward make it that night. Doreen gets pregnant, *so they marry and live unhappily* [1] *until Doreen runs off with the air-conditioning man* [2]. Edward turns into an alcoholic.

(The first passage is coded for CYN– because the author paired something which is usually a happy event – a marriage – with an unhappy outcome.)

Nonreciprocated Affiliation (NRA–)

This category is scored when an affiliative relationship depicted in the story is in trouble due to the feelings or behaviors of one or both parties. Stories about friends, lovers, spouses, and immediate family members (e.g., father, mother, siblings) can be scored for NRA– because these relationships are usually affiliative in nature, or have been at some point. Do not, however, automatically score NRA– for fights between more distant relatives (e.g., cousins) unless it is clear they have been close. The problem must be within the relationship; external factors that threaten the relationship (e.g., parents who do not approve of the match) are not scored.

Score NRA– when one person wants to end an affiliative relationship. In addition, score when anger, fights, or major disagreements seriously disrupt or end relationships. Behavior that threatens a relationship (e.g., husband who is labeled a workaholic drives wife to consider divorce) is scored as well. However, do not score when fights are "playful" or described in jest.

Nonreciprocated affiliation is also scored when one person makes affiliative overtures that are refused or totally ignored, for example, "John asked, would she go to Maine with him for the weekend? She said 'absolutely not.'"

Additional scoring guidelines are as follows:

1. Score NRA– when the criteria already outlined are met, even if the problem is resolved by the end of the story. The characters' attempts to

overcome the problem in their relationship would be scored SA+ if it is successfully worked through during the course of the story. Stories like this are rare, but would be scored for both NRA− and SA+ if criteria for both coding categories are met.

2. This category can be coded more than once per story. If both people have internal blocks against their relationship, both blocks are mentioned, and both people do not want the relationship to continue, score NRA− for each person. If the two people are "not getting along" or "have decided to end the relationship" and each person's reason is not spelled out, score NRA− only once. Also score NRA− once when one character wants to end a relationship, has fallen out of love, etc.

Examples of stories that are scored for NRA−:

Mom and dad wanted me to live as them and their kind – the Amish of Pennsylvania. . . . I was the first in our family to ever decide other than maintaining and accepting the Amish way. *It has hurt them deeply, but I can not live for something that is not part of me.* I've always felt displaced in their environment. Someday they may understand.

(NRA− is scored here because the author is rejecting parental values in a way that seriously threatens their relationship.)

Father and son in the son's office. . . . Harry is proud that his boy is doing well but it's hard for him to say so. His standard communication to David consists of why haven't you done this or I would have done that differently and where did you get that suit from anyway. David wants his father to leave. He is annoyed but mostly frustrated that *no matter what he does this man whom he loves is never satisfied regardless of how much he tries.* . . . He wants them to show love to each other.

A man and a woman are meeting after work and are talking about their relationship. *They have been arguing lately about the oddest things now that they are working together.* The man doesn't think that there is a problem and laughs it off. *The woman will quit her job and stop seeing the man.*

The couple at the bench are Anne-Marie and Bernie. They are living together, *but Anne-Marie is already having troubles.* . . . He's pretty scared too – he's afraid that Anne-Marie will leave, but he's not quite sure why she shouldn't, or even, why he wants her to stay. She'll stick around for awhile, but most of their time will be spent talking about why they should or shouldn't be together. *Their relationship will end collapsing inwardly like a black hole in space.*

This couple is going through a divorce and they are discussing the children and what should be done about their custody and visiting rights. This is not a bitter divorce and they love their children very much so the whole situation hurts them very much but *they just cannot live together anymore. They have realized that they are really two very different people and they are just not getting along. The only problem, really, is that they married each other for the wrong reasons to begin with.* . . . *They were never really in love.*

(NRA− is scored twice here because the internal blocks of both people are described. Even though the blocks are the same, they are described in sufficient detail to warrant scoring NRA− twice.)

CALCULATING SCORES

Scores are determined in the following manner. The trust subscale score represents the total number of positive categories coded from a subject's stories. The mistrust subscale score is the sum of all the negative categories coded. Overall trust–mistrust is obtained by subtracting the mistrust subscale score from the trust subscale score. Scores calculated in this way typically range from −5 to 6, with a mean of around 1. Scores usually range from 0 to 6 on the trust subscale and from 0 to 5 on the mistrust subscale.

Occasionally a sample of subjects may produce stories with very little imagery that is scorable for CYN− and NRA−. This may be true of particularly well-adjusted, content adults, or people administered the measure under unusual conditions (e.g., self-administration, noisy or otherwise distracting surroundings, etc.). As a general rule of thumb, imagery codable for CYN− or NRA− should occur somewhere in the stories of at least a quarter of the subjects in a given sample in order for Mistrust scores to be considered valid. If the mistrust scale is used separately and less than half the subjects in a sample receive scores of greater than 0, it probably makes more sense to use the subscale as a dichotomous measure (e.g., mistrustful imagery present: yes or no) rather than as a continuous measure.

It is also possible for subjects to pile up extremely high mistrust scores (>6) by writing stories full of imagery that is coded for CYN−. The recommended way for dealing with such outliers is to lower their scores to equal those of the subjects with the next highest scores.

19 *Power motivation*

JOSEPH VEROFF

The beginning ideas for the development of a thematic analysis of power motivation in projective stories emerged from speculations that Roger Heyns, Jack Atkinson, and I had when we were refining the thematic assessment of need for affiliation (see chapter 14). In 1952 we were discussing reasons why minimal affiliation imagery came through in stories written about a picture of two men of equal status, a picture that we had assumed would elicit a considerable amount of affiliative imagery. What alternative type of thematic material might emerge, we asked? We immediately turned our attention to issues of power. And it was the hope of developing a companion measure to the study of affiliation motivation that prompted a systematic analysis of power motivation. We thought of power as being an alternative to affiliation.

These original speculations about power motivation were founded primarily on the thinking of Adler (see Ansbacher & Ansbacher, 1956). Adler was quick to see that a general social interest was basic to people's humanity and that social interests often implied assertive concerns with power. Much of his elaborations about social interests focused on early learned feelings of inferiority in connection with the family situation. He assumed that a child innately fears being overwhelmed not only by more powerful parents but also by older siblings. Such speculations made him focus on the concern about influence that comes from having been strongly influenced by others. We also gave some consideration to the possibility that power motivation may be linked to the dynamics of the authoritarian personality (Adorno, Frenkel-Brunswick, Levinson, & Sanford, 1950).

Rather than speaking of feelings of inferiority, however, the research initially focused on the concern about controlling the means of influence. By that conception the person with strong power motivation does not constantly seek dominance or assertiveness over others, but rather is concerned only with making sure that, if the person did want to influence, the means by which influence could occur was in that person's control.

THE INITIAL STUDY

In a search for the kind of thematic imagery that would differentiate one group as opposed to another on the dynamics of controlling the means of influence, I assumed that people who were seeking political office and were aroused to think about whether they had won an election would be prototypic of the concern of controlling the means of influence (Veroff, 1957). Thus, I used a group of candidates for student government who were gathered on the night of an election to await returns. I asked them to tell stories in response to pictures. This group was assumed to be highly aroused for power. A contrasting group was a group of students who were in an ordinary classroom. It should be noted that this paradigm contrasting an aroused versus a neutral group, the paradigm that has been used in developing scoring schemes for a variety of motives (achievement, affiliation, and sex, see Atkinson, 1958a), was not purely followed in this case. The procedure used to derive the power scoring system confounded both the situation and the persons. A group of people running for office was the aroused group, and an ordinary classroom was the control group. Imagery that differentiated these two groups can be attributed to either the person difference or the situation difference, or both. Very likely both were involved in the study. Nevertheless, this study did accentuate the concern about controlling the means of influence presumed to underlie the power motive.

The major thematic material that did emerge in these comparisons, and thus formed the basis for the coding scheme for the power motive, was content that explicitly stated concern about influence: trying to influence someone, trying to convince another person of a point of view, or some affective concerns about establishing or controlling the means of influence. In addition, imagery in which some type of role relationship was stated that indirectly implied that someone had control over the means of influence of another also differentiated the groups (e.g., a statement of a boss–worker relationship going on). In the initial study the "need for power scores" based on these kinds of imagery related to other aspects of people's lives in a way that validated the measure as a concern over controlling the means of influence. Most important of these findings was the fact that college men who were high in need for power were those who were seen by their instructors as argumentative in the classroom. Also found were clear results that the power motive was higher among men who had older siblings than among those who had only younger siblings (Veroff, 1957).

FOLLOW-UP STUDIES

When this measure of the power motive became available for general use, a number of researchers found it helpful in understanding social phenomena. Veroff and Veroff (1972) argued that these new results showed that in social settings, where the focus is directly on how successfully a person exercises influence, people with high power motives are not necessarily assertive. Where the focus is away from the influence, then people with high need for power scores become particularly assertive. Browning (1961), for example, demonstrated the importance of the motive in distinguishing politically active from politically inactive businessmen. Veroff and Veroff argued that the spotlight is not on businessmen to be political. Thus, they can take the lead if they have high power concerns. Browning and Jacob (1964) found that only at the local level are politicians with higher power motive scores more likely to be successful than those who had lower scores. Again the spotlight is not on local people as much as it is on leaders at the state or federal level. McKeachie (1961) found that college students with high power motive scores compared with those with low scores received better grades in classrooms where student volunteering was common. This was not true in other classrooms. Terhune (1968) found that the measure of power motivation was useful in isolating those people who were exploitative in the setting of a prisoner's dilemma game. Furthermore, in a type of international game setting they were also more likely to be retaliatory. These latter results were beginning to auger the fact that although the power motive as measured was related to assertive behavior under certain conditions, it also could be a reflection of a negative type of insecure motivation.

There are other clear results about the negative aspects of high power motivation. Rudin (1965) found that societies in which children's readers were high in references to power imagery had higher homicide and suicide rates than societies in which these references were lower. Barrett and Franke (1970) confirmed these results only with regard to homicide. McClelland (1971b) found that societies with high power motivation in combination with low affiliation motivation were more likely to presage the rise of authoritarianism. In a national survey of motives Veroff, Atkinson, Feld, and Gurin (1960) found that high power motives were particularly strong in black men and in poor and less educated people. A subtler negative experience of high power motivation came in S. Mueller's (1975) study of the power motive in music students. She found that those who were high in the power motive were unsatisfied as teachers but much more satisfied as performers. She argued that the teaching role was one in which there was some concern about whether the person taught would reflect what the teacher had wanted to control. It is only in one's own performance that a person could control the impact. In S. E. Hunt's (1972) study, people with high power motive scores were less willing to compromise in a two-person influence setting. Thus power motivation can get in the way of smooth conflict resolution.

The bulk of the early literature using the power motive measure suggested the idea that the motive reflected fear of weakness, more than a positive approach to power. As such it bore some resemblance to reactance motivation, or the motivation to reassert one's freedom to choose, theorized by Brehm (1966), to occur whenever another person limits one's alternatives. Both fear of weakness and reactance reflect a concern about being influenced by others, about being in a weak position and unable to control one's fate. Veroff and Veroff (1972) in a reconsideration of the meaning of the power motivation measure suggested that this security-oriented aspect of power motivation often puts highly motivated people into a position of *not* seeking power, of avoiding public scrutiny. It was their contention, therefore, that power motivation as measured in the thematic analysis would not necessarily have a direct correspondence to whether people actually were powerful in social situations, because people with high power motivation often resisted being in situations where public appraisal of power was occurring. These conclusions were especially supported by the results of studies by Berlew (1961) and Lindman (1958).

The fact that the power motive assessment emphasized the fearful side, and the fact that its initial experimental validation confounded the person differences with social arousal differences, led both Uleman (1972) and D. G. Winter (1973) to develop other assessments of the power motive, ones that would reflect the more positive concerns that power motivation may have. Winter's assessment (see chapter 21) supplanted Uleman's and it largely supplanted the use of the initial measure. Winter's assessment was highly correlated with the other two and seemed to be more inclusive and more responsive to positive experimental procedures. It is suggested here that Winter's revised measure of the power motive (see chapters 21 and 22) can be considered a companion measure of power motivation to the one discussed in this chapter. The Winter measure of the power motive is more oriented toward having positive impact. For example, where S. Mueller (1975) found, with the original measure of the power motive, that teachers with high power motive scores were dissatisfied, D. G. Winter (1973), by contrast, found with his more inclusive measure a distinct orientation toward teaching in people who scored high on the power motive.

TWO NATIONAL STUDIES OF THE POWER MOTIVE

Thus, beginning in the mid-1970s it was assumed that the original measure of power motivation was a measure of fear of weakness. New substantial results with this measure, primarily stemming from two national surveys, further confirmed this assumption. The major results from one survey were reported in Veroff and Feld (1970), a study in which motive assessments in interaction with various life roles were seen as important predictors of psychological well-being. Results from that work are too numerous to mention. Two of them can be highlighted to demonstrate how the measure of power motivation as fear of weakness has been useful in thinking about social role analysis. College-educated men and women who are high in the power motive are more likely to experience marital problems than people who are low in the motive. It is difficult to know in this research whether the motive was the basis of their problems, or whether once marital problems are generated, people's motive for power becomes particularly strong. In either case it is clear that the power motive as a fear of weakness is the best interpretation of these data. Another result from Veroff and Feld's work deals with parenthood. Compared with those with low power motivation, fathers with high power motivation felt some disruption in their feelings about parenthood as their children reached adolescence and adulthood. The results are interpreted to mean that when children grow up and are often rebellious, then men as parents become more uneasy about their role if they have high power motivation. And once again we could reinterpret the results to mean that when children become rebellious and disrupt parental feelings, then men have their power motives strengthened.

The first national study of motives was done in 1957; the second, in 1976. Both were cross-sectional samples of American adults. The differences between 1957 and 1976 with regard to the measure of the power motive as fear of weakness were estimated (Veroff, Depner, Kulka, & Douvan, 1980). In both men and women the power motive was higher in 1976 than in 1957. A group for whom there was a decrease rather than an increase, however, was black males. The intervening time between 1957 and 1976 saw the civil rights movement emerge. Perhaps this could make the difference in the fear-of-weakness scores. There was greater recognition of black influence in the society, which undoubtedly became transmitted in the socialization of black children.

From the 1976 survey results relating the fear-of-weakness measure to various reactions people had about their lives, Veroff (1982) suggested a new facet to fear of weakness. It may reflect a concern about sexual identity. Evidence for this conclusion was offered for both men's and women's results. Men who were high in measured power motivation were particularly striking in their low self-esteem and drinking problems and, at the same time, were extremely positive about their sexual lives and social relationships. I read this as a protest about masculinity among men with high power motives. This syndrome comes very close to the results of McClelland, Davis, Kalin, and Warner (1972) with regard to power concerns of alcoholics. The results for women were also interesting with regard to considering power motivation as a concern about sexual identity. Women with high power motive scores were women who seemed to be comfortable about their autonomy in the business world, but not in the image that that type of behavior creates for others. They seemed to be concerned about the gender attribution of their autonomous behavior.

RECOMMENDATION FOR THE USE OF THE MEASURE OF
POWER MOTIVATION

A different pattern of results emerged in the national survey when the power motive was defined in terms of Winter's scoring, which is presented in subsequent chapters. While most of the research on the power motive in the last two decades has largely been with Winter's revised scoring, a return to measuring fear of weakness as an accompaniment to the Winter assessment seems appropriate. One would get considerable mileage from assessing both motives, and discover whether a person is positively oriented (low fear of weakness – high hope of power), negatively oriented (low hope of power – high fear of weakness), ambivalent (high in both positive and negative orientations), or very low (low in both). Such a typology would be important to consider in future research.

The coding scheme presented in the following chapter has generally been applied to stories told or written in response to pictures. It has been used in coding thematic material gained from myths (Child, Storm, & Veroff, 1958), and children's readers (McClelland, 1961), but by and large it has been applied to adults' reactions to stories told in response to pictures.

The pictures that are used to elicit the stories cover an assortment of interpersonal settings. It is recommended that the following assortment be in any set that is used: (a) a group scene depicting people of the same sex as the subjects; (b) a same-status two-person scene of the same sex as the subject; (c) an older–younger scene, the same sex as subjects; and (d) a man and woman scene. These are very different settings for the concern about weakness. When the motive measure cuts across situations as in such a battery, there are sufficient opportunities for particular power concerns to be channeled. The set of stories that were obtained from the national survey includes pictures as recommended above (see appendix II). Except for the picture of the man and woman, each sex should have its own set of pictures depicting women for women and men for men.

Standard instructions for the administration of the thematic apperceptive measure are presented in chapter 37 along with a discussion of other methodological issues.

Stories should be elicited in neutral settings, in hopes of obtaining the measure of the power motive that is characteristic of the person under ordinary conditions. If stories are elicited from a very heterogeneous population, there probably should be some correction for story length. In the national survey, for example, the number of words used in the story was found to be moderately correlated with motive scores. Some correction that removes that correlation is in order (see chapter 37 for further discussion of this issue).

The power motive scoring system has been used for both men and women. The original validity study was cross-validated on a group of women who were running for office in contrast to women who were in the college classroom. By and large the results were replicated (Corban, 1956).

With what population can this measure be used? Because the results for blacks in the national survey were congruent with ideas about black power motivation between 1957 and 1976, it is suggested that the measure may be valid for blacks even though the pictures used did not depict blacks. The fact that McClelland (1961) in the assessment of children's readers in *The Achieving Society* had measures of the power motive based on different cultures, and found intriguing and meaningful results, suggests that this measure may be useful cross-culturally. And the fact that it has been used meaningfully in a national population survey (see chapter 6) suggests that it can be used for people of different ages and different educational statuses.

One difficulty with the measure has been its comparatively low coding reliability. Some studies report correlations for intercoder agreement only in the .70s which is generally lower than users of thematic measures aspire to. This coding unreliability results from some leeway given to the coder about what "influence" is under certain circumstances. One of the major coding criteria has to do with identifying role relationships that exemplify power strivings. The parent–child relationship is somewhat difficult to code in this respect because there are some obligatory activities requiring parents to teach, which is sometimes coded for power motivation and sometimes not. There has been some difficulty in unraveling the nature of power strivings in such role relationships. Researchers are encouraged to spend time working out explicit general criteria for this problem and others with the specific stories of the particular group studied.

CONCLUSION

Power motive scores were correlated with other motive measures in the 1976 national survey, and these are reproduced in Table 19.1. It is clear that the original idea that stimulated the measure of the power motive is still apparent in the correlations. Need for affiliation is negatively correlated with need for power for both men and women. It is as if needs for affiliation and power are two incompatible strategies for dealing with interpersonal relationships. While both concerns can coexist, it is more likely that one or the other predominates. McClelland (1975) has advocated that both motives be assessed, that those who are high in need for power but low in need for affiliation are more unsocialized in their concerns about power than those who are high in need for power but also high in need for affiliation. (See chapter 5 for McClelland's discussion of such motive patterns.) Although McClelland uses Winter's measure of the power motive, no doubt the assessment of the power motive as fear of weakness with the same kind of typological analysis should have considerable payoff.

Table 19.1. *Intercorrelations among measures of motives used in 1976 national survey (by gender)*

	Motive measures			
	Power (FOW)[a]	Affiliation	Achievement	Power (HOP)[b]
Power (fear of weakness – FOW)		−.13**	.05	.42****
Affiliation	−.14**		−.09*	.01
Achievement	−.01	.10*		.03
Power (hope of power – HOP)	.32****	−.04	.08*	

Note: Pearson *r*s from Veroff, Depner, Kulka, and Douvan (1980). Men ($N = 508$) above the diagonal; women ($N = 700$) below. Motive scores are corrected for correlations with story length.
[a] Veroff power measure (see chapter 20).
[b] Winter power measure (see chapter 22).
* $p < .05$.
** $p < .01$.
**** $p < .0001$

The assessment of fear of weakness through this measure of power motivation has already yielded important information about interpersonal behavior, ways men and women cope with their lives and with each other. It has also yielded information about how earlier socialization in families and in society at large affects this fear of weakness. Nevertheless, much more needs to be explored for developing a comprehensive theory about the nature of power motivation as fear of weakness. Its use in conjunction with the measures of need for affiliation and the Winter method of assessing power motivation is highly recommended.

LEARNING TO SCORE FOR *N* POWER

The following chapter presents the scoring manual for *n* Power. See chapter 37 for a discussion of scorer training. The practice stories provided in appendix I of this volume do not include sufficient *n* Power imagery to be useful for learning the present system. Instead, for practice stories and expert scoring see appendix I of *Motives in Fantasy, Action and Society* (Atkinson, 1958a). See also appendix III of this volume about ordering additional practice materials.

20 *A scoring manual for the power motive*

JOSEPH VEROFF

The method of scoring stories written in response to pictures for power motivation closely parallels the pattern established for the hunger, achievement, and affiliation motives. Essentially what has been involved in measuring these motives and what will be involved in measuring power motivation is a content analysis of the written protocols for evidence of thought processes related to a conceptual behavioral sequence.[1] In order to analyze a story for power motivation, therefore, a person has to decide that the story presents some evidence of concern with the satisfactions characteristic of the motive, as it will be defined, and then must understand how the motive is manifested in imagery relevant to the analysis of the behavioral sequence.

It is of crucial importance for scoring stories for power motivation that the scorer understand the behavioral sequence. Once a person is able to identify the presence of imagery in a story that is related to power motivation, then the subcategory system of coding logically follows from the behavioral sequence. The means of identifying Power Imagery in a story will be discussed in the following section, as will the way in which Power Imagery is manifested in the categories derived from the behavioral sequence. Once a scorer decides that a story is unrelated to power motivation, he no longer has to be concerned with the subcategories. If he decides that a story does contain the category Power Imagery, then he must check over the story for imagery that can be subcategorized according to the behavioral sequence. A story is scored either Power Imagery (Pow Im) or Unrelated (U Im). One additional category not falling in the behavioral sequence analysis is the Thema category. The latter is a category which is scored if the story con-

This scoring manual was adapted from Veroff, J. (1955). *Validation of a projective measure of power motivation.* Unpublished doctoral dissertation, University of Michigan, Ann Arbor. It was originally published as Chapter 14 in Atkinson, J. W. (Ed.). (1958a). *Motives in fantasy, action and society* (pp. 219–233). Princeton, NJ: Van Nostrand. It is reprinted here by permission (copyright by J. W. Atkinson).

taining Power Imagery is saturated with imagery relevant to the power motive.

DEFINITION OF POWER IMAGERY (POW IM)

In order for the overall code of Power Imagery to be scored, there has to be some reference to the thoughts, feelings, and actions of one of the characters in a story which indicates that the character is concerned with the control of the means of influencing a person. Power Imagery can be indicated in the imagery about any character mentioned in the story. Evidence of concern can come from any one of three sources.

I. *There is some statement of affect surrounding the maintenance or attainment of the control of the means of influencing a person.* A character can be feeling good about winning an argument or feeling bad because he was unable to have his way about something. Also statements about wanting to win a point or show dominance, gain control (such as by a political or executive position), convince someone of something or put a point across can be interpreted as implicit statements of affective concern about the control of the means of influence. Affective concern can also be found in *statements of wanting to avoid weakness.* Examples of this are being humiliated in a status position, being ashamed of an incapacity to assert one's self or become dominant, resenting the influence of another and wanting to overcome this.

Special considerations under Criterion 1. Some very weak statements of concern over control of the means of influence are scored. Statements of desires to teach another person something, to inspire another person, to interest another person in something – although apparently weak in obvious power significance – should be scored. The only times when statements like those above would not be scored would be in cases where the teaching or inspiring or interesting is solicited by the person being influenced, such as statements of teachers wanting to answer questions that students have raised. Solicited advice or opinion would be scored if there is evidence for Power Imagery over and above mere mention of answering requests. A person "trying to put across a point" within a solicited advice-giving story would make the story scorable for Power Imagery.

Statements of a person wanting another person to gain control of the means of influence – such as a person wanting someone else to win an election – will not be scored as Power Imagery. The only case like this which can be scored is where there is a very clear identification of the person wanting and the candidate. This kind of imagery may appear in election stories where John *wants to win* the election, although John is not the candidate.

Examples of Criterion 1

1. It is a family scene of "The Late George Apley" type. The patriarch of the family is explaining a business decision to his son. The son has *resented* his father's maintaining his position as head of the business in his old age. The son wants an explanation of why he does not have control of the procedure and still must let his father decide. The father will maintain the family business and will be in charge of all investments, 'till his death at which time his son will take over.

(The statement of the son's resentment of his father's position is an example of direct affective concern about the means of influence.)

2. Father and son. The son has just told his dad that he has enlisted. The father is not pleased. The son has been dominated by his parents since his youth and *wants to get away from it*. The father can't understand it. The son wants understanding. The son will come out a better man. The parents will have reconciled themselves to the fact that the son is able to stand on his own two feet.

(Here is an example of a statement of *wanting* to avoid the influence of someone else, from which affective concern over control of the means of influence is inferred. This is a sufficient reason for scoring this story under Criterion 1. Note that there is a close tie between feelings of dependence and feelings of being dominated. These feelings will be hard to separate in stories and should be scored for evidence of Power Imagery.)

3. It has been proposed at a board of directors meeting that Jones Paper Clips, Inc. be merged with Acme Wire Products Co. Both companies started out following World War II, competed stiffly for local control of the paper clip market. Both companies are deep in debt, losing money. Joe White who has dreamed of being a big executive has sunk his life's savings in Jones P. C., Inc. *He doesn't want to lose control*. The merger will be accomplished. Joe will be V.P. of a new company which will prosper. He will later sell out, found new company which will run old one out of business.

(Again, the direct statement of need for maintaining control is an indication of affective concern that can be scored for Power Imagery.)

4. A group of boys, possibly those who are on some committee, are in the process of holding a meeting. The chairman who is at the table has asked a question and two boys are debating heatedly. Probably, one boy *feels strongly that his point of view should be recognized* while the boy standing opposite him objects. The boy at the window is disgusted by this bickering and the boy on the left side of the table *wants his ideas to be accepted*. There will be a confusing and heated discussion among the boys because the argument is apparently startling and vital. Probably a compromise between the two boys will result if disgust can be avoided with the members.

(There are many instances of affective concern about the control of the means of influence in this story.)

5. Students in some classroom with the instructor asking questions. A discussion probably started the class off and then the teacher started asking questions to get the points of his lecture across. The instructor *wants to teach the class.* Information is wanted by the students. The information wanted will be gotten by answering questions.

(The italicized phrase makes this story scorable for Power Imagery.)

6. Two men are talking. One is a teacher. The other is his student. The student has a problem in choosing a career and has come to the teacher for advice. The student wants sound advice. The teacher *wants to advise him correctly,* and is thinking about how to put his suggestions. They will come up with a temporary idea which the student will try out.

(Although the italicized imagery seems to meet Criterion 1, it is not used as evidence for Power Imagery because the advice in this story was solicited. The story is *not* scored for Power Imagery.)

2. *There is a definite statement about someone doing something about maintaining or attaining the control of the means of influencing another person.* Something that the character is actually doing is the only kind of imagery that can qualify as Power Imagery under this criterion. The character has to be disputing a position, arguing something, demanding or forcing something, trying to put a point across, giving a command, trying to convince someone of something, punishing someone (and theoretically any activity) in order to obtain control of the means of influencing someone. Statements that are either in the passive voice or in the past or future tense are scorable. But the mere mention of dissension or of a shift in opinion in a story is not sufficiently explicit for it to be scored. Someone must be explicitly dissenting or trying to influence opinion in these cases. Physical power can be used as a means of influencing, but does not by itself imply power concern. Power Imagery would not be scored, for example, if it were clear that the utilization of physical power was mainly in the service of expressing hostility.

Three special considerations should be noted under Criterion 2. The two special considerations noted under Criterion 1 are applicable to Criterion 2 also. Trying to interest, teach, inspire someone will be statements that are scorable for Power Imagery under Criterion 2. Trying to win an election for someone else would not be scored unless there is a close identification of the person campaigning and the person up for office. A third consideration should be recognized. Sometimes it will be clear that the activity of the characters in the stories, although it meets the criteria listed in the previous paragraph, is *only* for the purposes of arriving at the goal of some other motive. When this is so, the story should not be scored for Power Imagery. However, *if it is not clear* whether power motivation or some other motivation is the ultimate concern of the imagery, *score the story for Power Imagery.*

Examples of Criterion 2

7. These two men are planning a break from the political party to which they both belong. The elder man is the instigator. Noticing the disapproval the young man has shown with the party policy, *he is convincing him to join with him. The elder man was pushed into the party*. At first, he thought it was a good idea. As he saw the workings of it he became more against it. The elder man is going to break from the party and wants the younger man to join. He is convincing the younger man. *The two will start a new opposition party*. Both will prove workers and a steadfast friendship will evolve.

(This story contains many instrumental activities with someone actually doing something in order to control the means of influence. Hence, it would be scored under Criterion 2 for Power Imagery. *Convincing someone* is perhaps the best example of the kind of imagery which is to be scored by this criterion.)

8. It is a board meeting of a large corporation. The characters are the chairman and the board of directors. It is a crucial meeting because a minority group *is trying to seize control*. The minority group, under the direction of a young, able, financial wizard, *has been gaining strength in order to upset the old-wing control of the corporation*. The leader of the new revolutionary group is mad because he has first been thwarted by a neat parliamentary trick of the "old guard" chairman. The new group *will take control*, unseating the old guard because they represent progress and initiative. The new always wins out over the old.

9. It seems as if two men are having a discussion of a very important problem and the older of the two seems to find it hard *to convert* the other. A long argument must have happened to account for the expression of the man. *The older seems to be trying to get a favorable answer from the reluctant younger man*. I believe the older man who seems the most calm will *win the argument*.

(The above two stories are filled with statements of specified instrumental acts in the service of power concerns, as defined.)

10. These are students in a classroom. *A student is expounding* on a theory which he thinks is correct. This is a physics class. The teacher has asked a question, and this student thinks he has the answer. The rest of the students are waiting for the teacher's reaction. Some do not think the answer given is correct. The teacher will say this is almost the correct answer, and then he will give the complete answer.

(In this story the only statement which makes the story scorable is the italicized one. A term "expounding" should be taken as a behavior implying an influence attempt.)

11. This looks like a political rally with campaigners present. Time has come for town elections. They are preparing for candidates and the campaign. Ideas and suggestions are being given for publication, etc. Dates will be set for speeches, etc. The election will be held after all the campaigning and publicizing. *One of the men will win*.

(This story is entirely composed of instrumental behavior for an election. It would not be scored if the last sentence were not present. The statement that one of the men will win implies that he was doing the campaigning also. Without this statement one would not know whether one of the campaigners was a candidate or not. And in that case the story would not have been scored.)

12. Four older men are lounging in the living room telling sea stories. They were all at a dinner party with their wives and have retired to smoke while the wives clear the tables and wash the dishes. The man on the left is a republican unknown to the others who are democrats. He will blast Truman and the others except the one with his back toward us will *pounce on him verbally*. The one with his back toward us is a Commie who will agitate the rest until they find out what he is saying. All *will pounce on the Commie* and the wives' nice bridge-dinner party will end up in a fight and the cops are called.

(The term "pounce on" used in this story stands for behavior directed toward controlling the means of influence. Often aggressive statements will appear in the context of power imagery. Again it might be difficult to separate aggression and power. Aggressive statements would not be scored if the aggression is obviously just for the sake of destruction without any regard to its implications for controlling the means of influence.)

13. Four top union men are meeting at one of the men's home. *They are arguing on a policy*. There has been intense friction between the union and the management at the factory over a wage dispute. The man sitting at the left in the picture *is demanding the other's support* in the backing of a venture. They will meet the next day with management and *have a bitter quarrel over settling the wage dispute*. The appearance of their faces indicates that they are firm in their convictions and *will stand up for the union*.

(This story contains many statements of instrumental activity that service the means of control of influence. One might question whether the instrumentality is directly related to the control orientation. But there is enough evidence here that it is when one notes that the imagery has to do essentially with a dispute for the control of decisions.)

14. *Old maid is trying to get her way with her supporting nephew*. The man's parents were killed when he was young and the aunt raised him. She was an old maid. The aunt thinks that her nephew owes her more than respect. She wants devotion. He wants a release from it all. He wants to get married and she doesn't appove. He will assert himself and get married, but he will always wonder whether he did the right thing.

(The only imagery in this story scorable for Power Imagery is the first sentence. It is an example of Criterion 2.)

15. Seems to be a classroom; either a discussion or lecture is taking place. Persons involved are students and one instructor. The student seems to be answering or asking a question of the instructor. This has been done and now the student is responding. An answer to the question is being thought by student or instructor, as the case may be. An answer will be given and possibly the whole class will assume a more wide awake feeling.

(This story is not scored for Power Imagery. Although it is a teaching situation, no one is trying to teach, inspire, put a point across. It is only a matter of getting answers to questions that were asked.)

16. Two men are discussing something seriously. The persons are a middle-aged man and a very elderly gentleman. It is possible that the middle-aged man is seeking advice from the elderly gentleman about some family business as they appear well-to-do. They are thinking about a problem. The younger man wants advice from the elderly gentleman. The older gentleman will give the young man advice and he will accept it or he might not.

(This story is not scored for Power Imagery either. Although one person is giving advice to another, it was solicited advice and, hence, does not meet Criterion 2.)

3. A story can be scored for Power Imagery *if there is a statement of an interpersonal relationship which in its execution is culturally defined as one in which there is a superior person having control of the means of influencing another one who is subordinate.* Examples of these are: boss–worker, judge–defendant. Mere mention of a superior–subordinate relationship is not enough. There has to be some mention of the activity involved in carrying out this relationship. Indeed, if a story about a boss and a worker goes on to elaborate about the affiliative bond between the two men, the story should not be scored. Mere mention of the fact that a given person was influential would be enough to allow the story to be scored. For a story to be scored Power Imagery under this criterion, there has to be some mention of the subordinate as well as of the superior position. Either the subordinate is directly involved in the imagery, or the effect of the superior on the subordinate has to be clear, for the story to be scored. The parent–child relationship is not in itself considered a power relationship. The use of culturally defined channels of influence by the subordinate in a story of a superior–subordinate relationship will be scored.

Examples of Criterion 3

17. A campaign headquarters with the big boss talking with the people who are to do the heavy campaigning for "their man." The campaign means a lot to the man running, for in the past years their side has lost by very few votes. If the campaign is carried out with the utmost in ideas and enthusiasm, they will be able to win. But, however, the campaign is not an easy one to win. All are considering this viewpoint. The big boss will lead the others in a big band box campaign so that they will be victors. That campaigning is to be considered as one of the most important parts.

18. A boss is talking to her secretary, telling her what has to be done. The secretary came in to find out what there had to be done for the day. She is thinking that she ought to do the work promptly. She wants to do a good job. She will carefully do what is expected of her.

(In both of these stories, the main reason for scoring these stories for Power Imagery is the statement of the role relationships which are culturally defined as power-related, viz., relationships between bosses and workers. Furthermore, the activities in the stories bear out the underlying power relationships.)

Subcategories

These categories unless otherwise specified are scored only once per story. If Unrelated Imagery (U Im) is scored, no subcategory will be scored. Any sentence can be scored for more than one subcategory. The same phrase may be scored for Imagery and any other category, but the same phrase may *not* be scored for *two* subcategories.

NEED (N)

If in the story there is an *explicit* statement of someone wanting to attain or maintain control of the means of influence, then the story should be scored for Need. Most of these statements will be prefaced by such phrases as "he wants to," "he wishes to," or "he would like to." However, some phrases such as "is determined to" can be taken as implying a state of need. One should be careful to code stories Need only if the goal state related to power is the one which is inherently connoted by the condition or object which is wanted in the statement. For example, if a story is about a person trying to convince someone of doing something in order to attain money and, if within the story the imagery "he wants money" appears, then this story would not be scored for Need. It would be scored for Need if the subject had written "he wants to convince this person." The person in the story can be wanting either to attain the goal of control or to avoid the feeling of weakness or being dominated.

Examples of need

19. Two men are discussing a situation. They apparently disagree. The man on the right is trying to convince the other of something. They have realized they disagree on something. And now they are arguing it out. The man on the right is trying to convince the other. The other man by the window seems not to be convinced. *The man on the right wants to convince him* and the other is unwilling to be convinced. They won't reach a decision. The man by the window refuses to be convinced.

20. Two boys have met after taking a law test. They are discussing various problems on the test and the answers they gave. Debating their own answers as most logical. They are now arguing. They have just come from this previously mentioned law test for which they have both studied hard and have both interpreted a question differently. One thinks that his answer was correct while the other also believes his is. *They both wish their point to be recognized by the other*. Probably both boys will end up saying, "Well, we'll see when we get those tests back," meaning there will be no compromise of ideas at this meeting.

(In the two examples above the italicized phrases are clear statements of Need.)

21. The younger man is the son of the older, a prominent lawyer. (The young man wishes to get out and start a practice of his own.) The father does not approve. The father has taken great pride in the son and always assumed he would carry on his name. The father is telling the son how silly it is to go out on his own. Although *the son would like to get out from under his father's rule*, he is being swayed. The son will remain in business with his father. He will, however, never feel completely independent of his father. He will not be a forceful person.

(This story is likewise scored for Need. Note, however, that it is not scored on the basis of the second sentence in the story. This is not a statement of need for control of the means of influence. The italicized phrase is what makes this story scorable for Need. It is a statement of need to avoid being dominated or influenced.)

INSTRUMENTAL ACTIVITY (I)

This category is scored for a story if there is a statement in the story about someone actually *doing something* to control the means of influence. Actually any kind of behavior can theoretically be scored if there is a connection between that behavior and the attainment or maintenance of control within the context of the story. Usually the kind of behavior scored as Instrumental Activity is someone trying to convince someone, put a point across, teach something, interest someone in something. Many times thinking behavior is scorable. For example, someone is thinking of the best means to convince his audience.

One should be careful to avoid scoring stories that imply Instrumental Activity but by the nature of the wording merely describe situations. One would not score, "There is an argument going on," but one would score "Jim is arguing with Bill over a point of view."

The Instrumental Activity is further scored I+, I−, or I?. It is scored I+ if the total activity is *ultimately* successful in arriving at a goal. The Instrumental Activity is scored I− if it is unsuccessful and I? if it is questionable in attaining the goal (e.g., "He *probably* will win"). If there are several instrumental activities mentioned and they vary in the sign one can attribute to them, they are scored I?. This is also true if there is more than one character who shows power concern in the story, and one wins and the other loses out. If there is a compromise, score I?. Activities occurring in the past, present, or future can be scored for instrumental activity.

Examples of Instrumental Activity

22. The man with the brief case has come as a salesman to see the elder man, a prominent businessman. The elder man hardly notices him because he is thinking

thoughts of his own. The elder man has always been dominant in the firm. In the board meeting the other day he was opposed by a new board member. *He is thinking of how he is going to overcome this obstacle*, a situation in which he has been often. *He will continue to plot against the man who opposes him until he gets his resignation.* After the man has resigned, the elder man will find no satisfactions in his group of yes men.

23. Fellow at the window is a college president, the other guy is a regent *demanding in a friendly way that some policy be carried out*. Seems the students are disturbed by a proposed new form of student government. The regent wants the president to quiet them down somehow. President feels he must concur, although it may be against his moral convictions. Regent wants non-interference from lowly students. Actually he thinks that president is capable but too liberal. President will give in. *Regent will invite him to his house for dinner.* President forgets incident and again becomes willing pawn.

(The two stories above would be scored I+ because of the italicized phrases in them.)

24. A college undergrad, a senior, *is speaking to a neophyte and presumably a freshman about his fraternity and its glories*. He hopes to get the guy to pledge his fraternity. The freshman has been to this fraternity, but wonders whether he should pledge it. *The senior has been badgering him for a few days.* The freshman is wondering if what the senior is saying is bull. The senior hopes he is getting his points across. The freshman will give the question a lot of thought and won't get too much sleep. *The senior and the other brothers will continue to hound the guy.* Eventually he will say no to them.

(All the italicized phrases are examples of the instrumental acts. The story is scored I− because the acts were not successful.)

GOAL ANTICIPATION (GA)

Goal Anticipation (Ga) is scored for a story if within the story there are statements of characters thinking about the goal – controlling the means of influence – or thinking or anticipating about whether they will or will not be successful in reaching the goal. It should be noted carefully that this means that a *character in the story* has to be doing the thinking. Comments by the author of the story about whether or not the goal will be reached are not scorable.

Examples of Ga are someone worried about whether he is going to win an election, someone thinking about the fact that he is going to win an argument, someone merely thinking about winning a point or showing superiority.

Ga can be scored Ga+ if the anticipation is goal attainment (he thinks he will win the election), and it is scored Ga− if the anticipation is either doubt about goal attainment (he is worried about his chances of winning the election) or concern about losing (he thinks he will lose the election). Both Ga+ and Ga− can be scored for the same story.

Examples of Goal Anticipation

25. It is a business meeting. The members are officials of a board with equal standing. The man (left, standing, clenched fist) is angry. The board has voted on a measure and the angry man has lost a former supporter, so his plan is thwarted. The angry man wants them to reconsider *as he thinks that their plan will be disastrous to his plans.* The opposition, seemingly quite friendly, will not back down. The rest of the group are non-committal.

(The man thinking that their plan will be disastrous to his is a negative goal anticipation. The story would be scored Ga−.)

26. There is a boy and a young man. The man is telling the boy something rather serious. Perhaps they are talking about school or one of the boy's friends. The man has stopped the boy to talk with him. He wants to convince him of something. Perhaps about doing his schoolwork. The boy is listening patiently maybe a little annoyed at having to listen to what the man says. He is listening though and will probably remember some of what the man says. The man will leave *feeling that he has accomplished something.* The boy will probably learn from what was said but not necessarily follow it.

(This story would be scored for Ga+. In this story the word "feeling" seems to mean "thinking." The phrase "feeling that he has accomplished something" is interpreted to mean "thinking about the goal." Thus it is scored Ga+. Although the term "anticipation" is used to define this category, the goal does not have to be in the future. The goal can be in the past or present, as in this example. That is, a statement about a goal already accomplished which the character is thinking about is scored Ga.)

BLOCKS IN THE PERSON OR IN THE WORLD (BP AND BW)

If within a power-related story, there are instances of disruptions to ongoing behavior toward attaining or maintaining control of the means of influence, then the story is scored for Block. It will be important to make a distinction between ongoing disruption and disruption which in fact establishes the power-related concern to begin with. Almost all power-related stories contain blocks in the sense that people are to be convinced or taught or influenced in some way. This kind of imagery is not scored for Block because it is too intimately connected to the power concern. What is scored for Block, however, is an instance of further disruption to the power-seeking behavior in a story already established as a power-related story. For example, one would not score an argument in which one is trying to convince another of a point of view if all that was mentioned was that there was this kind of argument going on. If, however, the story goes on with the argument situation and elaborates the difficulties encountered by the first person in convincing the second, then the story would be scored for Block. Mere failure to obtain the goal would not be scored for Block.

If the obstacle lies in some weakness or difficulty of the person concerned with establishing the control of the means of influence, then the story is scored Block Person (Bp). If the obstacle lies in the world – either in another person or in a given situation – then the story is scored for Block World (Bw). Both Bp and Bw can be scored within the same story. Each can be scored only once per story.

Example of Block Personal

27. The secretary has come in for an appointment with the boss. She has been a little slow in her work and the boss has called her in for a pep talk. He wants her to get on the ball and is trying to persuade her to do more work on time. *He is not very tactful* about it, which the secretary resents. She finally quits the job to take on a better one.

Example of Block World

28. These men are gathered together for a discussion. They are trying to work out a solution to the best means of handling their failing business in which they are partners. Business has turned for the worse so the leader of the partners has called a meeting at his home. The man on the left is trying to convince the others that they need a new sales force. The other men are dubious. He wants them to accept his plan. *The man standing will disagree violently with this man.* No decision will be reached.

AFFECTIVE STATES: POSITIVE (G+) AND NEGATIVE (G−)

Affective states associated with the reaching or not reaching the goal of control of the means of influence are scored G. When someone in the story experiences happiness with having convinced someone of something, dominated some situation, and influenced another person's behavior, then the story is scored for Positive Affect (G+). There has to be an explicit statement of these feelings, and they should not be inferred from mention of successful outcome alone. A story is scored for Negative Affect (G−) if someone feels upset or angry about either being weak or not having successfully influenced someone. These affective statements can appear in the sequence preceding final goal attainment or frustration. But the distinction between anticipations of future events which can contain some affective words (e.g., being worried about an election or being satisfied that he will gain control of the business) should be kept clear from immediate affective statements (e.g., he is glad to have won the argument). The former are scored Ga and the latter are scored G.

An important thing to remember in scoring a story for Affect is that the affective statement has to be *connected to the power concern*. Just because clear affective imagery appears within a story scorable for Power Imagery, it does not mean that this affective imagery is scorable for G. A story in which there is a character who is depressed and who at the same time shows power concern scorable for Power Imagery is not automatically scored for G−. The depression has to be related to lack of power satisfaction.

On occasion there will be no direct affective statements surrounding control of the means of influence, but the story still should be scored for G because the statement of the outcome is so vivid that the implication of affect is obvious. For example, if a man were to be running for office and he wins and becomes the most influential governor the state ever had, then the scorer should feel free to score the G+ category because of this statement. Note that becoming a *good* governor would not be scored. This is a statement which has no direct relevance to the power concern. Both G+ and G− can be scored in the same story.

Examples of affective states

29. An older and younger man are conversing. They are talking about the young man's future. He has reached a point in his career where he has to decide whether he should take a job that holds no interest but pays well or take a job that holds his interest but is financially inferior. The older man is trying to talk the younger man into taking the poorer paying job. He wants him to take the job. The younger man cannot decide about it. Under the guidance of the older man the younger man takes the poorer paying job. The older man *feels satisfied* that he was able to convince him into this decision.

30. A teacher is instructing a class in political science. It is an ordinary classroom in a leading university. The teacher has prepared himself for the class, having gone over the points that he wanted to get across for that day. The students want clarification of his lecture. They do not understand what the teacher has talked about. *The teacher is disgruntled because he thinks he has been ineffective.* He will try to go over the points one by one. The students may or may not understand this time.

(The first example is scored for G+; the second for G−.)

THEMA (TH)

Thema is a subcategory which requires a judgment independent of the scheme of the behavioral sequence. When the behavioral sequence of the power concern is the central plot of the story and does not have competition from other concerns for being the predominant source of imagery in a story, then the subcategory Thema should be scored. That is, when the power concern is elaborated in such a way that most of the story deals with attaining or maintaining control of the means of influence, then Thema is scored. In a sense, the judgment of presence of Thema is a judgment of the intensity of the power motivation concern in a given story. The assumption in regard to this judgment is that the stronger the motive the less likely will other motive thoughts appear in the story.

Scoring Thema should be independent of the number of subcategories scored. Although it is likely that a story containing elaborations of many of the subcategories would be unidimensional with respect to showing power concern predominantly, the scorer should not use the frequency of subcategories as the criterion for scoring Thema. Indeed, a story can be written in such a way that few of the subcategories are scored, and yet it would be obvious that the power motivation concern is the *leitmotif* of that story. And what is more, a story can contain a number of subcategories in one or two sentences, but the rest of the story can be unrelated to power motivation. In that case, then, Thema would not be scored. Do not score Thema if there was some question of scoring Power Imagery to begin with.

Examples of Thema

31. Two college students are conversing somewhere on campus. They are discussing whether or not ———— State College should be titled a university. The one speaking is trying to convince the other that it should. He is pointing out that it has many various colleges. He is a logical and sensible person. His friend, however, will never be convinced simply because he thinks ———— is better than ———— State and, thus, cannot give up the idea that ———— State should not become a university. The two persons will go on being friends. The first student will always be the more open-minded.

(Although this story can be scored for only one subcategory, I−, the story is still scored for Thema, because there are no other predominant behavioral sequences in the story.)

32. Here are a number of workers for the Republican party. They have gathered together to outline the campaign. Each of them has been nominated for a post in the City Elections. Since they want to win the election, they have come together to plan the campaign. They are thinking of their chances for election and would like to win very much. After careful planning they win the election. To celebrate they throw a party.

(This story has very little reference to anything outside the behavioral sequence related to the election. Hence, it would be scored for Thema.)

33. An older man is trying to convince the younger man into running for office in the coming election. The older man has lost his power in the party, and since the younger man is very popular in town, he wants to persuade the man to run for mayor, because he thinks he can maintain some of his influence behind this man. The younger man is very enterprising. He recently moved to town, set up his business, and would like to settle down to a comfortable life. The prospects of being in politics do not intrigue him. The younger man likes talking with the older man and he just would like things to be on a friendly basis. The older man cannot convince the younger man to run, which makes the older man unhappy. The younger man settles down, has lots of children and lots of friends.

(Although this story is scored for Need, I−, Ga+, G−, it would not be scored for Thema, because the competing imagery about the desires and thoughts of the younger man cuts down the saliency of the Power Imagery in this story.)

If Power Imagery is scored, then the greatest possible number of sub-categories which can be scored in a single story is: Need (+1); I, either I+, I?, or I−, (+1); Ga+ (+1); Ga− (+1); Bp (+1); Bw (+1); G+ (+1); G− (+1); and Th (+1). Together with +1 for Imagery, this would make the maximal score possible +10.

NOTE

1 See the introductory passage of the scoring manual for the achievement motive, chapter 10.

21 *Power motivation revisited*

DAVID G. WINTER

THEORETICAL AND EMPIRICAL BACKGROUND

Definition

The power motive is the desire to have impact on other people, to affect their behavior or emotions. This broad and general definition includes a whole family of overlapping concepts such as influence, inspiration, nurturance, authority, leadership, control, dominance, coercion, and aggression. Although these concepts have varying connotations of legitimacy, morality, and implied reaction of the other person (the "target" of power), they share a core meaning of one person's *capacity to affect the behavior or feelings of another person* (see D. G. Winter, 1973, chapter 1).

As a class of goal striving, the power motive is to be distinguished from other power-related psychological and sociological concepts, such as roles and statuses permitting power, skill at using power, feelings of power, and values and beliefs about the exercise of power – ranging from authoritarianism to Gandhi's nonviolent *satyagraha* or "leverage of truth" (see Erikson, 1969, pp. 410–440). For all of its conceptual and empirical distinctiveness, the power motive does not exist in isolation. These other concepts determine how it is channeled into specific behaviors and are thereby essential to a complete understanding of the striving for power.

Conceptual framework

The idea that humans have a drive for power or "will to power" is prominent in many cultural and intellectual traditions. In the Western "patriarchal" tradition, the ideas of Machiavelli, Hobbes, Nietzsche, and Adler quickly come to mind; but power strivings also play a prominent role in feminist thought (J. B. Miller, 1982; Ruddick, 1983) and traditional Asian political thought (Pye, 1986).

The present measure of power motivation, the revised *n* Power scoring system, was developed within the McClelland–Atkinson tradition of

301

motives as (a) relatively stable dispositions to strive for certain classes of goals, which are (b) reflected in mental contents of "associative networks," and therefore (c) most appropriately measured through content analysis of verbal material (see Atkinson, 1958a; McClelland, 1985b). These content analysis systems, in turn, are (d) developed by comparing the verbal material (or thematic apperception) produced by people in whom the motive has been experimentally aroused with that of people in a more neutral state of arousal.

Power motivation is probably learned, perhaps through the kinds of early experiences discussed by McClelland and Pilon (1983). At its core, however, the power motive may grow out of innate biological bases such as an incentive system for having "impact" or the "flight–fight–fright" response of the sympathetic nervous system (McClelland, 1982; 1985b, pp. 320–325). The motive may be conscious or unconscious, depending upon values, defenses, and other cognitive factors such as self-schemata or ability to monitor inner thoughts and wishes. In the United States, for example, *power* is a topic especially hedged with suspicions, doubts, and denials. Leaders almost never say that their actions are motivated by a desire for power; instead they talk of "service" or "duty." As a result, one might expect Americans to be defensive or unaware of their power motivation. (In contrast, many Asian cultures are more open, direct, and positive about the role of power in human affairs; see Pye, 1986.) This is one important reason for measuring power motivation indirectly, through content analysis of verbal material, rather than by direct questioning.

The power motive itself is conceived as a stable disposition, but its actual expression in behavior depends on a host of other personality and situational factors. Other motives may combine with power (see McClelland, chapter 5) or compete with power (Atkinson, 1982; also reprinted as chapter 2 in this book). Other psychological variables such as expectancies and incentives (Atkinson & Feather, 1966), responsibility (D. G. Winter & Barenbaum, 1985b), and probably self-control, habits, and styles channel the power motive just as they do other motives. Finally, social structural variables such as class (D. G. Winter & Stewart, 1978, pp. 400–402) and race (Greene & Winter, 1971) may have important effects, either directly (through "real" opportunities and constraints) or indirectly (through expectations and other cognitive elements).

Background

Veroff (1957) developed the first content analysis measure of the power motive, and in fact this scoring system continues to be a useful measure of the fearful or avoidance-tinged aspects of the power motive (see chapters 19 and 20). In other words, the original Veroff scoring system is now considered to measure fear of weakness (see Veroff, 1982; Veroff & Veroff,

1972; also chapter 19). Uleman (1972) developed another measure, which he later called the "influence motive." The revised power motive measure, described here, is considered to reflect power more as an approach motive or, in Atkinson and Feather's terminology (1966), the "hope of power."

MEASUREMENT INFORMATION

The scoring system

DESCRIPTION. The revised power motive measure presented in the next chapter is constructed within the traditional McClelland–Atkinson framework of a series of alternative categories reflecting basic motive-related imagery, and then a series of subcategories, reflecting emphasis or elaboration of that basic imagery. (Subcategories are only scored if basic imagery has been scored.) Basic motive imagery includes the following three alternative criteria: (1) *Someone shows power concern through actions that directly express power* (strong forceful actions, giving unsolicited help, trying to control or investigate, trying to influence or persuade, or trying to impress); (2) *one person's action arouses a strong emotional response in another*; or (3) *someone is concerned about reputation or position.*

Subcategories of elaboration include: positive and negative *prestige* of the actor, explicitly stated *need* for power, *instrumental activity*, world *block* or obstacle to getting power, *goal anticipations* of power, affective *goal states*, and *effect.*

In early research using the revised power motive measure, approach and avoidance power motives were distinguished (D. G. Winter, 1973, chapters 3, 5). If the material scored for power imagery contained altruism, doubt, or irony, then the entire score was classified as Fear of Power; if not, it was classified as Hope of Power. More recently, the approach–avoidance distinction has been conceptualized in terms of the entire revised power motive measure and the original Veroff measure (see chapter 19; also Veroff, 1982). Several other methods of partitioning power motive scores or combining them with other variables are described by McClelland, Davis, Kalin, and Wanner (1972, especially chapters 6, 8, and pp. 338–341, 348–356), McClelland (1975, chapters 8, 9), McClelland and Boyatzis (1982), and D. G. Winter and Barenbaum (1985b).

DERIVATION. The revised power motive measure was derived principally from a 1965 motive-arousal experiment with male business school students, in which aroused subjects saw a movie of President John F. Kennedy's inaugural address, while neutral subjects saw a movie about science demonstration equipment. D. G. Winter (1973, chapter 3) argued that such an experiment – at least for those subjects at that time – aroused power in its charismatic, traditional, and rational–legal sense, without at the same time arousing anxieties about power. The revised measure also took account of differences between aroused and neutral subjects in earlier experiments by Veroff (1957) and Uleman (1966, 1972). Further cross validation came from later studies where the power motive was aroused by improvised political activism role playing (Watson, 1969), and by a multimedia presentation of inspirational speeches (Steele, 1977).

Procedures for obtaining verbal material

The revised power motive measure can be used in a straightforward way to score thematic apperception material obtained in the traditional way, where pictures or verbal stimuli are used to elicit stories. There is no single "best" set of pictures or verbal cues. As a rule of thumb, researchers should select cues that have a moderately strong power theme, while at the same time suggest an alternative theme such as achievement or affiliation. Two or three such cues, in a total set of four to six, should provide an adequate basis for assessing power motivation (as well as many of the other content analysis variables discussed in this book). I have found the following three pictures especially useful for this purpose, for both women and men:

1. Ship's captain (McClelland, 1975, p. 385): strong power theme.
2. Couple on bench by river.
3. Women scientists (McClelland, 1975, p. 387): strong achievement and power themes.

These pictures are reproduced in appendix II. I have found the following verbal cues useful (adapted from Horner, 1968, and Lesko, 1974):

1. At the end of the day, Barbara is going back to the chemistry lab.
2. A father and his child look worried.
3. John is sitting on a chair with a smile on his face.
4. A mother is talking with her child about something important.
5. A brother and sister are playing. One is ahead.

Lundy (1988) has recently shown that the validity of thematic apperception measures is significantly higher when they are obtained in a relaxed, informal setting. This suggests that traditional thematic apperceptive instructions (reproduced, for example, in McClelland, 1975, p. 384) probably need to be changed. I suggest that written or oral instructions at the beginning of the thematic apperception task should be simple and emphasize spontaneity and imagination. Expressions such as "test" or "psychological test" should be avoided. Timing and instructions to go on to the next story should be casual; do *not* use a stopwatch or other formal "apparatus." The appendix of this chapter gives a sample instruction sheet that I have used with picture and verbal cues. (Modifications can be made as needed when pictures are projected on a screen instead of being bound into a booklet.)

It is very important that the thematic apperception task be given at the beginning of any testing session, before administering any other test, questionnaire, or procedure, in order to avoid inadvertent motive-arousal effects.

While traditional thematic apperception techniques are most commonly used to obtain motive scores, power motive imagery can also be scored from any imaginative verbal material such as speeches, interviews, or popular literature. In contrast to thematic apperceptive stories, these materials generally have no "natural" divisions into several-hundred-word scoring units. In such cases, researchers may wish to consider a new method of scoring motive imagery in continuous "running text" (see D. G. Winter, 1991).

Power motivation in different populations

Although a good deal of the research on power motivation has been carried out with college students, usable scores have been obtained from junior high school students (Lesko, 1974) and the various demographic subgroups of a representative sample of the civilian adult population of the United States (Veroff, Depner, Kulka, & Douvan, 1980). Among less educated groups, though, the proportion of protocols not adequate for scoring may run over one-fourth.

SEX AND GENDER. Because the relationships between men and women have been largely stratified and structured around power, many people believe that men and women differ in the ways they establish, maintain, and express power. Whatever the truth of these beliefs, there is *no* evidence of any sex difference in the structure of the power motivation scoring system and procedures that arouse the motive (Stewart & Winter, 1976), or in the behaviors correlated with power motivation (D. G. Winter, 1988b; see also Stewart & Chester, 1982). Recent research suggests that apparent sex differences are really a function of socialization for responsibility (D. G. Winter & Barenbaum, 1985b).

RACE AND ETHNICITY. The revised measure of power motivation has been used with black U.S. college students (Greene & Winter, 1971), German university students (Schnackers & Kleinbeck, 1975; D. G. Winter, 1973, p. 136), and businessmen in India (McClelland & Winter, 1969, pp. 328–332; D. G. Winter, 1973, p. 115). Taken together, these studies show substantial convergence with the trend of validity results to be described, suggesting that the measure can be used with a wide variety of ethnic groups and cultures – but with one caution. Variations in resources, opportunities, and beliefs and values affect both what is considered to be "power" and what paths are used to attain power. (D. G. Winter & Stewart, 1978, p. 402, make this point with respect to social class.)

NORMS. Because power motive scores are strongly affected by the number and nature of the picture or verbal cues and the length of time subjects have to write or tell stories, there are no "norms" for the measure in the conventional sense, and it is not possible to compare scores obtained under different conditions. As a corollary, it is very important that all subjects in any particular study be tested under the same conditions, with the same cues. (See D. G. Winter, 1973, pp. 97–98, for a "second best" procedure that can sometimes be used where testing conditions have been heterogeneous.)

CORRECTION FOR LENGTH. In general, power motive scores are not significantly correlated with the length of the stories written; but significant correlations may occur when subjects range widely in intelligence, verbal fluency, or social class, when there is variation from subject to subject in the amount of time given to write each story (as in the standard clinically administered TAT), or when all subjects have either a very brief time (2 minutes or less) or a very long time (more than 5 minutes) to write each story. Such correlations are usually considered artifacts; their effects can be removed by a technique developed by D. G. Winter (1973, p. 146) as a generalization of previous techniques used by other researchers (Child, Storm, & Veroff, 1958; McClelland, 1961, pp. 64, 161, 461–463; Veroff, Atkinson, Feld, & Gurin, 1960). First, "predicted" scores, given length, are calculated on the basis of the overall regression of score on length. For each subject, this involves multiplying length by the overall correlation coefficient of length with motive score, times the ratio of the standard deviations of motive scores and length (SD of motive scores divided by SD of length; see D. G. Winter, 1989a). Subjects' predicted scores are then subtracted from their actual scores to give corrected scores that are exactly uncorrelated with length.

RELIABILITY. Test–retest correlation coefficients as an estimate of power motive reliability are confounded by many other factors, such as the implicit thematic apperceptive instructional set to tell "different stories," and the effect of fantasy expression of a motive on its subsequent level. When these contaminants are removed or controlled, test–retest correlations reach the psychometrically adequate level of around $r = .70$. Interested readers should consult Atkinson (1982; also reprinted as chapter 2 of this book) and McClelland (1981, 1985b, pp. 208–213) and, particularly for the power motive, D. G. Winter and Stewart (1977b) for further discussion.

KEY VALIDITY STUDIES

Major reviews of the validity of the revised power motive measure can be found in McClelland (1985b, chapter 8), D. G. Winter (1973, chapters 4–6; 1988), and D. G. Winter and Stewart (1978). I mention only the highlights here.

Formal social power

OCCUPATIONS AND OFFICE HOLDING. Evidence from several studies suggests that power-motivated men and women seek influence and formal social power in many different ways. Some choose power-related careers – for example, business executive, teacher, psychologist or mental health worker, journalist, and member of the clergy. They are especially likely to succeed as managers and executives in large corporations (McClelland & Boyatzis, 1982). Power motivation, especially among working-class people, also predicts activity in voluntary organizations and clubs.

What makes these particular occupations attractive? In each case, there is the opportunity (even the duty) to *direct the behavior of individual other persons* in accordance with some preconceived plan and to use *positive and negative sanctions* on others' behavior, all within a *"legitimate" institutional structure*. The kind of power that seems important to power-motivated people, then, is direct and legitimate *interpersonal* power. Careers such as science and law, which involve more indirect and abstract kinds of power, are not associated with power motivation. Thus a scientist, by inventing the transistor, may revolutionize the lives of millions of people, but that scientist's power is not nearly as direct and interpersonal as the power of executives in the transistor manufacturing company. And although many lawyers are involved in the mechanics of power, their role seems to be that of the hired expert rather than the actual power seeker.

Many political leaders seek power, but others are looking for love and acceptance, while still others may pursue excellence in politics. One study of local leaders found that those who sought positions of high power potential *and* who initiated their own candidacy scored higher in power motivation than other leaders and a control group (D. G. Winter, 1973, pp. 102–105). At-a-distance studies of American presidents and world leaders show that power motivation predicts rated greatness, an active and positive approach to politics, and propensity for war and aggression (D. G. Winter, 1991).

THE STRATEGIES OF POWER. How do power-motivated people get power? First, they are *visible* and get to be well known. For example, in gambling situations they like to take the kind of extreme risks that draw other people's attention (McClelland & Teague, 1975; McClelland &

Watson, 1973). College students high in power motivation become visible in subtler ways, such as by writing letters to the campus newspaper or having their names on their dormitory room door. Acquiring and using *prestige* and self-display also enhance visibility. Power-motivated people are likely to spend more money on prestige possessions (among college students, for such items as television sets, wine glasses, and framed pictures), and to have more credit cards. This concern with visibility suggests an essential difference between the power and achievement motives: In the words of the old proverb, people high in achievement motivation might "build a better mousetrap so that the world would beat a path to their door." In contrast, power-motivated people would try to get the world coming to their door without having to build the better mousetrap first.

Second, power-motivated people build *alliances* with others, especially with lower-status or less well known people who may feel they are outsiders and have nothing to lose. In groups, they are adept at defining the situation, encouraging others to participate, and influencing others. They are not especially well liked, however, nor are they viewed as working hard or offering the best solutions to the problem (see Jones, 1969, cited in D. G. Winter, 1973). Whether they are *personally* liked or not, they do create high morale among their subordinates (McClelland & Burnham, 1976).

Some costs of power

"GROUPTHINK."   Although it may be an important source of the leadership on which society depends, the power motive is not without its social and individual costs. Fodor and his associates (Fodor & Farrow, 1979; Fodor & Smith, 1982) found that power-motivated leaders are especially vulnerable to flattery and ingratiation by subordinates, while the groups that they lead are vulnerable to "groupthink" (cf. Janis, 1972) – cohesive and high in morale, but less effective in gathering and using information, and low in dealing with moral concerns.

Perhaps these studies help to explain why power so often seems to involve a fatal flaw: Power-motivated leaders wind up listening only to followers who tell them what they want to hear, with the result that they do not pay attention to important but unpleasant information. Here again is another difference from the achievement motive, which leads people to seek and use knowledge – even unpleasant knowledge – about results.

AGGRESSION AND THE "PROFLIGATE IMPULSE."   Under some circumstances, people who score high in power motivation are involved in fights, arguments, and other kinds of exploitative aggression. When they have the upper hand in negotiation or bargaining situations, for example, they are likely to break agreements and demand better terms (see Schnackers &

Kleinback, 1975; Terhune, 1968). Sometimes they also drink and use drugs, gamble, and exploit members of the opposite sex – behaviors that can all be labeled "profligate impulsivity" (see D. G. Winter, 1988b; D. G. Winter & Barenbaum, 1985b; D. G. Winter & Stewart, 1978, pp. 408–412). College-educated men high in power motivation are *less* likely to have wives with a career outside the home than are men low in power motivation (D. G. Winter, Stewart, & McClelland, 1977). Not surprisingly in view of all these findings, male power motivation is also associated with the breakup of relationships and divorce (Stewart & Rubin, 1976). Are these profligate behaviors an inevitable dark side of the power motive? Not necessarily. D. G. Winter and Barenbaum (1985b) found that people's sense of responsibility has a big effect on the way their power motivation is expressed. (See chapter 35 for a discussion of the responsibility measure.)

STRESS AND ILLNESS. In recent years, McClelland and his colleagues have gathered a chain of evidence illustrating another cost of power motivation to the individual (McClelland, 1982; 1984; 1985b, pp. 320–324). The essential relationships may be summarized briefly. High power motivation leads people to exaggerated and overaroused sympathetic nervous system activity, especially in response to stress. Over time, this reactivity reduces the effectiveness of the immune system, which in turn makes them vulnerable to infectious diseases, and also leads to cardiovascular problems.

Relation to other measures

The revised power motive measure has considerable discriminant validity. It is not consistently related to achievement, affiliation, or intimacy motivation. It is usually correlated with the "assertive" stance toward the environment (see chapter 31), as would be expected from the semantic overlap of some of the scoring categories.

In common with most thematic apperception measures (McClelland, 1980; McClelland, Koestner, & Weinberger, 1989; also reprinted as chapter 3 in this volume), power motivation does not consistently correlate with "objective" or self-report measures intended to reflect the "same" variable. Nor is it consistently related to authoritarianism, internal versus external control of reinforcement, or Machiavellianism. As suggested, these other variables involve beliefs or values about power, rather than the motivation or striving to acquire power (see also D. G. Winter & Stewart, 1978, pp. 393–396, 432–437.)

CONCLUSION

In combination with the original Veroff measure of power motivation (see chapter 19), we now have two measures of the power motive. The Veroff measure seems to reflect an *avoidance* orientation toward power – that is, power concerns derived from a fear of weakness (or even a fear of power itself). In contrast, studies with the revised measure described in this chapter suggest that it is an *approach*-oriented concern for having impact on others. Finally, the psychometric characteristics of the revised measure suggest that it is applicable to a wide variety of populations.

APPENDIX TO CHAPTER 21

Sample Instruction Sheet for Eliciting Thematic Apperception Stories

Telling Stories

Name _____

You are going to see a series of pictures [sentences], and I would like you to tell stories about the people shown [described] in the pictures [sentences]. Try to imagine what is going on. Then tell what happened before, what the people are thinking about and feeling, and what will happen next. Try to write a story, with a beginning and end, about each picture [sentence].

When I tell you to begin, turn the page and look at the picture for a few seconds. Then turn the page again and write your story. [When I tell you to begin, turn the page, look at the sentence at the top of the page, and think about it. Then write your story on the rest of the page.] You will find these questions spaced out on the page to help you write a story:

> What is happening? Who are the people?
> What happened before? How did the story begin?
> What are the people thinking about, and how do they feel?
> What will happen? How will the story end?

These questions are only *guides* for your stories; you need not answer each one specifically.

You will have about five minutes for each story. I will tell you when it's about time to go on to the next story.

There are no right or wrong stories. Write whatever kind of stories you like.

22 *A revised scoring system for the power motive*

DAVID G. WINTER

INTRODUCTION

This revised scoring manual for the power motive is parallel to the earlier scoring systems for the achievement and affiliation motives, as well as the original power motive manual developed by Veroff (1957; see chapter 20). Essentially two tasks confront the scorer. First, is there evidence that the story contains any concern about power? Thus the scorer first searches for evidence of power concern, according to the criteria listed in this chapter for scoring Power Imagery. Second, how extensive or elaborated is the power concern? If the story is concerned with power and has been scored for Power Imagery, the scorer then goes on to search for the presence of subcategories that elaborate the basic power concern. If Power Imagery has not been scored, then the scorer simply proceeds to the next story.

The subcategories are organized in a logical manner around a behavioral sequence. The scorer may find it helpful to keep the behavioral sequence in mind as an aid to scoring the subcategories. The power behavioral sequence originates in persons who experience a state of need or desire (*N*). They take action (*I*) toward a goal. Blocks or obstacles (*Bw*) may interfere with the action. They may anticipate attainment of the goal (*Ga+*) or failure (*Ga−*). If they actually attain the goal, they are likely to experience satisfaction or positive affect (*G+*); if they fail, they may experience negative affect (*G−*). The power-related aspects of the sequence may be further enhanced if they have, or associate themselves with, prestige (*Pa+*) or if they lack prestige (*Pa−*). The power theme is further enhanced if the actions create a significant or important effect (*Eff*). These subcategories increase the power of the act through increasing the "size" of the action and the "size" of the effect created. The power behavioral sequence is presented schematically in Figure 22.1.

This manual is a slightly modified version of the manual published in Winter, D. G. (1973). *The power motive* (pp. 249–264). New York: The Free Press. Reprinted with permission of The Free Press, a Division of Macmillan, Inc. (copyright © by David G. Winter, 1968, 1973).

311

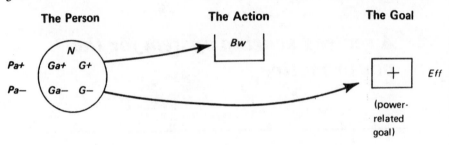

Fig. 22.1. Schematic representation of the power behavioral sequence.

DEFINITION OF POWER IMAGERY (POW IM)

Power Imagery is scored if some person or group of persons in the story is concerned about establishing, maintaining, or restoring their power – that is, their impact, control, or influence – over another person, group of persons, or the world at large. This power concern does not have to be the only theme, or even the major theme of the story, in order to be scored; it can be a peripheral theme. There are three more specific ways in which this power concern is expressed, or can be inferred from the stories; listed here are these three criteria for scoring Power Imagery.

1. *Someone shows power concern through actions that in themselves express power.* This person is called the "actor." These actions can be in the past or future tense, and in the passive voice. They can be wanted, fantasied, recollected, planned, or actually carried out in the story. They do not have to be successful. There are several types of such power actions:

a. Strong, forceful actions that affect others, such as assaults, attacks, chasing or catching (e.g., a criminal); verbal insults, threats, accusations, or reprimands; and sexual exploitation, where it is clear the action does not express mutuality or love. Crimes against persons or institutions (unless minor and of little effect) and gaining the upper hand or taking advantage of another's weakness in order to impose one's will on them are scored. Even such actions as begging or importuning can be scored, if they are intended to affect another's behavior or mental state. Do not score accidents. Examples include:

> They plan to attack an enemy supply area.
> The agents will catch the suspected people.
> The company representative has bawled out the captain.
> He is trying to seduce his secretary.
> The guy will go out to do some panhandling.

b. Giving help, assistance, advice, or support if it has not been solicited by the other person. However, solicited advice is scored where there is evidence for power concern beyond the mere answering of requests – for example, "He asked for advice, and in reply the mother tried to make the point that . . ." Teaching is scored, unless it is only a routine description of a teacher in a classroom. Examples include:

> The older woman protected the younger against others.
> The mother is interested in teaching her son basketball.
> Her husband went with her to help her, because she was stricken with grief.
> She is giving the kid advice.

c. Trying to control other persons through regulating their behavior or the conditions of their lives, or through seeking information that would affect another's life or actions: searching, investigating, checking up on, and so forth. Do not score routine requests for information or routine ordinary requests. Thus statements such as "The sergeant tells the men where to put the tent," "Anne wants Jim to lift the book," or "Anne asks Jim to lift the book," are not scored, because they are a part of everyday action and do not indicate any special concern for power. However, "Anne wants to influence Jim to lift the book," "Anne orders Jim to lift the book," or "The sergeant threatens the men . . ." are scored, because they go beyond routine actions and indicate a special concern for control. Examples include:

> The welfare worker arranged to transfer the kid to the country, to get him under a new influence.
> The executive is visiting the branch office to determine whether the agency should handle a new account.
> They are being sent to get information on the enemy troop build-up.
> The newspaper reporter is trying to get the lowdown on the politician.
> Complaints kept coming into the main office, so the manager was sent to get a first-hand report.

d. Trying to influence, persuade, convince, bribe, make a point, or argue with another person, so long as the concern is not to reach agreement or to avoid misunderstanding or disagreement. Mere mention of an argument or dissension would not, by itself, be scored; for example, the dissenters might come to a mutual resolution, or give up the argument in favor of affiliative activity. In other words, someone must be doing something, or wanting to do something, in order to change someone else's opinion. Examples include:

> His father tries to interest him in ranching.
> She tries to convince him to return home.
> The junior executive is trying to get her point across.

e. Trying to impress some other person or the world at large. Such actions as creative writing, making news or publicity, trying to win an election to office or identifying closely with someone else who is trying to win an election, and any action that will attract widespread attention is scorable. Trying to create a public effect or display, or gaining fame or notoriety, are scorable. The scorer should be careful to distinguish a concern for success as such from a concern for the fame or public attention that may result from success. Only the latter is scored for Power Imagery. Thus "She invents a better mousetrap" is not scored, but "... and the world beats a path to her door" is scored. Examples include:

> The reporter is interviewing the farmer about a feature story that he is going to write.
> An author is trying to gather thoughts for a bestseller.
> The guy is trying to impress his date.
> The man is urbane and sophisticated; he knows the right places in town to be seen in, and how to be seen in these spots.
> She is fed up with him and is putting on a scene.
> He was seen tearing hell through town in the family automobile.

(This last example shows a vigorous action and a suggestion of public attention.)

Not scored as Power Imagery: Generally actions are not scored for Power Imagery if they are described as wholly routine, or a wholly routine part of the role of the characters involved. Thus a teacher teaching or a soldier giving a routine command does not indicate a special concern for power; each is part of the routine roles of teacher or soldier. However, a parent teaching or an ordinary person giving a command is not routine and is therefore scored. Actions that are carried out *only* for the purpose of satisfying another motive are not scored for Power Imagery. Thus mention of extramarital sex would not be scored if the two people were in love, or were looking for companionship. Arguments are not scored if they are resolved as friendly discussions. Achievement-oriented actions that are successful are not scored, even if they are important and significant actions, unless the story also mentions that the actor will thereby become famous or achieve widespread public attention. In other words, the scorer should carefully distinguish the achievement and the power aspects of certain stories. Examples of things *not scored* for Power Imagery:

> They established one of the best thoroughbred farms in the world.

(This is only about achievement, not recognition.)

> A first date. Perhaps they will sleep together – they both want companionship and removal from reality.

(Sex is mentioned, but the concern is with affiliation and not power.)

> They are having a casual discussion. The man is explaining to the others about something they did not understand.

(This is routine.)

He helped his wife carry in the groceries.

(This "helping" is entirely routine.)

2. *Someone does something that arouses strong positive or negative emotions in others.* Here the person's power is shown by the emotional reaction of others: they feel pleasure, delight, awe, gratitude, respect, intense enjoyment; or fear, worry, despondency, strong jealousy, anger, or offense because of something the actor has done. Expressions of interest, such as "she was very interested" or "they listened intently," are not scored; but stronger expressions that indicate power or force are scored, such as "He was absolutely fascinated," or "Her words compelled their attention." The action that arouses the feelings must be intentional, or under the conscious control of the actor in order to be scored; but it does not matter whether the effect or emotional arousal is intended by the actor. Thus someone's response to natural disasters, accidents, economic depressions, and the like are not scored. Examples of Criterion 2 include:

> The professional player is giving a demonstration, and the boy is thrilled.
> She has taken him to a small cafe. He is enchanted by the atmosphere, and shows his delight.
> He told his mother what he had been doing. She broke down and cried.

3. *Someone is described as having a concern for reputation or position,* that is, about what someone else or the world at large will think of his or her power. The difference between this criterion and Criterion 1 is that under Criterion 1, some action at least has to be mentioned. Here, the person is concerned about reputation or others' judgment of his or her power, but no powerful actions are mentioned. The person may be concerned about being seen as superior, strong, or of high status; alternatively, he or she may be concerned about avoiding a reputation for weakness, inferiority, or low status. However, the scorer should carefully distinguish concerns for reputation as involving power from concerns about success or failure in achievement strivings, which would not be scored. Thus "John finished last and was sad" would not be scored; but "John finished last and was humiliated" would be scored. The difference is that the former case involves only an inner standard, while the latter case involves a concern about public evaluation. The desire for prestige is scored. The desire for money (being rich, having a large income, etc.) is not scored as such; but if the story makes it clear that money or income is closely related to prestige, then it is scored.

In addition, Power Imagery can be scored under this criterion if a character experiences positive or negative affect in regard to a position of high or low status or prestige. Thus a character may bask in the glory of high status, or be disappointed at an inferior position. Here again, the scorer should distinguish affect about position or prestige, which is scorable, from affect about successful or unsuccessful achievement strivings, which is not scorable. Examples of Criterion 3 include:

> The girl is thinking about the attention which is focused on her.
> He has taken her out because he likes her, but also because he wants to find out how his boss rated him on his last rating.
> He wants some money, so that he can move out of the small room to a luxurious resort, where he would have a rug on the floor and a maid at the door to clean up after him.
> The captain thinks she is not to blame, and wants to be vindicated.
> The mate knows that his job depends on the executive, but doesn't want to let the crew think he let a white-collar man tell him what to do.
> They are both slightly worried about the impressions they are making on each other.

Expressions *not scored* under Criterion 3 include:

> He wants a job. He wants to show he can handle himself in the world.

(There is no mention of public reaction or attention; the character may be trying to prove something to himself.)

> The woman has worked her way up through the company. She will prosper and live a happy life.

(This is an achievement theme; "working up through the company" and "prospering" do not explicitly refer to public acclaim.)

If Power Imagery could be scored under more than one criterion, the scorer should select the criterion that covers the major or the most important power-related aspects of the story. If several different characters in the story display concern about power, score the character with the most highly elaborated power concern for Power Imagery and subcategories. If other characters also express power concern, score additional subcategories as appropriate (i.e., considering them as actors), *so long as no subcategory is scored more than once per story*.

If Power Imagery is scored, then the scorer goes on to check for the presence of the subcategories, which are described subsequently. If Power Imagery is not scored, then the scorer ignores the subcategories and proceeds to the next story.

SUBCATEGORIES

Each subcategory can be scored only once per story. Any sentence can be scored for more than one subcategory. The same phrase can be scored both for Power Imagery and for any subcategory, but it cannot be scored for two subcategories. Any subcategory must be related to the power sequence or goal in the story in order to be scored. Sometimes a collectivity or group of characters is concerned about the power goal. In such cases, one or more of the subcategories can be scored on the basis of statements about one member of the group, and other subcategories can be scored on the basis of the other characters. In other words, the group may be split up for the purposes of scoring the subcategories, and the statements about each individual character may be considered to apply to the group as a whole.

Prestige of the Actor (Pa+, Pa−)

Prestige is scored if the character(s) concerned about the power goal is described in ways that increase (*Pa+*) or lower (*Pa−*) their prestige. Titles;[1] adjectives of status, reputation, fame, or skill; or an alliance or association with some prestigeful person, a large number of persons, or an institution (including government agencies) are all aspects of prestige that can be scored. Mention of the legal system ("taking a case to court") is scored *Pa+*. Prestige can also be scored if the setting of the story is described as exotic or prestigeful, such as with adjectives of status, fame, or prominence. Finally, prestige can be scored if a lower-status person is trying to exert power against a higher-status person. As an example, the prestige of David is increased when he defeats the powerful, prestigious Goliath. The prestige can be stated at the outset of the story, or it can be acquired during the story or as a result of the power-related action. Both *Pa+* and *Pa−* can be scored in a story, but each can be scored only once. Examples of *Pa+* and *Pa−* include:

> These are top-ranking military people. . . .
> She graduated from a leading educational institution. . . .
> They are sophisticated people at a very intimate, expensive, party. . . .
> The woman is a New York advertising agency executive. . . .
> The guy is a cheap punk. [*Pa−*]
> These men are Special Forces advisory units.

Stated Need for Power (N)

Need is scored if there is an explicit statement that some character wants to attain a power goal: to establish, maintain, or restore impact, control, or influence. Most of these statements will involve expressions such as "she wants to," "he wishes to," "they hope to," "she felt a need to"; or strong evidence of desire such as "he is very interested in," or "they are determined to." The goal may be broad and general, such as "she wants to persuade her son," or it may be a more specific subgoal, such as in the following: "The officer is planning an attack. The men want to get adequate information about the problems they will encounter." Here the desire for information is a specific part of the more general power goal, that is, the attack. However, Need should be scored only when the thing that is desired is related to the power goal. Statements of one person's wanting another to do something are not scored unless they are related to the power goal. Thus the following would not be scored for Need: "The boss is trying to convince the partners. One partner wants to break for lunch." *Need is not inferred from Instrumental Activity*, no matter how vigorous or forceful the action is. Thus "she demands . . ." is not scored. It may seem obvious to the scorer that characters who take strong forceful actions toward a power goal must want to reach the goal. Need is scored, however, only when there is a definite statement of need or desire on the part of one of the characters. Examples of *N* include:

> He would like to impress the girl.
> The inspector hopes to catch the smugglers.
> She wants to have an affair with him.

Instrumental Activity (I)

Overt or mental activity (such as planning) by characters in the story that indicates that they are actually doing something about attaining a power goal is scored as Instrumental Activity. There must be an actual statement of activity within the story, independent of both the original description of the situation and the final outcome of the story. Statements can be in the past or future tense or passive voice, so long as they are not simply descriptions of the outcome of actions. The scorer should be careful to avoid scoring statements that imply Instrumental Activity but, by the nature of the wording, merely describe situations. "There is an argument" is not scored, but "Helen is arguing with Jim" would be scored. Any action that is intended to lead to a power goal can be scored, even if the action is only a minor step toward the goal. However, the action must be related to the power goal and not to some other concern. Instrumental Activity is scored regardless of the outcome or success. Examples of *I* include:

> The man is trying emphatically to make a point.
> The crew will complete the attack mission.
> The captain is bitterly criticizing the other man.
> She is taking him to a small cafe to impress him.

Block in the World (Bw)

Block is scored if there is an explicit obstacle or disruption to the attempt to reach a power goal. It is not scored if the person merely fails to reach the power goal. Descriptions or counteractions after the goal is reached are scored for Effect. The scorer should carefully distinguish an obstacle or disruption to an ongoing activity from an obstacle that establishes the goal as power-related in the first place. Most power-related stories contain the suggestion of an initial block: There are people to be convinced, others to be impressed, or enemy troops to be attacked. Such initial obstacles merely define the power goal and are not scored. Only disruptions and obstacles that occur along the way to the goal and hinder ongoing action are scored

Bw. Thus if one character is trying to convince another character about something, then the other character's having an explicit counteropinion, or any characteristic of the other character or of the situation that suggests that the convincing is more difficult than is normally the case, could be scored for *Bw.* Sometimes there may be some doubt as to whether the obstacle is in the character seeking the power goal (not scored), or in the external situation. *Bw* is scored if the obstacle is at least partly in the external situation. Examples of *Bw* include:

> The commander is concerned about the mission, because the bridge is heavily guarded.

("Heavily guarded" goes beyond the routine resistance to attack that could be expected.)

> The inspector wants to look for contraband. The captain is trying to keep her off the ship.
> The girl resists his advances.
> The girl has to leave town and this will cost her the reputation as a star athlete.

Goal Anticipation (Ga+, Ga−)

Goal Anticipation is scored when some character in the story is thinking about the power goal – impact, control, or influence – or is anticipating the goal, or wondering whether he or she will attain it. This means that a character in the story has to be thinking or anticipating; comments by the author of the story are not scored. Goal anticipations are positive (*Ga+*) if the character is having positive anticipations; they are negative (*Ga−*) if the character has negative or doubtful anticipations. The word *thinking* is Instrumental Activity if it means planning, and is a Goal Anticipation if it means *thinking about* or *wondering about*. Examples of *Ga* include:

> The soldiers are weighing the odds of success in the coming attack. [*Ga−*]
> He is thinking ahead to future pleasures with his mistress. [*Ga+*]
> She is worried about the disgrace she will have to face. [*Ga−*]
> The man is thinking that he is convincing his boss. [*Ga+*]

Goal States (G+, G−)

Affective or feeling states associated with attaining or not attaining the power goals are scored *G+* or *G−*, depending on whether the affect is positive or negative. If a character is happy or pleased to have power (attacked, criticized, influenced another person), then *G+* is scored. If the actor is angry, upset, or dissatisfied about not having power (being weak or of low status, losing an argument, failing to impress someone), then *G−* is scored. Of course, the feelings have to be connected to the power goal;

mere elation or depression in a story that is scored for Power Imagery is not automatically scored for G. These statements of affect may or may not occur at the end of the story, when the final goal is reached or not reached. However, affective states $(G+, G-)$ should be distinguished from anticipations about the goal $(Ga+, Ga-)$. The former occur after the goal has been attained or lost; the latter occur in the mind of the character before the goal is reached, while the outcome is in doubt. $G+$ and $G-$ can also be scored for positive or negative affect about the attainment of minor goals that occurs along the way to the central power goal of the story. Negative emotional reactions to blocks are often scorable for $G-$. Examples of G include:

> Seeing the man smile serves to reassure her that she has impressed him. [$G+$]
> She is amazed that she is having such a hard time in the debate.

(Scored $G-$ because "amazed" is taken to connote that the woman is unhappy at having a hard time.)

> He will lose his reputation and become bitter. [$G-$]
> She is happy that attention is being focused on her. [$G+$]

Effect (Eff)

Effect is scored when there is some distinct response by someone to the power attempts or actions of a character in the story. There are three principal kinds of effects: (a) strong positive or negative emotions in one person as a result of the action of another (see criterion 2 for Power Imagery); (b) an overt counterattack, counterinfluence, escape, or similar counterreaction by one person to another's attack, influence, and so forth; or (c) some indication that the power action has produced a major, striking effect, such as widespread public acclaim, suicide, or the like. Responses have to be explicit in order to be scored for effect; they cannot be inferred. They have to be described as resulting from the power-related action, and not simply occurring by chance or for another reason. Resistance to another's power is scored; but compliance that goes beyond routine acceptance of power can also be scored, if the compliance or acceptance is enthusiastic, eager, or protesting. Effect, then, is scored if there is additional evidence of someone's power through elaboration of the effects of that power. Examples of Eff include:

> While the soldiers are searching, the enemy will capture the commanding officer.
> The inspector will find the contraband; however, the captain will escape and be smuggled out of the country.
> Jensen will solve the boy's problem and become endeared to millions.
> The girl takes her mother's advice, is successful, and frequently looks to her mother with respect.

FINAL NOTE

Power Imagery and each subcategory that is scored are counted +1. The total Power Motivation score for a story is the sum of scores for Imagery and subcategories. The maximum possible score for a story is +11. If there is no Power Imagery, then the story is scored 0.

ADDITIONAL SCORING FOR HOPE OF POWER AND FEAR OF POWER

If a story has been scored for Power Imagery and the appropriate sub-categories, then the scorer should proceed to make the following additional discrimination between *Hope* and *Fear*.

Fear of power is scored if one or more of the following are present in the story:

1. *The power goal is for the direct or indirect benefit of another* – either a specified other person or a cause (e.g., humanity, the Revolution, Justice, etc.). Examples include:

> She wants to be President so that she can lead the country out of chaos.
> He's fighting the champion – this is his chance to win a big purse. His kid is in the hospital and needs a big operation.

If more than one character is concerned with power, score Fear of Power if *any* of the characters has a power goal for the benefit of another.

Stories that involve soldiers, spies, agents of governments or companies, and reporters present a problem in the application of this criterion. In one sense, all such persons can be assumed to be carrying out a power action on behalf of their government, company, agency, newspaper, or the like. Fear of Power is scored if the country is mentioned (e.g., the country's name, "his country," "the country") in the case of soldiers and spies; Fear of Power is not scored if only "soldiers" or "the army" (navy, air force, armed forces, etc.) is mentioned. In the case of business persons, reporters, and agents for companies or agencies, Fear of Power is scored only if the power goal is for the benefit of a person, organization, or cause above and beyond the company, newspaper, or agency. Examples include:

> The executive checking to see whether her agency should take the new account. [Not scored.]
> The advertising executive is designing his agency's campaign for a new client company. [Scored.]
> The *Daily Planet* reporter is investigating a scandal for her paper. [Not scored.]
> The *Daily Planet* reporter is investigating a scandal; when her story is written, it will set off a campaign to restore good government to the city. [Scored.]

Finally, even if the power goal is for the benefit of another, but the character clearly and obviously derives extra, personal gratification from it, *Fear* is not scored. Thus a soldier fighting for his country who greatly enjoys killing would not be scored Fear of Power.

2. *Actors have doubt about their ability to influence, control, or impress others.* This does not have to be accompanied by actual failure, nor is mere failure sufficient to score Fear of Power under this criterion. Fear of Power is not scored if the actor doubts only the particular outcome; it is scored if there are basic doubts about ability to influence, control, or impress others. Thus not all cases of *Ga−* would be scored Fear of Power. Also scored under this criterion are stories in which the actor experiences confusion or emotional conflict about the power goal in the course of the story. Again, if there is more than one actor, Fear of Power is scored if any actor meets this criterion.

3. *The writer of the story suggests that power is deceptive or has a flaw,* as by the use of contrast, irony, or explicit statement. Here the editorial comments or the style of the writer can be scored, rather than the power goal or the characteristics of the actor. Fear of Power can also be scored under this criterion if the relationship between outcome and affect is reversed: if a character is happy after power failure, or sad after power success. Examples include:

> He fights the man and demolishes him, but he feels bad, because he lowered himself to the other guy's level. [Criterion 2 or 3 applicable.]
> When he finally got the girl, he was chagrined to learn that she was his sister.
> "Chet the Jet" – the world's greatest boxer – has lost to a ten-year-old.

All stories that are not scored for Fear of Power are considered as Hope of Power. The notation of *Hope* or *Fear* can be made in the margin of the scoring sheet, next to the total score for the story.

After all scoring is completed, the scorer should then add up the scores for each story in the protocol to get a total Power Motivation score; and then add the totals for those stories designated *Hope* to get a Hope of Power score, and those totals for the stories designated *Fear* to get a Fear of Power Score. The overall totals for *Hope* and *Fear* should add up to the total Power Motivation score. *Hope/Fear* is a *classification* of the score for each story; neither *Hope* nor *Fear* is given any additional points.

SELF-TEST: REVISED N POWER MANUAL

After reading the scoring manual, write out your answers to the following questions without consulting the manual. Then check the answers to see whether they are correct.

Imagery

What is the general basis for scoring Power Imagery? What are the three criteria for scoring Power Imagery? What kinds of statements would satisfy each of these criteria? What are the rules governing the scoring of Power Imagery in stories about solicited advice or help? Teaching or simple requests? Arguments? Success and great achievement? What is the procedure for scoring when several different characters in the story have power concerns?

Prestige

What general classes of words or phrases are scored for *Pa+* or *Pa−*? Can *Pa* be scored on the basis of prestige that is acquired by a character during the course of the story?

Need

What is the criterion for scoring *N*? What kinds of statements of desire are not scored *N*?

Instrumental activity

What is the criterion for scoring *I*? What are typical examples of *I*?

Blocks

What is meant by a Block? How is failure to obtain the goal scored?

Goal anticipation states

When is *Ga* scored? How are comments by the author dealt with? What is the difference between *Ga* and planning or thinking that is scored *I*?

Goal states

What is the distinction between *Ga* and *G*? What statements of affect or feeling are not scored *G*?

Effect

What are the three principal kinds of things that can be scored *Eff*? Is any reaction to a power attempt scored *Eff*?

Hope/fear

What is the rule for scoring cases involving an agent of a company (or government, etc.)? What is a reversed affect–outcome relationship? Do all cases of power that benefits someone else get scored for Fear of Power?

NOTE

1 As a scoring convention, the words *commanding officer* or any military rank of captain or below (captain, lieutenant, sergeant, corporal, private) are not scored in stories involving the military. Ranks of major, colonel, and general (field marshal) are scored. Equivalents for naval and air force ranks, as well as for ranks of other nations, should be determined by the scorer. "Captain" is not scored when it means simply the person in charge of a ship, unless the ship is named or described with an adjective (e.g., "newest ship," "big ship").

23 *Personal causation and the origin concept*

RICHARD DeCHARMS

The concept of personal causation brashly pairs the physical term *causation* with a human adjective *personal*, flying in the face of centuries of philosophical controversy. The reason is that personal causation is a human experience and is fundamental to understanding human behavior. It cannot be reduced to physical causation. We can only infer physical causation because we experience ourselves as causes. Personal causation is primary and fundamental; physical causation is secondary. (For more on this see deCharms & Shea, 1976; also, deCharms, 1968/1983, 1976, 1987a, 1987b.)

I have variously defined personal causation, first as a primary motivational propensity to be effective in producing changes in the environment (deCharms, 1968/1983, p. 269). Later, and more simply, "personal causation means doing something intentionally to produce a change" (1984). Personal causation is *not* the name of a motive, nor is it a personality disposition. Every human being "has" personal causation, that is, experiences herself, as a cause.

Origin is the term that is central to the content analysis system presented here. It is a locution invented not to name a newly discovered kind of personality or behavior, but rather to describe a *personal experience* that accompanies a behavioral episode of personal causation. A definition of *origin* is inadequate (like saying champagne tastes like your foot is asleep). We must describe how the concept is used (Ossorio, 1981; Wittgenstein, 1953). That is the purpose of the content analysis manual (see chapter 24).

It is misleading to use *origin* as a noun, except very loosely and crudely. People are not "origins" or "pawns." They have *origin experience* or experience originship. *Origin* is best used as an adjective to modify *experience*, *behavior*, *situation*, or *episode*. We know when we have origin experiences directly, immediately, just as we know when we are happy or sad. We can attribute origin experiences to others *without inference* by interacting with them and observing their behavior. Although origin experiences cumulate through learning, we *do not learn* the origin experience in one way and attribute it to others in another way. To posit this would lead directly to the

325

problem of other minds (Ryle, 1949). The developmental conceptualization has its roots in Macmurray's (1957) concept of agency and in Strawson's (1959) descriptive metaphysics and the ascription to others of states of consciousness. (See deCharms 1987b.)

But experiences are not solipsistic; they are elicited by environmental situations. So *origin* may also be used as an adjective to describe situations that elicit origin experiences. One must think of the person interacting with the environment. On one dimension a person may be more or less disposed to seek and experience originship; on another dimension situations may enhance or diminish the possibility of experiencing originship.

When a person has an origin experience she is highly motivated in the most positive, approach sense. She experiences herself as the cause of desired changes. But some people have more origin experiences than others. The origin concept is describing a personal disposition when it is used to describe the extent to which some people (more than others) seek origin experiences in which they can change their environment through personal causation.

The origin concept was developed to help people to have more origin experiences and to be more highly positively motivated. The measure (and the scoring manual) was developed primarily to gauge *changes* in experience, *not as a personality measure.*

The observable expression of the origin experience may take the form of many kinds of behavior. But the verbal, written, unselfconscious expression descriptive of others' behaviors in fantasy is one of the best ways to measure changes in the experience of originship. We derived the philosophical rationale for this from Bridgman's (1959) concept of operational analysis of "introspective words in the private mode" and Polanyi's (1958) concept of personal knowledge (deCharms, 1968/1983).

Although the thought sampling technique has roots in the concepts of the unconscious and projection, we avoid these terms in favor of construing the thought sample as a nonselfconscious description of the way a person experiences her world. As McClelland (see chapter 3) has noted, this is quite distinct from a self-attributed questionnaire measure.

In short, personal causation is not learned. To experience oneself as a cause is fundamental to human development. The experience of personal causation is an origin experience. Individual differences in seeking origin experiences and construing the world as a challenge constitute a personality disposition. The origin measure has been used more as a measure of change resulting from motivation enhancement than as a personality measure.

HISTORICAL BACKGROUND

The influence of McClelland's theory of motivation here is obvious. White's (1959) concept of competence was seminal. The term *personal causation* itself originated with Heider (1958) and Kelley (1967). The origin concept was first designed to capture Heider's "perceived internal locus of causality for behavior" – the self *originat*ing behavior. Setting out to enhance motivation, we were more interested in the *experience* of personal causation than the perception of it. We have tried recently to avoid the vague spatial metaphor contained in the internal–external distinction. Whereas it was used extensively in the original Plimpton manual (deCharms 1976), we have tried to expunge it from this one (see chapter 24), replacing *internal* with *personal* and trying to be more specific than the general term *external locus*.

RELATED CONCEPTS

Intrinsic motivation

I suggested that adding an extrinsic incentive to intrinsically motivated behavior would reduce the experience of personal causation (deCharms, 1968/1983; deCharms & Muir, 1978) about the same time that Kelley (1967) did. Deci (1975, 1980) has refined and researched the phenomenon using his concept of self-determination. Similarly, Lepper and Greene (1978), using the concept of overjustification, have proposed the "hidden costs of rewards." Deci and Ryan (1985) have been intensively investigating these concepts along with the notion of origin climate in the schools.

Flow

Csikszentmihalyi (1975) has described a highly positive motivated state that he calls *flow*. The flow experience may be the ultimate origin experience. Flow has been incorporated into the scoring definitions given in the next chapter. (See also Csikszentmihalyi & Csikszentmihalyi, 1988; Csikszentmihalyi & Larson, 1984.)

Locus of control of reinforcements

The locution *internal locus* causes confusion between Heider's "locus of causality for behavior" and Rotter's "locus of control of reinforcements" (Lefcourt, 1976; Rotter, 1966). Using the complete phrases including "for behavior" (Heider) and "of reinforcements" (Rotter), helps dispel this confusion. The theoretical foundation of the origin concept in Heider's notion and McClelland's motive theory stresses action itself. Rotter's concept derives from his social learning theory and stresses the reinforcing outcome of action. The origin measure is a content analysis of operant productions of fantasy stories. Rotter's measure is a self-report questionnaire. The two measures are not correlated (deCharms, 1981).

Efficacy

Bandura's concept of teacher efficacy has been related conceptually to the origin concept by Ashton and Webb (1986). There is no empirical demonstration of the relationship.

STUDIES OF THE ORIGIN CONCEPT

The major study for which the origin measure was developed was a 4-year, longitudinal, quasi-experimental treatment and control study reported in detail in deCharms (1976). The participants were inner-city elementary school teachers and pupils.

The project was designed to help teachers enhance personal causation in low-income, inner-city elementary school children. The experimental treatment involved training teachers who taught the children in sixth and seventh grade and used origin enhancing exercises in their classroom (for details, see deCharms, 1976). The treatment students experienced origin exercises plus the regular curriculum in their classrooms throughout the sixth- and seventh-grade year. Control children experienced only the regular curriculum from nontrained teachers.

The origin measure was administered to both treatment and control classes at the end of each school year for 3 years, from fifth grade (before any treatment) until seventh grade. Although teachers were assigned randomly to treatment groups, classes did not stay intact from sixth to seventh grade. This had the fortunate effect of giving four groups of pupils: (a) sixth- and seventh-grade treatment, (b) sixth-grade treatment only, (c) seventh-grade treatment only, and (d) no treatment.

Sensitivity to experimentally induced changes

Results of the above study demonstrated significant increases in origin scores (from means of about 5 to 12, $p < .001$) every year a group experienced the treatment (four different replications) and no increase in any of the four untreated groups. The groups comprised about 50 cases except for one small group of 27. (For more statistical detail, see deCharms, 1976, 1984.) In short, the origin measure proved highly sensitive to the effects of origin training in the classroom. Not only were the total origin scores increased but when broken down into the six individual scoring categories of goal setting, instrumental activity, and so forth, the scores for all six categories increased significantly.

THREE-YEAR FOLLOW-UP. H. Jackson (1976) readministered the origin measure to a sample of trained and control pupils in the eleventh grade. Four years after training there was still a significant difference between the means of the two groups. Jackson also devised a semistructured interview to measure life goals and responsibility orientation in these groups. The interviews of 79 pupils were content-analyzed using the same technique used for the stories. Again there was a significant difference between previously trained and untrained pupils. The correlation between the origin score on the stories and score on the interview protocols was not significant. In light of evidence reported subsequently this would be expected. The origin stories were third-person stories; the interviews were first-person self-reports.

HIGH SCHOOL GRADUATION FOLLOW-UP. A larger percentage of trained (37%) than untrained (27%) pupils graduated from high school ($p <$ .001, $N = 1199$). What made this finding stand up, despite the vagaries of follow-up data, was that a direct connection with the training origin score was found. For the boys only, the probability of graduating from high school was correlated with the amount of change in origin score attributable to training. Again this shows the sensitivity of the origin measure to change.

Other relationships

The origin score was related to a standardized measure of academic achievement (Iowa Test of Basic Skills). A median split of control pupils on the origin score produced higher mean achievement scores (adjusted for IQ) in the high origin pupils in two samples (sixth grade, $p < .06$, $N = 84$; seventh grade, $p < .03$, $N = 73$).

In one group of sixth-grade control children whose achievement motivation was measured, origin scores were not significantly correlated with achievement motivation ($r = +.22$, $N = 35$).

Data were also obtained on 85 black elementary school teachers (mostly female). The correlation between locus of control of reinforcements and the origin measure was nonsignificant ($r = +.11$).

There is some evidence of a relationship with power motivation. McClelland (1985b) analyzed some of the protocols written by untrained pupils. "In a sample of twenty-one pupils in deCharms's study who were high in Activity Inhibition, the correlation between the n Power and Origin scores is .36 ($p < .10$). Among an equal number of pupils low in Activity Inhibition, the correlation between these two measures is only .12" (p. 574). (See chapter 5 for a discussion of activity inhibition.)

CLASSROOM CLIMATE. A questionnaire measure of classroom climate was developed to assess whether the classroom was experienced as an origin or a pawn situation by the total class. It was not designed to measure individual differences but to be independent of the individual pupil's origin score. The correlations between origin climate scores and origin score in two samples were insignificant as measured by the phi coefficient (+.10, $N =$ 109; +.13, $N = 132$).

PARENT–PUPIL INTERACTION. Using a block-stacking game (Rosen & D'Andrade, 1959) to assess interaction between seventh graders and their mothers, K. Jackson (1973) showed a curvilinear relationship between the number of mother's directive statements to the pupil and the origin score of the child. The children with the highest origin scores were those whose mothers gave moderate amounts of help but did not dominate or ignore the child.

SEX DIFFERENCES. In all the analyses that have been described, boys and girls were initially analyzed separately. Yet sex differences were almost never found. Girls do write significantly longer stories and have slightly higher raw origin scores when not controlled for length of story.

ORIGIN AND PAWN SELF-PERCEPTIONS. Westbrook and Viney (1980) independently developed "unobtrusive measures of origin and pawn perception that could be applied to people's spontaneous verbalizations" (p. 167). Their origin categories were: self expresses intention, self expresses exertion, self expresses ability, self overcomes obstacles, self perceived as cause. They also scored for pawn categories.

Subsequently, Westbrook scored two samples of stories from the pupils in the longitudinal study discussed earlier. The Westbrook origin scores did not correlate significantly with the origin scores from the longitudinal study (sixth grade $r = +.19$, $N = 72$; seventh grade $r = +.26$, $N = 37$). The Westbrook pawn scores were slightly more highly correlated with the origin scores of the longitudinal study ($r = +.31$; $r = +.33$). These results may be attributable to at least two differences between the origin scoring manual presented here and that of Westbrook and Viney: (a) their scoring does not include any responsibility categories; (b) they developed their scoring categories on first-person, past-tense, self-report interviews. Fantasy stories are almost exclusively third person and usually include a statement about the future. In our scoring, past activity is not scored for the instrumental activity category.

SELF-REPORT VERSUS FANTASY. Story (1987) used cues to elicit stories written in the first person, for example, "You and another person working at a machine" rather than "Two men working at a machine." Origin scores from first-person stories were compared with origin scores from third-person stories written by the same high school students. Origin scores from first-person and third-person stories were moderately correlated. Both of these scores were compared to a self-report 12-item origin questionnaire (example: "In general, I control the activities in my life"). The origin scores from first-person origin stories were positively correlated with the self-attributed questionnaire measure; the regular third-person origin scores were not.

MEASUREMENT INFORMATION

The origin measure is a content analysis of (usually) six short stories written to verbal cues. Verbal cues were used rather than pictures since most pictures were of whites and most subjects were black.

The protocol

The protocol is made up of a face sheet for subject information (name, sex, etc.) and instructions as follows.

SHORT STORIES – INSTRUCTIONS

Today I want you to write some very short stories. To get you started I have given you a *suggestion* for each story. This suggestion is at the top of the pages that follow. I will read the suggestion out loud to you and then you can close your eyes and make up a story. Now I don't want you just to describe the suggestion – I want you to make up *your own story* about it.

Since we don't have very much time, I have also listed *four questions* which you should try to answer in your story. If you do this, you will have a complete story. Here is an example of a *suggestion and the four questions*:

A MAN IS LOOKING AT HIS DOG

(1) What is happening? (2) What happened before? (3) What is being thought or wanted? (4) What will happen?

On each page you will find one *suggestion* and the *four questions* like the example above. Write *one* story on each page. I will keep time and tell you which question you should be answering. You may not finish your story in time, but work as quickly as you can. When I tell you to, turn the page and then I will read the suggestion for the next story.

Don't worry if you can't think of a lot to write about. Just put down what you can so we will know what your story is like. If you make a mistake, just cross it out and go on. This will not count as part of your school work.

Remember: Make up your own stories, a different story for each page – thinking about the suggestion on that page only.

If you have any questions after we start, raise your hand but do not speak out. I will help you. Are there any questions?

These instructions are for school children. Timing (5 minutes per story) is relaxed and casual to avoid arousal. The setting is the school room, but avoiding pressure of tests and so forth.

STORY CUES.   Each cue is printed at the top of a separate page followed by the four questions equally spaced down the page allowing space to write in between.

> Cue 1. A father and son talking about something important.
> Cue 2. Two men working at a machine.
> Cue 3. A boy with his head resting on his hands.
> Cue 4. A mother and her child look worried.
> Cue 5. A young person sitting at a desk.
> Cue 6. Brothers and sisters are playing – one is a little ahead.

Of these cues only the first four are represented in the scoring manual in chapter 24. Cue 5 is a good cue that elicits stories much like Cue 3. Cue 6 has been dropped in recent studies due to scoring difficulties. Try "Two children playing in the yard" or "An adult handing something to a child." Both have produced scorable stories but have not been rigorously validated.

Six stories are recommended if time permits but four will be adequate, especially with large samples.

Some of the cues are descriptions of pictures used to measure motives with the advantage of being ambiguous as to race. The cues, and the stories and scoring in the next chapter are dominated by male figures. Stories have been collected as demonstrations using gender ambiguous cues, that is, "A young person sitting at a desk." Although this may avoid the criticism of sexism, a better approach for mixed gender populations might be to have a balance of masculine and feminine characters in the cues. There is no denying that the measure and scoring as described are predominantly male-oriented, despite the fact that the original manual and scoring were developed by women.

As mentioned, verbal cues can be changed to elicit first-person stories, for example, "You are sitting at a desk." This makes a big difference but more research is needed.

The subjects who provided most of the data discussed here were black inner-city fifth- to seventh-grade boys and girls or their teachers, who were predominantly female.

No rigorous norms have been established on the principle that cues, testing conditions, and so on vary widely. Each study should make only within study comparisons. Total score for a six-story protocol ranges from 0 to 36 but rarely exceeds 20. In one sample of eighth-grade inner-city children, the median origin score for six stories was 5.5 ($N = 70$). The scores are slightly skewed toward 0. They are significantly correlated both with number of words per story and with IQ. Usually controlling for either reduces the correlation with the other to insignificance. All correlations reported here were controlled for IQ (partial r or a transformed origin score). Mean differences were tested with analyses of covariance.

Reliability

SCORER RELIABILITY. Between two scorers reliability should approximate 90% agreement.

TEST HOMOGENEITY. Measured by odd-even split-half correlations (Spearman-Brown formula), test homogeneity ranged from $+.35$ to $+.91$ in four samples of approximately 50 cases each. (See deCharms, 1976, p. 129.)

Scott (1960) homogeneity ratios computed on intercorrelations between the six scoring categories were $+.22$ ($N = 53$) and $+.31$ ($N = 108$).

STABILITY OVER TIME. Measured by one year test–retest (fifth to sixth, and sixth to seventh grades), the correlations were $+.41$ ($N = 91$) and $+.38$ ($N = 49$).

24 *The origin scoring system*

RICHARD DeCHARMS AND
FRANZISKA PLIMPTON

INTRODUCTION TO ORIGIN CATEGORIES

The concept of a person acting as an origin involves two major components: a goal-setting sequence and responsibility.

The goal-setting sequence

When acting as an origin, a person independently determines his own goals, freely chooses the activity with which to pursue the goals, is realistic about his abilities and relationships with others and the environment, and is self-confident about his ability to initiate successful behavior leading to a positive conclusion to the goal-setting sequence.

Compare the following stories written in response to the verbal cue, "Two men working at a machine":

> 1a. (What is happening?) Bill and John are working together and fighting. (What happened before?) Before the machine broke down. (What is being thought or wanted?) John wants Bill to shut up. He thinks that Bill is dumb. (What will happen?) In the future they will be good friends again.
> 2a. Bill and John are working together and John is apologizing. Before they had a fight about the machine. John wants to make up and be friends with Bill. He thinks an apology will help. They will make up and be friends.

Story 1a has no origin-goal-setting sequence whereas Story 2a does.

Story 1a has no personally set goal and no sequence of activity leading to a positive outcome. In the last sentence miraculously they become friends but neither of them showed any activity to restore friendship or any involvement in attaining it. John wants Bill to shut up but that is not an origin goal. The story is devoid of any origin-goal-setting sequence.

In story 2a John wants to make up and be friends with Bill. This is a freely chosen affiliation goal. It is an example of the scoring category *goal setting*.

334

To the end of being friends, John is apologizing; he is actively doing something to reach his goal. This is an example of the scoring category *instrumental activity*. John realistically assesses the situation thinking that an apology is in order. This is an example of the scoring category *realistic perception*. That they will make up and be friends again is a direct result of John's goal and activity, and shows confidence in his ability personally to cause a change in his environment. This is an example of the scoring category *self-confidence*.

The responsibility sequence

When acting as an origin, a person assumes personal responsibility for his own actions and the consequences thereof. He also treats others as origins and shows concern for their welfare in a form of social responsibility.

Compare the following stories written to the verbal cue, "A mother and her child look worried":

> 1b. They are worried about father who is in the hospital.
> In the past he was in an accident.
> The daughter wants the father to get well and she is going to give blood to help him.
> The father will get well.
> 2b. They are worried that father doesn't come home.
> In the past the father had been in an accident.
> The girl wants the father to come home safe. The father will come home.
> 3b. The mother and son look worried.
> The father was in an accident.
> They wanted to go to a movie.
> The father will come home.

Story 1b shows the concern of the girl for the father and her determination to take personal responsibility to do something about it; she is going to give blood. This is an example of the scoring category *personal responsibility*. In addition to showing concern about the father (which is often just a repetition of the cue), she does something responsible to help. The positive outcome is an indication of the self-confidence that her actions will be successful and is an example of the category of *self-confidence*.

In story 2b the girl does not actually do anything but she shows her feeling of responsibility and concern for others by a statement of a desire for the father's welfare, she wants him to come home *safe*. This is a subtler form of the scoring category *personal responsibility*. As in story 1b the positive outcome is an example of *self-confidence* despite the fact that the girl did not actually do anything.

Story 3b is much the same as the others superficially. Concern appears, however, only in the repetition of the cue. It turns out that they want to go to a movie. They do not do anything about their worry, nor do they show affect or a desire for the welfare of the father. This story does not have *personal responsibility* in it.

Story 1b has both a goal-setting sequence and a responsibility theme. (Some of the other goal-setting sequence categories would be scored.) Story 2b is purely a responsibility story with no real goal-setting sequence. Story 3b is neither.

The division between the goal-setting sequence and responsibility sequence is a first step in deciding how to score a story but as we saw in the stories above any story can be one, the other, both or neither. The core of the goal-setting sequence consists of the following categories:

> Goal Setting (GS)
> Instrumental Activity (IA)
> Self-confidence (SC)

When Reality Perception (RP) and Personal Responsibility (PR) occur in a goal-setting sequence, they are scored and usually have to do with perception of self in the active situation and responsibility for actions and consequences.

The core of the Responsibility Sequence is Personal Responsibility (PR), very often accompanied by reality perception. PR here includes social responsibility and most often appears as concern for other persons.

There are six categories that have to be considered when scoring any story. Five have been mentioned. The sixth, *personal causation*, is more global as well as an attempt to capture aspects such as challenge and play that do not quite fit the goal setting sequence.

There are six components of the origin concept that constitute six independent scoring categories. Their brief titles are:

1. Goal Setting (GS)
2. Instrumental Activity (IA)
3. Reality Perception (RP)
4. Personal Responsibility (PR)
5. Self-confidence (SC)
6. Personal Causation (PC)

Categories 1 through 5 are often but not always encountered in that order in a story. The rarer appearance of PC is usually decided after the story has been considered for the other categories.

Each category has an origin aspect that may be compared with a pawn aspect, although no pawn categories have as yet been validated. Thus a self-determined goal is origin whereas an imposed goal is pawn; self-determined activity is origin, other-imposed is pawn; perceiving reality is origin, self-deception or not considering reality is pawn; responsibility is origin, irresponsibility is pawn; self-confidence is origin, lack thereof is pawn; seeing the world as a challenge is origin, reacting to threat is pawn. *Only the origin aspects constitute the scoring categories.*

CORE DEFINITIONS OF THE CATEGORIES

1. *Goal setting (GS)*

A character in the story sets a goal when he or she independently decides to behave, to act, or to attain a goal, that is, decides to get some thing or some state of affairs. The goal cannot be imposed by some other agency and the determination to do something to attain the goal must be clear through activity or other stated personal involvement. Mere wanting or wishing is not enough.

The goal may be concrete (bicycle, money), interpersonal (friendship, another's good, to influence another), a state of affairs (to be a success, to win, to pass a test, to be content), long term (to go to college, to become a doctor, lawyer, etc., to improve self or personal relationships).

Although GS is scored independently of activity, it should be clear that the person has chosen to behave or act specifically to reach the goal and is personally involved in the outcome. Dreaming of a million dollars is *not* GS unless it becomes a determination to do something to get it.

Words like *want* or *decide* should alert the scorer for GS, but not all want statements are scored. Physical wants or needs (food, drink, sleep) are not scored. "She wants him to hurry" or "they want him to come home" are not scored GS unless it is clear that the character sees it as a goal to be pursued.

GS is not scored for inferred goals; *the goal must be clearly stated.* If activity implies a goal *that is not stated*, GS is not scored but instrumental activity would be. As long as the above conditions are met, the goal may be past, present, or future goals.

The goal-setting decision that the scorer must make for each story may be worded as follows: Does a major character in the story freely set a nonphysical-need goal that is explicitly stated and followed by some indication of activity or personal involvement in attaining the goal? If so the story is scored 1; if not, 0.

Example where goal setting *is scored*. (Note: You must refer to the whole story as presented earlier):

Story 2a. John wants to make up. (And apologizes).

Example where goal setting *is not* scored:

Story 1a. John wants Bill to shut up.

2. *Instrumental Activity (IA)*

IA is any personally caused activity that is instrumental to attainment of a goal (either stated or inferred). IA must be explicitly stated, not inferred, and must be stated in *the present tense.*

Not all activity in a story is IA. Activity may merely set the stage ("They are making cars") and not be related to the rest of the story. "Thinking" by itself does not qualify unless it is deciding, that is, instrumental, whereas "planning" does qualify. Activity that is imposed or forced by another agency is not scored. If some other agency (parent, teacher) wants the child to do something, that is not scored unless there is a further indication that he personally decides to do it. The crucial aspects are the freedom of choice and the relation to the goal.

Past, future, or conditional activity statements are not scored.

The scoring decision that the scorer must make for each story is: Does a major character in the story engage in present, personally chosen activity to reach a goal? If so the story is scored 1; if not, 0.

Example where instrumental activity *is scored*:

Story 2a. John is apologizing.

Examples where instrumental activity *is not scored*:

Story 1a. Bill and John are working together. [But it is not toward any goal, just a descriptive statement. See the whole story.]
Story 1b. ". . . she is going to give blood." [Not present tense.]

3. *Reality Perception (RP)*

Reality Perception is a person's ability to understand his or her possibilities, strengths, weaknesses, and position in the environment–the capacity to analyze or understand the situation. It is critical with this category to consider the character's reality and not impose standards of our own. When "reality" is used here it is not the scorer's own but that of the character in the story. If the character is considering blocks to his goal, that counts as RP whether we think he is rational or not. If the character believes there is a cause–effect relationship between his behavior (not matter how bizarre) and the desired outcome, he is showing realistic perception.

RP can be recognized in the following ways.

CAUSES. The person recognizes *cause–effect* relations and his and/or other people's motives. The story indicates that the person is showing insight into his position and capabilities and his goals and activities are realizable.

Examples (some from the stories cited previously, others from short stories [ss] presented in an appendix to this chapter):

E2ss1. The boy broke their lawnmower. His father said, "since it was an accident, he wouldn't punnish him."
Story 1b. She "wants her father to get well and she is going to give blood." [She sees the cause–effect relationship between her action and her goal.]
Story 2a. John wants to be friends with Bill. *He thinks an apology will help.*

BLOCKS. The person sees obstacles that may interfere with goal attainment. Blocks are not used as excuses (pawn) but taken into account in planning and activity. The person is realistically considering the blocks to his activities or to attaining his goal and/or is considering appropriate means of overcoming blocks. (Actual overcoming of blocks is scored as Self-confidence.) Example:

E10ss1. John had asked his father if he could have a bicycle his father didn't have enough money so John had to get a job.

INTELLIGENT ADJUSTMENT, COMPROMISE, AND ACCEPTANCE OF EXPERT HELP OR ADVICE. If the person is in a situation beyond his control he shows realistic perception if he adjusts intelligently – an origin act in a storm is to protect oneself, not try to fight it. Another form is compromise with superior personal forces that is not just pawnish resignation. Still another is seeking or accepting expert help. Example:

E12ss1. The father is wanting his son to be something in life.
The boy makes up his mind that he is not going to be like his brother. [It is the comparison with brother that is scored RP. Making up his mind is scored PR.]

PLANNING. Planning in the present tense would be IA but in another tense it could be realistic perception. Example:

E2ss3. His said he would work for his money.

PERCEPTION OF SOCIAL INTERACTION. The individual shows indications of realistically seeing his place in social relationships and society. Example:

He is thinking that maybe if he were nicer he would be liked by more of his classmates.

PUNISHMENT, OBEDIENCE AND SOCIAL SANCTIONS. Probably because of the age of children in most of these stories, the relationship to authority plays a large role. A child can act as an origin by realistically assessing social sanctions, punishment, and obedience. This is really a form of intelligent adjustment. Example:

He will think about what his father said and he probably will obey.

Example where RP *is not scored* (compare with story 2a):

Story 1a. He thinks that Bill is dumb.

The scoring decision that the scorer must make for each story is: Does a major character in the story show evidence of reality perception, that is, does he realistically talk about causes in the environment, motives in self and other, or blocks to reaching goals and plan to overcome them? If so the story is scored 1; if not, 0.

4. *Personal Responsibility (PR)*

PR is the person's willingness to assume responsibility for the consequences of his or her actions, the attainment of goals, the fulfillment of desires, as well as a responsible concern for others. PR is shown in the following ways.

RESPONSIBILITY FOR ACTION AND GOAL ATTAINMENT. The person assumes active responsibility rather than wait for others or fate to attain his goals. Example:

> E12ss1. The father is wanting his son to be something in life.
> The boy makes up his mind that he is not going to be like his brother . . . An he's goin to work harder on his job. [Making up his mind is scored for PR. Recall that "not being like his brother" was scored for RP. It is often the case the RP and PR appear together.]

CONSEQUENCES. The person is willing to bear the consequences of actions, admit mistakes, and try to repair any harm he has done. Example:

> E2ss1. The boy said since he broke it he will pay for it to be fixed.

SOCIAL RESPONSIBILITY. The person shows awareness of responsibility or respect toward others or society in general. The person helps others. Example:

> E4ss2. One man will have to be layed off . . . The man who has two other jobs has volunteered.

CONCERN FOR OTHERS OR TO BE REUNTIED WITH ANOTHER. The person is worried about or sad for another or has a desire to reestablish a broken relationship. Concern must be explicit in a statement of activity, emotion, or wanting something to benefit the other. Examples:

> Story 1b. The daughter wants the father to get well and she is going to give blood. [Concern with proposed activity.]
> Story 1a. John is apologizing. . . . John wants to make up and be friends with Bill.

The scoring decision that the scorer must make for each story is: Does a character or the author show evidence explicitly stated of taking personal responsibility? If so the story is scored 1; if not, 0.

5. *Self-confidence (SC)*

The category SC is the person's confidence in his ability to succeed in goal striving, to effect desired changes in the physical or social environment, to control self and/or others. It is most often seen in a successful conclusion to goal striving at the end of a story. It may also be a confident statement or a statement of positive affect over goal attainment or pleasure in activity.

Self-confidence may appear in the following forms.

GOAL ATTAINMENT OR POSITIVE OUTCOME. The most ubiquitous form is usually found in a positive outcome to the goal-setting sequence stated in the last sentence of the story. It may of course also be an outcome of a responsibility story. The positive outcome must be related to the origin theme of the story and not just a miraculous ending from the "fairy godmother" or mere wish fulfillment. Goal attainment must result from the character's own personal effort so that he feels originship of the outcome. Example:

Story 1b. John is apologizing ... he wants to make up. They will make up and be friends. [Compare with Story 1a, which ends, "In the future they will be good friends again." This is not scored SC because it is merely a statement rather than the outcome of anything else in the story.]

OVERCOMING BLOCKS. The person succeeds in overcoming blocks, either self (tired, discouraged) or environmental (another person's demands or a physical obstacle or threat). The recognition of the block is scored RP, whereas the actual overcoming of it is SC. Example:

E1ss3. The boy is afraid of falling off the roller coaster. The boy will go but will not get on the roller coaster.

CONFIDENCE IN PERSONAL CAPABILITY. A character in the story shows his confidence in his own ability to do something. Example:

A3ss1. The son wants to drive the car.
The father thinks the son needs more experience. The son is convinced that he has had enough experience.

AFFECT OVER GOAL ATTAINMENT. A character shows a feeling of happiness or elation that he succeeded in a goal-setting sequence. This category ought to be the epitome of a statement of the experience of originship. Unfortunately, it occurs so rarely that there is not even an example to cite.

The scoring decision that the scorer must make for all stories is: Does a character in the story show self-confidence in his ability to attain a goal, state a positive outcome to a goal-setting sequence, or show emotion related to his originship? If so the story is scored 1; if not, 0.

6. *Personal Causation (PC)*

More often found in adults' stories than in children's, PC is a special category in two respects. First, it differs from the other categories in that it demands a higher level of inference of the scorer. It is more general, more global, and more difficult to define and to exemplify precisely. Hence, it is harder to score. Second, it is used arbitrarily to capture three rarely occurring aspects of originship known as self-investment, challenge, and play.

PC is only scored when the *whole story* shows evidence that the character(s) experiences himself as an origin, that is, that he is *experiencing himself as the personal locus of causality of his behavior*. "Whole story" means that the central plot centers on originship and that no other subplot or nonorigin elements exist in the story. Further, the origin theme must be elaborated extensively. The PC decision is usually made after all other categories have been considered.

The stress in the phrase "experienced personal locus of causality for behavior" is on "experience" and "behavior." The inference is that the character is "experiencing" the joyous feeling of connection between what he does (his behavior) and an intended change in his environment. Inferential level is great because people rarely say things like "Wow, I did it!" which would express it directly, so the feeling of personal causation and originship must be inferred.

The critical element in making the PC inference is that the character(s) totally chooses and directs his behavior. The chosen behavior may be instrumental to a self-chosen goal (the purest case) or the person may have reacted as an origin to an other-imposed situation or threatening physical environment. In the pure case the person experiences complete choice of both goals and behavior. He decides independently of other sources that he wants something (a bike, a friend) and chooses *what to do* to get it (get a job, give a gift). In the other-imposed situation the person may have a event forced on him (an examination, a broken machine), but he explicitly chooses the appropriate goal himself (to get a good grade, to fix the machine) and engages in the intended behavior (studies, takes the machine apart). Examples:

> E4ss3. The boy is thinking of a present to get his mother.
> The boy got three job no matter how long and hard to get the money he wants her the best present for her.
> He will get her something very meanful and lovely to her.
> E17ss3. There is a tornado warning out and he is the only one is class.
> He had to go back to school to get his homework and get his lunch box.
> The boy want someone to help him. He is thinking about what to do go home or stay in class.
> The boy will stay in class and the tornado will come. He will lay on the floor and keep his head down.

The subtlest forms of PC, rarely seen in these stories, are challenge, self-investment, and play.

CHALLENGE. A person acting as an origin experiences the world as a challenge. The person acting as a pawn sees it as a threat. Two students in the same graduate program exemplified this distinction. One, acting as a pawn, complained at length about the required courses. The other, acting as an origin, was puzzled at the first, claimed he never considered them as "required" but as an exciting challenge to master the content of his chosen field. The problem is that the second student would never have mentioned the challenge. "Isn't that the way everyone reacts?" As a result, the experience is not often stated; or, if it is, it is not couched in goal-setting terms; it must be inferred from subtler elaboration in the story. Example (a weak one at that):

E24ss3. The boy is trying to stand on his head until a 1 hour movie go off.
His brother told him that he can't stand on his head for five minutes
His brother thinks hes into for tring to stand on his head a hour
He will stand on his

SELF-INVESTMENT. This form is intended to capture any description of an experience similar to that described by Csikszentmihalyi (Csikszentmihalyi & Csikszentmihalyi, 1988) and dubbed "flow." Briefly, the experiential characteristics of the "flow" state include merging of activity and awareness, irrelevance of time, loss of self-awareness – the complete immersion in the activity to the exclusion of all other considerations. Not surprisingly, an example of this clearly expressed in these stories is rare. But it seems reasonable to infer it from the adult story that follows:

A4ss2. Two men are cutting a board to make a table.
The men bought the wood and decided what kind of table they wanted. (Also what shape and size.)
They want to make the table correctly so they are being very careful to follow the instructions they have and also to measure carefully.
They follow the instructions and make a beautiful cocktail table for their rathskeller.

PLAY. Casting most of the concept of PC in goal-setting terms excludes one of the most originlike activities – noncompetitive play. Such play has no goal, no instrumental activity. Yet a person engaged in play is most assuredly self-directed and experiencing himself as an origin. If a character in a story is engaged in play or anticipating it, the story may be scored PC. Example:

E23ss3. The boy his tired form working or running and playing now he is resting his head on his hand.
Before he was tired he was running and playing with his friends and having fun playing until he got tired of playing and stoped playing and he started resting hi head
He will be glad when he has rested so that he can start playing again.
soon he will be rested up and play again.

The scoring decision that the scorer must make for every story is: Does a character in the story show strong evidence of experiencing personal causation in the whole story in a freely chosen goal-setting sequence or in perceiving the situation as a challenge, or showing self-investment, or engaging in noncompetitive play? If so the story is scored 1; if not, 0.

PROCEDURES FOR SCORING

The "hero" problem. Most often the story has a central character. As in most of the stories used here, the author is a child and so is the "hero" or central figure. Given a central figure, *score only for the actions etc. of that figure.* Occasional stories are about several characters or a group. Here it is necessary to score for the group. Least often (and the instructions to the writers should warn against this) the author merely describes a situation and gives an opinion. Scoreable categories are usually scarce in such stories but an attempt should be made to score without falling into the trap of trying to imagine what the author was thinking. Never try to guess what the author was thinking; *score only what the story says about the characters in it.*

Disguise the identity, sex, and any other distinguishing characteristics of the author. A convenient way to do this is to have a separate face sheet on the protocol for such information that can be turned back while scoring the stories on the following pages.

Randomly mix all protocols to be scored. This makes it impossible for the scorer to know the author's gender, status, or experimental treatment. Assign numbers to the protocols that do not reveal subject characteristics. Write the numbers on the protocols and the scoring sheets.

It is convenient to divide the total set of protocols in a large study into batches of 10 or 20 protocols, turn all to story number 1 and proceed to score. Each batch *must* contain representatives of all types of subjects in the study (a random sample) to avoid trends in scoring from such things as fatigue from appearing as differences between groups or types of subjects. *Never* score, for instance, all males and then all females, or all trained and then all untrained subjects.

Score each story completely separately. The scorer should not know what the author wrote about in previous stories or the score of other stories in the protocol. The protocol (all stories) should never be viewed as a whole even if the author wrote it that way.

Score all number 1 cue stories together, then proceed to all the number 2 cue stories, and so forth. This promotes both reliability and validity and can be done by turning all protocols to Cue 1 and scoring all in a batch.

Each category is scored only once per story. No matter how often it may appear, a category is only scored once per story. An individual story may receive a score from 0 (no categories scored) to 6 (all categories scored). The latter is rare.

Even a simple sentence may contain more than one category and may be scored for more than one category. The scorer should always be able to identify exactly what led to the decision to score a category so that two scorers can compare exactly. The scorer may refer to specific words but remember that *fragments cannot be scored without taking into account the whole story*.

Make no marks on the protocol. Scoring reliability checks demand that the second scorer receives identical material as the first. Record the scores only on a separate scoring sheet.

Use separate scoring sheets, one for each story. Use a separate scoring sheet for Cue 1, Cue 2, and so on. All subjects' numbers in a batch will appear in order in column 1 of each of the scoring sheets. Six columns for the six categories run across the top. (See Table 24.1 after Practice Stories Batch B showing categories scored for each story.)

This technique makes it impossible for the scorer to check previous scores for any subject while scoring. It is convenient while scoring by stories but inconvenient for getting total scores. For recording all scores and total scores by story (but not by category) a similar sheet may be used with a column for subject number, total score on each story, and total score by subject.

If two scorers scoring independently use this technique, they will produce two sets of four pages (one for each story). Before arriving at a final total score, a coefficient of agreement between scorers must be computed. Differences between scorers must be resolved by discussing each discrepancy and agreeing on a final decision to score or not score the category. It is convenient to use the pages from one scorer to record all discrepancies and compute reliability. This can be done in a way, described shortly, that will preserve a complete account of each scorer's results on one set of pages, while the other set can be altered to reflect the final compromised scores to be used for further data analysis.

Say each scorer, while scoring, places an "X" in the appropriate box to record the scoring decision. When both scorers are through, page 1 (for Cue 1 stories) from each scorer can be placed side by side. With a colored pencil all Xs that appear on Scorer 2's page but not on Scorer 1's are penciled in color on Scorer 1's sheet. All Xs that appear on Scorer 1's sheet but not on Scorer 2's are circled on Scorer 1's sheet. Now Scorer 1's sheet can be read to see what each scorer did independently. Scorer 2's sheet has not been altered in any way.

To compute percentage of agreement one need only count the number of noncolored or noncircled Xs. These represent agreements. The original black Xs on Scorer 1's sheet, circled or not, represent the total categories scored by 1. The same can be obtained from looking at Scorer 2's unchanged sheet. These three numbers (number of agreements, number originally scored by 1, number originally scored by 2) are put into the simple formula for percentage of agreement.

$$\frac{2 \times \text{the no. of agreed upon categories}}{(\text{no. categories by Scorer 1}) + (\text{no. categories by Scorer 2})}$$

When learning to score it is useful to compute the percentage of agreement separately both by category and by cue. You may need practice on Cue 3, say, or on the reality perception category.

Hints on learning to score

THE ORIGIN CONCEPT. Learning to score for the origin concept is like learning to use any complex concept. One learns by using the concept. This is done by repeatedly engaging in the practice of scoring stories. Reading the manual is not sufficient.

IT TAKES TIME. Try to score for an hour or more each day. The goal is to reach 90% agreement before scoring protocols to be used as research data. To do this many scoring sessions are necessary. A week of this will only give minimal reliability (80% agreement).

IT TAKES TWO. Two scorers should study the manual and as soon as possible start scoring these and other stories independently and discussing disagreements. The value of independent scoring of two scorers followed by intense discussion of disagreements cannot be overemphasized.

A CARD FILE. Spend time writing down examples of disagreements and why the final decision was reached so that the next time a similar story is encountered consistency will be achieved. Keeping a file of index cards (3 × 5 inch) with a story on one side and categories scored and an explanation on the other side is very helpful. There is nothing like having to explain exactly why a category was scored.

WARM UP. A file has another advantage. Use it to warm up before scoring research protocols. Pull a few story cards at random and score them, before starting a session where reliability is needed for research purposes.

USE A CRIB SHEET. The origin concept is complex and hard to keep in mind. Make a crib sheet with the six major scoring decisions, each followed by subcategories to be remembered. Keep it at hand while scoring.

MAKE A GRAPH. For valuable feedback, make a graphic plot of percentage of agreement for each scoring session. As reliability increases, check individual categories or individual cues that may be most troublesome. Isolate these for special practice.

CRIB SHEET

Scoring decisions

1. *Personal Causation* (PC)
Perhaps score last.
Subcategories: Challenge, self-investment, noncompetitive play. Does a character in the story show strong evidence of experiencing personal causation in the whole story in a freely chosen goal-setting sequence or in perceiving the situation as a *challenge*, or showing *self-investment*, or engaging in *noncompetitive play*? If so, the story is scored 1; if not, 0.

2. *Goal Setting* (GS)
Does a major character in the story freely set a nonphysical-need goal that is *explicitly stated* and followed by some indication of *activity* or personal *involvement* in attaining the goal? Do not infer. Look for "want" statements. If so, the story is scored 1; if not, 0.

3. *Instrumental Activity* (IA)
Does a major character in the story engage in *present*, personally chosen activity to reach a goal? If so, the story is scored 1; if not, 0.

4. *Reality Perception* (RP)
Subcategories: Cause–effect, perceived blocks, intelligent adjustment, compromise, expert help or advice, planning, social reality, realistic obedience, and social sanctions.
Does a major character in the story show evidence of reality perception, that is, does he realistically talk about causes in the environment, motives in self and others, or blocks to reaching goals and plan to overcome them? If so, the story is scored 1; if not, 0.

5. *Personal Responsibility* (PR)
Subcategories: Consequences for action, social responsibility, concern for others.
Does a character or the author show evidence explicitly stated of taking personal responsibility? If so the story is scored 1; if not, 0.

6. *Self-confidence* (SC)
Subcategories: Positive outcome, overcoming blocks, confidence, affect over goal attainment.
Does a character in the story show self-confidence in his ability to attain a goal, state a positive outcome to a goal-setting sequence, or show emotion related to his originship? If so, the story is scored 1; if not, 0.

Appendix to Chapter 24

ORGANIZATION OF PRACTICE STORIES

The practice stories that follow are divided into three batches.
Batch A (40 stories) is made up of stories from 10 middle elementary

school children from the inner city. The subjects are identified by a letter and number (E1–E10) followed by the number of the cue (e.g., E1-1, E1-2). This section is arranged with all 10 stories from Cue 1 together, then those from Cue 2, and so on. Each story is immediately followed by an analysis and the scored categories. It is recommended that the beginning scorer, after reading through the 10 Cue 1 stories and the analyses, immediately try scoring them without reference to the analysis. A similar procedure should be used for the other 10 stories for each of the other 3 cues in Batch A.

Batch B is made up of stories from 5 similar children (E11, E12, E17, E23, E24). Again all Cue 1 stories appear before Cue 2 stories, and so on. But here the stories are not followed by the analysis. To facilitate learning to score, the stories all appear together and then the analyses appear. It is recommended that beginning scorers (using a score sheet) analyze the Cue 1 stories in the batch. Then check percent agreement with the written analyses. Similarly for Cue 2 and so on.

Batch C is made up of stories from 10 adult teachers (A1–A10), Cues 2 and 3 only. It is arranged in the same order as Batch B to facilitate scoring without reference to the analysis presented until all stories from one cue are scored.

Total number of practice stories with analyses is 80.

PRACTICE STORIES

Batch A, Cue 1

Subjects E1–E10.
Cue 1. A father and a son talking about something important.

Specific problems

Hero problem: This cue elicits stories where it is sometimes difficult to determine whether to score for the son or the father.

Solution: In order to obtain greater reliability an arbitrary decision has to be made. First, look for the goal-setting sequence categories (GS, IA, and SC). In stories written by children, score the goal-setting sequence categories for the son, only rarely for the father (exception E16ss1). If, however, clear origin categories occur for both characters, score for both (see E12ss1). If scoring adult protocols, score for either, depending on which is dominant. Second, look for the responsibility sequence (RP and PR) where you can score for the hero, a secondary character or even a mere statement by the author.

Goal problem: In scoring for Origin categories *any kind of goal* is acceptable. (Unlike scoring for motives like Achievement or Power where the goal determines the motive.) The problem is to eliminate something that is merely passively "wanted," "wished for," and so on, from a goal that the hero is willing to try to obtain and therefore shows origin characteristics. Further, one cannot judge what is an important goal to the character. The criterion, therefore, is the willingness to pursue the goal by taking action or affective involvment in it.

Solution: The goal is the beginning of the goal-setting sequence but the Origin aspect is the willingness to act and/or the confidence that the hero can attain the goal by his own efforts or affective involvement. Merely to want something is not enough, the hero must show a willingness or act to attain the goal or show some origin involvement. The best indication of this, of course, is a clear statement of instrumental activity (IA). But IA in past, future, or conditional is not scored for IA. Still, such nonscorable IA statements may be taken as indications of determination to reach the goal and if the goal is stated, GS may be scored. Conversely, if the goal can only be inferred it may not be scored as GS but it may be used to make a case for scoring instrumental activity (IA).

Note: A separate paragraph is used for the response to the four questions printed on the protocol but the questions are shown here only for E1ss1. Stories are reproduced as written.

E1ss1. (What is happening?) The son has broken a window by accident and ran. His bestfriend to the lady that he threw the rock. The father went over to talk to the lady about the window.
(What happened before?) The two boys had a fight and are mad at each other. His friend wants to get him in trouble
(What is being thought or wanted?) He wished that he had never met his friend and to beat him up.
(What will happen?) His father will make him pay for the window with his money.

E1ss1. This story has no goal-setting sequence but is descriptive of a responsibility situation. Here the son's behavior is mainly pawnish but the father holds him accountable – "His father will make him pay for the window." This is scored for the author's reality perception that this is the normal outcome (RP). Personal responsibility is not taken by the child so PR is not scored.
Scored RP.

E2ss1. The boys father is talking to him about important
The boy broke their lawn mower.
His father said, "since it was an accident, he wouldn't punnish him."
The boy said since he broke it he will pay for it to be fixed out of his allowance.

E2ss1. This story is descriptive of a responsibility situation. At first the boy seems in a pawn condition, but then he takes responsible action, "since he broke it he will pay for it," is scored for PR. RP is shown both in the father saying "since it was an accident" and in the son seeing the connection between his responsibility and paying for it. Completely on his own the son changes his pawn situation to one where he feels personal causation in restoring the situation of his doing. This is scored PC.

Scored PC, RP, PR.

> **E3SSI.** The son is asking his father can he have the car
> When then son took the car before he had an accident
> The boy is thinking and hopeing that his father will give in
> The father will probly give his son the car on certain conditions. He will be responsible for any damage.

E3SSI. The goal-setting sequence involved the inferred goal of having the car. GS is not scored because it is inferred rather than stated. However, in pursuing that goal "the son is asking his father . . ." This is instrumental to the goal and scored IA. "Thinking and hoping" would not be scored for IA. The outcome is only provisionally positive, "father will probly give his son the car," thus not scored for SC. The further condition, "be responsible for any damage," shows perception of reality and is scored RP but no one actually takes responsibility so it is not scored PR. There is no indication of the son experiencing personal causation so PC is not scored.

Scored IA, RP.

> **E4SSI.** The son is aksing the to spend more time with him
> The son was eggnored on father and son day
> The son wanted a little attention
> The father and son will be the champion of fathers and son day in most contests.

E4SSI. The goal sequence here derives from the statement "The son wanted a little attention." "The son is asking" is instrumental activity. These two sentences are scored GS and IA respectively. The last sentence is an objective statement that is too tenuously related to the sequence to be scored for SC. It is not clear that it is really the outcome of asking nor that it is totally positive. The statement that the son was ignored does not show reality perception by the boy, just a description of the situation; nor is there any clear evidence that the son felt that he caused a change, no PC.

Scored GS, IA.

> **E5SSI.** The father is telling the son about driving.
> The son complained that all his friends can drive now.
> The knowledge to drive.
> The son will learn to drive.

E5SSI. The goal setting sequence here is based on the statement the son wants "the knowledge to drive." Remember that the third paragraph usually answers the protocol sentence "what is being thought or wanted." This is scored GS. "The son complained" is past and not scored for IA but we can assume that the son approached the father to obtain the knowledge and can score RP as acceptance of expertise. "The son will learn to drive" is a positive outcome and shows SC.

Scored GS, RP, SC.

E6ss1. The father will not let the son go skating so the boy started to cry
last time he asked his father would not give him the money to go. so he started to
cry and went to his room
The father thought he had been a little selfish
So the father gave his son the money to go skating with

E6ss1. This is a good example of a goal sequence that is purely pawnish. The goal is to go skating but all the boy does is cry and remain totally under the control of his father. The outcome is positive simply because the father changes his mind and not through actions of the son.
Scored 0.

E7ss1. Jimmy wants a bicycle but his father says we need the money for something more important you need
we don't have any money to buy clothing or food and Jimmy wants a bicycle. the money is getting
Jimmy wants a bicycle so badly he crys when he sees someone else with one and keeps begging
Jimmy gets his bike and is so happy he rides it every day and promises to take good care of it

E7ss1. Here is a case where "Jimmy wants a bicycle" is repeated three times. He is certainly involved in the outcome, which is positive. These two aspects are scored GS and SC. "Promises to take good care of it" smacks of personal responsibility but does not actually show it; just a (possibly idle) promise (see also story A4ss3). "Keeps begging" is not scored IA.
Scored GS, SC.

E8ss1. Father and son lecturing about something Important.
Son forgot to mow the lawn before he to play.
Father is thinking of punishment, not too harsh and not too easy. Son wants to know what his punishment is going to be.
Father will say to Son that he will not be able to go outside for a week. Son says "Aw, Papa."

E8ss1. This is a situation where the son plays a totally pawn role. Even "wanting to know what the punishment will be" is not goal but rather occasioned by his impending decision.
Scored 0.

E9ss1. A man is talking to his son about the rent and bills that was over due.
Before that the man could aford the money but his wife died and all the money went to the hosiptile.
The man thought gettin a job will be the best thing to solve their problems.
The man will get a job and everything will work out fine.

E9ss1. The need for money to pay bills sets the scene here. The father shows reality perception in seeing that getting a job will overcome the block (RP). Then he takes the responsible action (future) of getting the job; scored for PR but not IA because it is not present tense. The outcome is positive showing self confidence (SC). The story does not show that the father experienced personal causation.

Scored RP, PR, SC.

E10ss1. John and his father are talking about gettin John a job. One that he could do after school. And on Sat.days.

John had asked his father if he could have a bicycle his father didn't have enough money So John had to get a job.

John wanted to get a job so that he can bicycle.

John's father will get him the job and he will buy the bicycle he wants.

E10ss1. The goal sequence here involves wanting a job in order to get a bicycle, "John wanted to get a job so that he can bicycle" (GS). "John and his father are talking" is instrumental to getting the job and bike, scored IA. The job is a realistic perception of the way of overcoming the block that the father didn't have enough money. Scored RP. That the father gets the boy a job is a positive outcome that does not show self-confidence, because the father did it and not the boy.

Scored GS, IA, RP.

Batch A, Cue 2

Cue 2. Two men working at a machine.

SPECIFIC PROBLEM. Cue 2 is fairly straightforward to score. The one imperative is not to score a repetition of the cue as instrumental activity.

The cue most often elicits goal-setting sequence stories about a broken machine. Responsibility stories about altercations between the two men or accidents where one is hurt are frequent. Occassionally, the men are inventors.

E1ss2. They are making cars and one man has a problem bout their boss

He caught his boss going into a bar and not coming out for some time.

The other man wanted no part in his partners problem.

Both men forgot about the problem and kept on working

E1ss2. This is a descriptive story with no goal-setting sequence involving personal causation. They are making cars but with no involvement. Therefore, PC, GS, IA, SC are not scored. "The other man wanted no part in his partners problem" shows a realistic perception of his own position – keeping out of something that is not his concern. Therefore it is scored RP. There is no statement concerning responsibility so PR is not scored.

This is an example where a "want" statement is not a statement of goal setting.

Scored RP.

E3ss2. The men are trying to fix the machine but one of the doesn't kno much about it because he just started working

His friend that work with him knew all about the machine and he home sick in the bed
The man is wanting his friend to get well so that he can return to work.
In about two weeks of the work of a new comer his friend will get well and return.

E3ss2. Here the nonstated goal is to fix the machine (it doesn't say someone wants to fix it) but they are "trying to fix" it. There is a goal-setting sequence but the characters are not personally invested in it so we do not score PC or GS. "Trying" being in the present tense is scored for IA. (Note that "wanting his friend to get well" is another wanting statement not scored for GS. He does nothing about it.) There is no statement of responsibility (no PR) nor is the outcome of the goal-setting sequence, fixing the machine, clear. No SC. However, "His friend that . . . knew all about the machine and" was "home sick" shows a perception and insight into one's position and an acceptance of expertness and is scored RP.
  Scored IA, RP.

E4ss2. The boss comes and says he must lay one man off one months
Business was going great he hired two men to do most his work.
One man will have to be layed off now one man this is his only job.
The man who has two other jobs has vollonted.

E4ss2. There is no goal-setting sequence in this story so we find no GS, IA, or SC. The story is descriptive of an imposed constrained situation. The constraints and consequences of the situation are clearly described – "Business was going great he hired two men" but now business slows down so "he must lay one man off." This is scored for RP. "The man who has two other jobs has [volunteered]" shows the personal experience of doing something – taking responsibility to alleviate the perceived situation. This is scored PR. The strong indication that the one man perceived the situation and experienced the feeling that he could do something about it is scored PC.
  Score PC, RP, PR.

E5ss2. Two men are trying to repair a tape recorder
One of the men broke the machine
The idea of making the machine run.
The machine will be repaired.

E5ss2. The goal-setting sequence is clear here – to fix the machine. The goal is stated as "the idea of making the machine run" and is scored GS. "Trying to repair" is scored IA and the outcome of overcoming the block of a broken machine is positive – "The machine will be repaired" is scored SC. There is no statement of perception of the situation or responsibility – not scored RP or PR. This is a *run of the mill* task where no strong personal experience of causal locus is stated – not scored PC.
  Score GS, IA, SC.

E6ss2. One man had let the gas out of the machine so they are arguing about it.
last time they got to fighting over who would run the machine
The other man thought that he needed a new partner
The man fired his partner and got him an other one and he felt verry sad

E6ss2. There is no goal-setting sequence here (no GS, IA). The theme is an interpersonal altercation apparently at the technical and personal levels. The "other man" sees that he needs a new partner (scored RP). He fires one and gets another but neither statement can be scored for IA because they are in the past tense. They do indicate the overcoming of blocks and are scored SC. There is no experience of strong PC, therefore PC is not scored.
Score RP, SC.

E7ss2. Joe and Harry argue about another job they say working in a beer factory isnt good.
they were content and liked the job because they got free beer but they now want to quit.
they want to get out of the factory and get a good job
they get what they want and were not satisfied because they come late every morning and get fired.

E7ss2. A goal is stated twice (in want statements) and is scored GS. But there is no subsequent goal-setting sequence involving initiated action (no IA) and positive outcome. They get a new job but then are fired – no SC. There is a clear perception of cause and effect – "they come late . . . and get fired," which is scored RP. Nothing indicated experienced personal cause, thus no PC, or responsibility, so no PR.
Score GS, RP.

E8ss2. Two men are working at a machine.
The machine conked out.
Onlooker wants the machine to be fixed so he can buy a candy bar. The two men wish the man would get lost.
The two men will fix the machine and say about the onlooker "one crackpot like that is enough."

E8ss2. This is basically a descriptive story. The repetition of the cue in sentence 1 is not scored IA. The "want" statement involving the onlooker is not related to the men who are working and not scored GS.
Score 0.

E9ss2. The men is working at a new machine that will do all the work.
Befor the men and t work hard and work late at night
The men wanted to no if the new michine would relly do all the work.
The men found out the machine can do the work just by pushing button.

E9ss2. This is an example where one inference can make a huge difference. If we infer that the men are "making" – that is, inventing – a new machine, then all six categories can be scored. But nowhere in the story is that clearly stated. If we assume that they are merely working at a new

machine supplied by someone else, then the story shows no investment, no PC, and the score is 0. The latter inference seems most prudent.
Score 0.

E10ss2. One of the men cut his hand very badly. And it began to bleed.
He was talking and was not playing any attention to what he was doing and the saw slipped and cut his hand.
The man wanted it to stop bleeding so he could get on with his work.
He will be sent to first-aid to get a patch on his hand.

E10ss2. This is not a story with a goal-setting sequence but rather a description of an accident. Despite the "want" phrase there is nothing scorable for GS nor is there any expression of experienced personal causation (PC). Nothing is done so there is no IA. However, the cause–effect relationship between "not paying attention" and "cut his hand" supported by "wanted to get on with his work" is scored for reality perception RP. The outcome is positive and scored SC despite the fact that the story is not centered around a goal statement or block to overcome yet shows faith in a positive result.
Scored RP, SC.

Batch A, Cue 3

Cue 3. A boy with his head resting in his hands.

SPECIFIC PROBLEMS. The thing to look out for in this cue is the difference between an origin set goal and a physical need. Many stories concern being tired, needing sleep, and so forth. Although such needs are not scored GS, such stories cannot be immediately dismissed as unscorable (see, for instance, E23ss3 where the boy is tired and resting in order to reenter an origin activity).

E1ss3. The boy is thinking about the school picnic. They are going to Holiday Hill.
The last year they went a boy fell off the roller coaster. He also broke his leg
He is thinking that the same thing will happen to him this year
The boy will go but he will not get on the roller coaster or other dangerous rides.

E1ss3. The inferred goal of this story is to go to the picnic but it is not scored GS. Knowing the goal makes it reasonable to score "thinking about the school picnic" IA, deciding whether to go or not. This is strengthened as an origin story because the boy is thinking of blocks, "he is thinking that the same thing will happen to him" (falling off the roller coaster). This is scored RP. "The boy will go but not get on the roller coaster" is a positive outcome and overcoming the block. Scored SC.
Scored IA, RP, SC.

E2ss3. A boy is tired from raking leaves
his mother told him she wasn't going to give him any more money

His said he would work for his money. Because it is hot and he wants an ice-cream cone.

After he finishes the man gives him a dollar. The boy buys his ice-cream and saves the rest for tomorrow.

E2ss3. This story has the self determined goal "he wants an ice-cream cone" (GS), but there is a block to be overcome. The boy "said he would work for his money," taking on responsibility (RP) for attaining his goal. He attains his goal by overcoming the block (SC). Then he even shows foresight (RP) in "saves the rest for tomorrow." The whole story is totally self-determined and shows the experience of personal causation (PC).

Scored PC, GS, RP, PR, SC.

> **E3ss3.** The boy is in school and hopeing that he could be out fishing or swimming.
> The boy played hookey and he got reported
> The boy is wishing that the summer vacation was here
> His father will take him fishing on a week end

E3ss3. This is a real fantasy story. Going fishing or swimming is the goal but it is followed by no activity or involvement in attaining the goal, so you cannot score "hopeing" GS. In E3ss1 the boy is "hopeing," but he is asking for and therefore doing something about the goal. Here the outcome is positive but not the result of the boy's activity or overcoming a block. Out of the blue – "fairy godmother" like – "His father will take him fishing." This is not scored SC. Essentially the story shows a pawnish reaction of wanting but not doing.

Scored 0.

> **E4ss3.** The boy is thinking of a present to get his mother
> The boy got three job no matter how long and hard to get the money.
> he wants her the best present for her.
> He will get her something very meanful and lovely to her.

E4ss3. This story presents all the aspects of the goal-setting sequence. The goal "he wants the best present for her" (GS). "The boy is thinking of a present to get his mother" is scored for IA. Although he is not thinking about getting the jobs, he is deciding about the present, that is, which is best. He "got three jobs . . . to get the money" shows reality perception of how to overcome the block of no money (RP) and also shows responsibility for overcoming the block (PR). Responsibility is also shown in the form of concern for others, "he wants the best present for her." Self-confidence is shown in overcoming the block and in the positive outcome, "He will get her something very meanful" (SC). The whole story is a self-determined goal with clear experience of causing a positive outcome (PC).

Scored PC, GS, IA, RP, PR, SC.

> **E5ss3.** The boy is trying to figure out a way to make money.
> He saw a model airplane he wanted at the store
> The boy wants money.
> The boy will get the money.

E5ss3. Here is another story of a self-determined goal but with less elaboration than E4ss3. The goal is the model airplane of sentence two, stated as a "want" statement and scorable for GS. "Trying to figure out a way to make money" is instrumental to that goal and scored IA. It also shows that he is taking responsibility for goal attainment (PR). The outcome, "The boy will get money" is clearly the result of his actions and not just incidental and is scored SC. Again goal and activity are self-determined and the elaboration of the story makes the inference of the experience of personal causation plausible (PC).

Scored PC, GS, IA, PR, SC.

E6ss3. The had been up all night and now he is trying to sleep
last time he had stayed up so late when he went to school he went to sleep in the classroom
The boy thought he was in bed but he had awaken and then went home and went to bed
Maybe the boy decided that he would not stay up so late.

E6ss3. Here we have an example of a descriptive story (with no goal-setting sequence) about a physical need – sleep. These are usually not scorable as origin stories. This one does not even mention the need or want of sleep. "Maybe the boy decided that he would not stay up so late" can be scored for RP because the author expresses the insight into the actions and consequences and it is not part of the physical need.

Scored RP.

E7ss3. tom was sad because his mother was ill. so he went to the church to say a prayer.
everything was allright before but when tom stopped going to church and fighting and skipping school his mother became ill.
toms mother wanted him to do right and kept after tom until he decided to do right
his mother became well and tom did better and was not ever going

E7ss3. It is difficult to decide about this story. On the one hand it can be chalked up to superstition related to going to church. But we must not impose any set of values on our judgment. Apparently Tom had faith in personal causal effect of prayer and stopping fighting. Here is a good case where the author's description shows a causal link. One cannot question the reality but score RP because the boy believes it. In addition, RP is scored for Concern for Others: "Tom was sad because his mother was ill." PR is scored for "he decided to do right" despite she "kept after him." It is stated as his decision. Outcome positive – SC.

Scored RP, PR, SC.

E8ss3. A Boy is resting his head on his hands.
The boy was running from two roughnecks woh tried to take his money.
The boy wishes the bruts would leave him alone. The Roughnecks are thinking about how much money they will get.

The boy will run home, tell his father and, and his father will get the police on the boys.

E8ss3. This is a descriptive story with no goal-setting sequence. However, considerable insight is shown by all the main protagonists. The boy wishes they would leave him alone and runs home, the father gets the police, and even the roughnecks are looking forward to money. The story is scored for RP only. "Boy wishes" is not GS because it is escape from physical harm. "Telling father" is future activity but acceptance of expert help (RP).
Scored RP.

E9ss3. A boy is thinking about the test he had to take the next morning.
Before that he didn't take any time to study.
The boy thought if he study that it may be a chance that he could past the test.
The next morning the boy pass the test just by studing and thinking.

E9ss3. The inferred goal here is to pass the test. "Thinking about the test" is usually scant evidence of instrumental activity but here the author tells us that he believes that it is, "the boy pass the test just by studing and thinking," so it is scored IA. "The boy thought if he study that it may be a chance that he could past the test" is scored RP. The outcome shows SC.
Scored IA, RP, SC.

E10ss3. Was thinking about a pony. He had one named Joca. He love his pony.
One day it jumped the fence and ran away. And Simon hasn't seen it sents.
Simon wanted his pony. And no other pony would do.
He will look all over the country untill he find Joca.

E10ss3. "Simon wanted his pony" is scored GS because it is supported by "he will look," which constitutes future activity. This shows responsibility for goal attainment and is scored PR (but not IA because it is future). The outcome is positive and scored SC.
Scored GS, PR, SC.

Batch A, Cue 4

Cue 4. A mother and her child look worried.

PROBLEMS *Scoring personal responsibility.* Story 4 is a cue that produces PR often because of the implied concern for others. It is often difficult to be sure that the concern is attributed to one of the characters. To be scored for PR under "true concern" the story must contain a statement of instrumental activity, of affect expressing concern, or of a goal that expresses concern through wanting something beneficial to the other person.

E1ss4 below shows a case where the concern is not attributed to anyone nor is there activity.

E2ss4 shows a case where "they want him to come home so they'll know he's alright," which qualifies for wanting something beneficial.

E3ss4 is another case where concern is clear because they tried (past, not IA) to contact him.

Scoring Goal Setting. Story 4 often has "want" statements that are not scored for GS. Statements like "They want him to hurry" (E2 ss4) are not goals that are set – not scored GS. If, however, they are the expression of concern as the second phrase, "so they'll know he' alright," shows, they can be scored PR.

Scoring Self-Confidence. Beware of positive outcomes that are not clearly the result of activity of the concerned persons. "The police found the boy" (E1ss4) or "later John comes home" (E2ss4) are not the result of activity or concern of the other characters.

E1ss4. Their brother was kidnapped and the police are looking for him.
The kidnapper said he was going to drive the boy home when getting out of school that day
The mother thought who ever the kidnapper is he will let him go
The police found the boy in an alley tied up

E1ss4. This is a descriptive story but it is not clear that anyone in the story is concerned enough to do anything. Did they call the police? That would be an unwarranted inference. Because there is no goal-setting sequence, none of those categories are scorable nor is there clear RP. The outcome is positive but is merely a factual statement unrelated to actions of the people – not scored SC.
Score 0.

E2ss4. A mother and her daughter is waiting for John to come home.
John was hit by a car after work.
They want him to hurry home so they'll know he's alright.
15 min. later, John, comes home. He went to buy some groceries.

E2ss4. This is a descriptive story that does show concern since "They want him to hurry home so they'll know he's alright." This is scored PR (not GS.) The positive ending is unrelated to anything done by the concerned persons and is not scored SC.
Scored PR.

E3ss4. The mother an child is worried because they can seem to contact her husben at the office
Her husben had to work late and they were worried
The mother and child is wanting him to come home right away
The father will get in about 12:00 and the mother and child will be sleep

E3ss4. From the first sentence it is clear that they tried to contact the father although it is not scorable for IA. It does show concern and willingness to act on it and may be scored PR. "Wanting him to come home right away" is not a set goal, not scored GS. The positive outcome is not a result of the concern or the activity and is therefore not scored SC.

Scored PR.

> **E4ss4.** The mother has seen her children with bad children.
> The bad children broke glass lited and other terrible thing you could thing.
> She doesn't want the child to practice bad habits.
> The mother will find that the child is keeping thos kids out of most there mischef

E4ss4. The negative want statement in this descriptive story qualifies it for the PR score. Again GS is not scored, nor is the positive ending related to anything done by the mother and is not scored SC.

Scored PR.

> **E5ss4.** The rent is due and they don't have any money.
> The was fired from her job.
> The rent money
> Friends will give her the money.

E5ss4. This is a simple story about wanting money to pay the rent. The need for money is completely imposed upon them and they do nothing about it. Perceiving the relation between needing money and the rent being due is not reality perception. The outcome is purely fortuitous, as friends give her money. A story totally lacking in experience of personal causation.

Scored 0.

> **E6ss4.** They dont have any food in the house to eat and they are starving
> last time they dind have any food on christmas the people collected money to buy them food
> The mother wish there was some way for them to eat because her little girl was hungry.
> Maybe they will get their food so they will not starve or the neighbors will feed them.

E6ss4. This is a unique story with weak indications that the mother is concerned about her daughter, but she does nothing and shows no affect. It cannot be scored for the mother's personal responsibility. It might be scored for perception of block under RP but again that is questionable, especially with physical needs. One might score the author for social responsibility (PR) but it certainly is not strong. When in doubt be conservative.

Scored 0.

> **E7ss4.** the father hasn't come home and the mother is so upset she calls the police
> he had been drinking and got drunk drove in his car and didn't come back
> she wishes he would stop drinking and the son wants the father to spend more time with him.
> the father gives up drinking but doesn't pay any attention to his son he goes out with other women

E7ss4. The major plot of this story involved the mother's concern for the father to come home and stop drinking. The fact that she "is so upset that she calls the police" qualifies the story for the score IA (calling the police) and affect (upset) or concern for the other (PR). The boy "wants the father to spend more time with him." We cannot score this GS because there is no elaboration and we scored the mother sequence. Because the further elaboration ends in a negative outcome, SC cannot be scored.

Scored IA, PR.

E8ss4. A mother and her kid look worried because father went out in a terrible storm to get the biggest child from a party.
A tree fell on their garage just before father had ridden away.
Mother and her child wants father to hurry home with the older child.
On the way home, father's car will crash against a tree and father and the kid will be hurt seriously. The kid will have to ware

E8ss4. "The mother and her kid look worried" is a repetition of the cue – not scorable for PR alone. But later they "want the father to hurry home with the older child." Although the want statement is not GS, it is support for PR shown in the first sentence. Putting the two sentences together gives a score of PR.

Scored PR.

E9ss4. A mother and he son was worried because they did not have the money to pay the doctor bill
Before that her hubson work and had money to pay the bills.
The lady though if she get a job that would be best
The lady got the job and was able to pay the bills.

E9ss4. Here the mother and son need money to pay the doctor bill, a situation similar to the story of E5ss4. Here, however, the lady does something about it. The perception that taking a job would solve the problem is scored RP. "The lady got the job" shows assumption of responsibility – scored PR. "and was able to pay the bills" shows confidence in a positive outcome and of overcoming blocks, and is scored SC.

Scored RP, PR, SC.

E10ss4. Father and son was expected to be home at 4:00 clock and it is now 5:30p.m.
Once when father was that late he was in an accident,
The mother and her child want their fathers to come home safely.
They will call the job to ask if they were still at work.

E10ss4. "The mother and her child want their fathers to come home safely" is a want statement not scored GS but rather PR for concern for others. "Safely" is the critical word. "They will call" further supports PR but is not scored IA (not present tense). The last statement also shows a correct perception of the possibility to do something and is scored RP.

Scored RP, PR.

Batch B Stories, Cue 1

Subjects E11, E12, E17, E23, E24.
Cue 1. A father and a son talking about something important.

E11ss1. A boy and his father is talking about marrage of his son it is very important that his son knows what his doing before getting married.
At first the boy was of his feauntsas house talkin about the plans.
He wants to marry her right away no back-ups are maybes in it.
So he is going to marry her any no matter what his dad says to him about it.

E12ss1. The father is talking to his son about getting a job.
Before, he had a job but he didn't keep it because he was never ontime.
The father is wanting his son to be something in life.
The boy makes up his mind that he is not going to be like his brother. He's going to get up in time to go to work. And he's going to work harder on his job.

E17ss1. They are talking about a car. The son told the father it was his friends
The son stole the car from someone he didn't know
The father want to know who his friend is and where do he live
The boy would have to go and show his father the friend and then he will have to tell the truth and take the car back and apologize

E23ss1. A father is talking to his son about something important
His son did something he wasn't suppose to do and his father is tellin him how important it is that he stop doing it
His father is trying to make him understand that he must stop acting like he do and start acting better
His son might stop acting like he do are he will just keep on doing it

E24ss1. The boy is going to
both was siting of them
They is thinking about they grandmother coming from out of town
They will all go to the bus station

Batch B Analysis, Cue 1

(Stories from E11, E12, E17, E23, E24)

E11ss1. The goal of this story is clearly stated, "He wants to marry her right away." This is scored for GS. Talking with his father is instrumental to this goal (IA). The outcome is clearly positive and shows confidence in goal attainment (SC). The boy shows determination to overcome any block to reach his goal demonstrating the urgency of feeling personal causation (PC).
Scored PC, GS, IA, SC.

E12ss1. This story poses the question, for whom do you score? The father apparently has an influence goal, he is "wanting his son to be something in life" (GS), and he "is talking to his son about getting a job" (IA). Taken together these two sentences also constitute PR. Then the plot turns to the son who "makes up his mind that he is not going to be like his brother" (RP) and "he's going to work harder on his job" (PR). The author of the story, though using two characters, is demonstrating all the categories above so they are all scored.

Scored GS, IA, RP, PR.

E17ss1. This is a responsibility plot. For the author's perception of social sanctions "he will have to tell the truth and take the car back and apologize" it is scored RP. Although the theme is responsibility it cannot be scored for PR since the boy does not freely assume the responsibility.

Scored RP.

E23ss1. This is a responsibility story but the boy does not make any origin response to taking responsibility nor can the father's actions be scored.

Scored 0.

E24ss1. This cryptic and descriptive story has no hint of an origin category.

Scored 0.

Batch B Stories, Cue 2

Cue 2. Two men working at a machine.

E11ss2. Mr. Bill and Mr. Evans is working together at a machine talking and appologizing to each other.

At first they had had a fight up in the bosses office about something that didn't matter.

So Mr. Evans thinks that they schould make up for it.

Mr. Bill & Mr. Evans a verry good friends agin now there talking together.

E12ss2. Two men are working this huge machine, with all sorts of buttons and levers.

Someone broke into the factory and stole the other machine, and all of the chemicals.

They want to make a solution that will make people strong & live longer.

The two men get into an argument. They drop the chemical. It starts a dangerous fire. The two men are trapped and unable to get out.

E17ss2. Both of the men or hurt. One leg of a man is broken and the arm of the other man is broken.

The men heard someone cry out watch for that brick and they both fell off of the machine.

The men are thinking they would never get any help because everyone is gone.

The janitor will come to help the men and then they would go to the hospital.

E23ss2. There two men who is worki on a machine trying to get it to work for its owner

Before the men came to fix it, it was working alright.

The men are wounder when they will be finish with the machine and get their money

Soon they will be finish with the machine so it will work right for its owner and they will get their money for doing the job

E24ss2. They is trying to figure out how to work the machine

They bose gave them a new job working with a machine.

The or trying to figure out how to work the machine
The bose is going to go and check

Batch B Analysis, Cue 2

E11ss2. The goal-setting sequence here is to make up and be friends again. It is, however, not explicitly stated so not scored GS. "Talking and appologizing" (present tense) is scored IA, that is, instrumental to making up. "Mr. Evans thinks that they should make up" is scored PR for being friends again. The insight that the fight was "about something that didn't matter" is scored RP. The two men overcome the block of the fight and the outcome is that they "are good friends again," scored SC. Mr. Evans correctly analyzes the situation, takes responsibility to initiate talking, all of which leads to a positive outcome. From this we can score PC from the inference that he experienced sequence and outcome as his cause.
Scored PC, IA, RP, PR, SC.

E12ss2. Here is an example of a goal-setting sequence gone wrong. The men have a goal "They want to make a solution" scored GS; they "are working this huge machine," present activity scored IA. Their goal is an innovation or an invention, "solution that will make people strong." which is scored PR. But everything goes wrong so there is no experience of PC, no reality perception on their part, and no self-confidence or positive outcome.
Scored GS, IA, PR.

E17ss2. There is no goal-setting sequence here, mere description. No PC, GS, IA, PR, or SC can be scored. The description does show reality perception. Scored RP in that they perceive their situation "because everyone is gone" they can't get help. Perception of Blocks.
Scored RP.

E23ss2. Here there is the goal-setting sequence of getting the machine to work. No goal is attributed to the characters, so no GS. But they "is working" so it is scored IA. The result of their action is positive and is scored SC. There is no expression of experiencing PC nor of reality perception or responsibility.
Scored IA, SC.

E24ss2. The goal of the goal-setting sequence is to figure out the machine but it is not explicitly attributed to the men with a want statement so we don't score GS. "Trying to figure out" occurs twice and is scored (only once) IA. There is no outcome or self-confidence or reality perception. "Trying" often connotes taking personal responsibility but here as in E23ss2 it is merely descriptive of activity in a run of the mill task rather than extra effort and responsibility.
Scored IA.

Batch B Stories, Cue 3

Cue 3. A boy with his head resting on his hands.

E11ss3. Byron is sitting in his class slotched over in his desk with his head on his hand thinking hard.

We had a test and Byron wants to know if he passed are fail the test so his thinking

He want to pass to the seventh grade so do we.

Report card day has come horay he says wev'e all passed. and the whole day goes alone fine.

E12ss3. A boy is thinking about his dog. It has just been ran over by a car.

His mother told him not to take the dog out for a walk without a chain.

The boy is wishing he had obeyed his mother.

His mother & father is feeling sad for him. So for his birthday, they buy him a puppy german sheperd dog that he's always wanted.

E17ss3. There is a tornado warning out and he is the only one is class

He had to go back to school to get his homework and get his lunch box

The boy want someone to help him. He is thinking about what to do go home or stay in class

The boy will stay in class and the tornado will come. He will lay on the floor and keep his head down

E23ss3. The boy his tired form working or running and playing now he is resting his head on his hand

Before he was tired he was running and playing with his friends and having fun playing until he got tired of playing and stoped playing and he started resting hi head

He will be glad when he has rested so that he can start playing again.

soon he will be rested up and play again

E24ss3. The boy is trying to stand on his head until a 1 hour movie go off

His brother told him that he can't stand on his head for five minuts

His brother thinks hes into for tring to stand on his head a hour

He will stand on his

Batch B Analysis, Cue 3

E11ss3. This is a typical test situation in school. There is a statement that Byron "wants to pass," which is scored GS. He is thinking but not in order to do well or pass, so this is not instrumental to passing. Not scored IA. The outcome of the test is passing showing SC. There is no statement of RP or PR or PC.

Scored GS, SC.

E12ss3. Here we have a responsibility story. The boy is apparently sorry for not obeying his parents. But he is not merely acting as a pawn, being sorry that the dog is dead, but rather is showing the capacity for intelligent adjustment in the form of a personal decision to obey rather than mere submission. This, "The boy wishes he had obeyed his mother," can be scored RP. "His mother & father is feeling sad for him" is an example of concern for others accompanied with affect (sad) and is scored PR.

Scored RP, PR.

E17ss3. In this descriptive story with no goal-setting sequence, the boy is subject to the threat of a storm over which he can have no control. Wanting help is not a goal, but "thinking about what to do" is instrumental activity. Scored IA. The boy does analyze the situation correctly and shows responsibility for problem solving. He "will stay in class . . . [and] lay on the floor and keep his head down" – scored PR. He overcomes the block – scored SC.

Scored IA, PR, SC.

E23ss3. This is a unique story where the physical need of being tired is related to an entirely different theme. You might infer that "wanted to play" is like being lazy or wanting to sleep and therefore totally pawnish. However, play is usually a totally self-determined, personally chosen activity and, in one sense, the epitome of originness. Yet it is rarely stated in goal-setting sequence terms because to reduce play to a set of goals and activity is to verbally transform the idea into a task or into work. Still it is clear that the boy, although tired, wants to play and is resting so that he can play. Resting cannot be seen as instrumental "activity" but it is instrumental to goal attainment, and can be scored PR. The outcome "he will be rested up and play again" is positive – scored SC for positive outcome. Play, when elaborated as an active process, is a subcategory of PC, so this is a rare case of that and is scored PC.

Scored PC, PR, SC.

E24ss3. This is the story of a challenge. The boy accepts the challenge of his brother. Apparently he feels confident, although this is not stated. He ups the time from 5 minutes to 1 hour. "Trying to stand on his head" can be scored IA. Accepting a challenge can be taken as feeling confident – scored SC. Because an Origin sees the world as an exciting challenge in which he can experience personal causation, it is scored PC.

Scored PC, IA, SC.

Batch B Stories, Cue 4

Cue 4. A mother and her child look worried.

E11ss4. Suzy and her mother is worried about her daddy.
at first when Suzy come home her mother said bad news daddy is gone over seas and every since then they're worried.
Suzy wants her father to come back to her and her mother.
Daddy will be home soon he's, he's home Suzy runs and grabs her daddy and hugs him tighter than tight.

E12ss4. They are worried about Kirk. The mother's son. He has went out to hunt a mountain lion. It's snowing very hard.
He has killed many cattles & horses.
They want Kirk to come home soon.
Kirk thinks he hears the lion but its only snow. He starts running fast. He slips &

fall. He can't stop. He falls off a cliff and Is killed. They find his body & has his funeral.

E17ss4. The mother and child or in the hospital worrying about father.
The father was in a car accident and they doctor said he was in serious condition.
The mother want to know is there any thing she could do. The child is thinking he is going to die.
The mother would give father some of her blood and a few more of her friends will, too. He will live.

E23ss4. Amother and her child is worried because her son has been hit by a car and is in the hospital.
Her son was playing ball and ran out in to the street to get a ball that was hit out into the street as he ran for it a car hit him.
His mother and sister is hoping he will be alright in the hospital.
Her son will pull through the acciedent but barly

E24ss4. They are trying to figure out what to fix
They got a letter saying there grandmother is coming over for dinner
They wont to tell There grandmother they didn't go get groceries yet
They grandmother is going to bring some food for the dinner

Batch B Analysis, Cue 4

E11ss4. Another case of personal concern, being worried (the cue) supported by "Suzy wants her father to come back." Scored PR. The outcome is positive and here it is directly related to the concern through affect (hugs) and is scored SC.
Scored PR, SC.

E12ss4. This is a descriptive story where the cue is repeated but not backed up by any activity and the "want" statement is merely for him "to come home soon" not "safely" or anything that is clearly beneficial to him. The want here does not qualify the story to be scored PR. Kirk is engaged in an originlike activity (hunting a mountain lion in the snow) but there is neither a goal statement nor a present activity statement, hence no GS or IA score. Still we can assume that Kirk experiences personal causation and score PC although the outcome is negative.
Scored PC.

E17ss4. This story is one of the rare cases in children's stories where the experience of personal causation and personal responsibility is clearly the dominant theme. The situation is an external threat to which the mother reacts with responsibility, insight, and confidence. The only category not scored is IA because of the arbitrary rule only to score present tense activity. GS is slightly questionable but can be justified for wanting "to know what she can do" as a goal contingent on the circumstances. To know what SHE can do is a personally chosen want. RP can be scored for perception of block, in the form of the accident and serious condition, and the perception of how to overcome the block by donating blood. PR is shown in her concern (worried) supported by "wanting to know" what to do, and doing it (giving blood). "He will live" is the outcome expressing confidence in one's capacity to overcome blocks and is scored SC. The whole story is one of the best examples of an explicitly stated experience of personal causation and scored PC.

Scored PC, GS, RP, PR, SC.

E23ss4. This story can be scored for PR, showing concern supported by the "hoping." It cannot be scored RP or SC because the positive outcome is qualified by "barly."

Scored PR.

E24ss4. The only puzzle here is whether "Trying to figure out what to fix" is instrumental to some kind of set goal. But they have not set a goal; they are just preparing for grandmother's visit. So neither GS nor IA can be scored. Clearly they are not concerned about Grandmother's well-being and the positive outcome has nothing to do with what the main characters are doing.

Scored 0.

Batch C Adult Stories, Cue 2

Subjects A1–A10.
Cue 2. Two men working at a machine.

A1ss2. Bob and Harry are making car parts for the Chevrolet company.
As they were working the machine became inoperable.
They were trying to decide whether on not the machine could be repaired by them, or should they avail the services of the maintenance department.
Being men of much ingenuity they repaired the machine and returned to the dull routine of making car parts, again.

A2ss2. Ted and Reggie are taking a book inventory and it is due that afternoon. The adding machine breaks.
They knew the inventory was due two weeks ago. Yet, they wait until the last minute.
They wanted to complete the inventory with least amount of work.
They will not get the machine fixed. The will have to make the computations with paper and pencil. Eventually they will finish.

A3ss2. John and Bill are making repairs on the plant machine. Bill is new and forgot to disengage a button before starting the machine.
John likes Bill even though he has had to help him in the past with his problems at the plant. Before John came along Bill did not know anyone. Bill had just gotten out of the Army and he and John became fast friends. John had been in the Air Force so their friendship had a common bond.
Bill is improving in his repairing so that John will not have to do everything. Both go with twin sisters.

A4ss2. Two men are cutting a board to make a table.
The men bought the wood and decided what kind of table they wanted. (Also what shape and size.)
They want to make the table correctly so they are being very careful to follow the instructions they have and also to measure carefully.

Table 24.1. *Categories scored in practice stories batches A and B, subjects E1–E24 (Cues 1–4)*

S#	Cue 1							Cue 2							Cue 3							Cue 4						
	PC	GS	IA	RP	PR	SC	Total	PC	GS	IA	RP	PR	SC	Total	PC	GS	IA	RP	PR	SC	Total	PC	GS	IA	RP	PR	SC	Total
E1	1						1				1			1			1	1		1	3							0
E2	1			1	1		3	No story						0	1	1		1	1	1	5					1		1
E3		1		1			2			1	1			2							0					1		1
E4	1	1					2	1		1		1		3	1	1	1	1	1	1	6					1		1
E5	1			1		1	3		1	1			1	3	1	1	1	1	1	1	5							0
E6							0				1		1	2						1	1							0
E7	1				1		2		1		1			2			1	1	1	1	3			1		1		2
E8							0							0			1				1					1		1
E9		1	1	1		1	3			1	1			2		1	1	1		1	3				1	1	1	3
E10	1	1	1				3			1	1	1	1	3	1	1			1	1	3				1	1		2
E11	1	1	1	1		1	4			1	1	1	1	5	1	1		1	1	1	3				1	1	1	2
E12	1	1	1	1			4	1		1		1		3			1		1	1	2	1			1	1		1
E17	1		1				1				1			1			1		1	1	3	1	1		1	1	1	5
E23							0		1	1			1	2	1			1	1	1	3					1	.	1
E24							0		1	1				1	1		1		1	1	3							0

They follow the instructions and make a beautiful cocktail table for their rathskeller.

A5ss2. One man is explaining to the other how the machine works and what the end product will look like.

The man not knowing much about the machine attempted to work on his own and destroyed some of the products.

The man wanted his supervisor to notice him and so proceeded without proper instructions.

The man realized that he could have injured himself as well as the products so he paid careful attention to the procedure and later was able to produce a perfect end product.

A6ss2. They are talking and they know they are not suppose to, because of the intense and dangerous job.

Only last summer a man got his hand cut off because he was not paying attention to his work.

One of the men is thinking if he can just talk to someone, his problem won't be as large.

If the man that is listening refuses to listen, the man that is talking will stop and know one will be hurt.

A7ss2. Willie and Joe are trying to retape the computer. Neither knows the full instructions for retaping. They are stumped.

They were working and the computer ran out of tape. The line was very long waiting to use the computer.

Willie and Joe are trying desperately to go step by step to make the computer work. Why wont someone who knows come.

Five minutes later, Roy – the supervisor came to their rescue. He showed them how to retape the machine. The machine was in operation again. The people in line could complete their work.

A8ss2. Bob and Tom looked at the engine. Neither one knew what had gone wrong.

The boss had taken a part to get it replaced without telling them.

Both Bob and Tom thought the engine was damaged by one of the other. They didn't know how to explain it.

The boss returned with the new part and both men continue work.

A9ss2. The men are trying to get the machine to work. It seems to be broken.

One man goes to get a manual of operating instructions.

They want the machine to work.

They read the instructions and find out that they forgot to thread the machine, a film projector, correctly. They re-thread the film projector and it works.

A10ss2. The machine is moving along a railroad track. The machine is a hand operated inspection car for the railroad.

The men have worked with the "hand-car" before and it has become routine for them to operate.

The men want to inspect the track for a two mile stretch.

The men will complete their run with no major difficulties.

Batch C Analysis, Cue 2

A1ss2. This story has a clear goal-setting sequence although the goal, to fix the broken machine, must be inferred and therefore not scored GS. "They were trying to decide" is past and therefore not scored IA. But it does show intelligent adjustment and is scored RP. "They repaired the machine" shows responsibility for goal attainment and is scored PR. It is also overcoming blocks and a positive outcome and scored SC. The choice to repair the machine is totally theirs and they succeed so we can infer that they experienced personal causation – scored PC.

Scored PC, RP, PR, SC.

A2ss2. This is a totally pawnish type story. The men are doing something that they obviously dislike and therefore did not choose, so neither the want statement nor the activity can be scored. They do eventually finish but that is not a positive ending to an origin episode. "They knew the inventory was due a week ago" does show reality perception but the fact that they did not act on it leaves them as pawns. However, the insight is that of the author and therefore can be scored RP.

Scored RP.

A3ss2. This story is an affiliative one yet there is never a clear statement of that goal or of either character doing anything (but working together) that is instrumental to that goal. Not scored GS or IA. The story can be scored PR, however, under the category of concern for others, because "he has had to help him in the past" (activity) and "John likes Bill" (affect). It is an origin story because John personally decided to help.

Scored PR.

A4ss2. This is a paradigm case of a goal-setting sequence with all the ingredients to score all of the categories. The men are doing a self-chosen activity to attain a self-chosen goal. In fact, here the goal and the activity are hardly discernible. Do they want a table or do they want to make a table? Obviously both – a real origin activity. The story is clearly a case of experienced personal causation – scored PC. The goal is clearly stated, "They want to make the table," scored GS. There are two examples of instrumental activity, "cutting the board," and "are being very careful," scored IA. "Decided what shape and size" and "being very careful to follow the instructions" are scorable for both RP and PR. Finally, the outcome is positive and scored SC.

Scored PC, GS, IA, RP, PR, SC.

A5ss2. In the story the stated goal is a power goal, "The man wanted his supervisor to notice him." This is scored GS. But his initial attempt failed so he adjusted intelligently by pursuing the unstated subgoal of learning the procedure. This as well as the phrase "the man realized" is scored RP. "He paid careful attention" is scored PR, responsibility for goal attainment. "Later was able to produce a perfect end product" shows self-confidence and is scored SC. The whole story indicates the experience of personal causation and is scored PC. The one questionable category is IA. If one man explaining to the other implies that the other is listening, then listening could be IA. But it is not spelled out. Conservative decision is not to score

IA. All other activities of the man, "paid careful attention" and so on, are not in the present tense.

Scored PC, GS, RP, PR, SC.

A6ss2. The implied goal of the one man is to lessen "his problem." To that end "they are talking," scored IA. ". . . thinking if he can just talk to someone, his problem won't be as large" is scorable for RP. There is no PR and the outcome is not scorable for SC.

Scored IA, RP.

A7ss2. The two men are trying to overcome a block although there is no goal-setting statement. There are two statements that constitute IA, they "are trying to retape" and they "are trying desperately." They show reality perception in knowing that they are stumped and in accepting expertness. Scored RP. Although they "are trying desperately" in the end, they are not responsible for the outcome so it is not scored PR or SC.

Scored IA, RP.

A8ss2. Because neither character has a goal stated or does anything, the only possibility for a score here would be perception of the block. But this is in a sense a negative instance of that. "Neither one knew." The conservative decision is not to score RP.

Scored 0.

A9ss2. "They want the machine to work" is scored GS even though it is an imposed goal due to the breakdown. It is stated as their choice. "They are trying to get the machine to work" is scored IA, as is "One man goes to get a manual." The latter phrase is also scored RP for perception of the means to overcome the block. "They read the instructions" and "re-thread the machine" are further instances of IA, and all of these activities show problem solving and responsibility for goal attainment – PR. They are successful in the outcome, showing SC. Overall it is evident that they feel personal causation in overcoming the block, scored PC.

Scored PC, IA, RP, PR, SC.

A10ss2. The only question in this story is the "want" statement. Have the men chosen this goal or is it imposed by their job? Because there is nothing to back up any origin involvement, the conservative decision is not to score GS.

Scored 0.

Batch C Adult Stories, Cue 3

Cue 3. A boy with his head resting on his hands.

A1ss3. Keith is pensively meditating at his desk in the drab room of his home. Yesterday, father had placed him on a week's punishment for leaving the neighborhood without permission.

As he mediates he ponders over the previous events which led to this moment. He keeps muddling them over and over in his mind.

Finally, Keith falls to sleep.

A2ss3. Larry is trying to decide on which job to take.

He has always had odd little jobs to earn spending money.

He doesn't know whether to take a job cutting grass, which is only during summer or whether to take the one selling papers, which is year round.

He takes the job selling papers because he can work year round. He would make more per hour cutting grass.

A3ss3. Bob is feeling bad because someone has stolen his bike. His mother had reminded him to lock when ever he left it alone.

He had seen some friend of his playing ball and he just got off the bike for a minute. The minute became 30 minutes and when he returned it was gone.

He now felt that his parents would be angry, he wouldn't find his bike and if he would have thought none of this would have happened.

Now he must go home and face his parents and tell them what happened.

A4ss3. A little boy is sitting at a kitchen table crying.

The boy has just asked his Mother to buy him a bike for his birthday which is one month away. His mother says she can not afford one.

Little boy wants the bike very much and tries to think of a way to get it.

The little boy gets a job helping in a corner grocery store and earns the money he needs to buy the bike himself. He gets it in time for his birthday.

A5ss3. The boy is sulking because he did not get to go where he wanted to go.

The boy went to the playground to play ball instead of cutting the grass as he promised.

The boy wants his father to give him another chance and promises that he won't let it happen again.

The father will take his son to the ball game after all because he has the tickets and was not able to get anyone to go with him because of such short notice.

A6ss3. He is discouraged because he can never answer the questions that the teacher is asking.

He was called on to recite and couldn't, but it wasn't that he didn't know the answer.

He wants to answer but something keeps telling him that he can't.

Unless the teacher finds out what is troubling him, he won't answer this time.

A7ss3. Reggie is worried. He must finish school. He doesn't know if his school or teacher will accept him. He has liked his school, teachers and classmates.

Reggie was having some problems at home with his father. He had been able to seek help from the class teacher, school social worker, and eventually professional help from a state institute. During the time of profess. help, he had to be temporarily withdrawn from school.

Many questions are in his mind? Why wouldn't the principal let him in school. Will people think I'm crazy because Ive been to a doctor. Will my friends and teachers still accept me.

A8ss3. James was very sick. He didn't know whether to continue working or go home.

Before he came to work that morning, he had problems. He didn't know who to turn to.

James wanted to tell someone, that he had hit a little boy, that was running across the street. What would he do.

Finally, James decided to call the hospital to see if he was alright. When he got to the phone he stopped and decided to go there instead. When he arrived at the hospital, the boys parents were worried. He finally admitted he did it.

A9ss3. The boy is worried about the future.

His grades were poor last marking period, and the teacher told him he would grow up to be a bum.

The boy does not want to be a bum but he is afraid his teacher is right. His father is a bum.

The boy drops out of school. After spending some time on the streets, he goes to night school because he wants to be able to get a good job. He finds that he likes night school. The work is hard, but everyone seems to be serious, including the teacher and himself.

A10ss3. The boy is reminiscing about the "great" times he has enjoyed in the past.

The boy had just talked with someone who has had similar experiences.

The boy wants to relate to himself about how happy and delighted(ful) his past life has been.

The boy's thoughts will continue until he has satisfied himself that life is as great as he has been thinking.

Batch C Analysis, Cue 3

A1ss3. The question here is whether to score RP, "father had placed him on a week's punishment." A descriptive story such as this is different from one where the boy is being punished and acknowledges it and does something about it. Here pondering leads to nothing.

Scored 0.

A2ss3. The unstated goal here is the job. "Trying to decide" is instrumental and scored IA. The third statement distinguishing between the advantages of the two jobs is scored RP. The outcome of the decision process is positive showing SC.

Scored IA, RP, SC.

A3ss3. Here we have a case of RP in that Bob sees the relationship between action and the consequences and "if he would have thought none of this would have happened." He is feeling guilty but this cannot be scored for PR because the guilt is not over a self-imposed standard.

Scored RP.

A4ss3. A strong origin story showing a boy "who wants the bike very much" – GS. He "Tries to think of a way to get it" – IA. He "Gets a job" shows both perception of means for overcoming a block (RP) and taking responsibility for goal attainment (PR). The outcome is positive showing SC. Overall the goal was self-determined, the means was self-determined, and the story clearly shows the experience of personal causation (PC).

Scored PC, GS, IA, RP, PR, SC.

A5ss3. This is a thoroughly pawnish story with some aspects that might be scored out of context. Wanting "his father to give him another chance" is not GS; the goal is to go to the ball game. The boy's means of attaining that goal are "sulking" and he "promises that he won't let it happen again" but there is no indication that this is more than an empty promise. Call it the "empty promises decision" – not scored IA. The outcome is totally unrelated to anything that the boy did – no SC.

Scored 0.

A6ss3. This is a weak story but the want statement sets a self-determined goal (GS) and there is a perception of a block, "something keeps telling him that he can't" (RP).

Scored GS, RP.

A7ss3. This story is mostly descriptive. Reggie "had been able to seek help" is scored both PR and RP because *he* sought the help and accepted expert help.

Scored RP, PR.

A8ss3. This is a social responsibility story. Wanting "to tell someone" is not a personally set goal, but deciding to go and "finally admitting that he did it" are clearly taking responsibility for actions and their consequences (PR). He has personally overcome the block of fear, showing SC.

Scored PR, SC.

A9ss3. This story, after a slow start, crams most of the categories into the last paragraph. "He wants to be able to get a good job" is scored for GS. He perceives that if "he goes to night school" he will attain his goal (RP), so he does (PR). He has both perceived the block (RP) and has overcome it (SC). The whole story shows a reaction to blocks that is wholly self-determined in setting an origin goal and acting independently to attain it (PC). There is no present-tense instrumental activity if you assume that all of the last paragraph in answer to the question (What will happen?) is in the future.

Scored PC, GS, RP, PR, SC.

A10ss3. This is truly a "fantasy" story and at first seems like pawnish wish fulfillment. Although fantasy, play, and such nonpractical, goal-directed activities seem the epitome of self-directed and origin activities, they are seldom encountered in these stories. It does some violence to put it into an in-order-to, goal-directed context, but we can score the boy for he "wants to relate to himself about how happy and delightful his past has been" (GS). Toward this goal he "is reminiscing" (IA). The outcome "satisfies" him (SC). This is clearly a unique story and stretches our categories to the limit.

Scored GS, IA, SC.

25 *Explanatory style*

CHRISTOPHER PETERSON

Psychologists have recently argued that an individual's causal beliefs relate to a variety of behaviors and outcomes. One approach by researchers concerned with the role of causal explanation is to ask if people show habitual patterns of explanation for good and bad events. If so, then *explanatory style* becomes an individual difference of considerable consequence. All the behaviors and outcomes affected by causal explanations per se may be under the more distal influence of a person's explanatory style, which helps to determine the particular causal explanations he or she offers in specific situations.

The reformulation of the learned helplessness model accords central status to causal explanations and explanatory style (Abramson, Seligman, & Teasdale, 1978). According to the original helplessness model, exposure to uncontrollable events produces passivity and low morale (Seligman, 1975). The reformulated model proposes that causal beliefs affect the nature of helplessness following uncontrollable events. Specifically, one can predict the potent psychological state of helplessness, which underlies failure, depression, illness and disease, and perhaps even death.

Both laboratory and field research demonstrate that the consistent determinant of this state of helplessness is uncontrollable events (Maier & Seligman, 1976; Peterson & Stunkard, 1989; Seligman, 1975; Thoits, 1983). However, sometimes the helplessness produced by uncontrollability is devastating – pervasive and enduring. Sometimes it is trivial – circumscribed and transient. What determines the character of helplessness following uncontrollable events?

According to the helplessness reformulation, the critical factor is the particular causal explanation made by the individual for the uncontrollable events (Abramson et al., 1978). Thus, when uncontrollability occurs, a person asks, Why? Certain answers to this question lead to debilitating helplessness, whereas other answers do not. Three dimensions of causal

I thank Lisa M. Bossio for her editorial advice.

explanations are considered relevant here. Causal explanations may refer to factors *internal* to the person ("it's me"), such as ability or effort, or they may refer to *external* factors, such as other people or chance. If one interprets uncontrollable events internally, the helplessness following these events tends to involve a loss of self-esteem.

Causal explanations may also refer to factors that are *stable* across time ("it's going to last forever") or *unstable*. The more enduring the attributed cause, the more long-lasting the helplessness following uncontrollability.

Finally, causal explanations may refer to *global* factors influencing a variety of domains ("it's going to undermine everything that I do") or to *specific* factors relevant only to circumscribed outcomes. Global causal explanations tend to result in generalized helplessness, whereas specific causal explanations do not.

The particular causal explanations made about uncontrollable events are determined by both the reality of the events and an individual's habitual explanatory style (Peterson & Seligman, 1984a). All things being equal, individuals with a pessimistic explanatory style are more likely to display helplessness deficits when confronted with a bad event than their counterparts with an optimistic style. That is, individuals who habitually explain the causes of bad events as internal, stable, and global should be more susceptible to helplessness deficits following bad events than those with the opposite style.

The helplessness reformulation is explicitly concerned with causal explanations for bad events. However, in much of our research applying the model to depression and other phenomena, we have also assessed causal explanations for good events (Peterson & Seligman, 1984a). Our findings suggest two general conclusions. First, explanatory style for good events is usually independent of style for bad events. Second, compared with explanatory style for bad events, explanatory style for good events usually shows the opposite relation with depression and helplessness; that is, internal, stable, and global explanations for good events predict the absence of deficits. Although we have no explicit theory about such explanations for good events, our intuitive sense is that they reflect hope and thus bolster optimism and self-esteem, perhaps by encouraging individuals to savor the good events that befall them.

Explanatory style can be measured with a self-report questionnaire developed for this purpose: the Attributional Style Questionnaire (ASQ; Peterson et al., 1982). The ASQ presents hypothetical events, good and bad, to respondents, who write down the "one major cause" of each event if it happened to them. Then, they rate each cause they have provided on 7-point scales in terms of internality versus externality, stability versus instability, and globality versus specificity. Ratings are averaged across events to yield estimates of a respondent's explanatory style.

Literally hundreds of studies have employed the ASQ to investigate the relationship of explanatory style to depression, school achievement, athletic performance, morbidity, and mortality. Despite the popularity of this questionnaire, it is obvious that the ASQ can be used only with subjects who are willing and able to complete the instrument. Given the range of topics to which explanatory style is potentially relevant, exclusive reliance on the ASQ to investigate explanatory style and its consequences is overly limiting. Consequently, we developed a content analysis technique to assess explanatory style in populations not accessible for administration of the ASQ (see chapter 26 in this volume).

Any spoken or written materials can be analyzed for spontaneously mentioned events and explanations. We have found causal explanations in such diverse material as newspaper quotations, therapy transcripts, diaries, political speeches, autobiographies, audiotaped diagnostic interviews, personal letters, and essays. In many cases, such materials are rich enough in naturally occurring good or bad events with accompanying explanations to assess an individual's explanatory style. We have encountered few difficulties in applying this content analysis technique, but no doubt boundaries exist. To date, we have used the procedure only with adults who speak English. Social class, gender, ethnicity, and psychopathology apparently present no barriers.

The purpose in this chapter and the next is to describe this content analysis method for assessing explanatory style, which we call the *CAVE technique*, an acronym for the Content Analysis of Verbatim Explanations. This description expands on previous statements, published (Peterson, Luborsky, & Seligman, 1983; Peterson, Seligman, & Vaillant, 1988; Schulman, Castellon, & Seligman, 1989; H. M. Zullow, Oettingen, Peterson, & Seligman, 1988) and unpublished (Peterson & Seligman, 1984b; Schulman, Castellon, & Seligman, 1988). In this chapter, I start by explaining why content analysis is an appropriate way to ascertain explanatory style. Then I describe some of the studies that provide validity evidence for our technique.

HOW TO REGARD THE CAVE TECHNIQUE

Content analysis of public records is not a new research technique. Other researchers have worked productively with such a strategy. Nevertheless, the technique is not used as often as it might be by "mainstream" psychologists, and not just because it can be painstaking. Instead, researchers are skeptical of content analysis because of connotations of bias and fuzziness. The CAVE technique involves two independent steps: (a) extracting verbatim causal explanations, and (b) rating them on 7-point scales according to their internality, stability, and globality. Both steps are done by researchers blind to outcome measures. Both steps have proved reliable.

Reasonable versus unreasonable uses of content analysis are not determined by the technique per se, but rather by the theory in which they are embedded. The CAVE technique is theoretically guided. Indeed, according to the helplessness reformulation and attribution theory in general, content analysis of verbal material is a particularly good assessment strategy, not a "second-best" procedure arising from compromise.

We view causal beliefs as hypothetical constructs, not as intervening variables (Peterson & Seligman, 1984a). They are a way for the theorist to make sense of what he or she has observed, and they can be assessed in a variety of ways. Because it has been convenient to do so, we have often administered the ASQ. However, there is no theoretical reason compelling the exclusive use of this or any other questionnaire to measure causal explanations.

Causal beliefs are part of an individual's naive psychology, the subject matter of attribution theory (Heider, 1958). Thus, unobtrusive research methods may be preferable to invasive techniques that run the risk of producing causal explanations not otherwise offered in the course of everyday living. Some critics have argued that people may not ordinarily explain events (Silver, Wortman, & Klos, 1982; Wortman & Dintzer, 1978). Quite simply, this argument is wrong. People offer causal explanations even when not specifically prompted to do so, and they do so particularly in response to aversive and surprising events (Wong & Weiner, 1981). The circumstances under which causal explanations are made without prompting are precisely those under which subjects are most likely to be mindful and thus most apt not to respond glibly or automatically as they might on a questionnaire (Weiner, 1985).

Reality may override style in determining explanations. In some cases, the event a person explains may be the primary determinant of its explanation (Peterson & Seligman, 1984a). The resulting explanation is irrelevant to estimating an individual's explanatory style. Here is an example. Over the years, we have often asked college students to explain the hypothetical event "You have been unsuccessful in looking for a job." Their answers often reflect the prevailing economic reality. When the job market is lean, that is the modal causal explanation. There is little variance in answers, and nothing "psychological" is revealed by them. In contrast, when opportunities for employment are more plentiful, so too is the variance in proffered causes, and the usefulness of these causes for estimating individual style is correspondingly enhanced. With regard to the CAVE technique, the researcher must be careful to apply it to material in which explanations are not mainly reality-driven.

Although we regard explanatory style as a trait, we do not expect people to show 100% consistency in the internality, stability, and globality of their explanations. This would be at odds with what is known about cross-situational consistencies in behavior. However, as a cognitive characteristic, more consistency can be expected for explanatory style than for other putative personality traits (Mischel, 1968).

To use the CAVE technique, it is imperative that at least several causal explanations be available for each individual under investigation. Explanatory "style" can only be assessed from multiple explanations. Individual consistency can only be ascertained if repeated explanations have been made. In some cases, explanations may not cohere into a style, because reality factors predominate. In other cases, style may not be apparent because individuals are inconsistent. "Style" should be reserved as a description of cross-event consistency in the various explanations that an individual offers.

The studies reviewed in the next section show that individuals are often consistent in the way they explain events. However, other studies also show that explanations change as a function of important events such as psychotherapy. And yet other studies show that individuals are consistent at one time and at another time, but not across time. We recommend a sophisticated view of explanatory style as a trait (Peterson & Seligman, 1984a). It should be treated as a dependent variable that can be modified by life events, as well as an independent variable that modifies future events.

CONSTRUCT VALIDITY OF THE CAVE TECHNIQUE

The CAVE technique makes possible research with all manner of interesting subjects, including those inaccessible with the ASQ – the quick, dead, famous, belligerent, sensitive, or remote. And although it is more labor-intensive than the ASQ, this technique allows the researcher to travel back and forth in time, conducting studies in a nonobtrusive way. If outcome measures are already available or can be obtained, and suitable verbatim material can be located from earlier in time, longitudinal research that would normally take many years to complete can be done in mere months. The CAVE technique is also likely to be far less costly than longitudinal investigations begun from scratch.

One of our first uses of the CAVE technique looked at transcribed psychotherapy sessions, in this case with a single patient noteworthy for his sudden mood swings, in and out of depression, which occurred during the course of a session (Peterson et al., 1983). We wondered if causal statements precipitated these shifts, and so the CAVE technique was an appropriate research strategy. We hypothesized that shifts *to* depression would be preceded by (relatively) internal, stable, and global explanations for bad events, whereas shifts *from* depression would be preceded by (relatively) external, unstable, and specific explanations.

We obtained transcripts from psychotherapy sessions in which mood shifts occurred, for both increased depression and decreased depression. For comparison purposes, we also obtained transcripts from sessions in which no mood shifts occurred. Causal explanations by the patient immediately before and after his mood shifted were extracted, rated, and combined into a composite by averaging across the three dimensions. Our hypothesis was supported. Highly internal, stable, and global causes preceded increased depression, and highly external, unstable, and specific causes preceded decreased depression. Causal explanations during sessions in which no mood shift occurred were intermediate.

In another early study, we asked 66 students on the University of Pennsylvania campus to write essays about the two worst events that had occurred to them during the past year (Peterson, Bettes, & Seligman, 1985). After writing these essays, subjects completed the ASQ and the Beck Depression Inventory (BDI), a frequently used measure of the extent and severity of common depressive symptoms (Beck, 1967).

We extracted and rated the causal explanations from the essays. These ratings were then collapsed across judges and then across explanations for the same event. Our results provided strong support for the validity of the CAVE technique. First, causal explanations were consistent across the two events. Second, explanatory style as assessed with the CAVE technique was correlated with depressive symptoms as proposed by the helplessness re-formulation. Third, scores of the extracted causal explanations converged with the corresponding scales of the ASQ.

However, convergence between the CAVE and the ASQ was not nearly so high as to suggest that these are simply alternative measures of explanatory style. This conclusion is supported by a more recent study by Schulman et al. (1989), who compared ratings by researchers of causes written on the ASQ by subjects with the ratings made by the subjects themselves. Researcher and subject ratings correlated highly, but subject ratings showed a stronger relationship to depression as measured with the BDI than did the researcher ratings. This may indicate that subjects are more sensitive to the meaning of their own causal beliefs than researchers are.

Burns and Seligman (1989) used the CAVE technique to investigate whether explanatory style is consistent over decades. Thirty subjects, averaging 72 years of age, provided diaries or letters written 50 years earlier. They also wrote brief essays about their current life. Both sets of material were CAVEd, and the researchers found that the composite measure (internality + stability + globality) of explanatory style for bad events proved highly stable ($r = .54$). Needless to say, these are impressive results, supporting both the validity of the CAVE technique and our conceptualization of explanatory style as traitlike.

The CAVE technique allowed Peterson et al. (1988) to undertake a 35-year longitudinal study of the psychological precursors of physical illness. Briefly, we assessed the explanatory style of 99 men who completed open-ended questionnaires in 1946 about their difficult wartime experiences. At that time, the subjects were approximately 25 years of age. Available for each subject at subsequent 5-year intervals were ratings of overall health, based on a physician examination abetted with medical tests. Pessimistic explanatory style predicted poor health from ages 45 through 60, even when initial measures of physical health and emotional well-being (taken at age 25) were held constant.

A final example of how the CAVE technique can be used to study subjects not accessible with the ASQ is H. M. Zullow et al.'s (1988) investigation of explanatory style among Democrat and Republican candidates for the presidency during elections between 1948 and 1984. Nomination acceptance speeches were CAVEd, and the resulting measure of explanatory style was combined with a measure of rumination also derived from content analysis of these speeches. The combination of pessimistic explanatory style for bad events and excessive rumination predicted the loser in 9 out of the 10 elections, even when popular poll results and incumbency were taken into account statistically.

We concluded that the voters respond to the degree of hope conveyed in a nomination speech. To the degree that a candidate can engender hopeful expectations in the electorate, that candidate will win an election; otherwise, the candidate will lose. Characteristic ways of explaining bad events reflect hopefulness or hopelessness, and so the CAVE technique is useful to the political prognosticator.

CAUTIONS

There are several drawbacks to the CAVE technique to which we draw your attention. First, to save time, researchers who have an opportunity to administer a questionnaire may prefer to use the ASQ. Second, the process of extracting causal explanations is the difficult step in the procedure, and we have not found all potential users of CAVE equally skilled or enthusiastic about doing extractions. Third, although we have started to map out the empirical relationship between the ASQ and the CAVE, the conceptual relationship between the two measures awaits a thorough treatment. We suspect that causal explanations for hypothetical events are not always interchangeable with those for actual events. Nonetheless, we expect the CAVE technique to be used widely in the future.

26 *The explanatory style scoring manual*

CHRISTOPHER PETERSON,
PETER SCHULMAN,
CAMILO CASTELLON, AND
MARTIN E. P. SELIGMAN

The actual Content Analysis of Verbatim Explanations (CAVE) technique has two steps: identifying and extracting causal explanations in verbatim material; and then rating these explanations along 7-point scales according to their internality, stability, and globality. We will describe these steps in order.

IDENTIFYING AND EXTRACTING CAUSAL EXPLANATIONS

Four or more events with explanations are ideally required to generate a valid style. Multiple events are the only way that a researcher can estimate a cross-situational style. Also, multiple events allow explanatory style to be more reliably measured. Peterson, Villanova, and Raps (1985) compared studies that disconfirm the reformulated learned helplessness model with those that support it, finding that the supporting studies had more attributions per subject than the disconfirming studies. Multiple events apparently minimize the effects of the reality of the situation, allowing the individual's habitual style to emerge.

In our research, we usually find bad events with explanations to be more abundant in verbatim material than good events with explanations. What this means is that researchers specifically interested in how people explain good events will have to search more diligently for suitable material for content analysis. When individuals describe events, good or bad, they often end up explaining them, if allowed or encouraged to elaborate their de-

This research was supported by grants MH-19604 and MH-40142 from the National Institute of Mental Health, grant AG-05590 from the National Institute on Aging, and by the MacArthur Foundation Network on the Determinants and Consequences of Health-Damaging and Health-Promoting Behavior. We thank the many members of the Helplessness Research Group for their assistance over the past decade in planning and conducting studies that used content analysis. We thank Lisa M. Bossio for her editorial advice.

scriptions. The briefer a description, the less likely it is to contain a causal explanation.

We define an event as any discrete occurrence that has a good or bad impact on the individual. Events can be wholly within the person ("I worked myself into a dither") or something imposed from without ("My neighbors made a colossal noise"). Events may occur in the past, present, or future. It is crucial that events be good or bad as the subject sees the matter. Ambivalent events ("My vacation was wonderful *and* terrible") or those that have good or bad elements in combination ("I made the best of an unfortunate situation, and I was successful") should not be analyzed. Neither should neutral events ("It was an ordinary phone call"), nor events that do not directly have an impact on the subject ("The Peruvian national soccer team has new uniforms, according to the paper") be considered.

We emphasize that the goodness or badness of an event must be judged from the point of view of the individual who has produced the verbatim material. For example, the researcher might decide that attending college is a good event, but the individual may instead regard this as a neutral or even a bad event. If there is any doubt about the valence of an event, it should not be extracted.

Once an event is located in verbatim material, one looks for an attributed factor that precedes and covaries with it, again from the perspective of the individual. Possible causes can include: (a) other events ("I was late for my appointment *because the car wouldn't start*"); (b) situational factors ("I failed the exam *because the room was freezing cold*"); (c) behaviors of the subject or others ("I bounced a check *because I forgot to keep my balance current*"); (d) dispositions ("I fought with my roommate *because I'm a perfectionist*"); (e) experience ("I was offered the job the second time I applied *because I'm older now*"); and so on – as long as the attributed cause precedes the event of interest and is seen by the individual as covarying with it. Sometimes the cause is transparent. And sometimes the cause must be inferred from clues, from statements such as "because . . . ," "as a result of . . . ," or "this led up to it." Only events that have explanations are extracted.

The individual should be offering his or her own explanation for the event in question, not merely agreeing with an explanation offered by another person, such as a therapist or interviewer. And similarly, we do not extract an explanation for an individual if he or she quotes someone else in explaining an event ("When you ain't got nothing, you got nothing to lose").

The process of extraction begins by searching through verbatim material, audiotaped or written, for events that have explanations. Hypothetical *events* are acceptable, such as:

E (Event): If I get admitted to medical school
A (Attribution): It would be due to my family's connections.

Hypothetical *explanations*, however, are usually not acceptable. For example:

> E: I would be thrilled
> A: If I hit the jackpot in the lottery.

The difficulty of rating the stability dimension (to be discussed) in these cases and the uncertainty of the cause ever occurring make hypothetical causes unextractable.

Bad events that have "good" explanations, or vice versa, should not be extracted. For example:

> E: I was fired
> A: Because I refused to do something unethical.

Although this sort of example satisfies all the previously stated criteria for an extraction, we have learned from experience that this will probably not be rated reliably. Further, an attribution such as this one has the effect of transforming a bad event into a good event (Peterson, 1983).

Here is another problematic example, a good event with a "bad" explanation:

> E: I have been less depressed lately
> A: Because my allergies are so bad I'm thinking only about them.

Here the "bad" attribution transforms what seems to be a good event into a bad one, creating ambiguity about how to regard this material.

In the best of circumstances, an identified event and explanation should include enough information for the rater to be able to rate the internality, stability, and globality of the cause. This may not always be possible, and if the extracted material contains so little information that raters need to guess about the status of the cause with respect to two or three dimensions, then it is best to pass over this material.

When an event has multiple explanations, we treat each explanation separately. For example, the phrase, "I didn't do well on my job because I didn't sleep well last night and because my ankle is sprained," would yield two extractions:

> E: I didn't do well on my job
> A: Because I didn't sleep well last night.
> E: I didn't do well on my job
> A: Because my ankle is sprained.

However, if the multiple explanations are interrelated and separating them removes important context and thereby makes it more difficult to understand the extraction, we prefer not to separate them.

A factor mentioned in one explanation may also be an event that itself is explained. For example:

> E: I haven't been sleeping well
> A: Because I'm worried about paying my bills.
> E: I'm worried about paying my bills
> A: [Because] the finance charge on my credit card is outrageous.

We suggest a stringent criterion in deciding that a causal statement should be extracted, granted the cascading problems caused by ambiguity of the event or the cause. Usually even brief samples of verbal material contain several acceptable causal explanations as characterized here, so a stringent criterion is not the limitation it might seem.

When a suitable event-attribution unit is located, we write it verbatim on an index card (along with an identifying code number). Both the event and attribution are presented to judges to be rated, along with enough contextual information to allow the raters to proceed sensibly. In this instance, added information is provided within brackets:

> E: I got it [a permanent job]
> A: [Because] I did an internship with him [the personnel director].

Note, though, that the event and the causal attribution should be copied verbatim.

We find that independent judges using the stringent criterion we suggest agree more than 90% of the time that a particular causal explanation is present (e.g., Peterson, Bettes, & Seligman, 1985). Thus, judges are able to reliably extract attributions from verbatim material. Because extraction is necessarily tedious, especially if a great deal of material must be scanned, we usually use but a single researcher to do the extractions.

RATING THE EXTRACTED CAUSAL EXPLANATIONS

When presenting a series of event-attribution units to raters, it is important to randomize the extractions within and between subjects. This is important so that the raters are not biased by previous ratings for the same subject and do not fall into entrenched rating patterns. We usually use four or five independent judges as raters, blind to each other as well as to outcome measures for the subjects.

Extracted attributions are rated by these judges on 7-point scales according to their internality versus externality, stability versus instability, and globality versus specificity. The "7" represents the most internal, stable, and global explanations, and the "1" the most external, unstable, and specific explanations. All of these ratings are made from the individual's point of view about the internality, stability, and globality of the cause of concern – not from the rater's perspective. Let us elaborate on some of the considerations that go into these ratings (Schulman, Castellon, & Seligman, 1989).

Internality versus externality

The reformulated learned helplessness theory proposes that this dimension is related to self-esteem. This dimension, therefore, is an attempt to measure the extent to which individuals blame themselves for bad events or credit themselves for good events. Other researchers have assessed related individual differences such as locus of control (Peterson & Stunkard, 1989), but we focus solely on the degree of blame or credit.

We see the 7-point scale for internality versus externality as divided into three regions:

A. Scale point 1, where the individual attributes blame or credit to someone or something completely external to the self.
B. Scale points 2 to 6, where the individual attributes the cause of an event to some combination or interaction of internal and external factors.
C. Scale point 7, where the individual attributes causality to a behavioral, physical, or mental characteristic solely internal to the self.

Examples of a 1 rating include causes that mention another person's actions or characteristics, the difficulty or ease of a task, time, a natural disaster, circumstances, the weather, and so on. Ratings between 2 and 6 are made when explanations divide blame or credit between the self and another person or between the self and the environment. Examples of a 7 rating include causes that refer to the individual's own traits, behavior, decisions, (in)ability, motivation, knowledge, disability, illness, injury, age, and social or political or demographic classifications (such as being a widow, conservative, old, or a Christian).

Following are some examples:
E: I did well on the paper
A: Because the assignment was easy. [Rating = 1]
E: I didn't get the job
A: Because they are disorganized. [Rating = 1]
E: I'm having problems with my wife
A: Because she can't accept my ambition. [Rating = 2 or 3]
E: We're getting a divorce.
A: We're just not made for each other. [Rating = 4]
E: I'm tongue-tied
A: When I get overheated. [Rating = 4]
E: I need surgery on my elbow.
A: It's getting worse from tennis. [Rating = 4]
E: I did well on the medical boards
A: Because I studied hard. [Rating = 7]
E: I didn't get the job
A: Because I'm too young. [Rating = 7]

Stability versus instability

This dimension reflects the persistence of a cause, whether it is chronic (stable) or transient (unstable). Remember that the stability of the cause is of interest, not the stability of the event. Given the event, whatever its nature, how long-lasting or transient is the attributed cause? We explicitly remind our raters of how the analogous question on the Attributional Style Questionnaire is phrased: "In the future when this event occurs, will this cause again be present?" Response choices range from 1 ("will never again be present") to 7 ("will always be present").

There are four related considerations that determine how this dimension is rated. First is the *tense* of the attributed cause. If the cause of an event is phrased in the past tense, then the rating should be less stable than if the cause is phrased in the present tense. Second is the *probability* that the cause will occur in the future (from the viewpoint of the subject). A cause unlikely to occur again should be less stable than a cause that is likely to occur again. Third is whether the attributed cause is *intermittent or continuous*. For example, bad weather is intermittent, and is therefore less stable than a continuous cause, such as a trait. Finally, is the attributed cause *characterological or behavioral* in nature (cf. Peterson, Schwartz, & Seligman, 1981)? Character traits (e.g., "I am smart, lazy, decisive") should be more stable than particular behaviors (e.g., "I did a smart thing, a lazy thing, a decisive thing").

Following are some examples, with annotations, of how extracted causes are rated on the stability–instability dimension:

> E: I can't attend the wedding
> A: Because I have to go to a conference. [Rating = 1]

(This cause is in the present tense but is unlikely to occur again.)

> E: I was depressed
> A: When my uncle died. [Rating = 2]

(This cause occurred in the past, cannot occur again, but may have some ongoing influence.)

> E: I have trouble sleeping
> A: When it's humid. [Rating = 3]

(This cause is likely to occur again but only intermittently.)

> E: My business is falling apart.
> A: Getting started so young was poor judgment on my part. [Rating = 3]

(This cause is in the past tense, has a small probability of future occurrence, and is behavioral rather than characterological.)

> E: I'm afraid to go out late at night
> A: Since I was mugged. [Rating = 4]

(This cause occurred in the past, has a small probability of a future occurrence, but may exert an ongoing influence on behavior.)

E: I can't restrain my appetite
A: When I see food on the table. [Rating = 4]

(This cause is in the present tense, is likely to occur again, and is intermittent, i.e., situation-specific.)

E: It's difficult for me to express gratitude.
A: That's just the way I was raised. [Rating = 5]

(This cause occurred in the past but still exerts an ongoing influence on behavior.)

E: I'm not doing well in my career
A: Because I'm such a lazy person. [Rating = 5 or 6]

(This cause is in the present tense, will probably occur again, and is characterological.)

E: I didn't get the job
A: Because I'm a woman. [Rating = 7]

(This cause is unalterable and continuous.)

Globality versus specificity

The third dimension we rate reflects the extent to which a cause affects an individual's life, whether it affects many areas (global) or just a few (specific). This dimension often proves the most difficult to rate because there may not be enough information to indicate how widespread the effects of the cause might be, granted the unique composition of an individual's life. A sprained ankle would have a greater impact for a professional athlete than a sportswriter, but we may not always know which profession a speaker has chosen.

In the absence of detailed knowledge about an individual, we ask how the attributed cause would affect the scope of a generic individual's life. We distinguish two broad categories of events in someone's life – achievement and affiliation. Each is obviously of numerous subcategories, and often these intermingle. So, this distinction is artificial and is not crisp. We do find it valuable heuristically because it helps the rater to avoid applying his or her idiosyncratic sense of globality versus specificity to other people's attributions.

Achievement, as we see it, subsumes occupational or academic success, one's acquisition of knowledge or skills, attainment of a sense of individuality or independence, and economic or social status. Affiliation includes the quality of intimate relationships, one's sense of belongingness or societal integration, sex, play, and marital or family well-being. These are just a few examples. Causes can affect some or many events in one or both of these broad categories. The greater the impact of the cause, the higher the globality rating.

It sometimes is helpful to look to the event itself for clues about the globality of the attributed cause; after all, the event is one of the possible effects. We do not, however, rate just the effects mentioned in the event, because the cause may have broader consequences. We primarily rate the globality of the cause and only secondarily look at the event as one of the effects of the cause.

Following are some examples, with annotations:

> E: I got a reckless driving ticket.
> A: I guess the cop had to fill his quota for the day. [Rating = 1]

(This cause affects one situation.)

> E: My relationships are handicapped
> A: By my fear of intimacy. [Rating = 2 or 3]

(This cause affects part of the affiliation category and possibly part of the achievement category.)

> E: My self-image has gotten worse
> A: Since my hair fell out. [Rating = 4 or 5]

(This cause affects parts of both categories.)

> E: I've had to cut back on my level of activity
> A: Because of my stroke. [Rating = 4 or 5]

(This cause affects parts of both categories.)

> E: I've lost all zest. I've felt devastated
> A: Since my wife died. [Rating = 6 or 7]

(Most of both categories are affected by this cause.)

General considerations

Here are some general pointers about rating, regardless of the particular dimension. First, if there is insufficient information to assign a rating, we deem the cause in question a 4, to avoid skewing the overall ratings. Second, each dimension should be rated independently of the other dimensions. Stability and globality, for example, often overlap in people's causal attributions (Peterson & Villanova, 1988), but they must be disentangled for rating. Third, our suggested guidelines are not inflexible rules. Grammatical nuances and each phrase's rich context must be taken into account. The particulars of an explanation may help in rating such ambiguous and difficult to rate causes as age, sickness, injury, and social classification. For example:

E: I couldn't finish the race
A: Because my body just gave up on me.

Although the individual quoted here is blaming her body, the way that she does implies a dissociation of herself from her body. She is not really blaming herself, just a "body" that is not who she is. Researchers who use the CAVE technique to study attributions concerning illness and injury must be particularly sensitive to such subtleties.

Our judges are given training and practice, as well as periodic calibration. Reading about explanatory style is important, as is seeing examples of extracted event-attribution units and how they are rated. We find that when the ratings of four or five judges are combined, reliabilities of the individual dimensions, as estimated by Cronbach's (1951) coefficient alpha, approach .90. Obviously, the more judges, the higher the reliability. Internality versus externality can usually be rated with greater reliability than the other two dimensions, because the endpoints have absolute meanings.

Once ratings are complete and reliability ascertained, we average them (within dimensions) across judges, then across events (keeping good and bad events separate). Depending on the purposes of the researcher, scores on the individual dimensions can be employed, or a further composite can be created by averaging across the three dimensions (cf. Carver, 1989).

SUMMARY

To sum up the most important points we have presented about the CAVE technique, we suggest that the researcher ask the following questions:

1. Are the extracted events clearly good or bad from the subject's point of view?
2. Do the extracted events directly affect the subject?
3. Are there clear cause-and-effect relationships between the extracted attributions and events?
4. When the event-attribution units are given to raters, do they have enough context to understand them?
5. Is there any doubt about the appropriateness of extracted units? *If in doubt, throw it out!*
6. Is there sufficient information for a particular rating?
7. Have the three dimensions been rated independently of one another?

RATINGS OF PRACTICE STORIES

We applied the CAVE technique to the practice stories that are included in appendix I of this volume. In appendix I, the "expert scoring" for explanatory style shows the extracted attributions for bad events, along with ratings by one of us (CP) of the stability and globality of these causes. Remember that these ratings are made on 7-point scales, where high numbers correspond to more stable and more global attributions, and low numbers to more unstable and more specific attributions.

Some qualifications are in order. The suitability of projective material for the CAVE technique is unknown. Causal explanations can readily be extracted and rated, but we do not know what the resulting scores reveal about the person who told the story. According to theory and research, attributions about events befalling the self are critical (cf. Sweeney, Shaeffer, & Golin, 1982). Which character in a story, if any, corresponds to the self? In a few cases, a research subject responds to pictures in the first person, but otherwise we are in the dark. This is why the internality rating was not made in the practice stories.

We are currently planning a study to look systematically at the relationship between explanatory style as assessed by the ASQ and causal attributions extracted from thematic apperceptive protocols and rated via the CAVE technique. Not all stimuli are equally successful at eliciting bad events, so we will use those cards that our pilot work has shown are rated highly by judges with respect to negative content. Pending the completion of this study, it is best to regard the examples in appendix I simply as illustrations of the CAVE technique rather than a recommendation that the CAVE technique be used with verbal responses to projective stimuli.

27 *Conceptual/integrative complexity*

PETER SUEDFELD, PHILIP E. TETLOCK,
AND SIEGFRIED STREUFERT

THE DEVELOPMENT AND CURRENT STATE OF THE CONSTRUCT

Theoretical origins

The conceptual/integrative complexity construct is a descendant of Kelly's (1955) personal construct theory. Generally, it fits within the cognitive styles approach. Because the emphasis of the work is on the structure of thought rather than on its content, the closest relatives of integrative complexity are cognitive complexity (Bieri, 1971) and cognitive structure (Scott, Osgood, & Peterson, 1979). More remote kinship – the remoteness being empirically demonstrated by low correlations (Schroder, Driver, & Streufert, 1967; Suedfeld, Tomkins, & Tucker, 1969; Vannoy, 1965) – exists with content-laden cognitive traits such as authoritarianism (Adorno, Frenkel-Brunswik, Levinson, & Sanford, 1950), dogmatism (Rokeach, 1960), and field independence (Witkin, Dyk, Faterson, Goodenough, & Karp, 1962). The direct line of development proceeds through conceptual systems (Harvey, Hunt, & Schroder, 1961), conceptual complexity (Schroder et al., 1967), interactive complexity (Streufert & Streufert, 1978; Streufert & Swezey, 1987), to integrative complexity (Suedfeld & Tetlock, 1990) and meta-complexity (Streufert & Nogami, 1989).

Briefly, the successive versions of the theory focus on the complexity of information processing and decision making, complexity being defined and measured (usually on a 1–7 scale) in terms of degrees of differentiation and integration (cf. Streufert, 1970). Differentiation refers to the perception of different dimensions within a stimulus domain, and to the taking of different perspectives when considering the domain. It is a necessary but not sufficient prerequisite for integration, which is the development of conceptual connections among differentiated dimensions or perspectives. Such connections are inferred from references to trade-offs between alternatives, a synthesis between them, a reference to a higher-order concept that subsumes them,

393

and the like. The next chapter will present examples that illustrate different levels of integrative complexity.

State and trait complexity

Conceptual systems theory and early conceptual complexity theory considered complexity to be a relatively stable personality characteristic or ability. The research concentrated on how this trait should be measured, and how individuals who differed in complexity behaved in various situations. *Systems theory* (Harvey et al., 1961) proposed that normal development progressed through four stages of increasing complexity (but characterized by content-related as well as structural factors), with different kinds of child-rearing practices fostering each one. Fixation at any level below Stage IV could occur as a result of particular developmental experiences. *Conceptual complexity theory* (Schroder et al., 1967) abandoned the idea of discrete stages in favor of a continuum, deemphasized developmental aspects, and began to focus on the relations between the information processing complexity exhibited by the individual and characteristics of the task environment.

Later versions of conceptual complexity theory (e.g., *interactive complexity* theories; see Streufert & Streufert, 1978; Streufert & Swezey, 1986) tend to view complexity as specific to various experiential domains. Further, they show increasingly more interest in environmental mediators between potential (i.e., trait) complexity and behavior, in refining the construct of complexity (e.g., into flexible and hierarchical integration), and in the relevance of complexity to social psychology (e.g., attitudes, social perception), industrial/organizational psychology, and health psychology. Explicit or implicit assumptions have held that complexity can be modified over the short run by concurrent experience and motivation (affecting primarily state complexity) or in the long run by certain experiences (including training in adulthood), as well as by organizational climates that foster one or another level of complexity. Thus, complexity may, in part, be a trait; but not necessarily an unchangeable one.

The *integrative complexity* viewpoint has to a great extent ignored the trait complexity question (not rejecting it, but holding it in abeyance) in favor of studying state complexity: the level of differentiation and integration shown in thought and behavior in a particular situation and context, and in the relations between such complexity and a wide variety of environmental, interpersonal, and internal factors. Here, complexity is seen as changing in response to fatigue, stress, intrapsychic conflict, social factors (such as accountability and self-presentation), audience characteristics, and so on. The extent to which such changes are unconscious adjustments to circumstances and/or deliberate adaptations is currently a controversial topic (Suedfeld & Tetlock, 1990).

The *metacomplexity* approach attempts to join various cognitive processes into a single, parsimonious theoretical structure. Metacomplexity theory applies differentiation and integration, as well as other concepts from the complexity theories, at three different levels of human functioning: (a) judgmental dimensions of individuals (cognitive complexity); (b) the interaction and interrelationship among cognitive processes such as styles, controls, abilities, and cognitive complexity (process complexity); and (c) dimensions of group and organizational functioning (organizational complexity). The theory also seeks to elucidate the interplay among these three levels of complexity (Streufert & Nogami, 1989). Both state and trait characteristics are considered. Somewhat related approaches have been suggested by Schroder (1989).

Higher-order strategies

Theorists have just begun to grapple with another interesting issue, that of state or trait characteristics related to the metastrategy of complexity. For example, are some people more flexible in changing their complexity level to fit a given situation (again, whether consciously or not); is such flexibility symmetrical for shifts toward and away from complexity; are there differences in perceiving that the environment will reward complex or simple behavior; to what extent are such differences learned or innate; and so on? The most recent research indicates that differences of this sort do exist and do significantly affect decisions and careers (e.g., Streufert, 1989; Streufert & Swezey, 1986; Tetlock & Boettger, 1989; Wallace & Suedfeld, 1988), but many of their parameters are as yet unknown.

Key studies

With the removal of the constraints imposed by the paper-and-pencil test format, the range of research applications has expanded enormously. In fact, so many problems have been addressed in complexity research that no summary can do justice to the literature. Nonarchival research has been directed toward the general topics of social perception, attitude and attitude change, attribution, cross-cultural communication, and interpersonal attraction; performance in complex simulation and actual work situations, word games, Peace Corps training, restricted environmental stimulation, preparing speeches for presentation to an audience, and solving real-life (e.g., organizational) problems; and attitudes concerning war crimes, social policy decisions, group leaders, capital punishment, and moral dilemmas. Archival work has addressed the prediction of international crises and their outcomes, the effects of social and political roles, the success and duration of leader careers, the impact of societal and personal stress, aging and the approach of death, theoretical positions in science, political ideology and political climate, and aspects of mass media.

A recent and very promising development is the interplay of archival, case study, and experimental research, deriving hypotheses from the one that can be tested by the other. This work began with Tetlock's (1979) attempt to use content analytic techniques, including the scoring of integrative complexity, to test the theory of groupthink. Since then, this convergent approach has been applied to the study of complexity, value conflict, and political ideology (e.g., Tetlock, 1983b, 1986) and the effects of accountability on complexity (Tetlock 1983a; Tetlock & Kim, 1987; Tetlock, Skitka, & Boettger, 1989).

MEASUREMENT

The Sentence/Paragraph Completion Test

In the early years of conceptual complexity studies, the Sentence Completion Test (SCT), another version of which is called the Paragraph Completion Test (PCT), became the method of choice (the test is described in more detail in the next chapter). The S/PCT has undergone several revisions. In its original version, it obtained from each subject six to nine brief essays, each written in 1 to 3 minutes and based on a "stem" (topic sentence) phrased so as to tap an important social domain (e.g., relations to authority). Because of various problems with the S/PCT format (e.g., the fact that in most studies the majority of scores were in the lower range of the scale, between 1 and 2), later versions have modified the number of paragraphs to be written, the amount of time allowed, or the topic sentences beginning the paragraphs. In some versions, topics were specifically selected to focus on diverse domains of cognitive functioning. Longer essays, written explicitly for the experiment and dealing with a specific topic (e.g., capital punishment: de Vries & Walker, 1988) have also been used. In general, we now advocate the use of longer time periods (up to 10 minutes per stem), with a reduction in the number of stems if that is necessary in order to avoid subject fatigue and excessive total time investment.

The S/PCT and its essay variant can be administered in either group or individual sessions. No special equipment is required, except for something to write on and something to write with. The measures have been used with both student (mostly secondary and postsecondary levels) and adult samples, both sexes, and all ethnic groups. Beyond obvious basic qualifications (e.g., literacy in whatever language is being used), there have been no particular prerequisites for taking the tests. Except for allowances in case of language or writing skill problems, instructions and stimuli can remain constant across subject groups.

Archival analyses

As the broad usefulness of this theoretical approach became more obvious, questions arose as to its generalizability to materials that were not necessarily written for the purpose of being scored for complexity. Suedfeld and Rank (1976) initiated the use of the 1–7 scale of differentiation and integration with archival materials, which is the basis of much of the current work on historical events, individual lives, and international relations. These studies have shown the scoring technique to encompass essentially any connected verbal discourse to which the researcher has access. This greatly extends the range of researchable sources, audiences, occasions, historical eras, topics, and cultures. The scoring of essays on complicated and controversial topics, written to present and defend one's opinions or to carry out some similar assignment, is a variant of this approach.

The materials used for archival studies are generally taken from books or newspapers. The number of paragraphs needed from each particular condition (e.g., from specific sources, from given time periods) is determined in advance. The library researcher selects each paragraph randomly from the total available and makes a photoduplicate. All information that could be used to identify the condition is removed insofar as possible, and the paragraphs are then scored blind by other researchers. In such studies, "conditions of administration" do not apply, and there are no data indicating that number of paragraphs scored, paragraph length, or similar variables influence the outcome significantly. Neither, apparently, does the scoring of the material in the original language versus an expert translation. Sources, both men and women, have been drawn from a varied pool: from the 16th to the late 20th century; from the Soviet Union, many European countries, North and South America, the Near East, and Asia; ages from the 20s to the 70s; and from among both successful and disgraced revolutionaries, victorious and defeated politicians, famous novelists, monarchs, scientists, judges, military officers, and the leaders who have governed and are now governing the world's superpowers.

Measurement of metacomplexity

Streufert (1989; Streufert & Swezey, 1986) has switched from written essays to a guided interview format, scored in accordance with his interactive complexity theory (see Streufert & Streufert, 1978). Respondents are encouraged to provide sufficient material (with time available determined by the interviewer) to permit scoring for complexity in multiple domains on a 25-point scale.

Streufert's research group has effected major changes in the early simulation scenarios (cf. Schroder et al., 1967). The current quasi-experimental simulation techniques permit continuous control of task environments and make it possible to measure multistyle determined complex functioning in task settings resembling the real world. A computer-assisted system provides sequences of information that permit multiple actions by participants. After 6 to 8 hours of task participation, 40 to 60 measures based on metacomplexity propositions are obtained. Some measures correlate highly with the S/PCT; others relate to other cognitive styles, controls, or abilities, or to their joint effects (Streufert, Pogash, & Piasecki, 1988). Research has been to a great extent directed toward performance in organizational settings.

Variables affecting complexity scores

One kind of variable that influences the complexity score is internal to the testing situation. For example, it is highly probable that time pressure, information overload, distraction, and some subject states (e.g., excessive or insufficient motivation, fatigue, or illness) will reduce scores. The exact stems used in the S/PCT, or the topic set for an essay, may also have some effect (see Reliability).

Another type of relevant variable is that which shapes the subject's expression. There has been a prolonged discussion of the extent to which writing style and related factors influence the score. Schroder et al. (1967) reported low to moderate correlations between verbal fluency, verbal IQ, and complexity. More recent research has shown the complexity score to be correlated significantly with the total number of words, sentence length, and words with more than three syllables. However, these associations were responsible for only a small portion of the total variance. Other stylistic variables were essentially unrelated to complexity (Coren & Suedfeld, 1990). Metacomplexity views base joint predictions of human functioning upon multiple stylistic constructs to increase predictive accuracy. Limited intercorrelations among those styles, however, suggest that complexity scoring cannot be replaced by mechanical assessments of writing style.

Comparisons of data-generating techniques such as PCT, essays, or guided interviews show only minor variations in mean complexity scores. In general, higher complexity scores are found in material that has been generated after some thought or planning has taken place and under conditions of little or no time constraint. Lower complexity scores are found in material that was generated with little prior thought and under strict time-limiting conditions. Written accounts tend to have higher scores than oral material (i.e., transcriptions of interviews).

In the scoring of prepared speeches, the question of who actually wrote the material – and therefore, of whose complexity is being assessed – appears to pose a problem for the validity of the score. However, there is reason to believe that (at least in the case of important speeches) "ghost-written" materials are not accepted for presentation unless they reflect the complexity of the speaker. For example, Ballard (1983) found no difference in mean complexity between prepared and spontaneous speeches given by Canadian prime ministers. Thus, the problem may not be as serious as has been feared. Nevertheless, it is obviously preferable to score passages known to have been written by the purported source, unless the goal is to obtain a score for an identified group – for example, the cabinet, or advisors to the president – rather than an individual.

Evidence for age and sex differences in integrative complexity is mixed. Porter and Suedfeld (1981) and de Vries and Walker (1988) found increases in complexity across the life-span (but only up to a point) and over various age groups. Other studies (by some of the same authors), however, found older participants to be more simplistic than younger participants. Each sex has been found to be higher in complexity in one or more studies, and no sex differences have been found in still others.

Implicit in the idea that verbal material can be scored for integrative complexity is the assumption that the source/author is linguistically competent. Otherwise, people who lack the ability to express themselves adequately in whatever language they are using may receive an invalid complexity score. Scores of English translations, incidentally, do not differ significantly from the scores assigned to the same passage in the original language.

Reliability

The issue of reliability is a difficult one when dealing with a construct that has both trait and state aspects. Schroder et al. (1967) report a split-half correlation of .70 for the S/PCT. Test–retest reliability differs for stems from the same domain as opposed to varied domains (in the .80s to .90s versus the .40s to .70s). Integrative complexity measures within the simulation-based metacomplexity approach show test–retest reliabilities of .62 to .94, as well as considerable predictive power. However, these results are obtained at the cost of an expensive methodology and an all-day measurement of participant (group or individual) functioning under a range of task demands (Streufert, Pogash, Piasecki, Nogami, & Swezey, 1988).

Interscorer agreement can be assessed without concern for the factors that may affect the source's complexity level. Coders are considered qualified when they reach 85% agreement or alternatively, a correlation of .85, with an expert. This usually occurs at the completion of a training workshop lasting up to 2 weeks and led by someone very experienced in both the theory and scoring of integrative complexity. In archival studies, the coder's familiarity with the historical context may influence the scores assigned; so may his or her reaction to the thoughts expressed – that is, the content. Concurrent complexity measurement and content analysis of the same materials need to be performed to assess this possibility (as well as the more important theoretical issue of the independence of structural and content variables).

28 *The conceptual/integrative complexity scoring manual*

GLORIA BAKER-BROWN,
ELIZABETH J. BALLARD, SUSAN BLUCK,
BRIAN DE VRIES, PETER SUEDFELD,
AND PHILIP E. TETLOCK

OVERVIEW

Integrative complexity is scored on a 1–7 scale. Scores of 1 indicate no evidence of either differentiation or integration. The author relies on uni-dimensional, value-laden, and evaluatively consistent rules for processing information. Scores of 3 indicate moderate or even high differentiation but no integration. The author relies on at least two distinct dimensions of judgment, but fails to consider possible conceptual connections between these dimensions. Scores of 5 indicate moderate to high differentiation and moderate integration. The author notes the existence of conceptual connections between differentiated dimensions of judgment. These integrative cognitions can take a variety of forms: the identification of a superordinate category linking two concepts, insights into the shared attributes of different dimensions, the recognition of conflicting goals or value trade-offs, or the specification of interactive effects and causes of events. Scores of 7 indicate high differentiation and high integration. A general principle provides a conceptual framework for understanding specific interactions among differentiated dimensions. This type of systemic analysis yields second-order integration principles that place in context, and perhaps reveal, limits on the generalizability of integration rules. Scores of 2, 4, and 6 represent transitional levels in conceptual structure. Here the dimensions of differentiation and integration are implicit and emergent rather than explicit and fully articulated.

This manual is based on previous versions developed by research teams at the University of British Columbia and the University of California (Berkeley). The order of authors is alphabetical.

401

Integrative complexity coding is difficult, in large part, because it does not rely on simple content-counting rules of the sort that some other content analytic approaches employ. Assessing integrative complexity requires the judgment of trained coders, who may have to make subtle inferences about the intended meaning of authors. Coders often make difficult judgments concerning whether differentiation or integration exists in particular statements.

For example, it is frequently difficult to say whether a qualification to an absolute rule has been sufficiently worked out to constitute an alternative or fully differentiated perspective. Passages may fall in the fuzzy boundary zone between scale values. Such cases frequently lead to the assignment of the transition scores 2, 4, and 6, indicating implicit as opposed to explicit differentiation or integration. It is not unusual for expert coders to disagree over score assignments for boundary zone cases, although the disagreements rarely exceed 1 point.

Coders must keep in mind several important aspects of the integrative complexity coding system. First, the system focuses on structure rather than content. There is no built-in bias for or against any particular position. One can advance simple or complex arguments for any of a variety of viewpoints; for example, in favor of or in opposition to capital punishment, choice on abortion, higher military spending, papal infallibility, and so on. The integrative complexity of a person's thoughts on an issue is determined not by the specific beliefs he or she endorses, but by the conceptual structure underlying the positions taken.

Second, it is essential not to allow the coder's personal preferences or biases on an issue to influence the conceptual assessment of a statement. Passages that take controversial moral or political stands may often challenge a coder's objectivity. In such cases, coders may be tempted to score passages with which they agree more highly than passages with which they disagree. Coders should keep in mind that the conceptual structure of the reasoning, and not the content, is being assessed here. Researchers may want to take additional precautions such as ensuring that coders with different political preferences agree in their complexity score assignments and following double-blind scoring procedures in which coders are kept unaware of both the hypotheses being tested and the sources of the text being analyzed.

Third, and as a corollary to the above point, the coder should not always assume that it is better to be more complex. Being complex in one's thinking is no guarantee of being correct. Indeed, it is not hard to identify examples of statements that are highly complex and, in hindsight, obviously wrong (e.g., some of the arguments of those who favored the appeasement of Nazi Germany prior to 1939). It is also not hard to identify examples of highly complex arguments that, in the light of present-day norms, are immoral (e.g., the arguments of anti-abolitionists in pre–Civil War America). The integrative complexity coding system does not rest on assumptions concerning the logical, pragmatic, or ethical superiority of any particular school of thought.

MEASUREMENT

The basic scoring unit refers to a section of material that focuses on one idea. Usually, but not always, this scorable unit consists of a single paragraph. Occasionally a large paragraph in the original material may be broken into two or more scorable units each having a single idea. On the other hand, several paragraphs in the original material may be collapsed into one scorable unit.

A variety of approaches exists for the generation (experimental) or designation (archival) of material that may be coded for integrative complexity. In essence, these approaches fall along a continuum of experimenter control and range from high (i.e., the Paragraph Completion Test, another version of the Sentence Completion Test) to low (archival documents).

The first step in sampling from archival material is to identify the complete pool of available and scorable units (see Unscorables section). From this pool at least five units should then be randomly chosen and scored. The mean of these scores represents the complexity score typically used in analyses. In the case of experimentally generated material, individuals should be instructed to generate at least five paragraphs so that the mean of the five can be calculated to determine the individual's score. If the generated material is all on one topic (e.g., a short essay), the researcher may prefer to use the entire essay as the scorable unit.

We have found that mean complexity scores vary not only as a function of situational variables, but also as a function of the type of population from which the sample is selected. For example, we found the mean complexity score in random college samples to be approximately 2. This differs in specialized samples (e.g., the mean complexity score was closer to 4 in materials from U.S. Supreme Court justices).

Experimentally generated material

The Paragraph Completion Test (PCT) was the method of choice in the early years of complexity research. This test has undergone several revisions. People are asked to complete six to nine brief responses, each written in 1 to 3 minutes and based on a sentence stem addressing important domains of the decision-making environment. The basic stems are:

> When I am criticized . . .
> When I don't know what to do . . .
> Rules . . .
> When a friend acts differently . . .

Confusion . . .
When I am in doubt . . .

Because of various problems with the PCT format (e.g., the fact that in most studies the majority of the scores were in the lower range of the scale, between 1 and 2), later versions modified the number of stems, the amount of time allowed, or the topics of the sentence stems.

The currently recommended procedure for the administration of the PCT is to extend the time limit to 10 minutes per stem. In order to avoid subject fatigue and boredom, and to retain a reasonable total time limit for the task, this format usually requires the use of fewer stems. We recommend three, preferably chosen to represent the major decision-making domains included in the original version, namely: relations to authority, interpersonal conflict, and informational uncertainty.

Alternatively, in particular experimental contexts the subject may be asked to write an essay on a topic relevant to the experiment. Such essays would be expected to contain several paragraph units, written with either no time limit or a very generous one, and can serve other research purposes (e.g., to assess attitudes or expectations) besides being coded for integrative complexity. In such cases, the instructions must make clear to the subjects that the composition should reflect opinions, evaluations, or judgments, and should not be merely a descriptive account (which would not be scorable for complexity).

The PCT and its essay variant, the Topic Completion Test (TCT), can be administered in either group or individual sessions. No special equipment is required, except something to write with and something to write on. The measures have been used with both student and adult community samples, both sexes, and many ethnic groups. Beyond obvious basic qualifications (i.e., literacy in whatever language is being used), there have been no particular prerequisites for taking the tests. Instructions and stimuli can remain basically constant across subject groups.

When coding materials are obtained experimentally, indications as to the author's gender, age, or race as well as condition and time of administration should be deleted before materials are ready for coding.

Archival material

The 1–7 scale of differentiation and integration can be used with any connected verbal discourse to which the researcher has access. The materials used for archival studies are generally taken from books or newspapers. The number of units needed from each particular condition (e.g., from specific sources, from given time periods) is determined in advance based on a minimum of five units per data point. The library researcher selects each unit randomly from the total available and makes a photoduplicate. Units should be scored in random order so that all material from one source or person is not scored sequentially. People or place names, and dates, should be deleted from the materials in order to avoid biasing the coder. The person who is coding the data set should be familiar with the topics addressed in the paragraphs. This is especially relevant when coding archival material of an historical or political nature, when knowledge of certain people and events may allow the coder to see different perspectives than would be obvious to a naive coder.

Reliability

Coders are considered qualified when they reach a correlation of at least .80 with an expert coder (i.e., the practice materials supplied in appendix I of this volume). Ideally, prospective coders would also reach a percentage agreement of 80%. These criteria have been difficult to meet without repeated practice and feedback from trained coders over a period of time. Learning to score texts for complexity has traditionally occurred in workshop training sessions lasting up to 2 weeks and involving detailed examination of problematic cases and group discussion of coding decisions.

This manual is designed to enable people to code integrative complexity by presenting detailed criteria for assigning each value on the 7-point scale. Clearly, it is best for beginners to discuss the issues raised in the manual with qualified scorers, or – if that is not possible – with other trainees. However, if the beginner has no access to other interested colleagues, we hope that the manual itself is sufficiently self-explanatory to permit the new coder to reach acceptable levels of reliability.

If an adequate level of agreement is not reached by the time the prospective coder has finished the practice materials, the authors of the manual can provide further samples (see appendix III for instructions on how to order additional practice materials). Learning to score integrative complexity is itself a complex task, and should be approached with the understanding that considerable time and energy will have to be devoted in order to become a qualified coder. Even after agreement with the practice materials has been obtained, qualified coders should reach an interrater reliability of .80 or 80% on a subsample of data (at least 15% of the data set) each time they begin coding new data.

GENERAL FORMAT OF THE MANUAL

With the exception of the section on Unscorables, the discussion of each scale score follows a common format. First, a general explanation of the score is given, identifying its unique characteristics. This is followed by the presentation of the critical indicator of that score, which is the aspect that must be identifiable in a passage for it to receive that score. Next, two specific indicators are presented and described, with an example of each. Specific indicators are a general guideline as to the types of passages that receive that score. However, it should be clear that the specific indicators are not all-inclusive and that the score can be assigned to materials that do not fit under one of the specific indicators.

For the lower scores (1–3), content flags are presented next. These are specific words or phrases that alert the coder to the possibility that a particular score may be appropriate. They must not be used to justify the score in and of themselves, because any individual word can be incorporated at any level of complexity. For this reason, content flags are not given for the higher-level scores (4–7), where excessive reliance on them is especially likely to be misleading. Explanations of scores given to examples are included for scores of 6 and 7 only, as they are often the most difficult scores for the new coder to learn to recognize.

We are interested in reactions that readers have to the manual and invite comments and suggestions.

UNSCORABLES

The identification and deletion of unscorable statements prior to selecting the final sample ensures the efficient use of the expert coder's time. Individuals who select the statements to be scored need not be reliable coders themselves, but should at a minimum understand this section on "Unscorables." Such knowledge will prevent the sample from being overloaded with unscorable material. Despite screening precautions, it should be realized that some statements in the sample will inevitably be judged unscorable. In coding, such paragraphs should be marked "X" and deleted from further data analyses.

General explanation

The main characteristic of an unscorable paragraph is that the author's rule structure for drawing inferences or making decisions is not evident. There are many reasons why the underlying rule structure might be obscure.

Specific indicators

CLICHÉS. A paragraph is unscorable if it consists solely of cryptic or glib remarks (e.g., Who cares? So what?) or of clichés (e.g., A stitch in time saves nine; a penny saved is a penny earned).

SATIRE AND SARCASM. When there is considerable ambiguity about either the object or thrust of a satirical passage, the passage is deemed unscorable.

QUOTATIONS. Scoring a paragraph that consists primarily of quotations may shed more light on the rule structure of the quotation than on that of the paragraph being scored. The key exception to this methodological rule is when the author comments on the quotations in sufficient detail to reveal the nature of his or her own thinking on the issue.

DESCRIPTIONS. When a paragraph is purely descriptive (i.e., it merely reports the occurrence of events and provides minimal clues concerning the author's perspective on those events), that paragraph is considered unscorable. Thus, a statement such as the following would be judged unscorable: "Mr. Reagan and Mr. Gorbachev met for four hours in Reykjavik and engaged in detailed discussion of a number of issues of mutual concern. They also discussed a number of regional conflicts."

There is, it should be stressed, no neat, nonarbitrary line that divides description on the one hand from evaluation and interpretation on the other. The previous statement, for example, becomes scorable by merely inserting a few key terms, such as "Mr. Reagan and Mr. Gorbachev engaged in detailed, sometimes acrimonious but often constructive discussions."

BREAKDOWNS IN UNDERSTANDING. Any paragraph that the reader cannot understand obviously cannot be scored. Breakdowns in understanding may arise for several reasons. Coders may decide to categorize a passage as unscorable if it requires a great deal of special knowledge that they do not possess, if it cannot be adequately understood out of context, or if it appears that the author does not have sufficient command of the language.

SCORER UNCERTAINTY. Occasionally the coder cannot decide which of two scores to assign to a paragraph. If the mathematical difference between them is 2 or greater, the paragraph should be categorized as unscorable and discarded. If the difference is less than 2, other qualified coders should be consulted. If no consensus is reached, the mean of the two possible scores can be assigned or the paragraph may be discarded.

SCORE OF I

General explanation

There is no sign of either conceptual differentiation or integration at this scoring level. The author relies, without qualification, on a simple, one-dimensional rule for interpreting events or making choices.

Critical indicator

Only one way of looking at the world is considered legitimate. The author either implies or explicitly states that there is one and only one reasonable approach to an issue. This position is typically expressed in the form of an absolute or categorical rule. These absolute rules are often, although not necessarily always, highly evaluative (e.g., "Only an immoral imbecile would believe . . ."). The end result of the application of an absolute rule is, however, always the same: the imposition of a dichotomous category structure (right vs. wrong, socialist vs. capitalist, determinism vs. free will) on the world, with little or no room for ambiguity or shades of gray. The author seeks rapid closure.

Specific indicators

Specific indicators are common ways in which the critical indicator manifests itself. They are not necessary for score assignment but are provided as guides for identifying critical indicators.

COMPARTMENTALIZATION AND REJECTION OF PERSPECTIVES OR DIMENSIONS. A common characteristic of a score of 1 is the evaluation of stimuli in an all-or-none fashion, without consideration of possible exceptions to, or qualifications of, the evaluative rule. Information is rigidly compartmentalized and, depending on the compartment into which it has been placed, included or excluded from consideration. The author implicitly or explicitly denies that reasonable others could disagree, or that an issue has aspects or dimensions that the author has not considered. Note that the author may go on at great length and provide detailed descriptions, explanations, or examples of the preferred rule. This additional content does not, however, justify a higher score. The author is elaborating on a dominant theme, not introducing alternative perspectives or dimensions.

The real reason why we are not competing effectively with the Japanese is the erosion of the work ethic in America. American workers do not take as much pride as they used to in the products they create in the plants and factories of this country. We hear too many stories of sloppy workmanship, absenteeism, drug addiction, alcoholism, and bad morale on the production lines and in the ranks of management. We won't be able to compete effectively until we regain the old-fashioned sense of pride in a job well done. Anyone who tells you something different just doesn't understand the world of business.

DOMINANCE OF A SINGLE EVALUATIVE RULE. Many statements distinguish a variety of specific issues or events, and then lump these issues or events together in a single overall evaluative category. The value judgments of the author permeate and dominate the discussion of specifics. Evaluative dominance of this sort can take many forms: lengthy lists of the costs of rejected options and the benefits of preferred options, protracted discussion of the vices of one's opponents and the virtues of one's allies ("My opponent is an opportunistic, deceitful, and malicious rascal"; "Comrade Brezhnev has selflessly, thoughtfully, and courageously guided our Party through many difficult times.")

As a traveler I got a glimpse of the misery that prevailed in the world. Poverty, hunger, mental illness – they were the inevitable result of life in this world. And as there was nothing I could do about it, I did not worry.

CONTENT FLAGS. The presence of one or more content flags alerts the coder to the possibility that the passage meets the criteria for a particular score. In using such flags as an aid in scoring, bear in mind that they do not in themselves justify any particular score. In many cases, it will be appropriate to assign a score of 1 to paragraphs that contain none of the "content flags," and in many other cases, it will be appropriate to assign higher scores to paragraphs that contain several of these content flags. In short, the mere presence of the words listed subsequently is neither a necessary nor a sufficient condition for assigning a score of 1. Integrative complexity coding cannot be reduced to a simple word count or word co-occurrence count content analysis system. It requires the judgmental process of linguistically competent human beings – a judgmental process that is extraordinarily difficult to capture, for example, in existing Artificial Intelligence programs. Content flags for the score of 1 are words or phrases connoting categorical, all-or-none thinking. Common examples include: *absolutely, all, always, certainly, constantly, convinced, definitely, entirely, forever, impossible, indisputable, irrefutable, irreversible, never, solely, surely, unconditionally, undoubtedly, unquestionably.*

SCORE OF 2

General explanation

In a statement assigned a score of 1, the author ignores or rejects alternative perspectives on an issue. In a statement assigned a score of 2, the author recognizes the potential for looking at the same issue in different ways or along different dimensions. Differentiations are, however, emergent rather than fully developed. The author may, for example, qualify a normative rule or causal generalization, or display an awareness of alternative futures. The author may also discuss past events in a way that suggests, but does not develop, new interpretations. On the whole, this scale value represents a transition level between the categorical structure of the score of 1 and the differentiated structure of the score of 3.

Critical indicator

The critical indicator for a score of 2 is the potential or conditional acceptance of different perspectives or dimensions. The author does not explicitly develop the alternate dimension or perspective; nor is it necessary that it be explicitly stated or named. Simple qualification, without elaboration, is sufficient evidence for a score of 2.

Specific indicators

CONDITIONAL ACCEPTANCE OF, OR EMERGENT RECOGNITION OF, OTHER PERSPECTIVES OR DIMENSIONS. The author implies or states that acceptance of a position or policy proposal need not be all-or-none, but a matter of degree that, in turn, hinges on the degree to which a particular condition or goal has been satisfied.

In regard to my own death, when it comes, I really think that my attitude will be influenced by circumstances. I don't want to die now because there are some obligations I want to fulfill but the day may come when I welcome death.

The author mentions that others may hold perspectives different from his or her own, but does not specify exactly how these perspectives are different. Or the author recognizes that an issue has several components or dimensions but does not elaborate on them.

I read that Haas has married Jarmila, which doesn't surprise me, for I always expected great things from Haas. But the world will be surprised. Do you know anything more about it?

EXCEPTION TO THE RULE. The author qualifies a generalization or stated perspective or dimension.

The letter said that he loved life but that this was not really living. He said that my mother, his friend, was calling him to her side. He hoped that we would forgive him.

CONTENT FLAGS. Conjunctions such as *but, nevertheless, while, however,* and *though,* and qualifier adjectives and adverbs (e.g., *probably, almost, usually*) may indicate a score of 2.

SCORE OF 3

General explanation

The crucial aspect of a score of 3 is the clear specification of at least two distinct ways of dealing with the same information or stimulus. The author recognizes that these different perspectives or dimensions can be held in mind simultaneously. The author may also specify conditions under which these perspectives or dimensions are applicable. However, there is no evidence of conceptual integration. Differentiation is the key element of a score of 3.

Critical indicator

The critical indicator for a score of 3 is the recognition of alternative perspectives or different dimensions, and the acceptance of these as being relevant, legitimate, justifiable, or valid.

Specific indicators

MULTIPLE ALTERNATIVES. One form of differentiation involves recognizing that "reasonable persons" can view the same problem or issue in different ways (the "truth" is not all on one side). Although the speaker may hold one viewpoint, he or she recognizes that others disagree and feels no need to disparage them. The author sees multiple perspectives.

Dear Sir,
I do not insist at all on speedy publication of this story, but do request you to inform me as soon as possible whether you can take it at all. Since you wish to avoid installments, finding room for my story must make problems; of course I realize that. If I nevertheless do not withdraw it of my own accord, my reason is solely that I am especially eager to see it published. But if it is completely out of the question, I could offer you another story, that I also have ready and that comes to only some thirty typewritten pages, so that it would be less dubious a matter, at least in regard to its size.

Differentiation can also take the form of recognizing more than one dimension of an event, situation, issue, person, or object.

I hope the gentle reader will excuse me from dwelling on Particulars, which however insignificant they may appear to grovelling vulgar minds, yet will certainly help a Philosopher to enlarge his thoughts and imagination, and apply them to the Benefit of Publick as well as Private Life, which was my sole design in presenting this and other accounts of my travel to the world.

The scorer must be confident that there are clearly two or more perspectives or dimensions to assign a score of 3. Sometimes the author may recognize two different views but only develop one of them. This would indicate the emergence of another perspective, which is given a score of 2. In other cases, the author may mention several characteristics of an issue but not elaborate any two of them to the point where they can be seen as distinct dimensions. This would be a list, and be assigned a score of 1.

In short, the scorer must feel certain that the author has clearly delineated two categories or rule structures in order to express the two (or more) perspectives or dimensions.

The score of 3 is given because of the evidence that differentiation exists, and is not related to the actual number of perspectives or dimensions that are differentiated. Including more than two alternatives does not increase the score.

INCREASED TOLERANCE FOR AMBIGUITY.   A score of 3 denotes greater flexibility than any lower score. Increased tolerance for ambiguity or conflict is shown when the author considers a number of parallel or contradictory perspectives or dimensions. A different perspective is no longer automatically wrong, bad, or identified with a disliked out-group. Good–bad or right–wrong judgments no longer require taking the all-or-nothing stances characteristic of the scale value of 1. The author recognizes that two views may operate simultaneously and that reasonable persons might favor either side. There is a reaction against absolutism in general.

I see myself as a watcher, a listener who aspires to understand (probably too much so) all of what I see and hear. I'm a people person who also demands a lot of time alone. In my solitary times, I think about almost every aspect of everything. I'm argumentative but also possess a good sense of humor to rescue myself when I've become too much the devil's advocate. I'm not psychic so I can only hope and not know if I've sufficiently answered the question of who I am.

CONTENT FLAGS.   All of the content flags characteristic of a score of 2 are also diagnostic of a score of 3. The same key words appear to signal both implicit and explicit differentiation. Additional content flags, specific to a score of 3, include *alternatively*, *either–or*, *on the other hand*, and *meanwhile*.

SCORE OF 4

General explanation

In the earlier levels, the major element determining a specific score was the presence or absence of differentiation. In the score of 4, we seek signs of the emergence of the second major scoring element, integration. That is, we begin to find indications of the ability to integrate different and sometimes conflicting alternatives. Conceptual integration is not clearly apparent at this level, however. Instead, the integration of alternatives is implicit.

A score of 4 must show two features. First, there must be a clear representation of alternatives. Second, there must be an implicit recognition of a dynamic relationship between or among them. The recognition of this relationship signifies the emergence of integration, although at this level it is expressed in a tentative and often uncertain manner. The clear description of the relationship is often withheld until further information is received.

In summary, there is only a suggestion that interaction exists between the alternatives; there is no overt statement specifying the nature of this interaction.

Critical indicator

The author must indicate that multiple perspectives or dimensions exist, and also that they could interact.

Specific indicators

TENSION BETWEEN ALTERNATIVES.   Occasionally, the manner in which alternatives are presented suggests that tension exists between or among them. It should be noted that the tension referred to here is not necessarily a negative factor, but is simply an indication that a dynamic relationship exists between the alternative perspectives or dimensions.

The recognition of tension may occur through a single clear-cut statement. For example, the author may state that resolution of a problem will be difficult because two groups hold different, somewhat contradictory views. This statement with respect to resolution implies that both groups are dependent on each other or must respect the other's standpoint, and will probably have to compromise – or, in other words, integrate their differing perspectives. In other paragraphs, tension between alternatives may not be stated so explicitly. A single statement that tension is present cannot always be found.

I have very treasured memories of Grandmother but for some strange reason I didn't feel a strong sense of loss at this time. I have had some guilt feelings about this. The nearest I can come to my attitude is that I felt that it was time for Grandma to die.

INTEGRATION EXPRESSED AS A SUPERORDINATE STATEMENT.   Sometimes a superordinate statement is given from which the two alternatives have been generated. It is usually the introductory statement in the paragraph. In this case, a broad statement encompasses the multiple perspectives or dimensions. This statement may also be presented as a single conclusion derived from the two (or more) alternatives.

I like to seek the help of the people around me. Sometimes I gain a lot of valuable information this way and sometimes it is more confusing. Even if I do become a little more confused at first, it is worth seeking advice. Information, like doubt, holds possibilities.

SCORE OF 5

General explanation

A score of 5 indicates the explicit expression of integration. Thus far, our explanation of the scoring technique has focused on various ways of delineating levels and indicators of differentiation. The one exception to this trend was the description of a 4, which may be viewed as the transition point between an expression solely defined by differentiation and one where evidence of integration appears. Whereas a score of 4 signifies the emergence of integration expressed in a tentative or uncertain manner, a score of 5 indicates that integration is clearly evident.

Critical indicator

The critical indicator of a score of 5 is that alternative perspectives or dimensions are not only held in focus simultaneously but also are viewed interactively. The author is not only able to see that multiple alternatives are all to some degree legitimate but is also able to delineate the relationship between them.

Specific indicators

MUTUAL INFLUENCE AND INTERDEPENDENCE. Sometimes, two or more alternatives are shown to be in a dynamic relationship with one another, in which each perspective affects and is affected by the other. The author must clearly recognize the reciprocity of the relationship for the passage to be scored a 5.

I like to seek the advice of the people around me. In talking with people I not only gain access to their opinions and ideas but I am also allowed to reanalyze my doubts. With time, this fusion of my reanalysis with other's ideas can often lead to a new approach to my initial conflict. Often this type of interchange can also help my advisors to clarify their own opinions on some important issues.

A relationship in which one alternative affects the other without consequence to itself is a one-way relationship and cannot be scored as a 5.

SYNTHESIS. The generation of a novel product is evidence of integration. This product may be explicitly related to the two alternatives in the paragraph, or the relationship may only be implied. The novel product may be expressed as an insight, a new policy, or the unexpected result of the interaction of the two dimensions.

I took such care of it that it lived and the leg grew well and as strong as ever; but by nursing it so long, it grew tame and fed upon the little green at my door, and would not go away. This was the first time that I entertained a thought of breeding up some tame creatures that I might have food when my powder and shot was all spent.

CONTENT FLAGS. Content flags are not appropriate for integrative statements, because in most cases specific words or phrases can be incorporated in simple as well as complex thoughts. However, such terms as *interplay*, *interaction, interdependency, mutual(ity), compromise, equilibrium, balancing,* and *trade-offs* are compatible with the score of 5.

SCORE OF 6

General explanation

In general, the score of 6 involves a high-level interaction indicating that the author is working with multiple levels of schemata. The alternatives at this level are dynamic: They are expressed as plans, processes, or courses of action made up of several moving parts, and as such we may often refer to them as systems or networks. One of the indicators of a score of 6 is the specific explanation of both the "moving parts" within a system and also how those parts affect each other or the system.

At this level alternatives are readily accepted, compared or contrasted, and integrated so as to present at least one outcome. Global overviews or organizational principles (temporal, causal, ideological) are often presented. The emergence of this type of principle is the second main indicator of the score of 6.

Critical indicator

For a paragraph to be given a score of 6, the author must be working across several levels of schemata and at least one of the indicators noted previously must be explicitly delineated. Thus, there may be an explicitly presented global overview with only an implicit indication of the specific dynamics of the alternatives. Conversely, there may be explicitly stated details about the dynamic interaction between alternatives and only an implicit communication of the global overview.

Specific indicators

COMPARISON OF OUTCOMES. The author is aware of two alternative courses of action and is able to compare their outcomes with regard to long-term implications. In comparing alternatives, the author may favor one over the other, but each is reasonably considered. Alternatives and outcomes may be actual or hypothetical.

One form of self-expression is influenced by our interpersonal relationships and experiences. My relations with my parents and friends have made me value honesty and intimacy. Another child's upbringing may have made independence a central concern. Unfortunately some children's social environment fosters mistrust and fear of rejection. By adulthood, if not earlier, we have all created a style of expressing ourselves, each subtly different, because of our varying backgrounds, which alter the paths we follow through life.

Explanation of Score: In the first sentence the author expresses a global overview of factors influencing self-expression. Different circumstances leading to the creation of various styles of expression are then compared.

Multiple levels of interactive schemata are present: the types of upbringing; styles of expressing ourselves; and paths we follow through life.

SYSTEMIC ANALYSIS. Any case in which the author describes how an existing relationship, network, or system can be affected by changes in an internal or external variable may be scorable as a 6. The effect that the active variable has on the system is often discussed in terms of the accommodation that the system makes to it at various hierarchical levels.

As for myself, I do not fear death, nor do I look forward to it. There is no appropriate time for death; if one conceives life as a dialectic, one realizes that issues are never settled once and for all. When every item on my list is completed a new list of items is generated. Relationships are never fulfilled; the deeper a relationship becomes the more nurturance and care it generates. In fact I'm not exactly in agreement with the choice points of Erikson's last stage – integrity versus despair. While despair is certainly the negative outcome, I'm uncertain that integrity – or acceptance of one's life as "good" – is the desirable resolution. For me, death simply means that the eternal struggle has ended.

Explanation of Score: The author gives the specifics but no global statement in describing a conceptualization of the relationship between life and death. Life and death are seen as unified opposites, a dialectic. Within this system issues and relationships are seen as ever changing. New inputs generate new feelings. The author can see places in which this system is commensurate with Erikson's hierarchy of stages and places where the two systems may differ.

SCORE OF 7

General explanation

The unique characteristic of a score of 7 is the presence of an overarching viewpoint pertaining to the nature (not merely the existence) of the relationship or connectedness between alternatives. In a score of 7, these alternatives are clearly delineated and are described in reasonable detail. How each alternative may be seen to be part of some overarching view, or how some overarching view encompasses these alternatives, is made evident.

Critical indicators

First, an overarching viewpoint is presented, which contains an explanation of the organizing principles (e.g., temporal, causal, theoretical) of the problem or concept.

Second, there is a discussion of the ways in which levels of the problem or concept interact and thus demonstrate the validity of the overarching viewpoint. The description of the ways in which levels of the system interact must be both specific and dynamic, demonstrating how each level is affected by the other.

Although these indicators are distinct, they are inextricably linked. The overarching view encompasses the components of a system, and in fact may have developed as a result of the author's simultaneous consideration of these levels or components.

Specific indicators

COMPARISON OF OUTCOMES. The author takes a global view of the events in the situation and relates these events to an organizing principle. At the same time, the specific nature or dynamics of at least one of the events is outlined in some detail. The possible outcomes of events are compared and related to this global view.

As is the case of the many movements led by our party over the last years and more, there are always shortcomings among great achievements. So there are always at least two ways to approach the resolution to these inherent shortcomings. The outstanding contradiction with which we are now faced in our work is the tension and strain in various quarters caused by disproportions. Due to the party's achievements both in development and investment, resources are finally available. Now we must concern ourselves with the intricacies of distribution. The development of unequal distribution has affected the social and working relationships between citified workers and their rural peasant counterparts. The rural workers are hesitant to maintain long work hours when they perceive that the citified workers benefit more than they do themselves. The citified workers believe that the rural life is far easier than their own and that the government farm subsidies are a waste of funds that could be better used in industrializing the cities. Further, within the cities themselves we even have disruption among the various strata there, between merchants and workers, between land-owners and renters. Likewise, the various strata among the peasants are at odds with one another. This is a political problem. The key to whether we can mobilize the broad masses to continue the great leap forward into the future that our party wishes to achieve is the extent to which we can ensure, by whatever means we now develop, the fair distribution of resources. If we are not able to establish an equitable system, and to convince the various strata among the population that this has been achieved, hostility and competition will continue to grow. Disproportionate distribution of resources is a problem which can be solved with a well-planned strategy, but hostility among the people is a problem which may change the entire face of our country.

Explanation of Score: The author takes a global view of the multiple controversies in this example, relating them all to the disproportionate distribution of resources. At the same time, the specific nature of the controversies is outlined (e.g., between urban and rural workers, among several city strata). Notice that it is not necessary for every part of the system to be delineated; for example, no specific statement is made concerning the friction that is developing among the peasant strata. The author also sees the distribution system as related to two organizing principles: although equivocal distribution of resources is basically an economic problem, it will also have political ramifications. Two possible outcomes are presented, both dependent on the party's ability to distribute resources fairly.

SYSTEMIC ANALYSIS. In general, this type of highly integrative passage explores specific complex interactions within a complex system, using an overarching global view as a way of uniting these observations. The author begins by taking a global view of the problem and then provides examples for the particular interpretation. The effect of one action on other levels throughout the system is then clearly explained. The general and specific consequences of this "ripple effect" are delineated.

Social relationships permeate every aspect of our lives: our family and friends, our culture, and our global community. The family is the primary source of the development of our social bonds. This extends to new and different people as we make and remake friendships throughout life. The unique experiences that we take away from our varied relationships influence our form of self-expression which is, itself, a component of our social interactions with family and friends and with our extended community.

Explanation of Score: The author makes clear reference to multiple, specific, embedded levels of "our lives" within the context of an overarching global network of social relationships. The varied relationships we have with others in these family, friendship, cultural, and global community spheres have an impact on our "self-expression," which, as a consequence, influences the interactions we have in these social spheres. This dynamic, rippling effect is the hallmark of systemic analysis in the score of 7.

29 *Uncertainty orientation*

RICHARD M. SORRENTINO,
CHRISTOPHER J. R. RONEY,
AND STEVEN E. HANNA

In the past decade or so, social psychology and psychology in general have been dominated by research and theory on cognition and social cognition. Motivational theories have either been ignored or cognitive alternatives substituted. Our research program has attempted to integrate both areas, pointing out the importance of each to the other. This work has resulted in what is now a continuing series of volumes entitled *The Handbook of Motivation and Cognition* (vol. 1: Sorrentino & Higgins, 1986a; vol. 2: Higgins & Sorrentino, 1990). In those volumes, contributors from both camps were forced to think about these issues in depth. We also presented our research and development of the construct we present in this chapter, uncertainty orientation (see Sorrentino & Higgins, 1986b; Sorrentino, Raynor, Zubek, & Short, 1990; Sorrentino & Short, 1986). Our feeling is that this construct could serve as a stepping-stone for a more complete integration of the areas of motivation and cognition.

Uncertainty orientation was originally designed to examine individual differences in cognition related to achievement behavior (see Sorrentino, & Hewitt, 1984; Sorrentino & Roney, 1986; Sorrentino, Short, & Raynor, 1984), but it is now seen as related to many areas of general psychology. Unlike much of the research in cognition and social cognition, however, we do not assume a "rational" model of human behavior. We do agree that many people are interested in understanding themselves and the world around them, and that they process information accordingly. However, we also believe that there are many others, perhaps a majority of those in society, who place little emphasis on this type of behavior.

CONCEPTUAL FRAMEWORK

Our construct of uncertainty orientation incorporates both types of people just described. People who conform to the rational model are people we

419

call uncertainty-oriented; people who do not are people we call certainty-oriented. The uncertainty-oriented are assumed to be primarily motivated to seek clarity through mastery of uncertainty, whereas the certainty-oriented are motivated to maintain clarity by adhering to what is already known (Raynor & McFarlin, 1986; Sorrentino & Short, 1986).

The uncertainty-oriented are curious about the unknown, open to new and possibly inconsistent information, and have a high tolerance for ambiguity. They experience positive information value from the process of thinking, discovering, and finding out. They derive little satisfaction from knowing without working through the challenge of uncertainty. This cognitive functioning is consistent with the notion of "human the scientist" and hypothetical-deductive reasoning (see Sorrentino & Roney, 1990).

The certainty-oriented are assumed to be dominated by a need to ignore changes to existing cognitions and a need to maintain clarity. They are attracted to the familiar and predictable, have an authoritarian and dogmatic way of knowing, and have a low tolerance for ambiguity. They experience positive information value from the product of thinking – knowledge – but are threatened by the process of thought in any situation that entails confusion about the self or the environment. Their cognitive functioning features adherence to a particular viewpoint and resistance to alternatives or change. Uncertainty is to be avoided. It provides negative information value. The certainty-oriented are motivated to remove uncertainty when it is experienced. This is done by either ignoring or leaving the situation, or relying on past knowledge or others for solutions. The characteristics of uncertainty and certainty orientation resemble those of open-minded and closed-minded individuals, respectively (Rokeach, 1960).

Uncertainty orientation is assumed to be time-linked. The uncertainty-oriented seek out new ideas and explore previously unknown possibilities. They are presumed to be future-oriented. The certainty-oriented cling to previously established ideas and are threatened by the uncertainty of the unknown. They are presumed to be past-oriented. We believe that individual differences in uncertainty orientation emerge early in life, either as a consequence of social-developmental factors, or as an interaction of these factors with genetic ones.[1] At present, it is safe to say that uncertainty orientation is an unconscious "screening device" for all situations. If the situation involves uncertainty about the self or the environment, uncertainty-oriented persons will be motivated to engage in that situation. This will be done in order to resolve that uncertainty in an attempt to discover new information about the self or the environment. If the situation continues to maintain clarity about what is already known or believed about the self or the environment, then certainty-oriented persons will be motivated to engage in that situation. This will be done in order to avoid confusion about the self or the environment and maintain clarity of thought and action.

BACKGROUND INFORMATION

Because of some confusing findings in our earlier research on achievement motivation (see Sorrentino & Short, 1977), we began to search for another individual difference variable that might moderate effects due to achievement-related motives. Our criterion was that this variable not be an extrinsic motive such as affiliation, fear of success, or power, but one that could be invoked in all situations. From this, we concluded that all situations differ from each other in some degree as to the amount of uncertainty in the situation. This includes all aspects of uncertainty, such as knowledge about the self, the environment, or the outcome of activity. Following from the Atkinson tradition (Atkinson, 1964; Atkinson & Feather, 1966; Atkinson & Raynor, 1974), we thought of uncertainty orientation as a resultant measure. That is, just as the motive to succeed and the motive to avoid failure could be independent, it was our belief that the preference for uncertain situations and the preference for situations of certainty could be independent. It is conceivable, for example, for someone to be filled with the desire to learn new things but to have been punished for past exploration of the unknown.

Also following the Atkinson tradition, our thought was to have a projective measure of the approach or uncertainty component and a self-report measure of the avoidance component.[2] Although we have tried to come up with other measures (for simplicity yes, but mainly in response to skeptics of projective measures – see Sorrentino & Higgins, 1986b; Weinberger & McClelland, 1990), this combination continues to produce the strongest and most consistent results (for reviews, see Sorrentino et al., 1990; Sorrentino & Short, 1986).

MEASUREMENT INFORMATION

The measure derived to infer one's need to resolve uncertainty about the self or the environment, *n* Uncertainty, is discussed here and in the scoring manual (see chapter 30). The measure derived to infer one's need to maintain past clarity about the self or the environment is adapted from Byrne and Lamberth's acquiescent-free measure of authoritarianism (see Cherry & Byrne, 1977). Our research has shown repeatedly that either component alone is not sufficient to assess one's uncertainty orientation. Rather, the resultant measure of uncertainty orientation, formed by transforming the total scores from each measure into Z-scores, and then subtracting the authoritarianism Z-score from the *n* Uncertainty Z-score, has been most successful.[3]

The projective measure of *n* Uncertainty is administered in exactly the same manner as the sentence lead version of the projective measure of *n* Achievement.[4] That is, under neutral testing conditions and with no other

Table 29.1. *Acquiescence-free authoritarianism measure.* (Adapted from Cherry & Byrne, 1977. In T. Blass (Ed.), *Personality variables in social behavior* (pp. 109–133). New York: Wiley. Copyright 1977 by Wiley and Sons. Reprinted by permission.)

The following is a study of what the general public thinks and feels about a number of important social and personal questions. The best answer to each statement below is your <u>personal opinion</u>. We have tried to cover many different and opposing points of view; you may find yourself agreeing strongly with some of the statements, disagreeing just as strongly with others, and perhaps uncertain about others; whether you agree or disagree with any statement, you can be sure that many people feel the same as you do.

Circle a number on the right margin of <u>each</u> statement to show how much you agree or disagree with it. Please mark each statement.

Circle +3, +2, +1, or -1, -2, -3, depending on how you feel in each case.

+1: I AGREE A LITTLE   -1: I DISAGREE A LITTLE
+2: I AGREE SOMEWHAT   -2: I DISAGREE SOMEWHAT
+3: I AGREE VERY MUCH   -3: I DISAGREE VERY MUCH

1. There is hardly anything lower than a person who does not feel a great love, gratitude, and respect for his or her parents.

2. An insult to our honour should always be punished.

3. Books and movies ought not to deal so much with the unpleasant and seamy side of life; they ought to concentrate on themes that are entertaining or uplifting.

4. What the youth needs most is strict discipline, rugged determination and the will to work and fight for family and country.

5. No sane, normal, decent person could ever think of hurting a close friend or relative.

6. Young people sometimes get rebellious ideas, but as they grow up they ought to get over them and settle down.

* 7. The findings of science may some day show that many of our most cherished beliefs are wrong.

*† 8. It is highly unlikely that astrology will ever be able to explain anything.

* 9. People ought to pay more attention to new ideas, even if they seem to go against the Canadian way of life.

10. If people would talk less and work more everybody would be better off.

11. A person who has bad manners, habits, and breeding can hardly expect to get along with decent people.

* 12. Insults to our honour are not always important enough to bother about.

* 13. It's all right for people to raise questions about even the most sacred matters.

14. Obedience and respect for authority are the most important virtues children should learn.

* 15. There is no reason to punish any crime with the death penalty.

* 16. Anyone who would interpret the Bible literally just doesn't know much about geology, biology, or history.

17. In this scientific age the need for a religious belief is more important than ever before.

* 18. When they are little, kids sometimes think about doing harm to one or both of their parents.

* 19. It is possible that creatures on other planets have founded a better society than ours.

* 20. The prisoners in our corrective institutions, regardless of the nature of their crimes, should be humanely treated.

21. The sooner people realize that we must get rid of all the traitors in the government, the better off we'll be.

* 22. Some of the greatest atrocities in history have been committed in the name of religion and morality.

The following scale appears next to each item: +3 +2 +1 -1 -2 -3.

*   These items are reversed-keyed.
†   This item is typically omitted because we have found that it is detrimental to the internal consistency of the scale and does not enhance prediction.

measure given prior to its administration. Although any sentence lead may be used, because the interest is in how one is concerned with or resolves the uncertainty in any given situation, we have been most successful with the following sentence leads:

1. Two persons are in a laboratory working on a piece of apparatus.
2. A person is sitting, wondering what may happen.
3. A young person is standing, a vague operation scene is in the background.
4. An older person is talking to a younger person.

Further details are presented in the scoring manual (see chapter 30). The measure of authoritarianism is administered next. It is shown in Table 29.1, along with a scoring key.

The measures presented here are for adult populations (academic or nonacademic). Children's versions are also available for children in grades 3–5 and 6–8. We have examined gender in nearly all of our research and have found no significant effects.[5] Figure 29.1 presents some data from various sample populations in Canada and the United States. They are presented for the resultant measure along with each of its components. These results are quite consistent with our belief that uncertainty-oriented persons should be more representative than certainty-oriented persons of university students (as opposed to factory workers of lower grade levels), and this representation should be greater in U.S. universities than Canadian ones. We also have data showing that Eastern cultures are lower in their uncertainty orientation (i.e., they are more certainty-oriented) than Western cultures (Lau, 1985). We believe this is because such cultures place less emphasis on the self and more on the group than Western cultures (see Sorrentino et al., 1990).

The *n* Uncertainty scoring manual yields high interrater reliability (all of our scorers yield above .90 with the scoring manual and with other expert scorers). Internal consistency (alpha = .12) and test–retest reliability (r = .35), however, are low. Percentage of imagery in the stories is also low (only about 20% in any single story) in our university (UWO) sample, but higher in some of the other samples shown in Figure 29.1. When used in conjunction with the authoritarianism component to form the resultant measure, predictive validity is high (see reviews listed earlier). Our research has shown reliable results as much as 7 months following assessment of the resultant measure (two studies in Sorrentino et al., 1984; and one by Roney & Sorrentino, 1990b).[6] We have not examined the effect of controlling for story length as yet. The authoritarianism measure has high test–retest reliability as well as high internal consistency (all above .86).

We recommend that analyses be performed by using only the upper and lower thirds of the resultant measure (i.e., uncertainty-oriented persons equal the upper third, certainty-oriented persons equal the lower third). Median splits and correlational analyses are not recommended as the middle

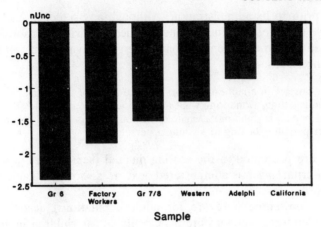

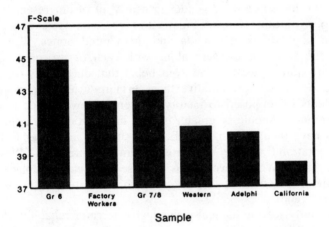

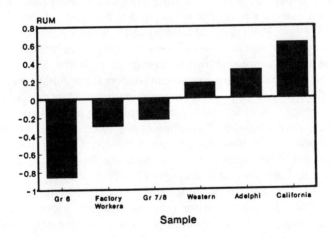

third has consistently been shown to be unreliable in our data and that of others on several projective and self-report measures (see Sorrentino & Short, 1977).

Finally, there does not appear to be a relation between uncertainty orientation and self-esteem (Rosenberg, 1979), or intelligence, as assessed by the progressive matrices task (J. C. Raven, Court, & Raven, 1977). Need for cognition (Cacioppo, Petty, & Kao, 1984) did correlate positively ($r = .20$) and reliably ($p < .05$) with uncertainty orientation in one of our studies but not in another ($r = .02$). The same was true for integrative complexity ($r = .21$, $r = .07$). As expected, certainty-oriented persons are more dogmatic (Trodahl & Powell, 1965; $r = -.44$, $p < .001$) and slightly more external (Rotter, 1966; $r = .18$) than uncertainty-oriented persons. Among some of the more interesting results, we found that uncertainty-oriented persons are significantly higher than certainty-oriented persons on theoretical and aesthetic values, but lower on religious values (Allport & Vernon, 1931), have higher private but not public self-consciousness (Fenigsteien, Scheier, & Buss, 1975) scores, and according to the telic dominance scale (Murgatroyd, Rushton, Apter, & Ray, 1978) they are more paratelic (process-oriented) than certainty-oriented persons who are more telic (goal-oriented). On subscales of this latter scale, certainty-oriented persons are also more planning-oriented and arousal-avoidant than uncertainty-oriented persons. Finally, as we also expected, whereas the Atkinson measure of achievement-related motives (see Atkinson & Feather, 1966) predicts differences in affective items on the Mehrabian Achievement scale (Mehrabian, 1969), that is, items that concern feeling good or bad about success or failure; our measure of uncertainty orientation predicts differences in what we call informational items (uncertainty about the outcome or one's ability). All of these results are consistent with our research and theory on uncertainty orientation.

KEY STUDIES – VALIDITY

The one study that influenced our thinking more than any other was our replication of Trope's (1979) study on reducing uncertainty in achievement

---

Fig. 29.1. *(facing)* Need for uncertainty (*n* Unc), authoritarianism (F-scale), and resultant uncertainty measure (RUM) scores for various samples.
Gr 6 = Grade six students from various schools near London, Canada (data collected as part of the Thinking Skills Project).
Gr 7/8 = Grade seven and eight students from a school near London, Canada.
Adelphi = Undergraduates from Adelphi University.
California = Undergraduates from the University of California at Santa Barbara.
Factory Workers = Workers in a factory in Rhode Island.
Western = Undergraduates from the University of Western Ontario.

tasks. Trope (1979) demonstrated that regardless of whether the task would yield potentially positive information about one's ability or potentially negative information about one's ability, subjects chose to engage in that activity over nondiagnostic tasks. We (Sorrentino & Hewitt, 1984) demonstrated that this result held only for uncertainty-oriented persons. Certainty-oriented persons, in fact, chose to engage in a task that would tell them nothing new about their ability, even though they knew that it was an important ability, and that they were potentially high in that ability. (They also did the same if they knew they were potentially low in that ability.) This was our first real evidence that: (a) theories that accept, as their basic premise, that all people have a need to know and understand aspects of the self and the environment may only apply to uncertainty-oriented people; and (b) certainty-oriented people simply do not want to know anything new about the self or the environment, regardless of the consequences.

Since then we have run a variety of studies in the areas of motivation and cognition, all of them consistent with these two basic assumptions. This includes our work on achievement behavior in which we have shown an additive or interactive effect with achievement-related motives on risk taking (Sorrentino, Hewitt, & Raso-Knot, 1990) and performance (three studies by Sorrentino et al., 1984; a study by Sorrentino & Roney, 1986; and two studies by Roney & Sorrentino, 1990b). It also includes our work on social cognition, in which we have addressed such issues as attitude change and persuasion (two studies by Sorrentino, Bobocel, Gitta, Olson, & Hewitt, 1988), social comparison theory (Roney & Sorrentino, 1990a), self-discrepancy theory (Roney & Sorrentino, 1990b; Roney & Sorrentino, 1990a; Sorrentino & Roney, 1990), social categorization (Roney & Sorrentino, 1987), and memory and recall (Driscoll, Hamilton, & Sorrentino, in press; King & Sorrentino, 1988). We are currently conducting research on dissonance theory and balance and consistency theory.

In all of these studies, the thrust of our research is that current theorizing in many of the areas mentioned only accounts for the behavior of uncertainty-oriented persons. Certainty-oriented persons behave quite differently and do not conform to the rational model of human behavior.

NOTES

1 As this chapter goes to press, we have in our hands data showing strong differences in classroom behavior as a function of uncertainty orientation and achievement-related motives as early as the third grade (the youngest group we have examined so far).

2 Whether certainty-oriented people actually avoid uncertainty, as opposed to ignoring it, is still at issue. Our current thinking is that uncertain situations motivate such people not to think or act in uncertain situations. Thus it is a combination of the two.

3 See Study 1 of Sorrentino, Short, and Raynor (1984) for an example of the breakdown and combination of the two components.
4 We use sentence leads instead of pictures as they are more conducive to testing of large audiences, but pictures may also be used.
5 We also find no gender differences with regard to our predictions for achievement motivation. We believe this is due to our use of "person(s)" as opposed to male or female leads. So far, however, this is only an assumption and not empirically tested.
6 Over 2 years later from the data reported in note 1.

30 *A manual for scoring need for uncertainty*

RICHARD M. SORRENTINO, STEVEN E. HANNA,
AND CHRISTOPHER J. R. RONEY

The projective measure of Need (*n*) for Uncertainty relies heavily in its conceptualization on J. Kagan's (1972) notions concerning modes of uncertainty resolution. It also utilizes a scoring system similar to those developed for *n* Achievement, *n* Power, and *n* Affiliation (see chapters 10, 14, and 20). Scoring procedures are the same for *n* Uncertainty as they are for these other measures, and chapter 37 and appendix I of this volume should be consulted for information regarding scorer training, obtaining verbal material for analysis, and other methodological considerations.

J. Kagan (1972) viewed the resolution of uncertainty as a primary motive; uncertainty was postulated to originate from incompatibility between (a) two cognitions, (b) cognition and experience, or (c) cognition and behavior. Kagan also suggested that a major source of uncertainty is one's inability to predict the future. These categories provided a basis for identifying the presence of uncertainty imagery in stories written to a sentence lead or picture.

NEED FOR UNCERTAINTY IMAGERY (NI)

The scorer's first task is to decide if the story contains any references to the goal of resolving or approaching uncertainty. This goal refers either to the desire to overcome or understand contradictory ideas, events, or behaviors, or to the desire and/or willingness to deal with an unpredictable future. Although the goal may or may not be attained in the story, concern over its attainment would be grounds to identify it as suitable imagery. In order for the story to be scored for imagery, one of the following criteria must be met. These criteria basically differ in terms of the sources from which uncertainty arises.

1. There is a *definite statement* in the story of a desired experience that has an uncertain possibility of being realized. The character must approach the experience.

In order to be scored under this criterion, the story must indicate some

428

doubt involving a desired outcome. This doubt will be most evident when the character is unsure of what behaviors or mental sets to activate in order to prepare for the future. This particularly applies when the doubt centers on potentially unpleasant circumstances that could result if the experience is attempted and not realized.

Mere mention of doubt over the future is not enough for scoring. The character must in some way seek to come to terms with the doubt through his or her own efforts. If the future is not under his or her control in any way whatsoever, then he or she must show some willingness to face and deal with the outcome whatever it may be. In most stories, however, the character will have some way of influencing the future. If the character desires an experience, then she or he must indicate a decision to approach and initiate that activity leading to a desire. Most important is that the mere mention of doubt is not enough for scoring the motive: the character must be willing to approach a desired experience even if a negative result will occur if the goal is not realized.

2. The character must seek to understand some "unknown."

The second criterion is intimately related with the first, except that it is more "present-oriented" and has fewer personal repercussions. It is designed for stories in which a character clearly expresses curiosity or wonder about an entity or phenomenon and actively seeks to clarify or learn more about it in order to satisfy this curiosity.

3. The character must express concern over an incompatibility between two ideas and seek to resolve the inconsistency.

Under this criterion, a character must express some concern over cognitions that conflict with one another. The character must come to terms with the conflict, either through direct examination or questioning of the sources with the end goal being resolution, or through an integrative approach that will reconcile the cognitions with each other.

Cases in which the inconsistency is denied or discounted or in which the problem is turned over to someone else should not be scored for imagery.

The source of the discrepancy may either be personally salient ideas, or ideas relating to a character's schemata of the objective world. Examples of the former would be conflicting ideas related to the self concept, and of the latter would be scientific curiosity aroused by inconsistencies in theories.

4. A character must express concern over an inconsistency between an experience or event and an established schema and seek to resolve the inconsistency.

The character encounters an event that is discrepant with an established schema. The source of the event may be internal (from within the character) or external (from the world). If the character is alerted by this discrepancy and seeks to interpret or act in the direction of resolving it in some way, then the story is scored. The discrepancy may be either personally salient or objective in nature.

By the word *schema* we mean an expectation or theory rather than a wish or ambition. For example, a discrepancy is present if a character expects a raise in salary that does not materialize, but not present if that character wishes for a raise in salary and does not get it. Wishes and ambitions are dealt with as doubtful outcomes under Criterion 1.

5. A character must express concern over the incompatibility between an idea and his or her behavior.

Once again mere concern over an inconsistency between an idea or schema and behavior is not enough to score this story for imagery. The character must indicate a willingness to actually do something to overcome the inconsistency. There must be an honest attempt to deal with the discrepancy or initiate activity that will change the inconsistency to the desired form of consistency.

DOUBTFUL IMAGERY (DI)

Stories that contain some reference to mastering uncertainty but which fail to reach one of the five given criteria should be scored as doubtful. If there is any doubt as to whether approach uncertainty imagery is present, DI should be scored. This doubt might arise for the following reasons.

When uncertainty is present and not avoided but not approached, score DI.

If the story has strong evidence in support of scoring for imagery but finishes with a bizarre or silly ending, it should be treated as DI. However, if the ending follows from essentially strange premises in the rest of the story, then it can be scored as NI.

Two minute rule: If you can not decide whether a story is DI or NI after 2 minutes, score NI but do *not* score any subcategories.

UNRELATED IMAGERY (UI)

This classification is chosen if there is no reference to the goal of mastering uncertainty in the story or if one of the following apply.

Stories in which a character is involved in a situation that is routine as inferred from the context of the story but which may involve an approach to uncertainty are scored UI unless the character clearly demonstrates affective concern as to the outcome.

If the character denies or actively avoids approaching uncertainty, then score UI.

If the character begins activity directed at resolving uncertainty and then gives up or hands the problem over to someone else in the story, then score UI.

If the character approaches uncertainty because he is required to or is coerced by someone else in the story, score UI.

Two minute rule: If you cannot decide if a story should be scored UI or NI after 2 minutes, score it DI.

If the story has been scored DI or UI, then no more scoring is possible. If the story has been scored NI, then examine it for the following possible subcategories.

Stated need to master (N)

Score N if a character in the story states a desire to reach the goal of mastering or approaching uncertainty. Most of the statements will contain a phrase such as "he wants," "he wishes," "he hopes," or "he is determined to." Often these phrases will be predicated by "to know" or "to understand." If there is any doubt as to whether such a phrase connotes a state of need, replace it by the phrase "needs to" and decide whether there is a similar connotation. For instance, "man must continue searching for an answer" could be changed to "man needs to continue searching for an answer" and retain its original connotation.

Care must be taken in determining whether such phrases relate to the goal of mastering doubt or inconsistency. *Statements that express a need that, having been reached, would satisfy the goal of mastering uncertainty would be scored.* If a scorer is unsure of how to score a phrase for need she or he should imagine what kind of goal would be attained if the desire were satisfied. If it is the goal of overcoming uncertainty, then the story would be scored N.

Need should not be inferred solely on the basis of goal-directed instrumental activity. There must be a definite statement of motivation within the story.

Need may be scored only once in each story.

Instrumental activity (I+/?/−)

This subcategory includes a character's overt or covert activities that are directed at or are the means of attaining the goal of either approaching or resolving uncertainty. Activity that would aim at increasing the probability of occurrence of a desired experience or doubtful outcome are examples of this. In the case of uncertainty that arises from inconsistent cognitions, any activity aimed either at solving or understanding the inconsistency should be scored. A phrase such as "he is seeking the answer to the problem" would be an example of this.

The instrumental activity is classified as being +, −, or ? depending on the net effect it has on the outcome of the story (successful, unsuccessful, or doubtful, respectively).

This category may be scored only once per story. If there is more than one activity and they have different effects, then the story should be scored I?.

By convention activity that falls in the initial and final sentences in a story may not be scored unless there is evidence that it is more than a mere statement of the situation or outcome. This occurs especially in the last part of the first sentence and the first part of the last sentence.

Statements in the past or future tense are scored so long as they offer more than the results of past actions or statements of future outcomes.

Goal anticipation (Ga+, Ga−)

For this subcategory, a character anticipates goal failure or attainment or may just be thinking about the goal. This especially includes thoughts about the implications of success or failure.

Ga+ is scored when someone in the story is thinking about a positive or desired outcome from the goal of mastering uncertainty. A direct expression of such a positive anticipatory goal state would be a statement such as "he thinks he can resolve his confusion" or "he is wondering if his decision will turn out for the best."

Ga− is scored when some character is either doubtful as to the final outcome or concerned over possible failure to reach a goal and/or negative consequences from this failure.

Care must be taken to distinguish these types of thoughts from instrumental thoughts such as those in which the character is thinking about how to obtain the goal.

This category need not refer only to the thoughts of the main character.

Ga+ and Ga− may be scored once each per story.

Blocks in the person (Bp) or in the world (Bw)

These subcategories are scored if the progress of goal-directed activity is hindered in some way and may be inferred from statements of frustration made during ongoing goal-directed behavior.

Score Bp if the block is a previous failure to overcome doubt or uncertainty or a present factor within the character, such as lack of confidence or skill.

Score Bw if the block comes from the environment such as interruptions from other people.

Care must be taken to distinguish between the source of uncertainty and obstacles that hinder the activity directed at resolving the uncertainty. *Bp may also be the source of the uncertainty.* Often personal shortcomings will be both a source of uncertainty and an obstacle in the path of resolving uncertainty. *Bw may not be both the source and the block.*

Bw may not be scored if it occurs in either the first or last sentence.

Each of these subcategories may be scored once per story.

If you are unsure of the source of the block (i.e., Bw or Bp), then score it Bw.

Nurturant press (Nup)

Score Nup when personal forces in the story aid the character in reaching a goal of resolving uncertainty. The assistance must be directly related reaching the goal.

It is important to distinguish between help from another person and handing the problem over to someone else. The latter constitutes avoidance behavior and should be scored UI.

Affective states: positive (G+) and negative (G−)

These subcategories include affective states that are associated with either the attainment or failure to reach the goal of resolving uncertainty.

If the character experiences such feelings as relief, confidence, or satisfaction with having approached and mastered uncertainty, the story is scored G+.

If feelings of depression, failure, or anxiety accompany failure to reach the goal or blocks to progress toward the goal, then score G−.

The scorer must distinguish between feelings accompanying goal anticipations and those associated with goal achievement.

G+ can be scored during the attempt to attain the goal − for example, "he is fascinated by what he is learning." However, affective states that accompany goal-directed behavior must go beyond mere mention of instrumental activity.

Occasionally affective statements may be inferred from an outcome that is either so vivid and complete or in which the objective concomitants of reaching or not reaching the goal are so extreme that affect may be obviously implicated. However, these types of stories will be rare.

G+ and G− can each be scored once per story.

Thema (Th)

When the resolution of conflicting cognitions, behaviors, or events or the approach to a desired but unpredictable future is elaborated to the extent that it is the central plot or leitmotif of a story, then score for thema. In other words, the entire story must be an elaboration of the behavioral sequence involved in resolution of uncertainty. If there are any major counterplots or competing motivational sources (e.g., achievement or affiliation), then thema should not be scored. Thema is really a scorer's judgment of the intensity of the motivation expressed and, if there are no competing motives, then it can be assumed to be strong and thus scored.

Score thema independently of the number of subcategories that have already been scored. Occasionally stories may be scored only for NI and Th if the wording of the behavioral sequence has not allowed other categories to be scored. Conversely, stories that have a number of subcategories scored may not necessarily be scored for thema. In such cases the imagery may have been present in the first few sentences or there may be another source of motivation present.

NUMERIC VALUES

Assign numeric values once scoring for a story is complete. Stories scored UI should receive a value of -1. Stories scored DI should receive a value of 0. Stories scored NI should receive a value of $+1$ with an additional $+1$ assigned for each subcategory present.

STIMULUS MATERIALS AND EXAMPLES

We have developed and tested this manual using sentence leads rather than pictures. Subjects are required to respond to four such sentences and have 4 minutes to write each story. The sentence leads have been chosen to provide a compromise between the amount of imagery and the stability of the measure. They are as follows:

1. Two people are working in a laboratory on a piece of equipment.
2. A person is sitting, wondering about what might happen.
3. A young person is standing: A vague operation scene is in the background.
4. An older person is talking to a younger person.

At this point it seems wise to provide some examples of stories for each lead that contain typical themes and plots.

Lead line:

Two people are working in a laboratory on a piece of equipment.

Example 1:

1. Working in lab. – with equipment two people – one older, one younger.
2. Research is being done on a new chemical, previous research has created need for further experimentation. Many animals have been helped.
3. The older man is hoping the experiment in progress will be successful, but the younger is skeptical of cure for a disease.
4. The experiment will be successful but new ideas will be produced and further experimentation done. Hope is all but what is left.

Because "the younger man is skeptical," this story can be scored as a doubtful outcome (Criterion 1). It can also be scored as an approach to a phenomenon, under Criterion 2, because the researchers are interested in the disease (see the section on special examples). The final score is NI, N, I+, Ga− = +4.

In many cases, the researchers are inventing things rather than finding cures. These two types of stories often look the same, but see the section on special examples for a discussion of the differences.

Example 2:

1. The students are experimenting in Physics in one of the labs. These are students in first year. The students are very confused about what they are doing.
2. Before this the students were reading up on the experiment and trying to learn more about the equipment and the procedure they were to use. While preforming this . . .
3. The students are thinking of how they must complete the experiment in the required time. All of them want to hurry and finish with their work.
4. The experiment will be completed successfully and they will all do well on their lab report.

There is a doubtful outcome here, but the story is too routine to score NI. This is common for "school" stories. Score UI = −1.

Lead line:

A person is sitting, wondering about what might happen.

Example 1:

1. This person – female – Brenda is thinking about a critical issue. One that concerns her future career. She finds herself debating about what she really wants out of life.
2. This has happened because she has just started her university career and has found it not to be what she expected.
3. She wants to find her personal interest and is therefore thinking about how hard she will have to study in school to achieve her goal, that is to be a nurse.
4. She will work hard and as a result get good marks and recognition. Things will work out for her even if they are not what she expected.

Score this story NI, N, I+, Bw = +4 because her university experience is incongruent with her expectations of it (Criterion 4). The amount of studying required counts as a block in the world.

Example 2:

1. The person could probably be anybody on the surface of the planet. He/she is sitting in front of a window looking out.
2. Nuclear war has always been on the minds of everybody, a lot of paranoia, etc. The brink seems to be near.
3. The thought is of what will happen, the future possibly. But the person is wondering if the war is just an excuse or an easy way out.

4. What will happen doesn't really matter because the person sitting in the chair has already made up its mind.

Having "already made up its mind" is an example of need for certainty. Score this story UI = −1.
Lead line:

A young person is standing: A vague operation scene is in the background.

Example 1:

1. A young man in mid teens is standing by the glass of an emergency room. His best friend is surrounded by a mass of doctors trying to administer first aid.
2. He and his friend were out partying, got behind the wheel of the car, car went out of control, friend seriously hurt.
3. The young man is feeling extreme guilt, he was driving and it's his friend that's fighting for his life and he is unhurt.
4. His friend will live but be paralysed from the waist down. The young man will become a crusader/public speaker at schools against drinking and driving.

Stories about guilt should be scored under Criterion 5 as long as the character attempts to resolve the discrepancy between his behavior and his idea about himself. In this story, the young man becomes a "crusader/public speaker," so score NI = +1.
Example 2:

1. The student nurse is observing her first operation. She tried to stand at the back of the group so she would not have a direct view.
2. She had been warned her first observation may have a bad effect on her. She prepared herself by not eating anything earlier that day.
3. She is thinking and wondering if this sort of job is really what she wants out of life. She doesn't know if she could stand this every day.
4. She realized what was actually being done. The doctors were possibly saving a person's life. She then realized she did want a job like that and she forgot about the gruesomeness.

Stories about making decisions usually qualify for Criterion 3. This character is trying to decide if this job is right for her (or not) and she is able to make a decision by thinking about the value of medicine. Score NI, I+, Ga−, Th = +4.
Lead line:

An older person is talking to a younger person.

Example 1:

1. The old man is my grandfather. I, the young person, am sitting by his side. He is telling stories of the war. Stories I've heard a 100 times.
2. It is Thanksgiving. The family has all gathered together. A good dinner. but my grandfather cannot find peace. He sits me down and begins his tales.

3. I know he has memories, bad memories of the war. He doesn't tell me everything that happened. But I can see it all in his eyes. Somehow I think he wants to get back to those days. Even with all the pain.
4. Dinner is over, the day is done. The family will separate again. Each going their own way. My grandfather will stay there till the next holiday.

"Grandparent" stories are common for this lead and usually do not yield uncertainty imagery. There is no reference to uncertainty in this story, so score it UI = −1.

Example 2:

1. The people are a teacher and a student. The student is discussing problems he's having in the course. The teacher is trying to clear matters up for him.
2. The student has failed two tests and is concerned. The teacher also concerned is trying to be of help knowing the student has greater potential.
3. The student is thinking of dropping the course and taking something he will enjoy more. The teacher however thinks the student will eventually profit by remaining in the class.
4. The student remains in the class and passes the course eventually with help from tutors.

Stories about students are usually too routine to score NI, as was the case in Example 2 of the first sentence lead. However, there is an explicit statement of affect ("The student has failed two tests and is concerned"), so score it under Criterion 1. The final score of the story should be NI, I+, Bp, Nup, Th = +5. Score for blocks in the person because of the student's past failures. These failures are also the source of the uncertainty but this is acceptable for Bp (not, however, for Bw).

SPECIAL EXAMPLES

This section of the manual contains examples of problematic stories that we have found to be especially common. Many of these stories rely on scoring conventions that are not immediately obvious from the rules delineated previously and were developed over time as a response to these same stories. When these examples do not provide sufficient guidance for the scoring of marginal responses, remember the 2-minute rule.

Lead line:

A young person is standing: A vague operation scene is in the background.

Example:

1. It is a little boy named Bill. He is watching through a dirty window as his mother is being operated on.
2. His mom was in a car accident. She was badly hurt and now Bill is watching the doctors try to save her.
3. What is being thought is that she is going to die. Bill wants her to be all right but there isn't much chance.

4. There is nothing to do but hope. She will live but need a wheel chair.

There is uncertainty here under Criterion 1. Bill wants something that has an uncertain probability of being realized. Strictly speaking, because he does nothing about it, it could be scored DI. However, there is really nothing that he could do, so, by convention, score UI. This type of story is so common that to score DI would inflate the amount of doubtful imagery in the sample.

Lead line:

Two people are working in a laboratory on a piece of equipment.

Example 1:

1. The two are scientists working with a microscope. A male and a female. They are trying to cure cancer.
2. The two graduated from University and now have come back to work on a cure. The woman's father died of cancer.
3. They are looking in a microscope. The man is thinking this is it. The woman is thinking about being famous.
4. They find what they are looking for. It is a cure. The man and woman get married and buy a big house on an island.

Score NI in this example because, although there is no doubtful outcome (Criterion 1), finding a cure implies an approach to understanding the disease phenomenon (Criterion 2). This is true as long as the emphasis is on the discovery of a cure, rather than merely its implementation.

Example 2:

1. The two are scientist working with a piece of equipment. A male and a female.
2. The world needs a cleaner form of fuel and these two are trying to invent it. They have made a machine that turns brain waves into electricity.
3. The man thinks they should test it out on the woman so they hook her up. She thinks about pizza and lights a lightbulb.
4. They will sell their invention and make lots of money.

Stories about inventors often have similar structures as those about cures but should not be approached in the same way. Inventions do not necessarily imply an interest in any phenomenon in the same way that cures do. These stories must reach some other criterion, usually a doubtful outcome, to be scored: score this story UI.

It is often difficult to decide whether a story is too routine to be scored NI. In general, if the author explicitly mentions that the characters are functioning in an official capacity, are doing it because someone asked them to, or are doing it for a school project, then score the story UI, unless there is an explicit statement of affect or involvement to the contrary. The occupation of the characters is usually the best clue. If they are professionals like doctors or professors, then it is sensible to infer that they are emotionally involved in their projects. If the characters are students, laboratory technicians, or policeman, for example, then the work that they do is likely to be done primarily by rote or on behalf of someone else.

A story that included a statement like "they decided to do their science project on photosynthesis" should be scored as routine unless there is an explicit statement of affect. Compare the following statement to the previous example: "They were interested in plants and so they decided to do their biology project on photosynthesis." This story could be scored NI because it states clearly that they were interested in the project in spite of its routine nature.

31 *Assessing adaptation to life changes in terms of psychological stances toward the environment*

ABIGAIL J. STEWART
AND JOSEPH M. HEALY, JR.

THEORETICAL BACKGROUND

The conceptual framework associated with this measure has been developed and employed in the study of several normative life changes (e.g., school change, marriage, parenthood), and two negative life changes (divorce, death of a spouse). Development of this framework grew directly out of earlier research on stressful life events. During the 1970s a number of researchers demonstrated a consistent, modest relationship between experiencing life changes (assessed in terms of the overall readjustment they required) and a variety of indicators of physical and emotional health (Holmes, 1978; Myers, Lindenthal, & Pepper, 1971; Myers, Lindenthal, Pepper, & Ostrander, 1972; Paykel, 1974; Rahe & Arthur, 1978). Several important moderators of this relationship have since been suggested (hardiness, social support, gender; see Dohrenwend, 1973; Holahan & Moos, 1985; Kessler, 1979a, 1979b; Kessler & Cleary, 1980; Kobasa, 1982; Kobasa & Puccetti, 1983; Neff, 1985; Sarason, Johnson, & Siegel, 1978; Vinokur & Selzer, 1975; Wilcox, 1981). Career and family role life structure proved an important moderator of the relationship, at least for women (Stewart & Salt, 1981). However, a number of critics of the stressful life events approach (G. W. Brown, 1974; Hurst, 1979; Kellam, 1974; D. P. Mueller, Edwards, & Yarwis, 1977; Paykel, 1979) argued that it was important to supplement that approach with detailed study both of particular events, and of the processes underlying the relationship between life change and illness.

Our shift to the study of processes of adaptation and single stressful events began with a review of the crisis and role transition literatures (summarized in Stewart, 1982, and Stewart & Healy, 1985). The review pointed to some broad consistencies in the impact of life changes. Individuals' first internal responses to significant changes were dominated by shock and confusion, a certain "numbness," and behavioral paralysis. Individuals generally felt rather helpless, childish, and needy. The descriptive portrait of individuals who successfully coped with new situations suggested a gradually increased scope for autonomous action, culminating in vigorous assertiveness and ultimately transcendence of the need for assertion in a comfortable interdependent relation to the external environment.

In order to study similarities and differences in people's internal responses to life changes, Stewart derived a system for coding verbal content that could be used to assess alternate stances toward the external environment along four dimensions: relationship to authority, relations with others, feelings, and orientation to action. The scoring system was derived to differentiate the projective stories written by college students whose behavior seemed to reflect the preoccupations associated (according to Freud and Erikson) with dependency and Receptivity, Autonomy, Assertiveness, and Integration (see Stewart, 1982, for an account of the derivation of the scoring system as well as its psychometric properties). Each behavioral stance was reflected in the themes characterizing each group's stories. Thus, the students whose behavior seemed to reflect traditionally dependent and Receptive concerns told stories in which they felt lost and confused, and incapable of action, but in which other persons met their needs and authorities took care of them. Similarly, those students whose behavior was tightly structured (as with Freud's anal character type) told stories in which characters felt hesitant or uncertain, could take only limited actions to straighten up disorderly situations, but in which others did not meet their needs, and authorities were critical of them. Students who seemed to express Assertive impulses rather directly in their behavior also did so in their stories: characters felt angry, confidently attempted actions but failed at them, exploited other people, and opposed authority figures. Finally, those students who had formed relationships that seemed to combine "love and work" told stories in which characters felt ambivalent, were committed and emotionally involved with their work, formed mutual relations with others, and could recognize the human limitations of authorities. Thus, these behaviorally different groups of students also seemed to have quite different affective postures toward the social environment. (See Table 32.2, in the manual presented in the following chapter, for a summary of the themes differentiating the four groups.)

The four postures identified in this way also seemed to reflect an underlying dimension. Thus, the dependent or Receptive stance is one in which the environment is extremely salient and powerful. It is imagined to be the source of all aid and comfort, while the individual is immobilized and overwhelmed. The individual depicted in stories takes only limited and hesitant initiative in the Autonomous stance but the environment remains a powerfully salient and withholding context. In the Assertive stance, the individual is represented as angry, confident, and risk-taking, but others are merely objects for manipulation and opposition. Only in the Integrated stance are the self and the environment depicted in some balanced relationship.

In a sense, then, the four stances define a continuum at one end of which the individual is depicted as at risk of being entirely submerged in the environment, and at the other end of which the individual is depicted as in some stable and neutral relation to the environment. At the midpoints, the individual is viewed as struggling to master the environment, first in an overly narrow, then in an overly ambitious, sense. Clearly most people experience some of the concerns of each stance most of the time. However, the overall pattern of scores may indicate the predominance of one issue over others, and over time there may be shifts in an individual's overriding concerns.

The first-year college students whose data were analyzed in this initial derivation study may actually have been individuals who had been more or less successful in their attempt to adapt to the college environment over time. It is also possible that the four groups of students were defined by individuals with different types of personalities, rather than being individuals at different points in a process of adaptation to the college environment. (Of course, both could also be true.) Therefore, a series of longitudinal studies was designed and carried out, some studies assessing the initial impact of life changes, others the process of adaptation to changed circumstances, after the change had occurred.

STUDIES OF THE INITIAL IMPACT OF LIFE CHANGES

In order to assess the *impact* of life changes, we studied individuals before and after changes; we tested schoolchildren in the year before and after a school change (for example, to junior or senior high school), and college seniors before and after they graduated (see Stewart, Sokol, Healy, & Chester, 1986; Stewart, Sokol, Healy, Chester, & Weinstock-Savoy, 1982). Our prediction was that in both instances individuals would be more preoccupied, after the change, with Receptive-dependent issues relative to the other issues, than they had been before. Thus, we expected that there would be an increase in the salience and imagined power of the external environment and a reduction in the sense of agency and control of the individual. We expected these shifts to be reflected in a changed pattern of scores, with Receptive issues dominating. On the whole, results supported this conception.

Overall, schoolchildren and graduating college seniors did show the expected shift from before to after the change. However, there were some important moderators of these effects. Sex and social class operated to magnify or minimize these effects among schoolchildren, with middle-class girls most likely, and lower-class girls least likely, to adopt the Receptive stance after school changes. It is worth noting here that the Receptive stance was adopted by individuals ranging in age from 12 to 30. Thus, the affective response described here is, as predicted, part of a recurring process, which is not tied very directly to overall personality or cognitive development, though it may enable or facilitate it.

The studies described so far focused on the immediate response to a life change and give us some sense of the emotional impact of a change. Several other studies examined instead the process of adaptation during the post-change period and will be described later. One such study (described in Stewart, 1985; Stewart & Healy, 1985) examined adults' and children's responses to parental separation and divorce. The children's interview accounts of their reactions in the immediate postseparation period (within a few months of one parent's departure from the home) confirmed the pattern of results describing the impact of changes.

The children between the ages of 6 and 12 were asked, in the course of their account of how and when they learned of the separation, what they said and did in response to the news, and how they felt about it. Most children recalled themselves as having *done* nothing. Only 15% could remember any action, and half of those were distraction activities (watched television, did homework, etc.). Similarly, half of the children remembered saying nothing. Only 11% remembered objecting, and only 1% remembered asking logistical questions. The children clearly recalled the situation as one in which they were "acted upon" rather than acting. They also recalled themselves as having strong affective responses. In contrast to the relatively large number who did not remember what they did or said (15% and 21% respectively), only 4% did not remember how they felt, and only 3% remembered themselves as feeling nothing. The vast majority of children (84%) described themselves, on open-ended inquiry, as having felt "bad" or sad, with fewer than 10% reporting any other particular affect. When children were specifically asked whether they felt seven particular emotions "a lot," "a little," or "not at all," 83% still said they felt sad, but over one-third reported each of the other negative emotions. Feeling "glad" was reported by 26% of the children; however, even the vast majority (94%) of those few children who felt glad also reported at least one negative feeling.

In summary, the children experienced the news of the parents' impending separation as externally imposed and irresistible, and themselves as helpless and full of largely negative affective responses. This picture, obtained from a very different kind of data, confirms the broad outline of the impact of life changes assessed with the Stewart coding system. It suggests that conscious subjective experience of the impact of life changes is indeed an experience of helplessness, loss, and confusion, and therefore that the Receptive-affective posture does indeed pervade individuals' sense of themselves and their situation when they experience major life changes.

STUDIES OF THE PROCESS OF ADAPTING TO CHANGED CIRCUMSTANCES

Five cross-sectional and longitudinal studies of the process of adaptation to changed circumstances have been carried out on individuals making normative life changes. These include studies of children attending school for the first time, older children adapting to a new school, college students adapting to college, and young adults adapting to marriage and parenthood. Related studies have also been reported for 10 samples of college students (D. G. Winter, McClelland, & Stewart, 1981) as well as the course of short-term psychotherapy (Sokol, 1983).

Four of the five studies of normative life changes (reported by Stewart et al., 1982; and by Stewart et al., 1986) showed straightforward effects. When individuals were first tested immediately after a change, then again one or two years later, they showed a reduction in Receptive concerns and an increase in Autonomous and Assertive concerns. The one exception was the study of new parents. Here, only those mothers who had not experienced *additional* new changes (such as the birth of *another* child) in the postchange period showed the predicted effect. Reanalysis of the marriage data, taking account of additional changes in the "postchange" period, revealed that the moderating effect of additional change held there too. Thus, the adaptive shift appeared only for those individuals who did not face new adaptive demands in the postchange period.

Further analysis of the four groups showing unambiguous change aimed at identifying which of the 16 themes (i.e., four stances for each of four dimensions) shifted in frequency when the overall affective stance shifted. These analyses suggested that the affective movement in the postchange period lies substantially in *giving up the Receptive stance* (more than adoption of the less "primitive" ones). Thus, three of the samples showed a significant reduction in a needy view of others or authorities, and three also showed a significant decrease in felt confusion and helplessness. In addition, all four showed a reduction in the sense of authority figures as critical. In contrast, there were few commonalities across the four samples in those preoccupations that increased. This may in part reflect variations in the length of time postchange that passed before the second testing. Alternatively, it may be that the crucial, common experience in the initial period of adaptation is the reduced salience and power of the environment and the increased scope for action of the individual derived from giving up the Receptive stance. Precisely how, and how quickly, the other stances are adopted and abandoned may be rather strongly affected by individual and situational differences.

For example, D. G. Winter et al. (1981) explored the relationship between individual experiences in various institutions and adaptation to college. They showed that in two out of three comparisons between first-year students and seniors at different schools (an elite liberal arts college, a state teachers college, and a community college), seniors reflected a more advanced affective posture than did first-year students. In analyses of individual experiences at the liberal arts college that correlated with adaptation, they found that involvement in collegewide extracurricular and cultural activities (but *not* in dormitory or sports activities) was a positive predictor of adaptation. They then examined differences between first-year students and seniors at seven additional schools, selected for their divergence in educational goals. Students at schools with a strong emphasis on personal development as part of their educational goals showed the greatest adaptation to college. Moreover, diversity of the student body, and having more students live on campus, were related to positive adaptation across the seven schools. For students who have adopted a Receptive stance, exposure to diversity may enable broad-based integration, *if* the student is not simply overwhelmed and paralyzed. Thus, extracurricular and cultural activities may provide individuals with opportunities for successful initiative within a relatively small arena. These experiences outside of the classroom may in turn both reflect and provide some detached perspective on the educational situation.

One situation that may be viewed as providing such an opportunity is psychotherapy. In his study of the course of eight patients' short-term psychotherapy, Sokol (1983) argued that going into psychotherapy represents movement into a new situation, relationship, and role; thus, psychotherapy represents (in part) a situation demanding adaptation. Moreover, its novelty and demands for adaptation probably rearouse preoccupation with previous situations making the same kinds of demands. (Stewart & Healy, 1984, suggest that all changes may have this effect.) Thus, Sokol proposed that psychotherapy may permit successful adaptation (in our limited sense) for individuals who have been unsuccessful in particular adaptive attempts.

CONSEQUENCES OF POST-CHANGE ADAPTATION FOR COGNITIVE PERFORMANCE

We have seen that there is often a shift in affective stance in the period following a major change. But does this shift have any important consequences that go beyond emotional adaptation to the new situation? One possibility is that adoption and retention of the Receptive stance allows for cognitive processing of more information or "data," and therefore facilitates cognitive development. In addition, perhaps the affective disequilibrium provoked by external changes stimulates new efforts at self-definition.

Perhaps other aspects of cognitive and personality development are affected by the shift – and the rate of the shift – to other, more active, or Integrated stances.

To begin to test the possibility of cognitive advances stimulated by emotional adaptation, Stewart and Healy (1985) conducted a secondary analysis of data first analyzed by D. G. Winter et al. (1981). One of the cognitive tasks they administered, the Test of Thematic Analysis, demands that the subject analyze some verbal material and impose some kind of structure on it. Three of the categories that are scored within the usual scoring procedures (see D. G. Winter & McClelland, 1978) assess the degree to which the subject engages in true restructuring of the information: redefinition, subsuming of alternatives, and analytic hierarchy. We created an "information-structuring" score by summing these three categories.

As predicted, those individuals showing a *shift* between the first year and the senior year from a Receptive toward an Integrated stance showed the greatest gains in information-structuring over the same period. Interestingly, the most important predictor of *senior* structuring was not *senior* affective stance, but *first-year* Receptivity. Thus, adoption of the Receptive stance, with its attendant hypervigilance to the environment and lack of detachment, may be a crucial precondition for the development of new structures. However, because movement away from Receptivity, after a while, facilitates cognitive growth, identification of the factors that promote progress in the stances (as opposed to permanent Receptivity) is crucial.

Perhaps new integrations or structures are facilitated or demanded by the increased information absorbed by the individual adopting the Receptive stance. Thus, perhaps in new situations old constructs cannot be maintained, or are threatened by unassimilable information (see J. Block, 1982, for a discussion of this notion). Alternatively (and also consistent with Block's argument that the disequilibrium created by unassimilable information promotes cognitive change), perhaps individuals are motivated to new cognitive structuring by their discomfort with the Receptive stance. Thus, Receptivity may serve as a prod for cognitive development at least partly because it is unpleasant for adults and even older children, in our society, to feel helpless and dependent.

Healy (1985) further explored the relationship between emotional adaptation and cognitive performance in his dissertation. He employed a cross-sectional design that included a sample of parents in the process of adapting to marital separation and a matched sample of married parents who had not experienced any recent transitions. His aim was to test the idea that cognitive problem-solving skills that depend on a balanced and differentiated emotional stance would be impaired in individuals who had recently experienced a major life change, and who, therefore, should be early in the process of emotional adaptation. Comparisons of the two samples showed that, in fact, the samples differed as expected in emotional adaptation, and that the married sample scored higher on perspective taking, structured problem solving, and isolation of variables (a standard formal operations ability). Moreover, the married adults scored significantly higher, not surprisingly, on a composite cognitive performance score created by averaging scores for the three cognitive skills noted previously, as well as the fourth skill assessed in the study, the ability to brainstorm instrumental solutions to a problem. Within the sample of recently separated parents, parents who had adopted Assertive and Integrative stances scored significantly higher on this measure than the parents who were in the Receptive and Autonomous stances. Taken together, the evidence suggests that in the initial period of emotional adaptation, cognitive skills that involve simultaneously processing and synthesizing large amounts of information are impaired but that, in the long run, the Receptive stance may facilitate the development of increased information-structuring and synthesizing capacities.

STUDIES OF NEGATIVE CHANGES

Our recent research exploring life changes has focused on two negative changes: parental separation and divorce; and bereavement.

In order to study the process of emotional adaptation to marital separation, we recruited a sample of 128 recently separated mother–custody families from public divorce court dockets in five metropolitan Boston counties. Each family had at least one child between the ages of 6 and 12 and was separated 6 months or less at the time of initial contact. They were then followed up a year later. Our analyses focused on the process of emotional adaptation in children (Healy, Eisenstein, & Stewart, 1985). In the children of these separating families we did observe significant progress in the course of emotional adaptation over the first 18 months after the separation. It is important to note that although children showed decreased psychosocial adjustment difficulties over the same period, the two types of indicators (emotional stance and psychosocial adjustment) were not correlated within time. Thus, there seem to be two parallel independent processes taking place following major life changes.

In addition, other life change experiences moderated these results. Children who had had many past life change experiences maintained the Receptive stance for a longer period of time after the separation, and then progressed further in the sequence of stances over the next year than their peers with fewer previous changes. Moreover, the process of emotional adaptation was compromised for those children who experienced additional life changes after the separation. However, the amount of time since the separation moderated this effect. Children who experienced additional life changes shortly after the separation progressed significantly over time in the stance sequence while the process of adaptation was disrupted for those children who experienced subsequent changes much later. We concluded that, contrary to commonsense conceptions of change, negative life changes can have both positive and negative effects on the course of emotional adaptation. In fact, additional life changes following marital separation do not interfere with emotional adaptation as long as they occur shortly after the separation.

Other analyses have shown that past and concurrent life change experiences also influence the process of adaptation to marital separation in mothers. Like the children, mothers who had many past life changes remained in the Receptive stance longer after the separation and then adapted more quickly over the next year than their counterparts with fewer previous life changes. Moreover, additional life changes between the initial data collection and the follow-up 1 year later interfered with emotional adaptation. As we predicted, those mothers who did not experience any additional changes progressed significantly through the stance sequence. It is partly on the basis of these findings that we predict that additional post-transition life changes should play an important role in predicting the course of emotional processes taking place, following major stressful life events.

In order to extend the theory of emotional adaptation to another negative life change and to modify the emotional adaptation coding system for use with free response material, we undertook a secondary analysis of the Parkes and Weiss bereavement study data (Parkes & Weiss, 1983). This study tracked the course of bereavement in widows and widowers recruited in the metropolitan Boston area in the late 1960s. The widows and widowers were interviewed three or four times over the course of several years following the death of their spouses.

We included 30 men and women who were interviewed at least three times following the death of their spouses, and scored psychological stance in eight sections of the interviews (because thematic apperceptive stories were not available).

Analyses showed a strong overall increase in modal stance over the period of adaptation, but most of that increase occurred after the first year (during which scores were extremely low). There were, in addition, large differences in the stance scores obtained from material on different topics in the interview. Very low scores were obtained from participants' accounts of their spouses or their own adjustment, while much higher scores were obtained from participants' discussions of their children or their social life.

In general, analyses of the negative life change data suggest that psychological stances do shift in the postchange period, as is the case for positive changes. However, initial postchange stances are more exclusively Receptive, and the Receptive stance is given up more slowly. It is important to note, though, that psychological stances are not, apparently, always global or uniform; assessments of individuals' responses in one domain should not be assumed to reflect fully their stances in all other domains.

CHARACTERISTICS OF THE MEASURE

Each of the four emotional stances can be scored across four dimensions, yielding a total of 16 possible categories for which each story can be scored. The scores for each stance are corrected (if necessary) by regression for correlations with verbal fluency, standardized, and a subject's overall index score determined by the highest overall corrected score received. See chapter 37 for a more extensive discussion of adjusting scores to take account of story length. The scoring system possesses demonstrable inter-rater reliability and can be readily self-taught. *Self-trained* raters (see Stewart, 1982, for reports on these efforts) routinely obtain correlations above .85, often above .90, with expert scoring. Individuals using the scoring system without any direct training or contact with anyone connected with the manual's development (see, e.g., Rothman & Lichter, 1982; H. Zullow, 1983) report high interrater reliabilities. In addition, internal consistency figures are quite high (ranging from a low of .53 for Integration to .80 for Autonomy; see Stewart, 1982), despite the fact that TAT-like pictures are usually chosen to "pull" for different themes (which should lower internal consistency).

It must be conceded that test–retest reliability figures for this scoring system are not as high as those reported for traditional closed-ended tests. However, they are as high as those ever reported with projective tests (see Stewart, 1982). There are a number of arguments in the literature suggesting that test–retest reliability figures for projective tests do *not* set a ceiling on their validity, because of the special nature of projective tests (see Atkinson, 1982; Fleming, 1982; D. G. Winter & Stewart, 1977b, for general discussions of this issue). Some have suggested that all "unusual" tests result in a very different "psychology of the second test" than applies to the first test. Thus, the act of taking a thematic apperceptive measure a second time is simply not the same as the act of taking such a measure for the first time; the subject is, the second time, "prepared" for this odd experience (see Kenny, 1961; G. S. Lesser, 1961; Loevinger, 1957; McClelland, Atkinson, Clark, & Lowell, 1953). A second perspective is that the "demand charac-teristics" of some (perhaps most) projective tests lead subjects to assume that the task is in part to be "creative" (explicitly part of instructions for the thematic apperceptive measure) and therefore *not* to repeat themselves. In contrast, most standardized tests explicitly instruct subjects to "average" their moods, behaviors, reactions, and so on, and report the average, and not anything unique or unusual (see Heckhausen, 1963; and D. G. Winter & Stewart, 1977b, for full discussions of this argument). Finally arguments have been made (see Atkinson, 1982; McClelland, 1980) that writing or talking about a theme tends to "drain off" the tendency to write or talk about that theme at least for a period of time. Thus, short time-spans will tend to actually *minimize* test–retest reliability for tests of this kind; in fact, internal consistency will tend to be lower than stability over relatively long periods.

All of these arguments assume that projective test data are a valid source of information about individuals' internal states, and that those data are subject to lawful and predictable effects of time. They do not assume that test–retest stability of scores sets a limit on predictive validity, because retests are assumed to be subject to special problems not pertaining to initial tests. There is every reason to believe that scoring of open-ended interview and questionnaire responses, when scored for scoring systems developed on projective tests, produce much more stable scores (see, e.g., D. G. Winter, 1980, 1991, on the relatively high stability [.70s] of motive estimates based on scoring of naturally occurring verbal behavior).

It is important to note that this measure of emotional adaptation differs from measures of psychosocial adjustment. It derives from a conceptual framework that attempts to integrate existing literature on life changes and life crises, by focusing on common features of emotional response not limited to the domain of symptomatology. Thus, the focus is on internal but not necessarily distressed states. These internal states include elements of both affect (e.g., feelings of sadness and loss associated with the Receptive stance) and cognition (e.g., a view of authority figures as benevolent). They are, then, relatively coherent perspectives on the external world that commonly characterize individuals' postchange world view. Such perspectives are most reasonably assessed in terms of open-ended response formats (see, e.g., McClelland, 1980), despite the labor-intensiveness of such measures. In contrast, measures of psychosocial adjustment focus on levels of distress, or disturbances of ordinary effective functioning. An individual adapting to the Receptive stance might experience real distress (depression, stress symptoms, etc.), but it is quite feasible for such individuals to experience no disturbance of functioning. (Thus, an individual may experience a sense of loss, without being depressed). Similarly, individuals adopting other stances (e.g., Autonomous or Assertive) might experience distress (anxiety, anger), but they need not. In fact, in most of our research there has been no connection between emotional stance and any indication of emotional distress or psychosocial adjustment (Stewart, 1986; Stewart, Copeland, & Healy, 1987).

The next chapter presents the scoring system. To facilitate learning the scoring system, practice stories and expert coding are provided in appendix I.

32 *Scoring manual for psychological stances toward the environment*

ABIGAIL J. STEWART

INTRODUCTION

This manual is designed to facilitate scoring thematic apperceptive stories, or other imaginative verbal productions for a sequence of stances toward the environment. The scoring system was empirically derived as a measure of the psychological, or fantasy, characteristics of individuals who show behavioral evidence of preoccupation with the issues associated with the Freudian oral, anal, phallic, and genital psychosexual stages. The initial effort was to determine whether behavior that is conventionally recognized as indicative of these stage issues was associated with fantasy preoccupations that were predictable from Freudian theory in normal adults.

Derivation

Behavioral criteria for classifying individuals as oral, anal, phallic, or genital were selected. An individual was required to exhibit all of the criterion behaviors for one stage, and no more than one for any other. The behaviors were all chosen to be closely related to the Freudian zonal definitions of the sources of stage-related feelings and fantasies. That is, we chose to limit ourselves to strictly defined zone-related behavior. In a few cases we were unable to be quite so stringent, but in all cases we chose behaviors that even a superficial understanding of the Freudian stages would cause to be classified under one stage rather than another.

In brief, 6 college students who were part of a much larger sample given a variety of psychological and behavioral tests were selected as scoring highest on behavioral criteria for one and only one stage (thus, a total of 24 students were selected, 6 for each of four stages). These behavioral criteria are listed in Table 32.1.

This manual was prepared with the assistance of a grant from the Spencer Foundation. The author also wishes gratefully to acknowledge the advice and assistance of David C. McClelland, JoLynn Fallick, Patricia Salt, Mark Meterko, Sharon Jenkins, Augusto Blasi, and David Winter.

Table 32.1. *Criterion groups*

"Oral" behavior
1. Report a regular (not occasional) after-dinner snack
2. Which snack is more substantial than merely a "beverage"
3. Smoke more than 1/2 hour per day (more than 1 pipe, or more than 1 cigar, or 6+ cigarettes)
4. Eat breakfast on all class days

"Anal" behavior
1. Report more than 10 rituals performed each night before going to bed, including:
2. All rituals connected with cleaning
3. Report a regular time for getting up and for going to bed

"Phallic" behavior
1. Sex or enhancement of reputation reported as the principal motivation for dating
2. High school reported frequency of dating of 2–3 times/week or more often
3. Reported "playing the field" in high school dating (i.e., no one girlfriend)

"Genital" behavior
1. Have a "steady" girlfriend, and date only her (versus having a steady girlfriend but dating others also)
2. Studying and talking reported as major activities with steady girlfriend
3. "Making love" reported as major activity with steady girlfriend

Note: Subjects were required to meet all criteria for one group, and no more than one of the criteria for another group, in order to be included in a criterion group. In fact, no subject who met all the criteria for one group also met all criteria for inclusion in any other group.

Next, the thematic apperceptive stories written by the 6 subjects representing each stage were examined in order to test Freud's view that stage-related actions (the behavioral criteria) stem from a psychological substrate (which we might be able to identify in the fantasy material). Using the McClelland–Atkinson method of empirical analysis of fantasy described by D. G. Winter (1973, Chapter 3), we derived a scoring system that captured the differences in thought or fantasy patterns among the four groups and cross-validated it on an additional sample of 26 subjects. The actual content differences among the stories seemed strongly to confirm Freud's statements as well as those of later analysts, about the subjective fantasy life of persons with a given stage-related "character." These fantasy, or subjective, differences are described briefly in Table 32.2 and are embodied in the scoring system.

Briefly, individuals at all stages seemed to be concerned, in fantasy, with four major issues: relationships with authority figures, relationships with other people, inner feelings or affective responses, and orientation to action. Behaviorally oral individuals in fantasy showed a tendency to perceive authority figures as benevolent, and other persons as sources of immediate

Table 32.2. *Categories derived from and differentiating criterion groups*

	Categories			
Content areas	Receptive stance	Autonomous stance	Assertive stance	Integrated stance
Attitude to authority	Authority is benevolent	Authority is critical, reprimanding	Opposition to authority	Limitation of authority
Feelings	Loss, despair, confusion	Anxiety about competence, indecision	Hostility, anger	Ambivalence, complexity
Orientation to action	Passivity	Clearing of disorder	Failure, in face of confident attempt	Work and planning
Relations with others	Immediate gratification	Lack of gratification	Flight and exploitation	Mutuality, sharing, differentiation

gratification of their wishes. Their feelings showed a preoccupation with the issues of loss and abandonment including both confusion and despair, and their orientation to action was entirely passive-receptive. Behaviorally anal people, on the other hand, showed a fantasy view that other people in general would *not* gratify their wishes, and that authority figures would be critical and reprimanding. In addition, their predominant expressed affect was in the area of anxiety about competence, including both anticipatory anxiety and indecisiveness. Finally, fantasy characters' actions were oriented toward clearing up disordered or chaotic situations.

Behaviorally phallic people expressed an attitude of rebellious opposition to authority, and an attitude of exploitation or flight in relationships with nonauthority figures. In general, the approach to others seemed to involve a desire to "use" others for one's own purposes or to attempt to get away from them when using them was impossible. Finally, behaviorally genital people showed, in fantasy, a sense of the limited power of authorities, as well as an orientation to other people involving differentiation of others as clear external others, and a desire for sharing and mutuality in relations with others. In addition, they showed a tendency in the expression of feelings to express clearly ambivalent or apparently contradictory feelings, without any sense of tension about this ambivalence, and an orientation to actions indicating an emotional involvement in, or commitment to, work. The nature of the scoring system derived in this way was quite surprising in the extent to which it supported Freud's account of how people think and feel who are known to be oriented toward (or fixated at) various stages by actions he said were typical of that stage. The scoring scheme in Table 32.2 turns out to be almost a detailed description of Freud's or Erikson's "character types," although it was derived from actual significant differences in fantasies of individuals showing behavioral signs of stage preoccupation, not from theory.

Studying the psychological impact of transitions

Although some validational evidence for Freud's notions of stage pre-occupations in a sample of normal adults was of real interest, the long-range purpose of the development of the scoring system was for use in testing a theory of the psychological impact of transitions, especially transitions that involve major changes in an individual's personal environment. The theory takes the Freudian theory of psychosexual development as a starting point for the study of the adaptation of older children, adolescents, and adults to transitions. More specifically, it proposes that in later life new experiences and situations may lead individuals to reexperience the issues they first experienced as infants – issues of oral dependency, anal autonomy, and so forth – at a "higher level."

Thus, the human being may negotiate the issues of receiving and getting, taking and giving, and so forth, on one plane as an infant, and may be required by events of life to renegotiate these issues repeatedly at different levels throughout life. To be more precise, the initial experience that throws us all into the first negotiation of the stages, birth, can be operationally defined as the sudden and enormous increase in stimuli to be mastered, an onslaught of sensation or experience to be assimilated, in short, a "blooming, buzzing, confusion." It is possible, then, that later similarly radical increases in new stimuli to be mastered will force the individual into re-peated preoccupation, possibly on a different plane, with the issues of these stages again. Experiences that commonly may precipitate these renegotia-tions of the stage-related issues may be changes in schools, moves, marriage, new jobs, retirement, and so forth. Individuals no doubt differ in the number and kind of experiences like these that occur in their lives. In all of them, however, they must reorient their emotional relationship to the external environment, an external environment that has dramatically altered.

Because this scoring system does not assess literal zonal preoccupations (i.e., concerns with the mouth, genitals, etc.), we have attached descriptive labels to the fantasy clusters that seem better to describe the content of the fantasy than the strictly Freudian labels would. Moreover, although this scoring system may be seen as part of some validational evidence in favor of Freudian theory, the larger research effort involves the test of a theory that calls the Freudian notions of "character," fixation, and regression into question, at least in terms of their utility in the examination of normal personality. Our theory also in no way presupposes that the issues experi-enced by adults in adapting to transitions are directly tied to psychosexual zones; indeed, we take no position on the primacy of biological zones versus a natural sequence of psychological issues generated by the increasing competence of the child coupled with increased demands by the environment. The category clusters that differentiated the four zone-based criterion groups may be summed up as reflecting a preoccupation with *Receiving* (taking in, getting, incorporating), with *Autonomy* (holding on, maintaining, hanging on), with *Assertion* (expanding, reaching out, intruding), and with *Interaction* (relating, committing, connecting). The scoring system that follows, then, was derived from zonally defined behavioral clusters in the service of providing a measure of successive psychological stances toward the environment especially likely to be adopted by individuals undergoing major transitions.

Organization of the scoring manual

In Part I, the definitions of each category, organized by content area, are presented, and a sample protocol is used to illustrate the scoring procedure. In Part II, examples of correct scoring for each category are presented.

I. CATEGORY DEFINITIONS AND SAMPLE SCORED PROTOCOL

The scoring system presented here is organized around four separate issues or areas of content: Relationship to authority, Relationship to other people, Feelings, and Orientation to action. Within each content area, a story can be scored as reflecting a Receptive, Autonomous, Assertive, or Integrated stance toward the environment. A single story can be scored for more than one stance within a single content area (e.g., Autonomous and Assertive categories in Relationship to authority). In any particular story, usually only some categories (and even no category) may be scorable. Thus, the overall system contains 16 discrete scoring categories; none is mutually exclusive. The same phrase cannot be scored for more than 1 category; however, different parts of the same phrase can. For example, "Atlantic Ocean" can be scored for Differentiation ("Atlantic") and for Passivity ("Ocean"). A phrase that has been scored for 1 category may be used, *in conjunction with another phrase*, for scoring another category (e.g., Relationship to authority categories, which often require reference to several different phrases).

If a particular category is scored, it receives the score of $+1$; otherwise it is scored 0. Thus, each story receives a score of from 0 to 4 for each of the four stances toward the environment. The total scores for an individual are simply the four sums of scores across all stories. These are called the "raw" receptive, autonomous, assertive, and integrated scores. In addition, a single overall scale score can be computed by weighing each "Receptive" score 1, each "Autonomous" score 2, each "Assertive" score 3, and each "Integrated" score 4; then dividing the total of weighted scores by the unweighted total (sum of unweighted Receptive + Autonomous + Assertive + Integrated). The result is called the *Corrected Scale Score*. It will be seen that someone who is scored only for Receptive categories (however many) will have a Corrected Scale Score of 1, whereas someone who has half Receptive and half Autonomous categories will have 1.5, and so forth. Finally, an individual can be assigned to a *Modal Stage*. In this case, the individual's highest score defines that individual's modal stage. Normally this score is meaningful only when the person has written at least two scorable stories.

Relationship to authority

In applying these categories, an initial judgment of whether an authority figure or implicit authority figure (e.g., rules or laws) is present must be made. Common authority figures are bosses, parents, teachers, and leaders. If two characters seem to be of the *same* age, and to have *no* role-defined authority relationship, these categories are not scored. An example of a role-defined authority relationship is supervisor–worker. If two characters are children, an older child who is "admired" or appears to be assuming the role of authority can be scored as an authority here.

More than one authority figure in the same story may be scored if each would be scored in different categories. If a single figure carries out more than one action that would be scored under different categories, then all relevant categories may be scored. It is important to identify the sequence of actions by an authority and the outcome of each separate action in turn. Thus, one action may have a negative outcome, followed by another with a positive outcome. Each separate action should be examined separately. For any single story, however, each *category* can only be scored once, thus receiving a maximum score of 1.

BENEVOLENT AUTHORITY ("RECEPTIVE"). Score if authority figures (parents, teachers, counselors, bosses, leaders, etc.) implicitly or explicitly propose a course of action that is followed or carried out in the story, *and* which leads to a good outcome. (Do not score if this characterizes peer–peer interactions.) The course of action can be suggested; but Benevolent Authority is not scored if it is demanded. It can be assumed that an authority has implicitly proposed a course of action followed by a good outcome if the authority is pleased by the outcome, or if he or she has a positive response to an outcome (e.g., "His parents are elated at his graduation"). This includes situations in which authorities praise subordinates or are proud of them. It can also be assumed that the authority has been pleased by a positive outcome to an action proposed by him if the subject is pleased about the outcome.

Benevolent Authority can be scored if an authority helps, protects, or defends another character(s), so long as this help, protection, or defense is specified (involves a particular action) and so long as the help, protection, or defense does not have illegal or corrupt overtones. (Thus, "He will steal for his son" would not be scored.)

Do not score Benevolent Authority if the action is part of the minimal role definition of the authority. That is, parents consoling children, bosses talking to employees about a problem, policemen taking lost children home, and so forth, would not be scored. There must be evidence of actions or feelings beyond those required by the authority's role. However, if there *is* evidence of concern beyond role definitions, then *do* score (e.g., "The policeman bought the boy an ice cream cone").

Finally, Benevolent Authority can be scored if a character expresses positive feelings about an authority figure; for example, "He does not want to leave his parents," "He admires his boss," "The child hugs her mother," and so forth.

Occasionally stories occur in which a parent helps his or her child (who has now grown up to be an adult) in such a way that Differentiation (evidence of peer mutuality) would be scored. In such cases, where a parent–child relationship is described in peer–peer terms, do not score for Benevolent Authority. However, stories in which one child seems to act as a "benevolent authority" for a *younger* child may be scored here.

CRITICAL AUTHORITY ("AUTONOMOUS"). Score if authority figures are critical of other characters. That is, score if they reprimand, warn, threaten, punish, chastise, set straight, and so forth, *without* the positive outcome characteristic of Benevolent Authority and without any counterindication that the authority figure may be "right." If either the person being criticized, or the author of the story, indicates that the criticism is deserved, then do not score Critical Authority. Thus, while the following story involves a reprimand, it would not be scored Critical Authority because there is a clear indication that the authority is correct in reprimanding:

The teacher is reading varied abominations back to a student from the student's paper. . . . The student wrote it in one 24-hour session of coffee and Nodoz.

However, this exception applies only when there is direct evidence that the *specific* criticism of the authority is deserved. If there is evidence that the character is "bad" in a *general* way, or that some other specific criticism is deserved, then Critical Authority is scored.

Critical Authority is also scored if the authority figure shows concern (openly, or in her own mind) about the legality, morality, or "correctness" either of her own actions or the subject's actions. Here it does not matter whether this concern is justified or deserved. Thus, score for any evidence that an authority figure is concerned about the legality, morality, or "correctness" of any character's actions. If an authority causes a character to be put in jail, arrests a character, punishes someone, and so forth, it may be inferred that the authority is concerned about legality of actions. Finally, however, it is the authority herself who must have the concern about legality, and so forth, and not some other character in the story. Thus, if someone calls a police officer who escorts a delinquent home as a part of the job of the police, don't score for Critical Authority unless there is further evidence that the police officer is herself concerned, *or* that the person who called the police officer is an authority vis-à-vis the delinquent. Thus, if a boy "was caught shoplifting," but it is not clear *who* caught him, or what the concern was (legality, or property) then do not score Critical Authority. However, if an authority *on her own initiative* catches a boy shoplifting, do score unless there is evidence that the authority is simply "doing her duty" rather than genuinely concerned about the boy's behavior.

OPPOSITION TO AUTHORITY ("ASSERTIVE"). Score if the authority figure's interventions (including both suggestions and demands) are met with either the subject's outright refusal, or (without a direct response) if the subject ignores the intervention, either by not doing what the authority said or by doing what the authority said not to do. Also score if characters mock authorities, or show them disrespect or express hostility to them or about them. Group opinions or actions, which are critical or hostile vis-à-vis an authority figure, may be scored. If an individual initially opposes an authority's suggestions but ultimately capitulates, do not score Opposition. Thus, only score the outcome of the interaction with the authority, not the process.

Score Opposition to Authority if a character disobeys an abstract authority, such as a rule or a law. Thus characters who steal, break rules, murder, and so forth, should be scored here. Sometimes it is not clear whether an action involves daring and irresponsibility, but not opposition, from the character's point of view because it is not clear that an action is illegal (e.g., "he was breaking bottles down at the playground"). If it is clear that an action is illegal (murder, theft, etc.) then do score Opposition to Authority. If it is not clear, or if the action might best be seen as "mischief," then do not score here. If a character wishes or plans to remove an authority from power, directly (as by revolution) or indirectly (as by going over his head), it should be assumed that he in fact opposes it, and so Opposition to Authority should be scored. In general, all *wishes* to perform oppositional actions are scored, unless there is evidence that they are not serious wishes, or that there are equally strong positive feelings about the same authority.

Also score Opposition to Authority if an authority figure is described as being corrupt or immoral. Here the author's judgment of the authority may be taken as evidence of opposition; thus "He is trying to talk the boy into bumping someone off" would be scored for Opposition to Authority.

LIMITATION OF AUTHORITY ("INTEGRATED"). Score if an authority figure appears in the story, but is described as ambivalent, or unable or unwilling to give definitive help because it is impossible for her to do so. That is, score if there is some explicit recognition of the limitations of the power of authority. Do not score if there is any doubt about the reason for the authority's inability to help. Only score if there is a clear implication that the authority figure either does not know what to do, or cannot do anything. Do not score if there is any indication that the authority figure is indifferent or does not care. That is, score if the authority figure is *unable* to help, but not if she simply *refuses* to help.

Relationship to other persons

IMMEDIATE GRATIFICATION ("RECEPTIVE"). Score if someone in the story explicitly says that he or she "wants," "would like," or desires something *and* in the course of the story gets it, or has the want, and so forth, gratified. Wishes that occurred in the past may be scored here. The thing wanted may be anything – the arrival of a girlfriend, a job, help, and so forth. Any wish, no matter how apparently trivial, may be scored. Thus, "She wants to come inside. Her mother let her in" would be scored. However, *do not infer wants from activity*. "He is looking for a job" is not the same thing as "He wants a job"; only the latter can be scored Immediate Gratification (if he gets a job). Do not score if the story does not make clear what is in fact wanted, or whether in the end it is received or attained. However, if the character is very likely to get what he or she wants, then do score. Only score if it can be safely assumed that the person does get what he or she wants, for example, "She wants to marry him; she will probably get married" or "She wants to get a Ph.D. . . . Very likely in 5 years she will have her Ph.D."

If a character expresses a wish for something not to happen, for example, "I don't want a divorce" and it does not happen, then do score for this category. For example, "I don't want you to go. . . . He decided to stay" would be scored for Immediate Gratification. Do not score, however, in cases where characters attribute wants or desires to others; for example, "I know he wants me to . . ." or "I'm sure that's what she'd want me to do." Only score if the character is expressing his or her *own* wants, desires, or wishes.

Also do not score for fantasies or daydreams (e.g., "He's dreaming of being a fighter pilot") *unless* there is evidence that the character will take action to actualize the fantasy. Casual whims or free fantasy unrelated to concrete actions should not be scored, nor should hypothetical wishes; for example, "Now they can use this whenever they want."

Score this category when synonyms for want, wish, or desire are used; for example, "is determined to," "prays for," "hopes that," "is anxious to get." For example, this category would be scored for "She is determined to graduate," and for "He is praying for a victory," and for "He hopes he'll get a job." In this connection, the word "need" is somewhat problematical. If it is clear that the word is used as a synonym for "want," then do score Immediate Gratification, However, "need" is not scored when it is interpreted as "ought to have." In that case "need" is a judgment made by the author, for example, "These students have been studying in the library all day. They need to go outside and get some exercise." "Need" is scored in instances where "want" can be inferred, for example, "The boy needs help in putting together a model. He goes to his older brother for help. The brother gladly helps him." (Because he goes to get help, "need" can be taken to mean "want.")

LACK OF GRATIFICATION ("AUTONOMOUS"). Score if someone in the story wants something (as defined for Immediate Gratification) but does *not* explicitly get it by the end of the story. That is, score if it is unclear whether the wish is satisfied, or if it is clear that the wish is *not* satisfied. If a story would be scored for Immediate Gratification except that the want is *not* satisfied, then score Lack of Gratification. Example:

John wants peace. His parents want satisfaction. They will leave. John will go out and get drunk. [There are two instances of unsatisfied wants here, but Lack of Gratification can be scored only once per story for each content area.]

FLIGHT FROM OTHER PEOPLE AND SITUATIONS ("ASSERTIVE"). Score if someone in the story wants to escape or is relieved to have escaped from the control of some person (e.g., wife, friend, etc.). Also score if there is a generalized desire to escape (e.g., "He wanted to feel real freedom"), or if a character actually does escape or feels relieved after having escaped. Mental escape (e.g., daydreaming, or looking out of a window) may be scored, as can escape from situations (e.g., defection, truancy, emigration). Suicide, or thoughts of suicide, can be scored if it is clear that the goal is escape. Escape from another person or situation can also be inferred if a subject succeeds at something in spite of dire predictions of failure from the other. Flight should also be scored if a character "pulls back from" or "shies away from" another person.

Score Flight if a two-person relationship is described or referred to in such a way that one person seems to lack interest in, or concern about, the other. This criterion is met only if there is some relationship between the two people, not if they are thrown together accidentally. Lack of concern may be indicated by characters actually harming others without any indication of remorse or regret. However, lack of concern may also be inferred from: (a) exploitative relationships of any kind, including sexual ones; (b) concern about some third party other than the dyad (e.g., "The boy will get caught with her" or "The girl is thinking of her lover when she kisses her husband"); or (c) no indications of pleasure in the other person as a person (e.g., "They will have sexual relations and then freshen up"). Extramarital affairs, if they involve flight from a spouse or an effort to get revenge on a third party, may be scored here.

DIFFERENTIATION OF PERSONS AND OBJECTS ("INTEGRATED"). Score if characters in the story are identified by a name that *includes* a last name. That is, score if a first and last name are mentioned, or if only a last name is mentioned, but not if only a first name is used. Do not score if the last name is only an initial ("Mr. S."), or an obvious fake or label ("Joe Freshman"). Unusual or famous names however – no matter how strange – are scored (e.g., "Mr. Schicklegruber" or "Franklin Roosevelt"); but common undifferentiating names such as "Jones," "Smith," or "Doe" are not (unless a differentiating first name is added; thus, "Mr. Jones" and "John Doe" would not be scored, but "Harvey Smith" or "Steve Doe" would).

Also score if a character is identified as connected with a particular company, organization, ship, club, game, and so forth, that is identified by name (e.g., "The S. S. Virginia," "McBride Realty Co."). Names of geographic entities are scored if they are specific; for example, specific *named* rivers, states, cities, countries, nationalities ("Russian"), colleges, restaurants, or locations ("42nd Street and 7th Avenue"). However, do not score the names of the place or institution where the author of the story actually is. (Thus, in stories written by students at Ivy College, "Ivy" is not scored, and in stories written by IBM employees, "IBM" is not scored. Other specific named colleges or companies in these stories would be scored.)

Differentiation is also scored if a character indicates a full recognition of another character as a total person by either: (1) Helping the other character, *if* the help is by a peer and not by an authority. In this connection, parents helping children are assumed to be authorities unless there is evidence that the relationship is really a peer–peer one. (2) Describing a two-person relationship that involves mutual activity or feelings based on such activity. Thus, "They warmed each other up" and "The couple are planning their evening's activities together" would be scored. Evidence that the people enjoy *each other* is scored, but evidence that they enjoy an external activity for its own sake, rather than for the sake of the joint enjoyment, is not scored. Thus, "They are enjoying the guitarist" or "They both love working on this kind of thing" would not be scored. Only score if the pair is clearly mutually involved with each other and derives some positive feeling from this involvement. Do not infer or assume that activity is mutual unless it is clearly stated to be so. Thus, "They are celebrating their anniversary" or "They are giving a party" are not sufficiently clear as "shared" activities to be scored. Do not score if only one of the two characters in the dyad seems to feel emotionally involved or active toward another; or if the two characters "feel" involvement (e.g., "they are deeply in love") but there is no mutual *activity*.

Feelings

LOSS, DESPAIR, CONFUSION ("RECEPTIVE"). Score if there is explicit mention of words that suggest a sense of *loss*, of *sadness*, or of *confusion* about the nature of the world.

Characters may show a sense of loss by feeling grief, loneliness and abandonment. If someone in the story has died, only score Loss if there is evidence that another character feels a sense of loss; do not score on the basis of "objective" losses.

Characters may be sad, dejected, or disappointed. Sadness may also be inferred if characters feel futility, hopelessness, despair, depression, and so forth. It may also be inferred if characters are distressed, upset, disturbed, or worried (as long as they are not worried or upset about competence or work). However, it should not be scored for simple pity or for simply "feeling bad" where the negative feeling is not specified. Suicidal thoughts or actions are scored here only if they are clearly motivated by despair or hopelessness rather than by a desire to escape.

Finally, characters may show confusion or fear about the nature of the world. Thus score if characters are shocked, scared, startled, amazed, disoriented, surprised that things are the way they are, or feel disbelief; but do not score if a character is confused about a particular issue, or shows mild, transitory surprise over a particular event. If a character "gapes" or his mouth "hangs open," it may be assumed that he is amazed or shocked.

To summarize, only feelings, or indications of feelings, that are *strong* (e.g., "shock") or *global* (e.g., "disoriented" or "mixed up") should be scored here.

INCOMPETENCE AND INDECISION ("AUTONOMOUS"). Score any concerns about competence or efficacy when there are any references to feelings of foolishness, apprehensiveness, embarrassment, or indecisiveness and hesitation in decision making. Score any of these feelings unless there is evidence that they do not indicate any concern about incompetence or indecision. If it is unclear, *do* score Indecision. Do not score here if a character shows concern about a *past* performance; score only for concerns that are felt about *present* or *future* competence to perform adequately. Also, if a character is "worried about his work," only score if it is clear that the character is concerned about his or her *competence*, rather than about some other aspect of work (in which case Work Involvement might be scored in the "Orientation to Action" content area). Finally, uncertainty (including hesitation) on the part of a character is scored unless it is uncertainty about what the future holds (e.g., "They are uncertain as to whether they will get away in the future").

In general, when characters are uncertain in choice dilemmas, score this category. Such dilemmas normally involve at least two (and sometimes more than two) alternatives. For example, if a subject is in conflict about what he or she should do and wants to do, or if he or she is conflicted about two alternative positive choices (or even if conflicted about whether to make a choice), score this category. This category may be scored even if the subject does eventually solve the dilemma, so long as there was significant discomfort with the choice situation, or concern about competence before the decision was made.

It is important to note that Confusion and Indecision are not the same. Indecision is hesitation or anxiety in the face of a choice, not general confusion about reality itself.

Consider the following examples of Incompetence and Indecision:

These are two people in a suicide pact. Both are thinking that they can hesitate long enough to see the other jump first, then climb down and walk home.
He is trying to decide between *X* and *Y*.
He is torn.

HOSTILITY ("ASSERTIVE"). Score if there are references to feelings of bitterness, hostility, hatred, or resentment on the part of a character in response to some other person's action. Included here are instances where any character (including authority figures) is jealous, angry, furious, and so forth. Also included are situations in which a character feels bitterly about some person, even if that person did not do something that directly caused the problem. It is assumed that if a character feels bitterly or blames someone, he or she *believes* that the other person caused his or her problem, whether or not that other person actually did. Do not, however, score if someone is bitter about something that the other person did to a third party. (Example: "The father is bitter that the Navy kicked his son out.") Hostility may be inferred if one person or a group of persons *ridicules* or *humiliates* another person or group. Do not assume, however, that every fight, argument, or debate involves hostility unless it is explicitly so indicated (e.g., "heated debate" or "hot-tempered argument," etc., indicate hostility).

AMBIVALENCE ("INTEGRATED"). Score if there is evidence of ambivalence in the story. This may manifest itself in two ways: (a) A character makes mistakes but the mistakes do not determine the outcome. There is, then, evidence in the story that there is no simple relationship between performance and outcome, but rather a complex relationship. Example: "He was socially inept, but the boss gave him a raise anyway because he was such a good accountant." (b) Ambivalent affect is explicitly attributed to any character in the story. In these cases, a character feels two different and contrary emotions about the same thing. Examples: "He felt sorry for the boy, but felt that for his good he should prod him." "He wanted to please, but also wanted to do the right thing." "His parents were angry, but relieved to see him." Only score Ambivalence if a single character feels two *contrary* emotions, that is, two feelings that would normally lead to different actions. Thus, "angry and afraid" is scored, whereas "frustrated and dejected" is not scored, because the latter pair of adjectives would not necessarily have different behavioral consequences. Only score if a character feels the two contrary emotions simultaneously; if the two feelings are experienced in a series of nonoverlapping but contrary emotions, do not score Ambivalence. The following example would not be scored: "She was angry, but then felt relieved." Ambivalence is not the same thing as Indecision. Ambivalence is the recognition of two different emotions or desires about the same object, whereas Indecision is the alternation between two different behavioral choices, or the avoidance of any behavioral choice. Thus, "He is torn between going to college or joining the army" is scored Indecision whereas "He is both pleased and scared about going to college" is scored Ambivalence.

Orientation to action

PASSIVITY ("RECEPTIVE"). Score for explicit mention of feelings of calm, quiet, passivity. This includes any feelings suggestive of a generally placid, inactive state (e.g., sleep, dreams, daydreams, went to bed, rest) whether positive (e.g., bliss, relief, relaxed, pleased, content, leisurely, reassured, etc.) or negative (e.g., tired, bored, exhausted, listless, apathetic, etc.). Include references to characters who are unconscious or dead, but "sick" or "dying" characters are not scored unless there is further evidence that the character will actually become passive ("he will die," "he will lose consciousness," etc.). Also, do not score active words used to describe the process of causing another person to be dead (e.g., "killed," "murdered," etc.) unless the passive *state* words are also used. Score only for feelings or "states of being," not for a style or a tone of interaction or action. Thus, "he was gentle" or "he retired from a job" would not be scored; but "he was calm" would be scored. Also do not score if a term is not clearly used to indicate passivity (e.g., "He is pleased his friend came" may indicate gladness rather than peace, so Passivity is not scored). Do not score phrases that are so vague that it is not clear whether peace is implied. Thus "live happily ever after," "satisfied," "pleased," "pleasant" should not be scored.

Only score "retirement" if it appears that retirement is intended to involve passivity.

Symbols of these feelings or states can be scored as follows: (a) Marriage can be scored if it is a state in the future in which peace and calm will be attained (e.g., "He longs for the time when they're married," but *not* "He wants to marry her" or "They're happily married"). That is, score marriage only if it is a state in the future that is apparently imagined to be calm, pleasant, and conflict-free. Do not score other kinds of references to marriage. (b) References to bodies of water – puddle, river, ocean, harbor, canal, pool, and so forth. Specific bodies of water are scored only if the appropriate water word is added – thus "Charles" is not scored, but "Charles River" is; "Seine" is not scored, but "Seine River" is; "Pacific" is not but "Pacific Ocean" is, and so forth. Do not score for other forms of water, such as rain, snow, ice, steam, and so forth. Do score references to immersion (e.g., swimming, taking a bath), but activities such as washing face or hands are not scored. Do not score uses of terms in a metaphorical way that are sometimes used to describe water or "water activity" in other contexts. Thus "he is floating along in life" or "sailing along" would not be scored, because they really describe modes of locomotion rather than passive immersion.

ACTION TAKEN TO CLEAR DISORDER ("AUTONOMOUS"). Score if characters express concern about disorder. This concern can be manifested in several different ways.

1. They attempt to remove something from their environment that disturbs them (such as illegal cargo, people, etc.), but not something of which they are afraid. Do not score simple problem-solving efforts here. Only score situations in which there is some stimulus in the environment (including people) that is disturbing, and a character acts (or plans to act) to remove that stimulus. This stimulus must be specific to the individual; thus, general efforts to "cure" or "fix" general problems (e.g., the race situation, cancer) are scored only if the character is personally *affected*, and it is clear that the concern is disorder (i.e., not safety, death, etc.). Situations in which a character attempts to fix things that are broken, or resolves to do better or to stop making mistakes, are scorable here.

2. They attempt to leave a situation that is disorderly ("escape the hustle and bustle"); however, this should not be confused with Flight. In order to be scored here, the motive for escape must clearly be *the disorder* in the situation, and not simply any negative situation or negative aspect of the situation.

3. The "personal space" of one person is invaded (e.g., intrusions, trespassing, enterings, interruptions, being shot by a gun, being murdered, being bitten by a dog, etc.). This may include situations when a person spills on himself or hurts himself – that is, in some sense invading his own

personal space unintentionally. Injections or "shots" may be scored only if they are involuntarily or inappropriately administered. Thus, a person being given a shot of "truth serum" by the enemy, or a person who is "slipped a Mickey" should be scored, but medicine or injections given to help sick people are not scored. This idea of invasion also includes the broader sense of personal space (his office, home room) and not just his body. Thus, invasions into one's home are scored here.

4. The behavior of a character is "disordered" and thereby becomes a problem to himself or to others. Here someone may overdraw his bank account, oversleep, and so forth, and the consequences of that disorder become a problem. Thus, only score if, because a character's behavior has been disordered, some new problem is created for himself or another character; *do not* score simply because a character's behavior itself might be seen as disordered. Also score if a person's behavior is bizarre or unintelligible, and *therefore* a problem. Do not score, however, if a character's behavior is a problem to someone for some reason other than unintelligibility (e.g., wife upset about husband's affair, mother upset that child ran away, etc.). Simple references to a messy room, or house, or to dirt in general are not scored unless there is some indication that as a consequence there is a problem. Likewise, concern with neatness or messiness in general is not scored. Only score if there is a particular disturbance that is being straightened out, or which a character wants to straighten out, in the story. Do not score if action is taken to *prevent* anticipated disorder rather than to clear an existing disorder.

FAILURE OF ACTION ("ASSERTIVE"). Score if a character attempts an action, with confidence, but some error (not disorder, as for example oversleeping), especially an error in judgment, leads to failure. That is, a character tries to do something, in the (implicit) expectation that he or she can do it, and then fails through some error of his or her own. It may be assumed that a character has expected to succeed at an action if it has been undertaken and there is no evidence that he or she was doubtful of his or her ability to do it. Any kind of task may be scored here; for example, a criminal who tries to escape but gets caught would be scored, as would a salesman trying to sell to a customer who refuses to buy his product in the end, or someone trying to cheer up a friend. It must be clear that the *specific* action that was "tried" did not succeed. Thus, "He tried to steal the candy, but was caught with it in his mouth a block away" would not be scored because he did successfully steal the candy; he just didn't get away with it. If he were caught "with his hand on the candy in the store," then Failure would be scored.

However, if a character is attempting a task that almost necessarily and inherently involves failure – that is, a task at which the character cannot reasonably expect to succeed – then do not score Failure. Examples of these "inherently impossible" tasks might include finding a cure for cancer, writing the great American novel, and so forth. If the character is very young (e.g., a child learning to read), appropriate criteria for whether he can "reasonably expect to succeed" should be applied. Thus, a child of 6 trying to read the newspaper, but needing help with hard words, should not be scored for Failure, and so forth. If a story describes failures that occurred in the past, these failures may be scored here as long as there is no evidence that the character doubted his ability to perform at this (past) task.

Consider the following examples of Failure:

He went to the theatre to see the popular play, but found that the tickets were for yesterday and had to go home.

A man on the brink of discovery. Just beginning to understand.... He will run aground on the same mysteries and missing facts.

WORK INVOLVEMENT ("INTEGRATED"). Score if a character is thinking about, concentrating on, planning, or mentally preparing for work. Characters may be organizing their schedules in order to get work done, thinking about a work problem, or mentally drawing themselves together for work (e.g., "calming himself down," etc.). Also score if characters are anxious or worried about a work problem, but not if they are worried about their own competence. (In that case Incompetence would be scored.) Pride in work or ability at work is scorable here. Pride can be inferred if a character is proud of his or her company's product, team's success, and so forth. Group feelings about work may also be scored. In general, score any indication *of emotional involvement in work*. Involvement may be inferred from long time commitments (e.g., "he has worked for months to . . .").

However, *do not score simple evidence of working per se*, or of doing work for some instrumental purpose (including the planning that is simply part of the task). Thus, for example, the instrumental planning of meetings, or planning the strategy for a candidate's campaign on the part of his aide, would not be scored. Evidence of involvement in work is not indicated by characters working under external compulsion, or who are "making up time" in order to go on vacation. In addition, characters who are simply working or taking a routine break from work (without an instrumental goal of working better after the break), or who have doubts about the value either of their own work or of all work, are not scored here.

A concern with work in the future may be scored here, but not simply any concern with the future. Similarly, "work" may include any kind of work – including self-assigned tasks not tied to a job (e.g., "building a dream house for the family," "making a wonderful surprise dinner") but the involvement must be in an activity that is clearly a work activity and not simply any activity. Thus, "He wants to play a great game of tennis" would not be scored unless the character were a professional tennis player or was competing in a tennis competition.

If children are working on a task, then the scorer should think of a comparable situation in which adults are doing a task. If the adult situation would be scored for Work Involvement, then the children situation should be scored. Thus children who are "concentrating" or "proud" of their work (projects, etc.) are scored.

Example of a scored protocol

An individual thematic apperceptive protocol of four stories follows. A description of the picture about which the story was written is provided for each story. Within the story the italicized words or phrases are the basis for the scoring decisions that are indicated after each story. At the end of the protocol, the various kinds of summary scores for this protocol are illustrated and explained.

STORY FOR PICTURE I

The civilian seems to be asking information, with which the captain of the ship in the background is providing him. The civilian is not connected in any official way with the ship or the captain, but is just curious about something.

The ship has just docked, as the captain came down the plank he was asked a question by the civilian which he (the captain) is now attempting to answer.

The question probably concerned the ship and its operation. *The civilian wants the answer to his question. The captain seems to be answering* the question.

SCORING.   No Immediate Gratification for the civilian's request for information because "want" cannot be inferred from action.

Benevolent Authority is not scored in the first paragraph because the captain is not clearly an authority vis-à-vis the civilian, because the captain does not propose a course of action, because the captain is simply "doing his job," and because the civilian does not show positive feeling toward him.

Immediate Gratification is scored for the italicized wish and meeting of wish.

STORY FOR PICTURE 2

The young fellow is reading that newspaper. He seems rather *tired*, or perhaps even *despondent*. This is because *he has just been reprimanded by his parents* for being lazy. (Just look at that room. . . .)

He is *unhappy* because he and his parents have quarreled. *He would like to be reconciled* with them.

SCORING.   Passivity is scored for "tired."

Loss is scored for "despondent . . . unhappy."

Critical Authority is scored for "reprimanded" by parents even though the author indicates that something is wrong with the room, because "being lazy" may not be the cause of the state of the room.

Lack of Gratification is scored because the fellow "would like to be reconciled" but apparently is not.

STORY FOR PICTURE 3

A college senior is in love with a college junior. They are oppressed by the impracticality of marriage, for he is a scholarship student who will enter medical school in the fall. They have gone to the top of the building to get a *sense of freedom from worldly necessity*. They have frequently discussed the situation, and have made the rational decision that they must wait. *They each want each other*. The boy will remain steadfast. The girl will graduate, become exasperated with the apparent callousness of the boy, and will marry someone else.

SCORING.   Flight is scored for "sense of freedom."

Lack of Gratification is scored for "they each want each other." Differentiation is not scored because *mutual action* is not clearly involved.

"Exasperated" is not scored for Hostility because it is not clearly a *hostile* feeling.

Immediate Gratification is not scored for the girl's marriage because she does not see marriage as a placid future goal state, but rather takes action.

STORY FOR PICTURE 4

In the *Insurance Corporation of America*. *Al Peters* has been an employee for some forty years. Al *wants to retire* now with his wife and has a good pension plus a good bank account. When Al *retired*, the company missed him.

SCORING.   Differentiation is scored for Al's last name and the name of the company.

Immediate Gratification for Al's wish to retire followed by his actual retirement.

Passivity is scored for Al's state of being retired.

RAW SCORES

Receptive	5 times	scored @ +1 each = 5
Autonomous	3 times	scored @ +1 each = 3
Assertive	1 time	scored @ +1 each = 1
Integrated	1 time	scored @ +1 each = 1

MODAL STAGE.   "Receptive" has the highest total of any of the four stances. It is also possible to calculate the modal stance for each "issue." Thus, this individual is modally "Receptive" with respect to action, but "Autonomous" in relationship with authority.

CORRECTED SCALE SCORE

Receptive Component	5 times scored @ × 1 = 5
Autonomous Component	3 times scored @ × 2 = 6
Assertive Component	1 time scored @ × 3 = 3
Integrated Component	1 time scored @ × 4 = 4

Sum of Components

Corrected Scale Score   =   Sum of components divided by total
                                          number of categories scored

Corrected Scale Score   =   18/10 = 1.80

From the Corrected Scale Score, we would conclude that this individual was nearly Autonomous but toward the Receptive side of the stance marker.

II. EXAMPLES OF SCORING

Relationship to authority

BENEVOLENT AUTHORITY. The following stories are scored for Benevolent Authority:

1. The woman is speaking with the daughter of a friend. She listens to the girl who is sad and cannot speak with her own mother about what bothers her. The woman is very sympathetic and understanding. She wants to help the girl and is trying to figure out a diplomatic way to point out the girl's problems to her mother.
2. Ann was very sad because her father had just scolded her for fidgeting all through dinner [scored for Critical Authority]. She went to sit alone in the parlor. Just then her mother came in, kneeled beside the chair and in soothing tones reassured her daughter not to be upset because that's the way fathers are. Ann at first wasn't sure but then embraced her mother, smothering her with kisses. [Scored because of Ann showing affection to authority; the mother's reassurance is role-defined and is not therefore scorable.]
3. The younger girl is being comforted by her older sister. Her older sister is feeling concerned and is trying to help her get to the bottom of how she is feeling.

The following stories are *not* scored for Benevolent Authority:

1. Tommy is disappointed because he didn't make the little league team. His mother sits beside him patient and loving. She knows he feels worthless and tries to comfort him. She tries to give him strength which he finds difficult to accept. [She is performing a role-defined behavior in comforting him; also, there is no evidence that he follows her advice or feels warmly toward her.]
2. A businessman is making arrangements to take an overseas cruise. He is concerned about his wife, because she has a tendency to get seasick. He is feeling a little anxious and the captain's trying to put him at ease. From his facial expression I would say that the Captain is sympathetic. [There is no evidence that the Captain makes the man feel better.]
3. The picture shows a mother consoling her daughter who had a problem with school that day. The mother sympathizes with the child and will do all she can to make her feel better. [Role-defined behavior for the mother; no evidence of the outcome.]

CRITICAL AUTHORITY. The following stories are scored for Critical Authority:

1. A large smuggling ring has been operating in the New York Port Authority. A captain of one of the ships that has just docked is being questioned by a NYC detective. [Concern with legality.]

2. The mother has just beaten the child severely. The child is trying to think about what she'd done to deserve such a beating. This incident will occur in the future and the mother will end up hurting the child very badly, as is often the case in child abuse. [Punishment.]

3. "Susan, why do I have to keep telling you the same things over and over?" Susan was being scolded for playing in the mud with her nice clothes on. [Criticism.]

The following stories are *not* scored for Critical Authority:

1. The girl is performing an experiment while the teacher looks on. The professor appears to be concentrating very hard on her student. *She looks quite stern*, and it is hard to tell what she is thinking. [Although at first glance it may appear the teacher may be, or will be, critical, there is no indication that she actually is.]

2. The accountant's (Bob) work in the past few weeks has been steadily going downhill. Many careless mistakes have caused the company he is auditing several thousand dollars. The accountant's employer is disgusted and has criticized the accountant's incompetence. Bob realizes that his personal problems have been affecting his efficiency and will make a more concerted effort to concentrate solely on his job during office hours. [The criticism is just.]

OPPOSITION TO AUTHORITY. The following stories are scored for Opposition to Authority:

1. A business deal in which cocaine is being smuggled into the country is being transacted. The captain is discussing his terms of payment with an old businessman. The older man is thinking perhaps of not paying the captain. The captain is contemplating murder. [The authority is corrupt.]

2. The policeman found Albert under the railroad bridge with some members of a local club called the "Jets." He was smoking dope and drinking beer. Officer Smith let Albert off with a stiff warning. This was followed by a stern lecture from Albert's parents. The next day Albert was back with the "Jets." [Ignoring and disobeying authorities.]

3. Since the passenger on the ocean liner was displeased with captain's response to his complaints he took his grievances directly to the ship's owner. [Going over authority's head.]

The following stories are *not* scored for Opposition to Authority:

1. Mr. Grayson is advising his son to enter the business world upon completion of his college education. He is very happy in business and feels that his son will be also. Tom is not sure yet what line of work he wants to follow. He is considering several alternatives. [No sign of opposition here, only indecision.]

2. Mrs. Adams told Susan that she must be home by five o'clock to prepare dinner. While walking home from her friend's house at 4:30, Susan was the witness of a car accident. The police arrived quickly on the scene and detained Susan and a few others, inquiring about the details of the incident. Susan felt a civic duty to cooperate with the police since she was one of three witnesses. The next thing Susan

knew it was 5:30. The policeman escorted Susan home explaining to her mother why Susan (fearing her mother's reaction to her tardiness) was not home on schedule. [Extenuating circumstances: action was not deliberate opposition but the side effect of another action.]

3. The captain of the ship responsible for its entirety must face the task of telling one of its owners (now a passenger) that departure will be delayed due to weather conditions. The owner has a very important engagement and is in quite a hurry. The owner wants to depart on schedule and demands the captain's compliance. The argument arises when the captain tells the owner that it would be taking a great risk to travel in such conditions. He insists on the importance of the delay by saying that he was hired to run the ship as he alone sees fit. The conflict continues; finally, the captain sees no other alternative but to obey the owner's wishes. [*Not* corrupt or immoral, *and* the captain gives in in the end.]

LIMITATION OF AUTHORITY. The following stories are scored for Limitation of Authority:

1. The young woman confides in her mother to get advice about a certain problem. The girl is grateful she can unburden herself to her mother. The older woman is glad to have been confided in, but can't quite deal with the problem, as is indicated by her rigid posture.

2. The policeman is bringing the boy to his home after he caught him in some type of trouble. The boy will probably be involved in more mischief in the future. The mother is powerless to bring a halt to his mischief, which leads to enormous family difficulties.

3. The judge would like to make an exception for the man on trial but the law is the law and he lacks the authority to override the commonwealth's statutes.

The following stories are *not* scored for Limitation of Authority:

1. The student is totally confused by the material which will be covered in the final exam. In the past, this boy has been apathetic towards his schoolwork and disruptive in class. Two weeks before the exam he realizes that he must buckle down if he wants to pass. He asks the teacher for extra help, but to no avail. He turns the student away, saying that he should have thought of this earlier – now he will have to pay the consequences for his behavior. [The authority refuses to help; it is apparently in his power to do so, though.]

2. The boy is afraid to ask the professor to help him. He knows how many other things the teacher has to do. [There is no inherent limitation here, only the boy's belief.]

3. The girl's father stood there and said, "I could help you out of this ridiculous situation, but it would be wrong. The ball's in your court. . . ." [The father is refusing to help, not expressing a sense of limitation.]

Relationship to other persons

IMMEDIATE GRATIFICATION. The following stories are scored for Immediate Gratification:

1. This couple looked for a place where they could be alone and talk. The woman has a serious problem which is troubling her. She wants companionship and under-

standing. Her friend will sit and talk with her. The problem will be resolved because her friend deeply cares for her and will give her thoughtful advice.

2. This is Julia and Don. They've just started to school (college). They are at a party. Don would like to get to know Julia better, but he's sort of shy. Julia is an outgoing person, always smiling. Don came over to talk to her but he doesn't really know what to say because he's nervous and he wants to make a good impression because he likes her and also he wants and needs a friend. Don's home is far away in Detroit. Julia is from Atlanta (city where the school is located). They'll work it out. [Scored because the specific "wants" – "would like to know Julia," "wants to make a good impression," "wants a friend" – all seem to be generally satisfied in the final "They'll work it out."]

The following stories are *not* scored for Immediate Gratification:

1. Professor McNulty is leaving for his sabbatical at the end of the school semester. At this small party his colleagues are wishing him a good year. [The "wish" is not meant in the sense of a "desire" and is therefore not scored.]

2. Two women scientists are working on an experiment. They are feeling and thinking whether or not the results of the experiment will be what they hope, expect or want to see. [It is not clearly stated what precisely is wanted. Do not be tempted to score what you infer.]

3. Sam Bishop decided that for every man some sorrows must exist; he was still in good spirits, he would deal with the trouble of his mentally disturbed daughter when he needed to. [It is not clear here that "need" refers to a wish or desire, so it is not scored.]

4. They sat quietly in the romantic setting – talking and sipping their wine. Soon a Spanish guitarist waltzed over and began playing their song. Everything was like she had always dreamed it would be. The light, setting, music, mood. [Her "dream" may be a fantasy or imagining, rather than a wish, and therefore it should not be scored.]

LACK OF GRATIFICATION. The following stories are scored for Lack of Gratification:

1. They both want to retire to the ship's lounge and get a lemonade, but they ended up getting tequila sunrises instead.

2. The boat is about to depart and Sam has just remembered an important message he wishes to give to his wife. The Captain is emphatically trying to explain to him why it is too late to board the ship. He does promise however to relay the message to his wife. [It is not clear whether the message is actually received by the wife, so score Lack of Gratification.]

3. The woman asks the girl why she looks so sad. The woman wants to know the girl's problems, so that she can try to help her. The girl would explain her sorrow (problem) to the woman if she thought the woman could be trusted.

4. Judy, a student ambitious to become a dentist, works part-time and sometimes she is able to see Marvin. [Judy is "ambitious," but we do not know if she is successful.]

5. Bob and Mary have been going together since their freshman year in College. Mary was daily becoming worried as she approached her senior year and Bob had made her no promises. She was jealous of many of her friends as they all had plans of getting engaged or getting married after graduation. Surprisingly on Mary's day of graduation Bob showed up with a ring; he did not feel like the happiest of seniors though, even as he showed Mary the ring, who looked at it overjoyed. While Bob

seriously looked on knowing he was doing not what he wanted but what he thought she wanted. [Bob's action scores for *Lack* since he does something he doesn't want to do.]

The following story is *not* scored for Lack of Gratification:

1. The girl is unhappy because she can't have everything her friends have. [Do not infer a want when it is not explicitly and specifically expressed.]

FLIGHT.   The following stories are scored for Flight:

1. The mother has just scolded her daughter. After this the daughter is looking for a way to avoid speaking to her mother. She wants to be left alone. [Score for Flight, and for Lack of Gratification, because we do not know whether the girl gets her wish.]
2. The married couple can no longer tolerate living together. They plan to separate as soon as they can make new living arrangements.
3. Sam took Mary to a very "out of the way" place, figuring that neither his wife nor any of her friends would ever bump into him there.

The following stories are *not* scored for Flight:

1. Jim and Jeff, two students from Junior High, are now working in their wood shop class. The two boys like this class. It is a relaxed class unlike the more academically oriented classes in their schedules. It gives a break in their busy routines. [There is no real escape, or expressed desire for escape.]
2. Tom Grayson was on a business trip in Hawaii. He wished that his wife could have shared this trip with him, but the company sponsored executives only. One evening Tom went to a quiet bar to have a drink and relax. A beautiful Hawaiian woman approached his table and seductively asked if she may join him. He agreed though with some reservations, immediately aware of her intentions. He bought her a drink and they shared a lovely evening. [This is not scored because the encounter was not planned, because it was not designed as a flight from his wife, and because there is no clear exploitation in the story.]
3. The man on the right is the woman's boyfriend. He has just proposed at a "welcome home" party for the woman who has been away at school. The young lady responds by taking the proposal as a joke. She has been introduced to a fuller life while in college and she doesn't want to marry yet. The man is disappointed and hurt because he has waited for two years to ask her this question. He will probably lead a very lonely life. [This is not scored because, although the man is hurt, there is no *deliberate* harm involved.]

DIFFERENTIATION.   The following stories are scored for Differentiation:

1. Susan and Daniel are discussing plans for their upcoming marriage. They are sharing ideas and planning the details for the big event. [Joint activity.]
2. Alice and Stan have not seen each other in five years. They used to be high school sweethearts. They accidently met each other at the party of a mutual friend 500 miles away from their hometown. Here we see them at their reunion. They are very happy to see one another and are getting reacquainted. They are interested in finding out what has happened to each other in the last few years. They are also sharing their dreams and aspirations for the future. [Mutual activity and feeling.]
3. Karen Anderson was born in Paris, France, when her father was in the service.

Now that her father has retired she lives in Paris, Texas. [Specific name and location.]

The following stories are *not* scored for Differentiation:

1. Capt. Marvel has just come back from his trip and he is met by Mafioso Big Tony Cheese. [Joke names.]
2. These female chemists like each other but are so involved in their work they can't talk much. [No mutual activity.]
3. A man meets his friend who is now a successful businessman. By chance they met one afternoon in a restaurant. The two men begin to talk and make some sort of deal between them. [Although this is mutual activity, there is no indication of mutual concern involved, beyond what appears to be an economic plan.]
4. To them, marriage is sweet. They have been in love for quite some time. Now they have decided to tie the knot. They know not of the hardships of the married. They care not of them. They will think about them after the honeymoon. They will remember this day as the best idea they ever had or the worst mistake they ever made. But for now, they are happy. [Not scored; there is no mutual activity.]

Feelings

LOSS, DESPAIR, CONFUSION.   The following stories are scored for Loss, Despair, Confusion:

1. Mrs. Williams is shocked to see a policeman at the door with her son. Billy is very scared of the officer as well as of his mother's reaction when she finds out that he was caught shoplifting. [Score for Mrs. William's shock.]
2. Sam Evans is thousands of miles from home on a special assignment for his company. He looks longingly at the picture of his family which is sitting on his desk. He enjoys his work but regrets that it calls for frequent separation from his family. [Score for regret over separation.]
3. Little Billy gazed out his window before he went to sleep. He thought of how small he was in the huge universe. He thought about the vastness of space and the complexities of nature. He could not begin to answer the questions which he had but continued to gaze in wonderment. [Score for confusion about world.]
4. Susan decided to take a walk along the river to contemplate her life and its value. At present nothing is going Susan's way. She was laid off her job, her husband has left her, and she has just miscarried her first child. Susan has no one to turn to and feels she has nothing to live for. She is considering ending it all by casting herself into the river. [Score for despair.]

The following stories are *not* scored for Loss, Despair, Confusion:

1. Andy was anxious to get his chemistry test back, being sure that he had aced it. To his surprise he received a C rather than an A. He pledged to spend more time on his studies to insure higher grades in the future. [Do not score for this kind of surprise, only for surprise that suggests very strong feeling – such as shock – or which suggests naiveté about the workings of the world.]
2. Nothing was working out well for Joe at his job for the last month or so. The final blow came when he did not receive the promotion he felt he deserved. Joe was frustrated and here we see him deciding if he should stay with his company or look

for opportunity elsewhere. [Joe's feelings involve "frustration," which does not score here, and indecision, which would score for Indecision and not Loss.]

INCOMPETENCE AND INDECISION. The following stories are scored for Incompetence and Indecision:

1. Mary is considering several alternatives after matriculation from Boston University. She is not sure which path she wants to follow. She is a business major and there are several options available to her.

2. Scott Lawson is sitting at his drafting table taking a few moments to admire the picture of his family which is set on the corner of his desk. He loves his family very much and is proud of his successful wife and two promising children. He would love to be home with them right now. He wishes he could spend more time with them. However, he realizes that he should put many hours in at work to support them in the style he feels they deserve. [This is a conflict between what he should do and what he wants to do, so Indecision is scored.]

3. A student is performing an experiment. The look on the student's face shows her concerns of failure. [Feelings of incompetence.]

The following stories are *not* scored for Incompetence and Indecision:

1. Pamela realizes that there are several different ways of handling the recent problems she has been having with her boyfriend. Since she has been seeing Tom for close to two years she knows how to appeal to his better sense and make him "see the light." She immediately knows what plan of action to follow. [No hesitation in decision making.]

2. Saul enjoys his work very much and also loves being with his family. He would like to magically be both at home and at the office simultaneously. Realizing that this is an impossibility he makes the most of the time with his family and concentrates solely on his work while at the office. [This story indicates ambivalence, but not indecision or hesitation.]

3. Mr. Williams is wondering if all his hard work in college and in his job were worth it. [There is no hesitation or indecision here.]

HOSTILITY. The following stories are scored for Hostility:

1. Dr. Sarah Kingston, the emminent scientist, is so engrossed in her experiments that she doesn't notice much else in the lab. She didn't notice, for example the bitter calculating look in the eyes of her colleague Dr. Karen Hinsdale. Karen, however, was very aware of all of Sarah's movements. How she hated her, envied her success and fame. Somehow, someday, she would get even with her. Dr. Hinsdale just had to become familiar with Dr. Kingston's every habit and then she would strike.

2. To his dismay, Rob discovered that he flunked his French test. He turned his anger outward, blaming his failure on the teacher. He firmly believed that if she knew how to teach the course, it would be a pleasure rather than a struggle for him. He was also jealous of his friend Belinda, who received the highest mark in the class. [Both his anger and his jealousy would be grounds for scoring this story.]

3. Susan and Caroline are constantly competing with each other. Both have very negative impressions of the other. In fact, they have gone as far as to say they hate one another.

The following stories are *not* scored for Hostility:

1. Richie witnessed a young punk knock an old lady to the ground and steal her purse. Tom was outraged that someone would be so heartless. He quickly ran to the woman's aid. First, he helped the poor woman to her feet while attempting to calm her down. He than ran to call the police to describe the woman's assailant. [The outrage he feels is in response to a third-party's actions, and therefore does not score.]

2. A Naval officer is talking to a member of Congress concerning recent attacks on the military budget. Certain members of the military wanted to express their views on the matter. The officer is obviously angry and the Congressman is rather indifferent. [Anger is not specifically directed at the person addressed.]

3. Mr. Smith was furious. He had to be in England in six hours and now the ship was calmly rolling with the waves more than 500 miles from his destination. The passengers had been told that the delay was due to "engine trouble." The enraged Mr. Smith demanded to see the Captain. [It in not clear whether Mr. Smith will be enraged at the Captain; at the moment he appears to be enraged at the "engine trouble," so the story is not scored.]

AMBIVALENCE. The following stories are scored for Ambivalence:

1. These two women are research scientists trying to find a safer, more effective form of birth control. They had many difficulties while doing their experiments and also messed up the formula. As a consequence they accidentally invented the cure for the common cold. [Mistakes do not determine the outcome; instead, there is a complex relationship between performance and outcome.]

2. A new discovery is about to be made. For years two women scientists have been competing with each other for the satisfaction of making the discovery. Finally the search was over. The one scientist, with pride written over her face, shows the other the strain which she has obtained. The other appears rather happy, but her expression is also one of sorrow and envy.

3. Paul sat in his glassed-in office, gazing at the picture of his family. He was very proud of his beautiful wife and children. Suddenly Paul lifted his chair and tossed it through one of the large glass windows. Paul looked at the picture one more time and then followed the chair by diving through the broken window. Paul plunged down 18 stories. When he hit the street, he got up, dusted himself off, and went home. [Complex relationship between performance and outcome.]

The following stories are *not* scored for Ambivalence:

1. Tommy's mother was relieved to see him. Then she realized how angry she really was. [The conflicting feelings were in series, not simultaneous.]

2. Bob was frustrated and disappointed that he didn't get a home run. [The two feelings are not really in conflict, and in any case would not lead to different behavioral outcomes.]

Orientation to action

PASSIVITY. The following stories are scored for Passivity:

1. The ocean liner is called *Queen of the Isles*. ["Ocean."]
2. An older woman is facing the routine of daily life. She is bored and lacks life in her eyes. ["Bored."]

The following stories are *not* scored for Passivity:

1. The ship will sail on to its destination. [No reference to immersion.]
2. Tomorrow he is departing on a cruise to the Bahamas. [No reference to immersion.]
3. He is looking forward to the activities he has planned for his retirement. [Retirement is not presented as passive here.]
4. Sandra and Tom are getting married in June. They are very much in love and it seems likely that this is a couple who will live happily ever after. ["Happily ever after" is not scored for Passivity.]

ACTION TAKEN TO CLEAR DISORDER. The following stories are scored for Action Taken to Clear Disorder:

1. A grad student is trying to conduct a chemistry lab but feels pressured by his professor who is watching her diligently. [The personal space of the girl is invaded by the professor.]
2. After a heated argument in the restaurant, Caroline slapped Ted [invasion of personal space] for making some snide remark. On the way out she trips and stumbles into the guitar player who falls on his guitar and smashes it into pieces. [Invasion of personal space; disordered behavior leading to a problem.]
3. The boys will have a big fight over the toy and it will break during the argument. [Disordered behavior becomes a problem.]

The following stories are *not* scored for Action to Clear Disorder:

1. "Boy, this has been a rough day," Henry thought. That meeting with Bob, his supervisor, sure was a disaster. After all those extra hours on those designs for the project there were still so many problems to be worked out. He would now have to travel around the country for another round of meetings to iron out the problems. [The problems do not seem to involve disorder.]
2. The president wants to entertain some diplomats on his ship. Unfortunately, the ship is being overhauled so he is in a jam, he has already invited a couple of ambassadors. He sends out his appointments secretary to try to remedy the situation by talking with the captain of another ship. He will attempt to make some type of alternative arrangements. [He is solving problems, but not clearing disorder.]
3. A man and woman are standing together in a crowd viewing a well-known speaker. The man, a young intelligent architect, and the woman, a shy school teacher, are absorbing the dynamic speaker to such an extent that he in his applause bumps into her. He's mumbling an apology and also notices her reticent manner. Finding her attractive, however, the young man is determined to draw her from her shell and succeeds in doing so. This is quite evident by the brilliant smile shown on her face. After 14 months the couple is happily married! [Not scored – there is no evidence that bumping is seen by her as invasion.]

FAILURE OF ACTION. The following stories are scored for Failure of Action:

1. It's March in Boston and the Charles River is still frozen. Mary Robson is sitting on a bench, catching the first rays of sun as they try to melt the ice. Along comes Jim Revere who Mary knows and doesn't particularly like. Jim sits down and

tries to warm her heart, but to no avail. His efforts fail to melt Mary's heart and the Charles is frozen for another week. [He tries, in apparent confidence, but fails.]

2. Captain O'Neill is the captain of an ocean liner who is being confronted by the owner of a large business. Mr. Dunn is trying to talk the captain into carrying some of his cargo on the next voyage. Captain O'Neill refuses to transport this cargo, asserting that his ship is not a cargo ship and he will not endanger his passengers by carrying cargo. Mr. Dunn is attempting to intimidate the captain by flaunting that he knows important people in powerful positions who could easily have Captain O'Neill removed from his position. The captain held his ground and sailed. Mr. Dunn was unsuccessful in threatening Captain O'Neill. [Dunn tried in confidence but failed.]

3. Karen is working on a research project for her chemistry class. She is very nervous. Her experiment was a failure. [Karen tried; though she was nervous, this is *not* evidence that she expected to fail; but she did.]

The following stories are *not* scored for Failure of Action:

1. The two boys are putting together a battery-operated airplane. Before this the boys looked in every store in town for a battery-operated plane but could only find this kit. [They did not fail; even if they had, it probably would not have been as a result of an error of judgment.]

2. Jack and John are extremely excited about the outcome of their project. Because of improper materials, however, their project fails. [Failure not due to error in their judgments but external factors beyond their control.]

WORK INVOLVEMENT. The following stories are scored for Work Involvement:

1. Dr. Rose Waterman and Dr. Karen Nicholson have been working diligently for five years on finding a cure for muscular sclerosis. They have just completed the last series of tests and they got a positive result. Both are overjoyed with their discovery. They have worked hard and now feel a sense of accomplishment. [Both their "joy" and their "sense of accomplishment" indicate emotional involvement in work.]

2. Kevin and Harry worked all day in their cellar. In school they learned about the prehistoric age and now they wanted to learn more. Their curiosity urged them to buy a dinosaur modeling set. Together they will build a dinosaur and see more closely what these animals looked like. [Work beyond the necessary is described, due to a great, extra interest in the work.]

3. Bill Cochran entered into the architectual business this year. He is ever ready to work late and take long trips in order to advance himself. He is very dedicated to his career. [Emotional involvement.]

The following stories are *not* scored for Work Involvement:

1. These technicians are performing some experiments and concentrating on their work. Next they will evaluate their work and write down how their experiment turned out. [Although they are concentrating, there is no indication that this concentration is internally motivated; it may be externally demanded, and therefore should not be scored for this category.]

2. The man is working at his desk. He is married and has a family. He works hard in order to provide for them. And he will continue to work diligently in order to provide a good home for them. [His work is not motivated by emotional involvement.]

3. Two fifth grade boys are working on a science project. As they work they take great care in fitting every piece together, remembering that only a good project will win the science fair. They want very much to win because their sisters are working together also and they don't want to be outdone by the girls. [Motivation is not involvement in work as such, but rather to win.]

33 *Self-definition and social definition: personal styles reflected in narrative style*

ABIGAIL J. STEWART

Most of the measures described in this book assess the content in verbal material. In contrast, the measure to be described here assesses aspects of the narrative style, under the assumption that the way in which an individual tells a story reflects a broader "personal style." Stylistic characteristics of personality have been considered a part of both normal and abnormal personality from the beginning (see, e.g., Allport, 1961; Allport & Vernon, 1933; D. Shapiro, 1965), but they have captured the interest of psychologists less consistently than have thematic or content characteristics. Perhaps one reason for this is that exploration of content-based characteristics and stylistic characteristics requires completely different strategies. A researcher seeking to establish the validity of a content-based measure is usually in a position to choose a relatively narrow domain of human activities, and assess correlates in that domain. In contrast, a researcher seeking to establish the validity of a stylistic measure generally hopes to establish that the style unifies behavior in many different domains. The research strategy must be to cast a relatively wide net, and to identify stylistic similarities underlying substantive, or domain, differences.

Self- and social definition are concepts derived from Sartre's (1946/1965) analysis of the problem of identity formation for Jews in the context of anti-Semitism, and de Beauvoir's (1949/1953) application of the same reasoning to the problem of identity formation in women in the context of constraining social definitions of women. Both Sartre and de Beauvoir point out that social definitions provided by a cultural environment can either be adopted by the individual (i.e., simply taken over as defining the self) or resisted. Both specify different forms of resistance as well. The measure of self- and social definition simply aims to assess the degree to which an individual is inclined to accept social definitions, or to attempt to create personal self-definitions; it does not aim to identify different techniques or strategies of self-definition (though this would be an interesting project), nor does it

I am grateful to Sharon Rae Jenkins for her helpful feedback on this chapter.

481

attempt to assess the different identities or self-concepts actually created. It is, then, the general stance toward social or external definitions – accepting or resisting – that is assessed. The precise behavior predictable from self-definition will, therefore, depend completely on the strength and content of cultural or subcultural norms. As the norms for a given group change, or as the norms differ for different groups, so too should the correlates of self-definition.

DEVELOPMENT OF THE MEASURE

The measure was derived by comparing the thematic apperceptive stories of female college students planning careers in the early 1970s with those planning marriage and a family without a career (a full account of this process is presented in Stewart, 1971; Stewart & Winter, 1974). It was assumed that women planning careers at that time were more likely to be "defining themselves," whereas women planning marriage and family without careers were more willing to accept the then-prevailing social definition of women. (It is important to note that we would not expect these two groups to reflect self- and social definition in the same way today.)

Using the traditional empirical method of deriving thematic scoring systems (McClelland, Atkinson, Clark, & Lowell, 1953; D. G. Winter, 1973), we identified characteristics that differentiated the stories of a small number of women drawn from each criterion group, and then cross-validated them using another sample of undergraduate women from a different college. The scoring system derived and cross-validated in this way assessed the narrative style of the story, regardless of its content.

Stories told by the "self-defining" criterion group were characterized by explicit causal statements, and by a sequence of "reasons" (or causes) resulting in effective actions or plans for action. (This sequence refers to the actual plot or temporal sequence, not necessarily the narrative sequence.) Stories told by the "socially defined" criterion group were characterized, in contrast, by causelessness (actions occurred without explanations), a sequence of actions resulting (again, temporally) in feelings or mental states, and ineffective actions. These differences seemed to result in stories that were, on the one hand, depictions of characters faced by explicable tasks, goals, or difficulties, who were capable of meaningful action (or plans for actions) to confront them, versus depictions of characters filled with thoughts and feelings, detached from actions and faced by inexplicable events, beyond meaningful personal intervention.

It should be noted that both sets of stories included references to both actions and feelings. It was the temporal sequence – ending with resolving action versus ending with feelings – and the degree of felt efficacy of the actions, that was differentiating. Comparison of stories written about the same picture may help clarify the differences.

The first story is characteristic of self-definition: Events are depicted in terms of their causes and consequences, and the main characters take instrumental actions that resolve the problem presented in the story.

There are two men standing in front of a ship. The captain of the ship is telling the business man that he cannot get a ticket because they are totally booked. The man is pleading with the captain that he must get on the ship because there is an important meeting going on and he must attend. The man is panicky because he feels he must be at the meeting. His plans were changed at the last minute. The captain finally has the other men tracked down and one is willing to share his room with the desperate man. The captain lets the man on the ship.

In this story characters have strong feelings, and difficult, upsetting things happen. However, the things that happen are presented in a relatively logical way, as if they are intelligible; and the people in the story are able to address the difficulties that arise.

In contrast, the following story, written in the socially defined style about the same picture, involves events that are unexplained (although causal words do occur) and ends without any resolution, but a "mental state" ("knew"):

The Captain is being questioned about the murder that has taken place on his ship. Charlie Chan has been put on the case because he was a passenger. Since the Captain's alibi was phoney Mr. Chan knew he was the one who murdered Dr. Who.

Stories in a socially defined style sometimes involve almost no plot at all. For example:

The fellow with the uniform appears to be the captain of the ship, and the other person in the picture would appear to be a passenger about to board ship. The captain appears to be explaining something about the trip they are about to embark on. The captain appears to be in a pleasant frame of mind. The other person, you can't see his face, so you assume he is in a happy frame of mind also. As far as what will happen next it appears that they are going on a trip. And they are anticipating it will be a pleasant one.

In this story very little happens, the outcome is unresolved, and characters are depicted as having thoughts and feelings, but not as taking actions that resolve the ambiguities in the situation.

The initial validational study (Stewart & Winter, 1974) included an assessment of the independence of this measure from other confounding, or apparently related, measures. Thus, self- versus social definition (scored on a continuum) was found to be unrelated to achievement, power, or affiliation motives, internal versus external control of reinforcement, traditional indexes of "femininity," SAT scores, age, family social class, and verbal fluency. Later studies (Chester, 1981; Grossman, 1983; Jenkins, 1982; Smits, 1980) have confirmed this general pattern of independence, although significant correlations between self-definition and other measures have been obtained in particular studies. For example, although it was unrelated to California

Psychological Inventory (CPI) Femininity in Stewart & Winter's initial study, and to Minnesota Multiphasic Personality Inventory (MMPI) scales in Grossman's (1983) sample of cancer patients, self-definition was correlated with Spence and Helmreich's (1978) scales for masculinity and androgyny in Chester's (1981) study of new mothers. Overall, there is strong evidence that the measure is distinct from other, existing measures.

Stewart and Winter's initial study also explored background and behavioral correlates of the measure. Women high in self-definition tended to have had employed mothers; self-employed, or professional, fathers; to be eldest or only children; and not to have older brothers. A number of studies of women from that and earlier cohorts have indicated that these variables were associated with high achievement, or freedom from the traditional female role (see, e.g., Almquist & Angrist, 1970; Hennig & Jardim, 1976). In terms of behavioral correlates, self-defining women reported engaging in more instrumental activities (political action, office holding), and more activities at that time counternormative for women (e.g., telephoning men, having loud arguments, swearing, majoring in the sciences or social sciences versus the humanities).

In that initial study the reported sources of pleasure, fears, and secrets of the two groups of women were explored. Overall, analyses suggested that self-defining women took pleasure in autonomy and achievement, and in intimate relationships, whereas socially defined women took pleasure in rather global aspects of the external environment (variety, nature), and the social world (friends, acceptance by others). Self-defining women reported more fears of social problems, failures in terms of their own standards of performance ("not living up to my potential"), and social isolation. In contrast, socially defined women reported fears of death and violence to them, being defined as a failure by others ("flunking out"), and the actions of others ("being left by my boyfriend").

Finally, self-defining women reported that their "secrets" were their "real" dependency and inferiority, despite their apparent competence and independence. Socially defined women's "secrets" were their hostile and other tabooed feelings (e.g., "murderous jealousy"). Overall, these differences suggested that the inner lives of these two groups of women indeed reflected different felt relationships of the self and the social environment.

PREDICTING LIFE PATTERNS IN WOMEN AND MEN

Two different longitudinal studies of women educated during the 1960s have demonstrated a link between self- and social definition in college and later career patterns. Thus, both Stewart (1975, 1980) and Jenkins (1982, 1990) have demonstrated that self-definition was associated not only with career aspirations but generally with nontraditional and successful careers over time in women drawn from this cohort. Social definition, in contrast, was associated with more felt conflict between work and family roles (see especially Jenkins, 1990), and less early pursuit of career achievement. It is important to note, though, that self-defining women were no more or less likely than socially defined women of this cohort to establish and maintain families. Jenkins (1982) also explored the value of using self-definition as a moderator variable in assessing the relative power of personality variables versus situational variables in predicting life outcomes. She found (as predicted) that personality variables predicted achievement aspirations and behavior among self-defining women (those above the median on the total self-definition score), and social support predicted the same variables among socially defined women (those below the median on the total score). This analysis suggests, then, that self-definition may not only be a valuable predictor of life patterns, but an important moderator of the relative impact of situations, and of individual personality.

In a longitudinal study of men parallel to Stewart's study of women, D. G. Winter, McClelland, and Stewart (1981) found that self-definition in college predicted later involvement in voluntary organizations, self-description as "focused" and "energetic," and dual-career marriage among men with children. Thus, men high in self-definition (like their female counterparts) seem to be inclined to engage in counternormative behavior (dual-career families, for this cohort). They also appear to lead vigorous, relatively unconflicted lives. Interestingly, self-definition among these men was also negatively correlated with blood pressure indicators, suggesting that among men self-definition might be related to stress management.

SELF-DEFINITION AND COPING ABILITY

Although the expression of self-definition in life patterns must be expected to depend on changing cultural and subcultural norms, the relationship between self-definition and coping ability may apply more broadly. There is considerable evidence that among women self-definition is related to coping capacity, or the ability to manage complex lives and difficult times in those lives. Stewart (1980) found that among women constrained by caring for small children, self-definition was associated with the creation of imaginative outlets for entrepreneurial or artistic energy. Similarly, Jenkins (1990) found that self-definition was associated with management of multiple roles, and with the assumption of organizational leadership roles among mothers. Moreover, Stewart (1978) found that self-defining women were more likely to define stressful times in their lives in terms of problems located outside themselves, framed within a broad (not merely domestic) context, but were also more likely to describe the solutions as within themselves. In turn, they were more likely than socially defined women to report having taken effective instrumental actions in an effort to cope with their problems in these times. Thus, the tendency to see the individual (self) as capable of effective action, while at the same time not taking inappropriate personal responsibility for events, seems to facilitate taking instrumental action in the face of difficulties or stressors. In related research, Stewart, Chester, Lykes, and Sloman (1981) reported a significant correlation in five samples of high school students between self-definition and a projective measure of composite locus of control that assessed the capacity to invoke both internal and external causality, rather than only one or the other.

Three studies of coping in adults included both men and women. Chester (1981) found a positive relationship between self-definition and reports of instrumental coping strategies among women in a sample of new parents, but not among men. Chester suggested that the lack of relationship among men was probably due to their overwhelming adoption of an instrumental coping strategy (80%) in handling difficulties with their young children. This difference between men and women in their modal coping strategy points up the importance of consideration of sample and situational characteristics when assessing coping strategies. It may be that in some other arena men might be found to adopt more widely varying coping strategies; alternatively, perhaps men are so strongly socialized to adopt instrumental coping strategies that subtler distinctions among these strategies must be made in studying men's coping. In this instance, for example, it might be suspected that "instrumental" strategies might not always have been the most effective ones for handling problems with young children. Perhaps some distinctions could be made between instrumental strategies that are also interpersonally responsive and those that are not.

Similarly, Smits (1980) found that among liberal arts college seniors self-definition was positively associated with an instrumental career decision-making style. However, self-definition tended to be negatively correlated with instrumental decision making for undergraduate students in "professional" schools (engineering and business). (Students in the two types of schools did not differ in level of self-definition, only in its correlates.) He argued that for students in the professional schools, "instrumentality" (active efforts to seek out independent information and perspectives) might be either unnecessary (because choice of the school really implied career choice) or even dysfunctional, because the school took significant responsibility for "placement," and the career choice was already made.

Finally, Grossman (1983) examined the degree to which self-definition might help lower emotional distress in patients with cancer, under the assumption that better coping strategies might help such patients manage their anxiety about their illness. He found that overall self-definition was associated with lower emotional distress in patients with cancer, even after controlling for sex, ego strength, socioeconomic status, site of the cancer (his sample included five sites), staging (degree of metastasis), and defensive denial. In separate analyses by cancer type (or site), he found that self-definition was associated with lower distress for all groups, except the group with lung cancer. These patients, who were also all men, actually showed the reverse pattern, with lower emotional distress associated with social definition. Because men in general did not show this reversal, Grossman concluded that coping with lung cancer – which may often include coping with a sense of partial responsibility for the illness due to smoking behavior – may indeed be enhanced by social definition, unlike coping with the other cancers.

CHANGE IN SELF-DEFINITION

Finally, there is evidence that self-definition may itself change, as a function of life experiences. D. G. Winter et al. (1981) reported that self-definition was higher among seniors than first-year students in several very different college environments, but this difference was greatest at the competitive liberal arts colleges. Interestingly, participation in varsity sports was associated with increases in self-definition for both women and men at the one college studied in depth. Although varsity sports have a reputation as imposing a powerful normative "culture" that might seem antithetical to self-definition, perhaps (at least at small liberal arts institutions that do not emphasize sports) those norms so strongly support individual effort and instrumentality that they encourage growth in self-definition.

Other evidence from this same sample suggested that participation in "sex-role transcendent" activities in college encouraged the growth of self-definition for both men and women. Thus, for women, participation in math and science and in political or academic interest clubs was associated with larger gains, whereas involvement in arts activities was associated with smaller ones. For men, participation in the humanities and voluntary service work was associated with larger gains, whereas science and traditionally male extracurricular involvements were associated with smaller gains. In an analysis across colleges, D. G. Winter et al. (1981) showed that self-definition increases were promoted by college environments that are larger and "encourage individual freedom of action" (p. 166), while increases in social definition were promoted by restrictive college environments.

Jenkins (1990) suggests that graduate education (like undergraduate) may tend to support and strengthen self-definition, as does successful, non-traditional career activity itself. Similarly, she suggests that self-defining women in routine, constraining situations may grow more socially defined over time.

CHARACTERISTICS OF THE MEASURE ITSELF

The self-definition score in all of the research reviewed here was a sum of the self-defining categories (causality and reason–action sequence) minus the socially defined categories (no causality, mental state ending, and ineffective action). This approach to creating a score assumes that self and social definition exist on a single continuum. An alternative scoring strategy would be to sum self-definition categories and social definition categories separately, and create four groups: those high in both; those low in both; and those high in one or the other.

The scoring system is relatively easy to learn, though it requires a capacity to focus on aspects of grammar and style. Scorers familiar with content-based scoring systems sometimes find the shift difficult to make. However, many scorers have learned the system from the manual alone and have attained interrater reliabilities above .85 quite readily. The classic psychometric characteristics of most scoring systems for TATs and TAT-like stories are difficult to assess, given the unique nature of the test itself, and the need to administer cues that are quite different from one another. Most factors, then, operate to produce low estimates of both over-time reliability and internal consistency reliability. Moreover, many estimates are based on samples of individuals undergoing major life transitions, and in these samples we would expect lower stability given the findings reported in chapter 31 for psychological stances toward the environment. Thus, stability estimates are low and many researchers do not report them at all (finding them relatively meaningless; see, e.g., Jenkins, 1990). However, Smits (1980) did report a test–retest reliability figure of .39 over three semesters with a sample of 500 students. Smits also reported that the internal consistency of the score, within his sample of graduating seniors, was .34, with category consistencies ranging from .00 to .47. Chester found test–retest reliabilities in her sample of new parents, tested three times over 30 months, averaged about .30. Finally, Stewart (1978) pointed out that the correlations between self-definition in college and the rated clarity of articulation of the problem described as occurring in "the most unhappy or upsetting time that you've lived through" fourteen years later, as well as the causes of the problem, could be taken as estimates of the stability of self-definition. These correlations were .64 and .73.

The next chapter presents the scoring system. To facilitate learning the scoring system, practice stories and expert coding have been provided in appendix I.

34 *Revised scoring manual for self-definition and social definition*

ABIGAIL J. STEWART

GENERAL INSTRUCTIONS

This scoring manual is designed to be used to score thematic apperception stories. It involves evaluating the presence or absence of five stylistic characteristics of stories. Two of these characteristics (Causality and Reason-Action Sequence) are scored +1; the other three (Uncaused Action, Mental State Ending, and Ineffective Actor) are scored −1 ("negative" and "positive" scores simply indicate positions along a bipolar continuum rather than evaluations). Each scoring category should be evaluated independently of each other category. Each category may be scored only once per story. Therefore, each story will receive a score ranging from −3 to +2.

In preparation for scoring a story, a scorer must make a number of judgments. These judgments involve two general issues: First, what are the essential components of the narrative? That is, the scorer must identify the story plot and separate that plot from any editorial commentary by the author that is irrelevant to the story. Typically "editorial comments" include comments on the picture used to elicit the story ("that's very dated," "that's too dark," etc.), political statements ("this is elitist"), and evaluations or judgments ("I don't like her," etc.). However, if a story is *nothing but* such editorial comment, and involves no narrative at all, then Uncaused Action (UA) is scored. Probabilistic statements that do sustain the plot (e.g., "I think she'll give in" or "probably he'll agree") should be scored as if they had been stated in definite terms. In these cases, the scoring would have been Reason–Action Sequence (RA), since the likelihood is for an action, in both cases.

Next, the scorer must identify the *temporally* last element in the story sequence. This last element will then be scored for various stylistic qualities. However, many stories written for research purposes end with a sentence fragment rather than a complete sentence (due to time limits). If the frag-

I am grateful for the help of Robert Oresick and Gerard Smits in the preparation of this revision of the scoring manual.

489

ment contains a main clause (subject and verb), it should be included as part of the story for scoring purposes (e.g., a story ending, "she left home to . . ."). If it does not contain a complete main clause ("he will . . ."), or if it ends with a main clause that is an incomplete thought ("He will see . . ."), the fragment should be ignored and the preceding full sentence should be taken as the end of the story.

SCORING CATEGORIES

Causality (Scored +1)

Causality is scored for any word(s) that explicitly indicate a causal relationship, or any expression that could properly be replaced by the phrase "in order to" or the word "because." This causal connection must be explicit and not merely implicit in the close juxtaposition of two seemingly related sentences.

Expressions frequently used in this way, which should *always* be scored, are *because, cause, effect, result, is due to, for that reason, therefore, thus.*

Expressions that are often used to express causal relations are:

by: "He gained his position in the corporation by pulling strings." (It could be rephrased, "In order to gain his position in the corporation, he pulled strings.")

stems from: "Her actions stem from feelings of inadequacy."

since: "Since he is only 17, he cannot drink in Connecticut." (Do not score where since is used in a time expression: "I have not had anything to drink since I was 17.")

means to an end: "I took him to lunch as a means to (the end of) winning his favor." (It must be possible to insert the words "to an end" without doing violence to the meaning but may involve use of means with particular end stated.)

if . . . then; unless . . . then: "He knew that if he went to college (then) he could become a wealthy man."

for: "she is feeling sad, for her husband has left her." (Do not score "for" when it is used to indicate direction, duration, or amount; do score when it is used to indicate intention or aim or could be replaced by "because").

as: "He is weeping as his dog was just run over by a car."

to: "He went into the building (in order) to find his wife." (This judgment should be cautious. Thus, "the opportunity to make it big," "the chance to go there," and "the right time to do this," are *not* scored because they are not *necessarily* causal.)

so; so that: "He is going to school so that he can become a garage mechanic."

consequently; as a consequence of: "as a consequence of their fight, they avoided one another."

through (by): "through his hard work, he achieved a great deal."
why: "Why he did this is that he needed help."

In general, score a story for this usage if it contains any expressions that can be replaced, without altering the meaning, by "because," "in order to," or "for this reason." In all cases, the goal (the thing caused) should be separate and distinct from the instrumental action or feeling. Do not score "He went to the store to shop." The two actions are not separate; that is, it is not possible to shop without going to the store. On the other hand, "He went to France to learn French" is scored, because "learning French," and "going to France" are two separate acts, *connected only by the intentionality of the actor*. One can learn French without going to France, or go to France for some other purpose. Thus, "to" is used here to express a causal, purposive connection.

The following are examples of causality:

> As they are members of an insurance company they are discussing no-fault insurance.
> They are in a happy mood because the business firm is going to have a vacation.
> Since I am in college, I prefer to look at it this way.
> Due to economic hardship, the two firms have joined together.

The following are examples of statements *not* scored for causality:

> As they both stared at the thermometer, different thoughts passed through their minds. [Here "as" has time, and not a causal, referent.]
> Two biochemists have decided to get together. [Here "to" could not be replaced by "in order to," so we conclude that it is not used to indicate a causal relationship.]
> He wants to know if the solution will boil. [Here "if" is not used as in "if . . . then," but rather could be replaced by "whether" which does not indicate causality.]

Reason–Action Sequence (RA) (Scored +1)

"Actions" occur in most stories. They may be initiated by individual or by collective "actors." We are concerned here with a particular kind of action: those actions which are consequences of feelings, thoughts, or external events; thus, they are actions given justification in terms of "reasons." In general, stories that have the following sequence, *when the narrative is ordered chronologically*, are scored: "reasons," *followed by* actions or purposeful plans for action.

Stories that have *no* actions or have *only* actions without related "reasons" (preconditions that could be viewed as causes) are scored for "Uncaused Action," while stories which have the following sequence are scored for "Mental State Ending": actions or events *followed by* feelings, thoughts, speculations.

The main criteria for whether a story should be scored for Reason–Action Sequence are whether the final element in the story is an action which (a) is phrased in active (not passive) voice and (b) uses an active main verb.

The "final element" is either the last whole sentence or the last independent clause, that is, "I arrived and told him off." "I told him off" is the last independent clause, linked to another independent clause, by a conjunction. On the other hand, in "I was sad, leaving home," "was" is the main verb, and "leaving home" is a dependent clause, not scorable. Active verbs (which are scorable) may refer to physical actions (goes, walks, consoles, etc.) or to instrumental thoughts (decides, plans, etc.). Verbs in the infinitive form (to be, to have, to go) are not scored, because they are dependent or auxiliary verbs (e.g., "I decided *to be* a dancer"; "I divorced my husband, *thinking* he *was* a rat" – the italicized verbs here are not main verbs of independent clauses and are therefore not scorable).

A few verbs are problematic; they are not always either active or passive. Here the scorer must be guided by the implicit meaning of the author of the story. Thus, *find* may refer to a chance event or realization, not an active search as in "She found she was pregnant," *or* to purposeful action, as in "She found her son, after a long search." The scorer must be guided by his or her judgment of the meaning of the verb in these cases. Other problematical verbs are *live, have* (as in "have fun," "have an affair"), *reach, get, make it, handle, proved,* and *listen.* Examples of scored and nonscored usages will be listed at the end of this section. In general, the crucial issue for all these verbs is the extent to which they describe a purposeful action under the control of the actor versus a state of being or a passive reaction.

Stories should not be scored for this category if the story ends with a speculative fantasy, rather than a purposeful plan for action. Some plans for action clearly will result in action; some in all probability will. According to this principle, orders or commands for others to take action should be scored, for example, "go to x." Similarly, answers to questions, if they imply an intention to act, for example, "Yes, I'll go dancing," may be scored here. If it is unclear whether the plan will lead, or is seriously intended to lead, to action, then do not score. Stories that end with states of being ("They lived happily ever after," "They were successful") should not be scored for this category.

Stories should not be scored for action if the actions that occur are "meaningless." This can occur when the action at the end is merely ritual or routine (eating breakfast, turning on the stereo, going to bed) or when the action is stated to be devoid of meaning or power to change the situation. That is, if an action is taken solely to satisfy a need, or out of a "need to act," but has no power to resolve the situation, do not score. For this reason, also do not score actions that are "ritual repetitions"–reliving, or redoing, past experiences, with no purpose or probable effect.

Stories that end with "instrumental thought" should be scored (as in "he attempts to clear his confusion") where it is clear some specific mental effort is being made, but not where mental effort is more meditative or less goal-directed (as in "sifting through thoughts"). Similarly, score threats of and plans for action only where it is clear that action will probably result. "Looking forward" and "expecting" may be scored if they are essentially plans, as in "she expects to leave for Madrid June 12." In seduction scenes, "plans" may be slightly less explicitly stated and still scored, as in "he watched her to see when to make his move." In this example, the character is clearly calculating the best moment to take his action, so RA should be scored.

Actions clearly predicted to be futile are not scored (e.g., "He will try, but he will fail"). Failures, however, if they are phrased as *actions*, can sometimes by scored, for example, "She runs and comes in last." If the emphasis is on the *action*, score RA (as well as Ineffective Actor – see later sections). Actions that have unintended consequences but are nonetheless carried out are also scored (e.g., "He gets what he wants, though by then it's unimportant to him" vs. "He is unable to get what he wants," which would not be scored). Equally, actions that are continuing ("He keeps trying") are scored even though they may not end within the story, as long as they are relevant and potentially resolving.

A calculated refusal to act in most cases is scored as an action. That is, a refusal to act that is intentional, purposeful, directed is in itself a form of instrumental action, and is scored (e.g., "I wanted to hold on to him, so I did not tell him how I felt"). Do not score decisions not to decide what to do (e.g., "I decided to just wait and see"). Finally, suicides are considered in the context of this scoring system to be purposeful actions, unless other-wise indicated, and are scored.

The following are examples of threats and plans for actions, which are scored:

> I'll teach him a lesson.
> He seriously considered sending him away.
> He resolved to work hard.
> He determined to go to Canada.
> He hopes to buy a car with his new found money.

(In this case, "hopes" indicates plan.)
The following are examples of threats and plans for actions, not scored:

> He is thinking of leaving home.
> He imagined what it would be like to go away.

The following are examples of simple scorable actions:

> He resigns.
> She storms out of the room angrily.

(When an action and an emotion are simultaneous, the action is still scored; it merely indicates the person's feeling *while* acting, which is not the same as the person's feelings *after* acting.)

> He went to Paris for the year.
> He divorced his wife.

Some examples of problematical verbs follow:

> He arrives at the office and *finds* a mistake has been made.
> He arrives home and *finds* his wife with another man.
> He *finds* his son in the garage.

(In the first case, it is not clear that the man makes any effort; rather, it appears that he "is told," which is passive voice; thus, not scored. In the second case, it is by *chance*, not effort, that he finds his wife, so not scored. In the last case, purposeful action is clearly being taken, so it is scored.)

> He *lives* a fulfilling life.
> She *lives* through it.

(In both cases, though the verb is in "active voice" the implication is not really of action, but of survival or a state of being, so not scored.)

> He *has* a good time at the party.
> They *have* an affair.
> He *has* a hernia.
> He *has* a great success.

(The verb "to have" often connotes implicit ownership, which is really a special case of a state of being, of being the owner [as in the hernia, the success], so they are not scored. To "have" a good time and to "have" an affair do not suggest *explicitly* purposeful action, so they are not scored. To *decide* to have an affair is scored, because the operative verb is "decide," which is instrumental thought or action.)

> He *has* the doctor examine him.
> He *has* to go to the hospital.

(In the first case, it is suggested that he "allows" or "permits" or "asks" the doctor to examine him, which is scored RA. In the second, the suggestion is that he is under some compulsion, external or internal – that is, that the action is not deliberately chosen, so it is not scored.)

> He *listens* for evidence of pathology in the patient's story.
> They *listen* to the speaker.

(In the first case, deliberate instrumental attention is being paid; here listening is instrumental action. In the second case, no such indication is made, and we assume that they are passively receiving the stimulus of the speech, so RA is not scored.)

Uncaused Action (UA) (Scored −1)

There are a number of ways in which this category may be scored. They are as follows:

1. The story is the mere description of a "scene," a setting of a stage, on which nothing happens. The occurrence of any discrete temporal shift in the story would preclude scoring UA. The change may involve a shift from the past to the present or a shift from the present to the future, or both. This way of scoring UA is reserved *only* for cases in which there is absolutely no plot movement (temporal shift).

Stories that include references to past actions or states can still be scored UA. This is true wherever there is a blurring of time boundaries so that there is no clear separation of past and present. There is, then, no discrete shift of events. Such "blurring" is often (though not always) conveyed by the use of the present-perfect tense ("He has learned," "She has trained her son"). It is also sometimes conveyed by a description of generic actions that transcend time boundaries ("She shows love," "He gives him room to grow," etc.).

Cues useful in determining whether a temporal shift has occurred:

(a) "He has been working for hours. He is exhausted." Do not score UA as it is reasonable to assume that the exhaustion has followed, or is a logical consequence of, the hours of work.

(b) "He has been working for hours. He is sharpening his pencil." Here, UA would be scored as the sharpening of a pencil does not follow as a logical or necessary consequence of working for hours.

(c) Stories with no apparent temporal movement, which contain an "If . . . , then . . ." sequence ("If all goes well, she'll win"; "If things go on this way, she'll leave"; etc.) are sometimes problematic. If the specified "if" condition is likely to occur, then UA should not be scored. However, if the "if" condition is *unlikely* or if it is unclear what the probability is, then score UA.

(d) Words such as "now" or "presently" often indicate a temporal shift, as in, "He has traveled throughout the world. Now he lives in France."

(e) Temporal change is indicated by such phrases as, "This is the meeting *after* yesterday's session," or "The political rhetoric *continues* to irritate him."

Temporal shifts may occur in stories that are scored UA, for the reasons given in paragraphs 2 through 6.

2. Score UA if actions or events "occur," but there is no way to account for them. Do not score here for "compulsions," but rather if all action in the story is unaccounted for. Thus, sometimes stories recount a series of actions but these actions cannot be accounted for or explained within the terms of the story.

Also score UA if the action that does occur is not "active" – if it rep-

resents an unwilled, unplanned "event," not caused by the actor intentionally. Examples of these kinds of actions are "seizures," "sneezes," and
so forth.

3. Score UA if the last temporal element is "irrational," given the context
of the story, or if it is an action or event which is a highly unlikely occurrence. ("The bag he picked up at the supermarket had a million dollars in
it.")

4. Score UA if the story is *all* editorial comment or political rhetoric.

5. Score UA if the story presents *only* an account of "consciousness" –
the thoughts or feelings or dream of one or more characters, who do not act
in any significant way (thus, "he turned his head" is not an important
action).

6. Score UA if the story is all dialogue in which no action occurs or is
planned at all. If the only action that occurs is expressive (e.g., "smiles,"
"laughs," "hugs"), also score UA (and Mental State Ending if it is the last
temporal element).

The following are examples of uncaused action:

> After three years of marriage the young couple is back at the place where they
> met. She remembers how it was three years ago, and so does he, but their thoughts
> are different. She remembers how romantic it all was, and he remembers the
> thoughts that had gone through his mind about the sweet young girl.

> All night and all day the girl and her brother had waited at the train station for the
> night train. They think of how they should never have let their brother go alone into
> the city to find a job. But they needed the money. But he had promised to be home
> yesterday, and trains came and went and he was nowhere to be seen." [All thinking
> – past actions simply elaborate present description.]

> He went to a night club and took with him all the ribbons his father had won for
> his cattle. He handed the ribbons to the topless dancers. [Scored because no reasons
> are given for his actions; he simply "does" them.]

> Joyce and Bill will stop seeing each other for a year. Eventually, they will resume
> their relationship. [No reasons are given for either action.]

> We ran and ran seemingly for miles through the grass. We finally stopped, and
> Romero seduced me. I suddenly remembered to go meet my husband. [No reasons
> are given for the running, or for the "suddenly remembering."]

Mental State Ending (MSE) (Scored −1)

When the sequence of the story is arranged chronologically, Mental State
Ending is scored if the story *ends* with the feelings or thoughts of a character, and not with action or purposeful plan for action. Stories are also scored
that end in "states of being" rather than acts ("they were happy," "they
were successful," "they lived happily ever after"), as long as these states
are phrased either in the personal form ("they were successful") or refer
to emotions ("it was a sad time"). Also scored are actions which are
noninstrumental but are rather "expressive," that is, merely serve to

demonstrate feelings – for example, "they applauded," "he hugged her." Sometimes expressive statements are made in an impersonal form, for example, "it was a happy day," "the atmosphere was supportive." Do score these instances MSE, because it must be assumed that the relevant "feeling states" are experienced by people. Do not score if impersonal statements do not *clearly* refer to emotional experience; thus, "the atmosphere was sticky" would *not* be scored because it is not clear whether this refers to the physical or the emotional/interpersonal environment. Stories in which the verb in the final element is *grow* should be scored, as "growing" is essentially a "being" state, rather than an intentional action.

If a sentence involves a main and dependent clause, one of which expresses action and the other a simultaneous feeling, do not score MSE even if the mental state is described in the main clause, (e.g., "they are scared, as they rob the bank"). Thus, where action and feeling are described as simultaneous do not score MSE unless the feeling is expressed in a final unmodified independent clause (e.g., "they rob the bank and are scared").

Examples of scoring for mental state ending follow:

Johnny's father had died. His mother is trying to distract him. Thus, staring blindly at a book, both try to concentrate. [The story ends with instrumental thought – concentration – thought that is in the service of the end of taking the boy's mind off his father's death. Seriously instrumental thought should *not* be scored as mental states, but rather as actions.]

Bill and Mary have had a fight. Mary does not understand why Bill is leaving for another girl. She can't bring herself to ask him. Mary cries to herself. Bill, on the other hand, lazily sits down and tries to figure out how to get out of the room. [It is unclear, and indeed at best improbable, that Bill's thoughts are instrumental, or will lead to action. We are left with Mary crying and Bill thinking, so do score Mental State Ending.]

I went to meet my lover, then ran back to the plaza where I was supposed to meet my husband. Drunk with exhaustion I collapsed in front of a majestic building. I was too tired to move, but was worried m,y husband would soon arrive. [The final scorable element – main verb – is "was worried," a mental state.]

Ineffective Actor (IA) (Scored −1)

There are two general categories which make it possible to score for Ineffective Actor: the futility of acting, and impersonality.

FUTILITY OF ACTING, OR INABILITY TO ACT ON WISHES. The overall guiding principle for this section of Ineffective Actor is any indication that the action that occurs should not properly be viewed as intended, instrumental, resolving action. Score a story if there is the prediction that whatever actions will or do take place will make no difference, have no effect. This can take many forms:

(a) the prediction by the author or a character that the action will have no effect;

(b) the expression by the author or a character of a belief that all action is merely a "playing out of roles" – that there is no "genuine" behavior occurring; or that the characters are "false" or faking their feelings;

(c) an assertion that the action is meaningless or the situation hopeless;

(d) an assertion of the inability or reluctance or fear of acting (this occurs when the desire for action is expressed, but the character then rejects the possibility of action);

(e) an assertion that the character is trapped and *unable* to act – that he or she is forced into some position, and there is no possibility of escape;

(f) the situation at the end of the story is unchanged. The end point is merely an "end point" and not a resolution; this occurs when the story ends before a resolving action has been taken, or where a potentially resolving action occurs but has no effect. The final situation is one of irresolution and a sense that the characters are at least to some extent in limbo. ("They are on the brink of finding the answer to their question.");

(g) the ability to act in the story is determined by external events. That is, score where an action is taken (or prevented) that is caused only by the occurrence of the external event. ("Then the Depression came and all the banks closed, so the banker sold apples.");

(h) falls, diseases, accidents, or chance events control the final outcome of the story, not instrumental actions of characters ("She fell, so the show folded."). (Do not score if a chance event is mentioned and/or sets the scene for the story but does *not* control the *final outcome*. The final outcome is not necessarily the final scorable element. It refers to the final state arrived at by one or more of the main characters in the story.);

(i) cycles of non-resolving actions, without the possibility of resolution. (That is, if effort will be made "over and over" or "again and again" but may ultimately be fruitful, the category is not scored. It is scored only if there is no expectation of resolution.);

(j) all action or resolving action is in the form of fulfillment of ritual or routine. That is, the actions have no instrumental significance; score also where routine is seen as inescapable and a "trap." (E.g.: "He was upset. He finished dinner and went to bed.") If a sentence involves a main and dependent clause, one of which expresses action or instrumental thought (which would be scored as RA) and the other a routine action, do not score IA even if the routine action is described in the main clause (e.g., "They drink coffee, as they plan the job"). Therefore, where instrumental action (or thought) and routine actions are described as simultaneous do not score IA unless the routine action is expressed in a final unmodified independent clause (e.g., "They plan the job and they drink coffee.");

(k) actions fail, that is, abort. (They do not come to their logical conclusion. This is especially relevant for seductions, robberies, murders, suicides, and so forth.);

(l) an action or series of actions merely allows the characters to recoup forces and return to the old situation as it was (e.g., "After the happy affair, he returns to his unhappy marriage.");

(m) the final scorable element is an answer to a question which is routine ("ok") or simply a passive response to orders. Note that simple responses such as "ok" or "sure" are not scorable final elements as they are not main clauses. The answer must be a main clause to score; if it is not, the previous sentence should be used for scoring purposes. Of course, answers such as "ok" do provide information and should be taken into consideration especially when evaluating a story for lack of resolution. (Do not score if the answer is implicitly an action or proposal for action, e.g., "Yes, I'll marry you.")

IMPERSONALITY. Score a story if the final element of the story is phrased in passive voice or impersonal construction. Score also if resolving actions are phrased as inner compulsions rather than chosen, willed actions. Included here should be expressive statements (scored under MSE) that are put in impersonal form ("It was a happy day").

The following are examples of IA:

> They will be reconciled.
> They will hold out and then peace comes.
> It turns out that . . .
> He must go home.
> That was the only thing that made her not want to be a derelict.

35 *Responsibility*

DAVID G. WINTER

THEORETICAL AND EMPIRICAL BACKGROUND

Definition

In everyday language, *responsibility* has several related meanings, all involving the control of behavior by internal mechanisms. "Responsible" people feel an *inner obligation* to do what is right. They are dependable and can be "counted upon" (Barnard, 1938, chapter 17; Blasi, 1980, 1983). When parents exhort young people to "show a little responsibility," they are trying to instill *self-control* and *awareness of the consequences* of action. To a lawyer or philosopher, responsibility means acknowledging or *"owning" one's behavior* (Sartre, 1947), such that the results are a kind of judgment upon the self. Finally, many prosocial behaviors involve *taking responsibility for others* (Gilligan, 1982; Hoffman, 1982). The scoring system described in this chapter was designed to reflect the concept of responsibility in all these different senses.

While the word *responsibility* is rarely found in personality research studies or textbooks, the underlying concept is clearly reflected in such diverse topics as political leadership (Weber, 1919/1948, pp. 115–117); moral judgment (Gilligan, 1982) and moral action (Blasi, 1980, 1983); ego control (J. H. Block & Block, 1980) or impulse control (Pulkkinen, 1986); prosocial versus antisocial behavior (Olweus, Block, & Radke-Yarrow, 1986); delay of gratification (Mischel, 1974; 1986, chapter 16); and the Socialization scale of the CPI (Gough, 1987).

Conceptual framework

The present responsibility measure was developed in the McClelland–Atkinson tradition, in which the thematic apperception protocols of contrasting groups, assumed to differ in some personality characteristic, are used to derive an empirically based content analysis measure of that characteristic. In the present research, "high" and "low" responsibility groups

500

were defined by using naturally contrasting groups rather than by experimental arousal.

Responsibility measured in this way is conceived as a stable disposition. It is not a motive, because it does not energize and direct behavior toward particular broad classes of goals or natural incentives. Rather, it is a complex cluster of cognitions (beliefs and values) that act to channel, shunt, or even block the ways in which all motives are expressed. Although there is no direct evidence as yet, responsibility may well have some foundation in temperament factors such as reflectivity or inhibition (J. Kagan, 1966, 1989), conscientiousness (McRae & Costa, 1987; Norman, 1963), or even introversion (Eysenck & Eysenck, 1985). As suggested later in this chapter, however, learning and socialization experiences (perhaps throughout life) are also critical.

Background

The responsibility measure grew out of repeated efforts to distinguish "good" expressions of the power motive, such as organized social power and leadership, from "bad" expressions such as drinking, drug use, and aggression – collectively termed "profligate expansive impulsivity" (see McClelland & Boyatzis, 1982; D. G. Winter, 1973, pp. 161–163). In the most recent effort, a review and analysis of power motivation in women, D. G. Winter (1988b) found that having a younger sibling (for college students) or having children (for adults) seemed to moderate or channel women's – and men's – power motivation into "leadership" rather than profligate behaviors. Drawing on cross-cultural research (Whiting & Edwards, 1973; Whiting & Whiting, 1975), Winter suggested that these two variables reflect differences in the amount of socialization for responsibility. On this basis, D. G. Winter and Barenbaum (1985b) then developed the present responsibility scoring system as a direct measure of the results of this socialization.

MEASUREMENT INFORMATION

The scoring system

DERIVATION. Winter and Barenbaum first selected two groups of five subjects each, from a larger sample of 240 male college graduates who had written thematic apperceptive stories at the beginning of their first year of college, 15 years before: (a) Men scoring at least one-half *SD* above the mean in power motivation and who later had at least one child (at least three also had younger siblings) were the "responsible power" group. (b) Men scoring at least one-half *SD* above the mean in power motivation and who did not have children (at least three also did not have younger siblings) were the "profligate power" group.

Comparison of the thematic apperceptive stories of these two groups suggested several themes that were present more often in the "responsible power" group. Five of these themes were then cross-validated on other pairs of groups assumed to differ in responsibility: (a) new fathers who also had younger siblings, versus M.B.A. candidates who had neither children nor younger siblings; (b) male high school students with younger siblings, who also performed many household chores, versus male high school students with no younger siblings and few chores; and (c) eldest sixth-graders with two or more younger siblings, versus youngest sixth-graders with two or more older siblings. After further analysis of the cross-validation results and reflection on the theoretical literature previously mentioned, these themes were refined into the following five categories, which define the thematic apperceptive measure of responsibility (see the full scoring system in the following chapter):

1. Moral standard: Reference is made to an abstract standard involving morality or legality.
2. Obligation: Someone is obliged to ("has to") act, either out of inner obligation or impersonal imperatives.
3. Concern for others: Someone helps or shows sympathetic concern for another.
4. Concern about consequences of own action.
5. Self-judgment: Someone critically evaluates or judges own character.

Although all five categories differentiated the high- and low-responsibility groups in the same direction, the intercorrelations among the five categories are usually low (as is true of many thematic apperceptive measures). Several factor analyses with larger samples, carried out in the course of research with the new responsibility measure (e.g., D. G. Winter, 1990a, 1990c, in press; D. G. Winter & Barenbaum, 1985b) suggest that *standards*, *obligation*, and *self-judgment* often go together in one cluster, while *concern for others* and *concern for consequences* make up a second cluster unrelated to the first. This suggests that responsibility has two components: a self-critical "must" that is focused on present and past outcomes, and an altruism that is oriented toward the consequences of the future. Perhaps the "must" component comes first, with altruism and awareness of consequences developing later, along with general cognitive growth.

Psychometric and other considerations

PROCEDURES FOR OBTAINING VERBAL MATERIAL. The responsibility measure can be used to score thematic apperception material obtained in the traditional way, using either picture or verbal cues. The procedural and other suggestions given in chapter 21 on "Power motivation revisited" (including the correction of scores for any correlation with overall length of thematic apperceptive stories) also apply to responsibility.

RELIABILITY AND NORMS. There are no data on the temporal reliability of responsibility scores. Because responsibility scores are strongly affected by the number and nature of the picture or verbal cues and the length of time subjects have to write or tell stories, there are no "norms" for the measure in the conventional sense, and it may not be possible to compare scores obtained under different conditions.

SEX AND GENDER. On grounds of common sex-role socialization, we might expect women to score higher in responsibility than men. Usually they do, but so far the differences are small and not statistically significant. There are some gender differences in the antecedents and expression of responsibility, as discussed in the following review of validation research. There are no data on race or ethnicity effects.

KEY VALIDITY STUDIES

Moderating power motivation

The responsibility measure was originally conceptualized as a moderator of power motivation. D. G. Winter and Barenbaum (1985b) reanalyzed data from several samples of college students and adults. They found that among women and men high in responsibility, power motivation usually predicted office holding, effective and "conscientious" functioning, and openness to new experience. Among women and men low in responsibility, however, power motivation predicted "profligate" behaviors such as drinking, reading sex-oriented magazines, and sexual possessiveness. Several further studies confirm this moderating effect of responsibility on the expression of power motivation.

ORGANIZATIONAL LEADERSHIP. In a sample of 141 men newly hired as ATT nontechnical managers, McClelland and Boyatzis (1982) found that the "Leadership Motive Pattern" (or LMP, consisting of high power motivation, which is greater than affiliation motivation, and high Activity Inhibition) predicted subsequent managerial success after 8 years. D. G. Winter (in press) rescored these stories for responsibility and found that the combination of high power motivation and high responsibility predicted managerial success at about the same level as did the LMP.

In fact, these two ways of moderating the power motive share considerable empirical variance as well as theoretical overlap. The dichotomous variable "responsible power" (above the median on both variables) is highly correlated with the dichotomous LMP classification ($r = .42$, $p < .001$). However, in this sample responsibility is uncorrelated with LMP components of Activity Inhibition or affiliation motivation, and only weakly correlated with power motivation ($r = .15$, $p < .05$).

PROSOCIAL AND ANTISOCIAL AGGRESSION. Two findings from D. G. Winter and Barenbaum's (1985a) secondary analysis of data from the Sears, Maccoby, and Levin (1957) child-rearing study provide further validation of the moderator role of responsibility. Responsibility and power motivation were scored from thematic apperceptive stories collected by McClelland and Pilon (1983) when the subjects were 30 years of age. A subgroup of children from the original study was tested by Sears (1961) at age 12 with attitude scales measuring prosocial aggression ("aggression used in a socially approved way for purposes that are acceptable to the moral standards of the group," with "appropriate rules" and "socially acceptable controls," p. 471) and antisocial aggression (acts or sentiments "that are normally unacceptable socially in the formal pattern of our culture").

Among women and men high in responsibility, power motivation correlated positively ($r = .60$, $p < .05$) with the "prosocial aggression" scale and is unrelated to the "antisocial aggression" scale at age 12. Among participants low in responsibility, however, power motivation correlates positively with antisocial aggression ($r = .46$, $p < .05$) but is unrelated to prosocial aggression.

DIVORCING MOTHERS. Barenbaum (1987) studied mothers in the process of separation and divorce. She found that among mothers high in responsibility, power motivation was associated with better management of conflict with a former spouse, whereas among mothers low in responsibility it predicted open expression of such conflict (blaming former spouse, verbal aggression and litigation, and involvement of children in the conflict).

Responsibility as a "freestanding" personality variable

Apart from its effects on the expression of power motivation, what else does responsibility predict? Barenbaum (1987) found that high-responsibility mothers were more likely to consider their children when making decisions about custody and living arrangements. They were also less likely to report using verbal aggression in conflict situations.

D. G. Winter (1990c) rescored thematic apperceptive stories collected at age 30 from 60 male participants in the Grant Study of Adult Development (Vaillant, 1977). Responsibility scores were modestly but significantly correlated with an overall measure of adaptation to career and family roles ($r = .30$, $p < .01$), though unrelated to a composite measure of successful self-maintenance.

How does the sense of responsibility develop? As a part of their initial validation studies, D. G. Winter and Barenbaum (1985b) found relationships to reported parental expectations in such areas as performing chores, doing well at school, and being polite and well mannered. From the secondary analysis of the Sears et al. (1957) study discussed earlier, D. G. Winter and Barenbaum (1985a) found that assigning many specific chores was necessary to develop responsibility in boys, whereas reasoning and verbal discipline were enough for girls.

D. G. Winter (1990a) further found, somewhat surprisingly, that neither a summer program at an elite private boarding school (described in D. G. Winter, Alpert, & McClelland, 1963) nor 4 years of liberal education at the elite "Ivy College" (described in D. G. Winter, McClelland, & Stewart, 1981) had any overall effect on responsibility scores. However, among college men, participation in organized activities promoted responsibility and participation in informal social life retarded responsibility; among college women, involvement in academic life increased responsibility.

Relation to other measures

Studies carried out to date have found no consistent relationships between responsibility and achievement or affiliation motivation. Nor has responsibility been found to relate to Self-definition, Activity Inhibition, or Fear of Success. (Correlations in the .20s are sometimes found with power motivation.) Finally, there are no consistent relationships with demographic characteristics, although this topic has not been studied systematically.

Responsibility has long been an important concept in philosophical and psychological thought. My own interest in this concept grew out of my research on power motivation, in which I made several different attempts to discover factors that channeled power into what I would now call "responsible" or "irresponsible" directions. Perhaps the scoring system originally developed for this purpose will in the long run give us a clearer understanding of the broader concept of responsibility.

36 *Scoring system for responsibility*

DAVID G. WINTER

The Responsibility scoring system, first used in a study by D. G. Winter and Barenbaum (1985b), consists of five categories: Moral–Legal Standard of Conduct, Internal Obligation, Concern for Others, Concern about Consequences, and Self-judgment. These categories are used to score imaginative verbal material, including both individual thematic apperceptive stories and also other verbal materials such as speeches, fiction, open-ended questions, and so forth, collectively known as "running text" (see D. G. Winter, 1991).

The scoring system can be applied in either of two ways: First, *individual thematic apperceptive stories can be scored in the usual way* (cf. Atkinson, 1958a). Here each story is treated as a separate unit and scored for the presence or absence of each category. A category is scored only once per story, no matter how many times it occurs in that story. Each category counts as +1, so that the total score for a story is the sum of categories scored as present in that story. A person's total score is the sum of scores on all stories. (See chapter 21 and also D. G. Winter, 1973, p. 146, for a discussion of how to handle situations where total scores are significantly correlated with the length of the thematic apperceptive stories.)

Second, running text verbal material of variable length (or TAT stories considered as running text) *can be scored*. Here each sentence can be scored for whatever categories are present, with the proviso that consecutive sentences cannot be scored for the same category (unless some other category occurs between the two occurrences). Each occurrence of each category is scored +1, and the total score is divided by the number of words in the text to give a score per 1,000 words.

After carefully studying this manual, scorers should score the Picture 1 practice stories (see appendix I) and then check their results against the

Copyright © 1984, 1986, 1989 by David G. Winter. I am indebted to Nicole Barenbaum, Janet Malley, Tracey Oberg, Stacey Pawlak, and Abigail Stewart for advice and assistance in the development of the Responsibility scoring system and the preparation of this manual.

expert scoring. For each category as well as for the overall score, scoring reliability can be computed according to the following formula:

$$\text{Percentage Agreement} = \frac{2 \times \begin{pmatrix} \text{no. of agreements between self} \\ \text{and expert on presence of a category} \end{pmatrix}}{\begin{pmatrix} \text{no. of presence scores by self} \end{pmatrix} + \\ \begin{pmatrix} \text{no. of presence scores by expert} \end{pmatrix}}$$

The "consecutive sentences" rule (mentioned earlier) can affect calculations of scorer agreement on running text. When two consecutive sentences could be scored for the same category, and one scorer scores the first and the other scorer scores the second, it can be counted as an agreement.

Reliability should always be calculated for each practice set, and errors noted and understood before going on to score the next practice set. For research purposes, an *overall* percentage agreement figure of .85 is a minimum standard. (For infrequently scored categories, percentage agreement figures may run lower, so long as the overall figure is .85 or higher.)

CATEGORIES OF THE RESPONSIBILITY SCORING SYSTEM

Moral–Legal Standards of Conduct (Standard)

Standard is scored when actions, people, or things are described in terms of some abstract standard or principle that involves (at least to some extent) legality, morality, or virtuous conduct.

The standards must be *moral* or *legal*. Actions that are described in positive ways (e.g., "appropriate," "polite," "successful," or "wise") should not be scored unless the morality or virtue of the standard is specifically mentioned. Many words have positive connotations; but Standard is scored only when the specific underlying moral or legal standard is mentioned.

The following are some typical standards: right/wrong (when referring to morality and not accuracy), good/bad, legal/illegal, lying and cheating, and honest. Sometimes a word or phrase can be confusing. *Good*, for example, is scored when it means "morally good," but it is not scored when it means "successful" or "excellent." (In ambiguous cases of this kind, scorers should ask themselves whether the adjective or phrase could be taken as a synonym for "morally good/morally bad" or "right/wrong.")

These moral or legal standards must be mentioned *explicitly*. They *cannot* be inferred from either the action itself or the consequences. Thus even though "mass murder" is a crime, and even though a murderer is caught, convicted, or punished, Standard would not be scored unless words like *crime* or *illegal* were used. Negations ("not good") can be scored, so long as the standard that is negated is a clearly scorable one.

Examples of Standard:

> The man has entered the country illegally.
> Their relationship has not been immoral.

Not scored for Standard:

> She is trying to do the test right.
> The man applied for a respectable job. ["Respectable" suggests social status more than morality.]
> They were drinking beer. Nothing too bad about that. [Negation, but the standard being negated is not clearly moral because it seems to involve style or status.]
> He wants to appear knowledgeable. ["Knowledgeable" does not involve morality or virtue.]
> Every citizen has the right to vote. ["Right" here means "privilege," not a moral or legal standard of conduct.]

Internal Obligation (Obligation)

Obligation is scored when a person (group, nation, or other collectivity) or a character in a story is described as obliged to act (or not act), because of internal or impersonal forces – *not* in response to the act of another person or group. Typically characters feel that they "have to" or "must" act. To be scored, however, this feeling of obligation or compulsion must be an end in itself and not part of an explicitly stated, instrumental means–end relationship. (Thus "she felt she had to finish writing the paper" would be scored, but "she had to finish writing the paper in order to pass the course" would not be scored.) Statements that a character's action was the result of an internalized moral code would also be scored.

Obligation also includes rules, regulations, orders, instructions, responsibilities, duties, and similar imperatives, *so long as they are impersonal in origin* and are not established by some specific other person. Thus imperatives that are part of a threat in response to some other person's act or threat are not scored. Rules, responsibilities, and so forth that come from some corporate or institutional source, or from "society" in general, *are* scored. The rule or imperative must be explicitly mentioned and must affect (or potentially affect) the person's action; but it does not have to be endorsed by that person.

Finally, Obligation is scored when characters are "instructed," "ordered," or "forced" to act, if no specific other person is mentioned as the source of the instruction, order, command, and so forth. (Obligation is scored in these cases even if the characters do not have an inner feeling of obligation.)

The rationale for these different criteria is that impersonal imperatives and inner feelings of obligation are two of the stages in the process by which external demands – coming from specific others – are transformed into an internal sense of responsibility.

Negations of obligation (e.g., "she didn't have to") are not scored, but breaking obligations (e.g., "they broke the rules") are scored.

Examples of Obligation:

> The boy was following the rule.
> The captain has been instructed to allow no one on board.
> The girl must get back to her dorm.

Not scored for Obligation:

> The young man was forced by his father to apply for the job. [Father is the explicit source of the obligation.]
> She threatened ruin if he didn't pay off. [His "having to" pay is only the *means* to avoid the *end* of ruin.]
> The man's car broke down. He will be forced to borrow money to fix it. [Here, "forced" applies to a means–end relationship.]
> The man is telling him he will have to leave. [Explicit source.]
> If you turn up the music, I will be forced to call the police. [Imperative is part of a threat in response to another's act.]

Concern for Others (Others)

Others is scored when a person (group, nation, etc.) or character in a story is described as helping someone else (whether this help is solicited or not) or is sympathetically concerned about another person.

"Help" includes all ordinary helpful actions, and in fact *any* action or planning that is either intended or received as helpful, so long as there is no explicit counterindication that the helper had some other intention or that the act was not helpful. Routine actions such as teaching, answering questions, or responding to requests are not necessarily scored, unless there is some indication that the action is helpful or has a helpful effect.

Bringing about some general good condition is not scored unless the theme of help or positive effect on others is explicit. For example, "John showed concern for preserving world peace" is not scored, but "John helped the people by preserving world peace" would be scored.

Sympathetic concern about someone else can be scored even if there is no overt helpful act, so long as the concern is clearly on behalf of the other person. On the other hand, scorers should be careful to distinguish Others from intimacy or affiliation. By themselves, close intimate relationships, or friendly conversation, are not scored for Others unless there is some explicit helpful act or sympathetic concern.

Examples of Others:

> The parents are upset and worried about their daughter's future.
> The boss will understand his problem, and give him a raise.
> She's teaching him. He will feel good, because then he can be a doctor like her. [The helpful effect is elaborated here, so that Others is scored.]
> He wants to help his country.

Not scored for Others:

The boy is in trouble. His father is too upset to think clearly. [It is not clear whether the father is upset on his own behalf, or is genuinely concerned about the son.]

She's teaching him, but his mind is on something else. [Here a teaching attempt is apparently not helpful.]

Concern about Negative Consequences (Consequences)

Consequences is scored when a person (group, nation, etc.) or character in a story is described as having some inner concern (worry, anxiety, being upset, or even just reflecting) about the possible negative consequences of his or her *own* action (or inaction), either in anticipation or in retrospect. Scorers should be careful to distinguish reasons for actions (which are not scored) from consequences of actions (which are scored). Reasons refer to events in the past that evoke or cause an action; consequences refer to anticipations of future events. Of course, Consequences is scored when anticipated consequences are the reason for an action.

Hypothetical actions, implied actions, and actions taken to avoid negative consequences that might occur as the result of inaction, can be scored so long as there is concern about consequences. Consequences is often expressed in the form of "If . . . then . . ."

In order to score Consequences, the person showing the concern must be the same as the person whose action (or inaction) has the consequences. Thus: "Mary was concerned about her action" would be scored, but "Mary was concerned about John's action" would not be scored. Finally, "Mary said that 'John was concerned about his action'" would be scored because the person who acts (John) is the same as the person who has the concern, even though we only know this through Mary's words.

Concern about success or failure of an action is scored only when there is concern about subsequent effects or consequences of this success or failure. Mere concern about success or failure by itself is not scored.

Examples of Consequences:

The captain is hesitant to admit the reporter, since she has been instructed to allow no one on board. [Concern is shown about consequences of an anticipated act.]

The boy broke a rule, and is worried about being thrown out of college.

Mary said that John now regrets his haste.

Not scored for Consequences:

He wishes to apologize for his unkindness to her. [Character does not necessarily feel inner regret or similar concern.]

The son has some misgivings about his first real encounter with the group. [Concern is about success or failure, rather than about the consequences of success or failure in the encounter.]

He looked on regretfully as she left. [Concern is about the consequences of someone else's action.]

Mary said that John regrets Martha's haste.

Self-judgment

Self-judgment is scored when a person (group, nation, etc.) or character in a story is described as critically evaluating his or her own character (wisdom, morality, self-control, good sense, etc.). Examples would include shame, guilt, or embarrassment at an action, or even the simple realization of having done wrong.

The sentiments must refer to the self, or to the action itself, not to the outcome or the results of the action. Thus regret at failure would only be scored if it involved self-criticism.

Sometimes, character judgments are expressed indirectly or "editorially" by the writer of the story, instead of being directly expressed by a character in the story. If the editorial judgment is strong and goes beyond description of action or the results of action, then Self-judgment can be scored in such cases.

Examples of Self-judgment:

> The young man realizes he has done wrong. [The last word in this sentence is also scored for Standard.]
> A friend will see what he is reading, and he will be very embarrassed.
> They are amused at the ridiculousness of their behavior. [Borderline so far as the characters' self-evaluation goes, but "ridiculousness" does involve a clear editorial judgment by the writer of the story.]

Not scored for Self-judgment:

> She's going to do it wrong, and then she feels unhappy. [Character's feeling relates to the outcome, not necessarily to the self.]
> The man lost his job because he was found inebriated on duty. [No self-criticism, and "inebriated" is a weaker editorial judgment than "ridiculousness" in the previous example.]
> The boy is thinking that he shouldn't have done it. [No sign that the boy feels self-criticism as a result of what he did.]

Finally, a scoring sheet may be made as follows:

Set _____   Scorer _____   Date _____

Story	STD	OBL	OTH	CON	S-J	Total

PART III

*Methodology, scorer training,
data collection*

37 *Methodological considerations: steps in research employing content analysis systems*

CHARLES P. SMITH, SHEILA C. FELD,
AND CAROL E. FRANZ

Research involving the analysis of verbal material for content and/or style involves the following steps: (1) deciding what type of verbal material (and subject population) to sample, (2) choosing a method for obtaining the material, (3) collecting the material, (4) learning a content analysis system, (5) learning how to measure intercoder agreement, (6) coding (scoring) the material, and (7) analyzing the data. This chapter presents information and recommendations regarding these steps in research.

Following this chapter, appendix I provides practice stories with "expert scoring" for a number of the scoring systems included in this book. Anyone who wishes to learn to use one of these systems should read the chapters on that system and the section in this chapter on scorer training and then follow the directions in appendix I for using the practice materials.

STEP I. DECIDING WHAT KIND OF VERBAL MATERIAL TO OBTAIN

The nature of the verbal material to be obtained is determined by the following considerations: the *type of variable* to be measured (e.g., content or style, individual or group characteristic); the *number of variables* to be measured from the same sample of verbal material; and the *time period* to be dealt with (past or present).

To measure a *content* variable or variables (e.g., achievement, intimacy, power), one typically samples thoughts aroused by situations representative of the content domain or domains (see chapters 5, 6, and 7). To measure a *style*, one needs a sample of material that permits the expression of *consistency in mode of thought* across occasions or domains (see chapters 25 and

This chapter is based, in part, on previous chapters by Feld and Smith (1958) and Smith and Feld (1958). We are indebted to David Winter for permission to use material from two unpublished papers that deal with measuring motivation and adjusting scores for differences in the length of verbal samples.

33). For example, to measure explanatory style one needs descriptions of how a person accounts for a number of negative events.

To study individuals, groups, or societies from a previous historical period, it is obviously necessary to use preexisting verbal materials, whereas either verbal material produced for other purposes (e.g., letters, speeches) or specially collected materials may be used to study the present. Group or societal characteristics have usually been studied by means of preexisting materials, such as folktales or children's stories (see Child, Storm, & Veroff, 1958; McClelland, 1961, 1975; D. G. Winter, 1973, appendix V), but they may also be studied by means of survey research (see chapter 6).

STEP 2. SELECTING A METHOD OF OBTAINING VERBAL MATERIAL

Clearly, the method to be used is determined, in part, by the type of variable to be measured. Perhaps the first decision involves whether to use verbal materials produced for other purposes or to collect new materials. Preexisting verbal materials, or those produced for other purposes (e.g., personal documents, speeches, transcriptions of television programs or therapy sessions), have been used to measure many of the variables included in this book. Such materials may be available when individuals or groups are not willing or able to provide special material for research purposes. Because the use of preexisting materials is described extensively by McClelland (1975, appendix 4), and by Winter (chapter 7), Peterson (chapter 25), and Suedfeld, Tetlock, and Streufert (chapter 27), the discussion of Steps 2 and 3 will deal primarily with specially collected material.

Elicited material may take various forms, such as thematic apperceptive stories, essays (see chapter 25), or paragraph completion (see chapter 27). The advantages of collecting material include control over the characteristics of the subject population (e.g., age, sex), the conditions under which the material is produced, the range and amount of material sampled, and the number of occasions on which verbal samples are obtained.

Collected material may be obtained orally, as in survey research (see chapter 6), or in written form in individual or group testing sessions. Written materials may be obtained by self-administration or by the researcher. Most research with specially collected material has employed written material obtained by means of group testing. Research suggests that individual and group testing produce similar thematic apperceptive stories (Lindzey & Heinemann, 1955; Murstein, 1963), although Sarason and Sarason (1958) found that TAT stories obtained by means of group testing were sadder than those obtained by individual testing. Eron and Ritter (1951) found that individually obtained oral stories were similar in content to group written stories but that there were some formal differences in the two types of stories. Oral stories were longer and contained more alternate themes;

written stories contained more humor and tended to be somewhat more flippant. From a research viewpoint, one disadvantage of individual testing is that the one-on-one relationship of the storyteller to the test administrator makes it difficult to establish consistently the same rapport and testing situation for all subjects.

Methods for obtaining appropriate verbal material are described for each of the scoring systems included in this volume. The most extensive body of information concerns methods of obtaining thematic apperceptive stories. To elicit such stories, one can use picture cues or verbal cues.

Picture cues for thematic apperceptive stories

Picture stimuli are major determinants of thematic apperceptive story content (see, e.g., Alper & Greenberger, 1967; Kenny, 1964; Murstein, 1965d). Holt (1978) and Murstein (1972) review information concerning the frequency with which various themes occur in response to different TAT pictures. The early assumption that the Murray (1943) TAT pictures would serve as general purpose stimuli in nonclinical research has been largely abandoned, and the Murray TAT pictures are rarely used today in the type of research reported in this volume, primarily because they were chosen, in part, to elicit content of interest to the clinician.

Although stories written about pictures may be coded for many kinds of variables (e.g., motives, orientations, styles), most research on picture cues has dealt with the measurement of motives. Consequently, the following discussion most often refers to the literature on the selection of pictures for motive measurement.

The use of pictures as stimulus cues for stories requires decisions about picture content, stimulus pull or "cue strength" (the average amount of imagery of a particular type elicited), ambiguity, the number of pictures to be used, and the order in which they are to be presented. Criteria for picture selection are discussed by Birney (1958), Haber and Alpert (1958), Jacobs (1958), Murstein (1965c, 1965d), Reitman and Atkinson (1958), Veroff (chapter 6, this volume), and Veroff, Atkinson, Feld, and Gurin (1960).

Sets of pictures developed for research on motives by McAdams, by McClelland, by Veroff, and by Winter are included in appendix II along with references for sources of other pictures that have been used in research. As explained in appendix II, the McAdams, McClelland, and Veroff sets permit the measurement of several different motives from the same stories. A researcher may reproduce and use these established sets or develop new pictures as needed for new purposes or new populations.

For the researcher who wishes to develop a new set of pictures, we now present a general discussion of the issues involved in picture selection. This discussion is followed by separate recommendations for the selection of pictures to be used to measure a *single* motive and the selection of pictures for *multimotive* assessment.[1] For additional suggestions regarding cue selection, the reader should consult the chapters in this volume dealing with the particular variables of interest.

GENERAL CONSIDERATIONS. First, one must decide whether to use special pictures for particular groups of subjects. One key issue here is how similar to the subjects the depicted characters need to be. Most investigators have used different pictures for males and females, or pictures that include both male and female characters (see, e.g., chapter 6; also Murray, 1943). Evidence reviewed by Murstein (1965d), however, suggests that it is probably not necessary to use pictures of black persons to obtain valid stories from black subjects. Pictures developed for various cultural or socioeconomic groups are reviewed by Bellak (1975) and by Murstein (1965d).

Another consideration is selecting pictures that elicit the subjects' current concerns. For this reason, it may be advisable not to use pictures showing only characters younger than the subjects (Reitman & Atkinson, 1958) as they may elicit recollections of past events rather than thoughts that reflect current concerns (see McClelland, Atkinson, Clark, & Lowell, 1953, pp. 197ff.). Pictures that are out of date with respect to such features as clothes and hair styles also may not elicit stories that are characteristic of current experiences. Therefore, it may be necessary to update standard pictures from time to time (cf. Henry, 1956, p. 51; Murstein, 1972).

Second, one must decide how many pictures to use. Unfortunately, the relationship between test length and reliability is more complicated for thematic measures than for objective measures. There is a limit to the number of stories subjects will cooperate in producing in one session, and, furthermore, if as many as eight stories are obtained in a single session, the later stories may be less valid than the earlier ones according to the results of Reitman and Atkinson (1958, pp. 676–677; see also Atkinson, chapter 2, and the subsequent discussion on the dynamics of action).

A review of reliability issues (chapter 8) leads to the recommendation that at least six stories be obtained from each subject (see also Crandall, 1951). This means using six pictures if testing is done on a single occasion or alternate forms of four to six pictures each (see Haber & Alpert, 1958; Lundy, 1985; Smith, Krogh, & McMahan, 1991) if testing can be done on more than one occasion under comparable circumstances within a relatively short period of time (e.g., 1 week).

Third, usually pictures are selected to be representative of common situations in which the motives or dispositions of interest are aroused (cf. chapter 6; Crandall, 1951). For example, to obtain achievement imagery one might use pictures of work, school, and other performance settings. A number of studies have indicated that it is feasible to measure more than one motive (or other variable) from the same set of verbal material (see chapters 5, 6, and 7; also Reitman & Atkinson, 1958, pp. 677–678; Veroff et al., 1960). For this purpose pictures representative of the various relevant situations are selected. (See picture sets assembled by McAdams, by McClelland, and by Veroff in appendix II.)

If one wishes to measure *fears*, or variables that are not normally accessible to consciousness, then considerations concerning picture content and ambiguity become more complex (see, e.g., J. Kagan, 1959; Karon, 1981; Murstein, 1965d; also Fleming & Horner, chapter 11, this volume).

Fourth, in addition to selecting pictures on the basis of *content* that will elicit thoughts representative of the variable to be measured, it is necessary to consider picture ambiguity and cue strength (stimulus pull). By *ambiguity* we mean the tendency of a picture to evoke alternative themes. (For a broader conception of ambiguity as well as a procedure for assessing ambiguity, see Murstein, 1972.) By *cue strength* we mean the percentage of subjects who produce imagery of a particular type in response to a picture.

A procedure for rating picture content and ambiguity is described in an impressive reliability study by Haber and Alpert (1958). One of their criteria for picture selection was low ambiguity: "A picture had to be primarily concerned with the achievement motive and could not have any significant number of cues pertaining to other motives" (p. 647). They obtained a substantial correlation of .58 ($p < .001$) between *ambiguity ratings* of 30 pictures by one group of subjects and *cue strength* measured by percentage of achievement imagery in stories written to those pictures by a different group of subjects. Using comparable 6-picture forms, they also found greater test–retest reliability for pictures with high cue strength ($r = .59$) than for pictures with low cue strength ($r = .36$).

Fifth, depending on their cue strength and ambiguity some pictures elicit stories that are more easily scored than other pictures (Feld & Smith, 1958, p. 241).

RECOMMENDATIONS. To develop a set of pictures to measure only a *single* motive, we recommend the following steps:

1. Select pictures whose content constitutes a reasonably representative sample of motive-relevant situations that have similar significance to all members of the population to be tested – that is, the situations should be as nearly universal as possible so as to arouse the same kinds of expectancies in all individuals. As Atkinson (1958b) put it, "To infer differences in the strength of motive . . . we need only assume that *average strength* of a particular expectancy (e.g., the expectancy of achievement . . .) aroused by *all* of the pictures in the series is approximately equal for all subjects" (p. 609).[2] In addition, to measure motives the selected pictures should permit or encourage future-oriented, goal-anticipatory thought rather than recollections of past events (McClelland et al., 1953, pp. 197–214).

2. Select pictures whose cue strength (i.e., the average amount of motive-

relevant imagery) will produce the greatest differentiation among subjects and yield distributions of scores that are not badly skewed. This criterion implies that pictures with cue strength in an intermediate range may be best. We will reconsider this issue after our discussion of ambiguity. (In early research on the achievement motive [McClelland et al., 1953, p. 206], the tentative suggestion was made that subjects might be differentiated most effectively by administering low cue-value pictures under achievement-orienting instructions. This suggestion has long since been abandoned in favor of using neutral instructions to tap *characteristic* levels of motive arousal.)

Clearly pictures that elicit imagery from either very few subjects (low cue) or nearly all subjects (high cue) do not differentiate. As Murstein (1965c) puts it: "Apparently, the high cards had such an overwhelming pull for n Ach, that subjects responded with achievement regardless of their own achievement motivation, whereas the low cards did not possess sufficient cue strength to trigger off n Ach" (p. 286). Murstein also found that pictures of medium-scaled stimulus value had greater validity than those of low or high value.

3. Select pictures whose ambiguity is relatively low. This will permit all subjects to express motive-relevant content. Individual differences in amount of motive-relevant content are then more likely to be attributable to individual differences in motive strength. (As noted, low ambiguity was one criterion of picture selection used by Haber and Alpert, 1958.) In a review of the literature on projective assessment, Singer (1981) reaches a similar conclusion: "For picture story material, ambiguity *per se* is not quite as desirable as was thought. If anything, the weight of current evidence in the measurement of motives such as aggression suggests that special pictures depicting some aggression are more useful than the traditional set of [TAT] cards" (p. 306). (See also Epstein, 1966.)

The addition of an ambiguity criterion complicates matters because of the correlation between ambiguity and cue strength. Two findings of Haber and Alpert (1958) are relevant to a resolution of the matter. First, they found that high cue pictures had better reliability than low cue pictures. Second, there was at least as good a distribution of scores for high cue as for low cue pictures. *Therefore, our recommendation is for the selection of pictures with relatively low ambiguity and relatively high cue strength (i.e., approximately 50% to 80% imagery).* Fortunately, these two considerations can be satisfied reasonably well by selecting pictures only on the basis of cue strength, because, as Haber and Alpert showed, ambiguity tends to decrease as cue strength increases. Obviously additional empirical evidence is needed to put this recommendation on firmer footing.

4. Order of presentation should be determined by several considerations. The first is whether the order in which a picture is presented affects its cue strength. Although this may be the case for some motives such as sex

(Clark, 1952), it may not be the case for more socially acceptable motives. Studies employing Latin Square designs showed no significant effects of picture order on achievement motivation (McClelland et al., 1953, p. 188) or on achievement, affiliation, or power motivation (Veroff et al., 1960). If significant order effects are discovered by means of pretesting a new set of pictures, then either an optimum ordering can be determined or picture scores can be adjusted for order effects.

In the absence of specific knowledge about order effects, the researcher is advised to space apart pictures that are likely to elicit similar themes, and begin with a picture that will draw subjects into the task and not make them defensive or uncooperative. An example to the contrary is provided by a recent pilot study of highly educated women in which one of us was involved (C.F.). The first two cues depicted men and apparently aroused antipathy toward the task.

To develop a set of pictures to measure *more than one motive*, modified procedures are called for. A model study to consider is that of Veroff et al. (1960) in which pictures were *pretested* for cue strength and order effects before a final selection was made. In general, the following procedures have been followed:

1. Pictures are selected whose content reflects a sample of relatively universal motive-relevant situations.

2. With respect to cue strength and ambiguity, Veroff et al. (1960) "tried to select pictures in which one kind of motivation was rather strongly suggested, but at least one or the other kinds of motivation was weakly suggested" (p. 3). D. G. Winter (1989d) recommends a similar approach: "Researchers should select cues that suggest different motives, while having a moderately strong 'pull' for the motive(s) they want to study" (p. 1). The final selection of pictures in the Veroff et al. (1960) study produced "an adequate balance of scores for the three motives" (p. 3).

3. Pictures are ordered so as to intersperse those with the strongest pull for different motives.

IMPLICATIONS OF THE DYNAMICS OF ACTION. It is interesting to consider the implications for picture selection of the theory of the dynamics of action (Atkinson, chapter 2, this volume). A simplified interpretation of that theory suggests that if one wanted to measure the *relative* strength of two motives, say achievement and affiliation, one should use a high ambiguity picture (permitting either achievement or affiliation themes). If, however, a single motive (e.g., achievement) is to be measured, then it would be best to select a picture low in ambiguity, that is, interpreted fairly universally as a situation that permits the expression of achievement motivation and *only* achievement motivation. Such a picture should increase only the strength of achievement tendencies in all or most subjects and permit the expression of individual differences in the strength of those tendencies to be expressed in associative thought. This conclusion is consistent with our recommendation for the selection of pictures for the assessment of a single motive. So far so good. However, if one wishes to select pictures to elicit imagery for *several different motives*, there are two possible alternatives. One is to select a few low ambiguity pictures for each separate motive, the other is to select pictures with greater ambiguity that permit the expression of either one or another kind of motivation. The latter approach appears to have been followed in the selection of the picture sets described previously. The dynamics of action suggests the possibility, however, that such pictures may be more likely to measure the *relative* strength of each motive than the *absolute* strength of each motive.

The dynamics of action also has implications for the order of presentation of pictures. It assumes that expressing imagery reflective of a particular motive reduces the strength of that motivational tendency. Such a reduction will eventually permit the expression of a competing tendency. Thus, there may be some value in alternating pictures that have high cue value for different motives. However, the reduction of tendencies and the expression of competing tendencies is likely to occur *at a different rate for different individuals*, so that it may be theoretically possible to devise an ideal picture order for a single individual but not for a group of individuals. Research on ambiguity and picture order exploring implications of the dynamics of action should advance our understanding of these issues.

PRETESTING. One implication of the foregoing discussion is that it is advisable to *pretest* new pictures, or old pictures used with new populations, in order to establish cue strength and ambiguity. Through pretesting one can also establish the amount of interscorer agreement for each picture in order to identify any scoring difficulties that may arise when scoring stories dissimilar to those used as examples in coding manuals and practice materials.

Verbal cues for thematic apperceptive stories

Murstein (1965d) has reviewed studies that compared stories obtained in response to verbal descriptions of TAT pictures with stories obtained in response to the pictures themselves. Both methods appear to yield similar data, although verbal cues, being less complex, probably tend to be lower in ambiguity. Verbal cues, in the form of story topics, have been used in a number of studies to elicit stories. Of the systems included in this book, those by Horner and Fleming (see chapters 11 and 12), deCharms (chapters 23 and 24), and Sorrentino, Hanna, and Roney (chapters 29 and 30) employ verbal cues, and such cues have been used in the study of other motives as well.

Verbal cues are easier to work with than pictures and less expensive. Subjects tell a story about a suggested topic – for example, "A student sitting in a classroom" – as readily as about a picture of a student sitting in a classroom. Furthermore, the student in the verbal cue could be male or female, black or white, in grade school or college. The student is not characterized by a specific form of dress or setting, hence, such cues may be advantageous for cross-cultural comparisons. It may also be easier to develop alternate forms with verbal cues than with pictures (cf. Smith et al., 1991). If one wishes to ensure that the subject will write about a person of his or her own sex, it is easy to specify the sex of the character. For example, one of the cues used to elicit fear-of-success imagery was "After first term finals, Anne finds herself at the top of her medical school class" (see chapter 11).

Verbal cues that have been used in research, and instructions for their administration are given in chapters 11, 23, and 29. In addition, Winter (chapter 21) lists five verbal cues that he has found useful in research on power motivation. Each verbal cue is usually printed at the top of each page on which a story is to be written.

Most of the previously mentioned considerations regarding content, stimulus pull, number of stories, order of presentation, and so forth that apply to pictures as stimuli also apply to verbal cues. One difference between verbal and picture cues that might not occur to the reader has been identified by deCharms (see chapter 23). Whereas picture cues almost always elicit third person stories, it is possible with verbal cues to elicit either third person stories, as with the cue given previously, or first-person stories (e.g., "I am sitting on a chair with a smile on my face."). These two types of cues do not evoke comparable responses, and deCharms recommends the use of third-person cues. As with picture cues, pretesting of verbal cues is strongly advised to establish cue strength and scorability.

STEP 3: COLLECTING VERBAL MATERIAL

Methods of collecting preexisting verbal material are described in chapters 7, 25, and 27. For methods of collecting elicited material other than stories, see chapter 25 on explanatory style and chapter 27 on conceptual/integrative complexity. The remaining measures included in this book, whether they deal with motives, styles, or orientations, have typically been based on the analysis of stories. Consequently, the balance of this section will deal with procedures for collecting stories.

Because of the sensitivity of thematic apperception to situational factors, the story measure should come first or near the beginning of the data collection session. That is, it should not be preceded by questionnaires, tests, instructions or activities that might alter mood or motivation or arouse evaluation apprehension, defenses, desire to please the administrator, and so forth.

To assess a person's *characteristic* thought processes, the story measure should be administered under *neutral* conditions (see chapters 9 and 21, this volume; Lundy, 1988; Smith, 1966). The thematic measure should not be referred to as a "test." The experimenter's manner should be relatively informal (though not to the point that subjects do not take the task seriously); a prestige or authority relationship between the administrator and the subjects should be avoided. Timing should be played down in order to avoid a testlike and evaluative atmosphere. D. G. Winter (1989d) suggests that "Timing and instructions to go on to the next story should be casual: do *not* use a stop-watch or other formal 'apparatus'" (p. 3).

Instructions

The instructions for the thematic measure are either read to or read by the subjects. Several versions of the instructions will be presented. They have been adapted from the original instructions for the Thematic Apperception Test (Murray, 1943). We will begin with the instructions that have been used most frequently over the years:

Picture Interpretations
You are going to see a series of pictures, and your task is to tell a story that is suggested to you by each picture. Try to imagine what is going on in each picture. Then tell what the situation is, what led up to the situation, what the people are thinking and feeling, and what they will do.

In other words, write as complete a story as you can – a story with plot and characters.

You will have 20 seconds to look at a picture and then 4 minutes to write your story about it. Write your first impressions and work rapidly. I will keep time and tell you when it is time to finish your story and to get ready for the next picture.

There are no right or wrong stories or kinds of pictures, so you may feel free to write whatever story is suggested to you when you look at a picture. Spelling, punctuation, and grammar are not important. What is important is to write out as fully and as quickly as possible the story that comes into your mind as you imagine what is going on in each picture.

Notice that there is one page for writing each story. If you need more space for writing any story, use the reverse side of the paper. (Atkinson, 1958a, p. 837)

With respect to timing, Atkinson (1958a) states:

Four minutes are allowed for writing the story. At the end of each minute, the investigator says informally, "It is about time to go on to the next question." About 30 seconds before the end of the fourth minute, the investigator says, "Will you try to finish up in about 30 seconds?" At the end of four minutes he says, "All right, here is the next picture." (p. 837).

A modified set of instructions, entitled "Telling Stories," that may be used *with either picture or verbal cues* is given by Winter in an appendix to chapter 21. A third set of instructions entitled "Storytelling" is given in appendix I. These instructions for *self-administration* were used in research by David McClelland to elicit the stories that are provided for practice scoring. (McClelland more often uses the heading "Picture Story Exercise.") *Because his subjects had taken the thematic apperceptive measure previously*, the McClelland instructions contain the sentence: "It makes no difference if the stories are similar to or different from ones you have written previously." Research by D. G. Winter and Stewart (1977b) and by Lundy (1985) suggests that a sentence of this kind improves test–retest reliability by making it explicit that subjects are not expected to write stories that are *different* from those they wrote before. (Test–retest instructions are described in more detail in chapter 8 on Reliability Issues.)

Note that the Winter and McClelland instructions omit any reference to writing quickly in order to avoid putting too much pressure on the subject, and they allow 5 minutes for writing each story (a time interval employed in many published studies that may be especially appropriate for samples of persons who may not write as quickly as college students). For most populations allowing more than 5 minutes per story appears neither necessary nor desirable (cf. Atkinson, 1958a, p. 677). On the other hand, allowing only two and one half minutes per story may accentuate the effects of verbal fluency and introduce an unwanted correlation between scores and story length (Atkinson, 1958a, p. 837). If 4 or 5 minutes are allowed for each of six stories, approximately 30 to 35 minutes should be provided for administration of the thematic apperceptive measure.

If picture cues are used, the usual procedure for group testing is to show a slide for 15 to 20 seconds and then ask subjects to write a story about it. Subjects may also be given a booklet which contains a copy of each picture followed by a page for writing each story. Lindzey and Silverman (1959) recommend "the use of individual sets of cards with 20 second exposure of the stimulus material" (p. 322).

On each story sheet are printed the four questions listed here (from Atkinson, 1958a, p. 837):[3]

    1. What is happening? Who are the persons?
    2. What has led up to this situation? That is, what has happened in the past?
    3. What is being thought? What is wanted? By whom?
    4. What will happen? What will be done?

The procedures employed by Winter (chapter 21) and by McClelland (in appendix I) modify the wording of these guiding questions. Most investigators have spaced the four questions evenly apart on the page provided for each story. McClelland, however, has put the questions at the top of each page as reminders in the hope of obtaining a sustained story line rather than short segmented answers to questions. It is a good idea to provide a space at the top of each page for the story number and the subject's identification number.

Instructions for the use of a thematic measure in survey research are given by Veroff in chapter 6, and still other versions of the basic thematic apperceptive instructions are given by some of the authors whose content analysis systems are presented in this volume (e.g., deCharms, chapter 23). If stories are obtained orally due to the nature of the subjects or the data collection conditions, it is advisable to tape record the stories and to limit interventions by the administrator, following the instructions, to reminders about the guiding questions. Procedures should be agreed upon for dealing with questions from the subject, or responses from the subject such as "I don't know." (see chapter 6; also Veroff et al., 1960).

In survey research or other occasions for individual administration of a thematic measure, the subject may be shown an individual copy of each picture (as a TAT card is shown), or the pictures may be printed in a booklet and shown to the subject one by one. Pictures printed in a booklet or prior to each story sheet may also be used for self-administration of the measure.

All these variations may be somewhat unnerving to a researcher new to this approach who wishes to employ a standard and correct methodological procedure. Obviously there is no standard procedure. However, there is substantial agreement on the kinds of changes that should be made in the 1958 instructions given previously. For example, do not refer to the thematic measure as a test, make timing unobtrusive, omit reference to writing quickly, allow 5 minutes for noncollege populations, and, if retesting, tell subjects that it is all right to tell either the same or different stories. A researcher would also be safe in using the instructions provided in chapter 21, or in appendix I, or by the author(s) of the scoring system to be used.

STEP 4: LEARNING A CONTENT ANALYSIS SYSTEM

A reasonable *goal* for learning most of the coding systems included in the volume is to attain a degree of agreement with the "expert scoring" of practice materials of approximately .9 and interscorer agreement of .85 or better in published research. Persons who have already become adept with the coding manual they wish to use may wish to skip to Step 5.

Scorer training

To learn a new scoring system one may receive training from an expert, train oneself, or experience some combination of the two methods. By "expert" we mean someone who has thoroughly mastered a particular scoring system and who has had extensive experience in using the system in research.

Many of the chapters in this volume that deal with particular coding systems make suggestions concerning ways of learning those systems. In chapter 23, for example, deCharms provides a particularly thorough discussion of how to learn and use the Origin scoring system. For most of the systems, practice materials for self-training are provided in appendix I. Special practice stories are provided following the scoring manuals for Intimacy (chapter 16) and the Origin scoring system (chapter 24). In addition, for some of the systems there are supplementary practice materials that may be obtained in publications or from the authors of the systems (see appendix III on how to order additional practice materials).

EXPERT TRAINING. Typically an expert conducts a seminar in which trainees who have read the coding manual receive clarification regarding the meaning of coding categories. Trainees then score practice materials, compare their scoring with that of the expert, and discuss differences between their scoring and that of the expert in order to further clarify their understanding of the coding categories (cf. Reitman & Atkinson, 1958, p. 680; Suedfeld, Tetlock, & Streufert, chapter 27, this volume). A helpful discussion of training coders for the analysis of a large amount of data obtained in survey research is given in Veroff et al. 1960.

SELF-TRAINING. For a number of the systems included in this volume it is possible to attain sufficient mastery of the scoring system without the benefit of expert training. In essence, one first reads the coding manual several times and then scores practice materials until a sufficient level of agreement is attained with the expert scoring for the practice materials. Feld and Smith (1958) developed a set of practice materials for learning to score *n* Achievement, *n* Affiliation, and *n* Power. Their procedures involved a "self-test" on the scoring manual followed by approximately 12 hours of scoring of seven sets of practice stories. Trainees were urged to review their errors before going on to a new set of stories, and the absence as well as the presence of each category was specifically noted. Feld and Smith found that the rank-order correlations between graduate student trainees and the expert scoring on a criterion set of stories written to the pictures used for the practice materials ranged from .83 to .90 for *n* Achievement (Mdn = .87), .86 to .92 for *n* Affiliation (Mdn = .87), and .73 to .89 for *n* Power (Mdn = .78). For stories written to new pictures, the attained correlations were somewhat lower (.80 to .84, .78 to .86, and .68 to .91, respectively). In the Feld and Smith study, at the conclusion of self-training, approximately 75% of the trainees were ready to score research materials with very little additional practice. D. G. Winter (1973) developed a similar self-training procedure for his revised *n* Power scoring system. He reports that six scorers trained by this method attained somewhat higher levels of agreement with the expert scoring than those reported by Feld and Smith (1958).

The Feld and Smith (1958) results, and our subsequent experience, indicate that not all trainees make equally good scorers. Some persons take longer than others to obtain scoring proficiency, and a few never do, even though they may possess high intelligence and verbal aptitude. Feld and

Smith noted that persons with prior coding experience learned the motivation coding systems more quickly than those without prior experience. We recommend that persons who do not attain high and consistent agreement with the expert scoring of practice materials should leave the scoring of research materials to those who have attained the requisite level of agreement.

RECOMMENDATIONS FOR SELF-TRAINING:

1. Begin by reading the scoring manual several times. Make sure you understand each illustrative example given in the manual. It is a waste of time to begin scoring if you have not mastered the criteria for each coding category.

2. Take the "self-test" for the manual if one is provided with the manual or practice materials.

3. You may want to make a summary sheet of key points to bear in mind as you score (cf. "cribsheet" for Origin scoring in chapter 23).

4. Before scoring, look at the picture used to elicit the story (or a description of the picture) or read the verbal cue used to elicit the story.

5. In scoring thematic apperceptive stories, keep in mind the questions used to guide the writing of the stories. A single word may be scored if it is an answer to a guiding question. For example, if the words "An A." or "Companionship." represent answers to the question "What is wanted?" then they would be scored for *Need* in the achievement and affiliation systems. That is, the story writer is saying "The student *wants* an A." "The girl *wants* companionship."

6. Score the first batch of practice material and compare your scoring with that of the expert. *Make a record of your errors* so you can review them before scoring the next batch of stories.

7. Record the presence *or* absence of each category. This requires an explicit decision about each category.

8. When you encounter difficulties in scoring, *consult the manual and the expert scoring of the practice stories* for help in reaching a decision. Expect to refer to the manual frequently as you score the practice stories.

9. Be able to justify each decision by being able to point to specific phrases that meet the criteria for a particular scoring category. Even if it seems as though a category may be present, if you cannot point to specific words that meet a scoring criterion, do not score the category. This conservative procedure insures higher interscorer agreement. In other words, if in doubt, don't. (Do not underline phrases or write on the *original* story materials so that your response will not affect that of others who may read the same material.)

10. Before each scoring session, warm up by reviewing the manual and your record of the errors you made in previous stories.

It may help to know that learning is slow at first and rather laborious, but it becomes easier and much faster as you gain experience. Allow at least 12 hours for practice. Score a set of materials, then wait a day or two, and score some more. You can evaluate your progress and determine whether you are ready to score research materials by using the following indexes of interscorer agreement.

STEP 5. MEASURING INTERSCORER AGREEMENT

The most commonly used indexes of interscorer agreement have been (a) category agreement or the percentage of agreement between two scorers on the *presence* of a category and (b) rank-order correlation (*Rho*) between total scores. The formula for the percentage of Category Agreement (CA) is given below. Scorers 1 and 2 (S1 and S2) could be a trainee and an expert, or two scorers of research materials. To calculate CA, count the number (no.) of times the category (cat.) was scored as *present* by each scorer and the number of times they *agreed* on its presence.

$$CA = \frac{2(\text{no. of agreements between S1 and S2 on } \textit{presence} \text{ of cat.})}{(\text{no. of times S1 scored cat.}) + (\text{no. of times S2 scored cat.})}$$

Because some categories are scored very infrequently, an index that includes agreement about the *absence* of a category could be misleading. For example, if the expert scored a category as present in 2 out of 100 stories and the trainee scored it as present in none, they agree 98 percent of the time, yet the trainee has missed the category altogether. Although publications usually report CA for only a primary category (e.g., whether or not achievement imagery is present), it may be helpful when learning a system to compute CA for each coding category to discover specific coding problems. The CA index is less meaningful, however, when few instances of a category are present in the material. For further discussion of measures of intercoder agreement, see J. Cohen (1960), Holsti (1968, p. 66), and Scott (1955).

Ideally, publications should include a report of the degree of interscorer agreement (CA and *Rho*, or, at least, *Rho*) obtained with the research materials and *not just with practice materials*. Even if a researcher has attained a high degree of agreement with the expert scoring of practice materials, we believe that reporting that fact in published research is not a good substitute for having at least a sample of the research stories scored by a second person to permit a report of interscorer agreement.

STEP 6: PREPARATIONS FOR CODING, AND CODING

Preparations

WARM-UP. Regardless of their experience and degree of agreement with the expert scoring of practice materials, *all scorers* need to reread the scoring manual carefully before starting to score research materials. We strongly recommend that at least one set of practice materials be scored as a warm-up before coding verbal material for research purposes.

UNFAMILIAR MATERIAL. Interscorer reliability will almost certainly decrease if verbal material with which the scorer is not familiar is scored (see S. Feld & Smith, 1958). Such material can take the form of stories written in response to cues other than those used to elicit the examples in the manual or the practice stories. However, even stories written to familiar pictures by different subject populations may pose this problem. For example, stories written by college students differ from those of younger or less well educated persons, whose stories may be shorter or different in content. The problem of reduced interscorer agreement may also occur if one applies the coding manual to nonstory material. For example, Child et al. (1958) discuss this problem in connection with their analysis of folktales.

Ultimately one may have to settle for somewhat lower interscorer reliability for unfamiliar than for familiar material. However, it is extremely important to attain the highest possible degree of agreement. To that end, the following things can be done. If possible, a pretest sample of the new material should be obtained and scored by two experienced scorers. They can discuss their differences, consult the manual, and agree on conventions to be applied to the new material. If pretest material is not available, a sample of the obtained research material may be used for initial discussion, and agreed upon conventions can then be applied to the scoring of the remaining material. Veroff (chapter 6) discusses how this problem has been dealt with in survey research. Examples of agreed upon conventions that supplement the scoring manuals for achievement, affiliation, and power motivation for a nationwide survey sample may be found in *Marriage and Work in America* (Veroff & Feld, 1970, pp. 370–371).

SCORING SHEET. Develop a procedure for recording all the information you need. One method is to provide a *row* for each subject and a column for the subject identification number, each coding category, the total score, and component scores (if any). If each coding category has a specific numerical value, that information can also be given at the head of the column. Space at the end of the row may be used for comments. Make provision at the top of each page for such information as the name of the scorer, the date of scoring, and the cue being scored. An example is given at the end of chapter 36.

PREPARATION OF MATERIALS TO BE SCORED. It is important to score the materials blind with respect to such information as sex, age, or race of subject, condition of administration, and so forth. *After all data are collected*, information of this kind should be removed from the story pages so that the coder knows only the subject identification and the cue for the story. If, for example, males and females wrote stories to the same cues, their stories should be shuffled together so that the scorer will not know the sex of the story writer. The same procedure should be followed if materials obtained under different conditions of administration, or at different time periods, are to be scored. If the identification indicates sex or group, new identification numbers should be given.

PREVENTION OF "HALO" EFFECT.   When scoring a story, a scorer should *not* have in mind a subject's scores on other stories. The goal, obviously, is to score each story independently of the others. In order to accomplish this, score all the stories for one cue before going on to those for another cue, and shuffle the stories so that they are in a different order before going on to the next cue. After all stories have been scored, the scores for each story can be entered on a separate sheet to obtain a total score for all stories.

PRESERVATION OF SET.   Score stories for a particular picture in as few sittings as possible so as to preserve approximately the same set for that picture.

Things to do while scoring

1. Refer to the manual while scoring whenever necessary.

2. Unless you are working with a photocopy of the original material, do not make any marks on the story sheet, since they might influence another coder.

3. If a word or passage has been crossed out by the story writer, but is still readable, score it. It is as much a part of the sample of associative thought as the rest of the story.

4. Make a note of problem stories as you go along. Come back to them later when fresh and rescore them. It is a good idea to review the manual and practice materials before rescoring difficult stories.

5. Try to prevent "scorer drift." When a large number of stories is scored over a period of time, it is possible for a scorer to drift away from the coding manual definition of categories and develop personal idiosyncratic meanings for categories. It is also possible for a scorer to lose the ability to make discriminations as a result of fatigue or satiation. It is a good idea to structure scoring so that scoring sessions are not too lengthy. Refreshing of memory is helpful by regular review of the manual and practice materials. If possible, check interscorer reliability for subsamples of material (e.g., 30 stories) at periodic intervals to identify scorer drift. Arrange materials so that fatigue or boredom does not always affect the scoring of material from the same set of subjects.

Things to do after scoring

RECONCILING DIFFERENCES.   If another scorer has scored the materials, the two sets of scores can be compared, differences can be discussed and reconciled, and final scores can be agreed upon. If another scorer has not scored the materials, wait for a few days and then rescore the material. Compare your two sets of scores and reconcile any differences in order to obtain final scores. One possible, though costly, way of increasing relatively low scoring reliability is to have a third scorer, so that reconciled scores represent the best judgments of three coders (cf. Child et al., 1958).

POOLING SCORES FROM SEVERAL JUDGES.   If at all possible, try to avoid having more than one coder for a specific system, unless a second is needed for purposes of obtaining intercoder agreement and reconciling differences. However, if the number of subjects is very large, as in a nationwide survey, the stories may have to be coded by several different judges whose scores must then be pooled into one final distribution. Feld and Smith (1958, pp. 692–693) give recommendations concerning the assignment of material to judges and measures to take if scores from different judges must be pooled.

STEP 7: DATA ANALYSIS

Prior to data analysis decisions must be made about whether data from all subjects are usable, and whether scores must be adjusted for differences in story length.

When to drop subjects

Dropping subjects, or not using some of their data, is usually painful because it reduces sample size and introduces potential bias. Nevertheless, for reasons such as low verbal fluency, defensiveness, or lack of cooperation, subjects may write stories that are unusable or omit stories altogether. Data may not be usable if one or more stories are too short (e.g., Walker & Atkinson, 1958, found that stories containing fewer than 30 words were unscorable), if one or more stories are omitted, or if one or more subjects are clearly uncooperative.

A researcher must decide whether to drop a subject who has even a single unusable story, or to retain the subject and use an estimated score for one or more stories. We suggest that at least two-thirds of a subject's stories must be usable. Veroff et al. (1960) required at least half of a subject's stories to be complete and no more than one question omitted from any of the subject's other stories. In their survey sample loss of data was greatest among the least-educated groups. Veroff (chapter 6) describes similar criteria for data elimination.

An uncooperative subject may write an insult such as "Go to hell!" instead of a story, or copy a paragraph from an available book. It is often difficult to decide whether to include data when lack of cooperation is suspected. It is probably better to retain and score a clearly facetious story than to drop a subject. However, if it is clear that the subject's response is not appropriate, then one must drop the subject and report and explain that decision. If more than a few subjects in a group show lack of cooperation, there may have been some problem with the data collection procedures (e.g., an authoritarian administrator, or a bad time of day, that makes subjects resentful) and the entire group may have to be discarded. Obviously, that decision should be made before any analyses are carried out, that is, prior to knowledge of the results.

Controlling for differences in length of verbal sample

Early in research on achievement motivation, McClelland et al. (1953, p. 220) considered the possibility that two subjects might be equal in (true) motive strength, but if one was low and the other high in verbal fluency, the latter might produce more motive-relevant imagery. Consequently, to minimize differences in verbal output, all subjects were given the same amount of time to write their stories, and to minimize the effect of verbal output on motive scores, no coding category was scored more than once per story no matter how many times it appeared.

Reviewing the evidence on this issue, Atkinson (1958b) concluded that the relationship between length of protocol and motive scores has been "insignificant and negligible in homogeneous college groups when leading questions are employed and four minutes is allotted for each story. . . . However, when the same kind of instrument is employed in a very heterogeneous population . . . , or when a shorter time (two and one-half minutes) is allotted for writing stories without leading questions . . . a significant correlation between number of words per story and motives scores is obtained" (p. 837). As a result of these and subsequent findings, it has been "the regular practice to correct for verbal fluency by adjusting the motive score statistically for the total number of words in all the stories" (McClelland, 1985b, p. 193).

Studies by Child et al. (1958) and by Walker and Atkinson (1958) used similar procedures to adjust motivation scores for differences in story length. In the Walker and Atkinson (1958) study, raw fear scores were adjusted to give scores reflecting where subjects stood "in the distribution of scores obtained from protocols having nearly the same number of words as their own" (p. 152). Veroff et al. (1960) give a more extensive discussion of this method as applied to stories obtained in survey research. (See also Veroff and Feld, 1970, pp. 372–373.) Adjustment for length is also discussed in *The Achieving Society* by McClelland (1961, pp. 64, 161, 461–463).

Lindzey and Silverman (1959) and D. G. Winter (1973, p. 146) recommend a regression method to remove the effect of a correlation between motive scores and length of verbal samples:

First, "predicted scores," given length, are calculated on the basis of the overall regression of score on length. For each subject, this involves multiplying that subject's story-length by the following constant: the overall correlation coefficient of length with motive score, times the ratio of the overall standard deviations of motive scores and length (SD of motive scores divided by SD of length). Subjects' predicted scores are then subtracted from their actual scores to give corrected scores that are exactly uncorrelated with length. (D. G. Winter, 1989d, pp. 5–6)

RECOMMENDATIONS REGARDING STORY LENGTH. If one is sampling preexisting verbal material, in some instances one may be able to avoid a problem by selecting samples that are all approximately the same length. If this is not feasible, then with preexisting material or with elicited stories, one must first count the number of words in the verbal sample for each subject (or other unit of analysis, e.g., society). (Counting words is laborious, but unavoidable so far as we know unless one has transcribed the verbal material onto a computer, in which case one can use software, such as the spell-check feature of WordPerfect, to provide a word count.) If the correlation between length of material and variable score is statistically significant, an adjustment for length normally should be made (preferably for each story separately). An adjustment should *not* be made if length is an intrinsic manifestation of the variable being measured. Finally, if, for some reason, stories have been obtained under different conditions of administration, the effect of condition on story length should be ascertained before stories from different conditions are combined.

Suggestions for data analysis

ADDING STORY SCORES VERSUS MULTIPLE REGRESSION. It makes sense to sum items (i.e., story scores) to obtain a total score when items measure a single dimension and it is appropriate to give them equal weight. A thematic measure may not meet these criteria. Scores obtained from different pictures may be intended to sample the same broad domain, but the items are not likely to be equivalent. For example, pictures of two situations in which achievement-oriented behavior can occur, a classroom and an athletic field, may have different degrees of relevance to different subjects (arouse different expectancies). As Exner (1976) puts it, projective methods were not "designed with equivalence of the stimuli as a goal; rather, each part is expected to contribute to the whole, but not necessarily with the same weight or with the same impact for each subject" (p. 69).

In view of these considerations, an alternative to summing scores from different stories is to enter them into a multiple regression equation in which each picture can make its distinctive contribution to the prediction of a dependent variable. (If necessary, scores for each story can be adjusted for story length.) Fleming and Horner (chapter. 11) report on the use of this approach in their research on the Motive to Avoid Success. Since multiple regression assumes a linear relationship, if assuming linearity is inappropriate, variables may be transformed or nonlinear regression employed.

MULTIPLE DETERMINANTS OF ACTION. One may wish to relate scores for several different motives to some criterion variable. In chapter 5 McClelland discusses several ways of going about this including multiple regression and a configurational approach. McClelland also discusses ways of dealing with moderator variables (see also chapter 29 by Sorrentino, Roney, and Hanna).

CONCLUSION

In this chapter we have provided guidelines, based on accumulated experience, that should make it possible to conduct methodologically sound thematic research. However, these guidelines leave plenty of room for novel developments. Throughout the chapter we have identified interesting and challenging problems for future research that can improve our understanding and use of the thematic method. For example, information is needed about factors affecting the selection and ordering of cues, and factors affecting the reliability of scores. More specifically, how do stories differ when written in response to picture cues as compared with verbal cues? What is the optimal cue strength, ambiguity, and order of presentation for a set of pictures designed to measure several motives at one time? How do recent life changes (e.g., divorce, psychotherapy) affect stories and the stability of measures? Would scores be more reliable and equally valid if a greater number of stories were obtained in a session, with less time allowed for writing each story? One intriguing possibility for research would be to explore the implications of the theory of the dynamics of action (chapter 2) for these questions both by means of empirical studies and by computer simulation.

In conclusion, we believe that theory-based thematic research will continue to expand our understanding of personality, motivation, and behavior, and we hope that this volume will also encourage research on the method itself that will enable us to take even better advantage of its distinctive promise.

NOTES

1 The reader may also wish to consult different, though somewhat overlapping, sets of recommendations regarding picture selection given by Crandall (1951), Henry

(1956), and Murstein (1965d), whose concerns were somewhat different than ours.

2 This passage was written prior to the development of the theory of the dynamics of action, which puts a somewhat different perspective on the matter of making inferences about motive strength (see Atkinson, chapter 2, this volume).

3 It may be of interest to note that the Murray instructions put the first two questions in the reverse order: "Tell what has led up to the event shown in the picture, describe what is happening at the moment, what the characters are feeling and thinking; and then give the outcome" (1943, p. 3).

Appendix I: Practice materials for learning the scoring systems

CHARLES P. SMITH AND CAROL E. FRANZ

INTRODUCTION

An unusual feature of this book is the inclusion of scores for a number of different scoring systems for a common set of practice stories. Appendix I consists of a set of thematic apperceptive stories together with "expert scoring" for each of the scoring systems included in this book with the exception of the Veroff *n* Power scoring system (chapter 20), and the Origin scoring system (chapter 24). Because the picture cues used to obtain the practice stories did not elicit sufficient imagery of the type coded by these two systems, the reader is referred to appendix I of *Motives in Fantasy, Action and Society* (Atkinson, 1958a) for practice materials for the Veroff *n* Power system, and to the latter part of chapter 24 of this volume for practice stories and expert scoring for the Origin system. Appendix III tells how to order additional practice materials for the various scoring systems.

Before using these practice materials the reader is urged to read chapter 37, which makes recommendations about how to learn the scoring systems and how to evaluate one's progress. The remainder of this section of appendix I provides information about the practice stories and then presents the stories themselves. Following the stories are sections for each system consisting of suggestions for learning each system and the expert scoring for each system.

These practice materials were compiled with help from the contributors to this volume and others to be named. The stories were made available by David C. McClelland and Carol E. Franz who wish to acknowledge the assistance of Richard Koestner, Joel Weinberger, Joseph Healy, Jr., Elizabeth Vandewater, Elizabeth St. Lawrence, Stephen Kelner, Ruth Jacobs, and Caroline McLeod in the collection of the stories. Funding from the Seaver Institute made possible the follow-up study from which the stories were obtained. Expert scoring for *n* Achievement was provided by Caroline McLeod and Charles P. Smith, and for *n* Affiliation by Joseph Scroppo and Joel Weinberger. Expert scoring for the remaining scoring systems was provided by the authors of the scoring manuals.

Information about the practice stories

CUES.   Stories were written in response to the following pictures:

1. Ship captain
2. Architect (or draftsman) at a desk
3. A couple on a bench by a river
4. Two women scientists in a laboratory
5. Trapeze artists
6. Man and woman with two horses and a dog

These pictures are reproduced in appendix II. They were chosen so as to permit assessment of Power, Achievement, Affiliation, and Intimacy motivation as well as Psychological Stances and Activity Inhibition. Because this set of pictures was selected to elicit imagery for several different variables, *some of the pictures elicit very little imagery for particular variables.*

INSTRUCTIONS.   Most of the stories were collected by an interviewer who timed the stories as respondents wrote them. Materials were sent by mail to a few subjects who could not be interviewed; they self-administered the measure. Interviewers obtained stories as the first step in the interview. Subjects, *who had told stories to the same pictures 10 years earlier*, were given the following instructions for the storytelling task:

We would like you to look at some pictures one at a time. After you look at the picture, please make up a story about what might be going on in the picture. Try to imagine what is happening. Then tell what is going on now, what happened before, what the people are thinking and feeling, and what they will do. Write a story that is complete – a story that has a beginning, a middle, and an end.

There are no right or wrong stories, so write whatever story you think of when you look at the picture. Spelling, punctuation, and grammar are not at all important. IT MAKES NO DIFFERENCE IF THE STORIES ARE SIMILAR TO OR DIFFERENT FROM ONES YOU HAVE WRITTEN PREVIOUSLY. What is important is to write whatever story you think of as you imagine what is going on in each picture.

To help you remember what to tell about in your stories, we have put some reminders at the top of each page. They will ask if you have mentioned:

What is happening? Who are the people?
What happened before?
What are the people thinking about and feeling? What do they want?
What will happen next?

First look at the picture for about fifteen seconds. Then write your story, taking no more than five minutes. Then turn to the next picture, look at it briefly, write your story, and so on. There is one page for writing each story. If you need more space for writing any one story, use the back of the page.

As noted in the instructions, reminders were put at the top of each blank page that asked if the subject had mentioned the following: What is happening? Who are the people? What happened before? What are the people thinking and feeling? What do they want? What will happen next?

SUBJECTS. The subjects were 41-year-old adults who, as children, had been studied as part of the Sears, Maccoby, and Levin (1957) *Patterns of Child Rearing* sample. Stories were obtained from 89 white, middle-class adults from the metropolitan Boston area. All of the subjects had finished high school: 50% had at least some college, 42% pursued graduate degrees. Most (92%) were working at least part-time outside the home. Stories for 30 of the subjects (13 men and 17 women) are reproduced here. Because the sex of the story writer should not be known until after the stories are scored, information about the sex of the subjects is given on the page following the expert scoring section.

STORY CHARACTERISTICS. A few subjects have missing stories; some have unusually short stories. Information on how to deal with such problems is given in chapter 37. The stories are reproduced as written, with errors in spelling, grammar, and punctuation preserved. Some of the stories are written without paragraph breaks. When paragraphs appear they generally indicate a response to one of the four questions (What is happening? What happened before? What is being thought, felt, and wanted? What will happen next?).

Please turn now to the section of this appendix on the scoring system you wish to learn. Read the introductory material explaining how to learn that system. Following the introductory material is the expert scoring, which, of course, you should not look at until you score the stories in the manner suggested.

PRACTICE STORIES

Stories of 30 subjects are given for each of six pictures (although an occasional story is missing for a subject). The number of each story indicates the subject and the picture (e.g., 25-2 designates Subject 25, Picture 2). Before scoring look at the picture for each set of stories and keep in mind the questions given to guide the story writing (i.e., What is happening? etc.).

Picture 1

1-1. The captain of a ship belonging the gentleman in the picture is explaining why he hasn't met the owners expectations.

The ship is a passenger cruise ship which has gotten a poor reputation for service to passengers.

The captain is explaining what he'll need from the owner in order to provide better service in the future. He needs more competent help, better quality of food and better support from office staff.

2-1. This is the real Capt. Queeg telling Humphrey Bogart how to roll ball bearings between his fingers. Humphrey is blocking his dexterity with the bearings because of the blatant sexual imagery. Queeg has just explained that a bearing is a bearing is a bearing.

3-1. The Captain is explaining to George that his luggage will be found. It is not unusual for passengers to get to their room before the luggage arrives. Although George does feel frustration, he will wait as suggested by the Captain. The Captain will be available for George if the luggage does not arrive shortly.

4-1. It looks as if there is a senior officer talking with a person of lower rank. There is a conversation going on and judging by the face of the senior officer, who has a smile, it is a friendly conversation. They probably met in passing on the deck of a ship and perhaps were discussing something they had done the evening before. They will probably both continue on their separate ways – getting down to the days business.

5-1. The cruiseliner captain is talking with one of the passengers.

6-1. The captain of the ship is asking for a payoff for smuggling some items on his ship. The other man is an oriental man who asked for the smuggling, and is now meeting with the captain to iron out details about how the items will be loaded off the ship. They have done this before, but the captain knows that the smuggler is slow in paying for the "favor" and the captain is demanding payment now. The man will pay him at the end of the meeting, or else no "items" will be released to the shore.

7-1. Two people are having a conversation. One is the boat captain, the other is a passenger. The passenger booked a cruise. The captain is telling the passenger all about his ship.

He thinks the passenger wants information about the ship itself. The passenger wants information about the ship's speed, route, safety, etc.

They will take the cruise and have a good time. The weather will probably be good and the passenger will eat well, look around at all ports of call, and sunbathe a lot. He will have a nice vacation and arrive back home. Satisfied.

8-1. The captain of the cruise ship is making a point to a civilian (possibly a customer)

9-1. The captain and one of his passengers are talking about a problem the passengers having with his cabin. The water is leaking in his porthole.

The captain explains, that this happens at times and he will see its taken care of immediately. Mr. Smith, the passenger, say allright goes back to the cabin and waits for someone to come.

After a short wait, a man comes and fixes the porthole. As Mr. Smith trip continues he is pleased to find no more water coming in.

10-1. Two men are engaged in a Serious Conversation. One is the Captain of a Luxury liner about to set sail. The other, a private detective, who has just told the captain the ship must be detained. It is feared that an illegal passenger is on board, a passenger wanted very much by the police. The Captain is skeptical, and wants definite proof that there is such a dangerous person.

The proof give by the detective is not enough for the Captain to delay departure, and upset his passengers. The Luxury liner sails, along with the highly Sought after "Cat burgler."

11-1. It's 1952. The Captain of the cruise liner is smuggling drugs hidden in antique figurines from the South China Seas. Sort of a Maltese Falcon scenario. Captain is trying to make a deal with the man in the hat who is an undercover agent unbeknownst to the Captain, although he knows that someone is on his tail and he is in a hot spot. He's trying to get out of it and walking right into it. The man in the hat is just listening. Eventually the Captain will be caught. He will cook his own goose.

12-1. "Now, listen Bill. We found the cashmere sweaters in this little shop in Sydney. This little Kangaroo Lady actually taught me a new knit and purl stitch, two loops over and three under produces an iris pattern. Very pretty in ivory and purple with a green background."

"But what hope do we have of getting the diamonds in?"

Oh, see the rhinestones on the little, wide arm hole vest, just wash the glitter off. A few more are in my knitting-needles and I really found a good place. Use them as hem weights.

"Well, then we should have enough to go home to England forever."

Not forever, just until we know no one is chasing us.

13-1. I observe a ship's captain on the deck of a freighter speaking to a civilian. The civilian is a police officer investigating a crime which occurred aboard ship before it docked. One of the crewmen was found involved in the cargo hold. No one witnessed his death except, perhaps, the murderer.

The ship's captain is arguing with the police inspector that the crewman fell into the hold and died by accident. The Police inspector thinks it was a crime.

14-1. It appears that the Captain of this battleship is having a serious conversation with a public personality. Perhaps a leader in politics. The country has been at war and a serious mission is about to begin. The captain is explaining the complexities of this mission and how he sees the mission to be accomplished. His control in this conversation is needed.

15-1. This is a sea captain speaking to a detective. There has been a theft on his ship. The year is 1957. The captain is sternly explaining to the detective he must find the thief before they reach port. After much interviewing of passengers and crew the detective deduces that the thief is one of the crew he sets a trap using a diamond Ring and the thief springs for it a is caught Red handed.

16-1. It had been a real long summer. Captain Haver was more than ready to leave the Vineyard for the last roundtrip from Vineyard Haven after the Labor Day weekend. Then he'd have 2 weeks vacation, first a stop off in Falmouth to pick up his wife and their suitcases, and then a long but enjoyable ride to the coast of Maine.

Only problem was, he couldn't leave yet. The ferry had loaded real slow. 88° and lines of angry New Yorkers waiting in their cars for the last trip today. He knew only half of them would get on.

Then it happened. Someone noticed the gold coin on the ramp. Before Haver knew it, the cops, the newspaper and the Mayor were involved. Mayor Tisbury's bowler was stained through above the band, and sweat was pouring down his cheek. "You ain't movin' this ferry no place til we find out whose car contains more of that stolen loot from the Museum," he said gruffly.

Haver started to protest, raising his hand to emphasize a point, then dropped it slowly, realizing that it was no use arguing with this guy. He'd wait, the ferry would wait, his wife would wait, and best of all, Maine would wait.

17-1. An officer from a ship, that has just arrived at the dock, is approaching a customs official. The officer is answering questions from the customs' officer and is annoyed because he is loosing time. Both men know each other and have had problems in the past.

The ship's crew has not done anything illegal and after some time lost during the inspection, they will unload.

18-1. Two men are talking. One is the captain of the ship and the other is a visitor The visitor is going on a tour of the ship with the capt.

The Captain wants this visitor to be impressed with the "ship shape ship" The visitor will be favorably impressed with the capt. and his ship the visitor is a Senator and is capable of expanding funds for the Naval officers fleet.

19-1. The fellow with the uniform appears to be the captain of the ship, and the other person in the picture would appear to be a passenger about to board ship. The captain appears to be explaining something about the trip they are about to embark on. The captain appears to be in a pleasant frame of mind. The other person, you can't see his face, so you assume he is in a happy state of mind also.

As far as what will happen next it appears that they are going on a trip. And they are anticipating it will be a pleasant one.

20-1. There are two men standing in front of a ship. The captain of the ship is telling the business man that he cannot get a ticket because they are totally booked. The man is pleading with the captain that he must get on the ship because there is an important meeting going on and he must attend. The man is panicky because he feels he must be at the meeting. His plans were changed at the last minute. The captain finally has the other men tracked down and one is willing to share his room with the desperate man. The captain lets the man on the ship.

21-1. The two men are on board a ship at sea. One man is the ship's captain and the other is an agent of a foreign government. The agent is a mysterious person who is in charge of a secrete cargo in the ship's hold. The captain has delivered the cargo and is collecting pay for the task. The cargo, which has been transferred a great distance, will be removed from the ship and will disappear.

22-1. Telly Savalas (Kojak) is looking for a foreign crewman from this ship who is wanted for questioning in a robbery. Kojak doesn't know it, but the crewman is also čarrying the plague. The captain of the ship trys to help, but doesn't have any useful information. Kojak find the crewman eventually and saves the city from the plague.

23-1. A sea captain is talking to a male person who is probably a business man. They are on a freighter and they are having a difficult conversation. The sea captain is explaining to the business man a matter. Thus, the business man wants something from the sea captain. Based upon the captains hand position and the dress of the business man it seems the business man is in illegal business and the captain looks italian and about 60 years of age. I believe they will move illegal material on the ship distant to some port.

24-1. The Captain is explaining the ship's itinerary to a businessman who has cargo on board.

The situation is not without its confusions and the Captain is being mildly assertive as opposed to apologetic.

The businessman is not satisfied with the explanation, sensing undue delay or late delivery of his goods.

Stalemate will be the end of this discussion.

25-1. The man with his back to me has just asked the captain of the cruise ship directions to a local tourist spot. The captain is giving him directions and concerns about the area. Apparently there have been some gangs lurking around and have given some tourists a hard time. The captain is telling him to be very careful.

The man is a very aware individual who has done much traveling to remote areas of the world. He finds what he is looking for and does so quite safely.

26-1. The gentleman in the business suit is approaching the Captain of a cruise Ship. He has lost his passport and all identification. He is trying to convince the captain of the legitimacy of his request to board ship and continue on the cruise. The Captain is skeptical but willing to quickly check the ship's passenger list and verify the man's identification. He does this and allows the man to board. Also, he notifies the proper authorities that the passport and I.D.'s are lost and asks them to radio the ship if some are found.

27-1. There appears to be a question aboard ship. There is the captain and a passenger. The captain is explaining or clarifying to the passenger the direction which will be taken. Perhaps the passenger has misplaced his luggage or he could have a question regarding some sort of help.

28-1. This sea captain is being questioned by a New York City Police detective. There has been a crack down on drug smuggling in the city and all ship (cargo and pleasure) captains have been questioned.

This captain is stating that he has no reason to suspect any of his crew. He is still cooperative and willing to assist the police on this investigation in any way he can.

29-1. The Captain is being questioned about the murder that has taken place on his ship. Charlie Chan has been put on the case because he was a passenger. Since the Captain's alibi was phoney Mr. Chan knew he was the one who murdered Dr. Who.

30-1. The captain is talking to the owner of the ship about some problems with the cargo and he (the captain) didn't want anymore unmarked cargo as the ship was becoming inspected by the Federal Government and he (the captain) had to have everything opened. The captain said he had a problem in the past with drugs in the cargo and he had to spend a lot of time and money to clear himself. The owner said he was gone to check on the cargo and it wouldn't happen again.

Picture 2

1-2. An engineer working on an important project is in his office. He has stopped for a moment to look at the picture he has on his desk of his family. He realizes that he has not been able to spend the time he would like to with them. His work has taken up too much of his life and he would like to change that. He resolves to reassess his priorities and put his family in a higher spot.

2-2. This is a designer working on a concept called Stepford Wives. He is wondering if he should start with a modular frame that could produce an entire nuclear family or perhaps just one unit at a time. His doubt concerns an earlier career choice about working for Kenner products designing toys. In that capacity one of his models was elected President of the United States. Ultimately his Stepford model fails due to microwave exposure in the kitchen.

3-2. Lewis seems to always work late. It seems he never has enough time to be with his family. During these late hours his work quality suffers as his thoughts are with his family. Lewis will soon go home, leaving his work unfinished, to be with his family. Tomorrow is another day.

4-2. This man is at work. He looks as if he is looking at a picture of his family. He may be working on a project far from home and thinking of his family that he is missing. He may wish that he was back at home with them. He'll remember some of the happy things that have occurred when they are together. After a bit of daydreaming, he'll get back to work knowing that his family waits for him when he finishes.

5-2. A father/husband trying to do his job, but keeps thinking about his family.

He seems to be daydreaming. He may feel that he has chosen the wrong profession and wishes he could. He has a lot of responsibilities raising a family and at work. He cannot just quit and leave.

So he stays and continues as always.

6-2. This man is a architect for a large company who is having thoughts about leaving the company and opening his own architectural firm, to design homes, building, for his own clients, rather than buildings, complexes for his company. He is thinking of the security that his present company gives him financially and security wise, and for his family, but he thinks what would really make him happier at work and at home is being his "own" boss. He wants to do what's best for him and his family. What he now will do is tell his wife, and make plans to gradually go on his own, doing a few independent jobs on his own, and then when his own business is strong, will leave his present company.

7-2. This man is a draftsman of some sort and he is at work.

He prepared for this job by going to school – college – for many years. He likes his work.

The picture on his desk is his family, whom he loves. He is anticipating going home when work is done to his loving family.

He wants to get his work done soon.

He will finish his work and go home for dinner. After a nice evening with his family, he will be back at work tomorrow, doing the best job he can on his drafting.

8-2. A man (possibly a draftsman) at work in a plant. He appears to be a family man who is motivated by his work – He appears to have stable work–home life.

9-2. Mr. Jones, an architect is going to surprise his family by building them a new house.

As he gazes at their picture he trys to picture in his mind the kind of house they would love.

As the house come to mind he quickly sketches it down. That night he takes it home and tells his wife, next week we begin a new house.

His wife is very excited, but anxious, so much to do, how will we get it all done. Her husband exclaims, don't worry everything will work out.

10-2. A man deep in thought, being torn by a decision he must make. He is an Industrial architech working on plans to build a Nuclear Plant in his home town. It is a small town with good family people. People who need jobs which the plant would provide. The company planning to build the plant, he feels, is not a reliable one, and has made mistakes in the past. But the townspeople need jobs, and feel this is the best thing.

This architech will decide that although the plant will provide work for his fellow townsmen, it is far to dangerous to complete the plans and put his family in danger.

11-2. 1938 movie. This man is an architect whose business is in trouble. Someone from his black past has emerged and is trying to blackmail him. Not wanting to threaten the happy new life with wife and kiddies he has established since breaking free and changing his ways, he is now facing the torturous decision of whether or not to do something dishonest, (embezzle money) to keep the blackmailer quiet. He is torn. He tries to cover it up but eventually his wife suspects something is wrong, gets it out of him they take it on together and all works out in the end. (I feel a bit cynical about this ending – I like the idea, but it sounds a bit smarmy, like a 1938 movie, perhaps!)

12-2. Old photograph advertising Prince shirts. I knew the man before he lost his shape. God, I tried to marry him, but I wasn't rich and attractive enough to him. Now, he lives on Laurel just up from that nice white house with the green shutters. Bald as an egg, Gladys, and round as one. My Victor has not put on a pound since our marriage, but this guy Jack Fartheum really ballooned out. He doesn't seem to work, just sits in his back yard playing with a telephone or something.

13-2. I observe a man of about 40 years of age sitting at a drafting table taking a break from work. He is an architect. He is in the middle of a big project for the firm he works for. He is pleased by the way the job is going and he is pleased at his own work.

He is looking at a photograph of his wife and two children. He is thinking to himself what a lucky fellow he is to have such a family and a good job.

He has the look of self satisfaction. He is thinking of the vacation he has planned with the family as soon as the project is over.

14-2. Sometimes during the day when you're removed from a family situation, your mind tends to wander to that family. When at work, you can be distracted if the concentration isn't there. At home situations can make you feel happy or they can be seen for what they really are. It is good to be away from ones close to you so you can reflect on them with distance.

15-2. This is a man who is an Archectect from the 1940's. He has many drawings of a building he has designed. He spent many many hours on his building. But his plans have been rejected by the building. He's looking at the picture of his family, and thinking how many more hours he's going to be away from them as he has to redo all the plans to the building specifications again but he will do it and keep his job with the building.

16-2. Almost 40 and still pushing a pencil. The kids had grown so fast he could hardly believe it. The job sucked and the commute was enough to give him an ulcer.

Scott looked at the picture of his family again and had to catch his breath when he realized that the photo had been taken almost 15 years ago. If he didn't make the move soon, he'd be too old to start a new profession, not to mention too scared.

It was settled then! He and Michelle had talked it over many times and both agreed it had to be done soon. As soon as their youngest daughter started college, they would pack up their stuff, sell the house, and move west to Pennsylvania. They had managed to save a little money, their oldest daughter was on a free scholarship, and their youngest was on the coop plan at Northeastern. Pushing motorcycle sales would be tough too, but in a different way, and he was ready for it.

17-2. This fellow is pausing from a hard days work and thinking about his family. He seems to enjoy his family or he would "daydream" about something else to relax. It's possible that this is his last day of work before he goes on vacation with them.

He has a responsible job and provides for them adequately so I'm sure they are planning to go on a trip to Disney World.

18-2. The man is day dreaming at work as he looks at the photo of his family and realizes that the work that he does is for them in part. He wants to be happy at work and with his family. He will continue to do what he can for them.

19-2. The person in the picture appears to be a man who is hard at work; perhaps far away from his family as he looks at the picture in front of him. Perhaps he's wishing that he could be with his family instead of where he is now – working. As far as what happens next – he will probably pick up a telephone and call his family.

20-2. There is a man at his office working very late to meet a deadline. He is an architect and quite successful. He is tired and would like to be done and home. He looks at the picture of his family and wonders if it is all worth it – working so hard, so many late nights. He would rather be home having dinner with his family and then relaxing. He thinks about his responsibilities; all the things he wants to do for his family and what is expected of him at work. He knows he must finish his work. He stops, calls home to tell everyone he loves them and is thinking of them. Then he returns to work. He decides to take a day off when the project is done and relax.

21-2. The seated man is an archetect. He has designed many houses for many people over the years and is now planning a home for his own family. The people in the picture are his family and he is designing a very special home for them. He sits at his table thinking about what each person in his family would like to have in the new house. He will design the house so that each persons interests and dreams will be found in this house.

22-2. This man has had the same job for 10 years. He is good at his work but not aggressive and has not moved up in the company. He has just been laid off and wonders how he will tell his wife and how he will support his family. He feels sad and defeated.

23-2. A designer is looking at his family picture. The male of age 40 looking at his wife and two children. Hard work and he is taking a break. Something in the past or workload has caused him to take a mental break. What is wanted is a little TLC from wife, and this will probably happen when he gets home. A generally pleasant hard working guy with a good family.

24-2. The architect/developer has been working for some time on this project. Finally he has his approvals in place and is, and has been, studying blue prints of actual planned structures.

Although much is done, a year or more of painstaking attention will have to be devoted to actual construction. He looks at the picture of his family knowing that he faces a schism of thought. On the one hand, his successes are for them and their comfort and security. He is pleased to provide all this. On the other hand, his projects preclude him from having the kind of time with them that he would like. His priorities are necessarily in question.

25-2. The man is the husband and father of the people in the picture. They have gone to visit grandparents and he has stayed behind to work. He is in the middle of a project. It has been a week since they left and he is wishing they would come home soon. He sees the picture but then remembers the dog chasing his boy. His oldest girl and her first Christmas. A warm wonderful feeling fills his heart. Soon they will be home again.

26-2. The gentleman in the picture is fondly looking at a photo of his wife and children. He is working as a draftsman for the same company he has worked for the past 10 years. He is wishing that his company provided him with more opportunity for advancement and salary increment. He deeply loves his family and has decided to pursue his wish and applies for a job at another engineering Co. where he will be hired at a higher salary w/ more opportunity for advancement.

27-2. This is a draftsman or an engineer working late. He seems to be concentrating more on his wife and 2 children than on his plans.

I'm sure he'll finish up his work and head towards home.

28-2. This man is an advertising executive. He is working on a deadline as he always does on each project he undertakes.

It is early evening – his sleeves are rolled up – and he has already been on the job for 10 hours. He is anxious to finish up for the evening so that he can at least be home before his children go to bed – since he has already missed supper with his family.

29-2. The man is looking at the picture of his family and feeling depressed. It was Sunday and they called him in to finish the project. His family went to the beach and he was left home. Maybe if he hurries, he can still get there before dark.

30-2. The man works for a newspaper and is going abroad and his family is unable to go and he is upset. The job is in Iran and he is a little worried but want to go to work on his piece he hopes everything will go fine and he won't be captured by the government as a spy. He has been told by his boss our (US) government and foreign government everything will be ok.

Picture 3

1-3. Its winter in Boston, a couple in love are sitting together watching the ice form on the Charles. They have both taken the afternoon off from their jobs with the intent of spending the rest of the day together. They have been planning to get married as soon as George wins the lottery. He has been purchasing tickets for 4 years now and is trying to convince Zelda that his lucky # is coming up soon!

2-3. This is the bank of the Charles River where this young con artist is explaining to an innocent B.U. student how he has become the youngest full professor at M.I.T. She is unconvinced but enjoys the attention knowing he is oblivious to her highly infectious fatal disease. Shortly she will reject his advances and move on to another unsuspecting hustler.

3-3. Stephen is leaving. He does not know how to explain it to Sarah, his "significant other" for these past three year. It's a cold day in Boston and the frozen Charles River does not make parting any easier. In both their hearts, their love is still strong and they know they will never see each other again.

4-3. There is a man and a woman sitting on the banks of a river. They have some quiet time to just talk. They are enjoying the out of doors and the scenery. Talking together lets them know more about each others feelings.

5-3. Two people in love just taking a stroll and decided to sit and relax on the park bench.

Just light easy conversation. No hassles. A day off to relax and enjoy each other's company.

They will leave and have a nice quiet dinner outside in a restaurant.

6-3. This is a couple that works together in an office in Cambridge. He likes her very much, but he is kind of the office "nerd," someone that everyone gets along with, but who everyone kind of feels sorry for or thinks is a bother sometime. She has gone out for a walk in the early spring, during her lunch hour, to get some fresh air and exercise. He went out also, and followed her, to have a chance to talk away from the office. She is looking off in the distance, thinking that she would like to change jobs, move up, and yet is going on and on about his more immediate hopes and plans for his life. He will stay working there for a long time. She'll probably leave for another job in a year or so.

7-3. Two people are having a conversation in a park. They are a young couple – probably not married. They have been going together for a while and enjoy being together and discussing things they have in common and their goals in life. They want to get to know each other better. Each of them wants to know the plans and dreams of the other.

They will probably get married sometime in the future; they both seem too young now. They will finish schooling and get jobs and find a place to live.

8-3. Two people boyfriend and girlfriend spending some romantic time together – what apparently is wanted is a furtherance of the relationship by at least the male.

9-3. Janet asked her husband Fred to meet her on the river. She was so excited. How long they had waited for this to happen.

Fred appeared and she rushed to him, tears in her eyes. Fred she said, we're going to have a baby.

Fred was struck, speechless. He thought it would never happen. As he took her hand they sat on the bench. Fred was beaming from ear to ear.

This is the best news, what we've both waited for so long. I love you, Janet. I love you, Fred.

10-3. Two people sitting together, perhaps at lunch time break. They seem to know each other, and enjoy each others company. They both work for the same company, and have taken a walk after lunch. Now they are sitting, more likely discussing some work related matter.

11-3. By the Charles River, Harvard law student romances Radcliffe Art History major. He is entranced by her beauty, brains and eccentricity, though fearful that her questionable background might not be acceptable to his stuffy blue-blood family, in fact to himself. He is snotty and repressed. She is attracted and impressed but essentially frustrated that he is always a stick-in the mud. They are together for a couple of years but as she grows in herself she finally has the presence of self and mind (unlike myself) to realize that it will never work and goes on to marry an equally eccentric physicist from MIT.

12-3. Remember. Tell on me how flowers paled our lives, pedaling us in Vermont fields. The itch after the haying, you made me oatmeal baths to soothe the sores. Let's rob a bank or something, dump yesterday and today for tomorrow.

Remember the yellow floors in the summer house along the Costa Brava, near that single standing pine. We took turns looking at the floor arched like that old bridge. Row, row, row.

Too bad civilization has come to the Charles. Even ten years ago we could have walked down by the river and snuck a kiss and bumpadedump or two. Now, Helene, we almost need a private room in a special. Helene, now wake up. I know its cold, but it will be all right. I'll hold you. You have stopped shivering at least. Now talk to me a little, just say something . . .

13-3. The picture shows two graduate students sitting on a bench beside the Charles River.

They are in the same graduate course and have seen each other in class. Today, however, the are talking person to person for the first time.

After class he suggested to her that they take a walk together. She was ready for the invitation.

Although this is mid week he has just asked her if she would have dinner on Friday. He suggests his favorite pizza shop. She says o.k. but no anchovies. They both laugh.

14-3. On a warm, sunny day it is nice to escape from the everyday situations and sit alongside the water. Cambridge and Boston have many areas with benches to sit on while having your lunch. I'm reminded of home for the Charles River was in our back yard.

It is fun being with someone on this bench for the outside air seems to let the words flow easily.

15-3. There is a man and woman, who went for a walk on a winters day. They went to a quiet place with a lovely bridge over a part where it was quiet and free of distractors. They wanted to make plans for a trip to a warm climate. The winter here was pretty but harsh. The trip would take them to South america where they would work together in the warm climate catching birds to send to the zoo's in the states. It would be an exciting job.

16-3. Carol was always unhappy about something. If it wasn't her job, it was her love life. If those situations were going ok, she'd find something else.

But now she really had something to be unhappy about, and Jack was surprised at how well she was handling it.

December had been cold and dreary and it seemed that winter was far from over. During the holidays, Carol found out that her dad was dying of cancer. Ted would have expected that she would fall apart, but instead, she was sitting there on the banks of the Charles on a cold but sunny day in January, telling him about strength, about love, about real feelings. Things that Ted never realized were in her repertoire of thoughts.

Maybe it was just that people have more trouble dealing with day to day situations which were harder to assign feelings to than real issues.

17-3. This couple is enjoying one of the last nice days (good weather) before it gets uncomfortably cold to sit out doors. It looks as if they are in Boston by the Charles River.

Although they are not in a hurry, or have any appointments to meet, they are serious. This is one of the few chances they have to be alone. The man is discussing something of importance with his female friend. She appears to be listening and perhaps they will return "home" before dark.

18-3. The people are friends who are out for a stroll and stopped to take a rest. They come to this spot after and talk. They are enjoying each other and want to continue enjoying each other. Hopefully they will repeat this scene and stroll hand in hand into the sunset.

19-3. We have a young couple sitting happily apparently enjoying each other's company. Their surroundings appear to be very peaceful and enjoyable. Perhaps the next thing they will do is take a leisurely walk along the shores of the river.

20-3. It is a cold, brisk day in December. A man and woman are sitting on a bench by the Charles River. They are in love and happy. He is quite nervous because he has to tell her that he is being transferred to another city 1000 miles away and he wants her to marry him and come with her. He tells her and she is shocked. She loves him and wants to marry him but she does not want to leave her family, friends, job and security of her familiar surroundings. She is torn but knows that if he is going to go – she will go. She decides to tell him she needs time and they will talk more. She is hoping she can get him to change his mind, but if he won't, she will go.

21-3. It is winter on the Charles River in Boston. The two people sitting on the bench are students who have come to study and begin their careers. They have met and have found common interests in their careers and have found interest in each other. They are now planning their careers and their lives together. They will be married.

22-3. She has stopped to have a cigarette during her daily walk. The man has been trying to engage her in conversation, but he is boring and annoying. She is irritated that he has "trespassed on her space" and will get up and leave.

23-3. Two lovers male and female discussion some thoughts/feelings on the Charles River in the afternoon. They seem serious on their conversation, and she seems not to be listening well. I think the guy is smiling and looking for a response to the girl. Maybe he is asking her to do something for him, like a date etc. and she will probably accept. Girls in pony tails tend to be less conflicting personalities than girls with close groom looks. The guy looks out of control but happy.

PS: this sounds crazy

24-3. The two people on the bench recently met in Harvard Square. Each is single and desiring of meeting attractive counterparts, but here the fellow is much more desirous than the woman.

He is attempting to initiate/engage her in an interesting conversation of some mutual interest. His attempts are failing.

She is sitting placidly and by design, or circumstance, will be very hard to engage in such interchange.

I cannot predict the eventual result.

25-3. I hate doing this!

It is a cold windy day. This couple is dating and they have gone down to the river for a walk in the snow and ice. The have run thrown snowballs and are pleasantly sitting for a minute. They are getting to know one another. His thoughts – her thoughts. Eventually they will marry but not quickly. They will have many times together before that happens.

26-3. This couple is discussing the feasibility of their marrying one another. He is a Russian student on visa in the U.S. and she is a citizen here. They have fallen deeply in love and are weighing the red tape and bureaucracy involved in their pursuit of happiness as their desire to wed. They are truly in love and decide to wed, and he deflects to the US, renouncing his Soviet citizenship and giving up on any hope of seeing his parents and family anytime soon.

27-3. This seems to be a nice winter day in Cambridge along the Charles River. There appears to be ice on the water but I do think the temperature is above normal.

There is a couple sitting on a bench talking. Maybe they are friends or co-workers or even husband, or wife, brother or sister.

When they have finished their discussion, they'll back return to their cars and resume whatever they were doing before they met to talk.

28-3. Even though it is February in Boston it is still nice to get out at lunch time and enjoy the outdoors along the banks of the Charles River. It certainly helps to clear your head and keep you from getting drowsy after lunch.

These two people are from neighboring buildings and have come to enjoy each others conversation at the noon hour.

29-3. After a brief walk by the Charles River, Bob got up enough courage to ask Ann to marry him. Although he still had 2 yrs left at Harvard he wanted her for his wife. Ann said "yes" but only when he graduates.

30-3. This couple is at the Boston common and it is late fall and the girl is telling her boyfriend that she is going to have a child he is elated and can hardly wait to tell the world. She is very upset doesn't want the child but is unable to abort because of religious belief. She wants to stay in college and finish her degree and explore her life. She is only 20 years old. They both have different feelings and decide to see someone on a professional level and see from then.

Picture 4

1-4. Two employees of a medical test center are awaiting the results of an important test sampler from the president. The boss, standing on the right is checking that all necessary steps are followed.

The whole country's future could be in jeopardy if the test shows positive. The president had been bitten earlier that day by a rabid dog.

2-4. Madame Curie is concocting a elixir made of high grade radium which gives one a glowing sense of well being. The young assistant is curious about who will be the first human to test this wonder drug. Perhaps she will volunteer her bashful boyfriend who has been seeking illumination with Madame Blavatsky.

3-4. Gwen has been working for a cure to the disease ever since it started affecting most people in the city. She has been working day and night with her assistant Gail. It is a race against time with no clear winner in sight. She must go on.

4-4. A doctor and her assistant are doing some lab work. They may be analyzing specimens from a patient that has come in for test. They will get results and let the patient know their diagnosis. If there is a problem, they will offer remedies to help alleviate it.

5-4. Two female research scientists working in a lab.

They are trying to help find a cure for some disease.

Both always wanted to do this type of work and are very intense and serious about their profession.

They have a feeling of self-fulfillment and accomplishment and will continue to work in this field.

6-4. There are two research scientists who work in a lab doing medical research the woman on the left is the head of the program, and usually gets the publicity when any progress or results happen. The woman on the right does most of the background, hard, routine work, and doesn't get much credit for the work done. The woman on the left is the boss, and is somewhat autocratic – work is work, you do it and you get paid for it. The right side woman is rather shy and un-assertive, but proud of her work and accomplishments. She is going to ask her boss for a raise, because she knows she is good at her job. The boss will give her a raise, because she knows the other woman is the backbone of the program.

7-4. Two women are working in a lab. They are both researchers. They have studied and done research for a long time on this project and are thinking it would be nice to have a breakthrough and get good results.

They want the research to go well and be productive. They want to make a contribution to science.

They will get results, which will get them a step closer to a solution to the problem. They will continue doing research, searching for the truth in small pieces.

8-4. Teacher and student interacting in a scientific lab experiment.

9-4. They had been trying for days, months, years to find a cure for the deadly disease. Finally they were on the threshold of something.

As they stood and watched the chemicals mix, their breaths were held in anticipation. If this worked many people would be saved finally from Aids.

As she dropped the specimen into the test tube, what they had dreamed of for so long happened. It worked, as they looked at each other their eyes were full of tears and excitement. They had finally won.

10-4. Two women in a laboratory. Both seem to have knowledge and authority. The older one in the background is probably the Professor, and the other the Student. The Student is a mother and wife gone back to school to become a doctor. The professor feels this student has good potential, and observes her carefully. The professor wants this woman to succeed and will give her every chance she can, for she too is a wife and mother.

11-4. A Nobel-prize winning scientist (with test-tube) and her considerably lesstalented assistant who has always been jealous of her. In working on a cure for AIDS they have inadvertently discovered (or think they have) an antidote for advanced adolescent narcissism in men (guess who I'm angry at today). The assistant realizes that this could be a staggering breakthrough for mankind, stopping wars, death, destruction, pollution of the environment, unjust imbalance of wealth etc., but her personal grudge against her boss perverts her perspective and she is plotting to sabotage the experiments so that they never will be known to modern science. Her boss catches her in the lab one night trying to alter the results, understands what is going on, stops her, fires her, but not before explaining that, in fact the antidote only worked on brain cells up to the age of sixteen thereby only replicating a natural life process, and was therefore useless.

12-4. Ah, radon! I knew we could sell these young people a product. Protect your health, your children, your wife and mother. Buy a radon detector and for just 19.99 you can measure dust in the air in your basement.

13-4. I observe two biomedical chemists working in their laboratory. Both are tenured professors and have recently decided to work on a research project together.

The woman in the foreground is from Paris. She has been in the U.S. for 5 years. It was her idea to start the project. She is very intense in her belief that a certain gene can be identified. This intensity often gets in the way with the project. Her partner, a more reflective person, keeps the perspective. Together they make a good team.

14-4. There are so many diseases that we're aware of in the world that it is good to know that there are people who have dedicated themselves to science and healing. Becoming aware of your body and how you treat it is an awareness everyone should have and knowing that there is help for sickness can enable you to not feel as helpless.

15-4. This is a scientist and her assistant there working on a project to cure heartworm in dogs. They have been work on the project for six years. Today would be the day that there work could be called a success. The formula has been curing for several days. Now the assistant has checked ten of the twenty vials all of them are positive. The scientist checks the rest. They have done it. Now the project is over they have won.

16-4. Meg pipetted the chronoform carefully into the test tube. This extraction was the umpteenth one she had done, but the end was in sight. She would be glad to finish this project; glad because she was getting encouraging results, and glad because she wanted to move onto something else.

She was tempted to tell Chris some of the problems she had had during her years in the lab, but she was afraid that if she said too much, Chris would decide that she had taken a bad job, and leave. Then Meg would have to stay longer and train someone else.

It was a little selfish, but she felt that she had done her stint, and let Chris encounter her own problems, and deal with them in her own way.

17-4. A serious woman is working in her lab. She is thinking about her work or appears to be thinking of her work.

A coworker (possibly a male) appears to be interested in her and is about to tell her so. Although she will be polite, she will tell this person that although she may like him (or her) she is not interested in a serious relationship with this person.

She seems to have more interest in the work than in people (individuals).

18-4. Here we have two lab workers working on an experiment. They are anxious about doing the experiment and getting good results. They are wanting to do the work carefully and precisely. Hopefully they will find a miracle[?] cure for some dreaded disease.

19-4. The 2 people pictured appear to be Lab technicians performing some type of tests. They perhaps hope to find an answer to the causes of a patient's illness.

20-4. There are two women scientists in a lab conducting a very important experiment which could mean a breakthrough in the cure of a terrible disease. They are both tense and excited. They have been working for years and there have been so many disappointments along the way. One is watching and thinking how many hours, months, years have been tied up in this work, how her personal life has been second to her work. The other woman is thinking how her hands are shaking. The experiment is finished and it is a failure. They both look at each other, sigh and go back to work. They both pray that maybe tomorrow will be the day.

21-4. The two women are scientists. They are performing experiments in the laboratory with the hope of finding the cure for a disease that has defied a cure. The two have worked many long hours and will work many more hours without any real hope of being lucky and finding the cure. Their is some hope though and so they continue. Their hope is that the solution to the problem will be found and that they will bring relief to the many who suffer from the disease. They also hope for fame in their profession that will result when the cure is found.

22-4. These researchers have been conducting experiments for their university employer. They are half paying attention to what they are doing, and half discussing another research project they are working on. It is a day like any other.

23-4. A female/doctor pipetting out of a test tube while a male student observes. Looks like a serious lab test going on. Seems like the guy screwed up the test and the female doctor is saving the day. Student is learning and doctor is practicing the lab test very carefully. The doctor save the day, the student is happy, and I think the student will get right the next time.

24-4. The woman with the test tube in hand is an academic scientist demonstrating her work to a graduate student. This is a part of the laboratory training which accompanies a PhD program that the student is undertaking.

The scientist makes her point neatly and the student observes well.

25-4. This is a research laboratory. One woman is doing research, the other is her coordinator. The researcher is continuing her work and discussing what has happened and where she is going. She has just had a breakthrough and is telling her coordinator about it and what she expects she'll do next. Her coordinator is pleased and gives her some suggestions.

26-4. These 2 women are working in a research lab. The woman conducting the experiment is a woman in her 40's who has decided to get a graduate degree in Chemistry after a no. of years out of school. She is happy to have the opportunity to better herself but has doubts about her ability to work, raise a family and get a degree simultaneously. However, with determination and help from her family she will succeed in her goal and become a successful research scientist.

27-4. This is a laboratory in a hospital. The two women work together and one is in training to be a technician.

The technician testing the blood is explaining to the assistant different procedures necessary when testing blood.

In the future, the lab assistant will be doing her own testing and learning more about her job.

28-4. Hopefully a breakthrough will occur in the struggle to find a cure of AIDS. These two scientists are employed by an up and coming biogenetic firm in Cambridge.

They work tirelessly because they are truly devoted to their task and hope to bring it to a successful completion.

29-4. Mary is showing her sister, the new girl in the lab, how to run the blood test. Her sister has been very grateful for it was Mary who got her the job. Since her divorce, her life was in a mess. Mary has been very good.

30-4. The lady with the test tube is a doctor and the older woman looking on is the professor and they are working a new kind of medicine to help on checking for strokes and things are looking better and there will be new ways to find out why people are strike down with this terrible medical thing.

Picture 5

1-5. A circus act is underway. The two star performers are nearing the end of their performance. Just before the start of the act Wayne had found out that Sheila had been unfaithful to him. He wants to forget about the incident but can't.

He's decided to tell her he knows and that he forgives her if she'll never do it again. However, just as he is about to catch her on the last swing he misses, she falls and breaks her neck.

2-5. This photo is one of the rare surviving candid shots of my wife and I during our early married life. Often after dinner we would retire upstairs to our spacious bedroom for some stimulating foreplay. The photo captures the completion of a triple jump which was the highlight of our acrobatic fantasy phase. We might of been better off staying with the acrobatics since the high diving into a sponge was disastrous for our marriage.

3-5. Jane and Harry have been together, performing the same routine for 10 years. At first the excitement of show business and the traveling kept them together and happy. Now it is just a job. They have no other skills and are trapped in this existance. The strenuous physical requirement are becoming harder and harder. One day they will miss their connection and a new life will begin.

4-5. This is a circus event. A man is swinging on a trapeze. A woman swings from the other side, lets go and is caught by the man. Their timing has to be perfect. They both trust each other's skill. They will complete their act.

5-5. Two people are trapeze artists and consider their work as an art.

Both were born into families that did this for a living.

They both feel that this is what want to do for a living, but hope that this way of life (circus) doesn't get swept away.

6-5. The couple are practicing for a circus performance. They are in a second rate circus, that plays fairgrounds and is traveling from place to place all the time, a dirty, boring job, even though it requires their high skill and coordination to do a performance. She is bored with this life and wants to move to a better, more stable circus, he has been with the same circus all his life and wants to stay there, his family are in this circus too and partly own it. They are not married but are lovers. She will leave him and the circus shortly.

7-5. Two acrobats are doing a circus act. They studied gymnastics and found paying jobs at the circus.

They are concentrating on not making a mistake and falling. They have to concentrate very hard. They want to do a good job and put on a good show.

They will get through the routine and continue to perform for many years. Then they will train newcomers.

8-5. Two trapeze artists doing their thing – both have to have trust in one another to perform.

9-5. As the trapese swung her higher and higher, Faye realized she could never leave the circus. Chris had been after her for months to go. She had almost relented. But, now has she swung back and forth ready to swing a double sumersall. Daniel, her catcher waiting she knew Chris would have to love her life if he really loved her.

10-5. A young trapeze artist, who has always drempt of being the star of the show, now has her chance. The real star of the show had quit the circus that day, over a contract dispute. Now this young girl will have her chance to prove to them all, even the young man she is working with, and admires greatly that she is good!

She is unsure at first, but does prove to be a star after all!

11-5. The last performance of stunning trapeze artiste, known for her skill, body and hair. An orphan, found and brought up by a circus family has decided to run away from the circus go to Paris and find her roots. She gets work as a fashion model, where her face is seen and recognized by her mother's sister who contacts her, tells her her parents were killed in the war shortly after she had wandered away from them during a shelling attack. She quits modelling (after having made a lot of money) finding it shallow and boring. Thrilled to be reunited with what remains of her family she settles near them in Paris and pursues a writing career.

12-5. Supple gypsy spinners swinging from town to town, summer fair to winter carnival. Spinning upward and around, sometimes on trapezes tied to telephone poles while comrades sell cotton candy. Cokes, and caramel candy. No place to call home; no chance to return. To small towns near Budapest, Kracow, and Sophia from where they were driven by guns and tanks crashing down on their dreams. She was a doctor, and he wrote short stories about bow ties and high heels. She liked Tokaiazii, with onions and cheese on cafe chairs, talking to girl friends, flirting with every man. She likes Rochester with its broken down center. It feels like home. He likes Miami; sun and women unlike home.

13-5. These two trapeze artists have been working together for about 6 months. He had been working at the circus for about a year when she came along. He needed a new partner so he asked if she was interested.

Together they have been rehearsing the new act. It has taken a lot of time to get it right. Finally they feel they are acting as one.

Tonight they are performing in public for the first time. They have just completed a double spin and the crowd is applauding. This is what they have been waiting for.

14-5. Trusting is such a necessary element in people's lives to allow them to show all their skills and to develop healthy. When you trust in others and yourself you will always to continue to grow.

15-5. This is a husband and wife that are circus trapees proformers. They started training when they were very young under the husbands father. They have been training and working in small show for ten or more year. They were very good, but could not get a break. On this night a manager of a large circus saw them proform, and asked them to work in his circus. They would be rewarded for all they hard work after all.

16-5. This was really it! If Lisa had known 2 years ago how she would really fit in with this troupe, she wouldn't have been so nervous.

She felt really happy and in control of herself. Here she was flying 50 feet above the bigtop floor, attached to nothing, soaring thru the air, but confident to know that her partner would be there at exactly the right second to grab her and take her back to terra firma.

It was really a big change from her old self. She had been afraid to do anything – to change, to think, to move. But somehow she had managed to swallow her fears and take the job. It was unstable, it was chancy but boy was it enjoyable. She began to think that maybe it was the best thing she had ever done. She had taken action and in turn, taken control of her life, and even if the job ended suddenly, she would never again be afraid to go on and do something else.

17-5. This couple is performing at the circus. They are both well practiced and are confident that they can perform standard acrobatic feats with little difficulty.

Although they are good and professional, they are not creative showy and flashy which will be needed if they are to go anywhere in life.

Perhaps this will come with time.

18-5. These trapeze artists are performing in a circus. They are concentrating on their performance. They both want to give a good shows and not make any mistakes which in their line of work could be a bit of a problem. They will give a wonderful performance.

19-5. The 2 people pictured are circus performers. I think they're trapeze artists. They are concentrating on what move to do next, as they swing high above the circus floor. They've done this many times before and the thrill never decreases.

20-5. There is a man and a woman doing a trapeze act at a circus. They are married and have been together as an act for many years. He is looking at her and thinking how beautiful she is. She is looking at him and thinking how much she trusts him. He is so strong and reliable. She never fears he will not catch her. They both think what a good life it is. They have been talking about children and she knows he will have to find another partner if she gets pregnant. It is strange to her, but she doesn't worry. She knows he will be just as strong and reliable as a father and husband and they will always be together.

21-5. The two are aerialists. They are members of a great circus family who have been performing nightly as their parents and grandparents did for years. Their goal is to be the best at their profession. Their thoughts are on the task of completing the act without failure or injury and to please the crowd. They will complete the act with precision as they have for years. They have trained for years to complete the act safely and can perform with very little thought.

22-5. Nick and Olga are married trapeze artists. Just before the show they had a big fight, but now that they are working, they are only concentrating on staying alive! They often fight, but are able to put their emotions aside and cooperate/help each other when they perform.

23-5. Circus high wire act. Male on horizontal bar catch female in the air. Showtime at the circus and they have practice this act a lot, notice the precision of the body. The thought is will I make it, both by male and female and the act be successful. The act was successful and everybody applauded the performance.

24-5. The man and woman have been partners for years in this trapeze act. Today they are performing in a circus, being seen by thousands of young children.

Their attention is riveted on the split second timing necessary to their act. Total concentration is called for.

The catch, and the balance of the act, will be completed with absolute technical perfection. However, it will have demanded such intense concentration that it has no bearing whatsoever upon any other aspect of their existence/friendship/relationship.

It is rather as if time had momentarily stood still for their performance and resumed without acknowledging that performance.

25-5. Here are two performers from the circus. The girl is new and it is late at night – they are working out a new routine quietly by themselves. They are excited because they are very good. They are hoping to have a new act ready to present soon. They click and move together as one. Their performance is flawless. They soon will be the stars of the show.

26-5. These people are trapeze artists who have started to become romantically interested in each other after a year of working together. She is thinking of what the future will hold for them given the transient lifestyle their career demands of them and her desire for a family. She also realizes he is a trustworthy man in whom she has physically put her trust in every time they perform. They decide to wait a while longer before committing to each other.

27-5. There is a circus in town and many people have attended this gala affair. This is the acrobatic act of the program. Both the man and woman are also tightrope walkers. They are in the midst of their performance where he swings over and picks up the girl on the other side of the tightrope. He grabs her hands and they swing together performing different.

28-5. It is to bad that the circus is slowly becoming a thing of the past. Just imagine the skill that is required to perform this daring task.

This couple is married as are most successful Trapieze Teams. They work on refinement of skill constantly and their actual performance is merely the "Tip of the Iceberg" in the time and sweat that goes into this profession.

29-5. Sue tried to do a triple somersault and failed twice. Tom knew she could do it! She lift the bar, flew into the air and he caught her. She did it!

30-5. This artist are at a old fashion circus under a tent and are very happy to perform to a full tent. The music is just right and everything seems perfect then the light go out just has he was going to caught her. But by some ESP he does and the light go on and everyone is happy. The crowd claps.

Picture 6

1-6. A horse trainer, Mickey, is walking the princesses prize arabian stallions through a field of flowers. The princess has come along in the hopes of convincing Mickey to move to Egypt with her and the horses.

She needs his talents to run a huge stable in her homeland. Mickey, however, is not interested and is trying to convince her to bring the horses to the U.S.A. They continue back to the stable without reaching an agreement.

2-6. The border collie has once again located dear old drunken dad. This time he had fallen unconscious in a stable next to a team of horses. During the night he had a vision the horses would lead him to the hidden knowledge of Atlantis. Meg is trying to persuade Dad to return the horses to the barn which he borrowed them from.

The sad climax of this story is the collie leaves the farm in disgust for California. Happily the dog becomes a star in the movies and buys a house in Big Sur.

3-6. Sly has always taken care of the prize horses with great care. He was very proud of his training and grooming. Now there is a new owner of the stables; a Mrs. Rancraft. Although she is twenty years younger than he, she does appear to have the knowledge and experience to be a fine owner and boss. They both are looking forward to the relationship.

4-6. An older man is bringing two large horses in from the field. They look large enough to be work horses. A woman is walking alongside of him. They are talking together. They will bring the horses into the barns and perhaps sit down to lunch together.

5-6. Father and daughter are coming back from a walk on their farming estate.

They are talking about the future of farming, problems, solutions and the efficacy of staying in this business and passing on a tradition to the next generation.

They will keep the business in the family for as long as possible.

6-6. The man and the girl from India are talking a walk in the English countryside. She has moved to England from India after living there all her life. She married an English man. She is having a hard time adjusting to life in England, but he lives nearby and has become her friend. She likes him and feels comfortable talking to him and learning about the horses, and the way of life in England. She is thinking of feeding the horses what she has in her hand, but is a little scared. Eventually she will try to ride the horses and like it, and will adapt more to English ways of life and dress, but still taking pride in her Indian customs and background.

7-6. A man and woman are walking through a meadow with their horses. The man takes care of the horses all the time. The woman comes to visit regularly. She likes horses and riding, but has to live in the city, where she works.

The man is telling her facts about horses. She wants to know how her horse is doing and information about horses in general. The man enjoys talking about horses. It is a beautiful day to be outside. The woman and her dog will have a nice day and go back to the city, but they will be back next week. The man will come for the horses and feed them.

8-6. Daughter comes back to visit old homestead (possibly a holiday) she's interacting with her father – she is making an attempt to spend some quality time that perhaps she feels she didn't have as a child.

9-6. I have never seen such beautiful country as Ireland. It took my breath away. The rolling green hills, even the rain couldn't dampen my spirits.

Then I met a kind man who worked on a large farm. He love animals, especially horses. The two draft horses he had with him were superb.

I asked him to tell me some stories of this country of his. I'm sure he had many. As we walked along a mountain trail he told me of his childhood, and how he came to love his country and these animals so well.

I left Ireland a little freer and more hopeful knowing life could be so fulfilling.

10-6. A woman on a vacation, away from her hectic work schedule and city life, has taken a walk into a nearby field to pick wildflowers for her room. She meets a kind ol' Gentlemen his dog and two beautiful horses. They talk and walk together for a while. The little ol' man after hearing her story of why she is there, explaining that everyone needs a break, or rest from their work. Just like his beautiful animals need to be let loose each day to wander the fields.

11-6. By virtue of a time travel box, an Indian Maharanee from the 17th century travels forward and is dropped into a field in turn-of-the-century Northern England.

Totally confused she wanders over the fields till she runs into a local farmer whose wife has recently died. He is delighted to find a beautiful, exotic, cultured young woman wandering helpless on his land. He offers her a place to stay in exchange for help around the house (about which she knows not bing having had servants all her life). She is a bit put off at first but grows to be fond of him as they try to break the language barrier. They become great friends and she even begins to like country life, though missing the luxury and amenities of the Indian court. She is endowed with psychic powers and realizes she can send them both back to India for a little visit. He thinks this is swell and off they go. He loves the Indian court but after a while misses his horses and the countryside and knows he's getting old and his death is coming. She sends him back but comes to visit occasionally. When he dies she takes his dog back to India.

12-6. Father and daughter, home for a week, walking with the horses across the meadow where she used to play. He wants her to stay, but she has a home, a husband, children and his parents in the city. Yes, she misses the grape harvest with all the pickers. And she remembers her first kiss at the side of the maple tree that is gone now. Father's dog and Clydesdales never change, though. He wants her home. He wants her to bring the children more often. They should know horses.

She can't talk to him anymore, never could. Fathers are sweet to hug, but they know so little of life.

13-6. The picture shows a father and daughter together walking across the meadow on the family farm.

She has been away for several years following her career in the big city. She and her husband have been having marital problems for some time. Recently they decided to separate. She tried it alone but needed support. She called her father, a widower, and asked if she could come home for a visit. She has been there for about a week and feels very relaxed.

After talking to her father she feels it isn't so bad and she can face it.

14-6. We all need time off from our everyday lives to relax and ride the horses if this is our way of relaxing. To be with someone we enjoy and be out with nature.

15-6. This is an old man and his daughter. The old man still works his farm in the hills. He has horses and sheep. He still works the land the old way. His daughter has come to visit him from the city. She's be gone a long time. She's come back to the farm to stay. She's decided the city was not for her. She wants to work the land again like her father. He's happy at first but convinces her to go back to the city. The farming is to difficult for her.

16-6. Thistle climbed the hill methodically. She had been up and down this hill three times already today. She knew Gus was getting tired, too. She would have preferred to just stand in the field and chew on some clover. She also realized that if they had to do much more of this, Gus would be no fun tonite.

"Why does this jerk have to drag us along on his little walks, anyway?" she thought. He had company this weekend and Thistle knew that meant tours of the farm, rides. demonstrations of currying (and then of course the city human would try it and that hurt!), and finally they would allowed to have some time to themselves. The kids were too high spirited and not dependable for these little jaunts thru nature, so Thistle and Gus were it. "Oh well," she sighed, "We're almost back to the stall and we can relax, but damn I wish he'd stop pulling on that rope!"

17-6. A younger woman is interviewing an older man. Although he seems to have work horses, I don't think he is a farmer. Perhaps he is a horse breeder. He appears to have some money.

It looks like it is early morning on a fall day. He is enjoying the attention he is receiving from the younger woman and although he would like to make an advance, I doubt anything other than thoughts will occur.

He seems to be an honest type.

18-6. Two people are out for a horse ride. It was a wonderful day to be outside so they decided to get exercise for themselves and the horse. They are both thinking how nice it is to be in the fresh air and enjoying the day. They will have a wonderful outing.

19-6. There are 2 people strolling happily through the rolling countryside. The older gentleman is leading two horses as he chats amicably with a younger woman. The young woman appears to have cut some spring flowering bushes and is carrying them. They both appear to be enjoying spring and the reawakening of the countryside. Perhaps they're on their way back to the old gentleman's home, where they will have some tea and get further acquainted. I don't know.

20-6. It has been a long time since the woman has been home to visit her father. It feels so good to take a ride on the horses and then just walk along with the dog she loved so growing up. This place is her whole history and it's good to be back. Her father is happy to have his daughter there, but sad it's just for the weekend. It's been lonely since she went off to school. He knows he's lucky though. So many of the people he knows have terrible relationships and awful problems with their children. He knows he and his daughter will always be close and she will always be part of his life. He looks forward to grandchildren.

21-6. The two people are related. The woman on the right is the daughter of the person on the left. She has returned home to visit and to ride over the land that she once knew as she was growing up. They have reached a hill that was a favorite spot of the daughter many years ago. They have stopped to look closely at the spot and the daughter will walk the spot which was her favorite spot as a child. She will find that the spot is not quite what she had remembered. She will be disappointed and will sadly leave to go back to the present life.

22-6. She has gone for a walk and bumps into her neighbor, old Mr. Jones, who is bringing his horses in from the pasture. They chat for a while and she tells him she will come visit the next day with her children. He's happy to hear this and says the kids can ride the horses.

23-6. An old man with pipe with two Vermont work horses (I forgot the breed name) and a very beautiful girl. The dog belongs to the man and is a very old dog. The girl is young mid 20's and very stylish hand upon the trim look. The man is like the old salt in the sea and just enjoys a pretty lady's company. Nothing is really wanted but friendship and the old man loneliness being forgotten for a while. The girl felt good about herself, because she was able to give something precious to a person, with not price tag. They will part their ways both feeling good about the day.

P.S.: the dog just tagged along.

24-6. The Grandfather, his daughter, her dog, and their two horses have been out enjoying the pastoral splendor of their countryside.

It is a singularly precious time for the Grandfather who has long waited for her to have her college semester break. It is less meaningful to the granddaughter.

She no longer relishes the time spent with her Grandfather. She dresses, acts, and thinks in a "citified" way. The old relation cannot be rejuvenated. They will continue to love each other, but never again as *child* and grandparent.

25-6. It is a beautiful spring day warm and sunny after a long cold winter. The man has been out in the fields rounding up some work horses. The women has just been out for a walk in the foot hills with her dog. She has picked a bouquet of wild spring flowers. They great each other and are walking together for a time in pleasant conversation. Each is comfortable in the other presents. They will soon part and go on their way, each remembering the other.

26-6. This is a grandfather who is seeing his granddaughter for the first time in 10 years. She had reservations about visiting him, as he lives in a foreign country and felt that she would find the visit boring and confining. He in turn had feelings of being unable to provide a young, spirited girl with a happy visiting experience. While she is visiting she develops a deep affection and understanding of her grandfather which he returns. They become closer and will be sure to visit often in the years to come.

27-6. The scene is a farm in Ireland. Mary and her father are chatting on their way back to the barn. Mary was out in the field gathering some type of flower and she met her father and their family dog, Dusty, gathering up the horses at the end of day. All of them walked back to the barn on this lovely fall day.

28-6. This man has achieved his retirement goal of moving from a northeast suburban community into the natural-rural mountain setting in the rugged white mountains.

His daughter is in college (graduate school) but manages to get home to her family in this new setting which she uncomfortably calls home now.

29-6. Bill and Lucy are taking the horses back to the stable. They had been riding for an hour.

30-6. The older man is walking his wagon horses. The woman is from the city and is on vacation and went for a walk and bumped into the man as is talking about how great it is in the country. the man invite her to his home and she said ok. He will go take her on a wagon ride this will be her first wagon ride.

SCORING FOR *N* ACHIEVEMENT

Learning how to score involves three steps: mastering the scoring manual, coding practice stories, and comparing one's coding with that of the "expert scorer." First, read the two chapters (9 and 10) that deal with the achievement scoring system. Only after you have a good command of the content of the manual, take the self-test for the achievement manual that follows this section.

Next, read the introduction to appendix I for a description of the practice stories and how they were obtained. Make a scoring sheet on which you can record the coding categories for each story. Chapter 37 explains how to make a scoring sheet and gives a number of suggestions regarding how to learn a content analysis system and how to measure intercoder agreement. An example of a scoring sheet is given at the end of chapter 36.

If you have access to *Motives in Fantasy, Action and Society* (Atkinson, 1958a), begin by scoring the achievement practice stories in appendix I of that book. Otherwise, score the practice stories included in appendix I in this volume. Score all of the stories for each picture before going on to the next. Score the stories for 10 subjects and then compare your scoring with that of the expert. Then repeat the procedure for the next 10 stories, and so on. For each picture the expert scoring of the first 10 stories is accompanied by written explanations. Keep track of your errors, and review them before going on to a new picture. As you score, consult the manual as frequently as necessary. Compute the degree of interscorer agreement you attain (see chapter 37) picture by picture and/or using a total score for each subject based on all six pictures.

The achievement practice stories included in *Motives in Fantasy, Action and Society* were all written in response to pictures that elicited at least a moderate amount of achievement imagery. The pictures 'used for the practice stories included here were chosen to elicit imagery for several different motives, so the stories vary greatly from one picture to another in the amount of achievement imagery they contain. To obtain additional practice stories, consult appendix III.

The expert scoring follows the Achievement Self-test.

SELF-TEST: *N* ACHIEVEMENT MANUAL*

After reading the scoring manual (chapter 10), write out your answers to the following questions without consulting the manual. Then check your answers to see if you are correct.

Imagery. What is the goal of the achievement motive? What are the three general criteria for scoring Achievement Imagery? What are the specific kinds of statements that would satisfy each of these criteria? What kinds of stories are scored Doubtful Achievement Imagery?

Need. What is the criterion for scoring *N*? What two types of statements of desire are not scored *N*? What is the relationship between instrumental activity and the scoring of *N*?

Instrumental Activity. What is the criterion for scoring *I*? What types of statements of instrumental activity in the past tense would be scored *I* and what types would not be scored *I*? What determines whether *I* is scored +, ?, or −?

Anticipatory Goal States. When is *Ga* scored? What is done with anticipatory goal statements in which the outcome is doubtful or uncertain? What is the distinction between covert, or mental, activity that is scored *I* and that which is scored *Ga*?

Obstacles or Blocks. What is meant by obstacles or blocks? What is the distinction between *Bp* and *Bw*? What is done when it is doubtful whether a block is to be scored *Bp* or *Bw*? What "apparent environmental blocks" are not scored?

Nurturant Press. What is meant by *Nup*?

Affective States. What are the two criteria for scoring *G*? What is the distinction between *Ga* and *G*? What is the relationship between *I* and *G*?

Thema. When is *Th* scored? Can *Th* be scored if no other subcategories are scored?

* Reprinted with permission from pp. 693–694 of Smith, C. P., & Feld, S. (1958). How to learn the method of content analysis for *n* Achievement, *n* Affiliation, and *n* Power. In J. W. Atkinson (Ed.), *Motives in fantasy, action and society* (pp. 685–818). Princeton, NJ: Van Nostrand. (Copyright by J. W. Atkinson.)

EXPERT SCORING FOR ACHIEVEMENT MOTIVE*

Written explanations are provided for at least the first 10 stories for each picture.

Picture 1

Stories written to this picture frequently describe someone engaged in a task that seems to be an everyday part of his or her job. It is sometimes difficult to decide between TI and UI in borderline cases. If task involvement is mentioned only briefly, the story has been scored UI; if it has been elaborated, the story has been scored TI.

1-1. *AI.* The captain is engaging in an instrumental activity which has as its goal better service, implying concern for a standard of excellence.

I? The captain is explaining in order to provide better service.

No *Th.* Achievement concerns are expressed in a context that suggests other considerations such as a relationship of the accountability of an employee to an employer.

2-1. *TI.* One character is telling how to perform a task that requires skill. The other is unable to carry out the task with dexterity because of a block. To score for AI, more explicit evidence is needed that a character wishes to do better than someone else or attain a level of performance that would bring a feeling of pride in accomplishment. (Fanciful or facetious story content should not blind the scorer to the possibility of concern with standards of excellence.)

3-1. *TI.* Borderline UI. Although the focus is on the passenger, the Captain appears to be carrying out a routine responsibility in a conscientious manner.

4-1. *UI.* Primarily affiliative. At the end they get down to the day's business, but this is not sufficiently elaborated to be task imagery.

5-1. *UI.* Because of its brevity, for research purposes this story would probably have to be regarded as missing data (see discussion of when to drop a subject in chapter 37).

6-1. *UI.* The emphasis is on getting paid. If it were on doing a good job of smuggling, it could be scored for AI.

7-1. *UI.* Borderline TI. The captain, in providing information, is probably doing something called for by his job, but the elaboration of this routine task activity is minimal, with most of the story appearing unrelated even to routine job performance.

8-1. *UI.* No indication of AI. Not enough information is given to decide that this is routine task involvement.

9-1. *TI.* A routine problem is corrected. A hint of doing a good job is suggested, namely, the Captain will see that a problem is taken care of immediately. However, this action might be motivated by something other than achievement, such as forestalling further complaints. Working hard or fast is not necessarily indicative of achievement motivation.

10-1. *TI.* Both the Captain and the detective are doing their respective jobs. There is no explicit indication that they are trying to do them well.

11-1. *UI*

12-1. *UI*

13-1. *TI*

14-1. *TI*

15-1. *TI*

* Expert scoring by Caroline McLeod and Charles P. Smith.

16-1. *UI*
17-1. *TI*
18-1. *TI*
19-1. *UI*
20-1. *TI*
21-1. *UI*
22-1. *TI*
23-1. *UI*
24-1. *TI*
25-1. *UI*
26-1. *TI*
27-1. *UI*
28-1. *TI*
29-1. *TI*
30-1. *UI*

Picture 2

1-2. *TI*. A man working in his office. The fact that the project is important does not tell us that he is trying to do a good job.

2-2. *AI*. Unique accomplishment (refers to a movie plot about robots designed to replace housewives).

I−. He is thinking (wondering) how to go about it. Outcome: project fails.

Bp. Doubt (indecision) due to unfortunate outcome (tongue in cheek) of previous project.

Bw. Microwaves prevent the success of his efforts.

Th. The plot deals with carrying out an innovative project.

3-2. *TI*. Routine work. Mention of the quality of his work implies standards of performance, but there is no evidence of concern about doing better.

4-2. *UI*. Not enough elaboration of work for TI.

5-2. *UI*. Work not elaborated.

6-2. *AI*. Long-term involvement. He wants to open his own firm.

The statement "wants to do what's best for him and his family" is too ambiguous to score for *N*.

I+. Makes plans. Does independent jobs. Successful outcome: Own business becomes strong.

Ga+. Having thoughts about opening his own firm. Thinks what would really make him happier.

No *Th*. Thema is not scored because there are other themes reflecting concerns about security and family.

7-2. *AI*. Long-term involvement. Went to school and became a draftsman. Also concern about standards: "doing the best job he can on his drafting."

I?. He prepared by going to school. He will be back at work.

G+. He likes his work.

No *Th*.

8-2. *TI*. A man at work. "Motivated by his work" does not make it explicit that he is concerned about doing a good job. For example, he could be motivated for money or power.

9-2. *TI*. It is not clear that building the house is motivated by achievement concerns. Possibly it represents a unique accomplishment, or involvement in the attainment of a long-term achievement goal, but there is doubt about whether the imagery qualifies for these categories; therefore, score doubtful imagery.

10-2. *UI*. His work is secondary and not elaborated.
11-2. *UI*
12-2. *UI*
13-2. *AI, G+*
14-2. *UI*
15-2. *TI*
16-2. *AI, I?, Ga+, Th*
17-2. *UI*
18-2. *UI*
19-2. *UI*
20-2. *TI*
21-2. *TI*
22-2. *TI*
23-2. *UI*
24-2. *AI, I?* ("painstaking attention")
25-2. *UI*
26-2. *AI, N, I+*
27-2. *UI*
28-2. *TI*
29-2. *UI*
30-2. *TI*

Picture 3

1-3. *UI*
2-3. *UI*
3-3. *UI*
4-3. *UI*
5-3. *UI*
6-3. *AI, N*. She would like to change jobs, move up. Concern about career advancement. "Would like" is scored for *N*.
7-3. *UI*
8-3. *UI*
9-3. *UI*
10-3. *UI*
11-3. *UI*
12-3. *UI*
13-3. *UI*
14-3. *UI*
15-3. *TI*
16-3. *UI*
17-3. *UI*
18-3. *UI*
19-3. *UI*
20-3. *UI*
21-3. *AI, I?*
22-3. *UI*
23-3. *UI*
24-3. *UI*
25-3. *UI*
26-3. *UI*
27-3. *UI*

28-3. *UI*
29-3. *UI*
30-3. *TI*

Picture 4

1-4. *AI*. "Checking that all necessary steps are followed." This instrumental activity implies a concern about standards – doing the job properly.
　I?. The same phrase is scored for *I*.
2-4. *AI*. Concocting the elixir constitutes unique accomplishment, even if the story is told with tongue in cheek. No other categories are clearly related to achievement.
3-4. *AI*. Unique accomplishment.
　N. "She must go on." See Need section of manual – strong indications of the motive are scored as *N*.
　I?. Working day and night. Outcome not given.
　Th. There are no themes other than achievement.
4-4. *TI* Routine lab work. Nothing meets the criteria for scoring AI.
5-4. *AI*. Unique accomplishment.
　N. Always wanted to do this kind of work.
　I?. Trying to find a cure. Outcome not given.
　G+. A feeling of self-fulfillment and accomplishment.
　Th. Only achievement themes are present.
6-4. *AI*. The woman on the right is proud of her work and accomplishments.
　I+. She does most of the background work. The outcome is a raise.
　G+. Proud. Receives a raise.
7-4. *AI*. Concern over standards of excellence – they want the research to go well.
　N. They want the research to go well . . . want to make a contribution to science.
　I+. They have studied and done research. They will get results.
　Ga+. They . . . are thinking it would be nice to have a breakthrough . . .
　Th. Only achievement themes are present.
8-4. *UI*
9-4. *AI*. Unique accomplishment.
　I+. Dropped the specimen into the test tube.
　Ga−. Breaths held in anticipation (of the outcome). Since the outcome is in some doubt, score *Ga* minus.
　G+. Eyes full of tears and excitement.
　Th. Only achievement themes are present.
10-4. *AI*. Long-term involvement.
　No *N*. "The professor wants . . ." is not scored. If this want were satisfied, it would not represent a personal accomplishment for the professor.
　I?. Student has gone back to school to become a doctor.
　Ga+. Professor feels woman has good potential. See Example 39 in the scoring manual.
　Nup. Professor gives help and support.
11-4. *AI, I−*
12-4. *UI*
13-4. *AI, I?, Ga+, Bp, Th*. There is borderline evidence for scoring *I*. The phrases "have decided" and "start the project" suggest past activity rather than simply the outcome of past activity.
14-4. *UI*
15-4. *AI, I+, Th*
16-4. *AI, Ga+*

17-4. *TI*
18-4. *AI, N, Ga−, Th*
19-4. *TI*
20-4. *AI, N, I−, G−, Bw*
21-4. *AI, N, I?, Ga+, Ga−, Th*
22-4. *TI*
23-4. *AI, I+, Bp, Th*
24-4. *AI, I+, Th*
25-4. *AI, I+, G+, Th*
26-4. *AI, N, I+, Ga−, Nup, G+, Th*
27-4. *TI*
28-4. *AI, N, I?, Th*
29-4. *TI*
30-4. *AI, I?*

Picture 5

1-5. *UI.* Do not score for "star performers." The concern of the characters is not about achievement but about an interpersonal matter.

2-5. *UI.* There is no basis for scoring AI.

3-5. *UI.* "Now it is just a job." Rather than a possible source of achievement satisfaction, the job has become a source of unhappiness.

4-5. *AI.* Their timing has to be perfect. Concern about a standard of excellence.

I+. Man and woman are performing. Outcome: Will complete their act.

No thema. The story is marginally AI – too weak to be scored Th.

5-5. *AI.* "Consider their work as an art" implies a standard of excellence. Also concern with career – a long-term achievement goal.

N. This is what they want to do for a living.

No thema. Again the evidence of AI is marginal, and there is a theme unrelated to achievement about their way of life being swept away.

6-5. *TI.* Although the performers are practicing and the job requires skill, there is no evidence that they are concerned about doing a good job. Instead, the job is described as boring.

7-5. *AI.* Concentrating on not making a mistake. Want to do a good job.

N. Want to do a good job.

I+. They studied gymnastics. They are concentrating . . .

Th. The whole story deals with achievement-related concerns.

No *Nup.* "They will train newcomers" does not sufficiently describe the giving of help or support to a character or characters involved in an achievement-related activity.

8-5. *UI.* This story is not sufficiently descriptive of routine task activity to raise a question as to whether achievement concerns may be present. If the performers were "practicing hard," for example, the story could be scored for TI.

9-5. *UI.* The story does not deal with achievement-related concerns.

10-5. *AI.* ". . . drempt of being the star . . ." Also, she now has a chance to prove that she is good.

Ga+. "drempt of being the star"

Bp. Unsure at first. Refer to the section of the manual dealing with obstacles. She must overcome a lack of confidence.

G+. "prove to be a star after all!" An outcome that justifies the inference that pride in accomplishment would be felt. Sometimes an exclamation point reinforces the interpretation that affect is intended by signifying that "this outcome is really something!"

No thema. Themes other than achievement are mentioned such as the contract dispute.

11-5. *AI.* "Pursues a writing career" is scored for LTI, but no instrumental activity is scored because it occurs in the last phrase.

12-5. *UI*

13-5. *AI, I+*

Ga+. This is what they have been waiting for.

G+. A feeling of pride is inferred from the outcome, namely, applause for executing a difficult performance.

Th. A strong achievement story with no clear competing themes.

14-5. *UI*

15-5. *AI, I+, Bw, Th*

16-5. *TI*

17-5. *AI, Ga+, Bp, Th*

18-5. *AI, N, I+, Th*

19-5. *TI*

20-5. *UI*

21-5. *AI, N, I+, Th*

22-5. *UI*

23-5. *AI, I+, Ga−, G+, Th*

24-5. *AI, I+*

25-5. *AI, N, I+, G+, Th*

26-5. *UI*

27-5. *TI*

28-5. *AI, I+, Th*

29-5. *AI, I+, Ga+, Bp, Th*

30-5. *TI*

Picture 6

1-6. *TI*. Seeking Mickey's talents suggests concern that the stables be run well, but achievement goals are not sufficiently clear to score AI.

2-6. *UI*. Although the dog becomes a star, there is no evidence of *concern* about achievement. Do not score AI solely on the basis of outcome. However, a story with an animal as the hero may be scored AI if it meets one of the three criteria for scoring AI. For example, if a horse wanted to win a race, or a dog felt pride in becoming the best stunt dog in Hollywood.

3-6. *AI*. Has taken care of horses with great care.

G+. Very proud of his training and grooming. A clear example of pride in accomplishment.

Instrumental activity is not scored because it occurs in the first sentence.

4-6. *UI*. There is not sufficient task imagery to justify scoring TI. For purposes of scoring this and other stories written to this picture, refer to examples 16 through 22 in the achievement manual to get an idea of the kind of task involvement that is scored TI.

5-6. *AI*. Concern about the family business. Long-term involvement. They will keep it in the family as long as possible.

I?. Discussion of problems, solutions, and efficacy. They seem to be planning how to make a success of the business. Since the outcome is not a clearcut success, score I?.

No *Th*. When there is doubt about achievement being central to the plot, Thema is not scored.

6-6. *UI*

7-6. *UI* (See comment for story 4-6.)

8-6. *UI*

9-6. *UI*

10-6. *UI*

11-6. *UI*

12-6. *UI*

13-6. *UI*

14-6. *UI*

15-6. *TI* There is a suggestion of long-term involvement, but it is not made sufficiently explicit.

16-6. *UI*

17-6. *UI*

18-6. *UI*

19-6. *UI*

20-6. *UI*

21-6. *UI*

22-6. *UI*

23-6. *UI*

24-6. *UI*

25-6. *UI*

26-6. *UI*

27-6. *UI*

28-6. *UI*

29-6. *UI*

30-6. *UI*

SCORING FOR THE MOTIVE TO AVOID SUCCESS

Learning how to score involves three steps: mastering the scoring manual, coding practice stories, and comparing one's coding with that of the "expert scorer." First, read chapters 11 and 12. A self-test is given toward the end of the scoring manual in the section entitled Guide to Research with the Motive to Avoid Success Scoring System. This section of the manual also tells how to make a scoring sheet (see example following expert scoring for Picture 6) and how to calcuate intercoder agreement.

Next, read the introduction to appendix I for a description of the practice stories and how they were obtained. Score all of the stories for each picture before going on to the next. Score the first 10 stories and then compare your scoring with that of the expert. Then repeat the procedure for the next 10 stories, and so on. For each picture the expert scoring of the first 10 stories is accompanied by written explanations. Keep track of your errors, and review them before going on to a new picture. As you score, consult the manual as frequently as necessary. Compute the degree of interscorer agreement you attain picture by picture and/or using a total score for each subject based on all six pictures.

The pictures used to elicit the practice stories included here were cued for several different motives, but not for the Motive to Avoid Success, so the stories vary greatly from one picture to another in the amount of Motive to Avoid Success imagery they contain. Overall they contain relatively little. To obtain additional practice materials, consult appendix III.

EXPERT SCORING FOR THE MOTIVE TO AVOID SUCCESS*

Picture *1*

1-1. (0) "... explaining why he hasn't met the owner's expectations" constitutes instrumental activity, so that Absence of Instrumental Activity is not scored.

The captain, a gentleman, and passengers are mentioned so that Absence of Others is not scored.

No other imagery is present.

2-1. (0) No fear-of-success imagery is present.

"Queeg telling Bogart how" is instrumental activity, so that Absence of Instrumental Activity is not scored.

Queeg and Bogart are the characters so that Absence of Others is not scored.

3-1. (0) No fear-of-success imagery is present.

4-1. AIA (1) "talking with a person of lower rank" and "discussing something they had done" not sufficient indications of instrumental activity. Specific communications are required.

5-1. AIA (1) No purpose has been ascribed to the "talking" and thus Absence of Instrumental Activity is scored.

6-1. (0) No fear-of-success imagery is present.

7-1. (0) No fear-of-success imagery is present.

8-1. (0) Even this one sentence story has no fear-of-success imagery. Two people are mentioned and purposive behavior is indicated ("captain ... making a point to ... civilian), thus eliminating the most frequently scored categories.

9-1. (0) No fear-of-success imagery is present.

10-1. (0) No fear-of-success imagery is present.

11-1. (0) Negative consequences are contingent, and not scorable.

12-1. (0)

13-1. NC (1)

14-1. (0)

15-1. (0) Negative consequences are contingent, rather than noncontingent, and not scorable.

16-1. (0)

17-1. (0)

18-1. (0)

19-1. (0) Instrumental activity is borderline, but absence is not scored.

20-1. (0)

21-1. (0)

22-1. (0)

23-1. (0)

24-1. (0)

25-1. (0)

26-1. (0)

27-1. (0)

28-1. (0)

29-1. AIA (1) Negative consequences are contingent, and not scored.

30-1. (0)

*Expert scoring by Jacqueline Fleming and Matina S. Horner.

Picture 2

1-2. (0) No fear-of-success imagery is present.

2-2. NC (1) The Noncontingent Negative Consequence is "his . . . model fails due to microwave exposure in the kitchen."

3-2. IE (1) The scorable statement is "Lewis will soon go home, leaving his work unfinished, to be with his family."

4-2. AIA (1) Instrumental Activity is borderline in this case, but the preponderance of indefinite statements such as "he may be working on a project" are not sufficient.

5-2. (0) No fear-of-success imagery is present.

6-2. (0) No fear-of-success imagery is present.

7-2. (0) No fear-of-success imagery is present.

8-2. AIA (1) "A man at work" is not sufficient to score for purposive behavior.

9-2. (0) Interpersonal Engagement is not scored: All conditions are not met. The instrumental activity is project oriented. There is more excitement about the house than involvement on an interpersonal level.

10-2. (0) No fear-of-success imagery is present.

11-2. (0)

12-2. (0)

13-2. (0)

14-2. AIA (1)

15-2. (0)

16-2. (0)

17-2. (0)

18-2. AIA (1)

19-2. AIA (1)

20-2. IE (1)

21-2. (0) Interpersonal Engagement is not scored.

22-2. NC, AIA (2)

23-2. AIA (1)

24-2. (0)

25-2. (0) Interpersonal Engagement is not scored.

26-2. (0)

27-2. AIA (1) Absence of Instrumental Activity is borderline, but scored.

28-2. (0)

29-2. (0)

30-2. AIA (1)

Picture 3

1-3. IE (1) Scorable statements are ". . . taken the afternoon off with the intent of spending the rest of the day *together*" and "they have been planning to get married."

2-3. NC, IE (2) "fatal disease" is scorable for Noncontingent Negative consequences.

"enjoys the attention; rejects his advances" is scorable for Interpersonal Engagement.

3-3. AIA (1) Interpersonal Engagement is not scored: All conditions are not met. There is no instrumental activity toward an affiliative goal, even though actions are contemplated.

4-3. IE, AIA (2) "Talking together lets them know more about each others feelings" is sufficient instrumental activity for Interpersonal Engagement, but does not meet the purposive requirements of Instrumental Activity.

5-3. IE (1) "two people in love; have a nice dinner together" are scorable for Interpersonal Engagement.

6-3. (o) No fear-of-success imagery present.

7-3. IE (1) "enjoy being together . . . discussing things" are scorable for Interpersonal Engagement.

8-3. AIA (1) The absence of any activity at all makes this a clear case of Absence of Instrumental Activity. Interpersonal Engagement cannot be scored because of no activity toward an affiliative goal.

9-3. IE, R (2)

"I love you, Janet" is scorable for Interpersonal Engagement.

"we're going to have a baby; he thought it would never happen" are scorable for Relief. There is no mention of instrumental activity in trying to produce the long-awaited baby.

10-3. (o) No fear-of-success imagery is present.

"discussing some work related matter" is a borderline statement of instrumental activity, but was not scored.

11-3. IE (1)

12-3. IE (1)

13-3. IE (1)

14-3. AIA (1)

15-3. AIA (1)

16-3. NC, IE (2)

17-3. IE, AIA (2)

18-3. IE (1)

19-3. AIA (1)

20-3. IE (1)

21-3. IE (1)

22-3. IE (1)

23-3. IE, AIA (2)

24-3. (o)

25-3. IE (1)

26-3. IE (1)

27-3. (o)

28-3. (o)

29-3. IE (1)

30-3. IE (1)

Picture 4

1-4. NC (1) "President . . . bitten . . . by a rabid dog."

2-4. (o) No fear-of-success imagery is present.

3-4. (o) No fear-of-success imagery is present.

4-4. (o) No fear-of-success imagery is present.

5-4. (o) No fear-of-success imagery is present.

6-4. (o) No fear-of-success imagery is present.

7-4. (o) No fear-of-success imagery is present.

8-4. (o) No fear-of-success imagery is present.

9-4. (o) No fear-of-success imagery is present.

10-4. (o) No fear-of-success imagery is present.

11-4. IE (1)

12-4. AIA (1) Absence of Instrumental Activity is borderline, but scored.

13-4. (o)

14-4. AIA (1)

15-4. (o)

16-4. (o)

17-4. IE (1)
18-4. (0)
19-4. (0)
20-4. NC (1)
21-4. (0)
22-4. (0)
23-4. (0)
24-4. (0)
25-4. (0)
26-4. (0)
27-4. (0)
28-4. (0)
29-4. (0)
30-4. (0) Negative consequences are not scored.

Picture 5

1-5. NC (1) ". . . he misses, she falls and breaks her neck." The contingency is mixed but is scorable for Noncontingent Negative Consequences.
2-5. NC, IE, AIA (3) ". . . highdiving into a sponge was disastrous for our marriage" is scorable for Noncontingent Negative Consequences.

". . . often would retire upstairs . . . for some stimulating foreplay" is scorable for Interpersonal Engagement.

The instrumental activity in previous sentence is habitual and therefore Absence of Instrumental Activity is scored.
3-5. AIA (1) The activity is routine, and therefore not instrumental.
4-5. (0) No fear-of-success imagery is present.
5-5. AIA (1) Despite references to earning a living, there is no instrumental activity.
6-5. (0) No fear-of-success imagery is present.
7-5. (0) No fear-of-success imagery is present.
8-5. AIA (1) No instrumental activity is present.
9-5. IE (1) The activity toward an interpersonal goal is weak, but scored: "Chris had been after her for months to go."
10-5. (0) No fear-of-success imagery is present.
11-5. IE (1) Negative Consequences are not scored.
12-5. (0)
13-5. (0)
14-5. AIA (1)
15-5. (0)
16-5. (0) Relief is not scored.
17-5. (0)
18-5. (0)
19-5. (0)
20-5. IE (1)
21-5. (0)
22-5. IE (1)
23-5. (0)
24-5. (0)
25-5. (0)
26-5. IE (1)
27-5. (0)
28-5. (0)

29-5. (o)
30-5. R (1)

Picture 6

1-6. (o) No fear-of-success imagery is present.
2-6. (o) No fear-of-success imagery is present.
3-6. AIA (1) The instrumental activity is routine: "Sly has *always* taken care of the horses with great care."
4-6. AIA (1) This is a borderline case, but no purposive behavior is indicated for any of the actions.
5-6. (o) No fear-of-success imagery is present.
6-6. (o) No fear-of-success imagery is present.
7-6. (o) No fear-of-success imagery is present.
8-6. IE (1) "She's interacting with her father . . . to spend some quality time."
9-6. IE (1) "I met a kind man . . . life could be so fulfilling."
10-6. (o)
11-6. NC, IE (2)
12-6. AIA (1)
13-6. IE (1)
14-6. AIA (1)
15-6. (o)
16-6. (o)
17-6. (o)
18-6. (o)
19-6. AIA (1)
20-6. AIA (1)
21-6. NC (1)
22-6. (o)
23-6. AIA (1)
24-6. AIA (1)
25-6. IE (1) Interpersonal Engagement is borderline, but scored.
26-6. IE, AIA (2)
27-6. (o)
28-6. (o)
29-6. (o)
30-6. (o)

Scoring Sheet Format

S#	Noncont. Neg. Con. +1	Interper. Engage. +1	Relief +1	Abs. of Inst. Act. +1	Abs. of Others −1	Total

SCORING FOR *N* AFFILIATION

Learning how to score involves three steps: mastering the scoring manual, coding practice stories, and comparing one's coding with that of the "expert scorer." First, read the two chapters (13 and 14) that deal with the affiliation scoring system. Only after you have a good command of the content of the manual, take the self-test for the affiliation manual that follows this section.

Next, read the introduction to appendix I for a description of the practice stories and how they were obtained. Then, make a scoring sheet on which you can record the coding categories for each story. An example of a scoring sheet is given at the end of chapter 36. Chapter 37 explains how to make a scoring sheet and gives a number of suggestions regarding how to learn a content analysis system and how to measure intercoder agreement.

If you have access to *Motives in Fantasy, Action and Society* (Atkinson, 1958a), begin by scoring the affiliation practice stories in appendix I of that book. Otherwise, begin by scoring the practice stories included here. Score all of the stories for each picture before going on to the next. Score the stories for 10 subjects and then compare your scoring with that of the expert. Then repeat the procedure for the next 10 stories, and so on. For each picture the expert scoring of the first 10 stories is accompanied by written explanations. Keep track of your errors, and review them before going on to a new picture. As you score, consult the manual as frequently as necessary. Compute the degree of interscorer agreement you attain (see chapter 37) picture by picture and/or using a total score for each subject based on all six pictures.

The affiliation practice stories included in *Motives in Fantasy, Action and Society* were all written in response to pictures that were cued to elicit at least a moderate amount of achievement imagery. The pictures used for the practice stories included here were cued for several different motives, so the stories vary greatly from one picture to another in the amount of affiliation imagery they contain. To obtain additional practice stories, consult appendix III.

The expert scoring follows the Affiliation Self-test.

SELF-TEST: *N* AFFILIATION MANUAL*

After reading the scoring manual, write out your answers to the following questions without consulting the manual. Then check your answers to see if you are correct.

Imagery. Define the general basis for scoring Affiliation Imagery. What are the four other more specific bases for scoring Affiliation Imagery? What are the rules governing the scoring of Affiliation Imagery in stories which are about the following relationships: parent–child, marriage, dating, friendship?

* Reprinted with permission from pp. 735–736 of Smith, C. P., & Feld, S. (1958). How to learn the method of content analysis for *n* Achievement, *n* Affiliation, and *n* Power. In J. W. Atkinson (Ed.), *Motives in fantasy, action and society* (pp. 685–818). Princeton, NJ: Van Nostrand. (Copyright by J. W. Atkinson.)

Need. What is the criterion for scoring *N*? What two types of statements are scored *N* which do not meet the general criterion for scoring *N*?

Instrumental Activity. What is the criterion for scoring *I*? What are three fairly common types of actions usually scored *I*? When is giving advice or asking for advice scored *I*? What types of statements of Instrumental Activity in the past tense would be scored *I*, and what types would not be scored *I*? What determines whether *I* is scored +, ?, or −?

Anticipatory Goal States. When is *Ga* scored? What is done with doubtful or uncertain anticipatory goal statements? What is the distinction between covert, or mental, activity that is scored *I* and that which is scored *Ga*?

Obstacles or Blocks. What is meant by Obstacles or Blocks? What is the distinction between *Bp* and *Bw*? What is the most frequent type of statement scored *Bw*, *Bp*? Is the occurrence of a disruption of a relationship sufficient grounds for scoring Block?

Affective States. What are the two criteria for the scoring of *G*? What is the distinction between *Ga* and *G*? What is the relationship between *I* and *G*?

Thema. When is *Th* scored? Can *Th* be scored if no other subcategories are scored?

EXPERT SCORING FOR *N* AFFILIATION*

Picture 1

1-1. *U Im*: The imagery is not affiliative in nature.
2-1. *U Im*
3-1. *U Im*
4-1. *Aff Im*: "A friendly conversation"; this is the minimum evidence necessary to score *Aff Im*.
   I+: The characters are talking together in a friendly manner; this constitutes a convivial, companionate activity.
5-1. *U Im*
6-1. *U Im*
7-1. *U Im*
8-1. *U Im*
9-1. *U Im*
10-1. *U Im*
11-1. *U Im*
12-1. *U Im*
13-1. *U Im*
14-1. *U Im*
15-1. *U Im*
16-1. *U Im*
17-1. *U Im*
18-1. *U Im*
19-1. *U Im*

* Expert scoring by Joseph Scroppo and Joel Weinberger.

20-1. *U Im*
21-1. *U Im*
22-1. *U Im*
23-1. *U Im*
24-1. *U Im*
25-1. *U Im*
26-1. *U Im*
27-1. *U Im*
28-1. *U Im*
29-1. *U Im*
30-1. *U Im*

Picture 2

1-2. *Aff Im*: The engineer is expressing concern over maintaining and/or restoring a positive affective relationship; his primary motivation is his desire to spend time with his family, which strongly suggests an affiliative motive.

N: "He has not been able to spend the time *he would like to* with them." This is a stated desire to affiliate with others.

No I?: *I* is not scored because the instrumental act ("he resolves to reassess his priorities") occurs in the final sentence of the story and thus cannot be scored for this category.

Bw: The engineer's work interferes with his affiliative intentions.

No Th: Thema is not scored because affiliative themes are not the only ones included; concerns about work and achievement are also present.

2-2. *U Im*

3-2. *Aff Im*: The main character is concerned with restoring the affiliative relationship, which his work has impeded. The statements "his thoughts are with his family," and "[he will leave] his work unfinished, to be with his family" are the basis for this scoring.

I+: The main character goes home in order to be with his family; this is an act directed at fulfilling an affiliative motive.

Ga+: "His thoughts are with his family." The main character is thinking about the fulfillment of an affiliative motive (being with his family), which is scored as an anticipatory goal state.

Bw: His work (an environmental impediment) keeps the main character from his affiliative relationship.

Th: The entire story is concerned with the maintenance and/or restoration of the affiliative relationship; work is only mentioned as it relates to the affiliative theme.

4-2. *Aff Im*: "[He] is thinking of his family that he is missing. He may wish that he was back at home with them." This is expressed concern with restoring an affiliative relationship.

N: The main character misses his family and "he may wish that he was back at home with them." This is an expressed desire to affiliate with others.

Ga+: "He'll remember some of the happy things that have occurred when they are together." This is imagery concerned with the fulfillment of an affiliative relationship; it is scored *Ga+* even though it is in the past tense.

Bw: The physical separation between the main character at work and his family at home constitutes an environmental block in the affiliative relationship.

Th: The predominant theme is the affiliative relationship; other themes are presented only in relation to the affiliative relationship.

5-2. *U Im*

6-2. *U Im*

7-2. *Aff Im*: "He is anticipating going home when work is done to his loving family." This indicates a positive affective relationship and is thus scored *Aff Im*.

N: "He is anticipating going home when work is done to his loving family." This is a borderline case. Anticipating an affiliative activity, however, strongly implies a desire for affiliation.

I+: The act is to go home to dinner with his family. It is scored "+" because it successfully brings about a positive affiliative situation.

Ga+: The main character is anticipating a positive affiliative activity (going home to his family).

G+: "A nice evening with his family." This is a borderline scoring decision; "nice," however, strongly suggests a positive affective experience associated with the affiliative activity.

8-2. *U Im*

9-2. *Aff Im*: Mr. Jones wants to build a new house for his family, "the kind of house they would love." This is scored *Aff Im* because it is a friendly nurturant act that implies the desire to establish or maintain an affiliative relationship.

I+: Positive nurturant acts (building the house for his family) are scored *I*. It is scored "+" because the story emphasizes a successful outcome ("everything will work out").

10-2. *U Im*

11-2. *Aff Im, I+, Bw*

12-2. *Aff Im, I−, Bp*

13-2. *Aff Im, Ga+, G+*

14-2. *U Im*

15-2. *U Im*

16-2. *U Im*

17-2. *Aff Im, Ga+*

18-2. *Aff Im, N, I+*

19-2. *Aff Im, N, Bw, Th*

20-2. *Aff Im, N, I+, Ga+, Bw*

21-2. *Aff Im, I+, Th*

22-2. *U Im*

23-2. *Aff Im, N*

24-2. *Aff Im, N, I+, Bw*

25-2. *Aff Im, N, Ga+, Bw, Th*

26-2. *Aff Im*

27-2. *U Im*

28-2. *U Im*

29-2. *U Im*

30-2. *U Im*

Picture 3

1-3. *Aff Im*: Concern over marriage and the mention of "love" demonstrate a positive affiliative relationship.

I?: "Spending the rest of the day together," and "planning to get married" are instrumental acts intended to maintain and/or further an affiliative relationship. It is scored "?" because the outcome of these acts is unclear.

No Th: Thema is not scored because the discussion about playing the lottery does not directly relate to the affiliative theme.

2-3. *U Im*

3-3. *Aff Im*: The difficulty in parting implies concern with maintaining the affiliative relationship, and the statement that "their love is still strong" strongly suggests a positive affective relationship.

Bw: This is a difficult scoring decision. The impediment in the relationship cannot clearly be attributed to the actions or attributes of one of the characters. Consequently, *Bw* is scored.

Th: The entire story is focused on an affiliative relationship.

4-3. *Aff Im*: The characters "have some quiet time to just talk"; this is a convivial, companionate activity.

I+: Companionate activities are scored *I* ("they have some quiet time to just talk. . . . they are enjoying the out of doors and the scenery"). It is scored "+" because the act furthers the affiliative relationship ("talking together lets them know more about each other's feelings").

No G+: It is not clear that the enjoyment comes from the affiliative activity; in this story, the enjoyment could come from the pleasure of being in nature (rather than from being together).

No Th: The enjoyment of nature is a distinct theme from the affiliative story.

5-3. *Aff Im*: The characters are engaged in a friendly companionate activity ("a day off to relax and enjoy each other's company") and are described as "in love." These are both sufficient evidence to score *Aff Im*.

I+: Convivial companionate activities are scored *I*; the activity is described as relaxing and enjoyable and consequently is scored "+."

G+: "Relax and enjoy each other's company, . . . They will leave and have a nice quiet dinner." The affiliative activities are associated with positive emotional states.

Th: The entire story is devoted to an affiliative theme.

6-3. *Aff Im*: "He likes her very much . . . he went out also, and followed her, to have a chance to talk." This character is concerned with establishing an affiliative relationship.

I−: "He went out also, and followed her, to have a chance to talk." This is an act directed toward establishing an affiliative relationship. The indifferent behavior of the other character suggests that the act does not further the affiliative relationship; consequently, the act is scored "−."

Bp: "She is looking off in the distance, thinking that she would like to change jobs, move up, and yet [he] is going on and on about his more immediate hopes and plans for his life . . . he is kind of the office 'nerd.'" The story strongly suggests that the personal attributes of one of the characters impedes the affiliative relationship.

7-3. *Aff Im*: "They have been going together for a while and enjoy being together"; this strongly implies a positive affective relationship.

N: "They want to get to know each other better." This is an expressed desire for greater affiliation.

I+: The characters "enjoy being together and discussing things that they have in common and their goals in life." This is a companionate convivial activity; it is scored "+" because marriage is offered as the probable outcome.

Bp: The age of the characters prevents them from marrying immediately; this impediment emerges from the attributes of the characters rather than from an environmental block.

G+: "They enjoy being together."

Th: The entire story focuses on affiliative themes.

8-3. *Aff Im*: A borderline decision: "furtherance of the relationship" implies concern with maintaining an affiliative bond; moreover, the terms "boyfriend," "girlfriend," and "romantic time" imply an affiliative relationship.

9-3. *Aff Im*: The characters both feel love for each other; thus, affiliative concern is readily inferred.

I+: Scored because having a baby is presented as a positive nurturant act between the two characters.

Bw: "How long they had waited for this to happen . . . he thought it would never happen." This constitutes an environmental impediment in the interpersonal relationship, which, when overcome, furthers the affiliative bond.

G+: "Fred was beaming from ear to ear, . . . this is the best news." This statement and the love felt by both characters indicate a positive affective experience associated with the affiliative activity.

Th: The entire story focuses on an affiliative relationship.

10-3. *Aff Im*: "They enjoy each other's company." Although this story includes work-related themes, the relationship between the characters is a positive affective one.

I+: The characters are sitting together and enjoying each other's company; this constitutes a pleasurable companionate, activity and is thus scored *I+*.

G+: "They enjoy each other's company."

11-3. *Aff Im, I−, Bp, G−*
12-3. *Aff Im, I+, Ga+*
13-3. *Aff Im, I+, Th*
14-3. *Aff Im, G+*
15-3. *U Im*
16-3. *U Im*
17-3. *Aff Im, Bw*
18-3. *Aff Im, N, I+, G+, Th*
19-3. *Aff Im, G+, Th*
20-3. *Aff Im, N, I+, Bw, Bp, G+*
21-3. *Aff Im, I+*
22-3. *U Im*
23-3. *Aff Im, I?, Th*
24-3. *Aff Im, N, I−, Bp, Th*
25-3. *Aff Im, I+, G+, Th*
26-3. *Aff Im, N, I+, Bw, Th*
27-3. *U Im*
28-3. *Aff Im, I+, G+*
29-3. *Aff Im, N, I+, Bw, Th*
30-3. *U Im*

Picture 4

1-4. *U Im*
2-4. *U Im*
3-4. *U Im*
4-4. *U Im*
5-4. *U Im*
6-4. *U Im*
7-4. *U Im*
8-4. *U Im*
9-4. *U Im*

10-4. *U Im*
11-4. *U Im*
12-4. *U Im*
13-4. *U Im*
14-4. *U Im*
15-4. *U Im*
16-4. *U Im*
17-4. *Aff Im, I−, Bp*
18-4. *U Im*
19-4. *U Im*
20-4. *U Im*
21-4. *U Im*
22-4. *U Im*
23-4. *U Im*
24-4. *U Im*
25-4. *U Im*
26-4. *U Im*
27-4. *U Im*
28-4. *U Im*
29-4. *U Im*
30-4. *U Im*

Picture 5

1-5. *Aff Im*: "He's decided to tell her he knows and that he forgives her," implies concern with restoring an affiliative relationship.

I−: The character's decision to tell his partner that he knows about her infidelity and that he forgives her constitutes an instrumental act intended to restore the affiliative relationship. Scored "−" because it is unsuccessful due to the accident.

Bp: A past action clearly attributable to one of the characters (the woman's infidelity) has impeded the relationship.

Th: This is a borderline decision: While the final accident might be construed as a new theme, it appears to be a logical consequence of the disruption in the affiliative relationship, and thus is part of the predominant affiliative motif.

2-5. *U Im*
3-5. *U Im*
4-5. *U Im*
5-5. *U Im*
6-5. *U Im*
7-5. *U Im*
8-5. *U Im*

9-5. *Aff Im*: This is a confused story; the statement, "she knew Chris would have to love her life if he really loved her," however, implies concern with maintaining a positive affective relationship.

10-5. *U Im*
11-5. *Aff Im, I+, Bw, G+*
12-5. *U Im*
13-5. *U Im*
14-5. *U Im*
15-5. *U Im*
16-5. *U Im*

17-5. *U Im*
18-5. *U Im*
19-5. *U Im*
20-5. *Aff Im, G+*
21-5. *U Im*
22-5. *U Im*
23-5. *U Im*
24-5. *U Im*
25-5. *U Im*
26-5. *Aff Im, N, I?, Ga−, Bw, Th*
27-5. *U Im*
28-5. *U Im*
29-5. *U Im*
30-5. *U Im*

Picture 6

1-6. *U Im*
2-6. *U Im*
3-6. *U Im*
4-6. *Aff Im*: "They are talking together . . . they will . . . sit down to lunch together."
This convivial companionate activity implies an affiliative relationship.

I+: Companionate convivial activities, in this case talking and walking together, are defined as instrumental acts.
5-6. *U Im*
6-6. *Aff Im*: He "has become her friend." This is the minimum criterion for scoring this category; "she like[s] him" also implies affiliative concern.

I+: A borderline case. She "feels comfortable talking to him," suggests a convivial companionate activity.

G+: Also a borderline case. "Comfortable talking to him" indicates a positive affective experience associated with the affiliative activity.
7-6. *U Im*
8-6. *Aff Im*: "She's interacting with her father – she is making an attempt to spend some quality time." This implies concern with establishing/maintaining an affiliative relationship.

Not I?: "Spend some quality time" would normally score, but the first and last sentence of a story are not scored for *I*.

Bw: "Quality time that perhaps she didn't have as a child"; this is an impediment to the relationship that cannot be clearly attributed to one of the characters and is thus scored *Bw*.

Th: Predominant theme is concern with the affiliative relationship.
9-6. *Aff Im*: "I asked him to tell me some stories of this country, . . . as we walked along . . . he told me of his childhood." The entire story implies a companionate convivial activity between the two characters.

I+: Companionate convivial activities, such as walking together and telling stories, are scored as instrumental acts. It is "+" because of the positive affective outcome associated with the affiliative activity.
10-6. *Aff Im*: A borderline decision. "They walk and talk together," combined with the positive nurturant quality of the old man's comments to the woman, suggest the existence of a positive affiliative relationship.

I+: The acts of walking and talking together suggest acts intended to establish and maintain an affiliative situation.

11-6. *Aff Im, I+, Bw*
12-6. *Aff Im, N, Bp*
13-6. *Aff Im, N, I+, G+, Th*
14-6. *Aff Im, G+*
15-6. *U Im*
16-6. *U Im*
17-6. *Aff Im, N, G+*
18-6. *Aff Im*
19-6. *Aff Im, I+, Th*
20-6. *Aff Im, Ga+, Bw, G+, G−, Th*
21-6. *U Im*
22-6. *Aff Im, I+, G+*
23-6. *Aff Im, N, I+, G+, Th*
24-6. *Aff Im, N, I−, Ga+, Bp, G+, G−, Th*
25-6. *Aff Im, I+, G+*
26-6. *Aff Im, I+, Ga−, Bw, G+, Th*
27-6. *Aff Im, I+*
28-6. *U Im*
29-6. *U Im*
30-6. *Aff Im, I+*

SCORING FOR THE INTIMACY MOTIVE

Learning how to score involves three steps: mastering the scoring manual, coding practice stories, and comparing one's coding with that of the "expert scorer." First, read the two chapters (15 and 16) that deal with the intimacy scoring system. As chapter 16 explains, the practice stories included in appendix I do not provide as wide a range of intimacy imagery categories as might be desired. Therefore, a special set of practice stories for intimacy is included at the end of chapter 16. Begin by scoring those stories. Make a scoring sheet on which you can record the coding categories for each story. An example of a scoring sheet is given at the end of chapter 36. Chapter 37 explains how to make a scoring sheet and gives a number of suggestions regarding how to learn a content analysis system and how to measure intercoder agreement.

After you score the stories in chapter 16, read the introduction to appendix I for a description of the practice stories included in appendix I and how they were obtained. Score all of the stories for each picture before going on to the next. Score the stories for 10 subjects and then compare your scoring with that of the expert. Then repeat the procedure for the next 10 stories, and so on. For each picture the expert scoring of the first 10 stories is accompanied by written explanations. Keep track of your errors and review them before going on to a new picture. As you score, consult the manual as frequently as necessary. Compute the degree of interscorer agreement you attain (see chapter 37) picture by picture and/or using a total score for each subject based on all six pictures.

The pictures used for the practice stories included here were cued for several different motives, so the stories vary greatly from one picture to another in the amount of intimacy imagery they contain. To obtain additional practice stories, consult appendix III.

EXPERT SCORING FOR INTIMACY MOTIVATION*

Picture 1

1-1. 0
2-1. 0
3-1. 0
4-1. Dlg – A conversation
+A – "friendly"
Sr – "met in passing"
5-1. Dlg – A conversation
6-1. 0
7-1. Dlg – A conversation
+A – "They will take the cruise
and have a good time"
8-1. 0
9-1. 0
10-1. 0
11-1. 0
12-1. 0
13-1. 0
14-1. 0
15-1. 0
16-1. 0
17-1. 0
18-1. 0
19-1. 0
20-1. 0
21-1. 0
22-1. 0
23-1. 0
24-1. 0
25-1. 0
26-1. 0
27-1. 0
28-1. 0
29-1. 0
30-1. 0

Picture 2

1-2. 0
2-2. 0

* Expert scoring by Dan P. McAdams.

3-2. 0
4-2. +A – "missing" his family
5-2. 0
6-2. 0
7-2. +A – "loves" his family
8-2. 0
9-2. 0
10-2. 0
11-2. 0
12-2. 0
13-2. 0
14-2. +A, Sr
15-2. 0
16-2. 0
17-2. +A, CC
18-2. 0
19-2. Dlg.
20-2. +A, Dlg, Esc
21-2. 0
22-2. 0
23-2. 0
24-2. 0
25-2. +A, Ts
26-2. +A
27-2. 0
28-2. 0
29-2. 0
30-2. 0

Picture 3

1-3. +A – "a couple in love"
U – "planning to get married"
2-3. 0
3-3. +A – "their love is still strong"
Low – "the frozen Charles River
does not make parting any easier"
4-3. Dlg – talking
COW – "enjoying the out of doors
and the scenery"
5-3. Dlg – "light, easy conversation"
+A – "two people in love"
6-3. +A – "he likes her very much"
7-3. Dlg – A conversation
+A – "enjoy being together"
TS – "have been going together
for a while"
H – "things they have in common"
U – "get married"
8-3. +A – "boyfriend and girlfriend"
9-3. Dlg – a conversation
+A – "tears in her eyes"

TS – They have waited for a baby
"for so long"
10-3. +A – "enjoy each other's
company"
Dlg – a conversation
11-3. 0
12-3. +A, TS, COW, CC
13-3. Dlg, +A
14-3. +A, Esc, COW
15-3. 0
16-3. Dlg
17-3. +A, Dlg
18-3. Dlg, +A, TS
19-3. +A
20-3. +A, U, Dlg
21-3. 0
22-3. 0
23-3. +A
24-3. 0
25-3. Dlg, U, TS
26-3. Dlg, U, +A
27-3. Dlg
28-3. +A, Dlg, Psy
29-3. Dlg, U
30-3. +A, Dlg

Picture 4

1-4. 0
2-4. +A – "boyfriend"
3-4. 0
4-4. 0
5-4. 0
6-4. 0
7-4. 0
8-4. 0
9-4. 0
10-4. 0
11-4. 0
12-4. 0
13-4. 0
14-4. 0
15-4. 0
16-4. 0
17-4. Dlg
18-4. 0
19-4. 0
20-4. 0
21-4. 0
22-4. Dlg
23-4. 0
24-4. 0

25-4. 0
26-4. 0
27-4. 0
28-4. 0
29-4. 0
30-4. 0

Picture 5

1-5. 0
2-5. 0
3-5. 0
4-5. 0
5-5. 0
6-5. +A – "lovers"
7-5. 0
8-5. 0
9-5. +A – "he really loves her"
10-5. 0
11-5. 0
12-5. +A, Dlg
13-5. 0
14-5. 0
15-5. 0
16-5. 0
17-5. 0
18-5. 0
19-5. 0
20-5. Dlg, TS
21-5. 0
22-5. 0
23-5. 0
24-5. 0
25-5. 0
26-5. 0
27-5. 0
28-5. 0
29-5. 0
30-5. 0

Picture 6

1-6. 0
2-6. 0
3-6. 0
4-6. Dlg – "They are talking together"
5-6. Dlg – "They are talking . . ."
6-6. +A – "She likes him"
      Dlg – Talking
7-6. Dlg – Talking
8-6. 0

9-6. Dlg – "he told me of his childhood"
COW – "the beautiful
country . . . took my breath away"
Psy – "I left Ireland a little freer and
more hopeful knowing life could
be so fulfilling"
10-6. Dlg – "They talk and walk
together . . ."
Sr – An accidental meeting
Esc – Escaping "away from her
hectic work schedule" to intimacy
11-6. +A, U, TS, Sr
12-6. 0
13-6. Dlg, Psy
14-6. +A, Esc
15-6. 0
16-6. 0
17-6. 0
18-6. 0
19-6. +A, Dlg, COW
20-6. +A, U, TS
21-6. 0
22-6. Dlg, Sr, +A
23-6. 0
24-6. +A, COW
25-6. Dlg
26-6. +A, H, TS, U
27-6. Dlg
28-6. 0
29-6. 0
30-6. Dlg, Sr

SCORING FOR AFFILIATIVE TRUST – MISTRUST

Learning how to score involves three steps: mastering the scoring manual, coding practice stories, and comparing one's coding with that of the "expert scorer." Begin by reading the two chapters (17 and 18) that deal with the affiliative trust–mistrust scoring system. Next, read the introduction to appendix I for a description of the practice stories and how they were obtained. Make a scoring sheet on which you can record the coding categories for each story. Chapter 37 explains how to make a scoring sheet and gives a number of suggestions regarding how to learn a content analysis system and how to measure intercoder agreement. An example of a scoring sheet is given at the end of chapter 36.

Score all of the stories for each picture before going on to the next picture. Score the stories for 10 subjects and then compare your scoring with that of the expert. Then repeat the procedure for the next 10 stories, and so on. For each picture written explanations of the expert scoring are given for the first 12 stories. These explanations *follow* the list of scores for all six pictures. Keep track of your errors and review them before going on to a new picture. As you score, consult the manual as frequently as necessary. Compute the degree of interscorer agreement you attain (see chapter 37) picture by picture and/or using a total score for each subject based on all six pictures.

The pictures used for the practice stories included here were cued for several different motives, so the amount of affiliative trust–mistrust imagery varies from one picture to another. To obtain additional practice stories, consult appendix III.

EXPERT SCORING FOR AFFILIATIVE TRUST–MISTRUST*

Picture 1

Subject	Categories	T	M	T – M
1-1.		0	0	0
2-1.		0	0	0
3-1.		0	0	0
4-1.		0	0	0
5-1.		0	0	0
6-1.		0	0	0
7-1.		0	0	0
8-1.		0	0	0
9-1.		0	0	0
10-1.		0	0	0
11-1.		0	0	0
12-1.		0	0	0
13-1.		0	0	0
14-1.		0	0	0
15-1.		0	0	0
16-1.	CA+	1	0	1
17-1.		0	0	0
18-1.		0	0	0
19-1.		0	0	0
20-1.		0	0	0
21-1.		0	0	0
22-1.		0	0	0
23-1.		0	0	0
24-1.		0	0	0
25-1.		0	0	0
26-1.	AT+	1	0	1
27-1.		0	0	0
28-1.		0	0	0
29-1.		0	0	0
30-1.		0	0	0

* Expert scoring by James R. McKay.

Picture 2

Subject	Categories	T	M	T − M
1-2.		0	0	0
2-2.		0	0	0
3-2.		0	0	0
4-2.	SA+	1	0	1
5-2.		0	0	0
6-2.		0	0	0
7-2.	SA+	1	0	1
8-2.		0	0	0
9-2.	AT+	1	0	1
10-2.		0	0	0
11-2.	CA+	1	0	1
12-2.	CYN−, NRA−	0	2	−2
13-2.	CA+	1	0	1
14-2.		0	0	0
15-2.		0	0	0
16-2.	CA+	1	0	1
17-2.	CA+	1	0	1
18-2.		0	0	0
19-2.		0	0	0
20-2.	AT+	1	0	1
21-2.	AT+	1	0	1
22-2.		0	0	0
23-2.		0	0	0
24-2.		0	0	0
25-2.	AT+	1	0	1
26-2.		0	0	0
27-2.		0	0	0
28-2.		0	0	0
29-2.		0	0	0
30-2.		0	0	0

Picture 3

Subject	Categories	T	M	T − M
1-3.	SA+, CA+	2	0	2
2-3.	CYN−, CYN−, NRA−	0	3	−3
3-3.		0	0	0
4-3.	SA+	1	0	1
5-3.	SA+	1	0	1
6-3.	NRA−	0	1	−1
7-3.	SA+	1	0	1
8-3.	SA+	1	0	1
9-3.	SA+	1	0	1
10-3.	SA+	1	0	1
11-3.	NRA−	0	1	−1
12-3.	NRA−, AT+	1	1	0
13-3.	SA+	1	0	1
14-3.		0	0	0

Subject	Categories	T	M	T − M
15-3.	CA+	1	0	1
16-3.	SA+	1	0	1
17-3.		0	0	0
18-3.	SA+	1	0	1
19-3.	SA+	1	0	1
20-3.	AT+, SA+	2	0	2
21-3.	SA+, CA+	2	0	2
22-3.	NRA−	0	1	−1
23-3.	SA+	1	0	1
24-3.	NRA−	0	1	−1
25-3.	SA+, CA+	2	0	2
26-3.	AT+, SA+, CA+	3	0	3
27-3.		0	0	0
28-3.	SA+	1	0	1
29-3.	SA+	1	0	1
30-3.	NRA−	0	1	−1

Picture 4

Subject	Categories	T	M	T − M
1-4.		0	0	0
2-4.	CYN−	0	1	−1
3-4.		0	0	0
4-4.		0	0	0
5-4.		0	0	0
6-4.		0	0	0
7-4.		0	0	0
8-4.		0	0	0
9-4.		0	0	0
10-4.	AT+	1	0	1
11-4.		0	0	0
12-4.	CYN−	0	1	−1
13-4.		0	0	0
14-4.		0	0	0
15-4.		0	0	0
16-4.		0	0	0
17-4.	NRA−	0	1	−1
18-4.		0	0	0
19-4.		0	0	0
20-4.		0	0	0
21-4.		0	0	0
22-4.		0	0	0
23-4.		0	0	0
24-4.		0	0	0
25-4.		0	0	0
26-4.		0	0	0
27-4.		0	0	0

Subject	Categories	T	M	T − M
28-4.		0	0	0
29-4.	NRA−, AT+	1	1	0
30-4.		0	0	0

Picture 5

Subject	Categories	T	M	T − M
1-5.	CYN−	0	1	−1
2-5.		0	0	0
3-5.		0	0	0
4-5.		0	0	0
5-5.		0	0	0
6-5.	NRA−	0	1	−1
7-5.		0	0	0
8-5.		0	0	0
9-5.		0	0	0
10-5.		0	0	0
11-5.	AT+, AT+	2	0	2
12-5.		0	0	0
13-5.		0	0	0
14-5.		0	0	0
15-5.		0	0	0
16-5.		0	0	0
17-5.		0	0	0
18-5.		0	0	0
19-5.		0	0	0
20-5.	SA+	1	0	1
21-5.		0	0	0
22-5.		0	0	0
23-5.		0	0	0
24-5.		0	0	0
25-5.		0	0	0
26-5.	SA+	1	0	1
27-5.		0	0	0
28-5.		0	0	0
29-5.		0	0	0
30-5.		0	0	0

Picture 6

Subject	Categories	T	M	T − M
1-6.		0	0	0
2-6.		0	0	0
3-6.		0	0	0
4-6.		0	0	0
5-6.	CA+	1	0	1

Subject	Categories	T	M	T − M
6-6.	SA+	1	0	1
7-6.		0	0	0
8-6.	AT+	1	0	1
9-6.		0	0	0
10-6.		0	0	0
11-6.	SA+, CA+	2	0	2
12-6.	NRA−	0	1	−1
13-6.	NRA−, AT+	1	1	0
14-6.		0	0	0
15-6.	AT+	1	0	1
16-6.		0	0	0
17-6.		0	0	0
18-6.		0	0	0
19-6.	SA+	1	0	1
20-6.	NRA−, SA+	1	1	0
21-6.	AT+	1	0	1
22-6.	SA+	1	0	1
23-6.	SA+	1	0	1
24-6.	SA+	1	0	1
25-6.		0	0	0
26-6.	SA+	1	0	1
27-6.		0	0	0
28-6.		0	0	0
29-6.		0	0	0
30-6.	SA+	1	0	1

AFFILIATIVE TRUST−MISTRUST: EXPLANATION OF CODING OF
FIRST 12 STORIES FOR EACH PICTURE

Picture 1

1-1. No categories are scored.
2-1. No categories are scored.
3-1. No categories are scored.
4-1. No categories are scored.
5-1. No categories are scored.
6-1. No categories are scored.
　　Although the captain is described as "smuggling," there is no explicit mention of a good or moral front. Hence CYN− cannot be coded (see subsection "B" in CYN− section of coding manual).
7-1. No categories are scored.
8-1. No categories are scored.
9-1. No categories are scored.
10-1. No categories are scored.
11-1. No categories are scored.
　　CYN− is not coded here.
12-1. No categories are scored.

Examples of Picture *1* stories that are coded for something

16-1. CA+: Upcoming family vacation, which includes an "enjoyable ride."
26-1. AT+: Captain goes out of his way to help the passenger, in a manner that is clearly "above and beyond the call of duty."

Picture 2

1-2. No categories are scored.
2-2. No categories are scored.
   Despite the cynical feel, CYN− cannot be coded as criteria for A or B are not met.
3-2. No categories are scored.
4-2. SA+: Memories of the family being "happy together" qualifies as positive affect and shared feelings.
5-2. No categories are scored.
6-2. No categories are scored.
   Man who wants "to do what's best for him and his family" is not doing anything out of the ordinary, so AT+ is not scored.
7-2. SA+: Positive affect and shared feelings. Man loves his family who loves him back.
8-2. No categories are scored.
9-2. AT+: Whole story is about a man designing a house for his family and surprising them with his gift.
10-2. No categories are scored.
11-2. CA+: Man and wife work together on the man's problem, thus improving the relationship.
12-2. NRA−: Woman tries to attract and marry a man, but fails.
   CYN−: Attractive man becomes bald and fat (see B in CYN− section of coding manual).

Picture 3

1-3. SA+: Couple described as "in love."
   CA+: Couple is doing something special together, "taken the afternoon off."
2-3. CYN−: The young "con artist" is being deceitful.
   CYN−: A not so "innocent" B. U. student conceals her infectious illness, thus apparently dooming man.
   NRA−: She rejects his advances.
3-3. No categories are scored.
   Do not code NRA− as the couple is still in love and it is not clear why Stephen is leaving.
4-3. SA+: The couple is learning more about each other and sharing.
5-3. SA+: The two people are "in love."
   "Have a nice quiet dinner" does not score for CA+ as it is described in the last part of the last sentence.
6-3. NRA−: Woman ignores man's attempts to connect.
7-3. SA+: "Going together," "enjoy being together," and the discussions about

goals all qualify as shared affiliation. It can only be scored once per couple, however.

8-3. SA+: "Romantic " allows you to code this passage about a couple spending time together.

9-3. SA+: Coded for reciprocated expressions of love.

AT+ not coded as Janet asking Fred to meet her is the opening statement of the story.

10-3. SA+: They "enjoy each others company," which denotes warm, positive feelings.

11-3. NRA−: Woman ends relationship.

Although the story certainly has a cynical feel, CYN− is not scored because specific criteria are not met.

12-3. AT+: One character takes care of the other, "oatmeal baths to soothe the sores."

NRA−: Man attempts to comfort woman, but she offers no response whatsoever.

Picture 4

1-4. No categories are scored.

2-4. CYN−: Here, a scientist is taking advantage of the "boy friend."

The "glowing" and "illumination" are not about feeling good or enlightenment, as they are presented, but about dying from radiation poisoning. See Category "B" under CYN−.

3-4. No categories are scored.

4-4. No categories are scored.

5-4. No categories are scored.

6-4. No categories are scored.

7-4. No categories are scored.

8-4. No categories are scored.

9-4. No categories are scored.

10-4. AT+: The professor identifies with her student and goes out of her way to help her. See "d" in AT+ section of the coding manual.

11-4. No categories are scored.

Although this story has a cynical feel, it does not meet the criteria for CYN−.

12-4. CYN−: This example is also coded on the basis of category "B" in the CYN− section. People selling the product advertise it as a health-promoting product, when all it really does is "measure dust."

Other examples of Picture 4 stories that code for something

17-4. NRA−: The affiliative overture of the man is refused.

29-4. AT+: Mary got her sister a job.

NRA−: Sister was just divorced.

Picture 5

1-5. CYN−: Sheila was unfaithful. The last paragraph is ironic, but is not scorable for CYN− under Category A or B.

2-5. No categories are scored.

Although the couple engages in activity that looks like it could be coded for SA+ or CA+, the relationship is not enhanced, there is no mention of mutual enjoyment, and the outcome is negative. It is not clear what is meant by "disastrous for our marriage," so NRA− is not coded either.

3-5. No categories are scored.

4-5. No categories are scored.

5-5. No categories are scored.

6-5. NRA−: The woman leaves the man because she wants something different.

7-5. No categories are scored.

8-5. No categories are scored.

Although "trust" is explicitly mentioned, it is in the context of working together. In order to be scored for SA+ or CA+, this passage requires more elaboration about their relationship.

9-5. No categories are scored.

10-5. No categories are scored.

11-5. AT+: Mother's sister reaches out and contacts woman.

AT+: Woman decides to settle near her family and is "thrilled" about being reunited.

12-5. No categories are scored.

Other examples of Picture 5 stories

14-5. This does not code for anything. "Trust" mentioned in the abstract like this, without a description of two people trusting each other, does not code for SA+.

22-5. This does not code for CA+ because cooperation is described in the last clause of the story. See "a" in section on CA+ in coding manual.

Picture 6

1-6. No categories are scored.

2-6. No categories are scored.

3-6. No categories are scored.

4-6. No categories are scored.

5-6. CA+: Collaborative action in discussing the family business and making plans to pass it on to the next generation. This is seen as good for the family.

6-6. SA+: Affiliation is reciprocated here; he has become a friend and she likes him, etc.

7-6. No categories are scored.

8-6. AT+: Daughter's attempt to spend quality time is an example of someone trying to improve a relationship.

9-6. No categories are scored.

10-6. No categories are scored.

11-6. SA+: "They become great friends . . ."

CA+: The two go off on a vacation to India, which is seen as good for the relationship, "he thinks this is swell." Man's offer of a place to stay does not code for AT+ as this is a business deal.

12-6. NRA−: The father badly wants his daughter to stay (as is mentioned twice), but she does not and even finds it hard to talk to him at all.

Affiliative Trust–Mistrust Scores
(Total for 6 Pictures)

Subject	Mistrust	Trust	Positivity–Mistrust
1.	1	2	1
2.	4	0	−4
3.	0	0	0
4.	0	2	2
5.	0	2	2
6.	2	1	−1
7.	0	2	2
8.	0	2	2
9.	0	2	2
10.	0	2	2
11.	1	5	4
12.	5	1	−4
13.	1	3	2
14.	0	0	0
15.	0	2	2
16.	0	3	3
17.	1	1	0
18.	0	1	1
19.	0	2	2
20.	1	5	4
21.	0	4	4
22.	1	1	0
23.	0	2	2
24.	1	1	0
25.	0	3	3
26.	0	6	6
27.	0	0	0
28.	0	1	1
29.	1	2	1
30.	1	1	0

SCORING FOR POWER MOTIVATION (REVISED SYSTEM)

Learning how to score involves three steps: mastering the scoring manual, coding practice stories, and comparing one's coding with that of the "expert scorer." First, read the two chapters (21 and 22) that deal with the revised power scoring system. Only after you have a good command of the content of the manual, take the self-test given at the end of chapter 22.

Next, read the introduction to appendix I for a description of the practice stories and how they were obtained. Make a scoring sheet on which you can record the coding categories for each story. Chapter 37 explains how to make a scoring sheet and gives a number of suggestions regarding how to learn a content analysis system and how to measure intercoder agreement. An example of a scoring sheet is given at the end of chapter 36.

If you have access to *The Power Motive* (D. G. Winter, 1973) begin by scoring the practice stories in appendix I of that book. Otherwise, begin by scoring the practice stories included here. Score all of the stories for each picture before going on to the next picture. Score the stories for 10 subjects and then compare your scoring with that of the expert. Then repeat the procedure for the next 10 stories, and so on.

The expert scoring is given on the following pages. For each picture the expert scoring of the first 10 stories is accompanied by written explanations. *Keep track of your errors, and review them before going on to a new picture.* As you score, consult the manual as frequently as necessary. Compute the degree of interscorer agreement you attain (see chapter 37) picture by picture and/or using a total score for each subject based on all six pictures.

The pictures used for the practice stories included here were cued for several different motives, so the stories vary greatly from one picture to another in the amount of power imagery they contain. To obtain additional practice stories, consult appendix III.

EXPERT SCORING FOR POWER MOTIVE*

Picture 1

1-1. Total = 0 (There is no concern for prestige; the captain's concerns are elaborated in the achievement direction.)

2-1. Pow Im, Pa− ("Captain Queeg," taken to be negative prestige but could have been scored as positive prestige instead), I. Total = 3.

3-1. 0 (routine behavior)

4-1. 0

5-1. 0

6-1. Pow Im (captain is demanding payment), I. Total = 2.

7-1. 0

8-1. Pow Im, I. Total = 2.

9-1. 0

10-1. Pow Im, Pa+ ("luxury liner"), N (police "want" a subgoal), I. Total = 4.

11-1. Pow Im, I ("The captain will be caught"). Total = 2.

12-1. 0

13-1. Pow Im, Pa+, I. Total = 3.

14-1. 0 (Not clear that the "mission" involves power.)

15-1. Pow Im, I. Total = 2.

16-1. Pow Im, Pa+, I. Total = 3.

17-1. 0 ("Annoyed" not a strong enough emotion to score power.)

18-1. Pow Im, Pa+ ("senator"), N. Total = 3.

19-1. 0

20-1. Pow Im ("pleading"), (*not* I; no specific act mentioned). Total = 1.

21-1. 0

22-1. Pow Im, Pa+, Eff. Total = 3.

23-1. 0 (routine request from businessman to captain)

24-1. Pow Im ("assertive," a marginal case). Total = 1.

* Expert scoring by David G. Winter.

25-1. Pow Im (help). Total = 1.
26-1. Pow Im. Total = 1.
27-1. 0
28-1. Pow Im, Pa+. Total = 2.
29-1. Pow Im, Pa+ ("Charlie Chan"). Total = 2.
30-1. Pow Im, Pa+ ("Federal government"). Total = 2.

Picture 2

1-2. 0
2-2. 0
3-2. 0
4-2. 0
5-2. 0
6-2. 0
7-2. 0
8-2. 0
9-2. Pow Im, I, Eff (wife's excitement). Total = 3.
10-2. 0
11-2. Pow Im. Total = 1.
12-2. 0
13-2. 0
14-2. 0
15-2. 0
16-2. 0
17-2. 0
18-2. 0
19-2. 0
20-2. 0
21-2. Pow Im ("Each persons interests and dreams will be found in this house" suggests emotional effect), I. Total = 2.
22-2. Pow Im, Eff (man's reaction to being laid off). Total = 2.
23-2. 0
24-2. Pow Im, G+ ("he is pleased" at helping his family). Total = 2.
25-2. 0
26-2. 0
27-2. 0
28-2. 0
29-2. 0 (The man's negative emotions seem linked to the picture, not to the family's telephone call; however, this is a marginal case.)
30-2. 0

Picture 3

1-3. Pow Im. Total = 1.
2-3. Pow Im, Pa+ ("full professor at M.I.T."), Pa− ("con artist"). Total = 3.
3-3. 0
4-3. 0
5-3. 0
6-3. 0
7-3. 0

8-3. 0
9-3. Pow Im (Fred's reaction to Janet's announcement), Eff. Total = 2.
10-3. 0
11-3. 0 (As elaborated in the story, the student's "romancing" suggests affiliation, with no overtones of power.)
12-3. Pow Im. Total = 1.
13-3. 0
14-3. 0
15-3. 0
16-3. 0
17-3. 0
18-3. 0
19-3. 0
20-3. Pow Im, I, Ga+ (she is anticipating an influence attempt), Eff. Total = 4.
21-3. 0
22-3. Pow Im, Pa− ("boring"), Eff. Total = 3.
23-3. 0
24-3. 0
25-3. 0
26-3. 0
27-3. 0
28-3. 0
29-3. 0
30-3. Pow Im, Eff. Total = 2.

Picture 4

1-4. Pow Im (dog's biting), Eff. Total = 2.
2-4. 0
3-4. 0
4-4. Pow Im (Offering remedies is help). Total = 1.
5-4. 0
6-4. 0 (A borderline case: Prestige is mentioned, but the concern is weak; "autocratic" does not describe any actions).
7-4. 0
8-4. 0
9-4. Pow Im, Eff (many people saved). Total = 2.
10-4. Pow Im (professor's help), Pa+. Total = 2.
11-4. Pow Im (many images: breakthrough could have great effect, firing, sabotage), Pa+ ("Nobel-prize winning scientist"), I (firing), Ga+ (plotting sabotage), Bw (assistant's sabotage is obstacle to the "breakthrough" and great effect). Total = 5.
12-4. 0
13-4. 0
14-4. 0
15-4. 0
16-4. 0
17-4. 0
18-4. 0
19-4. 0
20-4. 0
21-4. Pow Im, N ("Their hope is" could have been scored Ga+ instead). Total = 2.

22-4. 0
23-4. Pow Im, ("Saving the day" is help, and has positive emotional effect), I, Eff. Total = 3.
24-4. 0
25-4. 0
26-4. 0
27-4. 0
28-4. 0
29-4. Pow Im (Sister is grateful for Mary's act), Eff. Total = 2.
30-4. 0

Picture 5

1-5. 0 (No evidence his miss was intentional).
2-5. 0
3-5. 0
4-5. 0
5-5. 0
6-5. 0
7-5. 0 ("Good show" here suggests achievement).
8-5. 0
9-5. Pow Im (Chris's urgings), Bw (Faye puts up more than routine resistance to Chris's urgings). Total = 2.
10-5. Pow Im, Pa+, Ga+. Total = 3.
11-5. Pow Im (parents "were killed in the war" by "shelling attack"). Total = 1.
12-5. Pow Im ("driven by guns and tanks"). Total = 1.
13-5. 0
14-5. 0
15-5. 0
16-5. 0
17-5. 0
18-5. 0
19-5. 0
20-5. 0
21-5. Pow Im (pleasing the crowd), Ga+. Total = 2.
22-5. 0
23-5. Pow Im, Eff. Total = 2.
24-5. 0
25-5. 0
26-5. 0
27-5. 0
28-5. 0
29-5. 0
30-5. Pow Im (Crowd claps at their action), Eff. Total = 2.

Picture 6

1-6. Pow Im, Pa+ ("princess"). Total = 2.
2-6. Pow Im. Total = 1.
3-6. 0
4-6. 0

5-6. o
6-6. o
7-6. o
8-6. o
9-6. o
10-6. o
11-6. Pow Im (while her psychic powers suggest capability more than influence, they do have an effect on him), Pa+ ("Maharanee"), I. Total = 3.
12-6. o
13-6. o
14-6. o
15-6. Pow Im, I. Total = 2.
16-6. Pow Im ("this jerk dragging us along"), Pa− ("jerk"). Total = 2.
17-6. Pow Im ("enjoying the attention"), Pa+ ("appears to have some money"), G+ ("enjoying the attention"). Total = 3.
18-6. o
19-6. o
20-6. o
21-6. o
22-6. o
23-6. Pow Im (her help), G+ ("feeling good about herself" as the result of a power act). Total = 2.
24-6. o
25-6. o
26-6. o
27-6. o
28-6. o
29-6. o
30-6. o

SCORING FOR EXPLANATORY STYLE

Learning how to score involves three steps: mastering the scoring manual, coding practice stories, and comparing one's coding with that of the "expert scorer." First, read the two chapters (25 and 26) that deal with the explanatory style scoring system. Study the scoring manual carefully. It is a waste of time to begin scoring before you have a thorough grasp of the coding categories and the illustrative examples.

Next, read the introduction to appendix I for a description of the practice stories and how they were obtained. Chapter 37 gives a number of suggestions regarding how to learn a content analysis system and how to measure intercoder agreement.

Score all of the stories for each picture before going on to the next picture. Score the stories for 10 subjects and then compare your scoring with that of the expert. Then repeat the procedure for the next 10 stories, and so on. The expert scoring is given on the following pages. For each picture written explanations are given for the stories that are scored for explanatory style. The expert scoring shows the extracted attributions for bad events as well as the stability and globality of these causes. Keep track of your errors, and review them before going on to a new picture. As you score, consult the manual as frequently as necessary.

The pictures used for the practice stories were chosen to elicit imagery for several different variables, so the stories vary from one picture to another in the frequency of coding categories for explanatory style. To obtain additional practice stories, consult appendix III.

EXPERT SCORING FOR EXPLANATORY STYLE[*]

Picture 1

1-1. E: The captain . . . hasn't met the owner's expectations.
A: [he has not had] more competent help, better quality of food, and better support from office staff. Rating: x-5-5
2-1. E: Humphrey is blocking his dexterity with the [ball] bearings
A: because of the blatant sexual imagery. Rating: x-7-1
3-1. E: George does feel frustration.
A: [because] his luggage [has been lost]. It is not unusual for passengers to get to their room before the luggage arrives. Rating: x-2-3
9-1. E: The water is leaking in his porthole.
A: This happens at times. Rating: x-4-2
10-1. E: The ship must be detained.
A: It is feared that an illegal passenger is on board, a passenger very much wanted by the police. Rating: x-4-7
11-1. E: He is in a hot spot.
A: [because] someone is on his tail. Rating: x-2-7
13-1. E: One of the crewmen was found involved [dead?] in the cargo hold.
A: [He] died by accident. Rating: x-1-1
A: It was a crime. Rating: x-2-6
16-1. E: He couldn't leave yet.
A: The ferry had loaded real slow. 88° and lines of angry New Yorkers waiting in their cars for the last trip today. He knew only half of them would get on. Rating: x-4-6
17-1. E: The officer . . . is annoyed
A: because he is losing time. Rating: x-2-5
A: Both men know each other and have had problems in the past. Rating: x-5-5
20-1. E: The business man . . . cannot get a ticket
A: because they are totally booked. Rating: x-4-4
E: The man is panicky.
A: He fells he must be at the meeting. Rating: x-4-7
23-1. E: They are having a difficult conversation.
A: The businessman wants something from the sea captain. Rating: x-2-3
24-1. E: The businessman is not satisfied with the explanation.
A: [because he is] sensing undue delay or late delivery of his goods. Rating: x-2-4
25-1. E: The captain is giving him areas and concerns about the area.

[*] Expert scoring by Christopher Peterson.

A: There have been some gangs lurking around and have given some tourists a hard time. Rating: x-4-7

27-1. E: There appears to be a question aboard ship.

A: Perhaps the passenger has misplaced his luggage or he could have a question regarding some sort of help. Rating: x-3-3

28-1. E: All ship (cargo and pleasure) captains have been questioned.

A: There has been a crackdown on drug smuggling. Rating: x-3-5

29-1. E: He was the one who murdered Dr. Who.

A: Since the Captain's alibi was phony. Rating: x-3-4

30-1. E: Problems with the cargo.

A: He had a problem in the past with drugs in the cargo, and he had to spend a lot of time and money to clear himself. Rating: x-5-3

Picture 2

1-2. E: He realizes that he has not been able to spend the time he would like with them [his family].

A: His work has taken up too much of his life. Rating: x-5-6

2-2. E: His doubt concerns an earlier career choice about working for the Kenner products designing toys.

A: [because] in that capacity one of his models was elected President of the United States. Rating: x-2-6

3-2. E: It seems he never has enough time to be with his family

A: [because he] seems to always work late. Rating: x-7-4

4-2. E: He is missing [his family].

A: He may be working on a project far away from home. Rating: x-2-2

5-2. E: A father/husband trying to do his job, but keeps thinking about his family.

A: He may feel that he has chosen the wrong profession. . . . He has a lot of responsibilities raising a family and at work. He cannot just quit and leave. Rating: x-6-6

10-2. E: A man . . . torn

A: by a decision he must make. Rating: x-2-6

11-2. E: This man if an architect whose business is in trouble.

A: Someone from his black past has emerged and is trying to blackmail him. Rating: x-5-5

12-2. E: I tried to marry him [but he refused].

A: I wasn't rich and attractive enough to him. Rating: x-7-3

14-2. E: You can be distracted

A: if the concentration isn't there. Rating: x-2-3

22-2. E: This man . . . has not moved up in the company.

A: He is good at his work but not aggressive. Rating: x-7-4

E: He feels sad and dejected.

A: He has just been laid off. Rating: x-2-7

24-2. E: [He does not have] the kind of time with them [his family] that he would like.

A: His projects preclude him. Rating: x-5-4

29-2. E: The man is . . . feeling depressed.

A: It was Sunday, and they called him in to finish the project. Rating: x-1-2

30-2. E: He is upset.

A: His family is unable to go [abroad with him]. Rating: x-2-3

E: He is a little worried

A: [because] he [may] . . . be captured by the government as a spy. Rating: x-2-6

Picture 3

11-3. E: She is . . . essentially frustrated
A: [because] he is always a stick-in-the-mud. Rating: x-7-5
16-3. E: Carol was always unhappy about something.
A: If it wasn't her job, it was her love life. If those situations were going okay, she'd find something else. Rating: x-7-6
E: But now she really had something to be unhappy about.
A: During the holidays, Carol found out that her dad was dying of cancer. Rating: x-2-4
20-3. E: She is shocked.
A: She loves him and wants to marry him, but she does not want to leave her family, friends, job, and security of her familiar surroundings [and move away with him]. Rating: x-6-4
22-3. E: She is irritated.
A: He has "trespassed on her space." Rating: x-2-2
30-3. E: She is very upset.
A: [She] doesn't want the child but is unable to abort because of religious belief. Rating: x-6-5

Picture 4

1-4. E: The whole country's future could be in jeapordy.
A: The president was bitten earlier in the day by a rabid dog. Rating: x-1-7
11-4. E: [Her assistant] has always been jealous of her.
A: [because the assistant is] considerably less talented. Rating: x-7-4
E: . . . wars, death, destruction, pollution of the environment, unjust imbalance of wealth.
A: [because of] advanced adolescent narcissism in men. Rating: x-5-7
E: She is planning to sabotage the experiments.
A: Her personal grudge against her boss. Rating: x-6-4
13-4. E: This intensity often gets in the way of the project.
A: She is very intense in her belief that a certain gene can be identified. Rating: x-7-3
23-4. E: A serious lab test going on.
A: Seems like the guy screwed up the test, and the female doctor is saving the day. Rating: x-2-2
26-4. E: She . . . has doubts
A: about her ability to work, raise a family, and get a degree simultaneously. Rating: x-6-7
29-4. E: Her life was in a mess.
A: since her divorce. Rating: x-2-6

Picture 5

1-5. E: She falls and breaks her neck.
A: Just as he is about to catch her on the last swing, he misses. Rating: x-1-1
2-5. E: . . . disastrous for our marriage
A: [was] the high diving into a sponge. Rating: x-2-4
3-5. E: Trapped in this existence
A: [because] they have no other skills. Rating: x-7-7

6-5. E: She is bored with this life
    A: [because it is] a second-rate circus. Rating: x-5-6
11-5. E: She quits modelling
    A: (after having made a lot of money), finding it shallow and boring. Rating: x-6-4

Picture 6

2-6. E: Dear old drunken dad . . . had fallen unconscious in a stable next to a team of horses.
    A: During the night he had a vision the horses would lead him to the hidden knowledge of Atlantis. Rating: x-1-2
6-6. E: She is having a hard time adjusting to her life in England.
    A: She has moved to England from India after living there all her life. Rating: x-5-7
13-6. E: Recently they decided to separate.
    A: She and her husband have been having marital problems for some time. Rating: x-6-5
15-6. E: He . . . convinces her to go back to the city.
    A: The farming is too difficult for her. Rating: x-6-5
16-6. E: Thistle and Gus were it [for the walk].
    A: The kids were too high spirited and not dependable for these little jaunts through nature. Rating: x-7-2
20-6. E: It's been lonely
    A: since she went off to school. Rating: x-4-4
21-6. E: She will be disappointed and will sadly leave to go back to her present life.
    A: She will find that the spot is not quite what she remembered. Rating: x-7-2
26-6. E: She had reservations about visiting him.
    A: as he lives in a foreign country and felt that she would find the visit boring and confining. Rating: x-6-3
    E: He in turn had feelings of being unable to provide . . . a happy visiting experience
    A: [because she is] a young, spirited girl. Rating: x-7-3

SCORING FOR CONCEPTUAL/INTEGRATIVE COMPLEXITY

Learning how to score involves three steps: mastering the scoring manual, coding practice stories, and comparing one's coding with that of the "expert scorer." Begin by reading the two chapters (27 and 28) that deal with the conceptual/integrative complexity scoring system. Study the scoring manual carefully. It is a waste of time to begin scoring before you have a thorough grasp of the scoring categories and the illustrative examples.

Next, read the introduction to appendix I for a description of the practice stories and how they were obtained. Make a scoring sheet on which you can record your coding decisions for each story. Score all of the stories for each picture before going on to the next picture. Score the stories for 10 subjects and then compare your scoring with that of the expert. Then repeat the procedure for the next 10 stories, and so on.

The expert scoring is presented on the following pages. For each picture written explanations of the expert scoring are provided for the first 10 stories. Following the written explanations is a table that gives scores for all subjects for all stories. Keep track of your errors, and review them before going on to a new picture. As you score, consult the manual as frequently as necessary.

The pictures used to obtain the practice stories were chosen to elicit imagery for several different variables, so the stories vary from one picture to another in the kinds of imagery they contain. To obtain additional practice stories, consult appendix III.

EXPERT SCORING FOR CONCEPTUAL/INTEGRATIVE COMPLEXITY*

Picture 1

1-1. The author clearly delineates multiple dimensions (3, in this case) of what the Captain needs in order to provide better services (i.e., more competent help, better quality of food, better support).

2-1. The author presents ideas in a plain manner; no attempt is made to qualify or expand the perspectives of the characters or the dimensions of their actions.

3-1. The author's statement that George will wait for his luggage (as suggested by the Captain) is qualified by the frustration George feels.

4-1. The author discusses all of the activities/actions of the participants within a single dimension. Although the paragraph is not rigid (i.e., the use of "probably"), there is no attempt at differentiation.

5-1. More than one sentence is required for scoring as the minimum scoring unit for complexity. This is also a description without any personal judgment or evaluation.

6-1. This paragraph is largely descriptive (i.e., minimal evaluation). Although the content flag for a score of 2 is used (i.e., "but"), it does not represent the qualification of an absolute rule in this case and therefore does not merit the higher score.

7-1. The author clearly provides the perspectives of both the Captain and the passenger with the former focusing on information about the ship itself and the latter focusing on the qualities/capabilities of the ship.

8-1. A single sentence is insufficient for the scoring of integrative complexity.

9-1. This paragraph is largely descriptive with minimal evaluation (i.e., "pleased to find"). Different perspectives are not provided for the two characters nor are different dimensions about the "problem" given.

10-1. The author provides the two perspectives of the Captain and the private detective. The private detective fears that an illegal passenger is on board and wants the ship detained. The Captain is skeptical and believes that the private detective's proof is insufficient to warrant upsetting his passengers.

---

* Expert scoring by Gloria Baker-Brown, Elizabeth J. Ballard, Susan Bluck, Brian de Vries, Peter Suedfeld, and Philip E. Tetlock.

Picture 2

1-2. The author recognizes the existence of multiple alternatives (multiple priorities: work and family) and some tension is expressed between these (i.e., "he would like to change that") and a superordinate statement is provided (i.e., "He resolves to reassess his priorities").

2-2. The author recognizes that there are at least two ways of achieving the goal of creating "Stepford Wives": producing an entire nuclear family or one unit at a time.

3-2. The author presents two alternatives in his life: work (evaluated in terms of diligence and quality) and family (evaluated in terms of time and thought). These alternatives are in conflict with each other thereby leading to the assigned score.

4-2. The author differentiates between what the character is doing and what the character may be thinking. Actions concerning work and thoughts about family are kept parallel.

5-2. The author recognizes that the father/husband is dissatisfied with his profession (work dimension) but recognizes his responsibilities to his family (family dimension). There is no tension between these alternatives as seen in the final sentence.

6-2. The author presents and discusses the various levels of thought associated with opening "his own architectural firm" (i.e., financial and personal security, as well as personal and professional contentment). The author also presents a course of action, again in multiple steps, originating in telling his wife, taking an extra job, then leaving his present company for his own independent firm under the condition of strong business. The specifics of a system of thought are presented as a plan for safely developing a new business.

7-2. The author evaluates both family and work according to a single dimension of like/love. Everything (i.e., both home and work life) is positively valued.

8-2. This paragraph is largely descriptive with minimal evaluation (i.e., "motivated by his work," "appears to have"). The dimensions of work and family are not elaborated and, in fact, are collapsed into a single dimension (i.e., "work–home life").

9-2. The excitement expressed by the architect's wife is qualified by her anxiety. Qualification is the hallmark of a score of 2.

10-2. The author explicitly presents the conflicts between the alternatives that are being considered (i.e., the unreliability and dangerousness of the plant/company, and the needs of the townsfolk including his family).

Picture 3

1-3. The author does not recognize that the two characters may have different perspectives. Most of the paragraph considers "them" as a single unit.

2-3. The male con artist believes he is conning an innocent student but the student's perspective is quite different. She realizes she is being conned and, in fact, is conning him (possibly transmitting a fatal disease).

3-3. Stephen and Sarah continue to love each other while at the same time recognizing that they will never see each other again. Their feelings and thoughts, although incongruous, are held simultaneously.

4-3. The "out of doors" and the "scenery" are too similar to be considered as even emergent dimensions. The author's "rule" is that talking together lets them know more about each other's feelings. Although this "rule" could easily be elaborated to examine each character's perspective on the other (which may not differ), this is not done.

5-3. The underlying theme of the paragraph is relaxation and enjoyment (both of which are evaluatively positive) and no exception to this theme is introduced.

6-3. In this paragraph there are two sets of two perspectives. The "nerd's" office mates all get along with him and at the same time see him as bothersome and feel sorry for him. Later in the paragraph, the woman is thinking about changing her job while he talks about his future.

7-3. There is evidence of emergent perspectives and dimensions in this completion. "Each wants to know the plans and dreams of the other," each wants to see the other's perspective. Their relationship is seen as having three potential dimensions although these are somewhat similar and are unelaborated, that is "they enjoy being together, discussing things they have in common and their goals in life."

8-3. If not rated as unscorable (because it is a single sentence), the completion would be given a score of 1 as it states the male's perspective straightforwardly and does not mention the female's view.

9-3. Both characters are seen as "in love" and happy to have conceived a child. Their emotions are not seen as multidimensional or different from one another.

10-3. The author has a unidimensional interpretation of the characters and events in the story.

Picture 4

1-4. There is no recognition by the author that the two employees may have different thoughts or feelings about the situation. The information given is not qualified or expressed conditionally.

2-4. Although the author is not extremely rigid or evaluative in interpreting events, no differentiation is evidenced.

3-4. The author sees one fundamental dimension to the story – that Gwen has been, is, and will continue trying to find a cure for the disease.

4-4. The author lists a straightforward sequence of events.

5-4. The author does not differentiate between the two research scientist's feelings but the feelings which are attributed to both of them show recognition of emergent dimensions. The women are seen as intense and serious about their careers as well as self-fulfilled and accomplished.

6-4. The author delineates the two scientists' perspectives both in terms of responsibilities and status at work, and feelings toward asking for/granting a raise.

7-4. The author recognizes two dimensions of the researchers' goals: for the research to "go well and be productive" as well as to "make a contribution to science." These are two different levels of research, as evidenced in the last paragraph in which the author separates the solution of this specific problem from the larger goal – the search for truth.

8-4. This is unscorable as it is only one sentence and is also a description showing no evaluation.

9-4. This paragraph is scored for emergent recognition of two dimensions. The researcher's eyes were filled with tears and excitement.

10-4. The author shows several instances of minor differentiation but does not actually specify two alternatives (perspectives or dimensions). Emergent recognition is evidenced in the unelaborated view of the women as having both knowledge and authority, and the view of the student as a mother/wife/potential doctor, and the professor's empathy for the student.

Picture 5

1-5. Differentiation takes the form of a qualification. "He wants to forget about the incident, but can't."

2-5. The author outlines a series of events that are linked together into a story but shows no exploration of the character's thoughts or feelings, or alternative ways to interpret events.

3-5. The author recognizes dimensions of the acrobat's job limitations (they are unskilled for other work and have increasing physical demands put on them) and emergent dimensions of the job's benefits (the excitement of show business and the traveling).

4-5. The paragraph begins as a straight description. When some interpretation is given it is reported as a factual account. The author seems to be seeking closure.

5-5. The two characters in the story are not considered as having different perspectives, nor are their backgrounds or futures seen as multidimensional. This lack of response differentiation is evidence of a simple structure.

6-5. The two characters are seen as having distinct, parallel perspectives on their work as entertainers. The work itself is also seen as multidimensional; it is both a dirty, boring job and one that requires great skill and coordination.

7-5. The paragraph consists of a series of events that are basically unrelated. When evaluation occurs, it is unidimensional. "They want to do a good job and put on a good show."

8-5. This completion is unscorable as only one line of text was produced.

9-5. Although Faye makes a decision to stay in the circus the decision is qualified by her having "almost relented."

10-5. The fact that the young trapeze artist proves to be a star is qualified by her initial unsureness.

Picture 6

1-6. The author clearly presents the differing perspectives of the characters in the story: the princess who hopes to convince Mickey to relocate to manage a stable and Mickey who hopes to convince the princess to bring the horses to the USA.

2-6. Although various characters are mentioned, they are not provided with different perspectives on a single event. The story comprises a set of otherwise disconnected statements.

3-6. The youth (and implied inability) of Mrs. Rancraft is qualified by her apparent knowledge and experience. "Owner" and "boss" also imply different dimensions along which Mrs. Rancraft may be evaluated, although they are insufficiently elaborated and therefore a score of 2 is assigned.

4-6. The author presents a story in a series of otherwise disconnected statements. There is no evidence of differentiation.

5-6. Differentiation is provided in the statement about the future of farming and the efficacy of staying in the business (economic considerations) and passing on the tradition to the next generation (personal concern).

6-6. Differentiation is evident in the simultaneous acceptance of the "English ways of life and dress" while "still taking pride in her Indian customs and background." The sentence immediately preceding the last is an example of a qualification (score of 2); however, paragraphs are always awarded the score reflecting the highest level of integrative complexity evident.

7-6. The author provides a qualification of the woman's fondness of horses and riding by the restriction that she "has to live in the city." Implicit differentiation is also provided in her desire to know more about horses in general.

8-6. Although there is evidence of some flexibility (i.e., "possibly," "perhaps"), the author shows no signs of differentiation.

9-6. The final sentence has evidence of implicit differentiation ("a little freer" and "more hopeful") and thus a score of 2 is assigned.

10-6. This paragraph has no evidence of differentiation; neither character has a unique perspective on the situation and moreover, everyone, including the animals, needs a break.

Table I.1. *Conceptual/integrative complexity scores by subject and stimulus*

Subject	Stimulus					
	1	2	3	4	5	6
1	3	4	1	1	2	3
2	1	3	3	1	1	1
3	2	4	3	1	3	2
4	1	3	1	1	1	1
5	×	3	1	2	1	3
6	1	6	3	3	3	3
7	3	1	2	3	1	2
8	×	1	1	×	×	1
9	1	2	1	2	2	2
10	3	4	1	2	2	1
11	3	2	4	3	1	3
12	2	2	2	1	1	3
13	3	1	2	4	1	2
14	1	3	1	3	2	2
15	1	2	2	1	2	3
16	2	3	4	4	4	3
17	1	1	2	2	3	2
18	1	1	1	1	1	1
19	1	1	1	1	1	1
20	1	3	4	3	3	3
21	1	4	3	3	3	1
22	2	3	2	3	3	1
23	1	1	2	2	1	3
24	3	4	3	1	3	2
25	3	1	2	3	1	1
26	2	1	4	4	4	4
27	1	1	2	2	1	1
28	2	1	1	1	2	1
29	1	1	3	1	1	1
30	1	2	4	1	2	1

Note: × = unscorable

SCORING FOR NEED FOR UNCERTAINTY

Learning how to score involves three steps: mastering the scoring manual, coding practice stories, and comparing one's coding with that of the "expert scorer." First, read the two chapters (29 and 30) that deal with uncertainty orientation. Next, read the introduction to appendix I for a description of the practice stories and how they were obtained. Make a scoring sheet on which you can record the coding categories for each story. Chapter 37 explains how to make a scoring sheet and gives a number of suggestions regarding how to learn a content analysis system and how to measure intercoder agreement.

Score all of the stories for each picture before going on to the next picture. Score the stories for 10 subjects and then compare your scoring with that of the expert. Then repeat the procedure for the next 10 stories, and so on. The expert scoring gives the categories scored for each story for all pictures. This information is followed by a section on Annotated Scoring of Selected Practice Stories. Therefore, after you check the categories scored for a story, look to see if there are additional comments on that story. *Keep track of your errors, and review them before going on to a new picture.* As you score, consult the manual as frequently as necessary. Compute the degree of interscorer agreement you attain (see chapter 37) picture by picture and/or using a total score for each subject based on all six pictures.

The pictures used for the practice stories included here were cued for several different motives, so the stories vary greatly from one picture to another in the amount of uncertainty imagery they contain. To obtain additional practice stories, consult appendix III.

EXPERT SCORING FOR NEED FOR UNCERTAINTY[*]

Picture 1

1-1. UI = −1	14-1. UI = −1
2-1. UI = −1	15-1. UI = −1
3-1. UI = −1	16-1. UI = −1
4-1. UI = −1	17-1. UI = −1
5-1. UI = −1	18-1. UI = −1
6-1. UI = −1	19-1. UI = −1
7-1. DI = 0	20-1. UI = −1
8-1. UI = −1	21-1. UI = −1
9-1. UI = −1	22-1. UI = −1
10-1. UI = −1	23-1. UI = −1
11-1. UI = −1	24-1. DI = 0
12-1. UI = −1	25-1. UI = −1
13-1. UI = −1	26-1. UI = −1

[*] Expert scoring by Steven E. Hanna, Christopher J. R. Roney, and Richard M. Sorrentino.

27-1. UI = −1   29-1. UI = −1
28-1. UI = −1   30-1. UI = −1

Picture 2

1-2. NI = +1   16-2. NI, I?, Ga+ = +3
2-2. UI = −1   17-2. UI = −1
3-2. UI = −1   18-2. UI = −1
4-2. UI = −1   19-2. UI = −1
5-2. DI = 0   20-2. NI, I? = +2
6-2. NI, N, Ga+, Th = +4   21-2. UI = −1
7-2. UI = −1   22-2. (#316)
8-2. UI = −1   23-2. UI = −1
9-2. UI = −1   24-2. DI = 0
10-2. NI, Th = +2   25-2. UI = −1
11-2. DI = 0   26-2. UI = −1
12-2. UI = −1   27-2. UI = −1
13-2. UI = −1   28-2. UI = −1
14-2. UI = −1   29-2. UI = −1
15-2. UI = −1   30-2. UI = −1

Picture 3

1-3. UI = −1   16-3. UI = −1
2-3. UI = −1   17-3. UI = −1
3-3. DI = 0   18-3. UI = −1
4-3. UI = −1   19-3. UI = −1
5-3. UI = −1   20-3. NI, N, I? = +3
6-3. UI = −1   21-3. UI = −1
7-3. NI, N, I? = +3   22-3. UI = −1
8-3. UI = −1   23-3. UI = −1
9-3. UI = −1   24-3. UI = −1
10-3. UI = −1   25-3. UI = −1
11-3. NI = +1   26-3. NI, N, I+ = +3
12-3. UI = −1   27-3. UI = −1
13-3. UI = −1   28-3. UI = −1
14-3. UI = −1   29-3. UI = −1
15-3. UI = −1   30-3. NI, N, G− = +3

Picture 4

1-4. UI = −1   10-4. UI = −1
2-4. UI = −1   11-4. NI, I+ = +2
3-4. NI, N, I? = +3   12-4. UI = −1
4-4. UI = −1   13-4. NI = +1
5-4. NI, N, I?, G+   14-4. UI = −1
6-4. UI = −1   15-4. NI, I+ = +2
7-4. NI, N, I+, Th = +4   16-4. UI = −1
8-4. UI = −1   17-4. UI = −1
9-4. NI, N, I+, Ga+, G+ = +5   18-4. NI, N, Ga− = +3

19-4. UI = −1
20-4. NI, N, I−, Ga−, G−, Bp = +6
21-4. NI, N, I?, Ga− = +4
22-4. UI = −1
23-4. UI = −1
24-4. UI = −1

25-4. UI = −1
26-4. NI, Ga−, G+, Nup = +4
27-4. UI = −1
28-4. NI, N, I? = +3
29-4. UI = −1
30-4. NI = +1

Picture 5

1-5. UI = −1
2-5. UI = −1
3-5. UI = −1
4-5. UI = −1
5-5. UI = −1
6-5. UI = −1
7-5. UI = −1
8-5. UI = −1
9-5. UI = −1
10-5. NI, N, Ga− = +3
11-5. UI = −1
12-5. UI = −1
13-5. UI = −1
14-5. UI = −1
15-5. UI = −1

16-5. NI, I+, Ga−, G+, Bp = +5
17-5. UI = −1
18-5. UI = −1
19-5. UI = −1
20-5. UI = −1
21-5. UI = −1
22-5. UI = −1
23-5. UI = −1
24-5. UI = −1
25-5. UI = −1
26-5. DI = 0
27-5. UI = −1
28-5. UI = −1
29-5. UI = −1
30-5. UI = −1

Picture 6

1-6. UI = −1
2-6. UI = −1
3-6. UI = −1
4-6. UI = −1
5-6. UI = −1
6-6. UI = −1
7-6. NI, N = +2
8-6. UI = −1
9-6. UI = −1
10-6. UI = −1
11-6. UI = −1
12-6. UI = −1
13-6. UI = −1
14-6. UI = −1
15-6. UI = −1

16-6. UI = −1
17-6. UI = −1
18-6. UI = −1
19-6. UI = −1
20-6. UI = −1
21-6. DI = 0
22-6. UI = −1
23-6. UI = −1
24-6. UI = −1
25-6. UI = −1
26-6. UI = −1
27-6. UI = −1
28-6. UI = −1
29-6. UI = −1
30-6. UI = −1

ANNOTATED SCORING OF SELECTED PRACTICE STORIES FOR NEED FOR UNCERTAINTY

Picture 1

1-1. UI = −1: While it is true that the owner's expectations are violated (Criterion 4), this seems routine and is not clearly stated as a problem.
7-1. DI = 0: There is a definite statement of curiosity (Criterion 2) but it is not clear

enough that the passenger has approached the captain to get information about the ship.

10-1. UI = −1: The story resembles a conflict between two cognitions but fails to reach Criterion 3. On the one hand, the captain has a responsibility to his passengers. On the other hand, he has a responsibility to help the police. However, this second cognition is not internalized and he seems tempted to delay only because the private detective "has just told the captain that the ship must be detained." Score UI in any story in which the character is compelled to act by someone else.

12-1. UI = −1: In principal, it is permissible to score stories that are strange as long as they are internally consistent. However, the plot in stories like this is so unclear that we would not score NI unless it was obvious. One of the characters seems to mention a doubtful outcome (Criterion 1) but the other character already has a solution.

13-1. UI = −1: It is routine for detectives to "investigate" crimes and there is no actual statement of motivation in the story. If anything, this story argues for certainty orientation: Both the captain and the detective have firm opinions about the situation and neither seems willing to consider the other's interpretation.

24-1. DI = 0: There is some sense in the story that the businessman's expectations are being violated (Criterion 4) but he does nothing and this results in a "stalemate."

Picture 2

1-2. NI, N = +2: The source of the uncertainty is a discrepancy between an idea that he has about himself and his own behavior (Criterion 5). His resolution to change does constitute an attempt at resolution. The statement that "he would like to change that," although weak, does constitute Need. Do not score for Instrumental Activity because it falls in the last sentence and is really only a statement of outcome. Do not score for Thema because there is a strong affiliation theme.

2-2. UI = −1: The word "doubt" does not, by itself, constitute uncertainty imagery. In this story, it is not clear that there is a doubtful outcome, and so do not score DI.

6-2. NI, N, Ga+, Th = +4: This is not a doubtful outcome story. The source of the uncertainty is an incongruity between his personal needs and the needs of his family (Criterion 3). Score Need because "he wants to do what's best for him and his family." Score Goal Anticipation because he thinks that starting his own company will make him "happier." Thema is marginal because there is a strong current of affiliation in the story. The idea that he wants to be at home with his family is, however, closely enough related to the central uncertainty in the story that it does not constitute a significant subplot. Do not score Instrumental Activity because it falls in the last sentence and is a statement of outcome.

10-2. NI, Th = +2: This is a discrepancy between two cognitions (Criterion 3). Do not score Instrumental Activity because it falls in the last sentence. This is a good example of a story in which Thema is present with no other imagery.

11-2. DI = 0: This is a difficult story and we would have scored it as NI (Criterion 3) except for the last sentence. This sentence stands as a disclaimer for the rest of the story and dismisses it as sentimental and insincere.

16-2. NI, I?, Ga+ = +3: This story is somewhat subtle but should be scored as a doubtful outcome (Criterion 1). He wants to "make the move," which apparently means selling motorcycles. The character anticipates that this will be "tough," but does it anyway. He talks it over with his wife, so score Instrumental Activity. Score Ga+ because he describes himself as "ready for it."

20-2. NI, I? = +2: The source of the uncertainty in the story is not that the character "wonders if it is all worth it." Many people would rather be relaxing than working and he is not considering quitting his job. It is an incongruity between his commitment to his family and his responsibilities at work that contributes to the uncertainty in the story. He approaches and resolves this conflict by calling his family (I?) and by planning to take a day off work. Do not score Thema because the story is strongly affiliative. "Rather be home" is not an expression of Need because it does not reflect a motivation to reconcile the two cognitions.

26-2. UI = −1: This story illustrates an important point with regard to Criterion 4. A wish does not constitute an "established schema." Uncertainty under this criterion is generated by the violation of an expectancy or theory. The character in this story does not expect to advance in the company; he wishes it. Wishes usually must qualify as Criterion 1 to be scored NI and this one does not.

Picture 3

3-3. DI = 0: There is a desired experience with a doubtful outcome (Criterion 1) but it is not clear that he either tells her or avoids telling her.

7-3. NI, N, I? = +3: The scoring for this is rather subtle. Score NI because "they want to get to know each other better" and because "they want to know the plans and dreams of the other." These are statements of curiosity about a phenomenon (Criterion 2). A desire to learn about the self would also qualify. The word "want" qualifies the story for Need and score I? because they are "discussing."

11-3. NI = +1: There is a marginal amount of imagery from the perspective of both characters but hers is stronger. She is attracted to him but also repelled because he is boring (Criterion 3). She approaches the uncertainty by leaving him.

26-3. NI, N, I+ = +3: Although it is not stated clearly, there are two discrepant cognitions in this story (Criterion 3). They "are weighing the red tape and bureaucracy involved in their pursuit of happiness," presumably to decide if it is worth getting married. Score N because they have a "desire" to get married, and I+ because they are "weighing" the consequences.

30-3. NI, N, G− = +3: This is a difficult story because of the ending. Certainly Criterion 3 applies because the character cannot reconcile her religious beliefs with her desire to abort the child. The problem is that the couple is not able to decide for themselves and go to see a "professional." This may mean that they turn the problem over to someone else hoping that the professional will decide for them. That being the case, the story should be scored UI. An alternative explanation is that they are turning to the professional as Nurturant Press, hoping that this will help them make their own decision. We have chosen the latter interpretation, largely because of the last phrase: "and see from then," which seems to reserve the right to the final choice. Certainly, this scoring is tentative, and in a real scoring situation we probably would have used the 2-minute rule.

Picture 4

2-4. UI = −1: There is a weak case for scoring this story DI because the young assistant is curious but does nothing. However, the object of curiosity is trivial and routine, and so score UI.

7-4. NI, N, I+, Th = +4: This is not a doubtful outcome because there is no explicit statement of doubt about their ability to have a breakthrough. However, they are "searching for the truth" (Criterion 2). Score Thema because there are no other plots, and because motives like contributing to science and being productive are closely related to searching for the truth.

11-4. NI, I? = +2: All of the uncertainty imagery in this story can be found in the phrase "working on a cure for AIDS." An attempt to discover a cure implies an interest in the phenomenon that causes the disease. Score I? because they were "working." This story barely meets Criterion 2.

13-4. NI = +1: The search to "identify" a gene is an approach to a phenomenon (Criterion 3).

18-4. NI, N, Ga− = +3: Usually, a story involving people like "lab workers" is too routine for NI scoring. However, in this story, there is a direct statement of affect: "They are anxious about doing the experiment and getting good results," and so it qualifies as interest in the disease phenomenon (Criterion 2). Score Need because they "want" and Ga− because they are "anxious." Do not score Ga+ because the phrase "hopefully they will find a miracle cure" seems to be a statement by the narrator and does not necessarily reflect anticipation by the characters.

19-4. UI = −1: Here is an example of a case where the resolution of uncertainty is too routine (see Example 229) to score NI. They do want to cure a disease but they are lab technicians and, unless contradicted by a direct statement of affect, the scorer should assume that the tests they are doing are routine.

20-4. NI, N, I−, Ga−, G−, Bp = +6: Score this story as an approach to the phenomenon of disease (Criterion 2). Although it is unusual, it is reasonable to infer need from the fact that they both "pray" that tomorrow will be a better day. "Tense and excited" are expressions that are negative responses to anticipation (Ga−). Infer G− because they "sigh" when the experiment fails. Past failures like "so many disappointments along the way" constitute Blocks in the Person.

Picture 5

10-5. NI, N, Ga− = +3: She dreams of becoming a star and is "unsure at first." However, she tries anyway, so score NI (Criterion 1). "Unsure" constitutes Ga− and "drempt," although not a real word, constitutes N.

16-5. NI, I+, Ga−, G+, Bp = +5: There is a doubtful outcome because she took the job in spite of her fears. Score I+ because she took the job, Ga− because she was nervous about taking the job, and G+ because she feels "happy" and "confident." Score Bp because "she had been afraid to do anything."

26-5. DI = 0: There are two inconsistent cognitions here: She wants a family but knows that her career would make this difficult (Criterion 3). Deciding not to commit is not really a decision, so score DI.

Picture 6

6-6. UI = −1: That "she feels comfortable learning about horses" is not an expression of curiosity.

7-6. NI, N = +2: She is curious about horses (Criterion 2) and the implication is that she has asked him.

21-6. DI = 0: Her expectation of the place she remembers is violated (Criterion 4). There is not much that she could have done about the appearance of the spot but she could have tried to alter her schema to accommodate the new information: for instance, attempted to come to terms with the fact that things change.

SCORING FOR PSYCHOLOGICAL STANCES TOWARD THE ENVIRONMENT

Learning how to score involves three steps: mastering the scoring manual, coding practice stories, and comparing one's coding with that of the "expert scorer." Begin by reading the two chapters (31 and 32) that deal with Psychological Stances toward the Environment. Next, read the introduction to appendix I for a description of the practice stories and how they were obtained. Make a scoring sheet on which you can record the coding categories for each story. Chapter 37 gives a number of suggestions regarding how to learn a content analysis system and how to measure intercoder agreement.

Score all of the stories for each picture before going on to the next picture. Score the first 10 stories and then compare your scoring with that of the expert. Then repeat the procedure for the next 10 stories, and so on. On the following pages the expert scoring provides written explanations for each scoring decision for Picture 1. For Pictures 2 through 6, only the scored categories are given. *Keep track of your errors, and review them before going on to a new picture.* As you score, consult the manual as frequently as necessary. Compute the degree of interscorer agreement you attain (see chapter 37) picture by picture and/or using a total score for each subject based on all six pictures.

The pictures used for the practice stories included here were chosen to elicit imagery for several different variables, so the stories vary greatly from one picture to another in the kind and amount of imagery they contain. To obtain additional practice stories, consult appendix III.

EXPERT SCORING FOR PSYCHOLOGICAL STANCES TOWARD THE ENVIRONMENT*

Picture 1

1-1. None. It is not clear why the owner has not supplied what is necessary in the past, so no Authority categories can be scored. The captain's needs are not expressed as "wishes," but as necessary requirements.
2-1. Bogart is resisting the Captain's instructions, which might have scored for Opp, but since the Captain is not an authority vis-à-vis Bogart it does not.
   Diff.: Capt. Queeg and Humphrey Bogart are full, differentiating names.
3-1. None. Benevolent Authority does not score, because although the Captain apparently will help George if necessary it is not clear whether it is necessary, and even if it is, it is not clear what specific action the Captain would take. Moreover, although George is waiting, as recommended by the Captain, we do not know what the outcome of the waiting will be. Action to Clear Disorder does not score because

*Expert scoring by Abigail J. Stewart.

there is no intrusion or disruption, and no action is taken. George's "frustration" is not scorable for any of the Feelings categories.

4-1. None. This story comes close to suggesting "mutual activity," which would score for Differentiation. However, it is not clear that the preceding evening's activities were mutual, so it does not score.

5-1. Not scorable. Fewer than 50-word stories are rarely scorable.

6-1. Opp.: Corruption of the authority figure is implied in the captain requesting a payoff, and tolerating smuggling. It would also have scored for the other man asking to smuggle (for illegal action).

"Oriental" does not score for Diff. because it is not differentiating enough; a particular nationality would need to be specified.

7-1. Imm. Grat.: The captain seems to provide the passenger with the information he wants.

Pass.: Sunbathing is a "placid, inactive state."

8-1. Not scorable.

9-1. Ben. Auth.: The captain helps the passenger with his problem, and Mr. Smith feels good about the outcome.

10-1. Crit. Auth. does not score for authorities concerned about legality. It seems the private detective is not able to exercise authority over the captain.

Dis. does score, though, for the detective's efforts to capture the illegal passenger.

Lack: The police do not get the man they want. The captain also does not get definite proof.

Ben. Auth.: The captain protects his passengers from delay and upset by preventing the detainment.

Opp. scores for the illegal action of the "cat burglar" in stowing away.

Pass. does not score for "sailing" because the primary reference is to motion, not immersion.

11-1. Opp.: The captain is corrupt.

Flight: The captain is "trying to get out of" a "hot spot."

Diff.: "South China Seas."

Crit.: Because the captain will be "caught," it may be inferred that the undercover agent is concerned about the illegality of his actions.

Fail: Trying to get out of it, but failing, scores.

12-1. Opp.: It is clear that the two characters are breaking the law.

Diff.: Sydney, England.

13-1. Crit.: The police officer's investigation implies a concern with illegal action.

Opp.: The captain is objecting to the investigation.

Dis.: The captain invokes a "disorder" explanation of events (fell into the hole and died).

Pass.: The crew man actually died.

14-1. Work: The captain's emotional involvement is implied by the term "serious conversation," and by the fact that the captain is describing his personal vision of the mission.

15-1. Pass.: Sea.

Crit.: The captain wants to (and does) find the thief.

Opp.: The "thief" committed a theft and attempts a second one.

Fail.: The thief fails to steal the diamond ring.

16-1. Diff.: Captain Haver, Vineyard Haven, Falmouth, New Yorkers, Mayor Tisbury, Maine.

Host.: "Angry New Yorkers."

Dis.: Events interfere with the captain's plans.

Crit.: The mayor (and others) are concerned about the "stolen loot."

17-1. Host.: "Annoyed."

Dis.: "Time is lost" for no clear reason.

18-1. Imm. Grat.: The visitor is impressed, as the captain wants him to be.

Ben. Auth. does not score, because although the captain has the power to "expand funds," we do not know if he does so.

19-1. None. Ben. Auth. does not score because it is not clear that the passenger's happy state of mind was produced by anything the captain did.

20-1. Loss: "Panicky."

Imm. Grat. does not score, because the man's wish is never explicitly expressed as a wish (vs. "he feels he must be at the meeting").

21-1. Pass.: "Sea." Although there is an aura of mystery in this story, there is no specific disorder or illegal action.

22-1. Diff.: Telly Savalas.

Dis. does not score. Although Savalas saves the city from the plague, it is not clear that his concern is "disorder" – it seems more likely to be health.

Lim. Auth.: The captain tries to help but cannot.

Imm. Grat.: Savalas wants the man for questioning and finds him.

23-1. Pass.: "Sea."

Opp.: Business man is corrupt. Apparently the captain is too.

Lack does not score. Although the man "wants something" and we are not certain whether he will get it, the "want" is not specific.

Diff.: Italian.

24-1. None.

25-1. Dis.: Gangs have bothered tourists.

26-1. Dis.: The man lost his papers.

Crit.: The captain is concerned about the man's credentials.

27-1. None.

28-1. Crit.: The detective is questioning the captain about drug smuggling.

Pass.: Sea.

Diff.: New York City.

29-1. Diff.: Charlie Chan.

Opp.: The captain is a murderer.

30-1. Imm. Grat.: The captain wanted no more unmarked cargo. Apparently he got it.

Crit.: Government inspected ship.

Dis.: Clearing himself.

Picture 2

1-2. Lack.	16-2. Dis., Diff.
2-2. Diff., Work, Fail.	17-2. Pass., Diff.
3-2. None.	18-2. Pass., Lack.
4-2. Lack, Pass., Loss.	19-2. Lack.
5-2. Pass., Lack.	20-2. Lack, Indec., Pass.
6-2. Work, Imm. Grat.	21-2. Work, Immed.
7-2. Work, Imm. Grat.	22-2. Loss.
8-2. Work.	23-2. Imm. Grat., Pass.
9-2. Diff.	24-2. Work, Diff., Indec.
10-2. Indec., Work, Fail.	25-2. Lack.
11-2. Opp., Flight, Indec., Fail, Diff.	26-2. Imm. Grat., Lack.
12-2. Diff.	27-2. None.
13-2. Work, Diff.	28-2. Lack.
14-2. Dis.	29-2. Loss.
15-2. Work.	30-2. Loss, Lack, Diff.

Picture 3

1-3. Diff.
2-3. Diff., Pass., Dis., Flight.
3-3. Diff., Pass.
4-3. Pass., Diff.
5-3. Pass., Diff.
6-3. Diff., Dis., Lack, Imm. Grat.
7-3. Diff., Lack, Pass.
8-3. Lack, Diff.
9-3. Pass., Diff.
10-3. Diff.
11-3. Diff., Pass., Ambiv.
12-3. Flight, Diff., Pass.
13-3. Diff., Pass.
14-3. Flight, Pass., Diff.
15-3. Diff., Lack, Work.

16-3. Diff.
17-3. Diff., Pass.
18-3. Pass., Diff., Lack.
19-3. Diff., Pass.
20-3. Diff., Pass., Loss, Lack, Indec.
21-3. Diff., Pass., Work.
22-3. Dis., Fail, Flight.
23-3. Diff., Pass., Dis.
24-3. Diff., Fail, Pass., Lack.
25-3. Pass., Diff.
26-3. Diff., Flight, Lack.
27-3. Diff., Pass.
28-3. Diff., Pass., Dis.
29-3. Diff., Pass., Lack.
30-3. Diff., Loss, Lack.

Picture 4

1-4. Dis.
2-4. Diff.
3-4. Work.
4-4. None.
5-4. Work, Imm. Grat.
6-4. Work.
7-4. Work, Imm. Grat., Lack.
8-4. Unscorable.
9-4. Work, Imm. Grat.
10-4. Lack.
11-4. Opp., Host., Fail, Crit., Diff.
12-4. None.
13-4. Diff., Work, Dis.
14-4. None.
15-4. Work.

16-4. Work, Lack.
17-4. Work.
18-4. Work, Lack.
19-4. Lack.
20-4. Fail, Work, Lack.
21-4. Work, Lack.
22-4. None.
23-4. Dis., Ben. Auth.
24-4. None.
25-4. Ben. Auth.
26-4. Indec., Imm. Grat., Work.
27-4. None.
28-4. Work, Lack, Diff.
29-4. Diff.
30-4. None.

Picture 5

1-5. Flight, Lack, Dis., Ambiv.
2-5. None.
3-5. Ambiv.
4-5. None.
5-5. Imm. Grat., Lack.
6-5. Pass., Imm. Grat., Flight, Lack.
7-5. Work, Imm. Grat.
8-5. None.
9-5. None.
10-5. Work, Imm. Grat., Indec.
11-5. Flight, Diff.
12-5. Diff., Dis.
13-5. Diff., Work.

14-5. None.
15-5. Work.
16-5. Loss, Work.
17-5. Work.
18-5. Work, Imm. Grat.
19-5. Work.
20-5. Diff.
21-5. Work.
22-5. Work, Diff.
23-5. Indec., Work.
24-5. Work.
25-5. Work, Lack.
26-5. Lack.

27-5. None.
28-5. Work.

29-5. Fail.
30-5. Work.

Picture 6

1-6. Diff., Lack.
2-6. Pass., Diff., Dis.
3-6. Work, Diff.
4-6. None.
5-6. None.
6-6. Diff.
7-6. Imm. Grat., Work.
8-6. None.
9-6. Diff.
10-6. Diff., Flight.
11-6. Diff., Loss, Pass.
12-6. Lack.
13-6. Pass., Diff.
14-6. None.
15-6. Lack.

16-6. Pass., Lack, Dis.
17-6. None.
18-6. None.
19-6. Diff.
20-6. Loss, Diff.
21-6. Loss.
22-6. None.
23-6. Pass., Diff., Imm. Grat., Loss.
24-6. Diff.
25-6. Diff.
26-6. Diff.
27-6. Diff.
28-6. Pass.
29-6. None.
30-6. None.

SCORING FOR SELF-DEFINITION AND SOCIAL DEFINITION

Learning how to score involves three steps: mastering the scoring manual, coding practice stories, and comparing one's coding with that of the "expert scorer." First, read the two chapters (33 and 34) that deal with Self-Definition and Social Definition. Next, read the introduction to appendix I for a description of the practice stories and how they were obtained. Make a scoring sheet on which you can record the coding categories for each story. Chapter 37 gives a number of suggestions regarding how to learn a content analysis system and how to measure intercoder agreement.

Score all of the stories for each picture before going on to the next picture. Score the first 10 stories and then compare your scoring with that of the expert. Then repeat the procedure for the next 10 stories, and so on. On the following pages the expert scoring provides written explanations for each scoring decision for Picture 1. For Pictures 2 through 6, only the scored categories are given. *Keep track of your errors, and review them before going on to a new picture.* As you score, consult the manual as frequently as necessary. Compute the degree of interscorer agreement you attain (see chapter 37) picture by picture and/or using a total score for each subject based on all six pictures.

The pictures used for the practice stories included here were chosen to elicit imagery for several different variables, so the stories vary greatly from one picture to another in the kind and amount of imagery they contain. To obtain additional practice stories, consult appendix III.

EXPERT SCORING FOR SELF-DEFINITION*

Picture 1

1-1. C(ausality). "explaining why he hasn't met"; also, "in order" to would score.

R(eason)-A(ction Sequence). When the story is arranged in chronological order, the ending has the captain making an explanation about what he will need. It is clear why the captain needs to make this explanation.

2-1. C. "because" U(ncaused) A(ction). No context or reasons are given that would account for the somewhat odd scene portrayed in the story.

3-1. No C; although an apparent contingency is conveyed by the last phrase ("if the luggage does not arrive shortly"), it is purely hypothetical and does not convey any causality.

M(ental) S(tate) E(nding). The last element of the story is that George waits, feeling frustrated; so the story ends with a feeling state.

4-1. I(neffective) A(ctor). This story ends with a resumption of routine ("getting down to the days business"), rather than either an instrumental action (RA) or a mental state (MSE).

5-1. Not scorable; no real story.

6-1. C. "meeting with the captain [in order] to iron out details."

RA. The story ends with the man paying the captain.

7-1. MSE. The story ends with the passenger feeling "satisfied."

8-1. Unscorable.

9-1. MSE. The story ends with Mr. Smith feeling "pleased."

10-1. IA. The detective is unable to stop the captain from sailing; moreover, it is unclear precisely what the result of the "cat burglar's" presence on the ship will be.

11-1. IA. The captain fails to take effective action to get out of his "hot spot." In fact, he "cooks his own goose," a pretty clear statement of the inefficacy of his self-protective actions.

12-1. UA. The story is told in dialogue form.

13-1. MSE. The story ends with a mental state ("the inspector thinks it was a crime").

IA. The central issue of the story is unresolved at the end.

14-1. IA. The story ends with the plot unresolved; we are at the beginning of a mission, and have no idea how it turns out.

15-1. IA. The thief's efforts to steal the diamond ring result in his seizure.

16-1. C. The captain will stop in Falmouth [in order] to pick up his wife. Because he could stop for other reasons, we must construe this phrasing as conveying causality (he stops for this reason in this instance).

MSE. The story ends with the captain "realizing," a mental state.

IA. The story ends with the captain adopting a completely passive stance (waiting), because "it was no use arguing with this guy."

17-1. C. "because."

IA. The resolution of the story is a return to routine ("they will unload").

18-1. MSE. The story ends with the visitor being "favorably impressed."

IA. The ending is phrased in the passive voice ("will be impressed").

19-1. MSE. The story ends with the passengers' "anticipation."

IA. The story ends with the reader uncertain about how the trip actually turns out; thus, the central plot is unresolved.

20-1. C. "because."

---

*Expert scoring by Abigail J. Stewart.

RA. Although the man's panic and "desperation" are unexplained, most elements of the story are accounted for (the captain's behavior in particular), and the story ends with the captain taking an action ("lets the man on the ship"), for a reason ("the captain has the other men tracked down and one is willing to share his room with the desperate man").

21-1. UA. The story ends with completely unexplained events (the disappearance of the cargo). Moreover, earlier elements of the story are also unexplained (the mysterious person, the secret cargo, and the transfer of the cargo "a great distance").

IA. The ending is phrased in the passive voice ("the cargo will be removed").

22-1. RA. The story ends with a resolving, instrumental action.

23-1. UA. No reasons are given for the basic plot of the story (moving illegal material on the ship to some port).

24-1. IA. The story ends with an explicit stalemate and is phrased in the passive voice.

25-1. RA. The story ends with a resolving, instrumental action ("he finds what he is looking for").

26-1. RA. The story ends with resolving, instrumental actions (verifying the passenger's identification and notifying the authorities of the missing passport).

No UA. Although no explicit explanation is given for the loss of the identification, it is treated as an "accident," which requires no further explanation.

27-1. UA. No plot really emerges, so nothing really happens.

28-1. No C. Although the captain alludes to "reasons," it is in the context of indicating that he has no reason; thus, there is an absence of causality.

IA. The basic plot is completely unresolved at the end of the story.

MSE. The conclusion of the story describes the captain's mental state (his willingness).

29-1. C. "because."

MSE. The story ends with a mental state ("Mr. Chan knew").

IA. The central plot is unresolved by the end of the story.

30-1. C. "didn't want anymore unmarked cargo as [because] the ship was becoming inspected."

RA. The story ends with the owner agreeing to the captain's condition; this is resolving, verbal action.

Picture 2

1-2. MSE, UA.	16-2. RA.
2-2. C, IA.	17-2. UA, MSE.
3-2. C, IA.	18-2. IA.
4-2. IA.	19-2. RA, IA.
5-2. IA.	20-2. RA.
6-2. RA.	21-2. RA.
7-2. IA.	22-2. MSE, IA.
8-2. UA.	23-2. C, IA.
9-2. C, IA.	24-2. MSE, IA.
10-2. C, RA.	25-2. MSE, UA.
11-2. IA.	26-2. IA.
12-2. UA.	27-2. IA.
13-2. UA, MSE.	28-2. C, IA, MSE.
14-2. UA.	29-2. UA, MSE.
15-2. RA.	30-2. IA, MSE.

Picture 3

1-3. RA, IA.
2-3. UA, RA.
3-3. UA, MSE, IA.
4-3. UA, IA.
5-3. IA.
6-3. C, RA.
7-3. RA.
8-3. UA, MSE, IA.
9-3. MSE.
10-3. RA.
11-3. UA.
12-3. UA.
13-3. MSE.
14-3. UA, MSE.
15-3. IA.

16-3. MSE.
17-3. MSE, IA.
18-3. IA.
19-3. RA.
20-3. C, IA.
21-3. IA.
22-3. RA.
23-3. RA, UA.
24-3. MSE, IA.
25-3. RA.
26-3. C, RA.
27-3. IA.
28-3. C, MSE, IA.
29-3. RA.
30-3. C, RA, IA.

Picture 4

1-4. IA.
2-4. IA.
3-4. IA.
4-4. C, RA.
5-4. RA.
6-4. C, RA.
7-4. RA.
8-4. Uncodable.
9-4. C, IA.
10-4. RA, IA.
11-4. C, RA, IA.
12-4. UA.
13-4. RA, IA.
14-4. UA.
15-4. IA.

16-4. C, MSE, IA.
17-4. RA.
18-4. RA.
19-4. C, IA, MSE.
20-4. MSE, IA.
21-4. C, MSE, IA.
22-4. IA, UA.
23-4. MSE.
24-4. RA.
25-4. RA.
26-4. MSE.
27-4. RA.
28-4. C, RA, IA.
29-4. C, IA.
30-4. C, IA.

Picture 5

1-5. IA.
2-5. C, UA.
3-5. IA.
4-5. IA.
5-5. MSE.
6-5. RA.
7-5. RA.
8-5. Uncodable.
9-5. MSE.
10-5. IA.
11-5. RA.
12-5. UA, MSE.

13-5. C, RA.
14-5. UA.
15-5. IA.
16-5. C, MSE.
17-5. IA.
18-5. RA.
19-5. UA, MSE.
20-5. MSE.
21-5. IA.
22-5. MSE, IA.
23-5. RA.
24-5. IA.

25-5. C, MSE.
26-5. RA, IA.
27-5. RA, IA.

28-5. UA.
29-5. RA.
30-5. RA.

Picture 6

1-6. C, RA, IA.
2-6. RA.
3-6. MSE, IA.
4-6. IA.
5-6. RA.
6-6. RA.
7-6. RA, IA.
8-6. RA.
9-6. MSE.
10-6. C, RA.
11-6. UA.
12-6. UA, IA.
13-6. MSE.
14-6. UA.
15-6. RA.

16-6. MSE, IA.
17-6. MSE, IA.
18-6. IA.
19-6. IA.
20-6. MSE.
21-6. IA.
22-6. RA.
23-6. C, MSE, IA.
24-6. MSE.
25-6. MSE, IA.
26-6. C, RA.
27-6. IA.
28-6. IA.
29-6. IA.
30-6. RA.

SCORING FOR RESPONSIBILITY

Learning how to score involves three steps: mastering the scoring manual, coding practice stories, and comparing one's coding with that of an "expert scorer." Begin by reading the two chapters (35 and 36) that deal with Responsibility. Study the scoring manual (chapter 36) carefully. It is a waste of time to begin scoring before you have a thorough grasp of the scoring categories and the illustrative examples. Chapter 36 shows how to make a scoring sheet on which you can record the coding categories for each story.

Next, read the introduction to appendix I for a description of the practice stories and how they were obtained. Then begin to score. Score all of the stories for each picture before going on to the next picture. Score the first 10 stories and then compare your scoring with that of the expert. The expert scoring (on the following pages) gives the categories scored for each story. Then repeat the procedure for the next 10 stories, and so on.

Keep track of your errors, and review them before going on to a new picture. As you score, consult the manual as frequently as necessary. Compute the degree of interscorer agreement (Percentage Agreement) between you and the expert as explained in chapter 36.

The pictures used for the practice stories included here were chosen to elicit imagery for several different variables, so the stories vary greatly from one picture to another in the amount of Responsibility imagery they contain. To obtain additional practice stories, consult appendix III.

EXPERT SCORING FOR RESPONSIBILITY*

Picture 1

1-1. Standard, Obligation, Others, Consequences, Self-judgment. 0
2-1. 0
3-1. Others ("The Captain will be available for George"). Total = 1.
4-1. 0
5-1. 0
6-1. 0
7-1. 0 (*Not* Others; the captain's behavior is wholly routine.)
8-1. 0
9-1. 0
10-1. Standard ("illegal"). (*Not* Obligation; source of obligation is not impersonal.) Total = 1.
11-1. 0
12-1. 0
13-1. Standard. Total = 1.
14-1. 0
15-1. 0 (*Not* Obligation; the captain is the source of the detective's obligation.)
16-1. 0
17-1. Standard. Total = 1.
18-1. 0 (*Not* Others; the senator does not act and the captain is not helped.)
19-1. 0
20-1. Obligation ("he must attend"), Others (other man is "willing to share his room"), Consequences (man is aware of consequences of inaction – of not being on the ship). Total = 3.
21-1. 0
22-1. Others ("saves the city"). Total = 1.
23-1. Standard. Total = 1.
24-1. 0
25-1. Others (Not routine, since they are not on board ship). Total = 1.
26-1. 0
27-1. 0
28-1. 0
29-1. 0
30-1. Obligation ("he had to spend a lot of time"). Total = 1.

Picture 2

1-2. Consequences ("he realizes that . . ."). (*Not* Others; not clear that man's resolve is for his family rather than his own pleasure.) Total = 1.
2-2. 0
3-2. 0 (*Not* Others; no sign of concern for family.)
4-2. 0
5-2. Obligation ("he has a lot of responsibilities"). Total = 1.
6-2. Others ("he wants to do what's best for him and his family"). Total = 1.
7-2. 0
8-2. 0

* Expert scoring by David G. Winter.

9-2. o (*Not* Others; no sense that this shows concern or is for family's benefit. *Not* Consequences; man's concern is only about success vs. failure.)

10-2. Standard ("good family people"), Obligation ("a decision he must make"), Others (potential danger to family affects his decision), Consequences (awareness of danger of plant). Total = 4.

11-2. Standard ("black past" taken to imply immorality or illegality; also "dishonest"), Consequences (man's awareness of threat to family if he does not pay blackmail). (*Not* Others; wife's actions not necessarily for man's welfare rather than her interest.) Total = 2.

12-2. o

13-2. o

14-2. o (*Not* Standard; "good to be away" is not a legal or moral standard.)

15-2. Obligation ("he has to redo"), Consequences (thinking about being away from family as consequence of redoing). Total = 2.

16-2. Obligation ("it had to be done"), Consequences ("if he didn't make the move soon . . ."). Total = 2.

17-2. Obligation ("responsible job"), Others. Total = 2.

18-2. Others. Total = 1.

19-2. o

20-2. Obligation ("responsibilities"), Others ("he must finish"). Total = 2.

21-2. Others. Total = 1.

22-2. o (*Not* Others; no action and no clear concern for family.) Total = 1.

23-2. o

24-2. Obligation ("will have to be devoted"), Others ("his successes are for them"), Consequences ("his projects preclude him from having . . ."). Total = 3.

25-2. o (*Not* Others; he misses family but no sympathetic concern.)

26-2. o

27-2. o

28-2. o

29-2. o

30-2. Consequences. Total = 1.

Picture 3

1-3. o

2-3. Standard ("innocent," by contrast with con artist, suggests moral purity). Total = 1.

3-3. o

4-3. o (*Not* Others; this is intimacy, not help.)

5-3. o (*Not* Others; this is intimacy, not help.)

6-3. o

7-3. o (*Not* Others; no sympathetic concern; desire is only for intimacy.)

8-3. o

9-3. o

10-3. o

11-3. o (*Not* Standard; this is social status not morality. *Not* Consequences; her concern is about the failure of "it" and not the consequences of that failure.)

12-3. Others. Total = 1.

13-3. o

14-3. o

15-3. o

16-3. 0
17-3. 0
18-3. 0
19-3. 0
20-3. Obligation, Consequences. Total = 2.
21-3. 0
22-3. 0
23-3. 0
24-3. 0
25-3. 0
26-3. Consequences ("weighing the red tape"). Total = 1.
27-3. 0
28-3. 0
29-3. 0
30-3. 0

Picture 4

1-4. 0 (*Not* Consequences; the employee isn't worried.)
2-4. 0
3-4. Obligation. Total = 1.
4-4. Others. Total = 1.
5-4. 0
6-4. 0
7-4. 0 (*Not* Others; their contribution is to "science" not people.)
8-4. 0
9-4. 0
10-4. Others. (*Not* Standard; "authority" is expertise not morality.) Total = 1.
11-4. Standard ("perverts," a borderline image suggesting immorality). Total = 1.
12-4. 0
13-4. 0
14-4. 0
15-4. 0
16-4. Consequences. (*Not* Obligation; Meg's obligation is neither impersonal nor internalized.) Total = 1.
17-4. 0
18-4. 0
19-4. 0
20-4. Consequences. Total = 1.
21-4. Others. Total = 1.
22-4. 0
23-4. Others (marginal; doctor seems to have had good effect). Total = 1.
24-4. 0
25-4. Others (coordinator is "pleased," suggesting nonroutine sympathetic concern). Total = 1.
26-4. Others. Tota = 1.
27-4. 0
28-4. 0
29-4. Others. Total = 1.
30-4. 0

Picture 5

1-5. Standard ("unfaithful" suggests a moral standard). Total = 1.
2-5. Consequences. Total = 1.
3-5. Obligation. Total = 1.
4-5. Obligation (borderline; perfection may be only instrumental, but this is not spelled out). Total = 1.
5-5. 0
6-5. Obligation. Total = 1.
7-5. Obligation. Total = 1.
8-5. Obligation (borderline; some instrumentality suggested). Total = 1.
9-5. 0 (*Not* Obligation; "would have to" is instrumental, and not impersonal.)
10-5. 0
11-5. 0
12-5. 0
13-5. 0
14-5. 0
15-5. 0
16-5. 0
17-5. 0
18-5. 0
19-5. 0
20-5. 0 (*Not* Obligation. *Not* Consequences, since effects are described as not negative.)
21-5. 0
22-5. Others. Total = 1.
23-5. 0
24-5. Obligation. Total = 1.
25-5. 0
26-5. Obligation. Total = 1.
27-5. 0
28-5. 0
29-5. 0
30-5. 0

Picture 6

1-6. 0
2-6. 0
3-6. 0
4-6. 0
5-6. 0
6-6. Consequences. (*Not* Others; neither specific act nor sympathetic concern by the man.) Total = 1.
7-6. 0 (*Not* Obligation; "has to live in the city" has implied instrumentality.)
8-6. 0 (*Not* Others; not clear that "quality time" is for father's benefit rather than to make up for daughter's lack.)
9-6. 0
10-6. 0
11-6. Others. Total = 1.
12-6. 0

13-6. 0
14-6. 0
15-6. 0 (*Not* Others; not clear that father had intention or effect of help.)
16-6. Consequences ("if they had to do this"). (*Not* Obligation; the riders are the source.) Total = 1.
17-6. Standard. Total = 1.
18-6. 0
19-6. 0
20-6. 0
21-6. 0
22-6. 0
23-6. Others. Total = 1.
24-6. 0
25-6. 0
26-6. Consequences. Total = 1.
27-6. 0
28-6. 0
29-6. 0
30-6. 0

SEX OF PRACTICE STORY SUBJECTS

1. Male	16. Male
2. Male	17. Male
3. Male	18. Female
4. Female	19. Female
5. Female	20. Female
6. Female	21. Male
7. Female	22. Female
8. Male	23. Male
9. Female	24. Male
10. Female	25. Female
11. Female	26. Female
12. Male	27. Female
13. Male	28. Male
14. Female	29. Female
15. Male	30. Female

Appendix II: Pictures used to elicit thematic apperceptive stories

---

Fifteen pictures are included here for reproduction by researchers who wish to use any of these pictures for thematic apperceptive research. They will be referred to by means of the numbers given below.

1. Ship captain
2. Architect at desk
3. Couple on bench by river
4. Two women in lab coats in laboratory
5. Trapeze artists
6. Man and woman with horses and dog
7. Woman seated by girl reclining in chair
8. Four women
9. Kneeling woman fitting chair cover
10. Two women preparing food
11. Man with cigarette behind woman
12. Two men ("inventors") in a workshop
13. Four men seated at a table
14. Man and children seated at a table
15. Conference group: seven men around a table

The first six pictures, in that order, were used by David McClelland and his associates to obtain the practice stories included in appendix I. These pictures were chosen to elicit imagery for the achievement, affiliation, power, and intimacy motives as well as for Psychological Stances (see chapter 31) and Activity Inhibition (see chapters 5 and 9).

These pictures are not individually copyrighted so far as is known, so they may be reproduced individually or in any combination to obtain stories that may be coded according to the systems included in this book. However, McBer and Co. (137 Newbury St., Boston, MA 02116) has copyrighted a particular booklet entitled an *Exercise in Imagination*, which includes some of the pictures shown here. The booklet may be ordered from McBer. The company will also score it for a fee for *n* Achievement, *n* Affiliation, and *n* Power and provide a profile for these variables normed in terms of a large population of male and female adults. McBer may also be willing to score for these variables for stories obtained from other pictures in other combinations, although norms will not be available.

631

The same six pictures have been used by McAdams in the his research on intimacy. McAdams uses them in the following order: 3, 2, 1, 5, 4, and 6. In his research on power, Winter has used some combination of these pictures. In chapter 21, Winter recommends 1, 3, and 4 as being especially useful pictures in research on power motivation. For a four-picture set Winter recommends 1, 3, 4, and 5, in that order. For a six-picture set Winter would add 2 and 6, but would use 5 as the last picture.

The remaining pictures are those used by Veroff and his associates in survey research (see chapter 6). In the survey sets there are separate pictures for male and female respondents except for one common picture (11), which is the sixth picture in both sets. The pictures in the female set are 4, 7, 8, 9, 10, and 11. The pictures in the male set are 12, 13, 14, 2, 15, and 11. (The survey booklet shows the "architect" in Picture 2 looking to the left. Only the more frequently used version, in which the Architect is looking to the right, is reproduced here. A picture of the "architect" looking to the left may be found in Veroff and Feld, 1970, p. 44.)

Additional information on pictures is provided in *Motives in Fantasy, Action and Society* (Atkinson, 1958a, appendix III), which lists pictures that have been used in research on the achievement, affiliation, and power motives, and recommends sets of pictures for different purposes. Because it is difficult to obtain copies of pictures not reproduced here, sources of some of the pictures are listed *using the numbers assigned by Atkinson* (1958a, appendix III).

1. A few pictures, such as 1 (Father–son) and 7 (Boy with vague operation scene in background) are from the Murray (1943) Thematic Apperception Test.

2. Picture 2 (Inventors) is reproduced in McClelland, Atkinson, Clark, and Lowell (1953), as is Picture 8 (Boy in checked shirt).

3. In Veroff and Feld (1970) Picture 2 is reproduced as are the pictures used in the female and male survey sets that are also reproduced in this volume.

4. In McClelland (1985b, p. 191), Picture 8 is reproduced.

5. In McClelland (1975, appendix IB), four pictures are reproduced. They include three of the pictures reproduced here (Ship captain, Two women in a laboratory, and Trapeze artists) and a picture of a guitar, woman, and man with beer glasses.

6. The guitar picture is also reproduced in McClelland and Steele (1972) as are three of the pictures reproduced here (Couple on bench, Trapeze artists, and Architect) and two other pictures: Woman holding a flacon or flask, and Boxer.

Good copies of pictures not reproduced here may be difficult to obtain. If such a picture is needed for an important purpose, the editor of this volume may be able to be of assistance.

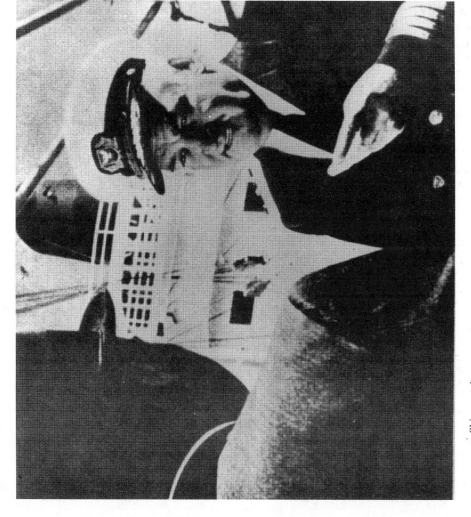

1. Ship captain

2. Architect at desk

3. Couple on bench by river

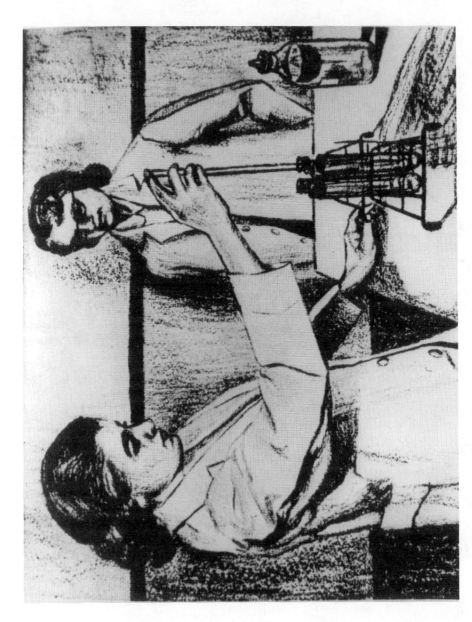

4. Two women in lab coats in laboratory

5. Trapeze artists

6. Man and woman with horses and dog

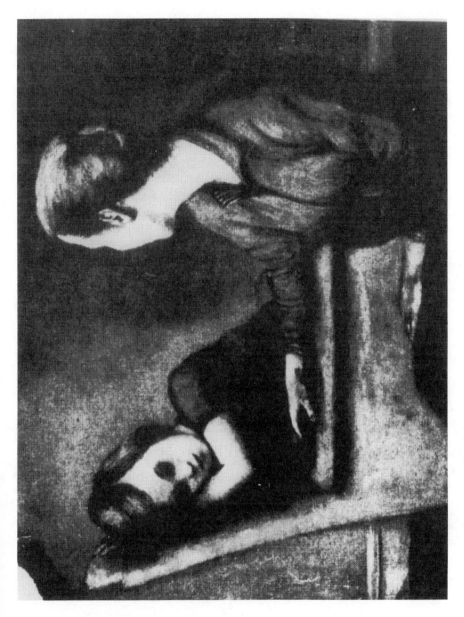

7. Woman seated by girl reclining in chair

8. Four women

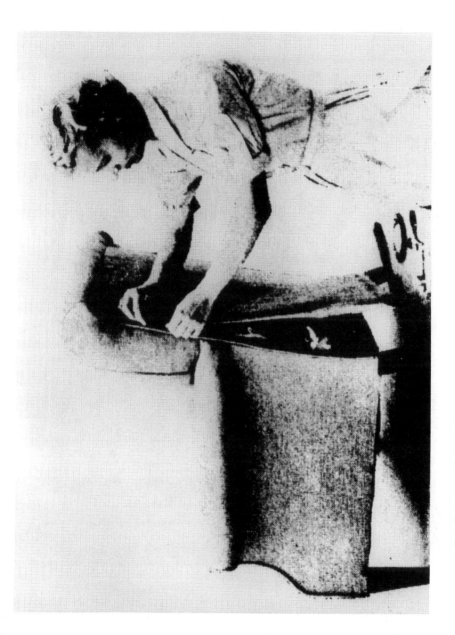

9. Kneeling woman fitting chair cover

10. Two women preparing food

11. Man with cigarette behind woman

12. Two men ("inventors") in a workshop

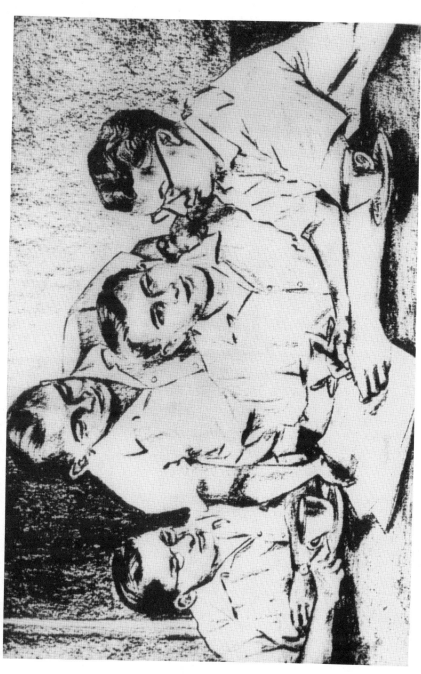

13. Four men seated at a table

14. Man and children seated at a table

15. Conference group: seven men around a table

Appendix III: How to order additional practice materials

For some indefinite period of time following the publication of this handbook, it will be possible to obtain additional practice materials for learning the scoring systems included in this volume. To inquire about obtaining further material for the system(s) in which you are interested, please write to the individuals listed. Their addresses are provided in the list of contributors that follows the table of contents. *Please include a stamped self-addressed envelope* with your letter. Thank you.

Achievement	Prof. Charles P. Smith
Affiliation	Prof. Charles P. Smith
Power (Veroff)	Prof. Charles P. Smith
Motive to Avoid Success	Prof. Jacqueline Fleming
Intimacy Motivation	Prof. Dan McAdams
Affiliative Trust–Mistrust	Dr. James McKay
Power (Winter)	Prof. David Winter
Explanatory Style	Prof. Christopher Peterson
Conceptual/Integrative Complexity	Prof. Peter Suedfeld
Need for Uncertainty	Prof. Richard Sorrentino
Psychological Stances	Prof. Abigail Stewart
Self-Definition	Prof. Abigail Stewart
Responsibility	Prof. David Winter

References

Abramson, L. Y., Seligman, M. E. P., & Teasdale, J. D. (1978). Learned helplessness in humans: Critique and reformulation. *Journal of Abnormal Psychology*, 87, 32–48.

Adler, G. (1985). *Borderline psychopathology and its treatment*. Northvale, NJ: Aronson.

Adorno, T. W., Frenkel-Brunswick, E., Levinson, D. J., & Sanford, R. N. (1950). *The authoritarian personality*. New York: Harper & Row.

Ainsworth, M. D. S., Blehar, M. C., Waters, E., & Wall, S. (1978). *Patterns of attachment: A psychological study of the strange situation*. Hillsdale, NJ: Erlbaum.

Ajzen, I., & Fishbein, M. (1970). The prediction of behavior from attitudinal and normative variables. *Journal of Experimental Psychology*, 6, 466–487.

Ajzen, I., & Fishbein, M. (1977). Attitude-behavior relations: A theoretical analysis and review of empirical research. *Psychological Bulletin*, 84, 889–918.

Ajzen, I., & Fishbein, M. (1980). *Understanding attitudes and predicting social behavior*. Englewood Cliffs, NJ: Prentice-Hall.

Alexander, I. E. (1988). Personality, psychological assessment, and psychobiography. *Journal of Personality*, 56, 265–294.

Aliotto, J. M. (1988). Social backgrounds, social motives and participation on the U.S. Supreme Court. *Political Behavior*, 10, 267–284.

Allport, G. W. (1937). *Personality: A psychological interpretation*. New York: Holt.

Allport, G. W. (1942). *The use of personal documents in psychological science*. New York: Social Science Research Council.

Allport, G. W. (1961). *Pattern and growth in personality*. New York: Holt, Rinehart & Winston.

Allport, G. W., & Vernon, P. E. (1931). *A study of values*. Boston: Houghton Mifflin.

Allport, G. W., & Vernon, P. E. (1933). *Studies in expressive movement*. New York: Macmillan.

Almquist, E., & Angrist, S. S. (1970). Career salience and atypicality of occupational choice in college women. *Journal of Marriage and the Family*, 32, 242–250.

Alper, T. G., & Greenberger, E. (1967). Relationship of picture structure to achievement motivation in college women. *Journal of Personality and Social Psychology*, 7, 362–371.

Andrews, J. D. W. (1966). *The achievement motive in lifestyle among Harvard freshman*. Unpublished doctoral dissertation, Harvard University, Cambridge, MA.

Andrews, J. D. W. (1967). The achievement motive in two types of organizations. *Journal of Personality and Social Psychology, 6*, 163–168.

Angelini, A. L. (1959). Studies in projective measurement of achievement motivation of Brazilian students, males and females: Proceedings of the 15th International Congress of Psychology, Brussels, 1959. *Acta Psychologica, 15*, 359–360.

Ansbacher, H. D., & Ansbacher, R. (1956). *The individual psychology of Alfred Adler*. New York: Basic Books.

Aron, B. (1950). The thematic apperception test in the study of prejudiced and unprejudiced individuals. In T. W. Adorno, E. Frenkel-Brunswik, D. J. Levinson, & R. N. Sanford, *The authoritarian personality* (pp. 489–544). New York: Harper.

Aronoff, J., & Wilson, J. P. (1985). *Personality in the social process*. Hillsdale, NJ: Erlbaum.

Aronson, E. (1958). The need for achievement as measured in graphic expression. In J. W. Atkinson (Ed.), *Motives in fantasy, action and society* (pp. 249–265). Princeton, NJ: Van Nostrand.

Ashton, P. T., & Webb, R. B. (1986). *Making a difference: Teachers' sense of efficacy and student achievement*. New York: Longman.

Atkinson, J. W. (1950). *Studies in projective measurement of achievement motivation*. Unpublished doctoral dissertation, University of Michigan, Ann Arbor.

Atkinson, J. W. (1953). The achievement motive and recall of interrupted and completed tasks. *Journal of Experimental Psychology, 46*, 381–390.

Atkinson, J. W. (1957). Motivational determinants of risk-taking behavior. *Psychological Review, 64*, 359–372.

Atkinson, J. W. (Ed.). (1958a). *Motives in fantasy, action and society*. Princeton, NJ: Van Nostrand.

Atkinson, J. W. (1958b). Thematic apperceptive measurement of motives within the context of a theory of motivation. In J. W. Atkinson (Ed.), *Motives in fantasy, action and society* (pp. 596–616). Princeton, NJ: Van Nostrand.

Atkinson, J. W. (1958c). Towards experimental analysis of human motivation in terms of motives, expectancies, and incentives. In J. W. Atkinson (Ed.), *Motives in fantasy, action and society* (pp. 288–305). Princeton, NJ: Van Nostrand.

Atkinson, J. W. (1964). *An introduction to motivation*. New York: Van Nostrand.

Atkinson, J. W. (1974). Motivational determinants of intellective performance and cumulative achievement. In J. W. Atkinson & J. O. Raynor (Eds.), *Motivation and achievement* (pp. 389–410). Washington, DC: Winston (Halsted Press/Wiley).

Atkinson, J. W. (1977). Motivation for achievement. In T. Blass (Ed.), *Personality variables in social behavior* (pp. 25–108). Hillsdale, NJ: Erlbaum.

Atkinson, J. W. (1980). Thematic apperceptive measurement of motivation in 1950 and 1980. In G. d'Ydewalle & W. Lens (Eds.), *Cognition in human motivation and learning* (pp. 159–198). Hillsdale, NJ: Erlbaum.

Atkinson, J. W. (1981). Studying personality in the context of an advanced motivational psychology. *American Psychologist, 36*, 117–128.

Atkinson, J. W. (1982). Motivational determinants of thematic apperception. In A. J. Stewart (Ed.), *Motivation and society* (pp. 3–40). San Francisco: Jossey-Bass.

Atkinson, J. W. (1983). *Personality, motivation, and action*. New York: Praeger.

Atkinson, J. W., & Birch, D. (1970). *The dynamics of action*. New York: Wiley.

Atkinson, J. W., & Birch, D. (1974). The dynamics of achievement-oriented activity. In J. W. Atkinson & J. O. Raynor (Eds.), *Motivation and achievement* (pp. 271–325). Washington, DC: Winston (Halsted Press/Wiley). Also in J. W. Atkinson & J. O. Raynor (Eds.), (1978), *Personality, motivation, and achievement* (pp. 143–197). Washington, DC: Hemisphere.

Atkinson, J. W., & Birch, D. (1978). *An introduction to motivation: Second edition*. New York: Van Nostrand.

Atkinson, J. W., Bongort, K., & Price, L. H. (1977). Explorations using computer simulation to comprehend TAT measurement of motivation. *Motivation and Emotion, 1*, 1–27.

Atkinson, J. W., & Feather, N. T. (Eds.). (1966). *A theory of achievement motivation*. New York: Wiley.

Atkinson, J. W., Heyns, R. W., & Veroff, J. (1954). The effect of experimental arousal of the affiliation motive on thematic apperception. *Journal of Abnormal and Social Psychology, 49*, 405–410. Also in J. W. Atkinson (Ed.), (1958), *Motives in fantasy, action and society* (pp. 95–104). Princeton, NJ: Van Nostrand.

Atkinson, J. W., & Litwin, G. H. (1960). Achievement motive and test anxiety conceived as motive to approach success and motive to avoid failure. *Journal of Abnormal and Social Psychology, 60*, 52–63.

Atkinson, J. W., & McClelland, D. C. (1948). The projective expression of needs. II. The effect of different intensities of the hunger drive on thematic apperception. *Journal of Experimental Psychology, 38*, 643–658.

Atkinson, J. W., & Moulton, R. (1969). *New methods of measuring achievement related motives* (Final report, Grant No. PS1399). Washington, DC: National Science Foundation.

Atkinson, J. W., & Raphelson, A. C. (1956). Individual differences in motivation and behavior in particular situations. *Journal of Personality, 24*, 351–363.

Atkinson, J. W., & Raynor, J. O. (Eds.). (1974). *Motivation and achievement*. Washington, DC: Winston (Halsted Press/Wiley).

Atkinson, J. W., & Raynor, J. O. (Eds.). (1978). *Personality, motivation and achievement*. Washington, DC: Hemisphere.

Atkinson, J. W., & Reitman, W. R. (1956). Performance as a function of motive strength and expectancy of goal-attainment. *Journal of Abnormal and Social Psychology, 53*, 361–366. Also in J. W. Atkinson (Ed.), (1958), *Motives in fantasy, action and society* (pp. 278–287). Princeton, NJ: Van Nostrand.

Atkinson, J. W., & Walker, E. L. (1956). The affiliation motive in perceptual sensitivity to faces. *Journal of Abnormal and Social Psychology, 53*, 38–41.

Bakan, D. (1966). *The duality of human existence: Isolation and communion in Western man*. Boston: Beacon Press.

Ballard, E. J. (1983). Canadian Prime Ministers: Complexity in political crises. *Canadian Psychology, 24*, 125–129.

Bandura, A. (1982). Self-efficacy mechanism in human agency. *American Psychologist, 37*, 122–147.

Bandura, A. (1986). *Social foundations of thought and action: A social cognitive theory*. Englewood Cliffs, NJ: Prentice-Hall.

Barenbaum, N. B. (1987). *Power motivation, responsibility, and conflict among divorcing parents*. Unpublished doctoral dissertation, Boston University, Boston.

Bargh, J. A. (1984). Automatic and conscious processing of social information. In R. S. Wyer, Jr. & T. K. Srull (Eds.), *Handbook of social cognition* (Vol. 3, pp. 1–44). Hillsdale, NJ: Erlbaum.

Barker, R. G. (1963). *The stream of behavior*. New York: Appleton-Century-Crofts.

Barnard, C. (1938). *The functions of the executive*. Cambridge, MA: Harvard University Press.

Barrett, G. V., & Franke, R. H. (1970). Psychogenic death: A reappraisal. *Science, 167*, 304–306.

Bartmann, T. (1965). *Denkerziehung im programmierten Unterricht*. Munich: Manz.

Bartrop, R. W., Lockhurst, E., Lazarus, L., Kiloh, L. G., & Penny, R. (1977). Depressed lymphocyte function after bereavement. *Lancet, 1*, 834–836.

Baruch, R. (1967). The achievement motive in women: Implications for career development. *Journal of Personality and Social Psychology, 5*, 260–267.

Beck, A. T. (1967). *Depression: Clinical, experimental, and theoretical aspects*. New York: Hoeber.

Beldner, J. (1979, April). *Fear of success in college women and its relation to performance in achievement situations*. Paper presented at the meeting of the Eastern Psychological Association, Philadelphia, PA.

Bellak, L. (1975). *The Thematic Apperception Test, The Children's Apperception Test and The Senior Apperception Technique in clinical use* (3rd ed.). New York: Grune & Stratton.

Berlew, D. E. (1956). *The achievement motive and the growth of Greek civilization*. Unpublished honors thesis, Wesleyan University, Middletown, CT.

Berlew, D. E. (1961). Interpersonal sensitivity and motive strength. *Journal of Abnormal and Social Psychology, 63*, 390–394.

Bickman, L. D. (1975). *Personality constructs of senior women planning to marry or to live independently soon after college*. Unpublished doctoral dissertation, University of Pennsylvania, Philadelphia.

Bieri, J. (1971). Cognitive structures in personality. In H. M. Schroder & P. Suedfeld (Eds.), *Personality theory and information processing* (pp. 178–208). New York: Ronald.

Biernat, M. (1989). Motive and values to achieve: Different constructs with different effects. *Journal of Personality, 57*, 69–95.

Birch, D. (1972). *Measuring the stream of activity* (Rep. No. MMPP 72–2). Ann Arbor: University of Michigan, Michigan Mathematical Psychology Publication.

Birch, D., Atkinson, J. W., & Bongort, K. (1974). Cognitive control of action. In B. Weiner (Ed.), *Cognitive views of human motivation* (pp. 71–84). New York: Academic Press.

Birney, R. C. (1958). Thematic content and the cue characteristics of pictures. In J. W. Atkinson (Ed.), *Motives in fantasy, action and society* (pp. 630–643). Princeton, NJ: Van Nostrand.

Birney, R. C. (1959). The reliability of the achievement motive. *Journal of Abnormal and Social Psychology, 58*, 266–267.

Blankenship, V. (1982). The relationship between consummatory value of success and achievement task difficulty. *Journal of Personality and Social Psychology, 42*, 901–914.

Blankenship, V. (1986). Substitution in achievement behavior. In J. Kuhl & J. W. Atkinson (Eds.), *Motivation, thought, and action* (pp. 186–202). New York: Praeger.

Blasi, A. (1980). Bridging moral cognition and moral action: A critical review of the literature. *Psychological Bulletin, 88*, 1–45.

Blasi, A. (1983). Moral cognition and moral action: A theoretical perspective. *Developmental Review, 3*, 178–210.

Block, J. (1982). Assimilation, accommodation, and the dynamics of personality development. *Child Development, 53*, 281–295.

Block, J., & Ozer, D. J. (1982). Two types of psychologists: Remarks on the Mendelsohn, Weiss, and Feimer contribution. *Journal of Personality and Social Psychology, 42*, 1171–1181.

Block, J. H., & Block, J. (1980). The role of ego-control and ego-resiliency in the organization of behavior. In W. A. Collins (Ed.), *The Minnesota symposia on child psychology* (Vol. 13, pp. 39–102). Hillsdale, NJ: Erlbaum.

Block, N. (Ed.). (1981). *Imagery*. Cambridge, MA: MIT Press.

Blumenthal, J. A., Lane, J. D., & Williams, R. B., Jr. (1985). Inhibited power motive, Type A behavior, and patterns of cardiovascular response. *Journal of Human Stress, 11*, 82–92.

Bongort, K. (1975). *Revision of program by Seltzer and Sawusch: Computer program written to simulate the dynamics of action* [Unpublished computer program]. Ann Arbor: University of Michigan.

Boyatzis, R. E. (1973). Affiliation motivation. In D. C. McClelland & R. S. Steele (Eds.), *Human motivation: A book of readings* (pp. 252–276). Morristown, NJ: General Learning Press.

Bradburn, N. M., & Berlew, D. E. (1961). Need for achievement and English economic growth. *Economic Development and Cultural Change, 10*, 8–20.

Bray, D. W., Campbell, R. J., & Grant, D. L. (1974). *Formative years in business: A long term study of managerial lives.* New York: Wiley.

Brehm, J. W. (Ed.). (1966). *A theory of psychological reactance.* New York: Academic Press.

Bridgman, P. T. (1959). *The way things are.* Cambridge, MA: Harvard University Press.

Brody, N., & Smith, C. P. (1972). *Reliability and validity of need for achievement: A reply to Entwisle.* Unpublished manuscript.

Brown, D. R., & Veroff, J. (Eds.) (1986). *Frontiers of motivational psychology.* New York: Springer-Verlag.

Brown, G. W. (1974). Meaning, measurement, and stress of life events. In B. S. Dohrenwend & B. P. Dohrenwend (Eds.), *Stressful life events: Their nature and effects* (pp. 217–243). New York: Wiley.

Brown, M. (1974). Some determinants of persistence and initiation of achievement-related activities. In J. W. Atkinson & J. O. Raynor (Eds.), *Motivation and achievement* (pp. 327–346). Washington, DC: Winston (Halsted Press/Wiley).

Brown, R. W. (1965). *Social psychology.* New York: Free Press.

Browning, R. P. (1961). *Businessmen in politics: Motivation and circumstance in the rise to power.* Unpublished doctoral dissertation, Yale University, New Haven.

Browning, R. P., & Jacob, H. (1964). Power motivation and the political personality. *Public Opinion Quarterly, 28*, 75–90.

Bruner, J. S. (1986). *Actual minds, possible worlds.* Cambridge, MA: Harvard University Press.

Buber, M. (1970). *I and thou.* New York: Scribner's.

Buck, R. (1985). Prime theory: An integrated view of motivation and emotion. *Psychological Review, 92*, 389–413.

Burns, M. O., & Seligman, M. E. P. (1989). Explanatory style across the life span: Evidence for stability over 52 years. *Journal of Personality and Social Psychology, 56*, 471–477.

Byrne, D. (1961). Anxiety and the experimental arousal of affiliation need. *Journal of Abnormal and Social Psychology, 63*, 660–662.

Byrne, D., & Lamberth, J. (1971). The effect of erotic stimuli on sex arousal, evaluative responses and subsequent behavior. *Technical reports of the*

Commission on Obscenity and Pornography (Vol. 8, pp. 41–68). U.S. Commission on Obscenity and Pornography. Washington, DC: Government Printing Office.

Cacioppo, J. T., Petty, R. E., & Kao, C. F. (1984). The efficient assessment of need for cognition. *Journal of Personality Assessment, 48*(3), 306–307.

Campbell, D. T., & Fiske, D. W. (1959). Convergent and discriminant validation by the multitrait-multimethod matrix. *Psychological Bulletin, 56*, 81–105.

Canavan-Gumpert, D., Garner, K., & Gumpert, P. (1978). *The success-fearing personality.* Lexington, MA: Lexington Books.

Cantor, N. (1990). From thought to behavior: "having" and "doing" in the study of personality and cognition. *American Psychologist, 45*, 735–750.

Cantor, N., & Langston, C. A. (1989). Ups and downs of life tasks in a life transition. In L. A. Pervin (Ed.), *Goal concepts in personality and social psychology* (pp. 127–167). Hillsdale, NJ: Erlbaum.

Cantor, N., Norem, J., Niedenthal, P., Langston, C., & Brower, A. (1987). Life tasks, self-concept ideals, and cognitive strategies in a life transition. *Journal of Personality and Social Psychology, 53*, 1178–1191.

Carlson, R. (1989, August). *Personology: The quest for theory.* Murray Award Address presented at the 97th Annual Convention of the American Psychological Association, New Orleans, LA.

Cartwright, D. P. (1953). Analysis of qualitative material. In L. Festinger & D. Katz (Eds.), *Research methods in the behavioral sciences* (pp. 421–470). New York: Holt, Rinehart, & Winston.

Cartwright, D. P., & Festinger, L. (1943). A quantitive theory of decision. *Psychological Review, 50*, 595–621.

Carver, C. S. (1989). How should multifaceted personality constructs be tested? Issues raised by self-monitoring, attributional style, and hardiness. *Journal of Personality and Social Psychology, 56*, 577–585.

Chaiken, S., & Stangor, C. (1987). Attitudes and attitude change. *Annual Review of Psychology, 38*, 575–630.

Cherry, E. F. (1977). *On success avoidance in women: A comparative study of psychoanalytic theories.* Unpublished doctoral dissertation, Adelphi University, Garden City, NY.

Cherry, F., & Byrne, D. (1977). Authoritarianism. In T. Blass (Ed.), *Personality variables in social behavior* (pp. 109–132). New York: Wiley.

Chester, N. L. (1981). *Coping with the stresses of new parenthood: A longitudinal study.* Unpublished doctoral dissertation, Boston University, Boston.

Child, I. L., Frank, K. F., & Storm, T. (1956). Self-ratings and TAT: Their relations to each other and to adulthood background. *Journal of Personality, 25*, 96–114.

Child, I. L., Storm, T., & Veroff, J. (1958). Achievement themes in folk tales related to socialization practice. In J. W. Atkinson (Ed.), *Motives in fantasy, action and society* (pp. 479–492). Princeton, NJ: Van Nostrand.

Clark, R. A. (1952). The projective measurement of experimentally induced levels of sexual motivation. *Journal of Experimental Psychology, 44*, 391–399.

Clark, R. A., & McClelland, D. C. (1956). A factor analytic integration of imaginative and performance measures of the need for achievement. *Journal of General Psychology, 55*, 73–83.

Cohen, J. (1960). A coefficient of agreement of nominal scales. *Educational and Psychological Measurement, 20*, 37–46.

Cohen, J. (1988). *Statistical power analysis for the behavioral sciences* (2nd ed.). Hillsdale, NJ: Erlbaum.

Cohen, N. E. (1974). *Explorations in the fear of success.* Unpublished doctoral dissertation, Columbia University, New York.

Cohen, S., & Wills, T. A. (1985). Stress, social support, and the buffering hypothesis. *Psychological Bulletin, 98*, 310–357.

Constantian, C. A. (1981). *Attitudes, beliefs and behavior in regard to spending time alone.* Unpublished doctoral dissertation, Harvard University, Cambridge, MA.

Corban, H. (1956). *Power motivation measured in women.* Unpublished senior thesis, Princeton University, Princeton, NJ.

Coren, S., & Suedfeld, P. (1990). A power test of conceptual complexity: Textual correlates. *Journal of Applied Social Psychology, 20*, 357–367.

Cortés, J. B. (1960). The achievement motive in the Spanish economy between the 13th and 18th centuries. *Economic Development and Cultural Change, 9*, 144–163.

Cortés, J. B., & Gatti, J. M. (1972). *Delinquency and crime: A biopsychosocial approach.* New York: Seminar Press.

Crandall, V. J. (1951). Induced frustration and punishment-reward expectancy in thematic apperception stories. *Journal of Consulting Psychology, 15*, 400–404.

Crockett, H. J., Jr. (1962). The achievement motive and differential occupational mobility in the United States. *American Sociological Review, 27*, 191–204.

Cronbach, L. J. (1951). Coefficient alpha and the internal structure of tests. *Psychometrika, 16*, 297–334.

Crowne, D. P., & Marlowe, D. (1964). *The approval motive.* New York: Wiley.

Csikszentmihalyi, M. (1975). *Beyond boredom and anxiety.* San Francisco: Jossey-Bass.

Csikszentmihalyi, M., & Csikszentmihalyi, I. S. (Eds.). (1988). *Optimal experience: Psychological studies of flow in consciousness.* Cambridge: Cambridge University Press.

Csikszentmihalyi, M., & Larson, R. (1984). *Being adolescent.* New York: Basic Books.

Cummin, P. C. (1967). TAT correlates of executive performance. *Journal of Applied Psychology, 51*(1), 78–81.

Davis, M. H. (1980). A multidimensional approach to individual differences in empathy. *JSAS Catalog of Selected Documents in Psychology, 10*, 85.

de Beauvoir, S. (1953). *The second sex.* (H. M. Parshley, Trans.) New York: Knopf. (Original work published 1949)

deCharms, R. (1957). Affiliation motivation and productivity in small groups. *Journal of Abnormal and Social Psychology, 55*, 222–226.

deCharms, R. (1968/1983). *Personal Causation.* New York: Academic Press. Paperback text ed., 1983, Hillsdale, NJ: Erlbaum.

deCharms, R. (1976). *Enhancing motivation.* New York: Irvington.

deCharms, R. (1980). The origins of competence and achievement motivation in personal causation. In L. J. Fyans, Jr. (Ed.), *Achievement motivation: Recent trends in theory and research* (pp. 22–33). New York: Plenum.

deCharms, R. (1981). Personal causation and locus of control: Two different traditions and two uncorrelated measures. In H. M. Lefcourt (Ed.), *Research with the locus of control construct* (Vol. 1, pp. 337–358). New York: Academic Press.

deCharms, R. (1984). Motivation enhancement in educational settings. In C. Ames & R. Ames (Eds.), *Research on motivation in education* (Vol. 1, pp. 275–310). New York: Academic Press.

deCharms, R. (1987a). The burden of motivation. In M. L. Maehr & D. A. Kleiber

(Eds.), *Advances in motivation and achievement* (Vol. 5, pp. 1–21). Greenwich, CT: JAI Press.

deCharms, R. (1987b). Personal causation, agency, and the self. In P. Young-Eisendrath & J. A. Hall (Eds.), *The book of the self* (pp. 17–41). New York: New York University Press.

deCharms, R., & Moeller, G. H. (1962). Values expressed in American children's readers: 1800–1950. *Journal of Abnormal and Social Psychology*, *64*, 136–142.

deCharms, R., Morrison, H. W., Reitman, W. R., & McClelland, D. C. (1955). Behavioral correlates of directly and indirectly measured achievement motivation. In D. C. McClelland (Ed.), *Studies in motivation* (pp. 414–423). New York: Appleton-Century-Crofts.

deCharms, R., & Muir, M. S. (1978). Motivation: Social approaches. *Annual Review of Psychology*, *29*, 91–113.

deCharms, R., & Shea, D. J. (1976). Beyond attribution theory: The human conception of motivation and causality. In L. H. Strickland, F. E. Aboud, & K. J. Gergen (Eds.), *Social psychology in transition* (pp. 253–267). New York: Plenum.

Deci, E. L. (1971). Effects of externally mediated rewards on intrinsic motivation. *Journal of Personality and Social Psychology*, *18*, 105–115.

Deci, E. L. (1975). *Intrinsic motivation*. New York: Plenum.

Deci, E. L. (1980). *The psychology of self-determination*. Lexington, MA: Heath.

Deci, E. L., & Ryan, R. M. (1985). *Intrinsic motivation and self-determination in human behavior*. New York: Plenum.

Deci, E. L., & Ryan, R. M. (1987). The support of autonomy and the control of behavior. *Journal of Personality and Social Psychology*, *53*, 1024–1037.

de Groot, A. D. (1969). *Methodology: Foundations of inference and research in the behavioral sciences*. The Hague: Mouton.

de Gruijter, D. (1980). A note on the correlation between strength of a motive and time spent expressing it in thematic apperception. Unpublished manuscript, University of Leyden.

Derogatis, L. R., Lipman, R. S., Rickels, K., Uhlenhute, E. H., & Covi, L. (1974). The Hopkins Symptom Checklist (HSCL): A measure of primary symptom dimensions. *Psychological Measurement in Psychopharmacology*, *7*, 79–110.

de Villiers, P. A., & Herrnstein, R. J. (1976). Toward a law of response strength. *Psychological Bulletin*, *83*, 1131–1153.

de Vries, B., & Walker, L. J. (1988). Conceptual/integrative complexity and attitudes toward capital punishment. *Personality and Social Psychology Bulletin*, *13*, 448–457.

Diaz, A. J. (1982). *An empirical study of the effects of CEO motives on intra-industry performance with examples drawn from U.S. and Japanese auto manufacturers*. Unpublished honors thesis, Harvard University, Cambridge, MA.

Dohrenwend, B. S. (1973). Social status and stressful life events. *Journal of Personality and Social Psychology*, *28*, 225–235.

Donley, R. E. (1968). *Psychological motives and the American presidency*. Unpublished honors thesis, Wesleyan University, Middletown, CT.

Donley, R. E., & Winter, D. G. (1970). Measuring the motives of public officials at a distance: An exploratory study of American presidents. *Behavioral Science*, *15*, 227–236.

Douvan, E. M., & Adelson, J. (1966). *The adolescent experience*. New York: Wiley.

Driscoll, D. M., Hamilton, D. L., & Sorrentino, R. M. (in press). *Uncertainty orientation and recall of descriptive information. Personality and Social Psychology Bulletin*.

Duncan, M. (1974). *An investigation into the evidence and nature of success avoidance in black college women.* Unpublished honors thesis, Harvard University, Cambridge, MA.

Edwards, A. L. (1954). *Edwards personal preference schedule manual.* New York: Psychological Corporation.

Elder, G. H., Jr., & MacInnis, D. J. (1983). Achievement imagery in women's lives from adolescence to adulthood. *Journal of Personality and Social Psychology, 45,* 394–404.

Emmons, R. A. (1986). Personal strivings: An approach to personality and subjective well-being. *Journal of Personality and Social Psychology, 51,* 1058–1068.

Emmons, R. A. (1989). The personal striving approach to personality. In L. A. Pervin (Ed.), *Goal concepts in personality and social psychology* (pp. 87–126). Hillsdale, NJ: Erlbaum.

Emmons, R. A. (in press). Motives and life goals. In S. Briggs, R. Hogan, & W. Jones (Eds.), *Handbook of personality psychology.* Orlando, FL: Academic Press.

Emmons, R. A., & King, L. A. (1988). Conflict among personal strivings: Immediate and long-term implications for psychological and physical well-being. *Journal of Personality and Social Psychology, 54,* 1040–1048.

Emmons, R. A., & King, L. A. (1989). On the personalization of motivation. In R. Wyer & T. Srull (Eds.), *Advances in social cognition* (pp. 111–122). Hillsdale, NJ: Erlbaum.

Emmons, R. A., & McAdams, D. P. (1991). Personal strivings and motive dispositions: Exploring the links. *Personality and Social Psychology Bulletin, 17,* 648–654.

Entwisle, D. R. (1972). To dispel fantasies about fantasy-based measures of achievement motivation. *Psychological Bulletin, 77,* 377–391.

Epstein, S. (1966). Some theoretical considerations on the nature of ambiguity and the use of stimulus dimensions in projective techniques. *Journal of Consulting Psychology, 30,* 183–192.

Epstein, S. (1979). The stability of behavior: I. On predicting most of the people much of the time. *Journal of Personality and Social Psychology, 37,* 1097–1126.

Erikson, E. H. (1963). *Childhood and society* (2nd ed.). New York: Norton.

Erikson, E. H. (1969). *Gandhi's truth: On the origins of militant nonviolence.* New York: Norton.

Eron, L. D., & Ritter, A. M. (1951). A comparison of two methods of administration of the Thematic Apperception Test. *Journal of Consulting Psychology, 15,* 55–61.

Espin, O., Stewart, A. J., & Gomez, C. (1990). Letters from V: Adolescent personality development in socio-historical context. *Journal of Personality, 58,* 347–364.

Esposito, R. P. (1976). *The relationship between fear of success imagery and vocational choice by sex and grade level.* Final report to the Spencer Foundation. Chicago.

Esposito, R. P. (1977). The relationship between the motive to avoid success and vocational choice. *Journal of Vocational Behavior, 10,* 347–357.

Exline, R. V. (1960). Effects of sex, norms, and affiliation motivation upon accuracy of perception of interpersonal preference. *Journal of Personality, 28,* 397–412.

Exline, R. V. (1962). Need affiliation and initial communication behavior in problem solving groups characterized by low interpersonal visibility. *Psychological Reports, 10,* 79–89.

Exner, J. E., Jr. (1976). Projective techniques. In I. B. Weiner (Ed.), *Clinical methods in psychology* (pp. 61–101). New York: Wiley.

Eysenck, H. J., & Eysenck, M. W. (1985). *Personality and individual differences: A natural science approach*. New York: Plenum.

Feather, N. T. (1961). The relationship of persistence at a task to expectation of success and achievement related motives. *Journal of Abnormal and Social Psychology, 63*, 552–561.

Feierabend, I. K., & Feierabend, R. L. (1966). Aggressive behaviors within polities, 1947–1962: A cross-national study. *Journal of Conflict Resolution, 10*, 249–271.

Feld, S. C. (1967). Longitudinal study of the origins of achievement strivings. *Journal of Personality and Social Psychology, 7*, 408–414.

Feld, S. C., & Smith, C. P. (1958). An evaluation of the objectivity of the method of content analysis. In J. W. Atkinson (Ed.), *Motives in fantasy, action and society* (pp. 234–241). Princeton, NJ: Van Nostrand.

Fenigstein, A., Sheier, M. F., & Buss, A. H. (1975). Public and private self-consciousness: Assessment and theory. *Journal of Consulting and Clinical Psychology, 43*, 522–527.

Feshbach, S. (1961). The influence of drive arousal and conflict upon fantasy behavior. In J. Kagan & G. S. Lesser (Eds.), *Contemporary issues in thematic apperceptive methods* (pp. 119–140). Springfield, IL: C. C. Thomas.

Festinger, L. (1943). Development of differential appetite in the rat. *Journal of Experimental Psychology, 32*, 226–234.

Fineman, S. (1977). The achievement motive construct and its measurement: Where are we now? *British Journal of Psychology, 68*, 1–22.

Fisher, S. (1967). Projective methodologies. *Annual Review of Psychology, 18*, 165–190.

Fleming, J. (1974). *Approach and avoidance motivation in interpersonal competition: A study of black male and female college students*. Unpublished doctoral dissertation, Harvard University, Cambridge, MA.

Fleming, J. (1976, April). *Fear of success in black women*. Paper presented at the meeting of the Eastern Psychological Association, New York.

Fleming, J. (1977). Comment on David Tresemer's "Do women fear success?" *Signs: Journal of Women in Culture and Society, 2*, 706–717.

Fleming, J. (1978). Fear of success, achievement-related motives and behavior in black college women. *Journal of Personality, 46*, 694–716.

Fleming, J. (1982). Projective and psychometric approaches to measurement: The case of fear of success. In A. J. Stewart, (Ed.), *Motivation and society* (pp. 63–96). San Francisco: Jossey-Bass.

Fleming, J., & Watson, R. I., Jr. (1980). *Examination of the new empirically derived scoring system for the motive to avoid success*. Unpublished manuscript, Barnard College, New York.

Fodor, E. M., & Farrow, D. L. (1979). The power motive as an influence on the use of power. *Journal of Personality and Social Psychology, 37*, 2091–2097.

Fodor, E. M., & Smith, T. (1982). The power motive as an influence on group decision making. *Journal of Personality and Social Psychology, 42*, 178–185.

Fontana, A. F., Rosenberg, R. L., Marcus, J. L., & Kerns, R. D. (1987). Type A behavior pattern, inhibited power motivation, and activity inhibition. *Journal of Personality and Social Psychology, 52*, 177–183.

Franz, C., McClelland, D. C., Koestner, R., & Weinberger, J. (1990). *The role of agency motivation in maintaining health over time: A longitudinal study*. Unpublished manuscript, Boston University, Department of Psychology, Boston.

French, E. G. (1955). Some characteristics of achievement motivation. *Journal of Experimental Psychology*, *50*, 232–236. Also in J. W. Atkinson (Ed.), (1958), *Motives in fantasy, action and society* (pp. 270–277). Princeton, NJ: Van Nostrand.

French, E. G. (1956). Motivation as a variable in work-partner selection. *Journal of Abnormal and Social Psychology*, *53*, 96–99.

French, E. G. (1958a). Development of a measure of complex motivation. In J. W. Atkinson (Ed.), *Motives in fantasy, action and society* (pp. 242–248). Princeton, NJ: Van Nostrand.

French, E. G. (1958b). Effects of the interaction of motivation and feedback on task performance. In J. W. Atkinson (Ed.), *Motives in fantasy, action and society* (pp. 400–408). Princeton, NJ: Van Nostrand.

French, E. G., & Lesser, G. S. (1964). Some characteristics of the achievement motive in women. *Journal of Abnormal and Social Psychology*, *68*, 119–128.

Frenkel-Brunswik, E. (1942). Motivation and behavior. *Genetic Psychology Monographs*, *26*, 121–265.

Freud, S. (1940). An outline of psycho-analysis. In J. Strachey (Ed.), *The standard edition of the complete psychological works of Sigmund Freud* (Vol. 23, pp. 144–207). London: Hogarth. (Original work published 1938)

Fyans, L. J., Jr. (Ed.). (1980). *Achievement motivation: Recent trends in theory and research*. New York: Plenum.

Gallimore, R. (1981). Affiliation, social context, industriousness and achievement. In R. H. Monroe, R. L. Munroe, & B. B. Whiting (Eds.), *Handbook of cross-cultural human development* (pp. 689–715). New York: Garland STPM.

Gilbert, S. C. (1986). *A sociocultural perspective of anorexia nervosa as related to fear of success*. Unpublished honors thesis, Harvard University, Cambridge, MA.

Giliberto, S. M. (1972). *Motivation and the Methodist revival*. Unpublished honors thesis, Harvard University, Cambridge, MA.

Gilligan, C. (1982). *In a different voice*. Cambridge, MA: Harvard University Press.

Gjesme, T., & Nygard, R. (1970). *Achievement-related motives: Theoretical considerations and construction of a measuring instrument*. Unpublished manuscript, University of Oslo, Oslo, Norway.

Glad, B. (1973). Contributions of psychobiography. In J. N. Knutson (Ed.), *Handbook of political psychology* (pp. 296–321). San Francisco: Jossey-Bass.

Gorsuch, R. L. (1983). *Factor analysis* (2nd ed.). Hillsdale, NJ: Erlbaum.

Gough, H. (1987). *California Psychological Inventory: Administrator's guide*. Palo Alto, CA: Consulting Psychologists Press.

Gough, H., & Heilbrun, A. (1975). *The adjective checklist manual*. Palo Alto, CA: Consulting Psychologists Press.

Gough, H., & Heilbrun, A. (1983). *The revised adjective checklist manual*. Palo Alto, CA: Consulting Psychologists Press.

Graham, J. A., Argyle, M. A., & Furnham, A. (1980). The goal structure of situations. *European Journal of Social Psychology*, *10*, 345–366.

Green, B. F. (1981). A primer of testing. *American Psychologist*, *36*, 1001–1011.

Greenberg, J. R., & Mitchell, S. A. (1983). *Object relations in psychoanalytic theory*. Cambridge, MA: Harvard University Press.

Greene, D. L., & Winter, D. G. (1971). Motives, involvements, and leadership among black college students. *Journal of Personality*, *39*, 319–332.

Griffore, R. J. (1977). Validation of three measures of fear of success. *Journal of Personality Assessment*, *41*, 417–421.

Groesbeck, B. L. (1958). Toward description of personality in terms of configuration of motives. In J. W. Atkinson (Ed.), *Motives in fantasy, action and society* (pp. 383–399). Princeton, NJ: Van Nostrand.

Grossman, R. A. (1983). *Self-definition vs. social definition as a predictor of emotional distress in cancer patients*. Unpublished doctoral dissertation, Boston University, Boston.

Gulliksen, H. (1950). *Theory of mental tests*. New York: Wiley.

Gurin, G., Veroff, J., & Feld, S. C. (1960). *Americans view their mental health*. New York: Basic Books.

Gutmann, D. (1975). Parenthood: A key to comparative study of the life cycle. In N. Datan & L. Ginsberg (Eds.), *Life-span developmental psychology: Normative life crises* (pp. 167–184). New York: Academic Press.

Haber, R. N., & Alpert, R. (1958). The role of situation and picture cues in projective measurement of the achievement motive. In J. W. Atkinson (Ed.), *Motives in fantasy, action and society* (pp. 644–663). Princeton, NJ: Van Nostrand.

Halberstam, D. (1986). *The reckoning*. New York: Morrow.

Hamilton, J. O. (1974). Motivation and risk taking behavior: A test of Atkinson's theory. *Journal of Personality and Social Psychology*, *29*, 856–864.

Hamm, R. J. (1977). Stability of self-concept and fear of failure. *Psychological Reports*, *40*(2), 522.

Hancock, J. G., & Teevan, R. C. (1964). Fear of failure and risk-taking behavior. *Journal of Personality*, *32*, 200–209.

Harvey, O. J., Hunt, D. E., & Schroder, H. M. (1961). *Conceptual systems and personality organization*. New York: Wiley.

Hayashi, T., & Habu, K. (1962). Research on the achievement motive: An experimental test of the "thought sampling" method by using Japanese students. *Japanese Psychological Research*, *4*, 30–42.

Hazan, C., & Shaver, P. (1987). Romantic love conceptualized as an attachment process. *Journal of Personality and Social Psychology*, *52*, 511–524.

Healy, J. M., Jr. (1985). *Emotional adaptation to life transitions and cognitive performance*. Unpublished doctoral dissertation, Boston University, Boston.

Healy, J. M., Jr., Eisenstein, J. L., & Stewart, A. J. (1985, March). *Past and post-separation change as a context for children's adaptation to parental separation*. Paper presented at the meeting of the Eastern Psychological Association, Boston.

Heckhausen, H. (1963). *Hoffnung und Furcht in der Leistungsmotivation* [Hope and Fear in Achievement Motivation]. Meisenheim, West Germany: Hain.

Heckhausen, H. (1967). *The anatomy of achievement motivation* (K. F. Butler, R. C. Birney, & D. C. McClelland, Trans.) New York: Academic Press. (Original work published in 1965)

Heckhausen, H. (1980). *Motivation und Handlung* [Motivation and action]. New York: Springer.

Heckhausen, H., & Halisch, F. (1986). *"Operant" versus "respondent" motive measures: A problem of validity or of construct?* Munich: Max-Planck-Institut für Psychologische Forschung.

Heckhausen, H., & Krug, S. (1982). Motive modification. In A. J. Steward (Ed.), *Motivation and society* (pp. 274–318). San Francisco: Jossey-Bass.

Heckhausen, H., & Kuhl, J. (1985). From wishes to action: The dead-ends and short cuts on the long way to action. In M. Frese & J. Sabini (Eds.), *Goal-directed behavior: Psychological theory and research on action* (pp. 134–160). Hillsdale, NJ: Erlbaum.

Heckhausen, H., Schmalt, H. D., & Schneider, K. (1985) *Achievement motivation in perspective*. New York: Academic Press.

Heider, F. (1958). *The psychology of interpersonal relations*. New York: Wiley.

Henley, N. M. (1967). Achievement and affiliation imagery in American fiction, 1901–1961. *Journal of Personality and Social Psychology, 7*, 208–210.

Hennig, M., & Jardim, A. (1976). *The managerial woman*. New York: Anchor.

Henry, W. E. (1956). *The analysis of fantasy: The Thematic Apperception Technique in the study of personality*. New York: Wiley.

Henry, W. E. (1961). Discussion of Dr. Veroff's paper. In J. Kagan & G. S. Lesser (Eds.), *Contemporary issues in thematic apperceptive methods* (pp. 112–118). Springfield, IL: C. C. Thomas.

Hermann, M. G. (1979). Who becomes a political leader? Some societal and regime influences on selection of a head of state. In L. S. Falkowski (Ed.), *Psychological models in international politics* (pp. 15–48). Boulder, CO: Westview Press.

Hermann, M. G. (1980a). Assessing the personalities of Soviet Politburo members. *Personality and Social Psychology Bulletin, 6*, 332–352.

Hermann, M. G. (1980b). Explaining foreign policy behavior using personal characteristics of political leaders. *International Studies Quarterly, 24*, 7–46.

Hermann, M. G. (1983). Assessing personality at a distance: A profile of Ronald Reagan. *Mershon Center Quarterly Report, 7*(6), 1–8. Columbus, OH: Mershon Center of the Ohio State University.

Hermann, M. G. (1987). Assessing the foreign policy role orientations of sub-Saharan African leaders. In S. G. Walker (Ed.), *Role theory and foreign policy analysis* (pp. 161–198). Durham, NC: Duke University Press.

Hermann, M. G. (1988). Syria's Hafez al-Assad. In B. Kellerman & J. Rubin (Eds.), *Leadership and negotiation in the Middle East* (pp. 70–95). New York: Praeger.

Hermann, M. G. (1989, March). *Personality profile data on Gorbachev*. Paper presented at the annual meeting of the International Studies Association, London.

Hermans, H., Petermann, F., & Zielinski, W. (1978). *LMT. Leistungsmotivationstest* [Achievement motivation test]. Amsterdam: Swets & Zeitlinger.

Heyns, R. W., Veroff, J., & Atkinson, J. W. (1958). A scoring manual for the affiliation motive. In J. W. Atkinson (Ed.), *Motives in fantasy, action and society* (pp. 205–218). Princeton, NJ.: Van Nostrand.

Higgins, E. T. (1990). Personality, social psychology, and person-situation relations: Standards and knowledge activation as a common language. In L. Pervin (Ed.), *Handbook of personality: Theory and research* (pp. 301–338). New York: Guilford.

Higgins, E. T., & Sorrentino, R. M. (Eds.) (1990). *The handbook of motivation and cognition: Foundations of social behavior* (Vol. 2). New York: Guilford.

Hoffman, M. L. (1982). The development of prosocial motivation: Empathy and guilt. In N. Eisenberg (Ed.), *The development of prosocial behavior* (pp. 281–313). New York: Academic Press.

Holahan, C. J., & Moos, R. H. (1985). Life stress and health: Personality, coping and family support in stress resistance. *Journal of Personality and Social Psychology, 49*, 739–747.

Holmes, D. S., & Tyler, J. D. (1968). Direct vs. projective measures of achievement motivation. *Journal of Consulting and Clinical Psychology, 32*, 712–717.

Holmes, T. H. (1978). Life situations, emotions and disease. *Psychosomatics, 19*, 747–754.

Holsti, O. R. (1968). Content analysis. In G. Lindzey & E. Aronson (Eds.), *The handbook of social psychology* (pp. 596–692). Reading MA: Addison-Wesley.

Holsti, O. R., (1969). *Content analysis for the social sciences and humanities*. Reading, MA: Addison-Wesley.

Holt, R. R. (1961). The nature of TAT stories as cognitive productions: A psychoanalytic approach. In J. Kagan & G. S. Lesser (Eds.), *Contemporary issues in thematic apperceptive methods* (pp. 3–43). Springfield, IL: C. C. Thomas.

Holt, R. R. (1978). *Methods in clinical psychology* (Vol. 1). New York: Plenum.

Hormuth, S. E. (1986). The sampling of experiences in situ. *Journal of Personality*, *54*, 262–293.

Horner, M. S. (1968). *Sex differences in achievement motivation and performance in competitive and non-competitive situations*. Unpublished doctoral dissertation, University of Michigan, Ann Arbor. (University Microfilms No. 69-12, 135)

Horner, M. S. (1972). Toward an understanding of achievement-related conflicts in women. *Journal of Social Issues*, *28*, 157–176.

Horner, M. S. (1973). *Success avoidant motivation and behavior: Its developmental correlates and situational determinants* (Final report, Grant No. OEG-1-71-1014). Washington, DC: Office of Education.

Horner, M. S. (1974). The measurement and behavioral implications of fear of success in women. In J. W. Atkinson & J. O. Raynor (Eds.), *Motivation and achievement* (pp. 91–117). Washington, DC: Winston (Halsted Press/Wiley).

Horner, M. S., & Fleming, J. (1977). *Revised scoring manual for an empirically derived scoring system for the motive to avoid success*. Unpublished manuscript, Harvard University, Cambridge, MA.

Horner, M. S., Tresemer, D. W., Berens, A. E., & Watson, R. I., Jr. (1973). *Scoring manual for an empirically derived scoring system for the motive to avoid success*. Unpublished manuscript, Harvard University, Cambridge, MA.

Howard, G. S. (1991). Culture tales: A narrative approach to thinking, cross-cultural psychology, and psychotherapy. *American Psychologist*, *46*, 187–197.

Hull, C. L. (1943). *Principles of behavior*. New York: Appleton-Century-Crofts.

Hunt, D. E. (1980). From single-variable to persons-in-relation. In L. J. Fyans, Jr. (Ed.), *Achievement motivation: Recent trends in theory and research* (pp. 447–456). New York: Plenum.

Hunt, S. M. (1972). *A comparison and validation of two thematic apperceptive measures of the need for power*. Unpublished doctoral dissertation, University of Michigan, Ann Arbor.

Hurst, M. W. (1979). Life changes and psychiatric symptom development: Issues of content, scoring, and clustering. In J. E. Barratt, R. M. Rose, & G. L. Klerma (Eds.), *Stress and mental disorder* (pp. 17–36). New York: Raven Press.

Inkeles, A., & Levinson, D. J. (1969). National character: The study of modal personality and sociocultural systems. In G. Lindzey, & E. Aronson (Eds.), *Handbook of social psychology* (rev. ed., Vol. 4, pp. 418–506). Reading, MA: Addison-Wesley.

Isaacson, R. L. (1964). Relation between *n* Achievement, test anxiety, and curricular choices. *Journal of Abnormal and Social Psychology*, *68*, 447–452.

Isen, A. M. (1987). Positive affect, cognitive processes, and social behavior. *Advances in Experimental Social Psychology*, *20*, 203–253.

Jackaway, R. (1974). Sex differences in achievement motivation, behavior and attributions about success and failure. *Dissertation Abstracts International*, *35*, No. 10, p. 5158-B. (University Microfilms No. 75–9624)

Jackaway, R., & Teevan, R. (1976). Fear of failure and fear of success: Two dimensions of the same motive. *Sex Roles*, *2*, 283–294.

Jackson, D. N. (1966). A modern strategy for personality assessment: The personality research form. *Research Bulletin*, *No. 33c*. London, Canada: University of Western Ontario.

Jackson, D. N. (1974). *Manual for the personality research form.* Goshen, NY: Research Psychology Press.

Jackson, D. N. (1984). *Personality research form manual.* Port Huron, MI: Research Psychologists Press.

Jackson, H. (1976). *An assessment of long-term effects of personal causation training.* Unpublished doctoral dissertation, Washington University, St. Louis, MO.

Jackson, K. (1973). *Maternal behavior correlates of child motivation in low income, black eighth grade children.* Unpublished doctoral dissertation, Washington University, St. Louis, MO.

Jacobs, B., Jr. (1958). A method for investigating the cue characteristics of pictures. In J. W. Atkinson (Ed.), *Motives in fantasy, action and society* (pp. 617–629). Princeton, NJ: Van Nostrand.

James, W. (1890). *The principles of psychology* (Vol. 1). New York: Holt.

Janis, I. L. (1972). *Victims of groupthink.* Boston: Houghton Mifflin.

Jemmott, J. B., III (1987). Social motives and susceptibility to disease: Stalking individual differences in health risks. *Journal of Personality, 55,* 267–298.

Jemmott, J. B., III, Hellman, C., McClelland, D. C., Locke, S. E., Kraus, L., Williams, R. M., & Valeri, R. C. (1990). Motivational syndromes associated with natural killer cell activity. *Journal of Behavioral Medicine, 13,* 53–74.

Jemmott, J. B., III, & Locke, S. E. (1984). Psychological factors, immunologic mediation, and human susceptibility to infectious disease: How much do we know? *Psychological Bulletin, 95,* 78–108.

Jemmott, J. B., III, & McClelland, D. C. (1989). Secretory IgA as a measure of resistance to infectious disease: Comments on Stone, Cox, Valdimarsdottir, and Neale. *Behavioral Medicine, 15,* 63–71.

Jenkins, S. R. (1979, August). *Fear of success, sex roles, and personal success goals.* Paper presented at the meeting of the American Psychological Association, New York.

Jenkins, S. R. (1982). *Person-situation interaction and women's achievement-related motives.* Unpublished doctoral dissertation, Boston University, Boston.

Jenkins, S. R. (1987). Need for achievement and women's careers over 14 years: Evidence for occupational structure effects. *Journal of Personality and Social Psychology, 53,* 922–932.

Jenkins, S. R. (1990). *Self-definition in thought, action, and life path choices.* Unpublished manuscript.

Jones, D. F. (1969). *The need for power as a predictor of leadership and exploitation in a variety of small group settings.* Unpublished honors thesis, Wesleyan University, Middletown, CT.

Kagan, J. (1959). The stability of T.A.T. fantasy and stimulus ambiguity. *Journal of Consulting Psychology, 23,* 266–271.

Kagan, J. (1966). Reflection-impulsivity: The generality and dynamics of conceptual tempo. *Journal of Abnormal and Social Psychology, 71,* 17–24.

Kagan, J. (1972). Motives and development. *Journal of Personality and Social Psychology, 22,* 51–66.

Kagan, J. (1989). Temperamental contributions to social behavior. *American Psychologist, 44,* 668–674.

Kagan, J., & Lesser, G. S. (Eds.). (1961). *Contemporary issues in thematic apperceptive methods.* Springfield, IL: C. C. Thomas.

Kagan, J., & Moss, H. A. (1959). Stability and validity of achievement fantasy. *Journal of Abnormal and Social Psychology, 58,* 357–364.

Kagan, J., & Moss. H. A. (1962). *Birth to maturity.* New York: Wiley.

Karabenick, S. A. (1977). Fear of success, achievement and affiliative dispositions, and the performance of men and women under individual and competitive situations. *Journal of Personality, 45*, 117–149.

Karabenick, S. A., & Yousseff, Z. I. (1968). Performance as a function of achievement levels and perceived difficulty. *Journal of Personality and Social Psychology, 10*, 414–419.

Karon, B. P. (1966). Reliability: Paradigm or paradox, with especial reference to personality tests. *Journal of Projective Techniques and Personality Assessment, 30*(3), 223–227.

Karon, B. P. (1981). The Thematic Apperception Test (TAT). In A. I. Rabin (Ed.), *Assessment with projective techniques: A concise introduction* (pp. 85–120). New York: Springer.

Kawamura-Reynolds, M. (1977). Motivational effects of an audience in the content of imaginative thought. *Journal of Personality and Social Psychology, 35*, 912–919.

Kellam, S. G. (1974). Stressful life events and illness: A research area in need of conceptual development. In B. S. Dohrenwend & B. P. Dohrenwend (Eds.), *Stressful life events: Their nature and effects* (pp. 207–214). New York: Wiley.

Kelley, H. H. (1967). Attribution theory in social psychology. In D. Levine (Ed.), *Nebraska symposium on motivation.* Lincoln: University of Nebraska Press.

Kelly, G. A. (1955). *A theory of personal constructs* (2 vols.). New York: Norton.

Kelner, S. P., Jr. (1990). *Interpersonal motivation: Positive, negative, and anxious.* Unpublished doctoral dissertation, Boston University, Boston.

Kennedy, P. (1987). *The rise and fall of the great powers: Economic change and military conflict from 1500 to 2000.* New York: Random House.

Kenny, D. T. (1961). Discussion of Dr. Murstein's paper. In J. Kagan & G. S. Lesser (Eds.), *Contemporary issues in thematic apperceptive methods* (pp. 274–287). Springfield, IL: C. C. Thomas.

Kenny, D. T. (1964). Stimulus functions in projective techniques. In B. A. Maher (Ed.), *Progress in experimental personality research* (Vol. I, pp. 285–354). New York: Academic Press.

Kessler, R. C. (1979a). A strategy for studying differential vulnerability to the psychological consequences of stress. *Journal of Health and Social Behavior, 20*, 100–108.

Kessler, R. C. (1979b). Stress, social status, and psychological distress. *Journal of Health and Social Behavior, 20*, 259–273.

Kessler, R. C., & Cleary, P. D. (1980). Stress, social status and psychological distress. *American Journal of Sociology, 57*(4), 309–314.

Kiecolt-Glaser, J. K., Fisher, L. D., Ogrocki, P., Stout, J. C., Speicher, C. E., & Glaser, R. (1987). Marital quality, marital disruption, and immune function. *Psychosomatic Medicine, 49*(1), 13–34.

Kiecolt-Glaser, J. K., & Glaser, R. (1986). Psychological influences on immunity. *Psychosomatics, 27*(9), 621–624.

King, G. A., & Sorrentino, R. M. (1988). Uncertainty orientation and perception: Individual differences in social categorization. *Social Cognition: A Journal of Social Personality, and Developmental Psychology, 5*(4), 369–382.

King, L. A. (1989, August). *Sex differences in motivation: A personal striving approach.* Paper presented at the 97th Annual Convention of the American Psychological Association, New Orleans, LA.

Kinsbourne, M. (1987). Brain mechanisms and memory. *Human Neurobiology, 6*, 81–92.

Klinger, E. (1966). Fantasy need achievement as a motivational construct. *Psychological Bulletin, 66*, 291–308.

Klinger, E. (1968). Short term stability and concurrent validity of TAT need scores: Achievement affiliation and hostile press. *Proceedings of the American Psychological Association*, *3*, 157–158.

Klinger, E. (1971). *Structure and functions of fantasy*. New York: Wiley.

Klinger, E. (1975). Consequences of commitment to and disengagement from incentives. *Psychological Review*, *82*, 1–25.

Klinger, E. (1977). *Meaning and void: Inner experience and the incentives in people's lives*. Minneapolis: University of Minnesota Press.

Klinger, E. (1978). Modes of normal conscious flow. In K. S. Pope & J. L. Singer (Eds.), *The stream of consciousness* (pp. 225–258). New York: Plenum.

Klinger, E. (1987a). Current concerns and disengagement from incentives. In F. Halisch & J. Kuhl (Eds.), *Motivation, intention, and volition* (pp. 337–347). New York: Springer-Verlag.

Klinger, E. (1987b). The interview questionnaire technique: Reliability and validity of a mixed idiographic–nomothetic measure of motivation. In J. N. Butcher & C. D. Spielberger (Eds.), *Advances in personality assessment* (Vol. 6, pp. 31–48). Hillsdale, NJ: Erlbaum.

Klinger, E. (1989). Goal-orientation as psychological linchpin: A commentary on Cantor and Kihlstrom's "Social intelligence and cognitive assessments of personality." In T. K. Srull & R. S. Wyer, Jr. (Eds.), *Advances in social cognition* (Vol. 2, pp. 123–130). Hillsdale, NJ: Erlbaum.

Klinger, E., Barta, S. G., & Maxeiner, M. (1980). Motivational correlates of thought content frequency and commitment. *Journal of Personality and Social Psychology*, *39*, 1222–1237.

Klinger, E., Barta, S. G., & Maxeiner, M. (1981). Current concerns: Assessing therapeutically relevant motivation. In P. Kendall & S. Hollon (Eds.), *Assessment strategies for cognitive-behavioral interventions* (pp. 161–196). New York: Academic Press.

Kobasa, S. C. (1982). The hardy personality: Toward a social psychology of stress and health. In G. S. Sanders & J. Suls (Eds.), *Social psychology of health and illness* (pp. 3–32). Hillsdale, NJ: Erlbaum.

Kobasa, S. C., & Puccetti, M. C. (1983). Personality and social resources in stress-resistance. *Journal of Personality and Social Psychology*, *45*, 839–850.

Koestner, R., & Franz, C. (1989, March). *Life changes and the reliability of motive assessment*. Paper presented at the meeting of the Eastern Psychological Association, Boston.

Koestner, R., Franz, C., & Hellman, C. (1991). *Life changes and the reliability of TAT motive assessment*. Manuscript submitted for publication.

Koestner, R., & McClelland, D. C. (1990). Perspectives on competence motivation. In L. Pervin (Ed.), *Handbook of personality theory and research* (pp. 527–548). New York: Guilford.

Koestner, R., Ramey, A., Kelner, S., Meenan, R., & McClelland, D. (1989). Indirectly expressed motivational deficits among arthritic adults. *Motivation and Emotion*, *13*(1), 21–29.

Koestner, R., Weinberger, J., & McClelland, D. C. (1991). Task-intrinsic and social-extrinsic sources of arousal for motives assessed in fantasy and self-report. *Journal of Personality*, *54*, 57–82.

Koestner, R., & Zuckerman, M. (1989). *Personality moderators of the effects of performance feedback on intrinsic motivation*. Unpublished manuscript, University of Rochester, Department of Psychology, Rochester, NY.

Korman, A. (1974). *The psychology of motivation*. Englewood Cliffs, NJ: Prentice-Hall.

Kreitler, H., & Kreitler, S. (1976). *Cognitive orientation and behavior.* New York: Springer-Verlag.

Kripke, C. F. (1980). *The motive to avoid success and its impact on vocational choices of senior college women.* Unpublished doctoral dissertation, Boston University, Boston.

Krogh, K. M., & Smith, C. P. (1986, August). *Reliability and validity of aggregated n Achievement scores.* Paper presented at the 94th Annual Convention of the American Psychological Association, Washington, DC.

Krol, T. Z. (1981). Heckhausen's thematic apperception test for measurement of achievement motivation. *Prezeglad-Psychologiczny, 24,* 565–572.

Krumboltz, J. D., & Farquhar, W. W. (1957). Reliability and validity of the n-achievement test. *Journal of Consulting Psychology, 21,* 226–228.

Kuhl, J. (1978). Standard setting and risk preference: An elaboration of the theory of achievement motivation and an empirical test. *Psychological Review, 85,* 239–248.

Kuhl, J. (1986). Integrating cognitive and dynamic approaches: A prospectus for a unified psychology. In J. Kuhl & J. W. Atkinson (Eds.), *Motivation, thought and action* (pp. 307–336). New York: Praeger.

Kuhl, J., & Atkinson, J. W. (Eds.). (1986a). *Motivation, thought and action.* New York: Praeger.

Kuhl, J., & Atkinson, J. W. (1986b). Motivational determinants of decision time. In J. Kuhl & J. W. Atkinson (Eds.), *Motivation, thought, and action* (pp. 265–287). New York: Praeger.

Kuhl, J., & Blankenship, V. (1979). The dynamic theory of achievement motivation: From episodic to dynamic thinking. *Psychological Review, 86,* 141–151.

Lansing, J. B., & Heyns, R. W. (1959). Need affiliation and frequency of four types of communication. *Journal of Abnormal and Social Psychology, 58,* 365–372.

Larson, R. S., & Csikszentmihalyi, M. (1983). The experience-sampling method. *New Directions for Methodology of Social and Behavioral Science, 15,* 41–56.

Lau, B. (1985). *Uncertainty orientation, learned helplessness, and cross-cultural differences.* Unpublished honours thesis, University of Western Ontario, London.

Lazarus, R. (1961). A substitutive-defensive conception of apperceptive fantasy. In J. Kagan & G. S. Lesser (Eds.), *Contemporary issues in thematic apperceptive methods* (pp. 51–71). Springfield, IL: C. C. Thomas.

Lefcourt, H. M. (1976). *Locus of control.* Hillsdale, NJ: Erlbaum.

Lepper, M. R., & Greene, D. (Eds.). (1978). *The hidden costs of reward.* Hillsdale, NJ: Erlbaum.

Lepper, M. R., Greene, D., & Nisbett, R. E. (1973). Undermining children's intrinsic interest with extrinsic rewards: A test of the "overjustification" hypothesis. *Journal of Personality and Social Psychology, 28,* 129–137.

Lesko, R. (1974). *Personality factors associated with academic achievement in junior high school students.* Unpublished honors thesis, Wesleyan University, Middletown, CT.

Lesser, G. S. (1961). Discussion of Dr. Murstein's paper. In J. Kagan & G. S. Lesser (Eds.), *Contemporary issues in thematic apperceptive methods* (pp. 274–287). Springfield, IL: C. C. Thomas.

Lesser, G. S. (1973). Achievement motivation in women. In D. C. McClelland & R. S. Steele (Eds.), *Readings in motivation* (pp. 202–221). Morristown, NJ: General Learning Press.

Lesser, G. S., Krawitz, R. N., & Packard, R. (1963). Experimental arousal of achievement motivation in adolescent girls. *Journal of Abnormal and Social Psychology, 66,* 59–66.

LeVine, R. (1966). *Dreams and deeds: Achievement motivation in Nigeria*. Chicago: University of Chicago Press.

Lifshitz, M. (1974). Achievement motivation and coping behavior of normal and problematic preadolescent kibbutz children. *Journal of Personality Assessment*, *38*, 138–143.

Lindman, H. (1958). *A study of motives and the vocational preferences of high school students*. Unpublished honors thesis, University of Michigan, Ann Arbor.

Lindzey, G. (1961). *Projective techniques and cross-cultural research*. New York: Appleton-Century-Crofts.

Lindzey, G., & Heinemann, S. H. (1955). Thematic apperception test: Individual and group administration. *Journal of Personality*, *24*, 24–55.

Lindzey, G., & Herman, P. S. (1955). Thematic apperception test: A note on reliability and situational validity. *Journal of Projective Techniques*, *19*, 36–42.

Lindzey, G., & Silverman, M. (1959). Thematic apperception test: Techniques of group administration, sex differences, and the role of verbal productivity. *Journal of Personality*, *27*, 311–323.

Littig, L. W. (1963). Effects of motivation on probability preferences. *Journal of Personality*, *31*, 417–427.

Little, B. R. (1983). Personal projects: A rationale and method for investigation. *Environment and Behavior*, *15*, 273–309.

Little, B. R. (1989). Personal projects analysis: Trivial pursuits, magnificent obsessions, and the search for coherence. In D. M. Buss & N. Cantor (Eds.), *Personality psychology: Recent trends and emerging directions* (pp. 15–31). New York: Springer-Verlag.

Locke, E. A., & Bryan, J. F. (1968). Grade goals as determinants of academic achievement. *Journal of General Psychology*, *79*, 217–228.

Loevinger, J. (1957). Objective tests as instruments of psychological theory. *Psychological Reports*, *3*, 635–694. Monograph Supplement 9.

Logan, G. D. (1980). Attention and automaticity in Stroop and priming tasks: Theory and data. *Cognitive Psychology*, *12*, 523–553.

Lowell, E. L. (1950). *A methodological study of projectively measured achievement motivation*. Unpublished master's thesis, Wesleyan University, Middletown, CT.

Luborsky, L. (1977). Measuring a pervasive psychic structure in psychotherapy: The core conflictual relationship theme. In N. Freedman & S. Grand (Eds.), *Communicative structures and psychic structure* (pp. 367–395). New York: Plenum.

Lundberg, U., & Frankenhaeuser. M. (1978). Psychophysiological reactions to noise as modified by personal control over stimulus intensity. *Biological Psychology*, *6*, 51–59.

Lundy, A. (1985). The reliability of the Thematic Apperception Test. *Journal of Personality Assessment*, *49*(2), 141–145.

Lundy, A. (1988). Instructional set and Thematic Apperception Test validity. *Journal of Personality Assessment*, *52*, 309–320.

Macmurray, J. (1957). *Self as agent*. New York: Harper.

Maehr, M. L. (1974). Culture and achievement motivation. *American Psychologist*, *29*, 887–896.

Maehr, M. L., & Kleiber, D. A. (1981). The graying of achievement motivation. *American Psychologist*, *36*, 787–793.

Mahone, C. H. (1960). Fear and failure and unrealistic vocational aspiration. *Journal of Abnormal and Social Psychology*, *60*, 253–261.

Maier, S. F., & Seligman, M. E. P. (1976). Learned helplessness: Theory and evidence. *Journal of Experimental Psychology: General*, *105*, 3–46.

Malley, J. E. (1989, August). *The importance of agency and communion for well-being: Individual differences in needs and experiences.* Paper presented at the 97th Annual Convention of the American Psychological Association, New Orleans.

Mandler, G., & Sarason, S. B. (1952). A study of anxiety and learning. *Journal of Abnormal and Social Psychology, 47,* 166–173.

Marshall, J. M., & Karabenick, S. A. (1977). Validity of an empirically derived measure of fear of success. *Journal of Consulting and Clinical Psychology, 45,* 564–574.

Martindale, C. (1990). *The clockwork muse: The laws of artistic change.* New York: Basic Books.

Maslow, A. H. (1954). *Motivation and personality.* New York: Harper & Row.

Maslow, A. H. (1968). *Toward a psychology of being.* New York: Van Nostrand.

Mason, A., & Blankenship, V. (1987). Power and affiliation motivation, stress, and abuse in intimate relationships. *Journal of Personality and Social Psychology, 52,* 203–210.

Masterson, J. F. (1988). *The search for the real self.* New York: Free Press.

McAdams, D. P. (1980). A thematic coding system for the intimacy motive. *Journal of Research in Personality, 14,* 413–432.

McAdams, D. P. (1982a). Experiences of intimacy and power: Relationships between social motives and autobiographical memory. *Journal of Personality and Social Psychology, 42,* 292–302.

McAdams, D. P. (1982b). Intimacy motivation. In A. Stewart (Ed.), *Motivation and society* (pp. 133–171). San Francisco: Jossey-Bass.

McAdams, D. P. (1984a). Human motives and personal relationships. In V. Derlega (Ed.), *Communication, intimacy, and close relationships* (pp. 41–70). New York: Academic Press.

McAdams, D. P. (1984b). Scoring manual for the intimacy motive. *Psychological Documents,* No. 2613. (Abstracted in Vol. *14*(1), 7.) San Rafael, CA: Select Press.

McAdams, D. P. (1985a). The "imago": A key narrative component of identity. In P. Shaver (Ed.), *Self, situations, and social behavior* (pp. 115–142). Beverly Hills, CA: Sage.

McAdams, D. P. (1985b). *Power, intimacy, and the life story: Personological inquiries into identity.* New York: Guilford.

McAdams, D. P. (1989). *Intimacy: The need to be close.* New York: Doubleday.

McAdams, D. P. (1990). Unity and purpose in human lives: The emergence of identity as a life story. In A. I. Rabin, R. A. Zucker, R. A. Emmons, & S. Frank (Eds.), *Studying persons and lives* (pp. 148–200). New York: Springer.

McAdams, D. P., & Bryant, F. (1987). Intimacy motivation and subjective mental health in a nationwide sample. *Journal of Personality, 55,* 395–413.

McAdams, D. P., & Constantian, C. A. (1983). Intimacy and affiliation motives in daily living: An experience sampling analysis. *Journal of Personality and Social Psychology, 45,* 851–861.

McAdams, D. P., Healy, S., & Krause, S. (1984). Social motives and patterns of friendship. *Journal of Personality and Social Psychology, 41,* 828–838.

McAdams, D. P., Jackson, R. J., & Kirshnit, C. (1984). Looking, laughing; and smiling in dyads as a function of intimacy motivation and reciprocity. *Journal of Personality, 52,* 261–273.

McAdams, D. P., Lester, R. M., Brand, P. A., McNamara, W. J., & Lensky, D. B. (1988). Sex and the TAT: Are women more intimate than men? Do men fear intimacy? *Journal of Personality Assessment, 52,* 397–409.

McAdams, D. P., & Losoff, M. (1984). Friendship motivation in fourth- and sixth-graders: A thematic analysis. *Journal of Social and Personal Relationships, 1,* 11–27.

McAdams, D. P., & Powers, J. (1981). Themes of intimacy in behavior and thought. *Journal of Personality and Social Psychology, 40,* 573–587.

McAdams, D. P., Ruetzel, K., & Foley, J. M. (1986). Generativity and complexity at mid-life: Relations among social motives, ego development, and adults' plans for the future. *Journal of Personality and Social Psychology, 50,* 800–807.

McAdams, D. P., & Vaillant, G. E. (1982). Intimacy motivation and psychosocial adjustment: A longitudinal study. *Journal of Personality Assessment, 46,* 586–593.

McClelland, D. C. (1942). Functional autonomy of motives as an extinction phenomenon. *Psychological Review, 49,* 272–283.

McClelland, D. C. (1951). *Personality.* New York: William Sloane.

McClelland, D. C. (1955). The psychology of mental content reconsidered. *Psychological Review, 62,* 297–302.

McClelland, D. C. (1958a). Methods of measuring human motivation. In J. W. Atkinson (Ed.), *Motives in fantasy, action and society* (pp. 7–42). Princeton, NJ: Van Nostrand.

McClelland, D. C. (1958b). Risk-taking in children with high and low need for achievement. In J. W. Atkinson (Ed.), *Motives in fantasy, action and society* (pp. 306–321). Princeton, NJ: Van Nostrand.

McClelland, D. C. (1958c). The use of measures of human motivation in the study of society. In J. W. Atkinson (Ed.), *Motives in fantasy, action and society* (pp. 518–552). Princeton, NJ: Van Nostrand.

McClelland, D. C. (1961/1976). *The achieving society.* Princeton, NJ: Van Nostrand. (Paperback edition, 1967, New York: Free Press. Reissued with a new preface, 1976, New York: Irvington)

McClelland, D. C. (1963). Motivational patterns in Southeast Asia with special reference to the Chinese case. *Journal of Social Issues, 19*(1), 6–19.

McClelland, D. C. (1965). N Achievement and entrepreneurship: A longitudinal study. *Journal of Personality and Social Psychology, 1,* 389–392.

McClelland, D. C. (1971a). *Assessing human motivation.* Morristown, NJ: General Learning Press.

McClelland, D. C. (1971b). *Motivational trends in society.* Morristown, NJ: General Learning Press.

McClelland, D. C. (1972). Opinions predict opinions: What else is new? *Journal of Consulting and Clinical Psychology, 38,* 325–326.

McClelland, D. C. (1973). Testing for competence rather than for "intelligence." *American Psychologist, 28,* 1–14.

McClelland, D. C. (1975). *Power: The inner experience.* New York: Irvington (Halsted Press/Wiley).

McClelland, D. C. (1979). Inhibited power motivation and high blood pressure in men. *Journal of Abnormal Psychology, 88,* 182–190.

McClelland, D. C. (1980). Motive dispositions: The merits of operant and respondent measures. In L. Wheeler (Ed.), *Review of personality and social psychology: 1* (pp. 10–41). Beverly Hills, CA: Sage.

McClelland, D. C. (1981). Is personality consistent? In A. I. Rubin, J. Aronoff, A. M. Barclay, & R. A. Zucker (Eds.), *Further explorations in personality* (pp. 87–113). New York: Wiley.

McClelland, D. C. (1982). The need for power, sympathetic activation, and illness. *Motivation and Emotion, 6,* 31–41.

McClelland, D. C. (1984). Motives as sources of long-term trends in life and health. In D. C. McClelland, *Motives, personality, and society: Selected papers* (pp. 343–364). New York: Praeger.

McClelland, D. C. (1985a). How motives, skills and values determine what people do. *American Psychologist, 40*, 812–825.

McClelland, D. C. (1985b). *Human motivation*. Glenview, IL: Scott, Foresman. (Paperback edition, 1987, New York: Cambridge University Press)

McClelland, D. C. (1987a). Biological aspects of human motivation. In F. Halisch & J. Kuhl (Eds.), *Motivation, intention and volition* (pp. 11–19). New York: Springer-Verlag.

McClelland, D. C. (1987b). Characteristics of successful entrepreneurs. *Journal of Creative Behavior, 3*, 219–233.

McClelland, D. C. (1989). Motivational factors in health and disease. *American Psychologist, 44*, 675–683.

McClelland, D. C., Abramson, L., Brown, D., Kelner, S. P., Jr., McLeod, C., Patel, V., & Silverstein, J. (1990). Affiliative arousal, alexithymia, dopamine release and blood sugar mobilization in healthy adults and adults with insulin dependent diabetes mellitus. Unpublished paper, Center for Health and Advanced Policy Studies, Boston University, Boston, MA.

McClelland, D. C., Alexander, C., & Marks, E. (1982). The need for power, stress, immune function and illness among male prisoners. *Journal of Abnormal Psychology, 91*, 61–70.

McClelland, D. C., & Apicella, F. S. (1945). A functional classification of verbal reactions to experimentally induced failure. *Journal of Abnormal and Social Psychology, 40*, 376–390.

McClelland, D. C., & Atkinson, J. W. (1948). The projective expression of needs: I. The effect of different intensities of the hunger drive on perception. *Journal of Psychology, 25*, 205–232.

McClelland, D. C., Atkinson, J. W., & Clark, R. A. (1949). The projective expression of needs: III. The effect of ego-involvement, success, and failures on perception. *Journal of Psychology, 27*, 311–330.

McClelland, D. C., Atkinson, J. W., Clark, R. A., & Lowell, E. L. (1953/1976). *The achievement motive*. New York: Appleton-Century-Crofts. (Reissued with New Introduction by John W. Atkinson, 1976, New York: Irvington)

McClelland, D. C., & Boyatzis, R. E. (1982). The leadership motive pattern and long-term success in management. *Journal of Applied Psychology, 67*, 737–743.

McClelland, D. C., & Burnham, D. H. (1976, March–April). Power is the great motivator. *Harvard Business Review, 54*, 100–110, 159–166.

McClelland, D. C., Clark, R. A., Roby, T. B., & Atkinson, J. W. (1949). The projective expression of needs: IV. The effect of need for achievement on thematic apperception. *Journal of Experimental Psychology, 39*, 242–255.

McClelland, D. C., Colman, C., Finn, K., & Winter, D. G. (1978). Motivation and maturity patterns in marital success. *Social Behavior and Personality, 6*, 163–171.

McClelland, D. C., Davis, W., Kalin, R., & Wanner, E. (1972). *The drinking man: Alcohol and human motivation*. New York: Free Press.

McClelland, D. C., Floor, E., Davidson, R. J., & Saron, C. (1980). Stressed power motivation, sympathetic activation, immune function and illness. *Journal of Human Stress, 6*(2), 11–19.

McClelland, D. C., & Franz, C. E. (in press). Motivational and other sources of work accomplishment in mid-life: A longitudinal study. *Journal of Personality*.

McClelland, D. C., & Jemmott, J. B., III. (1980). Power motivation, stress and physical illness. *Journal of Human Stress, 6*(4), 6–15.

McClelland, D. C., & Kirshnit, C. (1988). The effect of motivational arousal through films on salivary immunoglobulin A. *Psychology and Health, 2*, 31–52.

McClelland, D. C., Koestner, R., & Weinberger, J. (1989). How do self-attributed and implicit motives differ? *Psychological Review, 96*, 690–702.

McClelland, D. C., & Liberman, A. M. (1949). The effect of need for achievement on recognition of need-related words. *Journal of Personality, 18*, 236–156.

McClelland, D. C., Patel, V., Stier, D., & Brown, D. (1987). The relationship of affiliative arousal to dopamine release. *Motivation and Emotion, 11*, 51–66.

McClelland, D. C., & Pilon, D. (1983). Sources of adult motives in patterns of parent behavior in early childhood. *Journal of Personality and Social Psychology, 44*, 564–574.

McClelland, D. C., Ross, G., & Patel, V. T. (1985). The effect of an examination on salivary norepinephrine and immunoglobulin levels. *Journal of Human Stress, 11*, 52–59.

McClelland, D. C., & Steele, R. S. (1972). *Motivation workshops*. New York: General Learning Press.

McClelland, D. C., & Teague, G. (1975). Predicting risk preferences among power-related tasks. *Journal of Personality, 43*, 266–285.

McClelland, D. C., & Watson, R. I., Jr. (1973). Power motivation and risk-taking behavior. *Journal of Personality, 41*, 121–139.

McClelland, D. C., & Winter, D. G. (1969/1971). *Motivating economic achievement*. New York: Free Press. (Paperback edition with afterword, 1971)

McCrae, R. R., & Costa, P. T. (1987). Validation of the five-factor model of personality across instruments and observers. *Journal of Personality and Social Psychology, 52*, 81–90.

McKay, J. R. (1988). Trust vs. cynicism: The relationship of affiliative orientation to immunocompetence and illness frequency. *Dissertation Abstracts International, 48*, 11B. (University Microfilms No. 88-00821)

McKay, J. R. (1991). Assessing aspects of object relations associated with immune function: Development of the Affiliative Trust–Mistrust coding system. *Psychological Assessment: A Journal of Consulting and Clinical Psychology, 3*(4), 641–647.

McKeachie, W. J. (1961). Motivation, teaching methods, and college learning. In M. R. Jones (Ed.), *Nebraska Symposium on Motivation: 1961* (pp. 111–142). Lincoln: University of Nebraska Press.

McLeod, C., Hellman, C. J., Budd, M., & McClelland, D. C. (1990). *Personality characteristics which promote positive outcomes from behavioral medicine treatments*. Unpublished manuscript, Boston University, Boston, MA.

McNair, D. M., Lorr, M., & Droppleman, L. F. (1981). *Manual for the profile of mood states*. Educational and Industrial Testing Service: San Diego, CA.

Mehrabian, A. (1969). Measures of achieving tendency. *Educational and Psychological Measurement, 29*, 445–451.

Mehrabian, A. (1970). The development and validation of measures of affiliative tendency and sensitivity to rejection. *Educational and Psychological Measurement, 30*, 417–428.

Mehta, P. (1969). *The achievement motive in high school boys*. New Delhi: National Council of Educational Research and Training.

Meichenbaum, D., & Gilmore, J. B. (1984). The nature of unconscious processes: A cognitive-behavioral perspective. In K. Bowers (Ed.), *The unconscious reconsidered* (pp. 273–298). New York: Wiley.

Melton, A. W. (1952). Motivation and learning. In W. S. Monroe (Ed.), *Encyclopedia of educational research* (pp. 668–690). New York: Macmillan.

Mendelsohn, G. A., Weiss, D. S., & Feimer, N. R. (1982). Conceptual and empirical analysis of the typological implications of patterns of socialization and femininity. *Journal of Personality and Social Psychology, 42,* 1157–1170.

Miller, D. R., & Swanson, G. E. (1960). *Inner conflict and defense.* New York: Holt.

Miller, J. B. (1982). *Women in power.* Unpublished manuscript (No. 82-01), Wellesley College, Stone Center for Developmental Services and Studies, Wellesley, MA.

Miron, D., & McClelland, D. C. (1979). The impact of achievement motivation training on small business performance. *California Management Review, 21*(4), 13–28.

Mischel, W. (1968). *Personality and assessment.* New York: Wiley.

Mischel, W. (1974). Processes in delay of gratification. In L. Berkowitz (Ed.), *Advances in experimental social psychology* (Vol. 7, pp. 249–292). New York: Academic Press.

Mischel, W. (1986). *Introduction to personality* (4th ed.). New York: Holt, Rinehart & Winston.

Mitchell, J. V., Jr. (1961). An analysis of the factorial dimensions of the achievement motivation construct. *Journal of Educational Psychology, 52,* 179–187.

Morgan, C., & Murray, H. A. (1935). A method for investigating fantasies: The Thematic Apperception Test. *The Archives of Neurology and Psychiatry, 34,* 289–306.

Morgan, H. H. (1953). Measuring achievement motivation with "picture interpretations." *Journal of Consulting Psychology, 17,* 289–292.

Morris, J. C. (1966). Propensity for risk-taking as a determinant of vocational choice. *Journal of Personality and Social Psychology, 3,* 328–335.

Mücher, H., & Heckhausen, H. (1962). Influence of mental activity and achievement motivation on skeletal muscle tonus. *Perceptual and Motor Skills, 14,* 217–218.

Mueller, D. P., Edwards, D. W., & Yarwis, R. M. (1977). Stressful life events and psychiatric symptomatology: Changes or undesirability? *Journal of Health and Social Behavior, 18,* 307–317.

Mueller, S. (1975). *Motivation and reactions to the work role among female performers and music teachers.* Unpublished doctoral dissertation, University of Michigan, Ann Arbor.

Murgatroyd, S., Rushton, C., Apter, M. J., & Ray, C. (1978). The development of the Telic Dominance Scale. *Journal of Personality Assessment, 42,* 519–528.

Murray, H. A. (1938). *Explorations in personality.* New York: Oxford University Press.

Murray, H. A. (1943). *Thematic Apperception Test manual.* Cambridge, MA: Harvard University Press.

Murstein, B. I. (1963). *Theory and research with projective techniques: Emphasizing the TAT.* New York: Wiley.

Murstein, B. I. (1965a). New thoughts about ambiguity and the TAT. *Journal of Projective Techniques and Personality Assessment, 28,* 219–225.

Murstein, B. I. (1965b). Reliability. In B. I. Murstein (Ed.), *Handbook of projective techniques* (pp. 189–218). New York: Basic Books.

Murstein, B. I. (1965c). Scaling of the TAT for achievement. *Journal of Consulting Psychology, 29,* 286.

Murstein, B. I. (1965d). The stimulus. In B. I. Murstein (Ed.), *Handbook of projective techniques* (pp. 509–546). New York: Basic Books.

Murstein, B. I. (1972). Normative written TAT responses for a college sample. *Journal of Personality Assessment*, *36*, 109–147.

Mussen, P. H., & Jones, M. C. (1957). Self-conceptions, motivations and interpersonal attitudes of late- and early-maturing boys. *Child Development*, *28*, 243–256.

Myers, J. K., Lindenthal, J. J., & Pepper, M. P. (1971). Life events and psychiatric impairment. *Journal of Nervous and Mental Disease*, *152*, 148–157.

Myers, J. K., Lindenthal, J. J., Pepper, M. P., & Ostrander, D. R. (1972). Life events and mental status: A longitudinal study. *Journal of Health and Social Behavior*, *13*, 398–406.

Neff, J. A. (1985). Race and vulnerability to stress: An examination of differential vulnerability. *Journal of Personality and Social Psychology*, *49*, 481–491.

Norman, W. T. (1963). Toward an adequate taxonomy of personality attributes: Replicated factor structure in peer nomination personality ratings. *Journal of Abnormal and Social Psychology*, *66*, 574–583.

Noujaim, K. (1968). *Some motivational determinants of effort allocation and performance*. Unpublished doctoral dissertation, Massachusetts Institute of Technology, Cambridge, MA.

O'Connor, P. A., Atkinson, J. W., & Horner, M. (1966). Motivational implications of ability grouping in schools. In J. W. Atkinson & N. T. Feather (Eds.), *A theory of achievement motivation* (pp. 141–156). New York: Wiley.

Olds, J. (1977). *Drives and reinforcements: Behavioral studies of hypothalamic function*. New York: Raven Press.

O'Leary, V. E., & Hammack, B. (1975). Sex role orientation and achievement contexts as determinants of the motive to avoid success. *Sex Roles*, *1*, 225–234.

Olweus, D., Block, J., & Radke-Yarrow, M. (1986). *Development of antisocial and prosocial behavior*. Orlando, FL: Academic Press.

Ossorio, P. G. (1981). Conceptual-notational devices: The PCF and related types. In Davis, K. E. (Ed.), *Advances in descriptive psychology* (pp. 83–104). Greenwich, CT: JAI Press.

Pappo, M. (1972). *Fear of success: A theoretical analysis and the construction and validation of a measuring instrument*. Unpublished doctoral dissertation, Columbia University, New York.

Parkes, C. M., & Weiss, R. S. (1983). *Recovery from bereavement*. New York: Basic Books.

Parsons, J. E., & Goff, S. B. (1980). Achievement motivation and values: An alternative perspective. In L. J. Fyans, Jr. (Ed.), *Achievement motivation: Recent trends in theory and research* (pp. 349–373). New York: Plenum Press.

Paykel, E. S. (1974). Recent life events and clinical depression. In E. K. E. Gunderson & R. H. Rahe (Eds.), *Life stress and illness* (pp. 134–163). Springfield, IL: C. C. Thomas.

Paykel, E. S. (1979). Causal relationships between clinical depression and life events. In J. E. Barratt, R. M. Rose, & G. L. Klerma (Eds.), *Stress and mental disorder* (pp. 71–86). New York: Raven.

Patten, R. L., & White, L. A. (1977). Independent effects of achievement motivation and overt attribution on achievement behavior. *Motivation and Emotion*, *1*, 39–59.

Peterson, C. (1983). Clouds and silver linings: Depressive symptoms and attributions about ostensibly good and bad events. *Cognitive Therapy and Research*, *7*, 575–578.

Peterson, C., Bettes, B. A., & Seligman, M. E. P. (1985). Depressive symptoms and unprompted causal attributions: Content analysis. *Behaviour Research and Therapy*, *23*, 379–382.

Peterson, C., Luborsky, L., & Seligman, M. E. P. (1983). Attributions and depressive mood shifts: A case study using the symptom-context method. *Journal of Abnormal Psychology, 92*, 96–103.

Peterson, C., Schwartz, S. M., & Seligman, M. E. P. (1981). Self-blame and depressive symptoms. *Journal of Personality and Social Psychology, 49*, 337–348.

Peterson, C., & Seligman, M. E. P. (1984a). Causal explanations as a risk factor for depression: Theory and evidence. *Psychological Review, 91*, 347–374.

Peterson, C., & Seligman, M. E. P. (1984b). *Content analysis of verbatim explanations: The CAVE technique.* Unpublished manuscript, Virginia Polytechnic Institute and State University, Blacksburg, VA.

Peterson, C., Seligman, M. E. P., & Vaillant, G. E. (1988). Pessimistic explanatory style is a risk factor for physical illness: A thirty-five year longitudinal study. *Journal of Personality and Social Psychology, 55*, 23–27.

Peterson, C., Semmel, A., von Baeyer, C., Abramson, L. Y., Metalsky, G. I., & Seligman, M. E. P. (1982). The attributional style questionnaire. *Cognitive Therapy and Research, 6*, 287–300.

Peterson, C., & Stunkard, A. J. (1989). Personal control and health promotion. *Social Science and Medicine, 28*, 819–828.

Peterson, C., & Villanova, P. (1988). An expanded attributional style questionnaire. *Journal of Abnormal Psychology, 97*, 87–89.

Peterson, C., Villanova, P., & Raps, C. S. (1985). Depression and attributions: Factors responsible for inconsistent results in the published literature. *Journal of Abnormal Psychology, 94*, 165–169.

Piedmont, R. (1988). An interactional model of achievement motivation and fear of success. *Sex Roles, 19*, 467–490.

Polanyi, M. (1958). *Personal knowledge.* Chicago: University of Chicago Press.

Pollack, S., & Gilligan, C. (1982). Images of violence in Thematic Apperception Test stories. *Journal of Personality and Social Psychology, 42*, 159–167.

Porter, C. A., & Suedfeld, P. (1981). Integrative complexity in the correspondence of literary figures: Effects of personal and societal stress. *Journal of Personality and Social Psychology, 40*, 321–330.

Posner, M. I., & Snyder, C. R. (1975). Attention and cognitive control. In R. L. Solso (Ed.), *Information processing and cognition: The Loyola symposium* (pp. 55–86). Hillsdale, NJ: Erlbaum.

Powers, W. T. (1973). *Behavior: The control of perception.* Chicago: Aldine.

Pulkkinen, L. (1986). The role of impulse control in the development of antisocial and prosocial behavior. In D. Olweus, J. Block, & M. Radke-Yarrow (Eds.), *Development of antisocial and prosocial behavior* (pp. 149–175). Orlando, FL: Academic Press.

Purcell, K. (1961). Discussion of Dr. Feshbach's paper. In A. I. Rabin (Ed.), *Assessment with projective techniques: A concise introduction* (pp. 141–152). New York: Springer.

Pye, L. (1986). Political psychology in Asia. In M. G. Hermann (Ed.), *Political psychology* (pp. 467–486). San Francisco: Jossey-Bass.

Rahe, R. H., & Arthur, R. J. (1978). Life change and illness studies: Past history and future directions. *Journal of Human Stress, 4*, 3–15.

Raphael, T. D. (1982). Integrative complexity theory and forecasting international crises: Berlin 1946–1962. *Journal of Conflict Resolution, 26*, 423–450.

Raphelson, A. C. (1957). The relationships among imaginative, direct verbal, and physiological measures of anxiety in an achievement situation. *Journal of Abnormal and Social Psychology, 54*, 13–18.

Raven, J. (1988). Toward measures of high-level competencies: A re-examination of

McClelland's distinction between needs and values. *Human Relations, 41,* 281–294.

Raven, J., Molloy, E., & Corcoran, R. (1972). Toward a questionnaire measure of achievement motivation. *Human Relations, 25,* 469–492.

Raven, J. C., Court, J. H., & Raven, J. (1977). *Manual for Raven's progressive matrices and vocabulary scales.* London: H. K. Lewis.

Ray, J. J., & Singh, S. (1980). Effects of individual differences on productivity among farmers in India. *Journal of Social Psychology, 112*(1), 11–17.

Raynor, J. O. (1969). Future orientation and motivation of immediate activity: An elaboration of the theory of achievement motivation. *Psychological Review, 76,* 606–610.

Raynor, J. O. (1974). Future orientation in the study of achievement motivation. In J. W. Atkinson, & J. O. Raynor (Eds.), *Motivation and achievement* (pp. 121–154). Washington, DC: Winston (Halsted Press/Wiley). Also in J. W. Atkinson & J. O. Raynor, (1978), *Personality, motivation and achievement* (pp. 71–115). Washington, DC: Hemisphere.

Raynor, J. O., & Entin, E. E. (1982a). Future orientation and achievement motivation. In J. O. Raynor & E. E. Entin (Eds.), *Motivation, career striving, and aging* (pp. 13–82). New York: Hemisphere.

Raynor, J. O., & Entin, E. E. (1982b). *Motivation, career striving, and aging.* New York: Hemisphere.

Raynor, J. O., & McFarlin, D. B. (1986). Motivation and the self-system. In R. M. Sorrentino & E. T. Higgins (Eds.), *The handbook of motivation and cognition: Foundations of social behavior* (pp. 315–349). New York: Guilford.

Raynor, J. O., & Smith, C. P. (1966). Achievement-related motives and risk-taking in games of skill and chance. *Journal of Personality, 34,* 176–198.

Read, S. J., & Miller, L. C. (1989). Inter-personalism: Toward a goal-based theory of persons in relationships. In L. A. Pervin (Ed.), *Goal concepts in personality and social psychology* (pp. 413–472). Hillsdale, NJ: Erlbaum.

Reeve, J., Olson, B. C., & Cole, S. G. (1987). Intrinsic motivation in competition: The intervening role of four individual differences following objective competence information. *Journal of Research in Personality, 21,* 148–170.

Reitman, W. R., & Atkinson, J. W. (1958). Some methodological problems in the use of thematic apperceptive measures of human motives. In J. W. Atkinson (Ed.), *Motives in fantasy, action and society* (pp. 664–683). New York: Van Nostrand.

Reuman, D. A. (1982). Ipsative behavioral variability and the quality of thematic apperceptive measurement of the achievement motive. *Journal of Personality and Social Psychology, 43,* 1098–1110.

Reuman, D. A., Alwin, D. F., & Veroff, J. (1984). Assessing the validity of the achievement motive in the presence of random measurement error. *Journal of Personality and Social Psychology, 47,* 1347–1362.

Reuman, D. A., Atkinson, J. W., & Gallop, G. (1986). Computer simulation of behavioral expressions. In J. Kuhl & J. W. Atkinson (Eds.), *Motivation, thought, and action* (pp. 203–234). New York: Praeger.

Revelle, W., & Michaels, E. J. (1976). The theory of achievement motivation revisited: The implications of inertial tendencies. *Psychological Review, 83,* 394–404.

Rogers, E. M., & Neill, R. E. (1966). *Achievement motivation among Colombian peasants.* East Lansing: Michigan State University.

Rogers, E. M., & Svenning, L. (1969). *Modernization among peasants: The impact of communication.* New York: Holt, Rinehart & Winston.

Rokeach, M. (1960). *The open and closed mind.* New York: Basic Books.

Rokeach, M. (1973). *The nature of human values*. New York: Free Press.

Rokeach, M. (1979). *Understanding human values: Individual and societal*. New York: Free Press.

Roney, C. J. R., & Sorrentino, R. M. (1987). Uncertainty orientation and perception: Individual differences in social categorization. *Social Cognition: A Journal of Social, Personality, and Developmental Psychology*, 5(4), 369–382.

Roney, C. J. R., & Sorrentino, R. M. (1990a). *Individual differences in uncertainty orientation: Implications for theories of self-evaluation*. Unpublished manuscript.

Roney, C. J. R., & Sorrentino, R. M. (1990b). *Uncertainty orientation and self-discrepancy theory: The role of informational affective influences on performance*. Unpublished manuscript.

Rosen, B. C., Crockett, H., & Nunn, C. Z. (1969). *Achievement in American society*. Cambridge, MA: Schenkman.

Rosen, B. C., & D'Andrade, R. B. (1959). The psychosocial origins of achievement motivation. *Sociometry*, 22, 185–218.

Rosenberg, M. (1979). *Conceiving the self*. New York: Basic Books.

Rosenfeld, H. M., & Franklin, S. S. (1966). Arousal of need for affiliation in women. *Journal of Personality and Social Psychology*, 3, 245–248.

Rothman, S., & Lichter, S. R. (1982). *Roots of radicalism: Jews, Christians, and the new left*. New York: Oxford University Press.

Rotter, J. B. (1966). Generalized expectancies for internal versus external control of reinforcement. *Psychological Monographs*, 80, (Whole No. 609).

Ruddick, S. (1983). Maternal thinking. In J. Trebilcot (Ed.), *Mothering: Essays in feminist theory* (pp. 213–230). Totowa, NJ: Rowman & Allanheld.

Rudin, S. A. (1965). The personal price of national glory. *Transaction*, 2, 4–9.

Rushton, J. P., Brainerd, C. J., & Pressley, M. (1983). Behavioral development and construct validity: The principle of aggregation. *Psychological Bulletin*, 94, 18–38.

Russell, D., Peplau, L. A., & Cutrona, C. E. (1980). The revised UCLA Loneliness Scale: Concurrent and discriminant validity evidence. *Journal of Personality and Social Psychology*, 39, 472–480.

Ryan, R. M. (1982). Control and information in the interpersonal sphere: An extension of cognitive evaluation theory. *Journal of Personality and Social Psychology*, 43, 450–461.

Ryle, G. (1949). *The concept of mind*. New York: Barnes & Noble.

Sadd, S., Lenauer, M., Shaver, P., & Dunivant, N. (1978). Objective measurement of fear of success and fear of failure: A factor analytic approach. *Journal of Consulting and Clinical Psychology*, 46, 405–416.

Sarason, B. R., & Sarason, I. C. (1958). The effect of type of administration and sex of subject on emotional tone and outcome ratings of TAT stories. *Journal of Projective Techniques*, 22, 333–337.

Sarason, I. G., Johnson, J. H., & Siegel, J. M. (1978). Assessing the impact of life changes: Development of the life experiences survey. *Journal of Consulting and Clinical Psychology*, 46, 932–946.

Sartre, J. P. (1947). *Existentialism* (B. Frechtman, Trans.). New York: Philosophical Library.

Sartre, J. P. (1965). *Anti-Semite and Jew* (G. J. Becker, Trans.). New York: Schocken. (Original work published 1946)

Sawusch, J. R. (1974). Computer simulation of the influence of ability and motivation on test performance and cumulative achievement and the relation between them. In J. W. Atkinson & J. O. Raynor (Eds.), *Motivation and achievement* (pp. 425–438). Washington, DC: Winston (Halsted Press/Wiley).

Schmitt, D. (1990, July). *Measuring the motives of Soviet party General Secretaries and Soviet society: Congruence created or congruence reflected?* Paper presented at the annual meeting of the International Society of Political Psychology, Washington, DC.

Schnackers, U., & Kleinbeck, U. (1975). Machtmotiv und machtthematisches Verhalten in einem Verhandlungsspiel [Power motivation and power-related behavior in a bargaining game]. *Archiv für Psychologie, 127*, 300–319.

Schneider, K. (1978). Atkinson's "risk preference" model: Should it be revised? *Motivation and Emotion, 2*, 333–344.

Schroder, H. M. (1989). *Managerial competence: A key to excellence*. Dubuque, IO: Kendall/Hunt.

Schroder, H. M., Driver, M. J., & Streufert, S. (1967). *Human information processing*. New York: Holt, Rinehart & Winston.

Schroth, M. L. (1988). Relationships between achievement related motives, extrinsic conditions, and task performance. *Journal of Social Psychology, 127*(1), 39–48.

Schulman, P., Castellon, C., & Seligman, M. E. P. (1988). *Guidelines for extracting and rating spontaneous explanations*. Unpublished manuscript, University of Pennsylvania, Philadelphia.

Schulman, P., Castellon, C., & Seligman, M. E. P. (1989). Assessing explanatory style: The content analysis of verbatim explanations and the attributional style questionnaire. *Behaviour Research and Therapy, 27*, 505–512.

Scott, W. A. (1955). Reliability of content analysis: The case for nominal scale coding. *Public Opinion Quarterly, 19*, 321–325.

Scott, W. A. (1958). The avoidance of threatening material in imaginative behavior. In J. W. Atkinson (Ed.), *Motives in fantasy, action and society* (pp. 572–585). Princeton, NJ: Van Nostrand.

Scott, W. A. (1960). Measures of test homogeneity. *Educational and Psychological Measurement, 20*, 751–757.

Scott, W. A., Osgood, D. W., & Peterson, C. (1979). *Cognitive structure: Theory and measurement of individual differences*. Washington, DC: Winston.

Sears, R. R. (1942). *Success and failure: A study of motility*. New York: McGraw-Hill.

Sears, R. R. (1961). Relation of early socialization experiences to aggression in middle childhood. *Journal of Abnormal and Social Psychology, 63*, 466–492.

Sears, R. R., Maccoby, E. E., & Levin, H. (1957). *Patterns of childrearing*. Evanston, IL: Row, Peterson.

Seligman, M. E. P. (1975). *Helplessness: On depression, development, and death*. San Francisco: Freeman.

Seltzer, R. A. (1973). Simulation of the dynamics of action. *Psychological Reports, 32*, 859–872.

Seltzer, R. A., & Sawusch, J. R. (1974). Computer program written to computer simulate the dynamics of action. In J. W. Atkinson & J. O. Raynor (Eds.), *Motivation and achievement* (pp. 411–423). Washington, DC: Winston (Halsted Press/Wiley).

Shapiro, D. (1965). *Neurotic styles*. New York: Basic Books.

Shapiro, J. P. (1978). A new format for thematic apperceptive measurement of motivation. *Perceptual and Motor Skills, 47*, 744–746.

Shaver, P. (1976). Questions concerning fear of success and its conceptual relatives. *Sex Roles, 2*, 305–319.

Sheppard, H. L., & Belitsky, A. H. (1966). *The job hunt*. Baltimore: Johns Hopkins University Press.

Shinn, M. (1973). *Secondary school coeducation and the fears of success and failure*. Unpublished honors thesis, Harvard University, Cambridge, MA.

Shipley, T. E., Jr., & Veroff, J. A. (1952). A projective measure of need for affiliation. *Journal of Experimental Psychology*, *43*, 349–356.

Short, J. C., & Sorrentino, R. M. (1986). Achievement, affiliation and group incentives: A test of the overmotivation hypothesis. *Motivation and Emotion*, *10*, 115–131.

Silver, R. L., Wortman, C. B., & Klos, D. S. (1982). Cognitions, affect, and behavior following uncontrollable outcomes: A response to current human helplessness research. *Journal of Personality*, *50*, 480–514.

Simonton, D. K. (1981). The library laboratory: Archival data in personality and social psychology. In L. Wheeler (Ed.), *Review of Personality and Social Psychology: 2* (pp. 217–243). Beverly Hills, CA: Sage.

Simonton, D. K. (1987). *Why presidents succeed*. New Haven: Yale University Press.

Simonton, D. K. (1990). *Psychology, science, and history*. New Haven: Yale University Press.

Singer, J. L. (1981). Research applications of projective methods. In A. I. Rabin (Ed.), *Assessment with projective techniques* (pp. 297–331). New York: Springer.

Singer, J. L. (1988). Sampling ongoing consciousness and emotional experience: Implications for health. In M. Horowitz (Ed.), *Psychodynamics and cognition* (pp. 297–346). Chicago: University of Chicago Press.

Singer, J. L., & Kolligian, J., Jr. (1987). Personality: Developments in the study of private experience. *Annual Review of Psychology*, *38*, 533–574.

Sinha, B. P., & Mehta, P. (1972). Farmers' need for achievement and change-proneness in acquisition of information from a farm telecast. *Rural Sociology*, *37*, 417–427.

Skinner, B. F. (1938). *The behavior of organisms*. New York: Appleton-Century-Crofts.

Skinner, B. F. (1953). *Science and human behavior*. New York: Free Press.

Skolnick, A. (1966). Motivational imagery and behavior over twenty years. *Journal of Consulting Psychology*, *30*(6), 463–478.

Smith, C. P. (1963). Achievement-related motives and goal setting under different conditions. *Journal of Personality*, *31*, 124–140.

Smith, C. P. (1964). Relationships between achievement-related motives and intelligence, performance level, and persistence. *Journal of Abnormal and Social Psychology*, *68*, 523–532.

Smith, C. P. (1966). The influence of testing conditions on need for achievement scores and their relationship to performance scores. In J. W. Atkinson & N. T. Feather (Eds.), *A theory of achievement motivation* (pp. 277–297). New York: Wiley.

Smith, C. P. (Ed.). (1969a). *Achievement-related motives in children*. New York: Russell Sage Foundation.

Smith, C. P. (1969b). The origin and expression of achievement-related motives in children. In C. P. Smith (Ed.), *Achievement-related motives in children* (pp. 102–150). New York: Russell Sage Foundation.

Smith, C. P., & Feld, S. (1958). How to learn the method of content analysis for *n* Achievement, *n* Affiliation, and *n* Power. In J. W. Atkinson (Ed.), *Motives in fantasy, action and society* (pp. 685–818). Princeton, NJ: Van Nostrand.

Smith, C. P., Krogh, K. M., & McMahan, I. D. (1991). Reliability of n Achievement scores aggregated over occasions. Unpublished manuscript, City University of New York, Graduate School, New York.

Smits, G. J. (1980). *Individual differences in decision-making style*. Unpublished doctoral dissertation, Boston University, Boston.

Snare, C. E. (1990, July). *At-a-distance personality assessment of Iranian leaders since the Shah.* Paper presented at the annual meeting of the International Society of Political Psychology, Washington, DC.

Snare, C. E. (in press). Personality and foreign policy behavior: An examination of Muammar Kaddafi. In E. Singer & V. Harper (Eds.), *Political psychology and foreign policy.* Boulder, CO: Westview.

Sokol, M. (1979, April). *Facilitating adaptation: The psychotherapeutic process.* Paper presented at the meeting of the Eastern Psychological Association Convention, Philadelphia.

Sokol, M. (1983). *A content analysis of time-limited psychotherapy: Measuring emotional perspectives.* Unpublished doctoral dissertation, Boston University, Boston.

Sokol, M., Healy, J. M., Jr., & Oresick, R. J. (1980). *A content analysis method for assessing affective change in psychotherapy.* Paper presented at the meeting of the New England Psychological Association Convention, Boston.

Sorrentino, R. M. (1973). An extension of theory of achievement motivation to the study of emergent leadership. *Journal of Personality and Social Psychology, 26,* 356–368.

Sorrentino, R. M., Bobocel, C. R., Gitta, M. Z., Olson, J. M., & Hewitt, E. C. (1988). Uncertainty orientation and persuasion: Individual differences in the effects of personal relevance on social judgements. *Journal of Personality and Social Psychology, 55,* 357–371.

Sorrentino, R. M., & Hewitt, E. C. (1984). The uncertainty reducing properties of achievement tasks revisted. *Journal of Personality and Social Psychology, 4,* 884–899.

Sorrentino, R. M., Hewitt, E. C., & Raso-Knot, P. A. (1990). *Risk-taking in games of chance and skill: Individual differences in affective and information value.* Unpublished manuscript.

Sorrentino, R. M., & Higgins, E. T. (Eds.), (1986a). *The handbook of motivation and cognition: Foundations of social behavior.* New York: Guilford.

Sorrentino, R. M., & Higgins, E. T. (1986b). Motivation and cognition: Warming to synergism. In R. M. Sorrentino & E. T. Higgins (Eds.), *The handbook of motivation and cognition: Foundations of social behavior* (pp. 3–19). New York: Guilford.

Sorrentino, R. M., Raynor, J. O., Zubek, J. M., & Short, J. C. (1990). A theory of personality functioning and change: Reinterpretation of cognitive-development theories in terms of information and affective value. In E. T. Higgins & R. M. Sorrentino (Eds.), *The handbook of motivation and cognition: Foundations of social behavior* (Vol. 2, pp. 193–228). New York: Guilford.

Sorrentino, R. M., & Roney, C. J. R. (1986). Uncertainty orientation, achievement-related motives, and task diagnosticity as determinants of task performance. *Social Cognition, 4,* 420–436.

Sorrentino, R. M., & Roney, C. J. R. (1990). Individual differences in uncertainty orientation: Implications for the self-inference process. In M. P. Zanna & J. M. Olson (Eds.), *Social influence: The Ontario symposium* (Vol. 6, pp. 239–257). Hillsdale, NJ: Erlbaum.

Sorrentino, R. M., & Sheppard, B. H. (1978). Effects of affiliation-related motives on swimmers in individual versus group competition: A field experiment. *Journal of Personality and Social Psychology, 36,* 704–714.

Sorrentino, R. M., & Short, J. C. (1977). The case of the mysterious moderates: Why motives sometimes fail to predict behavior. *Journal of Personality and Social Psychology, 35,* 478–484.

Sorrentino, R. M., & Short, J. C. (1986). Uncertainty orientation, motivation and cognition. In R. M. Sorrentino & E. T. Higgins (Eds.), *The handbook of motivation and cognition: Foundations of social behavior* (pp. 379–403). New York: Guilford.

Sorrentino, R. M., Short, J. C., & Raynor, J. O. (1984). Uncertainty orientation: Implications for cognitive and motivational views of achievement behavior. *Journal of Personality and Social Psychology, 46,* 189–206.

Southwood, K. E. (1969). *Some sources of political disorder: A cross-national analysis.* Unpublished doctoral dissertation, University of Michigan, Ann Arbor.

Spence, J., & Helmreich, R. (1978). *Masculinity and femininity: Their psychological dimensions, correlates and antecedents.* Austin: University of Texas Press.

Spence, K. W. (1956). *Behavior theory and conditioning.* New Haven: Yale University Press.

Srivastava, N. (1979). Achievement motivation and self-concept in two settings. *Asian Journal of Psychology and Education, 4*(1), 5–9.

Star, S. (1955). *The public's ideas about mental illness.* Paper presented at the annual meeting of the National Association for Mental Health.

Steele, R. S. (1977). Power motivation, activation, and inspirational speeches. *Journal of Personality, 45,* 53–64.

Sternberg, R. J. (1986). *Intelligence applied: Understanding and increasing your intellectual skills.* New York: Harcourt, Brace, Jovanovich.

Stewart, A. J. (1971). *The nature of woman: A study of female responses to male definition.* Unpublished honors thesis, Wesleyan University, Middletown, CT.

Stewart, A. J. (1975). *Longitudinal prediction from personality to life outcomes among college-educated women.* Unpublished doctoral dissertation, Harvard University, Cambridge, MA.

Stewart, A. J. (1978). A longitudinal study of coping styles in self-defining and socially defined women. *Journal of Consulting and Clinical Psychology, 46,* 1079–1084.

Stewart, A. J. (1980). Personality and situation in the prediction of women's life patterns. *Psychology of Women Quarterly, 5,* 195–206.

Stewart, A. J. (1982). The course of individual adaptation. *Journal of Personality and Social Psychology, 42,* 1100–1113.

Stewart, A. J. (1985). *Children's adaptation to parental separation and divorce.* Unpublished paper.

Stewart, A. J. (1986). *Family transformation in the course of parental divorce* (Report No. R01-MH-38801). Washington, DC: National Institutes of Mental Health.

Stewart, A. J., & Chester, N. L. (1982). Sex differences in human social motives: Achievement, affiliation and power. In A. J. Stewart (Ed.), *Motivation and society* (pp. 172–218). San Francisco: Jossey-Bass.

Stewart, A. J., Chester, N. L., Lykes, M. B., & Sloman, J. (1981). *The development of career aspirations in adolescents* (Final report to the William T. Grant Foundation). Cambridge, MA: Radcliffe College, Henry A. Murray Research Center.

Stewart, A. J., Copeland, A. P., & Healy, J. M., Jr. (1987). *Children's adjustment to parental separation.* Unpublished manuscript, Boston University, Boston.

Stewart, A. J., Franz, C., & Layton, L. (1988). The changing self: Using personal documents to study lives. *Journal of Personality, 56,* 41–74.

Stewart, A. J., & Healy, J. M., Jr. (1984). Processing affective responses to life experiences: The development of the adult self. In C. Malatesta & C. Izard (Eds.), *Emotion in adult development* (pp. 277–295). Beverly Hills, CA: Sage.

Stewart, A. J., & Healy, J. M., Jr. (1985). Personality and adaptation to change. In R. Hogan & W. Jones (Eds.), *Perspectives in personality: Theory, measurement and interpersonal dynamics* (pp. 117–144). Greenwich, CT: JAI Press.

Stewart, A. J., & Rubin, Z. (1976). Power motivation in the dating couple. *Journal of Personality and Social Psychology, 34*, 305–309.

Stewart, A. J., & Salt, P. (1981). Life stress, life-styles, depression and illness in adult women. *Journal of Personality and Social Psychology, 40*, 1063–1069.

Stewart, A. J., Sokol, M., Healy, J. M., Jr., & Chester, N. L. (1986). Longitudinal studies of psychological consequences of life changes in children and adults. *Journal of Personality and Social Psychology, 50*, 143–151.

Stewart, A. J., Sokol, M., Healy, J. M., Jr., Chester, N. L., & Weinstock-Savoy, D. (1982). Adaptation to life changes in children and adults: Cross-sectional studies. *Journal of Personality and Social Psychology, 43*, 1270–1281.

Stewart, A. J., & Winter, D. G. (1974). Self-definition and social definition in women. *Journal of Personality, 42*, 238–259.

Stewart, A. J., & Winter, D. G. (1976). Arousal of the power motive in women. *Journal of Consulting and Clinical Psychology, 44*, 495–496.

Story, A. L. (1987). *A methodological study of impersonal versus personal and operant versus respondent measures of personal causation.* Unpublished honors thesis, Washington University, St. Louis, MO.

Straus, M. A., & Houghton, L. J. (1960). Achievement, affiliation, and cooperation values as clues to trends in American rural society, 1924–1958. *Rural Sociology, 25*, 394–403.

Strawson, P. F. (1959). *Individuals: An essay in descriptive metaphysics.* London: Methuen.

Streufert, S. (1970). Complexity and complex decision making: Convergences between differentiation and integration approaches to the prediction of task performance. *Journal of Experimental Social Psychology, 6*, 494–509.

Streufert, S. (1989). How successful executives think. *Boardroom Reports, 18*(12), 13–14.

Streufert, S., & Nogami, G. Y. (1989). Cognitive style and complexity: Implications for I/O Psychology. In C. L. Cooper & I. Robertson (Eds.), *International review of industrial and organizational psychology* (pp. 93–143). New York: Wiley.

Streufert, S., Pogash, R., & Piasecki, M. (1988). Simulation based assessment of managerial competence: Reliability and validity. *Personnel Psychology, 41*, 537–557.

Streufert, S., Pogash, R., Piasecki, M., Nogami, G. Y., & Swezey, R. W. (1988). Computer assisted training of complex managerial performance. *Computers and Human Behavior, 4*, 77–88.

Streufert, S., & Streufert, S. C. (1978). *Behavior in the complex environment.* Washington, DC: Winston.

Streufert, S., & Swezey, R. W. (1986). *Complexity, managers, and organizations.* New York: Academic Press.

Stricker, G., & Healey, B. J. (1990). Projective assessment of object relations: A review of the empirical literature. *Psychological Assessment: A Journal of Consulting and Clinical Psychology, 2*(3), 219–230.

Suedfeld, P. (1981). Indices of world tension in the "Bulletin of the Atomic Scientists." *Political Psychology, 2*(3/4), 114–123.

Suedfeld, P. (1985). APA presidential addresses: The relation of integrative complexity to historical, professional, and personal factors. *Journal of Personality and Social Psychology, 49*, 1643–1651.

Suedfeld, P., & Bluck, S. (1988). Changes in integrative complexity prior to surprise attacks. *Journal of Conflict Resolution, 32*, 626–635.

Suedfeld, P., Corteen, R. S., & McCormick, C. (1986). The role of integrative complexity in military leadership: Robert E. Lee and his opponents. *Journal of Applied Social Psychology, 16,* 498–507.

Suedfeld, P., & Piedrahita, L. E. (1984). Intimations of mortality: Integrative simplification as a precursor of death. *Journal of Personality and Social Psychology, 47,* 848–852.

Suedfeld, P., & Rank, A. D. (1976). Revolutionary leaders: Long-term success as a function of changes in conceptual complexity. *Journal of Personality and Social Psychology, 34,*169–178.

Suedfeld, P., & Tetlock, P. E. (1977). Integrative complexity of communications in international crises. *Journal of Conflict Resolution, 21,* 169–184.

Suedfeld, P., & Tetlock, P. E. (1990). *Integrative complexity: Theory and research.* Unpublished manuscript.

Suedfeld, P., Tetlock, P. E., & Ramirez, C. (1977). War, peace, and integrative complexity. *Journal of Conflict Resolution, 21,* 427–441.

Suedfeld, P., Tomkins, S. S., & Tucker, W. H. (1969). On relations among perceptual and cognitive measures of information processing. *Perception and Psychophysics, 6,* 45–46.

Sullivan, H. S. (1953). *The interpersonal theory of psychiatry.* New York: Norton.

Sundheim, B. J. M. (1962). *The relationships among n Achievement, n affiliation, sex-role concepts, academic grades, and curricular choice.* Unpublished doctoral dissertation, Columbia University, New York.

Sweeney, P. D., Shaeffer, D., & Golin, S. (1982). Attributions about self and others in depression. *Personality and Social Psychology Bulletin, 8,* 37–42.

Teevan, R. C., Diffenderfer, D., & Greenfeld, N. (1986). Need for achievement and sociometric status. *Psychological Reports, 58,* 446.

Terhune, K. W. (1968). Motives, situation and interpersonal conflict within prisoners' dilemma. *Journal of Personality and Social Psychology, 8* (Pt. 2, Monograph Suppl.).

Tessler, M. A., O'Barr, W. M., & Spain, D. H. (1973). *Tradition and identity in changing Africa.* New York: Harper & Row.

Tetlock, P. E. (1979). Identifying victims of groupthink from public statements of decision makers. *Journal of Personality and Social Psychology, 37,* 1314–1324.

Tetlock, P. E. (1981a). Personality and isolationism: Content analysis of Senatorial speeches. *Journal of Personality and Social Psychology, 41,* 737–743.

Tetlock, P. E. (1981b). Pre- to postelection shifts in presidential rhetoric: Impression management or cognitive adjustment? *Journal of Personality and Social Psychology, 41,* 207–212.

Tetlock, P. E. (1983a). Accountability and complexity of thought. *Journal of Personality and Social Psychology, 45,* 74–83.

Tetlock, P. E. (1983b). Cognitive style and political ideology. *Journal of Personality and Social Psychology, 45,* 118–126.

Tetlock, P. E. (1984). Cognitive style and political belief systems in the British House of Commons. *Journal of Personality and Social Psychology, 46,* 365–375.

Tetlock, P. E. (1986). A value pluralism model of ideological reasoning. *Journal of Personality and Social Psychology, 50,* 819–827.

Tetlock, P. E., Bernzweig, J., & Gallant, J. L. (1985). Supreme Court decision making: Cognitive style as a predictor of ideological consistency of voting. *Journal of Personality and Social Psychology, 48,* 1227–1239.

Tetlock, P. E., & Boettger, R. (1989). Cognitive and rhetorical styles of traditionalist and reformist Soviet politicians: A content analysis study. *Political Psychology, 10,* 209–232.

Tetlock, P. E., & Kim, J. I. (1987). Accountability and judgment processes in a personality prediction task. *Journal of Personality and Social Psychology*, *52*, 700–709.

Tetlock, P. E., Skitka, L., & Boettger, R. (1989). Social and cognitive strategies for coping with accountability: Conformity, complexity, and bolstering. *Journal of Personality and Social Psychology*, *57*, 632–641.

Thoits, P. A. (1983). Dimensions of life events that influence psychological distress: An evaluation and synthesis of the literature. In H. Kaplan (Ed.), *Psychosocial stress: Trends in theory and research* (pp. 33–103). New York: Academic Press.

Thorne, A. (1989). Conditional patterns, transference, and the coherence of personality across time. In D. M. Buss & N. Cantor (Eds.), *Personality psychology: Recent trends and emerging directions* (pp. 149–159). New York: Springer-Verlag.

Todd, J. A., Acha-Orbea, H., Bell, J. I., Chao, N., Fronek, Z., Jacob, C. O., McDermott, M., Sinha, A. A., Timmerman, L., Steinman, L., & McDevitt, H. O. (1988). A molecular basis for MHC Class II-associated autoimmunity. *Science*, *240*, 1003–1009.

Tolman, E. (1955). Principles of performance. *Psychological Review*, *62*, 315–326.

Tomkins, S. S. (1947). *The thematic apperception test: The theory and technique of interpretation*. New York: Grune & Stratton.

Tomkins, S. S. (1961). Discussion of Dr. Holt's paper. In J. Kagan & G. S. Lesser (Eds.), *Contemporary issues in thematic apperceptive methods* (pp. 44–50). Springfield, IL: C. C. Thomas.

Tomkins, S. S. (1987). Script theory. In J. Aronoff, A. I. Rabin, & R. A. Zucker (Eds.), *The emergence of personality* (pp. 147–216). New York: Springer.

Tresemer, D. (1976). The cumulative record of research on fear of success. *Sex Roles*, *2*, 217–235.

Trodahl, V. C., & Powell, F. A. (1965). A short-form dogmatism scale for use in field studies. *Social Forces*, *44*, 211–214.

Trope, Y. (1979). Uncertainty-reducing properties of achievement tasks. *Journal of Personality and Social Psychology*, *37*, 1505–1518.

Tulving, E. (1983). *Elements of episodic memory*. New York: Oxford University Press.

Tulving, E., & Schacter, D. L. (1990). Priming and human memory systems. *Science*, *247*, 301–306.

Uleman, J. S. (1966). *A new TAT measure of the need for power*. Unpublished doctoral dissertation, Harvard University, Cambridge, MA.

Uleman, J. S. (1972). The need for influence: Development and validation of a measure, and comparison with the need for power. *Genetic Psychological Monographs*, *85*, 157–214.

Uleman, J. S., & Bargh, J. A. (Eds.). (1989). *Unintended thought*. New York: Guilford.

Vaillant, G. (1977). *Adaptation to life*. Boston: Little, Brown.

Vannoy, J. S. (1965). Generality of cognitive complexity–simplicity as a personality construct. *Journal of Personality and Social Psychology*, *2*, 385–396.

Veroff, J. (1955). *Validation of a projective measure of power motivation*. Unpublished doctoral dissertation, University of Michigan, Ann Arbor.

Veroff, J. (1957). Development and validation of a projective measure of power motivation. *Journal of Abnormal and Social Psychology*, *54*, 1–8.

Veroff, J. (1961). Thematic apperception in a nationwide sample survey. In J. Kagan & G. S. Lesser (Eds.), *Contemporary issues in thematic apperceptive methods* (pp. 83–111). Springfield, IL: C. C. Thomas.

Veroff, J. (1969). Social comparison and the development of achievement motivation. In C. P. Smith (Ed.), *Achievement-related motives in children* (pp. 46–101). New York: Russell Sage Foundation.

Veroff, J. (1982). Assertive motivations: Achievement versus power. In A. J. Stewart (Ed.), *Motivation and society* (pp. 99–132). San Francisco: Jossey-Bass.

Veroff, J., Atkinson, J. W., Feld, S. C., & Gurin, G. (1960). The use of thematic apperception to assess motivation in a nationwide interview study. *Psychological Monographs, 74* (12, Whole No. 499). Also in J. W. Atkinson & J. O. Raynor (Eds.), (1974), *Motivation and achievement* (pp. 43–75). Washington, DC: Winston (Halsted Press/Wiley).

Veroff, J., Depner, C., Kulka, R., & Douvan, E. (1980). Comparison of American motives: 1957 versus 1976. *Journal of Personality and Social Psychology, 39,* 1249–1262.

Veroff, J., Douvan, E., & Kulka, R. A. (1981). *The inner American: A self-portrait from 1957–1976.* New York: Basic Books.

Veroff, J., & Feld, S. C. (1970). *Marriage and work in America.* New York: Van Nostrand–Reinhold.

Veroff, J., Feld, S., & Crockett, A. (1966). Explorations into the effects of picture cues on thematic apperceptive expression of achievement motivation. *Journal of Personality and Social Psychology, 3,* 171–181.

Veroff, J., McClelland, L., & Ruhland, D. (1975). Varieties of achievement motivation. In M. Mednick, S. Tangri, & L. Hoffman (Eds.), *Women and achievement* (pp. 172–205). New York: Holt, Rinehart & Winston.

Veroff, J., Reuman, D., & Feld, S. (1984). Motives in American men and women across the adult life span. *Developmental Psychology, 20,* 1142–1158.

Veroff, J., & Smith, D. (1985). Motives and values over the adult years. In D. Kleiber & M. Maehr (Eds.), *Advances in motivation and achievement* (Vol. 4, pp. 55–92). Greenwich, CT: JAI Press.

Veroff, J., & Veroff, J. B. (1972). Reconsideration of a measure of power motivation. *Psychological Bulletin, 78,* 279–291.

Veroff, J., & Veroff, J. B. (1980). *Social incentives: A life span developmental approach.* New York: Academic Press.

Vinokur, A., & Selzer, M. L. (1975). Desirable versus undesirable life events: Their relationship to stress and mental distress. *Journal of Personality and Social Psychology, 32,* 327–337.

Walker, E. L., & Atkinson, J. W. (1958). The expression of fear-related motivation in thematic apperception as a function of proximity to an atomic explosion. In J. W. Atkinson (Ed.), *Motives in fantasy, action and society* (pp. 143–159). Princeton: Van Nostrand.

Walker, E. L., & Heyns, R. N. (1962). *An anatomy for conformity.* Englewood Cliffs, NJ: Prentice-Hall.

Wallace, M. D., & Suedfeld, P. (1988). Leadership performance in crisis: The longevity-complexity link. *International Studies Quarterly, 32,* 439–451.

Watson, R. I., Jr. (1969). *Motivation and role induction.* Unpublished honors thesis, Wesleyan University, Middletown, CT.

Weber, M. (1930). *The protestant ethic and the spirit of capitalism* (T. Parsons, Trans.). New York: Scribners. (Original work published 1904–1905)

Weber, M. (1948). Politics as a vocation. In H. Gerth & C. W. Mills (Eds.), *From Max Weber: Essays in sociology* (pp. 77–128). London: Routledge & Kegan Paul. (Original work published 1919)

Weinberger, J., & McClelland, D. C. (1990). Cognitive versus traditional motivational models: Irreconcilable or complementary? In E. T. Higgins & R.

M. Sorrentino (Eds.), *The handbook of motivation and cognition: Foundations of social behavior* (Vol. 2, pp. 562–597). New York: Guilford.

Weiner, B. (1965). The effects of unsatisfied achievement motivation on persistence and subsequent performance. *Journal of Personality, 33,* 428–442.

Weiner, B. (1972). *Theories of motivation.* Chicago: Rand McNally.

Weiner, B. (1980). *Human motivation.* New York: Holt, Rinehart & Winston.

Weiner, B. (1985). "Spontaneous" causal thinking. *Psychological Bulletin, 97,* 74–84.

Weiner, B. (1986). *An attributional theory of motivation and emotion.* New York: Springer-Verlag.

Weinstein, M. S. (1969). Achievement motivation and risk preference. *Journal of Personality and Social Psychology, 13,* 153–172.

Wendt, H. W. (1955). Motivation, effort and performance. In D. C. McClelland (Ed.), *Studies in motivation* (pp. 448–459). New York: Appleton-Century-Crofts.

Westbrook, M. T., & Viney, L. L. (1980). Scales measuring people's perception of themselves as origin and pawns. *Journal of Personality Assessment, 44,* 167–174.

Westen, D. (1991). The clinical assessment of object relations using the TAT. *Journal of Personality Assessment, 56*(1), 56–74.

White, R. W. (1959). Motivation reconsidered: The concept of competence. *Psychological Review, 66,* 297–333.

Whiting, B. B., & Edwards, C. P. (1973). A cross-cultural analysis of sex differences in the behavior of children aged three through 11. *Journal of Social Psychology, 91,* 171–188.

Whiting, B. B., & Whiting, J. W. M. (1975). *Children of six cultures.* Cambridge, MA: Harvard University Press.

Wilcox, B. L. (1981). Social support, life stress, and psychological adjustment: A test of the buffering hypothesis. *American Journal of Community Psychology, 9,* 371–386.

Winter, D. G. (1973). *The power motive.* New York: Free Press.

Winter, D. G. (1976, July). Why the candidates run. *Psychology Today,* pp. 45–49, 92.

Winter, D. G. (1980). Measuring the motives of southern African political leaders at a distance. *Political Psychology, 2*(2), 75–85.

Winter, D. G. (1982). Motives and behavior in the 1976 presidential candidates. In A. J. Stewart (Ed.), *Motivation and society* (pp. 244–273). San Francisco: Jossey-Bass.

Winter, D. G. (1987a). Enhancement of an enemy's power motivation as a dynamic of conflict escalation. *Journal of Personality and Social Psychology, 52,* 41–46.

Winter, D. G. (1987b). Leader appeal, leader performance, and motive profiles of leaders and followers: A study of American presidents and elections. *Journal of Personality and Social Psychology, 52,* 196–202.

Winter, D. G. (1987c, April). *Power motive distortion in British and German newspapers and diplomatic dispatches at the outbreak of World War I.* Paper presented at the meeting of the Eastern Psychological Association, Arlington, VA.

Winter, D. G. (1988a). *Motive distortion during the Cuban Missile Crisis.* Unpublished manuscript, University of Michigan, Department of Psychology, Ann Arbor.

Winter, D. G. (1988b). The power motive in women – and men. *Journal of Personality and Social Psychology, 54,* 510–519.

Winter, D. G. (1988c, July). What makes Jesse run? [Motives of the 1988 candidates]. *Psychology Today*, pp. 20, 22, 24.

Winter, D. G. (1989a). *Correcting motive scores for the effect of length of text.* Unpublished manuscript, University of Michigan, Department of Psychology, Ann Arbor.

Winter, D. G. (1989b, March). *Gorbachev's motives: Opportunities, issues, and problems.* Paper presented at the annual meeting of the International Studies Association, London.

Winter, D. G. (1989c, May). *The power and affiliation motives and war.* Address presented at the annual meeting of the Midwest Psychological Association, Chicago.

Winter, D. G. (1989d). *Technical note on measuring motivation.* Unpublished manuscript, University of Michigan, Department of Psychology, Ann Arbor.

Winter, D. G. (1990a). *Childhood and young adult antecedents of responsibility.* Unpublished manuscript, University of Michigan, Department of Psychology, Ann Arbor.

Winter, D. G. (1990b). *Inventory of motive scores of persons, groups, and societies measured at a distance.* Unpublished manuscript, University of Michigan, Department of Psychology, Ann Arbor.

Winter, D. G. (1990c). *Predicting aspects of adult men's adaptation from a TAT-based measure of responsibility.* Unpublished manuscript, University of Michigan, Department of Psychology, Ann Arbor.

Winter, D. G. (1991). Measuring personality at a distance: Development of an integrated system for scoring motives in verbal running text. In A. J. Stewart, J. M. Healy, Jr., & D. J. Ozer (Eds.), *Perspectives in personality: Approaches to understanding lives* (pp. 59–89). London: Jessica Kingsly Publishers.

Winter, D. G. (in press). A motivational model of leadership: Predicting long-term management success from TAT measures of power motivation and responsibility. *Leadership Quarterly*.

Winter, D. G., Alpert, R. A., & McClelland, D. C. (1963). The classic personal style. *Journal of Abnormal and Social Psychology*, *67*, 254–265.

Winter, D. G., & Barenbaum, N. B. (1985a, July). *Developmental antecedents of a T.A.T. measure of responsibility.* Paper presented at the meeting of the International Society for the Study of Behavioral Development, Tours, France.

Winter, D. G., & Barenbaum, N. B. (1985b). Responsibility and the power motive in women and men. *Journal of Personality*, *53*, 335–355. Reprinted in A. J. Stewart & M. B. Lykes (Eds.). (1985). *Gender and personality* (pp. 247–267). Durham NC: Duke University Press.

Winter, D. G., & Carlson, L. (1988). Using motive scores in the psychobiographical study of an individual: The case of Richard Nixon. *Journal of Personality*, *56*, 75–103.

Winter, D. G., & Healy, J. M., Jr. (1983). *Coding the motive imagery content of television programs.* Unpublished manuscript, Wesleyan University, Middletown, CT.

Winter, D. G., Hermann, M. G., Weintraub, W., & Walker, S. G. (1991). The personalities of Bush and Gorbachev at a distance: Procedures, portraits, and policy. *Political Psychology*, *12*, 215–245.

Winter, D. G., & McClelland, D. C. (1978). Thematic analysis: An empirically derived measure of the effects of liberal arts education. *Journal of Educational Psychology*, *70*, 8–16.

Winter, D. G., McClelland, D. C., & Stewart, A. J. (1981). *A new case for the liberal arts.* San Francisco: Jossey-Bass.

Winter, D. G., & Stewart, A. J. (1977a). Content analysis as a technique for assessing political leaders. In M. G. Hermann (Ed.), *A psychological examination of political leaders* (pp. 27–61). New York: Free Press.

Winter, D. G., & Stewart, A. J. (1977b). Power motive reliability as a function of retest instructions. *Journal of Consulting and Clinical Psychology, 45*, 436–440.

Winter, D. G., & Stewart, A. J. (1978). The power motive. In H. London & J. Exner (Eds.), *Dimensions of personality* (pp. 391–447). New York: Wiley.

Winter, D. G., Stewart, A. J., & McClelland, D. C. (1977). Husband's motives and wife's career level. *Journal of Personality and Social Psychology, 35*, 159–166.

Winter, N. J. G. (1990). *The effects of the Hitler relationship on Mussolini's motive profile*. Unpublished honors thesis, University of Chicago, Chicago.

Winterbottom, M. R. (1958). The relation of need for achievement to learning experiences in independence and mastery. In J. W. Atkinson (Ed.), *Motives in fantasy, action and society* (pp. 453–478). Princeton, NJ: Van Nostrand.

Wise, R. A. (1980). Actions of drugs of abuse on brain reward systems. *Pharmacology, Biochemistry, and Behavior, 13* (Suppl. 1), 213–223.

Witkin, H. A., Dyk, R. B., Faterson, H. F., Goodenough, D. R., & Karp, S. A. (1962). *Psychological differentiation*. New York: Wiley.

Wittenborn, J. R. (1955). The study of alternative responses by means of the correlation coefficient. *Psychological Review, 62*, 451–460.

Wittgenstein, L. (1953). *Philosophical investigations*. New York: Macmillan.

Wong, P. T. P., & Weiner, B. (1981). When people ask "why" questions, and the heuristics of attribution search. *Journal of Personality and Social Psychology, 40*, 649–663.

Wortman, C. B., & Dintzer, L. (1978). Is an attributional analysis of the learned helplessness phenomenon viable? A critique of the Abramson-Seligman-Teasdale reformulation. *Journal of Abnormal Psychology, 87*, 75–90.

Zanna, M. P., Higgins, E. T., & Herman, C. P. (1982). *Consistency in social behavior: The Ontario symposium, 2*. Hillsdale, NJ: Erlbaum.

Zeldow, P. B., Daugherty, S. R., & McAdams, D. P. (1988). Intimacy, power and psychological well-being in medical students. *Journal of Nervous and Mental Disease, 176*, 182–187.

Zimmerman, D. W., & Williams, R. H. (1986). Note on the reliability of experimental measures and the power of significance tests. *Psychological Bulletin, 100*, 123–124.

Zuckerman, M., & Allison, S. M. (1976). An objective measure of fear of success: Construction and validation. *Journal of Personality Assessment, 40*, 422–430.

Zuckerman, M., Larrance, D. T., Porac, J. F. A., & Blanck, P. D. (1980). Effects of fear of success on intrinsic motivation, causal attribution, and choice behavior. *Journal of Personality and Social Psychology, 39*, 503–513.

Zuckerman, M., & Wheeler, L. (1975). To dispel fantasies about the fantasy-based measure of fear of success. *Psychological Bulletin, 82*, 932–946.

Zullow, H. (1983). *Women, self-focused power, and anorexia nervosa*. Unpublished senior thesis, Princeton University, Princeton, NJ.

Zullow, H. M., Oettingen, G., Peterson, C., & Seligman M. E. P. (1988). Explanatory style and the historical record: CAVEing LBJ, East versus West Berlin, and presidential elections. *American Psychologist, 43*, 673–682.

Zullow, H. M., & Seligman, M. E. P. (1990). Pessimistic rumination predicts electoral defeat in presidential candidates, 1900–1984. *Psychological Inquiry, 1*(1), 52–61.

Name index

689

Subject index